Houghton Mifflin Mathematics 10

Les Dukowski
Jerry Lunney
Walter Szetela
Robert G. Dearborn
R. Geoffrey Roulet
Edward Barbeau Jr.
George Scroggie

Houghton Mifflin Canada Limited

150 Steelcase Road West • Markham, Ontario • L3R 1B2

Houghton Mifflin Mathematics 10

Authors

Les Dukowski, Vice Principal, H.D. Stafford Jr. Secondary School, Langley, B.C.

Jerry Lunney, Vice Principal, St. Paul's High School, C.R.C.S.S.B., Nepean, Ontario

Walter Szetela, Faculty of Education, University of British Columbia

Robert G. Dearborn, Mathematics Dept. Head, Queen Elizabeth C.H.S., Edmonton, Alberta

R. Geoffrey Roulet, Special Assignment Teacher, Mathematics/Computers, Timmins (Ontario) Board of Education

Consultants

John Del Grande, Educational Consultant, Houghton Mifflin Canada

Charles C. Edmunds, Mathematics Department, Mount Saint Vincent University

Norman Rice, Dept. of Mathematics and Statistics, Queen's University

Linda L.B. Wheadon, Mathematics Teacher, Horton District H.S., Wolfville, Nova Scotia

Anne C. Vickers, Mathematics Consultant, New Brunswick

Ed Zegray, La Commission des Ecoles Catholique de Montréal

Additional Problem Solving material contributed by Steve Taylor, Richmond School District, B.C.

Canadian Cataloguing in Publication Data

Main entry under title:
Houghton Mifflin mathematics 10

For use in grade 10.
Includes index.

ISBN 0-395-42686-3

1. Mathematics — 1961– I. Dukowski, Les

QA107.H6893 1987 510   C86-094511-1

Editorial Advisers

Edward Barbeau Jr.
George Scroggie

Editors

Claire Robitaille
Fran Seidenberg

Assembly and Technical Art

Dave Hunter

Cover Art

Christopher Pratt, *Ocean Racer*
Design by Michael van Elsen

Printed in Canada

CONTENTS

1 Numbers and Variables

1-1 Algebraic Expressions

An electrician charges a $35 flat fee plus $21/h for a service call. The charge can be written using a formula.

$$\text{Charge} = \$35 + (\$21 \times t) \quad \text{or} \quad C = 35 + 21t$$

The right-hand side of the formula is an **algebraic expression**. Algebraic expressions are made up of sums and differences of **terms**. The terms of the expression above are 35 and $21t$. The letter t is a variable representing the number of hours spent on a service call.

The table shows some algebraic expressions and their parts.

Expression	Terms	Coefficients	Variables	Constants
$35 + 21t$	35			35
	$21t$	21	t	
$3abc + ab - 5bc$	$3abc$	3	a, b, c	
	ab	1	a, b	
	$-5bc$	-5	b, c	

EXAMPLE 1: What would the electrician charge if 4.5 h were spent on a service call?

Evaluate the expression $35 + 21t$ for $t = 4.5$.

$$35 + 21t = 35 + 21(4.5)$$ Substitute numbers for variables.
$$= 35 + 94.5$$ Simplify.
$$= 129.5.$$ 129.5 is the value of the expression when $t = 4.5$.

EXAMPLE 2: The electrician would charge $129.50.

Evaluate $ab + 2bc - 2$ for $a = 6$, $b = 2$, $c = 5$.

$$ab + 2bc - 2 = (6)(2) + 2(2)(5) - 2$$ Substitute.
$$= 12 + 20 - 2$$ Simplify.
$$= 30$$

EXERCISES

A **1.** Name the coefficient of each term.
   a. $3x$ **b.** $5ab$ **c.** mn **d.** $\frac{1}{2}k$
   e. $\frac{2}{3}xy$ **f.** xz **g.** $0.2mnq$ **h.** $8.35fmr$

2. How many terms are there in each expression?
   a. $3x + 12$ **b.** $5ab - 2b$ **c.** $2xy + 5x - 2$
   d. $3mn - 2r + 7$ **e.** $6x + z$ **f.** $3rs + 2s - 8 - 5r$

3. Name the variables in each expression in exercise 2.

B **4.** Evaluate the following expressions for the values of the variables given in the brackets.
   a. $x + 7$ $(x = 9)$ **b.** $x - 2$ $(x = 5)$
   c. $7 - x$ $(x = 3)$ **d.** $10 - y$ $(y = 5)$
   e. $8 - m$ $(m = 8)$ **f.** $x + y$ $(x = 8, y = 9)$
   g. $x - y + 7$ $(x = 10, y = 3)$ **h.** $b + y - 5$ $(b = 4, y = 8)$
   i. $11 - a + y$ $(a = 7, y = 0)$ **j.** $p + 7 - r$ $(p = 3, r = 10)$

5. Evaluate each expression for $m = 3$, $n = 8$, $p = 7$, $q = 1.5$.
   a. mnp **b.** $3m + q$ **c.** $13 - 2m$ **d.** $2m + 7$
   e. $7p + q$ **f.** $2mq$ **g.** $0.5n$ **h.** $m + nq - p$
   i. $2p + 9$ **j.** $4n - 4p$ **k.** $mp - 2n$ **l.** $6q + 2m - 2p$

6. **a.** An electrician uses the formula $(36 + 22.50t)$ to calculate the charge for a service call (t is time in hours). What is the charge for a 3.5 h service call?
   b. A plumber uses the formula $(32 + 24.60t)$ to calculate the charge (t is time in hours). Find the charge for a 5 h service call.
   c. A cab driver charges for a ride using the formula $(3.50 + 0.20d)$, where d is distance in 100 m units. What is the charge for a ride of 2.9 km?

2

C 7. Determine the values of the variables.
  a. $x + 10 = 14$ b. $5k = 25$
  c. $5k - 4 = 21$ d. $3x = 6$
  e. $3x + 8 = 14$ f. $2r - p = 7$ $(r = 5)$
  g. $5x + 2y = 23$ $(y = 4)$ h. $ab + 4 = 18$ $(a = 7)$
  i. $xy - 5 = 19$ $(y = 3)$ j. $2ab - a = 36$ $(a = 4)$
  k. $3xy + y = 49$ $(x = 2)$
  l. $3ab + 2bc = 46$ $(a = 5, b = 2)$
  m. $3xy - 2y + 8 = 36$ $(y = 7)$
  n. $2mn + 3np - 5 = 12$ $(m = 4, p = 3)$

8. Write a formula or an expression for each. Use the given variables.
  a. the perimeter of a square   c. the perimeter of a rectangle
  b. the area of a square   d. the area of a rectangle

  e. the area of a parallelogram   f. the surface area of a rectangular prism

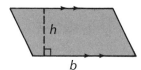
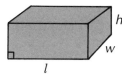

  g. a weekly salary for a worker paid by the hour (where r is the worker's hourly rate of pay)
  h. the amount a salesperson earns in commission when 2% commission is paid on all sales (where s is the salesperson's sales volume)

EXTRA

Economists, mathematicians, and scientists must often find formulas which fit patterns of data.

Study the pattern in each table of data below. Then write each variable in terms of the remaining one(s).

1.

P	a
12	4
15	5
21	7
30	10

$P = ?$
$a = ?$

2.

t	v	d
7	15	105
34	2	68
6	7	42
9	22	198

$t = ?$
$d = ?$

3.

C	p
23	3
43	7
58	10
68	12

$C = ?$
$p = ?$

3

1–2 Integers

When we count, we use the set of **natural numbers**.

$N = \{1, 2, 3, ...\}$

Many everyday situations require the use of the set of **whole numbers**.

$W = \{0, 1, 2, ...\}$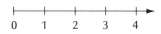

Some applications, however, cannot be described conveniently using the set of natural or whole numbers. For example, some bank accounts allow the customer to write cheques that are not covered by the customer's balance: their bank account goes into *overdraft*.

Situations like this require the use of negative numbers. If the account is overdrawn by $30, then the customer *owes* the bank $30. We say the balance is $(-30).

A number line is a good way to visualize this overdraft situation.

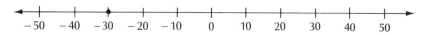

> The number line uses the set of **integers**, represented by *Z*.
> $Z = \{... -3, -2, -1, 0, 1, 2, 3, ...\}$

The distance between a point (x) and the point (0) on an integer line is the **absolute value** of x, written $|x|$.

EXAMPLE 1: Evaluate.

a. $|-30| = 30$ b. $|30| = 30$

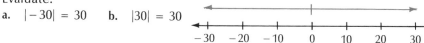

30 and -30 are **opposites**. They are the same distance from zero but in opposite directions.

c. $-|-45| = -(45)$ d. $|0| = 0$
$ = -45$

EXAMPLE 2: A customer with a bank balance of $(-30) deposited a cheque for $48. Find the new balance.

$(-30) + 48 = 18$

The new balance is $18.

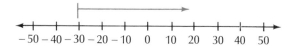

4

EXAMPLE 3:   A customer's account is $50 overdrawn. An incorrect debit of $40 had been made. This was corrected, that is, subtracted from the account. Find the new balance.

$$(-50) - (-40) = (-50) + 40 \qquad \text{To subtract, add the opposite.}$$
$$= -10$$

The new balance is (-10).

EXAMPLE 4:   The bank charges 15¢ for every cheque written during a month. One month, a customer wrote 7 cheques. What was the effect on the customer's balance?

$$(-15) \times 7 = -(15 \times 7)$$
$$= -105$$

The effect on the balance was (-105)¢ or $-\$1.05$.

EXAMPLE 5:   Evaluate.
   a. $6 \times (-5) = -30$ The signs are different so the answer is negative.

   b. $(-20) \div 5 = -4$

   c. $(-7) \times (-9) = 63$ The signs are the same, so the answer is positive.

   d. $(-38) \div (-2) = 19$

   e.   Evaluate for $k = -2, m = 3, n = -1$.
   $$(km) - n = (-2)(3) - (-1)$$
   $$= (-6) - (-1)$$
   $$= (-6) + 1$$
   $$= -5$$

EXERCISES

A   1.   Give the opposite.
   a. 7   b. -3 c. 10   d. -8 e. -6 f. 0

2.   Evaluate.
   a. $|-7|$ b. $-|9|$ c. $|0|$ d. $|-28|$ e. $-|16|$
   f. $-|-3|$ g. $-(-14)$ h. $-|(-8)|$ i. $-|-(-8)|$ j. $-|0|$

3.   Name the coefficients in each of the following terms.
   a. $-5ab$ b. $5mn$ c. $7rtu$ d. $-ab$ e. $-3xz$

4.   If n is a negative number, then what is the sign of $-n$?

5.   If n is a positive number, then what is the sign of $-n$?

6. Write an integer to represent each of the following situations.
   a. The change in the value of a stock which rose by $5 a share.
   b. The change in the value of a stock which fell by $5 a share.
   c. The temperature when it is 12 degrees below zero.
   d. The effect on a person's yearly budget when a promotion at work includes a raise of $4250/year.
   e. The effect on a person's monthly expenses when rent is increased by $58/month.
   f. The temperature when it is 4 degrees above zero.
   g. Three seconds before liftoff.
   h. An elevation of 60 m above sea level.
   i. A bank deposit of $450.
   j. Ten seconds after liftoff.
   k. An ocean depth of 60 m.
   l. A production increase of 40 units per day.
   m. A drop in sales of $50 000.

B 7. Write a sentence describing a situation that could be represented by each integer.
   a. -5 b. 27   c. -800 d. -45 e. -5904

8. Evaluate each integer expression.
   a. $(-8) + 3$ b. $(-7) + (-5)$ c. $(-7) - (-5)$ d. $15 + (-9)$
   e. $(-28) + (-37)$ f. $(-48) + 75$ g. $(-2) - 8$ h. $3 - (-10)$
   i. $12 - 15$ j. $(-6) - 9$ k. $14 - (-2)$ l. $(-21) - (-18)$
   m. $3 \times (-7)$ n. $(-4) \times (-8)$ o. $(-9) \times 6$ p. $(-5) \times (-7)$
   q. $0 \times (-18)$ r. $15 \times (-4)$ s. $26 \div (-2)$ t. $(-18) \div (-6)$
   u. $\frac{-21}{7}$ v. $\frac{14}{-2}$ w. $\frac{-35}{-7}$ x. $\frac{-25}{-5}$

9. Evaluate.
   a. $(-3) + 7 + (-15)$ b. $(-4) \times (3) \times (-2)$
   c. $(-2) \times 3 \times (-4) \times (-7)$ d. $(-8) - (-3) - 4 - (-5)$
   e. $14 + (-4) + (-7) + 5$ f. $4 \times (-9) \times (-2) \times (-1) \times (-1)$

10. Evaluate each expression for the values of the variables in the brackets.
   a. $x + 3$ $(x = -5)$ b. $x - 8$ $(x = 3)$
   c. $m - n$ $(m = -3, n = -7)$ d. $b + c - 3$ $(b = -4, c = 10)$
   e. $10 - a + b$ $(a = -8, b = -3)$ f. $p + 4 - r$ $(p = -11, r = 5)$
   g. $-mn$ $(m = -1, n = 1)$ h. $-3rst$ $(r = -10, s = -2, t = -4)$
   i. km $(k = -16, m = -5)$ j. $-3rxz$ $(r = -1, x = -3, z = -2)$
   k. $x\left(\frac{y}{z}\right)$ $(x = 3, y = 8, z = -2)$
   l. $\frac{ac}{b}$ $(a = 6, b = 5, c = -10)$
   m. $\frac{rm}{st}$ $(m = -6, r = -5, s = 10, t = -1)$
   n. $[x \div (y \div z)] \div t$ $(x = 120, y = 42, z = 14, t = -5)$

11. Write an integer expression to represent each situation. Then evaluate the expression.
  a. A stereo dealer received a delivery that cost $3509. On the same day, the store had sales of $8905.
  b. Kim signed a one-year lease for an apartment with a monthly rent of $468.
  c. A babysitter made $2 an hour from 17:00 to 24:00 and $3 an hour from 24:00 to 02:00.
  d. A sky diver fell 11 m each second during the first 4 s of a fall.
  e. A baker with 4 containers of flour on hand received a delivery of 15 more containers and, on the same day, used 12 containers of flour.
  f. A hot air balloon rises at 8 m/min for 15 min and then drops at 5 m/min for 6 min.

C 12. Evaluate.
  a. $|3 - 8|$
  b. $|(-5) + (6 - 8)| \times (-2)$
  c. $|3(-5) + 4|$
  d. $|(-8) - 5| - |3 - 7|$

13. a. For what numbers is it true that $|x| = x$?
  b. For what numbers is it true that $|x| = -x$?

14. Evaluate.
  a. $|x - y|$ $(x = 7, y = 10)$
  b. $|a + b|$ $(a = (-8), b = 7)$
  c. $|m - n|$ $(m = (-10), n = (-3))$
  d. $|3x|$ $(x = (-5))$
  e. $|5ab|$ $(a = (-3), b = (-2))$
  f. $|-rt|$ $(r = (-2), t = (-5))$

15. Find values for x that will make the following equations true.
  a. $|x + 2| = 7$
  b. $|x - 5| = 2$
  c. $|3x| = 15$
  d. $|2x + 1| = 7$
  e. $|x + 5| + 2 = 6$
  f. $|3x| - 2 = 10$
  g. $|4x - 2| + 3 = 9$

EXTRA

Polyominos are figures made up of unit squares touching edge-to-edge.

Dominos contain 2 unit squares.

Triominos contain 3 unit squares.

There is only one domino shape.

There are two triomino shapes.

1. *Tetrominos* contain 4 unit squares.
   Show all possible tetrominos with a sketch.
2. Pentominos contain 5 unit squares.
   There are 12 different pentominos. Sketch them.
3. The twelve pentominos can cover an 8-by-8 square leaving a 2-by-2 hole in the middle. Make a sketch of one of the 65 ways in which this can be done.

1–3 Order of Operations

Jamie and Leslie of Smalltown, Ontario have just won a lottery prize of $2000. But, before they can collect the money, they have to answer a skill-testing question, required by Ontario law. They are asked to evaluate $3 \times 9 - 7 + 5 \times 2$.

They feel that the question, as written, is ambiguous. The best thing to do would be to bracket the expression to make it precise. But, when this has not been done, there are conventions for evaluating such expressions.

EXAMPLE 1:   Evaluate $3 \times 9 - 7 + 5 \times 2$.

$$\begin{aligned} 3 \times 9 - 7 + 5 \times 2 &= 27 - 7 + 10 \\ &= 20 + 10 \\ &= 30 \end{aligned}$$

Multiply or divide before adding or subtracting.

Then add and subtract in order from left to right.

Some expressions will also contain grouping symbols, such as brackets, fraction bars, or absolute value signs.

EXAMPLE 2:   Evaluate $\dfrac{2ab + c}{5(c - b)}$ for $a = 4$, $b = -2$, $c = -4$.

$$\begin{aligned} \frac{2ab + c}{5(c - b)} &= \frac{2(4)(-2) + (-4)}{5[(-4) - (-2)]} \\ &= \frac{(-16) + (-4)}{5(-2)} \\ &= \frac{-20}{-10} \\ &= 2 \end{aligned}$$

Multiply before adding.
Work inside the brackets first.

Evaluate above the fraction bar first.
Then evaluate the denominator.

EXERCISES

A **1.** Evaluate.

    a. $13 - (8 + 4)$

    b. $5 \times 6 + 2$

    c. $5 \times (6 \div 2)$

    d. $5 - [6 - (3 + 2)]$

    e. $\dfrac{9 \times 5}{6 \div 2}$

    f. $\dfrac{3 \times 8 \div 2}{12 \div 4}$

    g. $\dfrac{36 \times (12 \div 6)}{24 \div (2 \times 3)}$

    h. $\dfrac{3 \times 8 \div 2}{12 \div 4} \times \dfrac{6 \div 3}{2 \times 7 - 13}$

    i. $(6 + 3) - (2 + 7)$

    j. $8 \div [(6 \div 3) \times 2]$

    k. $(6 + 5) \times [7 - (4 + 1)]$

    l. $[(6 + 8) \div 7] \times 2 + 3$

    m. $7 - \dfrac{4 \times 5}{12 - (4 - 2)}$

    n. $[6 - 5 \times (3 + 2) + 10] \times 3$

    o. $\dfrac{[19 - (3 \times 6)] \times 5}{2 \times 4 - 3 \times 3}$

    p. $\dfrac{8 + (3 - 7) \times 2}{4 + 6 - 6}$

    q. $24 \div \dfrac{3 \times (1 + 3) \times (2 + 2)}{2 \times 6 - (3 + 3)}$

    r. $\dfrac{18}{3 \times 3} + \dfrac{15}{7 \times 2 + 1}$

B 2. Evaluate for $x = -5, y = -2, z = 12$.
  - **a.** $2x + 1$
  - **b.** $5y - 3$
  - **c.** $7 - 3z$
  - **d.** $2x + 8$
  - **e.** $2x - 3y$
  - **f.** $3x + y$
  - **g.** $2x - 3z$
  - **h.** $-3y - z + 1$
  - **i.** $8x + 5 - z$
  - **j.** $8y - 2x + 1$
  - **k.** $x - 3y + 9$
  - **l.** $xy - 3z$
  - **m.** $2xz \div 3y$
  - **n.** $12z \div y$
  - **o.** $15zy \div 3x$
  - **p.** $xyz \div 15$

3. Evaluate each algebraic expression for $u = 5, v = -7, w = 2$, and $x = -3$.
  - **a.** $x - |u + v|$
  - **b.** $x(v + w)$
  - **c.** $xv + u$
  - **d.** $\dfrac{v + 14}{v} + 6$
  - **e.** $(u - v) + w$
  - **f.** $|xu| \div 3$
  - **g.** $(u - v) + (w + x)$
  - **h.** $(u - w) - |(x - v)|$
  - **i.** $x - [(u - w) + w]$

4. Evaluate each expression for the values of the variables in brackets.
  - **a.** $\dfrac{8a}{b + c} + \dfrac{3b}{3(c - a)}$ $(a = 3, b = 10, c = -2)$
  - **b.** $\dfrac{6 + (3x - 2y)}{(3x - y) - (z - 1)}$ $(x = 5, y = 3, z = 8)$
  - **c.** $\dfrac{(rf - g)t}{(t + 2g)(r + t)}$ $(r = 6, f = 3, g = 2, t = -5)$

C 5. Insert brackets to make each of the following expressions true statements.
  - **a.** $3 + 5 - 8 \times 2 + 7 \div 2 = -\dfrac{1}{2}$
  - **b.** $\dfrac{7 - 3 - 2}{4 + 8 \div 4} = 1$
  - **c.** $16 + 12 \times 18 - 20 = -8$
  - **d.** $5 \times m + n - 2 \times m = 30$ $(m = 5, n = 3)$
  - **e.** $3 \times p + 2 \times p - r - q = 0$ $(p = r = 1, q = 3)$

Using the Calculator
Bracket Keys

Scientific calculators usually allow you to calculate expressions with *nested* brackets quickly. Evaluate the following using the left and right bracket keys.

1. $10 - (9 - 8)$ 2. $10 - (9 - (8 - 7))$ 3. $10 - (9 - (8 - (7 - 6)))$
4. $10 - (9 - (8 - (7 - (6 - 5))))$ 5. $10 - (9 - (8 - (7 - (6 - (5 - 4)))))$

The bracket keys can be used to evaluate expressions with fraction bars.

For $\dfrac{6 - 6 \times 2}{5 + 4 - 3}$, press $(\; 6 \; - \; 6 \; \times \; 2 \;) \; \div \; (\; 5 \; + \; 4 \; - \; 3 \;) \; =$

  Note: Scientific calculators are usually programmed to follow the correct order of operations.

6. Check your answers for exercise questions 1g to 1r using the bracket keys on a scientific calculator.

1-4 Rational Numbers

How much would you pay for one orange? for one lime?

- One orange would be 99¢ ÷ 4,
  rounded to the nearest cent.

  $\frac{99}{4}$ or $4\overline{)99.00}$ $\quad\frac{24.75}{}$

  One orange would be 25¢.

- One lime would be 79¢ ÷ 6,
  rounded up to the nearest cent.

  $\frac{79}{6}$ or $6\overline{)79.000\ 00\ldots}$ $\quad\frac{13.166\ 66\ldots}{}$

  One lime would be 14¢.

Both $\frac{99}{4}$ and $\frac{79}{6}$ are rational numbers.

> A **rational number** is the result of dividing one integer by another. **Q** is used to represent the set of all quotients or rational numbers.
>
> $Q = \left\{ \frac{m}{n} \mid m, n \in Z \text{ and } n \neq 0 \right\}$
>
> Read: "**Q** is the set of all numbers which can be written in the form $\frac{m}{n}$, where m and n are integers and n is not zero."

Rational numbers can result in either a **terminating** or a **repeating decimal**. 24.75 is a terminating decimal. $13.1\overline{6}$ is a repeating or **periodic decimal**. The **period** is 6. The **length of the period** is 1.

EXAMPLE 1: Convert each terminating decimal to a fraction.

a. $0.38 = \frac{3}{10} + \frac{8}{100}$

$\quad\quad = \frac{30}{100} + \frac{8}{100}$

$\quad\quad = \frac{38}{100}$

b. $-0.0625 = -\left(\frac{6}{100} + \frac{2}{1000} + \frac{5}{10\ 000} \right)$

$\quad\quad\quad\quad = -\left(\frac{600}{10\ 000} + \frac{20}{10\ 000} + \frac{5}{10\ 000} \right)$

$\quad\quad\quad\quad = -\frac{625}{10\ 000}$

EXAMPLE 2: Convert the repeating decimal $0.\overline{36}$ to a fraction.

Let $n = 0.\overline{36}$

Or: $n = 0.363\ 636\ldots$ The period is 36. The period length is 2.

Then: $100\ n = 36.363\ 636\ldots$ Multiply both sides by 100 to bring one period to the left of the decimal point.

$\dfrac{-\ (n\ =\ \ \ 0.363\ 636)}{99n\ =\ 36}$ Subtract.

$n = \frac{36}{99}$ Solve for n.

$n = \frac{4}{11}$ $\therefore 0.\overline{36} = \frac{4}{11}$

EXAMPLE 3:   Evaluate $3a - b$ for $a = \frac{3}{7}$, $b = 0.4$.

$$3a - b = 3\left(\frac{3}{7}\right) - (0.4)$$

$$= \left(\frac{3}{1}\right) \times \left(\frac{3}{7}\right) - \left(\frac{4}{10}\right) \qquad \text{Convert decimals to fractions.}$$

$$= \frac{9}{7} - \frac{4}{10}$$

$$= \frac{90}{70} - \frac{28}{70} \qquad \text{The lowest common denominator is 70.}$$

$$= \frac{62}{70} \text{ or } \frac{31}{35}$$

EXAMPLE 4:   Evaluate $\dfrac{2ab}{c - a}$ for $a = 4$, $b = \frac{3}{5}$, and $c = \frac{1}{2}$.

$$\frac{2ab}{c - a} = \frac{2(4)\left(\frac{3}{5}\right)}{\frac{1}{2} - 4}$$

$$= \frac{\frac{24}{5}}{\frac{1}{2} - \frac{8}{2}} \qquad \text{The LCD is 2.}$$

$$= \frac{\frac{24}{5}}{-\frac{7}{2}}$$

$$= \frac{24}{5} \times \left(-\frac{2}{7}\right) \qquad \text{To divide, invert and multiply.}$$

$$= -\frac{48}{35}$$

Here is a shorter way to work example 4.

$$\frac{2ab}{c - a} = \frac{2(4)\left(\frac{3}{5}\right)}{\frac{1}{2} - 4}$$

$$= \frac{\frac{24}{5}}{\frac{1}{2} - \frac{8}{2}} \times \frac{10}{10} \qquad \text{Multiply by the LCM of 5 and 2 to clear the fractions.}$$

$$= \frac{48}{5 - 40} \qquad \begin{aligned}&\frac{24}{5} \times 10 \\ &\left(\frac{1}{2} - \frac{8}{2}\right)10\end{aligned}$$

$$= -\frac{48}{35}$$

EXERCISES

A   **1.**   How much for just one? Round up to the nearest cent as necessary.

a.    b.    c.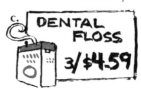

2.   Convert to decimals.

a. $\frac{37}{100}$ b. $\frac{3}{8}$ c. $-\frac{5}{16}$ d. $\frac{2}{9}$ e. $-\frac{7}{6}$

f. $\frac{15}{7}$ g. $-3\frac{8}{13}$ h. $4\frac{17}{24}$ i. $-4\frac{5}{9}$ j. $-6\frac{23}{45}$

3.   Convert to fractions.

a. 0.15 b. -0.008 c. 0.0375 d. -0.58 e. 1.39

f. -4.275 g. -15.001 h. 12.35 i. -4.0125 j. 3.925

B   **4.**   Add or subtract as indicated.

a. $\frac{2}{3} - \frac{1}{2}$ b. $\frac{5}{6} + \left(-\frac{1}{4}\right)$ c. $\left(-\frac{5}{8}\right) + \left(-\frac{1}{2}\right)$ d. $4\frac{8}{9} - \frac{11}{12}$

e. $\left(-\frac{8}{15}\right) + \frac{9}{10}$ f. $\left(-\frac{3}{7}\right) - \left(-\frac{1}{3}\right)$ g. $\left(-1\frac{3}{5}\right) - 2\frac{1}{2}$ h. $\left(-3\frac{1}{2}\right) + 1\frac{2}{3}$

5.   Multiply or divide as indicated.

a. $\left(-\frac{3}{5}\right) \times \frac{1}{2}$ b. $\left(-\frac{4}{7}\right) \times \left(-\frac{3}{8}\right)$ c. $\frac{1}{3} \div \frac{1}{6}$ d. $\left(-\frac{5}{9}\right) \div \frac{3}{10}$

e. $\left(-\frac{7}{12}\right) \div \left(-\frac{3}{4}\right)$ f. $1\frac{1}{2} \div \frac{2}{3}$ g. $\left(-\frac{3}{5}\right) \div \left(-2\frac{1}{2}\right)$ h. $-1\frac{3}{7} \times \left(-3\frac{1}{10}\right)$

6.   Evaluate.

a. $\frac{1}{4}\left(\frac{3}{5} - \frac{1}{2}\right)$ b. $\dfrac{0.7 + 0.5}{0.6}$ c. $\dfrac{(1.3 - 0.9)2.5}{0.8 - 0.6}$

d. $\left(\frac{5}{8} - \frac{1}{2}\right) - \left(\frac{2}{3} - \frac{1}{4}\right)$ e. $\dfrac{1.6(3.8 + 2.7)}{(4 - 2.25)4}$ f. $\dfrac{(0.8 - 0.4)(3.2 + 1.8)}{3[1.5 - (2.1 - 1.8)]}$

g. $\dfrac{\frac{2}{3} \times \frac{1}{2} + \frac{5}{6}}{\left(\frac{2}{3} + \frac{1}{2}\right) \times \frac{1}{3}}$ h. $\dfrac{1\frac{3}{4} - \frac{5}{8}}{\left(\frac{1}{2} + \frac{1}{3}\right)\frac{1}{5}}$ i. $3\left(\frac{2}{5} + 1\frac{1}{2}\right) - \left(1\frac{1}{2} + \frac{1}{5}\right)$

7.   Evaluate.

a. $0.8 + 3.5 \times \frac{1}{7}$ b. $\left(\frac{1}{2} - 0.1\right)\left(\frac{3}{8} + 0.25\right)$ c. $4.2 \times 3.1 - \frac{1}{3} \times 1\frac{1}{5}$

d. $7\left(3.8 + \frac{1}{4}\right)$ e. $6.25 \times \frac{1}{5} - \frac{5}{8} \times 4$ f. $3.7 - \left(1.5 - 2.8 \times \frac{1}{4}\right)$

g. $\dfrac{4\left(1\frac{1}{2} + 0.75\right)}{3.2 + 1.8}$ h. $\dfrac{(2.3 + 1.7)\left(5.6 - \frac{3}{5}\right)}{\frac{1}{2}}$ i. $\dfrac{\left(\frac{4}{5} - 0.1\right) - \frac{3}{10}}{\frac{1}{2}(2.5 + 2.3)}$

8. Given $a = \frac{1}{2}$, $b = \frac{2}{3}$, and $c = \frac{1}{4}$, evaluate each expression.

    a. $ab + c$ **b.** $3c + ab$ **c.** abc **d.** $\dfrac{ab}{c}$ **e.** $\dfrac{4a - b}{c}$

9. Given $x = 0.7$, $y = \frac{1}{2}$, and $z = 1.5$, evaluate each expression.

    a. $3x - y$ **b.** $\dfrac{x + y}{x - z}$ **c.** $x(y - z)$ **d.** $\dfrac{3x + y}{z}$ **e.** $\dfrac{xyz}{xy + zy}$

C   10. Convert each repeating decimal to a fraction.

    a. $0.\overline{4}$ **b.** $0.\overline{1}$ **c.** $0.\overline{81}$ **d.** $0.\overline{29}$ **e.** $0.\overline{385}$
    f. $-0.\overline{67}$ **g.** $1.3\overline{54}$ **h.** $-0.5\overline{431}$ **i.** $3.4\overline{52}$ **j.** $-0.\overline{9}$

11. Evaluate each formula for the given values of the variables.

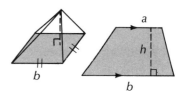

    a. Volume of a square pyramid $= \dfrac{b^2 h}{3}$

       $b = 12.5$ cm, $h = 8.1$ cm

    b. Area of a trapezoid $= \frac{1}{2}(a + b)h$

       $a = 4.2$ m, $b = 3.7$ m, $h = 5.6$ m

Review

1. Name the coefficients and variables in each.
    a. $7m$ **b.** $-2xy$ **c.** abc **d.** $-0.3p$ **e.** xy

2. Evaluate.
    a. $|-7|$ **b.** $|3|$ **c.** $|0|$ **d.** $-|-7|$ **e.** $-(-4)$ **f.** $-|9|$

3. Simplify each expression.
    a. $-15 + 3 \times (-8)$ **b.** $\left(\frac{2}{3} + \frac{1}{2}\right)\frac{3}{4}$ **c.** $[(-12) \div (-4)] \times (-5)$

    d. $\left(-\frac{3}{8}\right) \div \left[\frac{2}{3} \div \left(-\frac{1}{6}\right)\right]$ **e.** $(5.7 + 0.8 + 2.3)(-0.5)$ **f.** $\dfrac{3 \times (7 - 4)}{2 + 7 - 2}$

4. Evaluate each expression for $a = -2$, $b = 3$, $c = 0.7$.

    a. $a - b$ **b.** abc **c.** $ab + c$ **d.** $4c - b$ **e.** $\dfrac{4c - b}{ac + b}$

    f. $\dfrac{ab}{b + 9}$ **g.** $\dfrac{3c}{21}$ **h.** $\dfrac{10c}{ab + 1}$ **i.** $\dfrac{3c}{10}$ **j.** $\dfrac{9ab - 4}{10c}$

5. Convert each fraction to a decimal.
    a. $\dfrac{17}{1000}$ **b.** $-\dfrac{9}{125}$ **c.** $\dfrac{5}{18}$ **d.** $-2\frac{3}{11}$ **e.** $\dfrac{14}{45}$

6. Convert each decimal to a fraction.
    a. 1.76 **b.** -0.075 **c.** $0.\overline{54}$ **d.** $0.3\overline{21}$ **e.** $-4.\overline{36}$

1–5 Number Properties

The set of rational numbers has general properties that hold true for all the numbers in the set.

When two rational numbers are added or multiplied, their order can be reversed without changing the sum or product. Addition and multiplication are **commutative** operations.

$$0.8 + 0.4 = 0.4 + 0.8 = 1.2 \qquad \frac{1}{5} \times \frac{2}{3} = \frac{2}{3} \times \frac{1}{5} = \frac{2}{15}$$

> **Commutative Property**
> For all $a, b \in Q$, $a + b = b + a$ and $ab = ba$.

When three or more rational numbers are added or multiplied, the way in which they are grouped makes no difference to the sum or product. Addition and multiplication are **associative** operations.

$$(1 + 2.2) + 1.3 = 1 + (2.2 + 1.3) = 4.5 \qquad \left(\frac{1}{4} \times \frac{5}{6}\right) \times \frac{1}{3} = \frac{1}{4} \times \left(\frac{5}{6} \times \frac{1}{3}\right) = \frac{5}{72}$$

> **Associative Property**
> For all $a, b, c \in Q$, $(a + b) + c = a + (b + c)$ and $(ab)c = a(bc)$.

These properties can be used to make computations easier. Examine expressions before evaluating to select pairs of numbers that are easier to work with.

EXAMPLE 1: Evaluate. Apply the properties where appropriate to simplify computation.

a. $2.5 + 3.6 + 1.5 + 1.4$
$= 2.5 + 1.5 + 3.6 + 1.4$ Apply the commutative property.
$= (2.5 + 1.5) + (3.6 + 1.4)$
$= 4.0 + 5.0$
$= 9.0$

b. $\frac{1}{25} \times \left(\frac{7}{9} \times \frac{1}{4}\right)$ Look for an easy product.

$= \frac{1}{25} \times \left(\frac{1}{4} \times \frac{7}{9}\right)$ Apply the commutative property.

$= \left(\frac{1}{25} \times \frac{1}{4}\right) \times \frac{7}{9}$ Apply the associative property.

$= \frac{1}{100} \times \frac{7}{9}$

$= \frac{7}{900}$

Multiplication of rational numbers is **distributive** over addition.

$$3(5.5 + 2.2) \xrightarrow{\quad 3(7.7) \quad} 23.1$$
$$3(5.5) + 3(2.2) = 16.5 + 6.6$$

> **Distributive Property**
> For all a, b, $c \in Q$, $a(b + c) = ab + ac$, and $(a + b)c = ac + bc$.

The distributive property can also be applied to simplify some computations.

EXAMPLE 2: Evaluate each expression. Apply the distributive property where appropriate to simplify computations.

a. $36\left(\frac{1}{4} + \frac{5}{9}\right) = 36\left(\frac{1}{4}\right) + 36\left(\frac{5}{9}\right)$ It would be easier
$= 9 + 20$ to multiply each
$= 29$ addend by 36 first.

b. $(7 \times 1.6) + (7 \times 1.4) = 7(1.6 + 1.4)$ It would be easier to
$= 7 \times 3.0$ add 1.6 and 1.4 first.
$= 21.0$

EXERCISES

A **1.** State the property illustrated by each equation. Evaluate the left side and right side of each to show that they are indeed equal.

a. $3 + 18 = 18 + 3$ **b.** $3 + (27 + 8) = (3 + 27) + 8$
c. $6(10 + 15) = 60 + 90$ **d.** $8 + 7 + 2 = 7 + 8 + 2$
e. $5 \times (1.3 + 8) = (1.3 + 8) \times 5$ **f.** $12\left(\frac{1}{3} + \frac{1}{4}\right) = 12 \times \frac{1}{3} + 12 \times \frac{1}{4}$
g. $4 \times (16 \times 10) = (4 \times 16) \times 10$ **h.** $3.5 \times 0.9 = 0.9 \times 3.5$
i. $(-7) + (7 + 8) = [(-7) + 7] + 8$ **j.** $15 + [8 + (-6)] = 15 + [(-6) + 8]$

B **2.** Evaluate each expression, applying the properties where appropriate to simplify computation.

a. $39 + 28 + 11$ **b.** $4 \times 17 \times 5$
c. $23 + 48 + 27 + 12$ **d.** $4 \times 5 \times 1.5 \times 0.4$
e. $8\left(\frac{1}{2} + \frac{3}{4}\right)$ **f.** $3\frac{2}{3} + 5\frac{3}{8} + 2\frac{1}{3} + 2\frac{5}{8}$
g. $(-8) + 14 + 18 + (-6)$ **h.** $\left(\frac{7}{10} \times \frac{3}{8}\right) + \left(\frac{7}{10} \times \frac{5}{8}\right)$
i. $4.7 + 3.4 + 1.3 + 2.6$ **j.** $(4.5 \times 7.2) + (4.5 \times 2.8)$

15

3. Evaluate each expression. Use the number properties to make computations easier.

a. $\left(\frac{5}{7} - \frac{1}{2}\right)14$

b. $\dfrac{3.5 + 0.8 + 0.5}{5(12)}$

c. $\frac{3}{8}(15) + \frac{3}{8}(9)$

d. $\dfrac{(1.3 + 0.8 + 1.7)0.5}{0.3 - 0.5}$

e. $\left[\frac{5}{8} + \left(-\frac{1}{3}\right) + \left(-\frac{1}{8}\right)\right]$

f. $\dfrac{6\left[1\frac{1}{3} + \left(-\frac{1}{2}\right)\right]}{-0.8}$

g. $\dfrac{3.5(2.1 + 0.9)}{4[2.5 + (-1.2)]}$

h. $\dfrac{3\left(1\frac{1}{4} + 1 + 2\frac{3}{4}\right)}{(3.7 + 2.5 + 1.3)}$

i. $\dfrac{\frac{1}{6}[1.2 + (-3.6)]}{(1.8 + 0.5 + 0.2 + 1.5)}$

4. Evaluate each expression for the values of the variables given in brackets. Use the properties to simplify computations.

a. $3x(y + z)$ $\left(x = -5, y = \frac{3}{5}, z = -0.2\right)$

b. $ab + ac$ $\left(a = 7, b = \frac{3}{4}, c = -\frac{1}{4}\right)$

c. $m + n + p$ $\left(m = \frac{5}{7}, n = 0.3, p = -\frac{2}{7}\right)$

d. abc $\left(a = \frac{5}{7}, b = \frac{3}{4}, c = \frac{14}{15}\right)$

e. $y(z + t)$ $\left(y = 16, z = \frac{5}{8}, t = \frac{3}{4}\right)$

f. $4a(b + c)$ $\left(a = 3, b = \frac{3}{4}, c = \frac{1}{2}\right)$

g. $3ma - 2mb$ $\left(m = 7, a = \frac{2}{3}, b = \frac{1}{2}\right)$

h. $6f + 6g + 6h$ $(f = -3, g = 2, h = -4)$

i. $\dfrac{\frac{2}{3}a + \frac{2}{3}b}{2.5a}$ $(a = 0.8, b = 0.7)$

j. $\dfrac{(m + f + b)}{3m + 3b}$ $(m = 1.7, f = 0.6, b = 1.3)$

C 5. Show the pairs of expressions are equal by justifying the indicated steps.

a. $\left(\frac{1}{2}a + \frac{1}{2}b\right)h$

   $= (a + b)\frac{1}{2}h$ i. ?

   $= \frac{1}{2}h(a + b)$ ii. ?

b. $2\pi rh + 2\pi r^2$

   $= 2\pi rh + 2\pi r(r)$

   $= 2\pi r(h + r)$ iii. ?

c. $2sl + 4sr + 3sl$

   $= s(2l + 4r + 3l)$ iv. ?

   $= s(5l + 4r)$ v. ?

d. $\frac{1}{4}ms^2 + \frac{1}{12}l^2 + \frac{1}{4}mr^2$

   $= \frac{1}{4}ms^2 + \frac{1}{4}mr^2 + \frac{1}{12}l^2$ vi. ?

   $= \frac{1}{4}m(r^2 + s^2) + \frac{1}{12}l^2$ vii. ?

16

Application

Rational numbers may be expressed as fractions, decimals, or percents. Note the various forms in which the rational number $\frac{5}{8}$ can be written.

$$\frac{5}{8} \qquad 0.625 \qquad 62.5\%$$

There are many applications for which rational numbers must be rewritten in different forms to calculate the solutions to problems.

Banking

Rewrite the percents as decimals to solve each problem. A calculator may be used.

1. What is the interest earned on $380 deposited in a savings account at a rate of $8\frac{1}{4}\%$ for one year? (Use $I = Prt$, where I is interest, P is principal, r is annual interest rate, and t is time in years.)

2. The finance charge on a loan is $18\frac{1}{2}\%$ of the amount borrowed. If $1200 is borrowed, what is the total amount that must be repaid?

3. A savings account earns $6\frac{1}{2}\%$ interest per year calculated every six months and added to the balance. If $240 is deposited into a savings account, what is the total value of the account in two years?

Comparison Shopping

Find the better buy.

4. 500 g of bacon for $2.39 or 750 g of bacon for $3.45

5. 369 g of coffee for $3.29 or 275 g of coffee for $2.89

6. 375 mL of mouthwash for $3.29 or 200 mL for $1.69

7. 250 mL of jam for $1.69 or 325 mL for $2.09

Sports

8. Jay scored 11 out of 16 free throws during a basketball game. What percent of the shots were successful?

9. Sarah made 25 base hits in 63 times at bat. What is her batting average as a three-place decimal?

10. Doug has a 60% pass completion record. How many passes has he thrown if he has completed 24?

11. Jeanine scored goals in 21 out of 35 hockey games. In what percent of the games played has she scored goals?

1–6 Additive and Multiplicative Inverses

The rational numbers 0 and 1 have special properties.

Identity Properties For every rational number a:

$$a + 0 = a$$
$$0 + a = a$$
Identity property of addition

$$1 \times a = a$$
$$a \times 1 = a$$
Identity property of multiplication

Every rational number has an opposite or an **additive inverse**, which will add to it to give zero.

$$5 + (-5) = 0 \qquad\qquad (-7) + 7 = 0$$

Every rational number, except zero, has a **reciprocal** or a **multiplicative inverse**, which will multiply by it to give 1.

$$5 \times \left(\tfrac{1}{5}\right) = 1 \qquad\qquad (-7) \times \left(-\tfrac{1}{7}\right) = 1$$

Inverse Properties For every rational number a:

$$a + (-a) = 0 \qquad a \times \tfrac{1}{a} = 1$$
$$(-a) + a = 0 \qquad \tfrac{1}{a} \times a = 1 \qquad a \neq 0$$

Algebraic expressions also have opposites and reciprocals.

EXAMPLE 1: Find the additive inverse (opposite).

a. $3k$

$-(3k) = -3k$

b. $2x + 7$

$-(2x + 7) = -2x - 7$

c. $4mn - 5k$

$-(4mn - 5k) = -4mn + 5k$

EXAMPLE 2: Find the multiplicative inverse (reciprocal).

a. $\dfrac{3a}{xy}$

$\dfrac{1}{\left(\frac{3a}{xy}\right)} = \dfrac{xy}{3a}$

b. $\dfrac{2x + 7}{3k}$

$\dfrac{1}{\left(\frac{2x + 7}{3k}\right)} = \dfrac{3k}{2x + 7}$

c. 0

Zero has no reciprocal.

EXERCISES

A 1. Find the additive inverse (opposite) of each.

a. 3

b. -2

c. -5

d. 0.4

e. $4k$

f. $-\dfrac{3}{7}$

g. $-0.8m$

h. $-5.9j$

i. 0

j. -1

k. $xz + y$

l. $-3x + 7$

m. $-2xy - 5$

n. $-\dfrac{3}{mn}$

o. $1.3a + b$

2. Find the multiplicative inverse (reciprocal) of each.

a. a **b.** $\frac{3}{8}$ **c.** $\frac{a}{k}$ **d.** -9 **e.** $0.5b$

f. $3.5j$ **g.** $-2 + b$ **h.** $0.\overline{67}$ **i.** $-1.\overline{4}$ **j.** $1 + 4k$

k. $m + 5n$ **l.** $mn - 7j$ **m.** $6ab + 7c$ **n.** $-3xy$ **o.** $4a$

p. $-\dfrac{1}{xy}$ **q.** $\dfrac{-3ab}{2}$ **r.** $\dfrac{5x}{y}$ **s.** 0 **t.** $\dfrac{-13x}{4y + 9}$

B **3.** **a.** If the opposite of a is a positive number, what is the sign of a?
  b. If the reciprocal of b is a negative number, what is the sign of b?

4. Simplify.

  a. $5xy\left(-\frac{1}{5}\right)$ **b.** $8rt\left(-\frac{1}{4}\right)$ **c.** $\frac{1}{a}(4ab)$, $a \neq 0$

  d. $-6 + (-m + 2m + 6)$ **e.** $-(-r + 2) + 2$ **f.** $(3xy)\frac{1}{y}$, $y \neq 0$

C **5.** Solve for the variable.

  a. $x + 8 = 0$ **b.** $-3 + y = 0$ **c.** $x + \left(-\frac{2}{3}\right) = 0$

  d. $0.75 + r = 0$ **e.** $t + 1\frac{3}{8} = 0$ **f.** $k + (-5.9) = 0$

  g. $7x = 1$ **h.** $\frac{2}{3}y = 1$ **i.** $-0.3m = 1$

  j. $\frac{1}{n} = 5$ **k.** $0.777p = 1$ **l.** $5.999r = 1$

  m. $5x + (-1) = 0$ **n.** $-2x + 1 = 0$ **o.** $\frac{1}{2}x + 1 = 0$

  p. $0.8x + (-1) = 0$ **q.** $\frac{4}{3}x + (-1) = 0$ **r.** $\frac{1}{m} = 9$

EXTRA

Significant Digits

Recall that when doing calculations involving measurements, the result is rounded to the same number of *significant digits* as the least accurate measurement.

Solve the following. Round your result to the correct number of significant digits. Use a calculator.

1. The Cheops pyramid has a square base with a side length of about 230 m. Its height is about 145 m. Use the formula $V = \dfrac{b^2h}{3}$ to find the volume of the pyramid. (Note: The number 3 in the formula is not a measurement, it is an exact figure.)

2. An average two-storey house has a volume of about 1000 m³. The vehicle assembly building at the John F. Kennedy Space Centre in Florida has a volume of 3 666 500 m³. How many houses would fit inside the building?

19

1–7 Integral Exponents

To find the number of one-unit cells in the cube at the right, you would multiply the three dimensions of the cube.

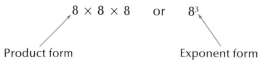

8 × 8 × 8   or 8^3

Product form   Exponent form

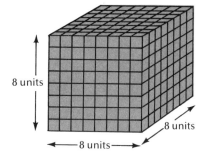

8 units

8 units

8 units

8^3 is a **power**: 8 is the **base**; 3 is the **exponent** and an integer and thus is the **integral exponent**.

EXAMPLE 1:   Evaluate each power.

a. $(-5)^4 = (-5)(-5)(-5)(-5)$
$= 625$

b. $-5^4 = -(5 \times 5 \times 5 \times 5)$
$= -625$

c. $6a^3$, for $a = 5$
$6a^3 = 6(a \times a \times a)$
$= 6(5 \times 5 \times 5)$
$= 750$

d. $(6a)^3$, for $a = 5$
$(6a)^3 = (6a)(6a)(6a)$
$= (6 \times 5)(6 \times 5)(6 \times 5)$
$= 27\,000$

e. $(9 + 3)^2 = (9 + 3) \times (9 + 3)$
$= 144$

f. $9 + 3^2 = 9 + (3)(3)$
$= 18$

Look for the pattern in the powers at the right to determine an appropriate meaning for 3^0 and 3^{-1}.

Exponents decreasing by 1.

$3^3 = 27$
$3^2 = 9$
$3^1 = 3$
$3^0 = ?$
$3^{-1} = ?$

Powers decreasing by a factor of 3.

Following the pattern would give $3^0 = 1$, $3^{-1} = \frac{1}{3}$, $3^{-2} = \frac{1}{3^2}$, $3^{-3} = \frac{1}{3^3}$, and so on.

EXAMPLE 2:   Evaluate each power, using the pattern established above.

a. $(-0.5)^0 = 1$

b. $\left(-\frac{2}{3}\right)^0 = 1$

c. $8^{-1} = \frac{1}{8}$

d. $-2^{-4} = -\frac{1}{2^4}$
$= -\frac{1}{16}$

In general, zero and negative exponents can be defined as follows:

For $a \neq 0$: $a^0 = 1$ $a^{-x} = \frac{1}{a^x}$

EXERCISES

A **1.** Write each of the following in exponent form.
    a. $8 \times 8 \times 8 \times 8 \times 8$ **b.** $6 \times 6 \times 6 \times 6 \times 6 \times 6 \times 6$
    c. $(-2)(-2)(-2)(-2)(-2)$ **d.** three squared

   2. Name the base and the exponent of each, then write in product form.
    a. 9^2 **b.** $(-4)^5$ **c.** -6^4 **d.** $(-3)^4$ **e.** seven cubed

B **3.** Evaluate each power.
    a. 2^5 **b.** 4^4 **c.** $(-3)^5$ **d.** 7^0 **e.** 0^3
    f. 1^5 **g.** -2^4 **h.** 10^{-3} **i.** -1^3 **j.** $(-1)^3$
    k. 3^{-1} **l.** 7^{-2} **m.** 5^1 **n.** -4^{-1} **o.** $(-3)^{-2}$
    p. -3^{-2} **q.** 4^0 **r.** -8^{-3} **s.** $(-5)^{-4}$ **t.** $(-3)^{-3}$

   4. Write each of the following as a power.
    a. 8   **b.** 27   **c.** 25   **d.** 100   **e.** 49
    f. 216   **g.** 32   **h.** 125   **i.** 10 000   **j.** 100 000

   5. Write each of the following as a power with a negative exponent.

    a. $\frac{-1}{25}$ **b.** $\frac{1}{8}$ **c.** 0.01   **d.** 0.000 001   **e.** $\frac{1}{625}$

C **6.** Jeff started a chain letter, sending 7 letters to 7 friends, asking them to send 7 letters to 7 friends, who would also send 7 letters to 7 friends, and so on. If the chain letter went through the first 7 links of the chain successfully, and Jeff received a post card from each recipient of the letter through its first 7 chain links, then how many post cards did he receive?

   7. Simplify and evaluate.
    a. $2^3 + 3^2$ **b.** $10^2 + 10^3$ **c.** $2^{-3} + 2^2$ **d.** $(2^3)(5^2)$
    e. $(2^{-2})(3^2)$ **f.** $-3^2 + 2^3$ **g.** $(-10)^2 + (-5)^3$ **h.** $(-6)^0(3^{-2})$
    i. $3^{-2} + 2^{-3}$ **j.** $(4^2 - 3^3)^{-2}$ **k.** $[(-5)^2 - 3^3]^{-2}$ **l.** $(5^0 + 3^2)^{-3}$

EXTRA

In photography, a filter is occasionally used for some special effect. Usually, the filter reduces the amount of light which is passed through the lens.

1. Suppose that a grey filter lets in only $\frac{4}{5}$ of the light. How much light would pass through 2 filters? 4 filters?

2. Write an expression that would describe the amount of light that would be let through by n filters.

3. Use a calculator to determine how many filters would be required to block 99% of the light.

21

1–8 Exponent Laws

When you multiply two powers having the same base, you add the exponents as shown below.

EXAMPLE 1:   Simplify.

    a. $8^2 \times 8^3 = (8 \times 8) \times (8 \times 8 \times 8)$ $2 + 3 = 5$
                   $= 8^5$

    b. $m^5 \times m^3 = (m \times m \times m \times m \times m) \times (m \times m \times m)$ $5 + 3 = 8$
                   $= m^8$

> In general, for all integers x and y: $b^x \times b^y = b^{x+y}$.

EXAMPLE 2:   Simplify.

    a. $4t^2 \times t^5 = 4 \times t^{2+5}$ **b.** $4y^3 \times 5y^8 = 4 \times 5 \times y^{3+8}$
               $= 4t^7$ $= 20y^{11}$

When you divide two powers having the same base, you subtract the exponents as shown below.

EXAMPLE 3:   Simplify.

    a. $10^7 \div 10^4 = \dfrac{10 \times 10 \times 10 \times \cancel{10} \times \cancel{10} \times \cancel{10} \times \cancel{10}}{\cancel{10} \times \cancel{10} \times \cancel{10} \times \cancel{10}}$ $7 - 4 = 3$
                $= 10^3$

    b. $m^3 \div m^5 = \dfrac{\cancel{m} \times \cancel{m} \times \cancel{m}}{m \times m \times \cancel{m} \times \cancel{m} \times \cancel{m}}$ $3 - 5 = -2$
                $= m^{-2}$
                $= \dfrac{1}{m^2}$

> In general, for all integers x and y, where b is a real number not equal to zero: $b^x \div b^y = b^{x-y}$.

EXAMPLE 4:   Simplify.

    a. $12m^8 \div 3m^6 = \dfrac{12m^8}{3m^6}$ **b.** $18a^3b^5 \div 2a^5b^{-2} = \dfrac{18a^3b^5}{2a^5b^{-2}}$
                     $= 4m^{8-6}$ $= 9a^{3-5}b^{5-(-2)}$
                     $= 4m^2$ $= 9a^{-2}b^7$
                                              $= \dfrac{9b^7}{a^2}$

To find the power of a power, multiply the exponents.

EXAMPLE 5: Simplify.

a. $(2^4)^3 = (2^4)(2^4)(2^4)$
  $= 2^{4+4+4}$ $\quad 4 \times 3 = 12$
  $= 2^{12}$

b. $(x^9)^4 = (x^9)(x^9)(x^9)(x^9)$
  $= x^{9+9+9+9}$ $\quad 9 \times 4 = 36$
  $= x^{36}$

In general, for all integers x and y: $(b^x)^y = b^{xy}$.

EXAMPLE 6: Simplify.

a. $(x^2)^{-5} = x^{2 \times (-5)}$
  $= x^{-10}$

b. $(3x^2y)^3(3x^2y)^2 = (3x^2y)^5$
  $= 3^5 x^{10} y^5$
  $= 243 x^{10} y^5$

An exponent outside of a pair of brackets applies to each factor within the brackets.

EXAMPLE 7: Simplify.

a. $(5x)^3 = (5x)(5x)(5x)$
  $= 5^3 x^3$
  $= 125 x^3$

b. $\left(\dfrac{3}{4}x\right)^2 = \dfrac{3^2 x^2}{4^2}$
  $= \dfrac{9x^2}{16}$

When evaluating algebraic expressions containing exponents, it is sometimes faster to simplify before substituting.

EXAMPLE 8: Evaluate each expression for $a = -5$ and $b = -2$.

a. $5ab^2 = 5(-5)(-2)^2$
  $= 5(-5)(4)$
  $= -100$

b. $(a^3b^{-1})(a^{-2}b^2) = a^{3-2}b^{-1+2}$
  $= ab$ $\quad$ Simplify first.
  $= (-5)(-2)$
  $= 10$

EXERCISES

A **1.** Simplify each product.

  a. $x^4 x^6$ **b.** $m^3 m^7$ **c.** $r^5 r^3$ **d.** $a^8 a^6$
  e. $y^5 y^7$ **f.** $z^8 z$ **g.** $n^1 n^3$ **h.** $m^6 m^0$

2. Simplify each quotient.

  a. $x^8 \div x^3$ **b.** $a^7 \div a^2$ **c.** $m^9 \div m^4$ **d.** $z^6 \div z$
  e. $r^5 \div r^4$ **f.** $a^4 \div a^2$ **g.** $b^{13} \div b^{13}$ **h.** $b^{10} \div b$

3. Simplify each power.
   a. $(a^3)^2$ b. $(x^2)^5$ c. $(b^2)^4$ d. $(z^4)^3$
   e. $(m^3)^3$ f. $(y^7)^2$ g. $(n^6)^0$ h. $(b^6)^2$

4. Simplify.
   a. $(st)^5$ b. $(mn)^8$ c. $(2a)^4$ d. $(5b)^3$
   e. $(-2xz)^4$ f. $(abc)^7$ g. $(bc)^0$ h. $(5xyz)^2$
   i. $\left(\dfrac{m}{n}\right)^4$ j. $\left(\dfrac{3a}{b}\right)^6$ k. $\left(\dfrac{2m}{3n}\right)^3$ l. $\left(\dfrac{xm}{3ab}\right)^3$

B 5. Evaluate each expression for $x = 3$, $y = -8$, and $z = -5$.
   a. x^5 b. y^2 c. $xz^2 + 3y$
   d. $\dfrac{5xy}{2z^2}$ e. $\dfrac{x^2}{yz}$ f. $\dfrac{25y^5}{xz^2y^4}$

6. Simplify each expression using positive exponents.
   a. $c^7c^3c^4$ b. x^2xx^4 c. $a^3b^2a^4b^{-1}$
   d. $(m^{-3}n^4)(m^5n^{-3})$ e. $x^4 \div x^6$ f. $x^{-3} \div x^6$
   g. $(a^2bc^3)(-4a^3bc^4)$ h. $(-6a^5b^2c)(-2a^4b^2c^2)$ i. $8m^3n^4 \div 2m^2n$
   j. $-6a^4b^8 \div 3a^2b^2$ k. $(x^{-4})^5$ l. $(b^{-4})^7$
   m. $(x^{-3})^{-2}$ n. $(a^6)^{-3}$ o. $(3m^2n)^3$
   p. $(-2m^3n^5)^4$ q. $(-4x^4z^5)^4$ r. $(3x^{-3}z)^{-2}$
   s. $\dfrac{x^3y^4z^2}{x^{-2}y^2z^{-1}}$ t. $\dfrac{12x^2y^{-3}}{6x^4y^2}$ u. $\left(\dfrac{-3m^4}{n^3x}\right)^3$

7. Evaluate each expression for the given values of the variables.
   a. $(x + y)^2$ $\left(x = \dfrac{2}{3}, y = \dfrac{1}{2}\right)$ b. $\dfrac{3x^2}{x + y}$ $\left(x = 0.5, y = 0.1\right)$

   c. $(m^2n)^{-1} + 3m^{-1}$ $\left(m = \dfrac{1}{2}, n = 3\right)$ d. $(x^2y^{-1}) + (x^{-1}y^2)$ $\left(x = -3, y = \dfrac{1}{3}\right)$

   e. $\dfrac{m^{-3}n}{p}$ $\left(m = 0.5, n = 3, p = \dfrac{1}{6}\right)$ f. $\dfrac{(a^{-1}b)^2}{c^{-1}}$ $\left(a = \dfrac{2}{3}, b = 6, c = 0.\overline{3}\right)$

   g. $\dfrac{(a - b)^{-1}}{(a + b)^{-2}}$ $\left(a = \dfrac{3}{4}, b = 0.15\right)$ h. $3x^{-1} + \left(\dfrac{2x}{y}\right)^{-2}$ $\left(x = 10, y = 8\right)$

8. Rewrite the following without using fractions.
   a. $\dfrac{x}{y}$ b. $\dfrac{m^3}{n^2}$ c. $\dfrac{2x^2}{y^4z^3}$ d. $\dfrac{10a^2b}{5c^3}$

   e. $\dfrac{30m^2}{m^5}$ f. $\dfrac{1}{x^{-3}}$ g. $\dfrac{m^{-3}}{n^{-2}}$ h. $\dfrac{5x^2y^{-3}}{z}$

9. Rewrite the following without using negative exponents.
   a. $a^{-3}b^2c$ b. $\dfrac{x^2y^{-3}}{z^5}$ c. $\dfrac{1}{x^{-4}y}$ d. $\dfrac{m^{-3}n^2}{x^{-2}y}$

10. Simplify using positive exponents.
   a. $(2a^2b)^3(ab)^2$
   b. $(5x^2y^3)^2(3y^4)^2$
   c. $(2a^3b)^3(-a^2b^2)^4$
   d. $(ab^3)^3(-2a^2b)^2(-b^3)^3$
   e. $(x^3y^{-2})^3$
   f. $(3xy^3)^2(2x^{-1}y^5)^3$
   g. $(-3a^4b^{-2})^{-3}$
   h. $(18x^5y^3)(9x^2y^8)^{-1}$
   i. $\dfrac{(-3a^2bc^3)^3}{-3ab^5}$
   j. $\dfrac{18x^2y^3}{9x^2y^8}$
   k. $\dfrac{m^4n^{-3}}{m^{-3}n^{-4}}$
   l. $\dfrac{(a^2b^3)^3}{(a^{-1}b^2c)^4}$

C 11. Simplify using positive exponents.
   a. $(3a^2b^2)^{-2}(2a^4b)^3$
   b. $(-3a^4b^{-2})^{-3}$
   c. $32x^5z \div (2x^2z^{-2})^{-3}$
   d. $12t^{-5} \div 4t^3 \times 3t^4$
   e. $\left(\dfrac{3x}{2y}\right)^{-2}$
   f. $\left(\dfrac{x^{-2}y}{z^2}\right)^{-3}$
   g. $(4ab^{-1})^{-2}(3a^2b)^3(2a^{-2})^3$
   h. $(6x^4z^3 \div 2x^3z^4)^{-2}$

12. Evaluate.
   a. $\left(\dfrac{2}{5}\right)^{-2}$
   b. $\dfrac{4}{3^{-2}}$
   c. $\dfrac{3^{-2}}{2^{-3}}$
   d. $\left(\dfrac{3}{4}\right)^{-1} \div \left(1\dfrac{1}{2}\right)^{-2}$
   e. $4^{-2} + 2^{-1}$
   f. $5^0 + 3^{-2}$
   g. $(1.5)^{-3}$
   h. $5^0 + (-4)^0$
   i. $\dfrac{1}{2x^0} + \dfrac{1}{3y^0}$
   j. $\dfrac{2}{(3x)^0} - \dfrac{1}{2y^0}$

13. Find the area of each shaded region.
   a.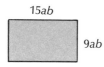
   b.
   c.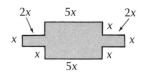

14. Find the volume of each solid.
   a.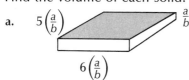
   b.

EXTRA
Mental Computation

Evaluate each of the following mentally. What pattern do you notice about each result?

1. $(0.1^4)^2$
2. $(0.3^2)^2$
3. $(0.2^4)^2$
4. $0.2^3 \times 0.2^5$
5. $0.1^5 \times 0.1^3$
6. $0.3^6 \times 0.3^0$
7. $(0.2)^9 \div (0.2)^7 \times (0.2)^4$
8. $(0.4)^{10} \times (0.4)^2 \div (0.4)^8$
9. $0.1^9 \times 0.1^4 \div 0.1^0$

25

1–9 Scientific Notation

Many applications involve numbers that are very large or very small. Such numbers can be rewritten using **scientific notation** to make them easier to read and to use.

A number in scientific notation is written as a number greater than or equal to 1, but less than 10, multiplied by an integral power of 10.

EXAMPLE 1:

a. The distance from the earth to the sun is 150 000 000 km.
   Write the distance in scientific notation.

   $150\ 000\ 000 \text{ km} = 1.5 \times 10^8 \text{ km}$

   The decimal point moved 8 places.

   Both measurements have 2 known significant digits.

b. The average mass of a cell is 0.000 000 005 g.

   $0.000\ 000\ 005 \text{ g} = 5 \times 10^{-9} \text{ g}$

   The decimal point moved 9 places.

   Both measurements have 1 known significant digit.

Calculations can often be simplified by writing numbers in scientific notation and applying the laws of exponents.

EXAMPLE 2:

Calculate. Use scientific notation.

$$38\ 000 \times 0.075 = (3.8 \times 10^4) \times (7.5 \times 10^{-2})$$
$$= (3.8 \times 7.5) \times (10^4 \times 10^{-2})$$
$$= 28.5 \times 10^2$$
$$= 28.5 \times 100$$
$$= 2850$$

Each factor has 2 significant digits.

Since there are 2 known significant digits in the two factors, the answer should be rounded to 2 significant digits: 2900.

EXAMPLE 3:

Calculate. Use scientific notation.

$$0.0275 \div 2500 = \frac{2.75 \times 10^{-2}}{2.5 \times 10^3}$$

0.0275 has 3 known significant digits.

2500 has 2 known significant digits.

$$= \frac{2.75}{2.5} \times \frac{10^{-2}}{10^3}$$
$$= 1.1 \times 10^{-5}$$
$$= 0.000\ 011$$

The answer has 2 known significant digits.

EXERCISES

A **1.** Express each number in scientific notation.

a.	5900	**b.**	0.006 27	**c.**	36 000 000
d.	0.049	**e.**	0.96	**f.**	59
g.	3.5	**h.**	62 000 000 000	**i.**	0.000 000 000 38
j.	460×10^3	**k.**	0.38×10^{-5}	**l.**	350×10^{-8}
m.	0.04×10^7	**n.**	0.37×10^{-1}	**o.**	710×10^{-4}

2. Express each number in decimal notation.

a.	1.1×10^6	**b.**	4.89×10^{-4}	**c.**	2.1×10^5
d.	3.411×10^{-2}	**e.**	9.6×10^0	**f.**	8.81×10^1
g.	47.4×10^{-3}	**h.**	86×10^3	**i.**	$0.002 87 \times 10^{-4}$

3. State the number of known significant digits in each measurement.

a.	390	**b.**	0.56	**c.**	10.3
d.	0.870	**e.**	0.004 86	**f.**	3.79×10^5
g.	4.90×10^{-3}	**h.**	2.807×10^{-1}	**i.**	16.0

4. Change each number to decimal notation.

  a. Canada's population is about 2.4×10^7.

  b. The population density of Nova Scotia is 1.56×10^1 people per square kilometre.

  c. The population density of the Northwest Territories is 1×10^{-2} people per square kilometre.

  d. There are 2.3×10^3 Inuit living mainly along Canada's north coast.

  e. The amount of land per person in the city of Vancouver is 2.7×10^{-4} km^2.

5. Write each number in scientific notation.

  a. Some scientists estimate that land masses first started to form on Earth 3 000 000 000 years ago.

  b. The North American continent is moving toward Asia at a rate of 0.000 000 000 32 m/s.

  c. The temperature of Earth's interior may be as much as 4000°C.

  d. The mass of a brontosaurus's brain was probably only 0.000 002 times the mass of the total body.

  e. What are believed to be the fossil bones of the oldest human ancestor were found in Ethiopia and are dated at 3 500 000 years.

B **6.** Supply the missing numbers.

  a. 38 000 × 21 000 000
   $= (3.8 \times 10^{\blacksquare}) \times (2.1 \times 10^{\blacksquare})$
   $= 7.98 \times 10^{\blacksquare}$

  b. 64 000 ÷ 250
   $= (6.4 \times 10^{\blacksquare}) \div (2.5 \times 10^{\blacksquare})$
   $= 2.56 \times 10^{\blacksquare}$

  c. 0.0056 × 175
   $= (5.6 \times 10^{\blacksquare}) \times (\blacksquare \times 10^{\blacksquare})$
   $= 9.8 \times 10^{\blacksquare}$

  d. 126 000 ÷ 0.028
   $= (\blacksquare \times 10^{\blacksquare}) \div (\blacksquare \times 10^{\blacksquare})$
   $= 0.45 \times 10^{\blacksquare}$
   $= \blacksquare \times 10^{\blacksquare}$

7. Calculate with pencil and paper. Use scientific notation.
   a. 3000 × 200
   b. 0.004 × 0.02
   c. 8 000 000 ÷ 400
   d. 0.009 ÷ 0.03
   e. 900 ÷ 0.003
   f. 2000 × 0.000 004
   g. 28 000 × 1500
   h. 0.000 36 ÷ 0.012
   i. 0.045 ÷ 1200
   j. 210 × 0.0025

8. Calculate. Use scientific notation. You may use a calculator.
   a. 3400 × 25 000
   b. 4750 ÷ 0.025
   c. 0.0275 × 0.000 16
   d. 0.000 48 ÷ 0.0125
   e. 0.0325 × 18 000
   f. (6300 × 0.026) ÷ 1800
   g. 0.0675 ÷ (0.0765 ÷ 425)
   h. (520 × 0.032) ÷ 12 500
   i. (4100 × 0.0035) × 0.000 16
   j. 384 000 × (4650 ÷ 0.062)

C 9. Calculate the solution in scientific notation. Then state your answer to the appropriate number of known significant digits.
   a. The volume of the Earth is about 1 080 000 000 000 km^3. The volume of a sugar cube is about 1 cm^3. How many sugar cubes would it take to get a total volume equivalent to that of the Earth?
   b. A regulation soccer field is 7300 m^2. The land area of Canada is about 9 200 000 000 000 m^2. How many soccer fields would it take to equal Canada's land area?

Biography

Helen Sawyer Hogg   1905–

Astronomer and professor emeritus, Helen Sawyer Hogg first began her study of globular star clusters and their variable stars as a graduate student in 1928. Her documentation of patterns of change in star clusters, in order to estimate such factors as a star's age and distance from the sun, has greatly contributed to knowledge of our galaxy.

Awarded her doctorate in astronomy in 1931, Dr. Hogg moved to Canada with her husband Frank, also an astronomer. In 1936, she joined the teaching staff at University of Toronto, becoming a full professor in 1957. In addition to her research and teaching, she contributed to numerous scholarly publications. After the death of her husband, Dr. Hogg assumed the writing of a weekly column on astronomy for *The Toronto Star*. The column, which ran for thirty years, culminated in the publication of the book, *The Stars Belong to Everyone*.

Among numerous awards and titles she has received is the Companion to the Order of Canada. Helen Sawyer Hogg's interest, dedication, and commitment to the field of astronomy over a period of almost sixty years have led to a well-deserved reputation as one of the world's foremost astronomers.

Review

1. Give the opposite and the reciprocal of each.
   a. -7 b. 0.75 c. $-1\frac{2}{7}$ d. a e. xy
   f. $\frac{3}{8}$ g. $-3\frac{1}{3}$ h. $8x$ i. $\frac{3m}{n}$ j. $0.8x$

2. Write an integer to represent each situation.
   a. The mine elevator descended 3 levels.
   b. Pat spent $28 on books.
   c. Chris made $21 babysitting.

3. Name the base and the exponent of each power.
   a. 7^6 b. $(-3)^3$ c. 2^{-5}

4. Write using exponents: $(-2)(-2)(-2)(-2)(-2)(-2)$.

5. Evaluate each power.
   a. 3^4 b. $(-2)^4$ c. -5^2 d. 7^{-2} e. -3^{-3}

6. Write each of the following as a power of an integer.
   a. 36 b. 32 c. $\frac{1}{100}$ d. $\frac{1}{25}$ e. 0.001

7. Use the laws of exponents to simplify using positive exponents.
   a. x^4x^{-2} b. $m^5 \div m^3$ c. $x^{15} \div x^{21}$
   d. $12x^8 \div 6x^4$ e. $x^{-3} \div x^{-8}$ f. $3x^5 \times 2x^8 \div 6x^6$
   g. $x^3y \times x^4y^2$ h. $(a^3)^5$ i. $(a^2b^4)^3$
   j. $(3a^2)^4$ k. $\left(\frac{2}{3}\right)^2$ l. $(2x^2)^3 \times 3x^5$
   m. $21m^3n^{-4} \div 7m^{-2}n$ n. $(5ab^2)(2bc^2)(-3a)$ o. $(5x^{-2}y)^2(3x^{-1}y^{-2})$

8. Rewrite without using fractions.
   a. $\dfrac{21m^8n}{7mn^5}$ b. $\dfrac{x^3y^{-4}}{x^7y^{-2}}$

9. Express in scientific notation.
   a. $36\ 000$ b. 18 c. $0.000\ 05$
   d. 360×10^{-8} e. 0.046×10^3 f. 0.393×10^{21}

10. Expresss in decimal notation.
    a. 3.7×10^{-3} b. 8.6×10^6 c. 4.3×10^{-1}
    d. 0.086×10^{-2} e. 439×10^2 f. $0.000\ 09 \times 10^{-3}$

11. Calculate and leave the answer in scientific notation.
    a. $600\ 000 \times 0.02$ b. $0.08 \div 0.0004$ c. $18\ 000 \times 250$
    d. $39\ 000\ 000 \div 0.0026$ e. $\dfrac{(0.003)^2}{150 \times 0.005}$ f. $\dfrac{0.036 \times 2400}{400^2}$

Applying Formulas

Use your algebraic skills to substitute into the given formula to solve each problem.

A 1. The total surface area of the walls of a room is $2h(l + w)$ where h is height, l is length of the floor, and w is width of the floor, all in metres. The cost of paint is $21.49 for a 4 L can or $5.99 for a 1 L can. One litre of paint covers about 40 m².
   a. How many litres of paint will it take to paint a room 4.5 m wide, 8.35 m long, and 2.6 m high?
   b. How much will it cost to paint the room?

2. The volume of a pyramid is given by the formula $V = \frac{1}{3}Bh$, where B is the area of the base. The formula for the area of a square is $A = s^2$. What is the volume of brass in a model of an Egyptian pyramid with a height of 12 cm and a square base with side length 15 cm?

B 3. The speed of an accelerating object is $v = at + v_0$, where a is acceleration, t is time, and v_0 is initial speed. A car travelling at an initial speed of 15 m/s pulls out to pass another car, accelerating at a rate of 2.5 m/s² for 3.5 s. What is the speed of the passing car after accelerating?

4. The distance travelled by an accelerating object is given by the formula $d = \frac{1}{2}at^2 + v_0t$. How far did the car in exercise 3 travel in 3.5 s?

5. The time a pendulum takes to swing across and back is its *period*. The period of a pendulum depends upon its length. The period (t seconds) and length (l metres) of a pendulum are related by the formula $l = \dfrac{t^2g}{4\pi^2}$. The variable g is a constant of gravity with a value of 9.8; the value of π is approximately 3.14. Find the length of the pendulum with these given periods.
   a. 1 s   **b.** 2 s   **c.** 5 s

C 6. When buying an item on an instalment plan, a customer pays more than its cash price. The additional amount, the *finance charge*, may not seem very high, but the interest rate may be much higher than current bank rates. Since the principal changes with each payment, calculating the interest rate using the simple interest formula is quite complicated. The *true interest rate* per year, r, on an instalment plan is given by the formula $r = [200NC \div P(n + 1)]\%$. N is the number of payment intervals per year; C is the finance charge; P is the principal (cash price less down payment); n is the total number of payments. Find the true interest rate for a sewing machine, cash price $329.78 (with tax), which can be bought for $80 down and $23/month for 12 months.

Using Scientific Notation

Calculate the solution in scientific notation. Then state your answer to the appropriate number of significant digits.

A 1. The sun is 150 000 000 km from Earth. Light travels at 300 000 km/s. How long does it take for light to travel from the sun to Earth?

B 2. A light year is the distance light travels in one year. If the speed of light is 3.00×10^5 km/s, calculate the length of one light year, given that there are 3.15×10^7 s in one year.

3. Alpha Centauri is the star nearest Earth. It is 4.3 light years away. How many kilometres is this?

4. Betelgeuse, one of the brightest stars in the sky, is a part of the constellation Orion. Betelgeuse is 520 light years from Earth. How many kilometres away is Betelgeuse?

5. The distance to the nearest galaxy is 1.5×10^{18} km. How many light years is this?

6. Canada's population is approximately 25 million. The total land area is 6.2×10^6 km². What is the average population density in people per square kilometre?

7. a. Earth's orbit is roughly circular. What is the approximate total distance travelled by Earth in one year? (The formula for the circumference of a circle is $2\pi r$, where $\pi \doteq 3.14$. Use data from question 1.)

   b. If there are roughly 9000 h in one year, what is the orbital speed of Earth? Use the formula for speed, $s = \dfrac{d}{t}$.

8. a. The radius of Earth is 6.4×10^6 m. What is the approximate volume of Earth? $\left(\text{The formula for the volume of a sphere is } V = \dfrac{4}{3}\pi r^3.\right)$

   b. The density of Earth is estimated to be 5500 kg/m³. That is, each cubic metre has a mass of 5.5 t. What is the mass of Earth?

   c. The density of styrofoam is 70 kg/m³. What would be the mass of an earth made out of styrofoam?

C 9. If your heart beats an average of 70 times per minute, how many times will it beat in one year? (Express your answer in scientific notation.)

10. A tap drips once every 5 s. Each drop of water contains 3×10^{22} molecules. How many molecules of water drip from the tap in one hour?

11. If a factory is producing 1500 pens every hour, operating around the clock (including weekends), then how many pens are produced in one year, given a 3-week shutdown during August?

Using the Calculator

Depending on your calculator you may have many ways of evaluating a power.

If your calculator only adds, subtracts, multiplies, and divides, then use the following keystrokes to evaluate 12^6.

| 1 | 2 | × | 1 | 2 | × | 1 | 2 | × | 1 | 2 | × | 1 | 2 | × | 1 | 2 | = |

There are only five multiplications.
12 is used as a factor six times.

| 2985984 |

If your calculator has a constant multiply key, sometimes marked | k | or sometimes done automatically, use the following keystrokes to evaluate 12^6.

| 1 | 2 | × | 1 | 2 | k | = | = | = | = | = |

| 2985984 |

There are five | = | used, not six.

Powers may also be evaluated using memory to reduce the number of keystrokes. Use the following keystrokes on a calculator with memory to evaluate $(1.25)^6$.

| 1 | . | 2 | 5 | M+ | × | MR | × | MR | × | MR | × | MR | × | MR | = |

The easiest way to evaluate powers on a calculator is to use the | x^y | key if you have one. The following keystrokes can be used to evaluate $(1.25)^6$.

| 3.8146973 |

| 1 | . | 2 | 5 | x^y | 6 | = |

| 3.8147 |

---

1. With the x^y key, you can enter exponents that are not integers. If you have a calculator with this key, determine the meaning of an exponent of $\frac{1}{2}$ by evaluating the following powers.

   a. $16^{\frac{1}{2}}$ b. $4^{\frac{1}{2}}$ c. $9^{\frac{1}{2}}$

   d. $10^{\frac{1}{2}}$ e. $2^{\frac{1}{2}}$ f. $20^{\frac{1}{2}}$

   g. $25^{\frac{1}{2}}$ h. $30^{\frac{1}{2}}$ i. $36^{\frac{1}{2}}$

2. What meaning would you expect for an exponent of $\frac{1}{3}$? Test your expectation.

3. Use your calculator to see if it evaluates powers with negative exponents correctly.

Application

There is a formula for finding the amount of an investment earning compound interest.

$A = P(1 + r)^n$ n is the number of compounding periods;

r is the interest rate over each compounding period;

P is the original amount invested.

If $100 is deposited in an account where it earns interest at 9% per annum compounded once per year, what amount is in the account at the end of three years?

Apply the formula.

$A = \$100(1 + 0.09)^3$ $n = 3$ (compounded once per year
$= \$100(1.09)^3$ over 3 a)
$= \$100(1.295)$ $r = 0.09$ (9%/a)
$= \$129.50$ $P = \$100$

At the end of three years, there is $129.50 in the account.

If the same $100 deposit were earning interest at 9%/a compounded quarterly, or four times per year, what amount would be in the account at the end of three years? Again, apply the formula, adjusting the values of n and r.

$A = \$100(1 + 0.0225)^{12}$ $n = 3 \times 4 = 12$
$= \$100(1.306)$ $r = 0.09 \div 4 = 0.0225$
$= \$130.60$

With interest compounded quarterly, the investment amounts to $130.60.

Use a calculator for these problems.

1. Find the amount available at the end of five years if $100 is deposited at each of the following interest rates compounded annually.
   a. 5%   **b.** 8%   **c.** 10%   **d.** 12%

2. What are the amounts in exercise 1 if the interest is compounded semi-annually? quarterly? monthly?

3. How long would it take for $100 to double at each of the above rates compounded annually?

33

Historical Note

René Descartes was the outstanding French mathematician of the seventeenth century. Our modern method of writing variable terms with exponents is credited to Descartes. Before Descartes's time, many different notations were used.

The Italian mathematician, Rafael Bombelli, in the last half of the sixteenth century, introduced the notation shown at the right. The exponent is placed in a small circular arc above the coefficient of the variable term.

$$\overset{1}{\underset{3}{\smile}} \quad \overset{2}{\underset{3}{\smile}} \quad \overset{3}{\underset{3}{\smile}}$$

$$\boxed{3x} \quad \boxed{3x^2} \quad \boxed{3x^3}$$

In about 1590, the mathematician, François Viète, used the letters N, Q, and C to represent powers so that $3N$ meant $3x$, $3Q$ meant $3x^2$, and $3C$ stood for $3x^3$.

Jobst Bürgi was a Swiss mathematician who, in about 1619, used Roman numerals for exponents, as illustrated in the examples at the right.

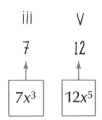

What shortcomings do you see with the notations of Bombelli, Viète, and Bürgi for writing variable terms with exponents?

EXTRA

By definition, a *paradox* is a seemingly contradictory statement that may be explained away with careful analysis. Below, a geometric paradox is shown. On the left is an 8-by-8 grid that has been divided into four regions. When these four parts are cut and rearranged to make the 5-by-13 rectangle on the right, the total area of the four regions appears to have increased by 1! Can you explain why?

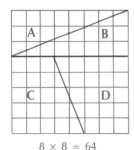

$8 \times 8 = 64$

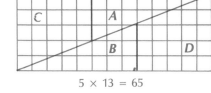

$5 \times 13 = 65$

Test

1. Evaluate each of the following for $a = 4$, $b = 6$, $c = -2$, and $d = 0.3$.
   a. $(a + b)c$
   b. $ad - bc$
   c. abc
   d. $ba + bd$
   e. $2ab + 7$
   f. $(a + 2b)(3b + 8)$

2. Convert each fraction to a decimal.
   a. $\frac{8}{100}$
   b. $-\frac{3}{75}$
   c. $\frac{7}{16}$
   d. $8\frac{7}{11}$
   e. $\frac{7}{15}$

3. Convert each decimal to a fraction.
   a. 3.68
   b. 0.055
   c. $0.\overline{38}$
   d. $0.3\overline{12}$
   e. $87.\overline{45}$

4. Give the additive inverse of each.
   a. 8
   b. $1.3x$
   c. $-\frac{1}{2}y$
   d. $4b - 5d$

5. Give the multiplicative inverse of each.
   a. $\frac{5}{7}$
   b. $-4\frac{2}{3}$
   c. x
   d. 1.5
   e. $\frac{3x}{2y}$

6. Use the laws of exponents to simplify each expression.
   a. x^5x^8
   b. $(3x)(x^2)(2x^3)$
   c. $(5a^3b)(6a)(-3b)$
   d. $(3x^{-5})(2x^4)$
   e. $27x^4 \div 3x$
   f. $(3a)^4 \div (3a)^7$

   g. $\left(\dfrac{x^2}{y}\right)\left(\dfrac{3x}{2y}\right)$
   h. $\dfrac{9x^4y^{10}z}{6x^7y^6z^4}$
   i. $\dfrac{(-3a^3bc^2)^3}{-3a^5b}$

   j. $-18a^{-7} \div -6a^{-4}$
   k. $(3y^2)^3$
   l. $(xy^3)^2(-2x^2y)^3(x^2)^4$

7. Express in scientific notation.
   a. 3
   b. 0.0068
   c. 423×10^4
   d. $0.000\ 81 \times 10^{-5}$

8. Express in decimal notation.
   a. 4.5×10^3
   b. 5.07×10^{-4}
   c. 6.40×10^{-8}
   d. 395.2×10^2

9. Simplify the calculation of each by using scientific notation.
   a. 7500×1200
   b. $30\ 666\ 000 \div 24\ 000$
   c. $\dfrac{0.18 \times 0.000\ 58}{0.0015}$
   d. $\dfrac{(12\ 000\ 000)^2}{25\ 000 \times 0.45}$

10. A rocket to the planet Mars travels 72 400 000 km at a speed of 40 000 km/h. How long would the trip take? Calculate the solution in scientific notation. Then state your answer to the appropriate number of significant digits.

Roots, Radicals, and Real Numbers

2–1 Square Roots

According to the label, a 4 L can of indoor paint will cover 36 m². What are the dimensions of the largest square that can be covered by the whole can of paint?

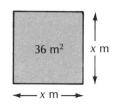

$$x^2 = 36$$
$$x = \sqrt{36}$$
$$x = 6$$

36 is a **perfect square** since its square root is an integer, 6. Other perfect squares are 1, 4, 9, 16, 25, and so on.

The largest square that can be covered by the can of paint is 6 m by 6 m.

The *inverse* of squaring a number is finding its **square root**.

The symbol $\sqrt{}$ is called a **radical sign** and $\sqrt{36}$ is called a **radical**. The expression below the radical sign, in this case 36, is called the **radicand**.

Every positive number has two square roots, one positive and the other negative, but the radical sign indicates the **principal**, or positive, square root of a number.

$$\sqrt{36} = 6 \qquad\qquad -\sqrt{36} = -6$$

Note: Negative numbers do not have square roots, since the square of any number is either a positive number or zero. $\sqrt{-36}$ is undefined.

$$\sqrt{6^2} = \sqrt{36} = 6 \qquad \sqrt{(-6)^2} = \sqrt{36} = 6$$

In general: $\sqrt{x^2} = |x|$

The radical sign is treated as a grouping symbol when evaluating expressions.

EXAMPLES: Evaluate.

$$\text{a.} \quad 3\sqrt{25} = 3(5)$$
$$= 15$$

$$\text{b.} \quad \sqrt{67 - 18} + 85 - 13 = \sqrt{49} + 85 - 13$$
$$= 7 + 85 - 13$$
$$= 79$$

$$\text{c.} \quad \sqrt{67 - 18 + 85 - 13} = \sqrt{121}$$
$$= 11$$

EXERCISES

A **1.** Which of the following are perfect squares?

a. 49	**b.** 15	**c.** 28	**d.** 100	**e.** 75
f. 34	**g.** 169	**h.** 40	**i.** 86	**j.** -400

2. Evaluate.

a. $\sqrt{16}$	**b.** $-\sqrt{25}$	**c.** $\sqrt{144}$	**d.** $\sqrt{36}$
e. $-\sqrt{81}$	**f.** $\sqrt{100}$	**g.** $\sqrt{121}$	**h.** $-\sqrt{1}$
i. $\sqrt{169}$	**j.** $\sqrt{9}$	**k.** $-\sqrt{64}$	**l.** $-\sqrt{196}$
m. $-\sqrt{49}$	**n.** $\sqrt{225}$	**o.** $-\sqrt{400}$	**p.** $\sqrt{256}$

B **3.** Evaluate each expression.

a. $7\sqrt{4}$	**b.** $-3\sqrt{100}$	**c.** $8\sqrt{121}$	**d.** $-5\sqrt{49}$
e. $-\frac{1}{3}\sqrt{9}$	**f.** $0.2\sqrt{25}$	**g.** $-0.3\sqrt{81}$	**h.** $-0.05\sqrt{0.01}$
i. $\sqrt{150 - 29}$	**j.** $\sqrt{49} - \sqrt{36}$	**k.** $\sqrt{25 - 9}$	**l.** $\sqrt{121} - \sqrt{64}$

m. $\sqrt{85 - 36} + \sqrt{49}$ **n.** $\sqrt{36} - \sqrt{169} - \sqrt{25}$

o. $\sqrt{25} - \sqrt{289} + \sqrt{36}$ **p.** $\sqrt{43 + 18 - 12} - \sqrt{75 + 6}$

q. $\sqrt{2^3 + 1} - \sqrt{36 - 11}$ **r.** $\frac{1}{3}\sqrt{81} + 1.6\sqrt{15 + 10} + \frac{3}{7}\sqrt{196}$

4. A square desk top has an area of 1.44 m². Find its dimensions.

5. Pat is tiling a floor area 4.5 m by 1.5 m. Each square tile has an area of 225 cm². How many tiles will Pat need?

6. A five-storey building with a square foundation has a total usable floor area of 6480 m². The outer walls are 0.5 m thick. Find the outside dimensions of the foundation.

7. Evaluate each expression for $a = 3$, $b = 6$, $c = 8$, $d = 2$.

a. $\sqrt{abd}$	**b.** $\sqrt{ac + 1}$	**c.** $\sqrt{cd} - \sqrt{a^2}$
d. $\sqrt{3bc}$	**e.** $5\sqrt{3bd} - 0.5\sqrt{2c}$	**f.** $\sqrt{a^2b + c + d}$
g. $\sqrt{bc + 1} - \sqrt{ac + 1}$	**h.** $\sqrt{0.5ab} - \sqrt{0.5c}$	**i.** $\sqrt{4a + c + 3d - 1}$

8. The time it takes a stone dropped off a bridge to fall to the ground is given by $t = 0.45\sqrt{h}$ (if air resistance can be neglected), where h is the height measured in metres and t is in seconds. How long will it take a stone to fall to the ground if dropped off a bridge 9 m high?

9. The speed at which a stone falling from a given height hits the ground is $v = 4.43\sqrt{h}$, where h is measured in metres and v is measured in metres per second. Find the speed at which the stone in exercise 8 hits the ground.

C 10. If x is any positive number, then simplify.

　　a. $\sqrt{x^2}$　　　　　　b. $-\sqrt{x^2}$

11. If x is any negative number, then simplify.

　　a. $\sqrt{x^2}$　　　　　　b. $-\sqrt{x^2}$

12. For what values of x are the following undefined?

　　a. $\sqrt{x}$　　　b. $\sqrt{-x}$　　　c. $\sqrt{10 - x}$　　　d. $\sqrt{x - 10}$

EXTRA

Any rational number can be an exponent. For example, the side length of the square shown can be expressed in three ways. To understand the meaning of this, consider the following.

Area = 4 × 4
= 16
The side length is:
4 or $\sqrt{16}$ or $16^{\frac{1}{2}}$.

If the laws for exponents hold for rational numbers, then:

$$\left(16^{\frac{1}{2}}\right)^2 = 16^{\frac{1}{2}} \times 16^{\frac{1}{2}}$$
$$= 16^{\left(\frac{1}{2}+\frac{1}{2}\right)}$$
$$= 16^1$$
$$= 16$$

Since $16^{\frac{1}{2}}$ is a number whose square is 16, then:

$$16^{\frac{1}{2}} = \sqrt{16}$$
$$= 4$$

Therefore, $16^{\frac{1}{2}}$ can be evaluated in two ways with a calculator.

| 1 | 6 | x^y | . | 5 | = | 　　4　　 | 1 | 6 | $\sqrt{}$ | 　　4　　 |

Evaluate. Then use your calculator as a check.

1. $9^{\frac{1}{2}}$　　　　2. $64^{\frac{1}{2}}$　　　　3. $100^{\frac{1}{2}}$　　　　4. $225^{\frac{1}{2}}$

5. $\left(49^{\frac{1}{2}}\right)^2$　　　6. $196^{\frac{1}{2}}$　　　7. $289^{\frac{1}{2}}$　　　8. $\left(2500^{\frac{1}{2}}\right)^2$

38

Using the Computer

The square root of a number, say $\sqrt{180}$, can be *approximated* by the following method developed by Sir Isaac Newton.

1. Make a *guess* at the square root.

   Try a guess of 13.5 since 180 is between $13^2(169)$ and $14^2(196)$.

2. *Divide* the number by the guess.

   $$\frac{180}{13.5} \doteq 13.333\ 333$$

3. *Average* the quotient and the guess.

   $$\frac{13.333\ 333 + 13.5}{2} \doteq 13.416\ 666 \quad \text{a new guess}$$

4. *Repeat* steps 2 and 3 until you reach the degree of accuracy you want.

   $$\frac{180}{13.416\ 666} \doteq 13.416\ 149$$

   $$\frac{13.416\ 666 + 13.416\ 149}{2} \doteq 13.416\ 408 \quad \text{an improved guess}$$

Newton's method is a step-by-step procedure for computing approximate values of square roots. Such a procedure is an **algorithm**. If a computer is to make a calculation, an algorithm to perform the calculation must be designed first. Then a program is written to follow the steps of the algorithm. The program below follows Newton's method to approximate $\sqrt{180}$, correct to three decimal places.

```
10  REM      THIS PROGRAM APPROXIMATES A SQUARE ROOT.
20  READ NUM: REM  READ IN NUMBER WHOSE ROOT IS TO BE APPROXIMATED
30  PRINT "THE ORIGINAL NUMBER IS ";NUM
40  INPUT "MAKE A GUESS AT THE SQUARE ROOT ";GUESS
50  TEMP = ABS (NUM / GUESS)
60  APPROX = (GUESS + TEMP) / 2: REM  CALCULATE A NEW GUESS
70  IF  ABS (GUESS - APPROX) < .001 THEN 100
80  GUESS = APPROX
90  GOTO 50: REM   REPEAT UNTIL ACCURATE TO THREE DECIMAL PLACES
100  PRINT "THE SQUARE ROOT OF ";NUM;" IS ";APPROX
110  END
120  DATA  180
```

1. Run the program. Compare the output to the answer derived above.

2. What line must change to estimate the square root of a number other than 180?

3. Modify and run the program to estimate the square roots of the following.
   a. 2   **b.** 20   **c.** 45   **d.** 73   **e.** 108   **f.** 125   **g.** 200   **h.** 500

2–2 Irrational Numbers

A **rational number** is any number that can be written in the form $\frac{m}{n}$, where m and n are integers and $n \neq 0$. If $\frac{m}{n}$ is rewritten as a decimal, it will either terminate or repeat. Some numbers, however, cannot be written in the form $\frac{m}{n}$ where m and n are integers and $n \neq 0$. They have decimal expansions that *neither* terminate *nor* repeat. They are **irrational numbers**.

Rational Numbers	Irrational Numbers
$\frac{4}{5}$ or 0.8	0.122 333 444 455 555 . . .
$\frac{1}{3}$ or $0.\overline{3}$	0.123 456 789 101 112 . . .
4.876 $\overline{326}$	1.121 231 234 123 451 . . .

If a whole number is not a perfect square, then its square root is an irrational number.

$$\sqrt{2} \doteq 1.414\,213\,562 \ldots \quad \text{irrational number}$$
$$\sqrt{4} = 2 \quad \text{rational number}$$

Between any two numbers, you can find both rational and irrational numbers.

EXAMPLE: Find a rational and an irrational number between 3.5 and 3.6.

- A rational number between 3.5 and 3.6 is 3.56.

- An irrational number between 3.5 and 3.6 is 3.512 112 111 211 . . .
  It was found by constructing a non-repeating pattern of numbers.

EXERCISES

A **1.** State whether the number is rational or irrational.

   a. 0.888 888 . . .   **b.** 0.181 181 118 111 18 . . .

   c. $\frac{4}{5}$ **d.** $\frac{28}{11}$

   e. 22.333 444 455 555 . . .   **f.** $-6.423\,751\,423\,751 \ldots$

   g. -13.5 **h.** 1.223 334 444 555 556 . . .

   i. $\dfrac{\sqrt{25}}{\sqrt{36}}$ **j.** $\dfrac{\sqrt{15}}{\sqrt{16}}$

 2. Is the number rational or irrational?

   a. $\sqrt{35}$ **b.** $\sqrt{49}$ **c.** $\sqrt{105}$ **d.** $\sqrt{121}$ **e.** $\sqrt{100}$

   f. $\sqrt{99}$ **g.** $\sqrt{50}$ **h.** $\sqrt{169}$ **i.** $\sqrt{200}$ **j.** $\sqrt{900}$

B **3.** Give the value of any rational square root among the given radicals.

    a. $\sqrt{0.25}$ **b.** $\sqrt{0.1}$ **c.** $\sqrt{0.8}$ **d.** $\sqrt{0.36}$ **e.** $\sqrt{0.81}$

    f. $\sqrt{0.75}$ **g.** $\sqrt{1.5}$ **h.** $\sqrt{1.44}$ **i.** $\sqrt{0.09}$ **j.** $\sqrt{0.05}$

4. Between each pair of numbers, find a number for each given type.

    Type i: a rational number with a terminating decimal expansion
    Type ii: a rational number with a repeating decimal expansion
    Type iii: an irrational number

    a. 0.6, 0.8   **b.** 8.3, 8.4   **c.** $-5.4, -5.7$

    d. 11.4, 11.45   **e.** 0.038, 0.0385 **f.** $-9.428, -9.4277$

5. For each expression, find the value of each square root to three decimal places. Then evaluate the expression to the nearest hundredth. A calculator may be used.

    a. $\sqrt{2} + \sqrt{5}$ **b.** $3\sqrt{6}$ **c.** $5\sqrt{2} + 2\sqrt{3}$

    d. $4\sqrt{10} - 3\sqrt{2}$ **e.** $7\sqrt{6} + 5\sqrt{2}$ **f.** $2\sqrt{5} - 4\sqrt{3}$

    g. $\sqrt{5} + \sqrt{2} - \sqrt{3}$ **h.** $\sqrt{6} - \sqrt{5} + \sqrt{4}$ **i.** $3\sqrt{5} - 2\sqrt{2} + 2\sqrt{3}$

C **6.** Use a calculator to evaluate each expression for $x = \sqrt{5}$. Round to the nearest hundredth if needed.

    a. $x^2 + 3x + 1$ **b.** $2x^2 - x + 4$ **c.** $3x^2 - 2x + 1$

    d. $x^4 + x^2 - 3$ **e.** $2x^4 - x^3 + 3x^2 - 2x + 1$

7. Enter any number into a calculator with a $\boxed{\sqrt{\ }}$ key and push the $\boxed{\sqrt{\ }}$ key repeatedly. What number is eventually reached? Does this always happen? Explain.

EXTRA

An irrational number of special interest is the **Golden Ratio**. A rectangle whose length and width fit the Golden Ratio is said to be the most artistically pleasing and is called a Golden Rectangle.

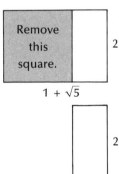

If a square is removed from a Golden Rectangle, like the one at the right, the resulting rectangle is also a Golden Rectangle. The ratio of the length to the width of any Golden Rectangle is $\dfrac{1 + \sqrt{5}}{2}$.

1. Find a decimal approximation of $\dfrac{1 + \sqrt{5}}{2}$ to the nearest thousandth.

2. Use a calculator to show that: $\dfrac{1 + \sqrt{5}}{2} = \dfrac{2}{\sqrt{5} - 1}$

3. Show that a rectangle with dimensions in the ratio 8 : 5 approximates the Golden Rectangle.

2–3 Product Property and Quotient Property

Compare the following calculations illustrating the square root properties.

$$\sqrt{25 \times 4} = \sqrt{100} \qquad\qquad \sqrt{25} \times \sqrt{4} = 5 \times 2$$
$$= 10 \qquad\qquad\qquad\qquad = 10$$

Product Property: For $a \geq 0$, $b \geq 0$: $\sqrt{a}\sqrt{b} = \sqrt{ab}$

$$\sqrt{\frac{100}{4}} = \sqrt{25} \qquad\qquad \frac{\sqrt{100}}{\sqrt{4}} = \frac{10}{2}$$
$$= 5 \qquad\qquad\qquad\qquad = 5$$

Quotient Property: For $a \geq 0$, $b > 0$: $\sqrt{\dfrac{a}{b}} = \dfrac{\sqrt{a}}{\sqrt{b}}$

The square root properties can be used to simplify expressions before evaluating them.

EXAMPLES: Simplify each expression.

a. $\dfrac{\sqrt{28}}{\sqrt{7}} = \sqrt{\dfrac{28}{7}}$ Quotient Property

$\qquad\qquad = \sqrt{4}$ The radicand is a perfect square.

$\qquad\qquad = 2$ The result is an integer.

b. $\sqrt{72}\sqrt{48} = \sqrt{36}\sqrt{2} \times \sqrt{16}\sqrt{3}$ Look for perfect squares: 36 and 16.

$\qquad\qquad = 6\sqrt{2} \times 4\sqrt{3}$

$\qquad\qquad = 24\sqrt{6}$ The result is an irrational number.

EXERCISES

A   **1.**   Apply the product property to simplify.

    a. $\sqrt{8}\sqrt{2}$ b. $(-\sqrt{6})(\sqrt{5})$ c. $\sqrt{12}\sqrt{3}$

    d. $(\sqrt{7})(-\sqrt{6})(\sqrt{2})$ e. $(-\sqrt{10}) \times \sqrt{2} \times (-\sqrt{5})$ f. $(-\sqrt{11})(-\sqrt{3})(-\sqrt{10})$

  2.   Apply the quotient property to simplify.

    a. $\dfrac{\sqrt{24}}{\sqrt{6}}$ b. $\dfrac{-\sqrt{72}}{\sqrt{8}}$ c. $\dfrac{\sqrt{75}}{\sqrt{5}}$ d. $\dfrac{-\sqrt{50}}{-\sqrt{5}}$ e. $\dfrac{\sqrt{60}}{-\sqrt{15}}$ f. $\dfrac{\sqrt{98}}{-\sqrt{2}}$

B   **3.**   Write as the product of two radicals, one of which has a perfect square under the radical sign.

    a. $\sqrt{12}$ b. $\sqrt{50}$ c. $\sqrt{99}$ d. $\sqrt{40}$ e. $\sqrt{90}$

    f. $\sqrt{300}$ g. $\sqrt{600}$ h. $\sqrt{160}$ i. $\sqrt{96}$ j. $\sqrt{176}$

4. Simplify.

a. $3\sqrt{5}\sqrt{3}$ b. $2\sqrt{7} \times 4\sqrt{3}$ c. $-7\sqrt{6} \times 9\sqrt{2}$

d. $2\sqrt{10} \times 4\sqrt{5}$ e. $(-4\sqrt{2})(-5\sqrt{50})$ f. $(12\sqrt{5})(-10\sqrt{7})$

g. $7\sqrt{12}\ 9\sqrt{11}$ h. $(11\sqrt{2})(-2\sqrt{12})$ i. $\dfrac{50\sqrt{55}}{10\sqrt{11}}$

j. $\dfrac{30\sqrt{18}}{3\sqrt{2}}$ k. $\dfrac{50\sqrt{12}}{-10\sqrt{3}}$ l. $\dfrac{40\sqrt{30}}{8\sqrt{6}}$

m. $(3\sqrt{2})(-2\sqrt{5})(\sqrt{7})$ n. $(\sqrt{8})(-5\sqrt{6})(-3\sqrt{3})$ o. $(\sqrt{11})(-3\sqrt{2})(5\sqrt{50})$

p. $\dfrac{-20\sqrt{20}}{-4\sqrt{5}}$ q. $\dfrac{-15\sqrt{32}}{3\sqrt{2}}$ r. $\dfrac{6\sqrt{12}}{6\sqrt{3}}$

C 5. Evaluate to two decimal places.

a. $\dfrac{\sqrt{12}}{\sqrt{15}} \times \dfrac{\sqrt{10}}{\sqrt{2}}$ b. $\dfrac{-\sqrt{18}}{\sqrt{6}} \times \dfrac{-\sqrt{5}}{\sqrt{3}}$ c. $\dfrac{3\sqrt{8}}{2\sqrt{5}} \times \dfrac{\sqrt{10}}{\sqrt{2}}$

d. $0.6\sqrt{2} \times 1.5\sqrt{3}$ e. $6\sqrt{0.5} \times 2.5\sqrt{8}$

f. $0.8\sqrt{2.5} \times 3\sqrt{20} \times 1.5\sqrt{0.5}$ g. $1.2\sqrt{3.5} \times 2.5\sqrt{0.2} \times 0.1\sqrt{0.2}$

6. Evaluate each expression for $r = 10$, $s = 2$, $t = 15$.

a. $\sqrt{rs}\sqrt{t}$ b. $\sqrt{5rs}$ c. $\dfrac{\sqrt{2s}}{\sqrt{5t}}$ d. $\dfrac{\sqrt{rs}\sqrt{rt}}{\sqrt{15r}\sqrt{6}}$

EXTRA

You can apply the product property of square roots to *estimate* the square roots of very large or very small numbers.

$$\begin{aligned}\sqrt{150\ 000\ 000} &= \sqrt{1.5 \times 10^8}\\ &= \sqrt{1.5} \times \sqrt{10^8} \qquad \sqrt{10^8} = 10^4 \text{ since } 10^8 = (10^4)^2\\ &\doteq 1.2 \times 10^4 \qquad\qquad \text{two significant digits}\\ &= 12\ 000\end{aligned}$$

$$\begin{aligned}\sqrt{0.003\ 28} &= \sqrt{3.28 \times 10^{-3}} \qquad \text{Adjust to an}\\ &= \sqrt{32.8 \times 10^{-4}} \qquad \text{even power.}\\ &= \sqrt{32.8} \times \sqrt{10^{-4}}\\ &\doteq 5.7 \times 10^{-2} \qquad\qquad \text{two significant digits}\\ &= 0.057\end{aligned}$$

Estimate the following to two significant digits.

1. $\sqrt{360\ 000}$ **2.** $\sqrt{0.000\ 049}$ **3.** $\sqrt{640\ 000\ 000\ 000}$

4. $\sqrt{0.000\ 000\ 562\ 3}$ **5.** $\sqrt{438\ 241}$ **6.** $\sqrt{37\ 562\ 408}$

2–4 The Set of Real Numbers

So far, you have worked with the following sets of numbers.

Set	Members
Natural numbers, N	$\{1, 2, 3, \ldots\}$
Whole numbers, W	$\{0, 1, 2, \ldots\}$
Integers, Z	$\{0, \pm 1, \pm 2, \ldots\}$
Rational numbers, Q	numbers such as $\frac{6}{5}$ and $-\frac{4}{1}$ that result when an integer is divided by a non-zero integer
Irrational numbers, $\overline{Q}$	numbers such as $\sqrt{2}$ with decimal expansions that neither terminate nor repeat
Real numbers, R	all rational and irrational numbers

The set of real numbers is included in the table above since you have already worked in both the set of rational and the set of irrational numbers.

The various sets of numbers can be represented in a Venn diagram like the one at the right.

Since no number can be both rational and irrational, Q and $\overline{Q}$ have no members in common: they are **disjoint sets.**

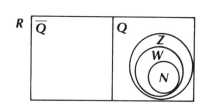

EXERCISES

A 1. Copy and complete the classification of each number.

		R	$\overline{Q}$	Q	Z	W	N
a.	6	Yes	No	Yes	Yes	Yes	Yes
b.	$\sqrt{5}$						
c.	$\frac{7}{8}$						
d.	$\sqrt{100}$						
e.	$3\frac{1}{5}$						
f.	-7.6						

g.	0	**h.**	$\sqrt{48}$	**i.**	$8.323\ 2\overline{32}$
j.	$0.312\ 131\ 4\ldots$	**k.**	4.8764	**l.**	$4.831\ 579\ 2\ldots$
m.	$\dfrac{\sqrt{5}}{2}$	**n.**	-1	**o.**	-12
p.	-4.6	**q.**	$-\sqrt{2}$	**r.**	$-0.\overline{12}$

44

B 2. True or false?
   a. All integers are rational numbers.
   b. Zero is a positive integer.
   c. All real numbers are integers.
   d. All rational numbers are real numbers.
   e. Some negative numbers are irrational numbers.
   f. No number is both rational and irrational.
   g. Any real number must be either a rational or an irrational number.
   h. All irrational numbers have decimal expansions with a pattern.
   i. All decimals which terminate are rational numbers.
   j. Zero is neither a rational nor an irrational number.

3. Can a calculator display an irrational number exactly? Why or why not?

4. The square roots of most integers are not rational numbers. Does this mean that they are not real numbers? Explain.

5. Which integer is neither positive nor negative?

Review

1. Evaluate to two decimal places.
   a. $\sqrt{20}$ b. $\sqrt{75}$ c. $\sqrt{53}$ d. $\sqrt{900}$ e. $\sqrt{68}$

2. Simplify.
   a. $\sqrt{36} + \sqrt{100}$ b. $\sqrt{153 - 32}$ c. $7\sqrt{16}$
   d. $-3\sqrt{25}$ e. $5\sqrt{49} - 2\sqrt{64}$ f. $5\sqrt{40} - 4$
   g. $0.8\sqrt{25}$ h. $1.5\sqrt{16} - \sqrt{81}$ i. $3\sqrt{15 + 10} - 2\sqrt{18 - 2}$

3. Evaluate each expression for $x = 2$, $y = 10$, $z = 5$.
   a. $\sqrt{xyz}$ b. $\sqrt{2y + z}$ c. $\sqrt{4y + z + 2x}$
   d. $\sqrt{x^2 z^2}$ e. $\sqrt{x^2 y - x^2}$ f. $\sqrt{xy + yz}$

4. Is the number rational or irrational?
   a. $0.314\ 311\ 431\ 114\ 311\ 114\ldots$ b. $-2.421\ 212\ 1\ldots$ c. $\sqrt{80}$
   d. 0 e. -5 f. π

5. Evaluate to one decimal place if needed.
   a. $\sqrt{0.36}$ b. $\sqrt{2.25}$ c. $3\sqrt{2} - \sqrt{5}$
   d. $2\sqrt{5} + \sqrt{3}$ e. $2\sqrt{2} - \sqrt{3} + 3\sqrt{5}$ f. $3(\sqrt{3} - \sqrt{2})$

6. Simplify.
   a. $\sqrt{7} \times \sqrt{5}$ b. $\dfrac{\sqrt{18}}{\sqrt{6}}$ c. $\dfrac{-12\sqrt{20}}{3\sqrt{2}}$
   d. $-4\sqrt{8} \times -3\sqrt{3}$ e. $2\sqrt{6} \times -3\sqrt{10} \times \sqrt{5}$ f. $\dfrac{-38\sqrt{46}}{-2\sqrt{2}}$
   g. $\dfrac{-7\sqrt{7} \times 4\sqrt{15}}{14\sqrt{5}}$ h. $\dfrac{4\sqrt{12}}{\sqrt{3} \times 2\sqrt{2}}$ i. $\dfrac{-\sqrt{32} \times -9\sqrt{5}}{3\sqrt{8} \times 3\sqrt{10}}$

2–5 Simplifying Radicals

The square root properties can be applied to write a radical in simplest form — the form in which the radicand contains no perfect-square factors.

EXAMPLE 1: Express each radical in simplest form. Assume all variables to be positive.

  a. $\sqrt{50} = \sqrt{25}\sqrt{2}$
          $= 5\sqrt{2}$

  b. $\sqrt{9b^4} = \sqrt{9}\sqrt{b^4}$
          $= 3b^2$

  c. $\sqrt{18a^5bc^6} = \sqrt{9a^4c^6}\,\sqrt{2ab}$
            $= 3a^2c^3\,\sqrt{2ab}$

$\sqrt{50}$, $\sqrt{9b^4}$, and $\sqrt{18a^5bc^6}$ are called **entire radicals** since they contain no coefficients outside the radical sign.

Any radical can be expressed as an entire radical.

EXAMPLE 2: Express each as an entire radical. Assume all variables to be positive.

  a. $3\sqrt{5} = \sqrt{9}\sqrt{5}$
          $= \sqrt{45}$

  b. $a^2\sqrt{ab} = \sqrt{a^4}\sqrt{ab}$
            $= \sqrt{a^5b}$

  c. $2x^2y\sqrt{3yz} = \sqrt{4x^4y^2}\,\sqrt{3yz}$
              $= \sqrt{12x^4y^3z}$

EXERCISES

All variables are assumed to be positive.

A **1.** Square the following.

  a. 5
  b. 7
  c. x
  d. z
  e. x^3
  f. y^5
  g. a^2
  h. $3b$
  i. $2b^5$
  j. $3ac$
  k. $10b^2$
  l. m^2n
  m. a^3bc^2
  n. $2xy^2$
  o. $5m^3n^2$
  p. ab^3c
  q. $4s^3t^5u$
  r. $11mn^2$
  s. $7u^3vw$
  t. $6r^2s^2t$

  2. Simplify.

  a. $\sqrt{81}$
  b. $\sqrt{121}$
  c. $\sqrt{a^2}$
  d. $\sqrt{x^2}$
  e. $\sqrt{m^4}$
  f. $\sqrt{p^6}$
  g. $\sqrt{4b^2}$
  h. $\sqrt{9m^8}$
  i. $\sqrt{100r^6}$
  j. $\sqrt{36m^{10}}$
  k. $\sqrt{a^4b^6}$
  l. $\sqrt{x^8y^2}$
  m. $\sqrt{m^2n^{10}p^{12}}$
  n. $\sqrt{16x^2y^2}$
  o. $\sqrt{25a^6b^2}$
  p. $\sqrt{144s^4t^2}$
  q. $\sqrt{49x^8y^6}$
  r. $\sqrt{81m^{10}n^8p^4}$
  s. $\sqrt{121u^2v^2w^2}$
  t. $\sqrt{225r^8u^{10}}$

  3. Express each as an entire radical.

  a. $3\sqrt{2}$
  b. $2\sqrt{5}$
  c. $2\sqrt{3}$
  d. $5\sqrt{6}$
  e. $4\sqrt{10}$
  f. $6\sqrt{5}$
  g. $10\sqrt{3}$
  h. $3\sqrt{10}$
  i. $3\sqrt{7}$
  j. $5\sqrt{11}$
  k. $4\sqrt{3}$
  l. $3\sqrt{11}$
  m. $6\sqrt{6}$
  n. $5\sqrt{5}$
  o. $7\sqrt{2}$

  4. Express in simplest form.

  a. $\sqrt{40}$
  b. $\sqrt{75}$
  c. $\sqrt{80}$
  d. $\sqrt{50}$
  e. $\sqrt{72}$
  f. $\sqrt{12}$
  g. $\sqrt{45}$
  h. $\sqrt{90}$
  i. $\sqrt{99}$
  j. $\sqrt{176}$

B **5.** Express each as an entire radical.

    a. $3\sqrt{x}$ **b.** $2\sqrt{y}$ **c.** $x\sqrt{5}$ **d.** $3\sqrt{5x}$

    e. $x\sqrt{y}$ **f.** $y^2\sqrt{y}$ **g.** $y^3\sqrt{x^2y}$ **h.** $3x\sqrt{xy}$

    i. $xy^2\sqrt{x}$ **j.** $x^2\sqrt{xy}$ **k.** $10mn^2\sqrt{3mnp}$ **l.** $5ab^2c^3\sqrt{2bc}$

6. Express in simplest form.

    a. $\sqrt{25x}$ **b.** $\sqrt{36y}$ **c.** $\sqrt{7y^2}$ **d.** $\sqrt{x^2y}$

    e. $\sqrt{11a^6}$ **f.** $\sqrt{m^6n^4p}$ **g.** $\sqrt{a^3b^5c^2}$ **h.** $\sqrt{18x^3y}$

    i. $\sqrt{75x^2y^6}$ **j.** $3x\sqrt{8x^3y}$ **k.** $2xy\sqrt{5y^2z}$ **l.** $10n\sqrt{9m^2n}$

    m. $xy\sqrt{18x^3y^5}$ **n.** $-5a\sqrt{12a^2b^3c^4}$ **o.** $7rt^2\sqrt{25rs^2t}$ **p.** $8x^2yz\sqrt{32xy^3z^2}$

7. Simplify.

    a. $\sqrt{6} \times \sqrt{8}$ **b.** $\sqrt{10} \times \sqrt{20}$ **c.** $3\sqrt{15} \times 2\sqrt{6}$

    d. $2\sqrt{5} \times 2\sqrt{20}$ **e.** $-2\sqrt{21} \times 4\sqrt{3}$ **f.** $3\sqrt{7} \times 5\sqrt{14}$

    g. $\sqrt{xy} \times \sqrt{x}$ **h.** $3\sqrt{mn^3} \times 5\sqrt{m^2n}$ **i.** $\sqrt{xy^2} \times \sqrt{x^2y} \times \sqrt{x^2y^3}$

C **8.** Express the volume of each right rectangular prism in simplest form.

a.

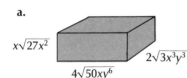

$x\sqrt{27x^2}$

$4\sqrt{50xy^6}$

b.

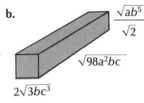

$\dfrac{\sqrt{ab^5}}{\sqrt{2}}$

$2\sqrt{3x^3y^3}$

$\sqrt{98a^2bc}$

$2\sqrt{3bc^3}$

c.

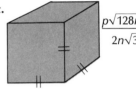

$\dfrac{p\sqrt{128m^5n^4}}{2n\sqrt{32p^3}}$

Using the Calculator

The length of one side of the cube at the right can be written as 4 or as the **cube root** of 64, $\sqrt[3]{64}$.

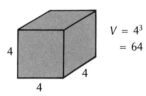

$V = 4^3$
$= 64$

$\sqrt[3]{64} = 4$ because $4^3 = 64$

The side length can also be expressed as $64^{\frac{1}{3}}$.

Since: $\left(64^{\frac{1}{3}}\right)^3 = 64^{\frac{1}{3}} \times 64^{\frac{1}{3}} \times 64^{\frac{1}{3}}$
$= 64^1$
$= 64$

Therefore: $64^{\frac{1}{3}} = \sqrt[3]{64}$
$= 4$

To evaluate $64^{\frac{1}{3}}$ or $\sqrt[3]{64}$ with a calculator, press:

Evaluate. You may use a calculator.

1. $\sqrt[3]{27}$ **2.** $8^{\frac{1}{3}}$ **3.** $343^{\frac{1}{3}}$ **4.** $\sqrt[3]{216}$

5. $1000^{\frac{1}{3}}$ **6.** $\sqrt[3]{125}$ **7.** $\sqrt[3]{512}$ **8.** $1331^{\frac{1}{3}}$

2–6 Rationalizing the Denominator

Simplifying an expression like $\dfrac{6}{\sqrt{2}}$ would require division by an irrational number. But it is usually preferable to divide by a whole number.

EXAMPLE 1: Rewrite $\dfrac{6}{\sqrt{2}}$ so that the denominator is not irrational.

$$\frac{6}{\sqrt{2}} = \frac{6}{\sqrt{2}} \times \boxed{\frac{\sqrt{2}}{\sqrt{2}}}$$

Multiply by $\dfrac{\sqrt{2}}{\sqrt{2}}$ (or 1) to make the denominator a whole number.

$$= \frac{6\sqrt{2}}{2}$$
$$= 3\sqrt{2}$$

The process of changing a denominator from an irrational number to a rational number, as done in example 1, is called **rationalizing** the denominator.

EXAMPLE 2: Rationalize the denominator and simplify if possible.

a. $\sqrt{\dfrac{5}{3}} = \dfrac{\sqrt{5}}{\sqrt{3}} \times \boxed{\dfrac{\sqrt{3}}{\sqrt{3}}}$

$= \dfrac{\sqrt{15}}{3}$

c. $\dfrac{6\sqrt{8}}{3\sqrt{50y}} = \dfrac{\overset{2}{\cancel{6}}\sqrt{\overset{1}{\cancel{4}}\cancel{2}}}{\cancel{3}\sqrt{\cancel{2}}\cancel{25}\sqrt{y}}$

$= \dfrac{\overset{1}{4}}{5\sqrt{y}} \times \boxed{\dfrac{\overset{1}{\sqrt{y}}}{\sqrt{y}}}$

$= \dfrac{4\sqrt{y}}{5y}$

b. $\dfrac{3\sqrt{10}}{8\sqrt{15}} = \dfrac{3\sqrt{\cancel{5}}^{1}\sqrt{2}}{8\sqrt{\cancel{5}}\sqrt{3}}$

$= \dfrac{3\sqrt{2}}{8\sqrt{3}} \times \boxed{\dfrac{\sqrt{3}}{\sqrt{3}}}$

$= \dfrac{\cancel{3}\sqrt{6}}{\cancel{24}_{8}}$

$= \dfrac{\sqrt{6}}{8}$

A radical expression is in simplest form when there are no square factors in any radicand, and there are no radicals in the denominator of any fraction.

EXERCISES

A **1.** Rationalize the denominator.

a. $\dfrac{1}{\sqrt{5}}$ b. $\dfrac{1}{\sqrt{2}}$ c. $\dfrac{3}{\sqrt{7}}$ d. $\dfrac{2}{\sqrt{5}}$ e. $\dfrac{1}{\sqrt{10}}$

f. $\dfrac{t}{\sqrt{3}}$ g. $\sqrt{\dfrac{8}{3m}}$ h. $\sqrt{\dfrac{a}{6}}$ i. $\dfrac{r}{\sqrt{5}}$ j. $\sqrt{\dfrac{3m}{n}}$

2. Rewrite in simplest form.

a. $\dfrac{2\sqrt{6}}{\sqrt{10}}$ b. $\dfrac{3\sqrt{7}}{\sqrt{14}}$ c. $\dfrac{\sqrt{13}}{2\sqrt{10}}$ d. $\dfrac{\sqrt{12}}{3\sqrt{8}}$ e. $\dfrac{5\sqrt{21}}{\sqrt{7}}$

f. $\dfrac{4\sqrt{5}}{\sqrt{35}}$ g. $\dfrac{\sqrt{16}}{3\sqrt{32}}$ h. $\dfrac{9\sqrt{45}}{\sqrt{15}}$ i. $\dfrac{3\sqrt{6}}{\sqrt{18}}$ j. $\dfrac{5\sqrt{7}}{\sqrt{50}}$

B 3. Rewrite in simplest form.

a. $\dfrac{3\sqrt{28}}{2\sqrt{63}}$ b. $\dfrac{10\sqrt{72}}{2\sqrt{45}}$ c. $\dfrac{8\sqrt{75}}{\sqrt{63}}$ d. $\dfrac{3\sqrt{48}}{5\sqrt{24}}$ e. $\dfrac{2\sqrt{32}}{3\sqrt{20}}$

f. $\dfrac{5\sqrt{50}}{7\sqrt{20}}$ g. $\dfrac{\sqrt{54}}{7\sqrt{8}}$ h. $\dfrac{3\sqrt{15}}{\sqrt{125}}$ i. $\dfrac{6\sqrt{32}}{5\sqrt{90}}$ j. $\dfrac{\sqrt{300}}{5\sqrt{21}}$

k. $\dfrac{6\sqrt{18}}{\sqrt{80}}$ l. $\dfrac{12\sqrt{48}}{3\sqrt{72}}$ m. $\dfrac{2\sqrt{63}}{3\sqrt{14}}$ n. $\dfrac{5\sqrt{90}}{9\sqrt{50}}$ o. $\dfrac{4\sqrt{45}}{3\sqrt{128}}$

4. Simplify. Assume all variables to be positive.

a. $\dfrac{3\sqrt{10x}}{\sqrt{5y}}$ b. $\dfrac{5\sqrt{3a}}{\sqrt{2b}}$ c. $\dfrac{3y\sqrt{x}}{\sqrt{y^3x}}$ d. $\dfrac{2a\sqrt{7b}}{\sqrt{bc^3}}$ e. $\dfrac{5\sqrt{8m}}{2\sqrt{n}}$

f. $\dfrac{6\sqrt{3x}}{15\sqrt{2y^2}}$ g. $\dfrac{\sqrt{27y}}{6\sqrt{x}}$ h. $\dfrac{3\sqrt{x}}{\sqrt{18y}}$ i. $\dfrac{3x}{5\sqrt{x}}$ j. $\dfrac{7y\sqrt{12}}{3\sqrt{27x}}$

C 5. Multiply and simplify.

a. $\dfrac{\sqrt{6}}{\sqrt{8}} \times \dfrac{\sqrt{3}}{\sqrt{5}}$ b. $\dfrac{\sqrt{12}}{\sqrt{8}} \times \dfrac{\sqrt{6}}{\sqrt{2}}$ c. $\dfrac{\sqrt{10}}{\sqrt{15}} \times \dfrac{\sqrt{6}}{\sqrt{7}}$

d. $\dfrac{\sqrt{35}}{\sqrt{7}} \times \dfrac{\sqrt{8}}{\sqrt{15}}$ e. $\dfrac{5\sqrt{2}}{\sqrt{18}} \times \dfrac{\sqrt{5}}{\sqrt{6}}$ f. $\dfrac{6\sqrt{5}}{2} \times \dfrac{-4\sqrt{10}}{\sqrt{15}}$

g. $\dfrac{\sqrt{27}}{\sqrt{10}} \times \dfrac{3\sqrt{5}}{\sqrt{8}} \times \dfrac{-\sqrt{2}}{4}$ h. $\dfrac{-3\sqrt{18}}{\sqrt{10}} \times \dfrac{\sqrt{12}}{5\sqrt{2}} \times \dfrac{-4\sqrt{7}}{\sqrt{6}}$

6. Evaluate each expression for $a = 2$, $b = 6$, $c = 8$.

a. $\dfrac{\sqrt{ab}}{\sqrt{c}}$ b. $\dfrac{7\sqrt{ab}}{8\sqrt{98}}$ c. $\dfrac{10\sqrt{bc}}{\sqrt{100c}}$

EXTRA

Number Trick

Think of a positive number.
Double it.
Increase the result by 1.
Add the square of your original number.
Take the square root of the result.
Subtract 1.
Your answer should be your original number. Can you explain why?

2–7 Combining Like Radicals

Radicals that have the same radicand are **like radicals**.

EXAMPLE 1: Select the like radicals in the set $\{5\sqrt{2}, \sqrt{x}, 3\sqrt{2}, 7\sqrt{3}, 3\sqrt{8}, 5\sqrt{x}, 3\sqrt{xy}\}$.

Like radicals: $\sqrt{x}$ and $5\sqrt{x}$ ← Both have x as the radicand.

$3\sqrt{2}$ and $5\sqrt{2}$ $3\sqrt{8}$ simplifies to $6\sqrt{2}$, also a like radical after simplification

$$3\sqrt{8} = 3\sqrt{4}\sqrt{2}$$
$$= 6\sqrt{2}$$

Like radicals can be combined in the same way as like terms.

EXAMPLE 2: Simplify.

$10\sqrt{7} + 3\sqrt{2} - \sqrt{2} - 4\sqrt{7}$

$= 10\sqrt{7} - 4\sqrt{7} + 3\sqrt{2} - \sqrt{2}$ Combine like radicals.
$= 6\sqrt{7} + 2\sqrt{2}$

EXAMPLE 3: Find an expression in simplest form to represent the perimeter of the trapezoid.

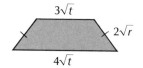

Perimeter $= 4\sqrt{t} + 3\sqrt{t} + 2\sqrt{r} + 2\sqrt{r}$ Combine like radicals.
$= 7\sqrt{t} + 4\sqrt{r}$

EXAMPLE 4: Simplify. Assume $x \geq 0$.

$2\sqrt{x^3y} - x\sqrt{16xy} + \sqrt{25x^3y}$

$= 2\sqrt{x^2}\sqrt{xy} - x\sqrt{4^2}\sqrt{xy} + \sqrt{5^2}\sqrt{x^2}\sqrt{xy}$
$= 2x\sqrt{xy} - 4x\sqrt{xy} + 5x\sqrt{xy}$ Combine like radicals.
$= 3x\sqrt{xy}$

EXERCISES

All variables are assumed to be positive.

A 1. Select pairs of like radicals.

a. $3\sqrt{6}, 6\sqrt{3}$ b. $2\sqrt{5}, -\sqrt{5}$ c. $7\sqrt{x}, -5\sqrt{x}$
d. $3\sqrt{y}, 3\sqrt{z}$ e. $2x\sqrt{xy}, 5y\sqrt{xy}$ f. $3\sqrt{mn}, -2\sqrt{mn}$
g. $\frac{5}{8}\sqrt{3y}, 0.8\sqrt{3y}$ h. $0.2\sqrt{mn^2}, 0.5\sqrt{m^2n}$ i. $2x\sqrt{y}, 2y\sqrt{x}$

2. Write three like radicals for each.

a. $5\sqrt{7}$ b. $3\sqrt{18}$ c. $4\sqrt{x}$ d. $8\sqrt{5x}$ e. $8k\sqrt{m^3n}$

B **3.** Simplify.

a. $7\sqrt{3} + 2\sqrt{3}$ **b.** $5\sqrt{8} - 3\sqrt{8}$ **c.** $2\sqrt{7} - 5\sqrt{7}$

d. $-6\sqrt{3} + 3\sqrt{3}$ **e.** $-5\sqrt{11} - 2\sqrt{11}$ **f.** $4\sqrt{y} - 7\sqrt{y}$

g. $\sqrt{x} - 3\sqrt{z} + 7\sqrt{x}$ **h.** $32\sqrt{6} + 3\sqrt{5} + 2\sqrt{5}$ **i.** $5\sqrt{x} + 3\sqrt{x} - 12\sqrt{x}$

j. $3\sqrt{b} - 2\sqrt{x} + 3\sqrt{x}$ **k.** $8\sqrt{r} - 3\sqrt{r} + 5\sqrt{tr}$ **l.** $3\sqrt{2} - \sqrt{4x} + 6\sqrt{x}$

4. Find an expression in simplest form to represent each perimeter.

a.

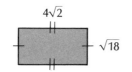

b.

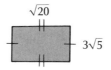

c.

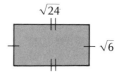

d.

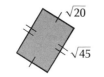

e.

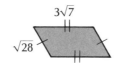

f.

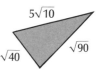

g.

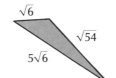

h.

i.

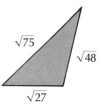

5. Simplify.

a. $3\sqrt{x} + \sqrt{16x}$ **b.** $\sqrt{25y} - 2\sqrt{y}$

c. $\sqrt{50m^2n} - \sqrt{18m^2n}$ **d.** $3\sqrt{ab^2} - 25\sqrt{4a}$

e. $\sqrt{200xy^2} + 5y\sqrt{16x}$ **f.** $3\sqrt{m^2n^3} - 2m\sqrt{n^3} + \sqrt{25m^2n^3}$

g. $7\sqrt{x^3y} - 3x\sqrt{xy} - 2\sqrt{4xy}$ **h.** $a\sqrt{12ab^2} + 25\sqrt{a^3} - \sqrt{75a^3b^2}$

6. Simplify.

a. $3\sqrt{2} - \sqrt{28} + 5\sqrt{7} + \sqrt{50}$ **b.** $\sqrt{20} - \sqrt{24} + \sqrt{54} + \sqrt{45}$

c. $2\sqrt{27} - \sqrt{75} + 3\sqrt{8} + \sqrt{18}$ **d.** $3\sqrt{5} + \sqrt{96} + \sqrt{80} - 2\sqrt{6}$

e. $5\sqrt{11} + \sqrt{72} + 3\sqrt{2} - 3\sqrt{11}$ **f.** $\sqrt{98} + 5\sqrt{2} + \sqrt{28} + \sqrt{63}$

g. $\sqrt{12} - \sqrt{40} + \sqrt{160} + \sqrt{27}$ **h.** $\sqrt{125} + \sqrt{72} - \sqrt{20} + \sqrt{18}$

i. $\sqrt{99} - \sqrt{60} - \sqrt{44} + 3\sqrt{11}$ **j.** $\sqrt{80} + \sqrt{108} - \sqrt{45} + \sqrt{75}$

k. $3\sqrt{2} + 2\sqrt{7} - \sqrt{32} + \sqrt{28} - \sqrt{12}$ **l.** $\sqrt{15} + 2\sqrt{6} - \sqrt{20} + \sqrt{54} + \sqrt{60} + 7\sqrt{5}$

C **7.** Simplify.

a. $\sqrt{16m} - \sqrt{9n} + 2\sqrt{n} + \sqrt{m}$ **b.** $\sqrt{28ab} + 3\sqrt{c} - 3\sqrt{7ab} + \sqrt{25c}$

c. $5x\sqrt{y} + \sqrt{15b} + 3\sqrt{x^2y} + \sqrt{60b}$ **d.** $\sqrt{75ab^3} - \sqrt{c^2d} - b\sqrt{3ab} + 5c\sqrt{4d}$

e. $3\sqrt{8xy^2} + \sqrt{x^2y} + y\sqrt{32x} + 2x\sqrt{y}$

f. $\sqrt{45a^3b} - \sqrt{12m^2n^3} + 3n\sqrt{48m^2n} + a\sqrt{125ab}$

51

2–8 The Pythagorean Theorem

The Pythagorean Theorem, named after the Greek philosopher, Pythagoras, is illustrated in an exhibit at the Ontario Science Centre in Toronto. The large plexiglass disc can be rotated so that fluid will flow from the smaller squares on the sides of the right-angled triangle to exactly fill the largest square on the hypotenuse (the longest side) of the triangle.

This shows that the sum of the areas of the squares on the sides is equal to the area of the square on the hypotenuse.

If c × c = c², and c = 5 units
5 x 5 = 25 sq. units
Then, if a² is equal to 16 sq. units,
how much is b²? How much is b?

The Pythagorean Theorem:
For a right-angled triangle, the square of the hypotenuse, c, equals the sum of the squares of the other two sides, a and b.

$$c^2 = a^2 + b^2$$

The Pythagorean Theorem can be applied to find unknown dimensions in right-angled triangles.

EXAMPLE 1:   Find the missing lengths.

a.

$$x^2 = 7^2 + 5^2$$
$$x^2 = 49 + 25$$
$$x^2 = 74$$
$$x = \sqrt{74}$$

b.

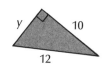

$$y^2 + 10^2 = 12^2$$
$$y^2 + 100 = 144$$
$$y^2 = 44$$
$$y = \sqrt{44}$$
$$= 2\sqrt{11}$$

There is a second part to the Pythagorean Theorem.

If the lengths a, b, and c of the sides of a triangle satisfy the equation $c^2 = a^2 + b^2$, then the triangle is a right triangle.

EXAMPLE 2: Which of the following are right triangles?

a.

b.

Test whether the lengths of the hypotenuse and of the two shorter sides satisfy the equation $c^2 = a^2 + b^2$ in each case.

a. $c^2 = 13^2$
    $\quad = 169$
    $a^2 + b^2 = 5^2 + 12^2$
    $\quad\quad\quad = 25 + 144$
    $\quad\quad\quad = 169$

Since $c^2 = a^2 + b^2$, the triangle is right-angled.

b. $c^2 = 10^2$
    $\quad = 100$
    $a^2 + b^2 = (2\sqrt{5})^2 + 8^2$
    $\quad\quad\quad = 4(5) + 64$
    $\quad\quad\quad = 84$

Since $c^2 \neq a^2 + b^2$, the triangle is not right-angled.

The Pythagorean Theorem can be applied to solve many problems involving unknown lengths or distances.

EXAMPLE 3: On an orienteering field trip, Kim hikes 8 km due north, 5 km due east, and then 2 km due south. How far is Kim from the starting point?

Let d be the distance in kilometres from the starting point.

Draw a diagram and then apply the Pythagorean Theorem.

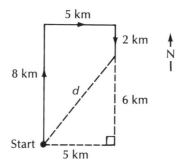

$d^2 = 5^2 + 6^2$
$d^2 = 25 + 36$
$d^2 = 61$
$\;d = \sqrt{61}$
$\quad \doteq 7.81$

To the nearest tenth, Kim is about 7.8 km from the starting point.

EXERCISES

A 1. Solve each equation. Round to the nearest tenth if needed.

- **a.** $3^2 + 4^2 = x^2$
- **b.** $5^2 + x^2 = 13^2$
- **c.** $7^2 + x^2 = 9^2$
- **d.** $x^2 + 10^2 = 15^2$
- **e.** $11^2 + x^2 = 12^2$
- **f.** $9^2 + 5^2 = x^2$
- **g.** $x^2 = 10^2 + 10^2$
- **h.** $3^2 + 6^2 = x^2$
- **i.** $7^2 + x^2 = 88^2$

2. Give the length of the hypotenuse for each triangle.

a.

b.
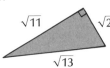

c.
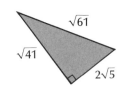

B 3. Which of the following are right triangles?

a.

b.
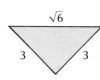

c.
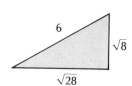

d.
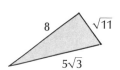

e.
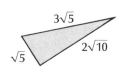

f.
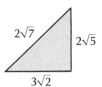

4. Find the length of each missing side to one decimal place.

a.

b.

c.
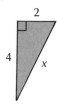

d.
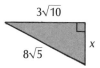

e.
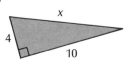

f.
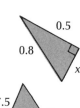

g.
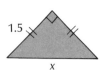

h.
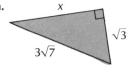

i.

54

5. A guy wire attached 7 m up a power pole is anchored 2 m from the foot of the pole. Find the length of the guy wire, correct to 0.1 m.

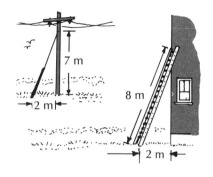

7 m

2 m

6. How far up a wall will an 8 m ladder reach, to 0.1 m, if the foot of the ladder is 2 m from the foot of the wall?

8 m

2 m

7. A rectangular gate 1 m by 2 m requires a diagonal brace. About how long should the brace be to the nearest 0.1 m?

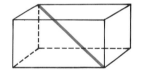

2 m

1 m

8. A pilot flies 300 km due north in a light plane, but the wind carries the plane 50 km to the west. How far, to the nearest kilometre, is the plane from its starting point?

C 9. Which of the following are right triangles?

a.

x
$\sqrt{2}x$
x

b.
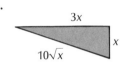
$3x$
x
$10\sqrt{x}$

c.
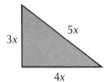
$3x$
$5x$
$4x$

10. Find the length of the diagonal of a rectangular box that is 20 cm by 8 cm by 10 cm, to the nearest 0.1 cm.

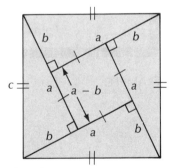

Historical Note

Pythagoras lived about 500 B.C. While he is generally credited with being the first person to prove the theorem that bears his name, there is no guarantee that Pythagoras did produce the first proof.

For example, the diagrammatic proof given at the right probably originated in the early history of China.

Use the diagram to show that the area of the large square c^2 is equal to the area of the triangles plus the area of the small square, or $c^2 = a^2 + b^2$. (Apply the distributive property in your proof to expand the area of the small square $(a - b)^2$.)

2–9 The Distance Formula

Andy is checking his cross-country ski trail map, shown below, to see how far he has left to go. He is now resting at the second warming hut located at $P(0,4)$. His ski tour ends where it started at $Q(5,1)$. To the nearest 0.1 km, how much farther must he ski?

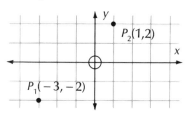

Find the distance PQ by applying the Pythagorean Theorem to the right-angled triangle made by the three warming huts.

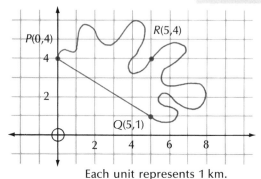

$PR = |0 - 5|$ or $|5 - 0| = 5$ km
$QR = |1 - 4|$ or $|4 - 1| = 3$ km

$PQ^2 = PR^2 + QR^2$
$\quad = 5^2 + 3^2$
$\quad = 25 + 9$
$\quad = 34$

$PQ = \sqrt{34}$
$\quad \doteq 5.8$

Each unit represents 1 km.

Andy has about 5.8 km left to go.

The method used above can be developed into a formula.

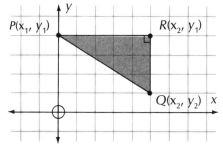

$PR = |x_1 - x_2|$ or $|x_2 - x_1|$
$QR = |y_1 - y_2|$ or $|y_2 - y_1|$

$PQ^2 = PR^2 + QR^2$
$\quad = (x_2 - x_1)^2 + (y_2 - y_1)^2$

$PQ = \sqrt{(x_2 - x_1)^2 + (y_2 - y_1)^2}$

The Distance Formula for two points $P_1(x_1,y_1)$ and $P_2(x_2,y_2)$:
$$P_1P_2 = \sqrt{(x_2 - x_1)^2 + (y_2 - y_1)^2}$$

EXAMPLE: Find the length P_1P_2 for points $P_1(-3, -2)$ and $P_2(1,2)$.

$P_1P_2 = \sqrt{(x_2 - x_1)^2 + (y_2 - y_1)^2}$
$\quad\quad = \sqrt{(1 - (-3))^2 + (2 - (-2))^2}$
$\quad\quad = \sqrt{4^2 + 4^2}$
$\quad\quad = \sqrt{32}$
$\quad\quad = 4\sqrt{2}$

In this text, "segment AB" is the same as "$\overline{AB}$". "AB" refers to the length of $\overline{AB}$.

EXERCISES

A 1. Find the length of each line segment. Use the Pythagorean Theorem if necessary. Leave each answer in radical form.

a.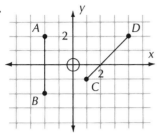
b.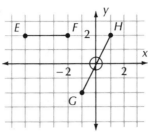
c.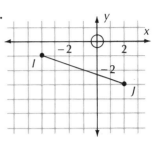

B 2. Plot each pair of points and find the distance between them. Round to the nearest tenth.

a. $A(2,5)$, $B(4,9)$
b. $C(-2,3)$, $D(5,-1)$
c. $E(0,2)$, $F(3,8)$
d. $G(-3,-5)$, $H(-5,-5)$
e. $I(3,0)$, $J(0,-5)$
f. $Q(-1,0)$, $R(3,-5)$
g. $P(8,-3)$, $T(-1,-4)$
h. $M(-4,-1)$ $N(-7,-5)$
i. $J(5,10)$, $K(5,-1)$

3. Find the perimeter of each polygon to the nearest tenth.

a.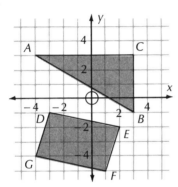
b.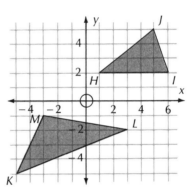

4. Find the distance between each pair of points to the nearest tenth.

a. $(3.5, 3.2)$, $(4.8, 1.6)$
b. $(2.7, 5.5)$, $(7.8, 3.2)$
c. $(-4.5, 1.9)$, $(1.6, -2.3)$
d. $\left(4\frac{1}{2}, 2.6\right)$, $\left(3\frac{1}{4}, 5.1\right)$

C 5. A line segment with length $\sqrt{65}$ has one endpoint at $(5,7)$. The other endpoint is at $(-2,y)$. Find the value of y. There are two possible solutions.

Using the Computer

Write a computer program that will accept the coordinates of two points and then calculate the distance between them.

Historical Note

The ancient Babylonians wrote on clay tablets, making marks in the soft clay in a script called cuneiform. The clay was then baked or dried to become a permanent record.

One of these clay tablets, dating from 1600 B.C. (over 1000 years before Pythagoras), contains columns of numbers which, upon inspection, prove to be the lengths of two sides of right-angled triangles where all dimensions are whole numbers. The three sides give sets of numbers which satisfy the Pythagorean Theorem and are called **Pythagorean triples**.

Further evidence indicates that the tablet was probably a mathematical table used to solve engineering problems. Historians think that, in order to generate these sets of numbers, the Babylonians had to be familiar with a formula for Pythagorean triples.

119	169
3367	11 521
4601	6649
12 709	18 541
65	97
319	481
2291	3541
799	1249
541	769
4961	8161
45	75
1679	2929
25 921	289
1771	3229
56	53

The clay tablet has four mistakes, probably copying errors.

1. Find the errors in the (translated) tablet at the right. Use the program below to check your answers.

```
10  REM  THIS PROGRAM WILL CHECK TWO
20  REM  NUMBERS OF A PYTHAGOREAN TRIPLE
30  FOR I = 1 TO 15
40  INPUT "ENTER THE FIRST NUMBER ";A
50  INPUT "ENTER THE SECOND NUMBER ";B
60  X = SQR ( ABS (A * A - B * B))
70  REM THIS ELIMINATES ROUNDING ERRORS BY THE COMPUTER
80  X$ = STR$ (X)
90  Y = LEN (X$):X$ = LEFT$ (X$,Y)
100 X = VAL (X$)
110 IF X ^ 2 = INT (X) ^ 2 THEN  PRINT "CORRECT": GOTO 130
120 PRINT "INCORRECT"
130 NEXT I
140 END
```

2. The following formulas will give Pythagorean triples if m and n are integers with $m > n$: $a = m^2 - n^2$; $b = 2mn$; $c = m^2 + n^2$. Write a computer program to give the Pythagorean triple corresponding to two integers input by the user.

58

Review

1. Simplify each radical expression. Assume all variables to be positive.

   a. $\sqrt{9x^3}$ b. $3\sqrt{24m^3n}$ c. $-0.2\sqrt{75a^5}$ d. $3.7\sqrt{m^7n^5p^3}$

2. Write as entire radicals.

   a. $2a\sqrt{b}$ b. $5\sqrt{7cd}$ c. $4k\sqrt{4k^2}$ d. $9bc\sqrt{5ab}$

3. Rewrite in simplest form.

   a. $\dfrac{5}{\sqrt{2}}$ b. $\sqrt{\dfrac{k}{7t}}$ c. $\dfrac{3\sqrt{6}}{4\sqrt{2}}$ d. $\dfrac{7\sqrt{3t}}{\sqrt{49t}}$

4. Write an expression in simplest form to represent the perimeter of each.

   a.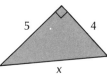

   b.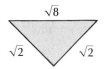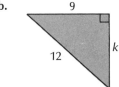

   c.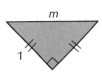

   d.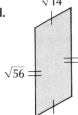

5. Find the length of each unknown side to one decimal place.

   a.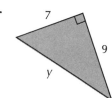

   b.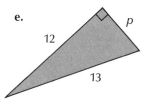

   c.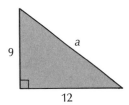

   d.

   e.

   f.

6. The steps in the stairway shown at the right are 20 cm high and 25 cm deep. The stairway has 14 steps in it. How long is the banister, to the nearest 0.1 cm?

   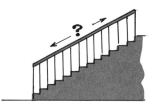

7. Find the perimeter of a figure with vertices $P(7,5)$, $Q(8,15)$, $R(0,15)$, and $T(0,9)$, correct to one decimal place.

8. A quadrilateral has vertices $A(4,1)$, $B(5,3)$, $C(3,2)$, and $D(2,0)$.

   a. Graph the vertices and join them.

   b. Show that the quadrilateral is a rhombus.

Formulas Involving Squares and Radicals

Solve, using a calculator and rounding to two decimal places where appropriate.

B 1. Police often use the length of skid marks to determine the speed a car was travelling when the brakes were applied. On dry pavement, the speed can be estimated using the formula:
Speed = $14\sqrt{l}$, where l is the length of skid.

Speed is measured in kilometres per hour and distance is in metres.

At what speed was a car travelling if it left skid marks of the following lengths on dry pavement?

a. 20 m   b. 10 m   c. 30 m

2. On wet pavement, the formula from exercise 1 becomes $S = 10\sqrt{l}$. At what speed was a car travelling on wet pavement if it left skid marks as given in exercise 1?

3. What will be the length of skid marks left by a car travelling at 50 km/h on dry pavement? on wet pavement? Use the formulas from exercises 1 and 2.

4. A motor vehicle bureau proposed that speeding fines be given according to the following formula: Fine = (Number of kilometres per hour over speed limit)^2 × $0.15.

What would be the fine for the following?

a. 60 km/h in a 30 km/h zone   b. 105 km/h in a 90 km/h zone
c. 62 km/h in a 50 km/h zone   d. 84 km/h in a 60 km/h zone

5. If a person is fined $135 for speeding in a 50 km/h zone, how fast was he or she driving? Apply the formula from exercise 4.

6. If a person is fined $216.60 for speeding in an 80 km/h zone, how fast was he or she driving?

7. The period of a pendulum is the time it takes to swing back and forth once. The formula $T = 2\sqrt{l}$ can be used to calculate the period of the pendulum in seconds, if l is the length in metres. Find the period of a pendulum with the given length.
a. 1 m   b. 2 m   c. 3 m   d. 10 m

8. Using the formula given in exercise 7, determine the length of pendulum that will have a period of one second.

Applying the Pythagorean Theorem

Make a sketch where necessary to help you visualize each problem, then solve. Use a calculator and round to one decimal place as necessary.

B **1.** The dimensions of a soccer field are 100 m by 73 m. How far is it from one corner flag to the opposite corner flag?

    2. A rectangular field measures 150 m by 80 m. Steve cuts across the field diagonally as a short cut on his way home. How much distance does he save on the short cut?

    3. You want to bring a sheet of glass 2.4 m by 2.1 m through a doorway that is 2 m high and 1.6 m wide. Will it fit?

    4. A rectangular gate is 3 m wide. The length of the diagonal brace is 3.4 m long. How high is the gate?

    5. The trusses in a garage roof span 6 m. The length of each rafter is 4 m. What is the height of the truss?

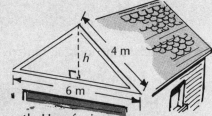

    6. Marie hikes 7 km north, 3 km east, and then 2 km north. How far is she from the starting point?

    7. Joe throws one end of a 40 m rope down to Angie at the foot of a sheer cliff. When Angie stretches the rope tight, it touches the ground 7 m from the base of the cliff. How high is the cliff?

    8. Oil wells are sometimes drilled at an angle. One well stands at the edge of the sea and is drilled so that it reaches oil at a depth of 2.7 km, at a distance of 0.6 km from the shore. What is the total length of the shaft?

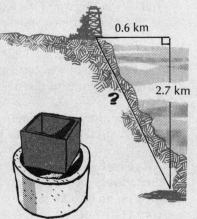

C **9.** A concrete cylinder used as an outdoor planter has an inside diameter of 45 cm. What is the largest square wood planter box that will fit inside the cylinder?

    10. What is the longest rod that will fit in a box measuring 10 cm by 20 cm by 30 cm?

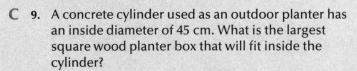

Test

Unit 2

1. Simplify.
   a. $\sqrt{49} + \sqrt{81}$
   b. $\sqrt{150 - 29}$
   c. $-3.2\sqrt{25}$
   d. $\sqrt{100} + 0.25\sqrt{36}$
   e. $0.6\sqrt{81} - 3\sqrt{25}$
   f. $5\sqrt{38 - 22} - 3\sqrt{3^2 + 4^2}$

2. Evaluate for $x = 6$, $y = 3$, $z = 5$.
   a. $\sqrt{yz - x}$
   b. $\sqrt{x + 2z}$
   c. $\sqrt{3xy + 2z}$

3. Classify the number as rational or irrational.
   a. 3.851
   b. $\sqrt{90}$
   c. -7
   d. $\sqrt{87}$
   e. $\sqrt{0.25}$

4. Evaluate to one decimal place.
   a. $\sqrt{0.67}$
   b. $\sqrt{1.69}$
   c. $2\sqrt{3} - \sqrt{6}$
   d. $5\sqrt{2} + \sqrt{3}$

5. Rewrite as entire radicals.
   a. $3\sqrt{7}$
   b. $8\sqrt{5}$
   c. $5\sqrt{x}$
   d. $x\sqrt{3x}$
   e. $2xy\sqrt{y}$

6. Write in simplest form. Assume all variables to be positive.
   a. $\sqrt{y^6}$
   b. $\sqrt{25x^2y^4z}$
   c. $\sqrt{50}$
   d. $\sqrt{98a^4}$
   e. $\sqrt{a^3b^2}$
   f. $\sqrt{\dfrac{5}{y}}$
   g. $\dfrac{6}{\sqrt{12}}$
   h. $\dfrac{\sqrt{36}}{\sqrt{2}}$
   i. $\dfrac{15\sqrt{54}}{5\sqrt{3}}$
   j. $\dfrac{\sqrt{2xy^2}}{\sqrt{6x}}$

7. Calculate the missing dimensions to one decimal place.

   a.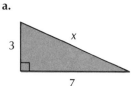
   b.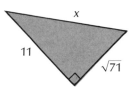
   c.
   d.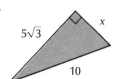

8. John was building a rectangular frame for a mirror. The length of the frame was 70 cm and the width was 40 cm. The length of a diagonal is 79 cm. Are the corners of the frame right angles?

9. A stream is 150 m wide. Joliette rows across and as she rows the current carries her 40 m downstream. How far from her starting point is she when she lands, to the nearest metre?

10. Find the distance between each pair of points, to one decimal place.
    a. $(3,8)$, $(7,12)$
    b. $(2, -3)$, $(-4,6)$
    c. $(-3,2)$, $(5, -4)$

11. A logging helicopter flies at a height of 150 m. It picks up logs and then travels 700 m north and 300 m west to drop off the logs. At the drop point, how far is the helicopter from the pick-up point? Answer correct to 1 m.

Cumulative Review

1. Evaluate each expression.
   a. $4 \times (-7) - 5(1 - 3)$
   b. $[36 - (-5)(-2)] \div 2$
   c. $(5 + 17) \div (-9 - 2)$
   d. $9 \div (-3) - 14 \div (-2)$
   e. $(4 + 7) \times (-9) - 90$
   f. $(5 \times 15) - (25 \times 3)$
   g. $(-1) \times 7 + (-1) \times 3$
   h. $(2)(-4)(-1) \div (-1)(-2)(-2)$

2. Evaluate for $a = -1$, $b = 7$, $c = -3$.
   a. ab
   b. $ac - b$
   c. $ab + c$
   d. $(2c + 1) \div 7$
   e. $2a - 7b$
   f. $4b - 5c$
   g. $a + b + c - abc$
   h. $|abc|$

3. Apply the exponent laws to simplify.
   a. $5x^2x^3$
   b. $3t^7 \div t^4$
   c. $(4k)^4$
   d. $(a^2b^3)^4$
   e. y^3y^7
   f. $x^3 \div x^4 \times x$
   g. $(t^7)^2$
   h. $z^8 \div z^6$

4. Express each number in scientific notation.
   a. 19 580 000 000
   b. 0.000 000 192
   c. 0.000 037
   d. 590 000 000 000

5. Calculate. Use scientific notation. You may use a calculator.
   a. $598\ 000 \times 196\ 000$
   b. $49\ 000\ 000 \div 6.90$
   c. $0.015 \div 0.000\ 005$
   d. $95\ 000\ 000\ 000 \times 24\ 000$
   e. $\dfrac{498 \times 25\ 000}{0.003}$
   f. $\dfrac{6200 \times 2900}{42\ 000}$

6. Find the length of each hypotenuse to one decimal place as needed.
   a.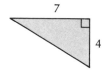
   b.
   c.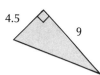

7. Which of the following are right-angled triangles?
   a.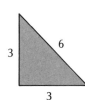
   b.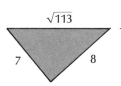
   c.

8. Find the distance between each pair of points to one decimal place as needed.
   a. $P(4,9)$, $Q(1,5)$
   b. $R(0,-2)$, $T(3,-1)$
   c. $A(-2,-7)$, $B(-2,8)$
   d. $J(2,4)$, $K(0,-4)$
   e. $M(-3,-9)$, $N(-10,-9)$
   f. $V(4,2)$, $W(-4,-2)$

A long-distance operator
working at a terminal.

3

Equations and Inequalities

3–1 Solving Linear Equations in One Variable

Andy has received a $10 long-distance gift certificate from his sister in Nanaimo. On Saturdays, from 12:00 to 23:00, a call to Nanaimo is $2.80 for the first 3 min and $0.80 for every minute or part of a minute after the first 3 min. What is the longest call Andy can make for $10?

Define a variable. Let *m* represent the number of minutes.

Unless otherwise stated, the variable is a real number.

Write an equation. $2.80 + 0.80(m - 3) = 10.00$ ← total cost, $10.00

cost of first 3 min

cost of $(m - 3)$ minutes (after first 3 min) at $0.80/min

Equations of this type are **linear equations**. The value of *m* that makes the equation true gives the length of time Andy could talk for $10. Before solving this equation, let's solve some simpler ones.

EXAMPLE 1: Solve each equation.

a.
$$x - 2 = 7$$
$$x - 2 + 2 = 7 + 2$$
$$x = 9$$

b.
$$x + 4 = -3$$
$$x + 4 - 4 = -3 - 4$$
$$x = -7$$

c.
$$5x = 15$$
$$\frac{5x}{5} = \frac{15}{5}$$
$$x = 3$$

d.
$$\frac{x}{7} = 3$$
$$7 \times \frac{x}{7} = 7 \times 3$$
$$x = 21$$

Performing the same operation on each side of the equation yields an **equivalent equation**. It does not change the value of *x*.

64

EXAMPLE 2:   Solve and check each equation.

a.
$$3x - 5 = 13$$
$$3x = 18 \quad \text{Add 5 to both sides.}$$
$$\frac{3x}{3} = \frac{18}{3} \quad \text{Divide by 3.}$$
$$x = 6$$

Check:
L.S. $= 3x - 5$
$= 3(6) - 5$
$= 13$
R.S. $= 13$
L.S. $=$ R.S. ✓

b.
$$5x + 7 - 2x - 3 = 8$$
$$5x - 2x + 7 - 3 = 8 \quad \text{Combine like terms.}$$
$$3x + 4 = 8$$
$$3x = 4 \quad \text{Subtract 4.}$$
$$x = \frac{4}{3} \quad \text{Divide by 3.}$$

Check:
L.S. $= 5x + 7 - 2x - 3$
$= 3x + 4$
$= 3\left(\frac{4}{3}\right) + 4$
$= 4 + 4$
$= 8$
R.S. $= 8$
L.S. $=$ R.S. ✓

EXAMPLE 3:   Now find the longest telephone call Andy can make for $10.00 by solving the equation $2.80 + 0.80(m - 3) = 10.00$.

$$2.80 + 0.80(m - 3) = 10.00$$
$$28 + 8(m - 3) = 100 \quad \text{Multiply each term by 10 to clear decimals.}$$
$$28 + 8m - 24 = 100 \quad \text{Apply the distributive property.}$$
$$8m + 4 = 100$$
$$8m = 96 \quad \text{Subtract 4 from each side.}$$
$$m = 12 \quad \text{Divide each side by 8.}$$

Andy can make a 12 min call for $10.

Check the answer in the original word problem:
$2.80 for the first 3 min, plus $7.20 for the next 9 min, is $10.00. ✓

A **formula** is an equation that states a rule about quantities represented by variables. **Isolating a variable** in a formula is solving for one variable in terms of the others.

EXAMPLE 4:   The formula for average speed, v, is $v = \frac{d}{t}$, where d is distance and t is time. Rewrite the formula to find distance in terms of speed and time.

$$v = \frac{d}{t}$$
$$v(t) = \frac{d}{t}(t) \quad \text{Multiply each side by } t \text{ to isolate } d.$$
$$vt = d \quad \text{or} \quad d = vt \quad \text{Note that } t \text{ cannot equal 0.}$$

65

EXERCISES

A **1.** Give the first step you would use to solve the following.

    a. $3x - 4 = 11$ **b.** $2q + 3q = 18$ **c.** $6j - 2j + 5 = 21$

    d. $14 = 4p - 6$ **e.** $5m = 3m + 24$ **f.** $3p + 4p + 8 = 15$

    g. $4.5x + 1.8 = 4.2x$ **h.** $3(x + 2) = 14$ **i.** $2.5(k - 3) = k - 1.6$

2. Solve each equation.

    a. $m - 3 = 5$ **b.** $t - 4 = -6$ **c.** $4x = 24$

    d. $15 + w = -6$ **e.** $4n = 32$ **f.** $7p = 49$

    g. $\dfrac{k}{7} = 8$ **h.** $\dfrac{z}{3} = -2$ **i.** $-6 = \dfrac{t}{-3}$

B **3.** Solve and check.

    a. $3m + 4 = 16$ **b.** $36 + 2r = 50$ **c.** $7k = 6 + 4k$

    d. $20y + 5 = 9y + 27$ **e.** $5s - 5 = 3s + 25$ **f.** $7w - 3w + 9 = 6w + 7$

    g. $24 + n = 15 + 4n$ **h.** $q + 5 - 2q = 13$ **i.** $3r + 12 - 5 = 8r - 3$

    j. $6y - 7 = 9 - 2y$ **k.** $4s - s = 2s - 7$ **l.** $5m - 11 = 13 - m$

    m. $2t + 3 - 3t = 12$ **n.** $4 - 3r + 6 = 1$ **o.** $2p - 5p + 6 = 5 - 4p$

4. Solve and check.

    a. $3(4n - 1) + 7 = 10$ **b.** $3(s - 1) - 5s = 5$

    c. $2(y - 2) = 3(y + 4)$ **d.** $3(t - 1) + 2(3t + 1) = 0$

    e. $3(r - 5) = 2r + 9$ **f.** $2(t - 4) + 15 = 13 - t$

    g. $5u - 3(u + 4) = 8 - 2u$ **h.** $4z + 7 - 5z = 2(z - 7)$

    i. $0.1v + 0.3v = 0.6(v - 5)$ **j.** $1.4 + 0.4r + 0.6 = 0.3(2r - 8)$

    k. $3(2 - m) + 5 = 7 - 2m$ **l.** $0.5(8x + 6) = 3x + 2.5$

    m. $0.2(4t - 8) = 0.6t$ **n.** $1.6 - 1.5(4y + 2) = 3.6$

    o. $2(3 + 4s) = 3(2 - 3s)$ **p.** $2(1.8 + 0.9x) = 1.2 + 0.8x$

5. Solve and check.

    a. $9.2 - 0.3t = 8.7 + 0.2t$ **b.** $6.5 + 0.7n = 0.2(n - 5)$

    c. $y - 2y + 3y = 4y + 9$ **d.** $5(2t + 8) - 9 = 7t - 11$

    e. $2x + 12 - 4x = 21$ **f.** $1.6 - 0.8x = 2.4x - 4.8$

    g. $5 - 3(2q + 4) = 7(2 - q)$ **h.** $4(3y - 8) + 7 = 5$

    i. $42 - m = 3(4 - 2m) + 6$ **j.** $3p - 17 + 2p = 4(2p - 3)$

6. One week, Bob earned a total of $475.80 for working 40 h at his regular hourly rate and 8 h at one and a half times his regular rate. What is Bob's regular rate? An equation to solve this problem is $40w + 8(1.5w) = 475.8$, where w is his regular hourly rate in dollars. Solve the equation to find his regular rate.

7. Maria earned her regular weekly salary of $295 plus 7% commission on sales for the week and earned $454.95. What were her sales for the week? An equation to solve this problem is $295 + 0.07s = 454.95$, where s is Maria's sales for the week in dollars. Solve the equation to find her sales for the week.

C **8.** Rewrite each formula, isolating the variable indicated.

	Basic Formula		Variable to Isolate	Rewritten Formula
a.	Area of a rectangle	$A = lw$	w	?
b.	Average of four numbers	$A = \dfrac{a + b + c + d}{4}$	c	?
c.	Interest	$I = Prt$	t	?
d.	Perimeter of a rectangle	$P = 2(l + w)$	l	?
e.	Intensity of light	$I = Ed^2$	E	?
f.	Volume of a cylinder	$V = \pi r^2 h$	h	?

9. Steve earns \$3.95/h plus tips as a waiter at a restaurant. One week he worked 36 h and earned \$267.20. How much did he earn in tips? Let t be his tips in dollars, and write an equation to represent the situation. Solve the equation to solve the problem.

10. Paula babysits for \$2/h before midnight and \$3/h for any time after midnight. On New Year's Eve, she babysat until 03:00 and made \$19. At what time in the evening did she begin babysitting? Let t be the number of hours she worked before midnight. Write an equation to represent the situation and solve the equation to solve the problem.

11. Solve and check.

a. $2(x + 3) - 7 = 3$ **b.** $x^2 + 2x - 1 = x(x - 3)$
c. $2x^2 - 3x = 2x(x - 2)$ **d.** $6(x^2 - x - 1) = 2x(3x + 4) - 6$
e. $2x(x + 2) = x(2x + 3) + 16$ **f.** $2x(x + 7) = x(2x + 5) - 27$

12. At the chalkboard, Dave solved correctly for w in the equation below. But one of the coefficients he wrote got smudged. What was the unseen coefficient?

$$■w + 2 = 3w + 14$$
$$w = 3$$

EXTRA

Using each digit only once, place one of the digits from 1 through 9 in each of the boxes so that the sum along each side of the triangle is 20.

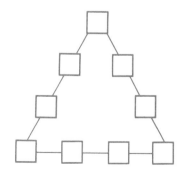

3–2 Equations Involving Fractions

Equations that contain fractions are most easily solved by clearing the fractions first.

EXAMPLE 1: Solve $\frac{3}{4}y = 18$.   Here is an alternative solution.

$$\frac{3}{4}y = 18$$

$(4)\frac{3}{4}y = (4)18$ Multiply each term by 4 to clear the fraction.

$3y = 72$

$y = 24$

$$\frac{3}{4}y = 18$$

$\left(\frac{4}{3}\right)\frac{3}{4}y = \left(\frac{4}{3}\right)18$ Multiply by the reciprocal of $\frac{3}{4}$ to clear the fraction.

$y = \frac{72}{3}$

$y = 24$

EXAMPLE 2: Solve and check.   Check:

$$\frac{x}{3} + \frac{x}{4} = \frac{7}{2}$$

$(12)\frac{x}{3} + (12)\frac{x}{4} = (12)\frac{7}{2}$ Multiply each term by 12, the LCD, to clear the fractions.

$4x + 3x = 42$

$7x = 42$

$x = 6$

L.S. $= \frac{x}{3} + \frac{x}{4}$

$= \frac{6}{3} + \frac{6}{4}$

$= 2 + \frac{3}{2}$

$= \frac{7}{2}$

$=$ R.S. ✓

EXAMPLE 3: Solve and check.

$$\frac{4x - 1}{4} + \frac{2x - 1}{5} = 2$$

$(20)\dfrac{4x - 1}{4} + (20)\dfrac{2x - 1}{5} = (20)(2)$ Multiply each term by the LCD, 20, to clear the fractions.

$5(4x - 1) + 4(2x - 1) = 40$ Apply the distributive property.

$20x - 5 + 8x - 4 = 40$ Combine like terms.

$28x - 9 = 40$

$28x = 49$

$x = \frac{49}{28}$ or $\frac{7}{4}$

Check: L.S. $= \dfrac{4x - 1}{4} + \dfrac{2x - 1}{5}$

$= \dfrac{4\left(\frac{7}{4}\right) - 1}{4} + \dfrac{2\left(\frac{7}{4}\right) - 1}{5}$

$= \dfrac{7 - 1}{4} + \dfrac{3.5 - 1}{5}$

$= \dfrac{3}{2} + \dfrac{1}{2}$

$= 2$

$=$ R.S. ✓

EXERCISES

A **1.** Solve the following equations.

a. $\frac{3}{5}x = 7$ b. $\frac{s}{4} = 9$ c. $\frac{3}{5}m = 9$ d. $-\frac{1}{3}x = \frac{1}{4}$

e. $\frac{-2}{3}t = -6$ f. $\frac{4}{5}y = -8$ g. $\frac{3}{2}k = \frac{1}{12}$ h. $14 = \frac{5}{7}z$

i. $-\frac{3}{4}q = 1$ j. $\frac{1}{5}x = 15$ k. $\frac{5}{8}j = \frac{5}{2}$ l. $\frac{-6}{5}t = \frac{1}{3}$

B **2.** Clear the fractions. It is not necessary to solve the equation.

a. $\frac{3s}{4} - \frac{2s}{3} = 6$ b. $\frac{3k}{5} - 6 = \frac{k}{3}$ c. $\frac{5z}{6} - \frac{3z}{8} = \frac{11}{3}$

d. $\frac{z - 2}{4} + \frac{z}{6} = \frac{16}{3}$ e. $\frac{2m}{3} - \frac{3m - 4}{8} = \frac{m}{6}$ f. $\frac{5}{2} - \frac{r}{9} = \frac{r + 2}{3}$

g. $\frac{4t}{5} + \frac{1}{2} = \frac{3t}{10} + \frac{4}{5}$ h. $\frac{-2k}{3} = \frac{-3k - 2}{6}$ i. $\frac{z - 3}{4} = \frac{z - 3}{3} - \frac{13}{24}$

3. Solve and check.

a. $\frac{5s}{3} + 1 - \frac{2s}{3} = 5$ b. $\frac{3m}{2} = 14 - \frac{m}{2}$ c. $\frac{5t}{6} + 1 = \frac{2t}{3} + \frac{3}{2}$

d. $-4r = r + \frac{5}{2}$ e. $\frac{2y + 3}{3} = y + 2$ f. $\frac{5x}{6} - \frac{x - 2}{4} = \frac{7}{2}$

g. $\frac{5(w + 1)}{4} = 3(w + 2)$ h. $\frac{4 - s}{2} = 4 + \frac{s}{2}$

i. $0.03s + 1.5 = 0.01s + 2.7$ j. $0.6y - 1.2 = 0.4y - 1.6$

k. $\frac{2m}{3} - \frac{3m - 4}{8} = \frac{m}{6}$ l. $\frac{a + 3}{3} + \frac{a - 2}{2} = 1$

m. $\frac{1}{3}(x - 5) + \frac{1}{4}(x + 1) - \frac{1}{6}(x - 4) = 1$ n. $\frac{2}{3}(x - 1) + \frac{3}{8}(x - 2) = 2$

o. $\frac{1}{5}(x - 2) + \frac{1}{10}(x + 2) + \frac{1}{5}(x + 2) = -10$ p. $\frac{1}{3}(x + 2) + \frac{1}{6}(x - 5) = -\frac{4}{3}$

4. Solve and check.

a. $3.5x + 4.5x - 8.2 = 7.8$ b. $2.3y - 18.3 = 1.3y + 17.4$

c. $1.25t - 3.48 = 6.24 - 0.25t$ d. $4.4z + 3.6z - 6.2 = 2.8z + 24.8$

e. $2.25n - 16.52 = 3.75n - 12.88$ f. $0.9t + 1.4 + 0.3t = 0.5t + 2.8$

g. $9.6 = 2.7r - 5.8r + 4.7$ h. $0.25(3s - 1) = 2.125$

C **5.** A container full of punch holds seven tenths ginger ale, two tenths orange juice, and 27 mL of lemonade concentrate. How much punch is there altogether? An equation to represent this situation is $0.7x + 0.2x + 27 = x$, where x is the total amount of punch in millilitres. Solve the equation to find the total amount of punch.

6. Find a non-algebraic solution to exercise 5.

3–3 Writing Expressions and Equations

Writing algebraic expressions and equations to represent given situations is a valuable skill in problem solving.

EXAMPLE 1: *Write an expression* to represent each phrase about the dimes and quarters saved in the jar. Let q be the number of quarters.

    a. the number of dimes if there are three more dimes than quarters: $q + 3$
    b. the value of the quarters in cents: $25q$
    c. the value of the dimes in cents: $10(q + 3)$
    d. the total value of the quarters and dimes in cents: $25q + 10(q + 3)$

With more information, expressions can be combined to write equations that solve problems.

EXAMPLE 2: Write an equation to represent each problem.

    a. If the total number of quarters and dimes in the jar is 17, how many quarters are there?

$$q + (q + 3) = 17 \quad \text{or} \quad 2q + 3 = 17$$

    b. If the value of quarters and dimes is $2.75, how many dimes are there?

$$25q + 10(q + 3) = 275 \text{ or } 25q + 10q + 30 = 275$$

    Note: The $2.75 is written as 275 so that the units in the equation are consistent (all in cents).

EXERCISES

A 1. Write an algebraic expression to represent each phrase. Let n be the number of nickels.
    a. three times the number of nickels
    b. the value of the nickels in cents
    c. the value of twice the number of nickels in cents

2. Let c represent Carl's age in years. Write an algebraic expression to represent each of the following, using the variable c only.
    a. Joanne's age in years, if Joanne is three years older than Carl
    b. Dean's age in years, if Dean is four years younger than Carl
    c. the age of Carl's teacher in years, if his teacher is twice as old as Carl

3. Using the expressions you wrote for exercise 2, write an equation to represent each problem. Use the variable c only.
   a. What is Dean's age in years, if four times Dean's age is three times Carl's age?
   b. If the sum of Joanne's and Carl's ages is 35 years, how old is Joanne?
   c. Eight years ago, Carl's teacher was three times as old as Carl. How old is Carl today?

B 4. Define a variable, using the appropriate units if necessary, and write an equation to represent the information given in each sentence.
   a. A number increased by seven is 26.
   b. My age decreased by six is 14.
   c. Five years from now Suzanne will be 23.
   d. Twice the length, decreased by 8, is 32.
   e. The sum of two consecutive numbers is 63.
   f. The number of some dimes and three more nickels than dimes is 21.
   g. The value of some dimes and three more nickels than dimes is $1.50.

C 5. Write an expression for each of the following phrases.
   a. the number of eggs in d dozen
   b. the number of tires on k automobiles
   c. the number of seconds in x minutes
   d. the cost in cents of p pears at thirty-five cents a pear
   e. the total cost in cents of b boxes of raisins at forty cents each and p packages of peanuts at fifty-five cents each
   f. the total cost in dollars of s shirts at $32 each and three more ties than shirts at $11 each

6. Whole numbers that follow each other are **consecutive** numbers.
   a. If x is a whole number, what is the next whole number?
   b. If x is the second of three consecutive numbers, what are the numbers?
   c. If y is an odd whole number, what is the next odd number?

7. For each problem, define a variable in appropriate units as necessary, and write an equation that could be used to solve the problem.
   a. Five times Tim's age is 85. How old is Tim?
   b. Melanie is three years older than Anna, and the sum of their ages is 35. How old is Anna?
   c. The number of nickels is twice the number of dimes, and there are 33 coins in all. How many dimes are there?
   d. In a basketball game with a total of 113 points, the Lions beat the Tigers by three points. How many points did the Lions score?
   e. Jay's father is three times as old as she is, and the difference of their ages is 26. How old is Jay?
   f. The sum of two consecutive numbers is 75. What are the numbers?
   g. The sum of two consecutive odd numbers is 88. What are the numbers?

Using Equations

For each problem, define a variable in the appropriate units, write an equation, and solve it to find the answer to the question.

A 1. At a movie theatre, 365 tickets were sold, some at $5 and the rest at $3.50. Total ticket sales amounted to $1763.50. How many of each price ticket were sold?

2. In the opening games of the season, the Torches scored 6 more goals than the Flames. Altogether the two teams scored 104 goals. How many goals were scored by each team?

3. A football costs three times as much as a basketball in the Hercules Sport Shop. In one month, the shop sold 41 basketballs and 13 footballs for a total of $1244. What is the price of a football?

4. In one season, the Canadiens played 80 games, 7 of which were ties. They won 17 more games than they lost. What was their win-loss record for the season?

5. Marc has read 148 pages in a book with 568 pages. If he reads 35 pages a day each day, how many days will it take him to finish the book?

6. A family spent $1260 on a trip to a resort. It cost them $504 to get to and return from the resort. If they spent 9 days at the resort, what were their average daily expenses while they were there?

B 7. A vending machine contains nickels, quarters, and dimes with a total value of $83.75. There are twice as many dimes as nickels, and 50 more quarters than dimes. How many of each coin are in the machine?

8. Louise, Michelle, and Penny worked for 38 h raking leaves. Louise worked twice as long as Michelle, and Michelle worked 2 h more than Penny. How long did each of them work?

9. The Hawks' performance improved in each quarter of their game. After being scoreless in the first quarter, they scored some points in the second quarter. They scored 6 points more in the third quarter than they did in the second quarter. In the fourth quarter they scored twice as many points as they did in the third quarter. Altogether they scored 46 points. How many points did they score in each of the last three quarters?

10. Two neighbours have back yards with equal areas of 576 m². One of the yards is square. The other is rectangular with the length twice as long as the width. Find the dimensions of each yard.

11. A side of a square is 8 cm more than a side of a regular hexagon. The square and the hexagon have equal perimeters. What is the perimeter of each polygon?

12. Linda earns $3.75/h and Larry earns $3.25/h. Larry works 4 h more each week than Linda does, but they both earn the same weekly pay. How many hours do Linda and Larry work, and how much do they earn per week?

13. A service station has 22 mufflers in stock, worth a total of $422. The premium mufflers are worth $23 each, $7 more than the standard mufflers. How many premium mufflers are in stock?

14. An airline with a fleet of 36 planes has 6 four-engine planes. The remaining planes have either two or three engines each. The total number of engines on all the planes is 100. How many two-engine planes does the airline have?

C 15. A submarine and a cruiser are 1200 km apart. The submarine can travel at 33 km/h under water and 39 km/h on the surface. The cruiser travels at 36 km/h. If the submarine, which is surfaced, and cruiser head for each other, can they meet in under 18 h?

16. Two cyclists leave the same point at the same time, in the same direction. One cyclist travels at 18 km/h, the other at 12 km/h. In how many hours will the cyclists be 27 km apart?

17. Paula is 20 years younger than her mother. Eight times Paula's age is three times her mother's age. How old is Paula?

18. A jet leaves Edmonton, flying at 750 km/h. One hour later another jet leaves, flying at 850 km/h in the opposite direction. How long after the first plane's departure will they be 4000 km apart?

EXTRA

Magic Squares

The sum of each row, column, and diagonal is the same. Copy and complete.

1.

2.5	1.5	2.9
?	?	1.9
1.7	?	?

2.

− 17	?	− 27
− 22	?	− 2
3	?	?

3.

− 1.6	?	?
?	?	− 1.4
− 0.8	− 1.8	− 0.4

Mixture Problems

A chemist has 100 mL of a 40% acid solution. She wants to reduce the strength of the solution to 25% acid by adding distilled water. How much water should she add?

Define a variable.
Let x be the amount of water to be added, in millilitres. Then the original acid solution with the added water will be $(100 + x)$ millilitres.

Write an equation.
The amount of acid in the new solution [25% of $(100 + x)$ millilitres] will be the same as the amount in the original solution [40% of 100 mL].

$$0.25(100 + x) = 0.4(100)$$
$$25 + 0.25x = 40$$
$$0.25x = 15$$
$$x = 60$$

The chemist should add 60 mL of water.

Check: 40 mL of acid in 160 mL of solution is 25% acid. ✓

The car radiator holds 20 L. It contains a 25% antifreeze solution. Since the weather is getting colder, the mechanic should make the solution 40% antifreeze. How much of the 25% solution should be drained and replaced with pure antifreeze to give a 40% solution?

Define a variable.
Let x be the number of litres of pure antifreeze to be added. Then $(20 - x)$ of the existing solution will be saved.

Write an equation.
The antifreeze added, along with that already in the tank [25% of the $(20 - x)$ litres], will have to result in a 40% solution [40% of the 20 L capacity].

$$x + \frac{25}{100}(20 - x) = \frac{40}{100}(20)$$
$$100x + 500 - 25x = 800$$
$$75x = 300$$
$$x = 4$$

Four litres of solution should be drained from the radiator (leaving 16 L) and then 4 L of pure antifreeze added.

Check: 4 L of pure antifreeze plus 25% of 16 L = 4 + 4 or 8 L;
8 L of antifreeze in 20 L of solution is 40% antifreeze. ✓

EXERCISES

A   1. A wholesale outlet has two grades of coffee, one selling for $8/kg and the other for $10/kg. The manager wants to mix the two grades to get 200 kg of coffee to sell at $8.75/kg. How much of each grade coffee should be mixed?

2. A clerk at a health food store is to enrich their granola by adding raisins. The plain granola sells for $5.00/kg and raisins sell for $7.00/kg. How many kilograms of granola and raisins should be mixed to make 120 kg of enriched granola to sell for $5.60/kg?

3. How many kilograms of peanuts and cashews should be mixed to make a mixture of 60 kg to sell at $6/kg, if peanuts sell for $4/kg and cashews for $12/kg?

B   4. A metallurgist has copper alloys, some of which contain 30% copper, and some with 48% copper. How many kilograms of each alloy should be mixed to make 240 kg of an alloy with 36% copper?

5. A chemist needs 200 mL of nitric acid of 30% strength. She has nitric acid solutions with strengths of 18% and 42%. How many millilitres of each acid should be mixed to produce the 200 mL of 30% acid?

6. How many millilitres of water should be added to 300 mL of a 30% sulfuric acid solution to dilute it to a 24% solution?

7. A car radiator holds 24 L of a 20% antifreeze solution. How much of the 20% solution should a mechanic drain and replace with pure antifreeze to give a 40% antifreeze solution?

8. How much water should a chemist add to 300 mL of a 42% sulfuric acid solution to dilute it to a 28% strength?

C   9. A broker invested $10 000, part earning interest at 8% per annum and the remainder at 10% per annum. If the investments earned $872 in one year, how much was invested at 10%?

10. A gardener at a greenhouse is combining two varieties of grass seed, one of which sells for $10/kg and the other for $6.00/kg. How much of each variety should be mixed to yield 120 kg of seed to sell for $7.50/kg?

11. How many millilitres of water should be added to 120 mL of a 15% acid solution to dilute it to a 10% acid solution?

EXTRA

The number 1 is both a perfect square and a cube. Find the next two such positive integers.

Using the Computer

In the science lab, students are combining an acid-water solution containing 20% acid with another solution containing 50% acid. They want 800 mL of a 32% acid solution. How much of each should they use?

The following program will solve this problem.

```
10  REM  SOLVE ANY MIXTURE PROBLEM
20  INPUT "WHAT IS THE TOTAL AMOUNT OF MIXTURE WANTED? ";F
30  INPUT "WHAT IS THE PERCENT STRENGTH OF THE MIXTURE WANTED? ";PF
40  INPUT "WHAT IS THE PERCENT STRENGTH OF THE FIRST SOLUTION? ";PA
50  INPUT "WHAT IS THE PERCENT STRENGTH OF THE SECOND SOLUTION? ";PB
60  PRINT "A = F*(PF - PB)/(PA - PB)"
70 A = F * (PF - PB) / (PA - PB)
80  PRINT "A = ";F;"*(";PF;" - ";PB;")/(";PA;" - ";PB;")"
90  PRINT "B = F - A"
100 B = F - A
110  PRINT "A = ";A", B = ";B
120  INPUT "DO YOU WISH TO CONTINUE? (Y OR N) ";C$
130  IF C$ = "Y" THEN  GOTO 10
140  END
```

```
]RUN
WHAT IS THE TOTAL AMOUNT OF MIXTURE WANTED? 800
WHAT IS THE PERCENT STRENGTH OF THE MIXTURE WANTED? 32
WHAT IS THE PERCENT STRENGTH OF THE FIRST SOLUTION? 20
WHAT IS THE PERCENT STRENGTH OF THE SECOND SOLUTION? 50
A = F*(PF - PB)/(PA - PB)
A = 800*(32 - 50)/(20 - 50)
B = F - A
A = 480, B = 320
DO YOU WISH TO CONTINUE? (Y OR N) N
```

The students should combine 480 mL of the 20% solution with 320 mL of the 50% solution.

Use the program to solve each mixture problem. Check your answers.

1. How much 80% pure gold should be mixed with 30% pure gold to obtain 400 g of 60% pure gold?

2. How much of a 15% acid solution should be mixed with a 25% acid solution to give 150 mL of an 18% acid solution?

3. If $9600 was invested, part at 6% and part at 9%, to obtain an average return of 7%, how much was invested at each rate?

Review

1. Solve each of the following equations.
   a. $4x + 9 = -11$
   b. $-1 = 3p - 7$
   c. $-2(a + 6) = 2a$
   d. $5 = 4(z - 2) - 3$
   e. $2x + 7 + 5x = -42$
   f. $-4(y - 3) = 2y - 6$
   g. $3(x - 4) = 2(3x - 1) + 5$
   h. $m(m - 4) + m^2 = 2(m^2 - 6)$

2. Solve and check.
   a. $\dfrac{m}{2} = 7$
   b. $16 = \dfrac{k}{3}$
   c. $\dfrac{2n}{3} + \dfrac{n}{2} = 14$
   d. $1 - \dfrac{x}{2} = \dfrac{x}{2}$
   e. $\dfrac{x - 5}{10} = \dfrac{1}{5}$
   f. $\dfrac{t + 1}{15} - \dfrac{t + 2}{6} = \dfrac{1}{3}$
   g. $\dfrac{s - 4}{3} - \dfrac{s - 3}{4} = \dfrac{5s}{12}$
   h. $\dfrac{r}{2} - \dfrac{r - 2}{3} = \dfrac{r + 3}{12}$

3. Write a phrase that might be represented by the given expression.
   a. $k - 7$
   b. $n + 5$
   c. $3m$
   d. $4t$
   e. $4t - 5$
   f. $25q$

4. Define a variable and write an expression to represent each statement.
   a. In the last game, Kay increased her point total by 11.
   b. Andy is earning half as much again as he did two years ago.
   c. The land value increased by 15%.

5. Ticket sales for a play amounted to $5760 for 800 tickets. Ticket prices were $5 and $10. How many tickets were sold for $10?

6. In the district track meet, Brock High School scored 52 points, winning 24 ribbons. Brock athletes won 6 first places worth 5 points each. The remaining points came from second places worth 3 points each and third places worth 1 point each. How many third places did Brock athletes win?

7. The Sea Breeze Motel has 72 units of single rooms and suites. One night all but 7 units were rented. Suites rent for $60 a night and single rooms for $40 a night. How many suites at $60 were rented that night if $2960 was collected?

8. A plane travelled 2197 km against a jet stream of 144 km/h. The trip took three and a quarter hours. What would be the speed of the plane in calm air?

9. Quarters and nickels are packed 40 to a container. Dimes are packed 50 to a container. After making his rounds to empty vending machines, a man had 49 full coin containers. Twelve of the containers had nickels. The remaining containers of dimes and quarters held a total value of $290. How many quarters were there?

3–4 Solving Linear Inequalities in One Variable

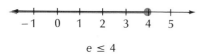

The maximum elevation on an island is 4 m. This statement can be represented by an inequality.

Let e be the elevation in metres.
Then: $e \leq 4$ Read, "e is less than or equal to 4."

The inequality can be graphed on a number line.

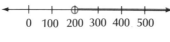

$e \leq 4$

The solid line indicates possible elevations like 0.1 or −1.3.
The solid dot shows that 4 is included as a possible elevation.

In this text, unless otherwise stated, the replacement set is R.

EXAMPLE 1:   For each situation given, define a variable and write an inequality to represent the situation. Graph the inequality on a number line.

a. Peg's chequing account allows her to write cheques without paying a service charge, provided her monthly balance stays above $200.
Let b be the balance in dollars with no service charge.

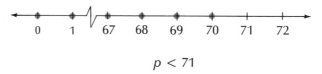

$b > 200$

The open dot indicates that 200 is not a part of the answer.

b. The winning basketball team scored 71 points.
Let p be the number of points scored by the losing team.

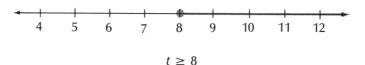

$p < 71$

c. Steve's project will take at least 8 h.
Let t be the time for Steve's project in hours.

$t \geq 8$

Inequalities can be solved in much the same way as equations.

EXAMPLE 2: At $30/h for labour and $60 for parts, the auto repairs will cost at least $150. How long will the repairs take? Let t be the number of hours needed.

$$30t + 60 \geq 150$$
$$30t + 60 - 60 \geq 150 - 60$$
$$30t \geq 90$$
$$t \geq 3$$

The replacement set is the set of non-negative real numbers.

$t \geq 3$

The repairs will take at least 3 h.

Multiplying or dividing an inequality by a constant requires extra care.

$$3 < 6$$
$$(-1)(3) > (-1)(6)$$
$$-3 > -6$$

Multiplying by -1 reverses the inequality.

$$-6 > -12$$
$$\frac{-6}{-2} < \frac{-12}{-2}$$
$$3 < 6$$

Dividing by -2 reverses the inequality.

> When multiplying or dividing an inequality by a negative number, change the direction of the inequality.

EXAMPLE 3: Solve $4 - 3n < 13$, where $n \in Z$. (Read, "n is a member of the set of integers.") Graph the solution set and check for one value.

$$4 - 3n < 13$$
$$-3n < 9$$
$$\frac{-3n}{-3} > \frac{9}{-3}$$
$$n > -3$$

Divide by -3 and reverse the inequality.

Check for $n = 1$:
L.S. $= 4 - 3n$
$= 4 - 3$
$= 1$
R.S. $= 13$
L.S. $<$ R.S. ✓

The solution set is $\{-2, -1, 0, 1, 2, 3, \ldots\}$.

$n > -3$

EXAMPLE 4: Solve $3(2 - x) < 2(2 - x)$, where $x \in R$.

$$3(2 - x) < 2(2 - x)$$
$$6 - 3x < 4 - 2x \quad \text{Subtract 6 from each side.}$$
$$-3x < -2 - 2x \quad \text{Add } 2x \text{ to each side.}$$
$$-x < -2 \quad \text{Multiply by } -1 \text{ and}$$
$$x > 2 \quad \text{reverse the inequality.}$$

Check for $x = 3$:
L.S. $= 3(2 - x)$
$= -3$
R.S. $= 2(2 - x)$
$= -2$
L.S. $<$ R.S. ✓

The solution set is the set of all real numbers greater than 2.

EXERCISES

A 1. For each situation, define a variable using the appropriate units and write an inequality to represent the situation.
   a. Tanya is less than 160 cm tall.
   b. A professional football player has a mass of more than 80 kg.
   c. In January, the rainfall was at least 120 mm.
   d. The elevator load limit is 1500 kg.
   e. A jet liner travels at more than 800 km/h.
   f. A good quarterback completes at least 50% of his passes.
   g. A batting average of at least 0.300 is excellent.
   h. After eating some chocolates, there were less than 20 left in the box.

2. Solve each inequality for $n \in Z$. Graph each solution set on a number line.
   a. $3n < 15$ b. $2n - 3 > 5$ c. $12 < 3n$
   d. $25n \geq 1$ e. $5n \geq -15$ f. $4n - 3 - 2n > -5$
   g. $4n + 7 \leq n - 3$ h. $-7n + 4 > 6 - 6n$ i. $-n - 1 \leq -2n - 3$

B 3. Define a variable and write an inequality to represent each statement. Solve and graph the solution on a number line.
   a. The $20 blouse plus a skirt will bring the total cost to over $50.
   b. If I drive for 4 h and stop for lunch and gas, I can complete the trip in less than 5.5 h.
   c. If it takes 6 min to type each page, it will take at least 90 min to type this report.
   d. The truck with a mass of 4 t and its load of bricks can have no more than a total mass of 7.5 t.
   e. Thawing the roast and then cooking it for 3 h will take at least 7 h.
   f. If I do not exceed the speed limit for 3 h, the farthest I can travel is 270 km.

4. Solve each inequality for $x \in Z$. Give the solution set and graph it on a number line.
   a. $\frac{x}{2} + 5 < 9$ b. $\frac{3x}{4} > -3$ c. $3x - 5 \geq 2 - x$
   d. $2(x - 3) \leq 5$ e. $\frac{x}{3} < 3(4 - x)$ f. $\frac{x}{2} + \frac{x}{3} \geq 4$
   g. $3.2x \geq 9.6$ h. $1.12x + 3.6 > 1.36$ i. $8.4x + 8.4 \leq 3.6x + 13.2$

5. Solve each inequality for $x \in R$. Match the inequality with the correct number line graph.
   a. $5 - 2x < 3$ b. $2(x - 3) \geq 3x$ c. $2.3x - 1.7x > 4.2$

A.
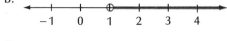

B.

C.

D.
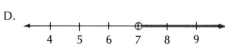

6. Match each number line solution with two correct inequalities.

a.

2 3 4 5 6 7

b.

0 1 2 3 4 5

c.

0 1 2 3 4 5

d.

4 5 6 7 8 9

A. $x \leq 4$
B. $x + 2 < 8$
C. $2.5x + 4.5 > 17$
D. $3x \leq 12$
E. $2x + 3 < 15$
F. $x - 2 > 3$
G. $3x < 12$
H. $x - 4 < 0$

C 7. Define a variable in the appropriate units and write an inequality to represent each problem. Solve each inequality and check for one value in the solution set.

a. In 15 games, the Jets scored over 50 goals. How many goals did they average per game?

b. A plumber charges a flat fee of $20 plus $30/h for service calls. How many hours did the plumber work on a service call for which the charge was over $100?

c. Michelle is saving for a school trip to Banff. She has $80 saved so far and wants at least $200. With her part-time job she can save $15 each week. How long will it take her to save up her money for Banff?

8. Solve each inequality for $x \in R$. Give the solution set and graph it on a number line.

a. $2(x + 3) \leq 3 - (x + 1)$
b. $x - 3(x + 5) \leq 3 - 2(x + 1)$
c. $x(x + 2) - 5(x + 2) - x(x - 1) \leq 0$
d. $4x^2 - 12x + 9 - 4x(x + 3) \geq 0$
e. $x(x - 7) \geq x^2 - 6 - x - 4$
f. $3(x^2 - 2x + 1) - 3x(x - 2) - (x - 2) \geq 4x$

9. A truck driver travelled more than 420 km. He drove part of the way at 80 km/h and for 2 h at 90 km/h. How long did he drive at 80 km/h?

EXTRA

Di stopped at a newsstand to pick up a copy of each of the local papers. The *Courier*, the *Clarion*, and the *Crier* together cost $1. A copy of the *Crier* costs more than 2 copies of the *Courier*. Three copies of the *Courier* cost more than 4 copies of the *Clarion*. Three copies of the *Clarion* cost more than a *Crier*. How much does each paper cost?

3–5 Solving Combined Inequalities

The weather forecast can be written using two inequalities. Let t be temperature in degrees Celsius.

$t \geq -2$ and $t \leq 4$

The word *and* indicates that t must satisfy *both* conditions. The two inequalities can be combined as shown below.

Today's Weather
Clear but cold
High 4° C
Low −2° C

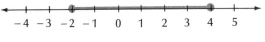

$-2 \leq t \leq 4$

Inequalities may also be combined using the word *or*, to indicate that either one condition, or the other, or both, must be satisfied in order for the combined inequality to be true.

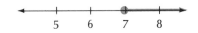

$x > 7$ or $x = 7$
compact form: $x \geq 7$

$x > 7$ or $x < 5$

EXAMPLE 1:   Solve $2m < -8$ or $m - 3 > 2$ for $m \in R$. Graph the solution.

$$2m < -8 \quad \text{or} \quad m - 3 > 2$$
$$m < -4 \qquad\qquad m > 5$$

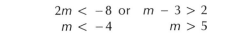

EXAMPLE 2:   Fiona, a fitness instructor, has her twenty-year-old students monitor their pulse rates regularly during their aerobics classes. A health guide indicates that a twenty-year-old's heart should beat 132 to 174 times per minute. The students take their pulse for only 10 s. How many beats should a twenty-year-old student have over 10 s?

Define the variable.
Let x be the number of beats in 10 s.
Then $6x$ is the number of beats in 1 min.

Write an inequality and solve it.
$132 \leq 6x \leq 174$
$22 \leq x \leq 29$ Divide by 6.

A twenty-year-old's heart should beat 22 to 29 times every 10 s.

EXERCISES

A 1. Write the solution set for each combined inequality, where $x \in Z$.

    a. $x > 2$ or $x < -3$ **b.** $-1 < x < 7$ **c.** $-6 \leq 2x \leq 4$

    d. $0 < x + 3 \leq 7$ **e.** $x \geq 0$ or $x < -4$ **f.** $-3 < x - 2 < 1$

2. Solve for $x \in R$. Graph each solution.

    a. $-3 < 3x < 9$ **b.** $-5 \leq 5x \leq 10$ **c.** $-6 < 3x < 0$

    d. $2 \leq 2x - 4 \leq 8$ **e.** $2x \geq 6$ or $2x < -6$ **f.** $3x > 6$ or $3x < -6$

B 3. Define a variable in the appropriate units and write a combined inequality to represent each situation.

    a. Rita is less than 18 but more than 14 years old.

    b. This classroom is between 5 m and 8 m long, inclusive.

    c. The temperature was within $3°$ C of $0°$ C all day long.

    d. My total cost for the concert was between \$30 and \$35.

    e. Having written cheques totalling \$429 during the month, Pat does not yet know which ones have come through.

    f. Liz drove at speeds from 80 km/h to 100 km/h on her trip.

    g. If Paul could double his earnings, he'd be making from \$30 to \$40 each week.

    h. The daily high temperature this month varied from $-5°$C to $9°$ C.

4. Solve for $x \in R$. Graph each solution which is not an empty set.

    a. $x - 3 > 2$ and $x - 3 < 5$ **b.** $2x + 1 \leq 5$ and $x \geq -4$

    c. $x - 2 > -2$ or $x + 5 < 1$ **d.** $-4 \leq 4x - 8 \leq 4$

    e. $2x > 8$ or $2x < 4$ **f.** $0 \leq 3x - 1 \leq 5$

    g. $6 \leq 3x - 9 \leq 12$ **h.** $x > -2$ or $-5x < 15$

    i. $3x < 6$ and $x > -2$ **j.** $-28 < 4x - 8 < 28$

    k. $x \geq 4$ and $x < -2$ **l.** $x > -2$ or $x < 5$

    m. $2x + 1 \geq -3$ and $2x + 1 \leq x + 3$ **n.** $-3x < 6$ and $4 < -2x$

    o. $4x + 1 < 0$ or $4x + 2 < 0$ **p.** $8 - 2x \leq 2 - x$ and $1 - 2x \geq -8$

    q. $3x + 6 < 0$ and $x \leq 4$ **r.** $2 - x < 4 + 2x$ and $4 - x \geq 5$

5. Write a combined inequality for each graph.

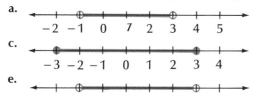
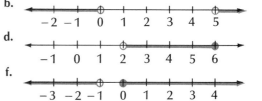

C 6. In their first 3 games, the Royals scored between 215 and 240 points, inclusive. If they continue to score at this rate over their remaining 12 games, what will be their point total for the entire season?

7. A broker invested some money which doubled in value after one month. The investment lost \$720 the next month. At that time, it was worth between \$3000 and \$3500. How much was originally invested?

3–6 Solving Inequalities Involving Absolute Value

A mathematical sentence containing a variable within an absolute value sign leads to two possible cases.

Absolute Value Sentence	Meaning	Graph	Two Possible Cases
$|k| = 2$	k is 2 units away from 0.	![graph -3 to 3 with points at -2 and 2]	$k = -2$ or $k = 2$
$|k| > 2$	k is more than 2 units away from 0.	![graph -3 to 3 with open circles at -2 and 2, arrows outward]	$k < -2$ or $k > 2$
$|k| < 2$	k is less than 2 units away from 0.	k is between -2 and 2. ![graph -3 to 3 with open circles at -2 and 2, segment between]	$k > -2$ and $k < 2$; that is: $-2 < k < 2$

An equation or inequality containing a variable within an absolute value sign can be solved by considering its two possible cases.

EXAMPLE 1: Solve and graph $|4x - 5| = 3$, for $x \in R$.

$$4x - 5 = 3 \quad \text{or} \quad 4x - 5 = -3$$
$$4x = 8 \quad \text{or} \quad 4x = 2$$
$$x = 2 \quad \text{or} \quad x = \tfrac{1}{2}$$

![number line from -2 to 2 with points at 1/2 and 2]

EXAMPLE 2: Solve and graph $|2x - 3| > 5$, for $x \in R$.

$$2x - 3 < -5 \quad \text{or} \quad 2x - 3 > 5 \qquad (2x - 3) \text{ is more than}$$
$$2x < -2 \quad \text{or} \quad 2x > 8 \qquad 5 \text{ units away from } 0.$$
$$x < -1 \quad \text{or} \quad x > 4$$

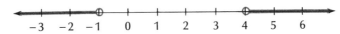

EXAMPLE 3: Solve and graph $|3x - 4| \leq 2$, for $x \in R$.

$|3x - 4| \leq 2$ means $3x - 4$ is between -2 and 2; that is: $-2 \leq 3x - 4 \leq 2$.

$$-2 \leq 3x - 4 \leq 2$$
$$2 \leq 3x \leq 6$$
$$\tfrac{2}{3} \leq x \leq 2$$

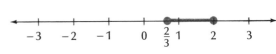

84

EXERCISES

A **1.** Give two possible cases for each of the following.
- **a.** $|b| = 7$
- **b.** $|a| > 2$
- **c.** $|m| \leq 3$
- **d.** $|a - 5| < 4$
- **e.** $|n + 3| \geq 9$
- **f.** $|5x - 7| = 3$
- **g.** $\left|\frac{m}{2}\right| \leq 10$
- **h.** $|7b + 4| = 5$
- **i.** $|2c - 8| \geq 6$

2. Draw the graph for each.
- **a.** $|m| = 1$
- **b.** $|z| \geq 3$
- **c.** $|t| < 5$

B **3.** Solve for $x \in R$ and graph the solution.
- **a.** $|x| \leq 4$
- **b.** $|2x| > 6$
- **c.** $|3x| \geq 6$
- **d.** $|2x - 3| < 1$
- **e.** $|3x - 1| \leq 5$
- **f.** $|2x - 5| > 7$
- **g.** $|2x + 7| < 7$
- **h.** $3 \leq |4x - 3|$
- **i.** $2 \geq |5x + 3|$
- **j.** $|x| + 8 \leq 15$
- **k.** $|2y| - 9 > 5$
- **l.** $|2y| - 9 > -5$
- **m.** $|2x - 3| = 5$
- **n.** $|x - 4| = 2$
- **o.** $|5x - 10| = 0$
- **p.** $|3x + 2| > 10$
- **q.** $|3x| - 4 \leq 8$
- **r.** $3 > |4x - 1|$

4. Write an equivalent sentence using absolute values.
- **a.** $-6 < 2b < 6$
- **b.** $j + 3 \leq -5$ or $j + 3 \geq 5$
- **c.** $k - 9 > -7$ and $k - 9 < 7$
- **d.** $5b + 1 > -2$ and $5b + 1 < 2$

5. Solve for $x \in R$ and graph the solution if it is not an empty set.
- **a.** $x - 3 > 5$ or $2x < -2$
- **b.** $3 - x > 5$ or $-2x < -2$
- **c.** $x - 3 > 5$ and $2x < -2$
- **d.** $3 - x > 5$ and $-2x < -2$
- **e.** $2x - 5 > -3$ or $3x - 2 > 4$
- **f.** $2x - 5 > -3$ and $3x - 2 > 4$

C **6.** Solve for $x \in R$ and graph the solution if it is not an empty set.
- **a.** $|4 - x| > 5$
- **b.** $|x - 4| > 5$
- **c.** $|4 - 2x| \geq 5$
- **d.** $|2x - 4| \geq 5$
- **e.** $|6 - x| < 3$
- **f.** $|2x - 3| \leq 0$

7. If Frank's bank balance were doubled and then increased by $15, the absolute value of the resulting balance would be less than $139. What is Frank's bank balance?

Using the Calculator

Patterns

Recall:
$$\sqrt{4} = 4^{\frac{1}{2}} = 2$$

Look for a pattern:
$$\sqrt{4^2} = (4^2)^{\frac{1}{2}} = 4^{2 \times \frac{1}{2}} = 4^{\frac{2}{2}} = 4$$
$$\sqrt{4^3} = (4^3)^{\frac{1}{2}} = 4^{3 \times \frac{1}{2}} = 4^{\frac{3}{2}} = 8$$

Keypresses:

$\boxed{4}\ \boxed{x^y}\ \boxed{.}\ \boxed{5}\ \boxed{=} \rightarrow 2$

$\boxed{4}\ \boxed{x^y}\ \boxed{1}\ \boxed{=} \rightarrow 4$

$\boxed{4}\ \boxed{x^y}\ \boxed{1}\ \boxed{.}\ \boxed{5}\ \boxed{=} \rightarrow 8$

Use the pattern you found to evaluate each. Then check with a calculator.

1. $\sqrt{4^6}$ **2.** $\sqrt{4^9}$ **3.** $\sqrt{4^{12}}$ **4.** $\sqrt{4^{15}}$ **5.** $\sqrt{4^{19}}$ **6.** $\sqrt{4^{25}}$

Using Inequalities

Mario's car has a fuel consumption of 12.5 L/100 km for city driving, and 8.5 L/100 km for highway driving. Last month, Mario drove 1800 km in his car. How much fuel did he use?

Define a variable.
Let n be the number of litres of fuel used.

Write a combined inequality.

fuel used on the highway $\leq n \leq$ fuel used in the city

$$1800 \times \frac{8.5}{100} \leq n \leq 1800 \times \frac{12.5}{100}$$
$$18 \times 8.5 \leq n \leq 18 \times 12.5$$
$$153 \leq n \leq 225$$

Mario used from 153 L to 225 L of fuel that month.

EXERCISES

A 1. Jim earns $6/h working part-time. He'd like to earn at least $50 a week. How many hours should he work each week?

2. A basket in basketball is worth two points and a foul shot is worth one point. Samantha scored 5 foul shots and some baskets. Her total point score was at least 21. How many baskets did she score?

3. A hockey team gets two points for a win and one point for a tie. Late in the season, the Maple Leafs had over 70 points and had won 34 games. How many games had they tied?

B 4. Tickets for a benefit concert were sold at $5 and $8. A total of 356 tickets were sold. How much money was taken in?

5. A plane flying at 800 km/h in calm air is aided by a jet stream which adds between 100 km/h and 200 km/h to the plane's speed. How long will it take the plane to travel 4500 km?

6. On a test with twelve problems, one mark was given for each problem that was attempted, and two additional marks were given for each correct solution. Roberta's mark was between 26 and 32 inclusive. She tried every problem. How many correct solutions did she get?

7. A plumber charges a flat fee of $20 plus $30/h for labour for home service. The bill for a service call was between $100 and $125. How many hours did the plumber work?

8. A 375 g package of Puff Curls costs $1.50. At what prices would the 525 g package be a better buy?

9. An elevator has a load limit of one tonne. Assuming an average mass of 56 kg for women and 70 kg for men, find the maximum number of adults that the elevator can carry.

10. A butcher sold a customer a total of 3200 g of meat and cheese. The meat cost $7.20/kg, and the cheese, $6.00/kg. The order amounted to more than $20. How much meat might the customer have purchased?

11. A total of 400 tickets was sold for a matinee performance, with youth tickets costing $3 each and adult tickets $5 each. Ticket sales amounted to less than $1700. What is the greatest number of adult tickets that could have been sold?

C 12. Pia can walk at 100 m/min and jog at 200 m/min. She walked and jogged for one hour, travelling no more than 8 km. What is the greatest amount of time she could have jogged?

13. Lou has two part-time jobs, one that pays $3.50/h, the other $4/h. One week he worked 21 h and earned at least $75. What is the greatest number of hours he could have worked at the lower-paying job?

14. Lisa owns $160 worth of tapes. Each tape cost from $8 to $10. How many tapes does Lisa own?

15. A family bought two types of new carpeting for their home, some at $24/m², some at $18/m². The total area covered was 40 m², all for no more than $900. What is the largest amount of the more expensive carpeting which could have been installed?

16. A taxi company charges $2.40 for the first kilometre or part of a kilometre, and $0.90 for each additional kilometre or part of a kilometre. How far could you ride if you had only $8?

17. A large factory pays its skilled workers an average wage of $130/day, while unskilled workers are paid an average of $90/day. What is the largest possible number of skilled and unskilled workers if there are three times as many unskilled workers as skilled workers, and daily labour costs are not to exceed $15 000?

18. Karl has to write a ten-page report. He estimates that the first page will take him an hour and a half, and the remaining pages will take from 15 min to 20 min. If his estimates are correct, how much time can he expect to spend writing the report?

EXTRA

Explore the odd-number triangle, given at the right.
Find at least one pattern involving perfect squares or perfect cubes.

```
              1
            3   5
          7   9  11
        13  15  17  19
      21  23  25  27  29
    31  33  35  37  39  41
  43  45  47  49  51  53  55
            . . .
```

Application

With the current high rate of heart disease among North Americans, there is an increasing awareness of the need for **cardiovascular fitness**, or having a healthy heart. The heart is a muscle. It can be exercised through **aerobics** like jogging, swimming, or brisk walking, which induce increases in heart and breathing rates.

Those who use aerobic exercise to achieve cardiovascular fitness can monitor their pulse rates during and after exercise to ensure maximum benefits from the exercise. They calculate their target heart rate by following the steps below.

1. Subtract your age from 220. This gives an estimate of your *maximum* heart rate per minute, *M*.

    This estimate is accurate for ages 20 years and over.

2. Categorize yourself.
    a. If you have been exercising regularly, your target heart rate is 75% of your maximum, or 0.75*M*.
    b. If you have not been exercising, your target rate is 70% of your maximum, or 0.7*M*.
    c. If you smoke or are 10 kg or more overweight, your target is 65% of the maximum, or 0.65*M*.

    For a 25-year-old of average mass who walks every day and does not smoke:
    $M = 195$ and $0.75M = 146.25$.
    The target rate over 1 min is 146.25.

3. Since, during exercise, it is easier to measure your pulse over a shorter time period than 1 min, divide by 6 to find the target heart rate over 10 s.

    a. $\dfrac{0.75M}{6}$ b. $\dfrac{0.7M}{6}$ c. $\dfrac{0.65M}{6}$ $\dfrac{146.25}{6} \doteq 24$ The target rate over 10 s is 24.

Note: It is dangerous to increase your heart rate to greater than 85% of your maximum. This is the basis of the *ranges* that help athletes assess whether they are pushing themselves too hard.

Copy the table, then complete it using the formulas above.

	Age	Maximum Heart Rate	Target Rate for Someone Who:		
			a. Has Been Exercising	**b.** Has Not Been Exercising	**c.** Is a Smoker
1.	20				
2.	25				
3.	30				
4.	35				
5.	40				
6.	50				
7.	60				

Review

1. Solve and check.
   a. $3x + 4 = 5x - 6$
   b. $2(3m - 4) = 5m + 7$
   c. $\frac{2z}{3} + 5 = \frac{3z}{2}$
   d. $2.5t + 6 = 0.5(2t + 6)$
   e. $2x(4x - 5) + 2x(4x - 1) + (4x - 1) = 10$
   f. $\frac{2}{3}(x - 1) + \frac{1}{2}(x + 3) = -1$
   g. $\dfrac{5x - 1}{6} - \dfrac{2x - 1}{3} = \dfrac{2}{9}$
   h. $6x(2x - 1) + 3(2x - 1) - 12x^2 - 7x - 1 = 5$

2. Rewrite the formula $A = \frac{1}{2}h(a + b)$ to isolate the variable h.

3. Solve each inequality for $x \in Z$. Graph your solution.
   a. $3x + 4 \le 16$
   b. $2x + 6 \ge x + 4$

4. Solve for $s \in R$. Graph your solution.
   a. $3s - 6 < s + 8$
   b. $2(s - 4) + 5 > 3s - 2$
   c. $s + 8 \le -5(s + 2)$
   d. $s(2s - 3) \ge 2s^2 + 6$

5. Write the solution set for each combined inequality for $x \in Z$.
   a. $x \ge 2$ or $2x \le 6$
   b. $2 < 3x + 5 < 14$

6. Solve and check each equation.
   a. $|t| = 11$
   b. $2|b| = 6$
   c. $|k - 7| = 14$
   d. $4|a + 3| = 15$
   e. $5|x| - 7 = 0$
   f. $3|q - 2| - 3 = 15$

7. Solve each inequality and graph its solution set if it is not an empty set.
   a. $|y| > 4$
   b. $|m| < 2$
   c. $|4n - 2| \ge 14$
   d. $4 > |2v + 3|$
   e. $-7 < |4 + u|$
   f. $|4 - x| > 3$
   g. $2|3k - 7| > 5$
   h. $15 \le 4 + 3|2 - w|$
   i. $12 \ge |2 - 5t|$

8. Keith has 100 coins, all quarters and dimes. The value of the coins is $19.60. How many of each coin does Keith have?

9. On a test worth 100 marks, there were 34 problems. Four of the problems were worth 5 marks each. The rest were worth 2 marks or 3 marks. How many problems were worth 2 marks?

10. A rock star received $0.75 per record for the first million records sold and $1 per record for each additional record. How many records must be sold for the rock star to earn at least $1 000 000?

11. Deb has saved $2000 for a European holiday. She needs $936 for air fare and has estimated that she will have daily expenses of $55. If her estimate is accurate, what is the greatest number of days she can spend on the holiday?

Test   Unit 3

1. Solve each equation.
   a. $3m = -6$
   b. $5s + 4 = 2s + 13$
   c. $1.5y - 6.4 = 2.6$
   d. $4.9t - 7 = 3.5t$
   e. $\dfrac{-4k}{5} = 8$
   f. $\dfrac{m}{6} - 2 = \dfrac{m + 1}{4}$
   g. $x(2x + 7) = x(2x - 1) + 16$
   h. $7x^2 - 9 = 7x(x + 1)$

2. Write the inequality or pair of inequalities suggested by each graph.
   a.

   b.

   c.

   d.

3. Solve each inequality. Graph each solution on the number line.
   a. $2x < -4$ b. $2x + 3 \geq -1$ c. $7 - 2x \geq 3$ d. $-2 < -3x - 1 \leq 7$

4. Solve each inequality and graph its solution set if it is not an empty set.
   a. $|x| \geq 3$
   b. $|2x + 3| < 7$
   c. $|3 - x| < 9$
   d. $|5 - x| \geq 4$
   e. $7 \leq |4x + 2| - 5$
   f. $|4 - x| + 7 \leq 15$

5. Describe a situation that might be represented by the following.
   a. $4t$
   b. $10d$
   c. $d - 7$
   d. $4t + 28$
   e. $10d + 20$
   f. $10d + 25(d - 7)$

6. Define a variable in the appropriate units and write an expression to represent the given information.
   a. There are 7 more pennies than quarters.
   b. The living room area is double that of the kitchen.
   c. Jan's salary was increased by $2800 per year.
   d. The 5 team-mates bought a pizza and shared the cost equally.

7. Anna averaged 90 km/h in highway driving and 50 km/h in city driving. She travelled 160 km, spending three times as long on highways as in the city. How much time did she spend on the highway?

8. Marc and Steve agreed to share their earnings of $147 based on the hours they worked. They worked a total of 42 h, but Steve worked 6 h more than Marc. How much should each receive?

9. How many millilitres of a 24% acid solution should be mixed with 60 mL of a 40% acid solution to make a solution that is 30% acid?

10. A soft drink machine contains 200 nickels, dimes, and quarters. Eighty of the coins are quarters and the rest of the coins are worth $10.20. How many of the coins are dimes?

Cumulative Review

1. Evaluate for $k = -5$, $m = 3$.
   a. km
   b. $km - 7$
   c. $km \div (-30)$
   d. km^2
   e. $m - k$
   f. $(km)^2$
   g. $-m^2$
   h. $km^2 - m^2$

2. Write the repeating decimal $0.\overline{45}$ as a fraction.

3. Simplify using scientific notation.
   a. $\dfrac{42\ 000}{395} \times \dfrac{1\ 200\ 000}{0.000\ 29}$
   b. $\dfrac{397\ 000\ 000 \times 250}{0.000\ 000\ 12}$

4. Evaluate.
   a. $\sqrt{400}$
   b. $\sqrt{225}$
   c. $\sqrt{1600}$
   d. $\sqrt{3 \times 27}$

5. Simplify each radical. Assume all variables are positive.
   a. $\sqrt{50}$
   b. $\sqrt{300}$
   c. $\sqrt{125}$
   d. $\sqrt{54}$
   e. $\sqrt{9x^3y^2}$
   f. $\sqrt{225a^5b^6}$
   g. $\sqrt{x^2y^4z}$
   h. $\sqrt{96km^2}$

6. Rationalize the denominator.
   a. $\dfrac{4}{\sqrt{2}}$
   b. $\dfrac{3}{2\sqrt{3}}$
   c. $\dfrac{x}{\sqrt{7}}$
   d. $\dfrac{t - 1}{3\sqrt{5}}$

7. The two shorter sides of a right triangle are 8 units and 15 units. What is the length of the hypotenuse?

8. Find the distance between each pair of points.
   a. $A(4,9)$, $B(5,2)$
   b. $U(0,9)$, $V(3,7)$
   c. $O(0,0)$, $J(3,-5)$
   d. $M(-5,-6)$, $N(-3,-11)$

9. Copy and complete the table.

t	$t \in R$?	$t \in \overline{Q}$?	$t \in Q$?	$t \in Z$?	$t \in W$?	$t \in N$?
2	Yes	No	Yes	Yes	Yes	Yes
$\sqrt{2}$						
$-\sqrt{2}$						
$\sqrt{-2}$						
$\dfrac{4}{7}$						
$\dfrac{5}{8}$						
π						
$\dfrac{3}{0}$						
5.92						
$3.\overline{1}$						
9.121 121 112 ...						
$\dfrac{\pi}{4}$						

4–1 Graphing Equations in Two Variables

Mick plays lacrosse with a community team. He earns 2 points for each goal scored and 1 point for every assist. After the first game of the season, Mick earned 6 points. How many goals and assists might Mick have scored?

Define the variables.
Let x be the number of goals Mick scored.
Let y be the number of assists Mick scored.

Write an equation to represent the number of points earned in the game.
$2x + y = 6$

Solve the problem by finding pairs of whole numbers that satisfy $2x + y = 6$. Make a table of the solutions.

Let $x = 0$:
$$2x + y = 6$$
$$2(0) + y = 6$$
$$y = 6$$
Solution: (0,6)

Let $x = 1$:
$$2x + y = 6$$
$$2(1) + y = 6$$
$$2 + y = 6$$
$$y = 4$$
Solution: (1,4)

x	y
0	6
1	4
2	2
3	0

The table shows all of the possible numbers of goals (x) and assists (y) Mick could have scored.

92

With the problem represented by the equation $2x + y = 6$, the solutions can be graphed in the coordinate plane.

For each point in the graph, the first number in its ordered pair is its **x-coordinate**. The second number is its **y-coordinate**.

The possible values for x and y are whole numbers. We say that the **replacement set** for x and y is the set of whole numbers.

We write: $2x + y = 6$, $x, y \in W$

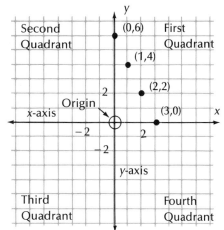

If the replacement set is not stated, it is the set of real numbers.

EXAMPLE 1:

List some solutions to $2x + y = 6$, $x, y \in R$. Draw its graph.

Let $x = 0$:	Let $x = 3$:
$2x + y = 6$	$2x + y = 6$
$2(0) + y = 6$	$2(3) + y = 6$
$y = 6$	$6 + y = 6$
	$y = 0$
Solution: $(0,6)$	Solution: $(3,0)$

Other solutions are given in the table.

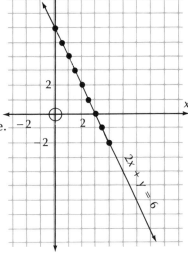

x	y
0	6
0.5	5
1	4
1.5	3
2	2
2.5	1
3	0
3.5	−1

Every increase of a half unit in x results in a decrease of 1 unit in y.

If we graphed *all* ordered pairs satisfying $2x + y = 6$, the result would be the straight line shown above, containing an infinite number of solutions.

The line crosses the x-axis at $(3,0)$.
The x-coordinate of this point, 3, is called the **x-intercept** of the line.

The line crosses the y-axis at $(0,6)$.
The y-coordinate of this point, 6, is called the **y-intercept** of the line.

Example 1 shows that the graph of $2x + y = 6$ is a straight line.

If an equation can be written in the form $ax + by = c$, with a and b not both 0, then its graph is a straight line $(x, y \epsilon R)$. Such an equation is called a **linear equation**.

Conversely, every straight line in the coordinate plane has an equation of the form $ax + by = c$, with a and b not both 0.

Linear: $2x - y = 5$ **Not Linear:** $2x^2 + y = 6$

$y = 3$ (or $0x + y = 3$) $xy = 16$

$3x - 6 = 0$ (or $3x + 0y = 6$)

EXAMPLE 2:   Graph $2x - y = 5$, $x, y \epsilon R$.

Since the equation is linear, its graph is a straight line. Two points in the solution are sufficient to graph a line. The two easiest points to find are related to the x- and y-intercepts.

To find the x-intercept,   To find the y-intercept,
let $y = 0$:   let $x = 0$:

     $2x - y = 5$ $2x - y = 5$

    $2x - (0) = 5$ $2(0) - y = 5$

        $2x = 5$ $-y = 5$

          $x = 2.5$ $y = -5$

The x-intercept is 2.5.   The y-intercept is -5.

The points $(2.5, 0)$ and $(0, -5)$ are in the line.

Find a third point as a check for your work.

Let $x = 1$:

     $2x - y = 5$

    $2(1) - y = 5$

      $2 - y = 5$

        $-y = 3$

          $y = -3$

x	y
0	-5
2.5	0
1	-3

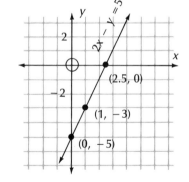

Solution: $(1, -3)$

The intercept method for finding two points in a line does not work when the line passes through $(0,0)$. Another point must be found. For example, the solutions $(0,0)$ and $(5,3)$ satisfy the equation $3x - 5y = 0$. A third point to check your work is $(-5, -3)$.

There are two special types of linear equations.

1. The graph of the equation $x = 3$ is a vertical line.

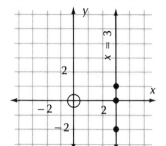

x	y
3	0
3	1
3	-2

Any ordered pair with 3 as its x-coordinate is a solution to this equation.

2. The graph of the equation $y = 5$ is a horizontal line.

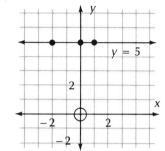

x	y
0	5
1	5
-2	5

Any ordered pair with 5 as its y-coordinate is a solution to this equation.

EXERCISES

A 1. Draw a coordinate grid with the x-axis and the y-axis each ranging from −10 to 10. Plot and label the following points.
   - a. $A(3,5)$
   - b. $B(9,3)$
   - c. $C(-2,8)$
   - d. $D(-5,-7)$
   - e. $E(0,5)$
   - f. $F(6,0)$
   - g. $G(2,-3)$
   - h. $H(-3,-8)$

2. Rewrite each equation in the form $ax + by = c$.
   - a. $x = 8$
   - b. $y = -2$
   - c. $2x - 8 = 0$
   - d. $3x - 4 = y$

3. Which of the ordered pairs listed satisfy the given equation?
   - a. $x + y = 7$ $(5,2), (7,7), (0,7), (-3,-4), (9,-2)$
   - b. $3x + y = 5$ $(0,5), (5,-5), (2,-1), (1,2), (3,2)$
   - c. $5x - 2y = 10$ $(2,0), (4,5), (0,5), (-2,-10), (2,5)$
   - d. $4x - 3y = 12$ $(3,4), (0,4), (3,0), (6,4), (-3,-8)$

B 4. Is the equation linear? If so, find 3 solutions and graph the line.
   - a. $5x - 2y = 20$
   - b. $x^2 + y = 16$
   - c. $\frac{1}{4}x + \frac{1}{2}y = \frac{1}{3}$
   - d. $4x^2 + 7 = y$
   - e. $\frac{1}{5}x - \frac{1}{2} = y$
   - f. $xy = 7$

5. For each equation, copy and complete the table of values and then graph the line represented by the equation.
   - a. $x + y = 5$
   - b. $x - 2y = 8$
   - c. $y = 2x + 8$
   - d. $x = 2y + 3$

x	y
0	?
?	0
3	?
?	-2

x	y
0	?
?	0
-6	?
?	3

x	y
0	?
-5	?
1	?
?	0

x	y
?	0
?	-2
?	3
0	?

6. Find the *x*- and *y*-intercepts of the line represented by each equation.
   a. $x + y = -2$
   b. $x + y = 16$
   c. $x - y = -4$
   d. $2x - 6 = y$
   e. $2y = 3x + 6$
   f. $4x + 3y = -24$
   g. $x = 3$
   h. $3x + 2y = 7$
   i. $y = -1$

7. For each equation, make a table of values with at least three ordered pairs, then graph the line represented by the equation.
   a. $x + y = 8$
   b. $x - y = 0$
   c. $2x + y = 7$
   d. $3x - y = 8$
   e. $2x - y = 7$
   f. $2x + 5y = 0$
   g. $6x = 2$
   h. $-x + 2y = 5$
   i. $2y = 5x - 3$
   j. $2x = 7y$
   k. $\frac{1}{3}y = \frac{1}{2}x - 1$
   l. $2x + 5y = 7$
   m. $x = 7$
   n. $y = 0$
   o. $3y = -2$

8. Graph each set of points. Draw a straight line through the points and name the *x*- and *y*-intercepts of the line.
   a. $(2,9), (1,6), (-2,-3)$
   b. $(1,-2), (3,2), (-3,-10)$
   c. $(6,-6), (-2,6), (-4,9)$
   d. $(-10,-2), (10,6), (5,4)$
   e. $(-3,0), (-2,-1), (0,-3)$
   f. $(-4,-1), (2,2), (4,3)$

9. Graph the line represented by the equation using the *x*- and *y*-intercepts. Find a third point in the line to check.
   a. $2x + 5y = 10$
   b. $6x + y = 0$
   c. $x - 3y = 12$
   d. $5x - 7y = 0$
   e. $3y = x - 9$
   f. $2x - 3y = 6$
   g. $y = -x - 2$
   h. $x = 7 - y$
   i. $y = 2x - 3$

10. Anne earns $8.90/h for a 40 h week and $13.35/h for overtime hours, or any time above 40 h for the week. If *x* represents the number of overtime hours worked and *y* dollars represents Anne's earnings, then an equation to represent her earnings is
    $y = (8.9)(40) + (13.35)(x)$, or $y = 13.35x + 356$. Make a table to find her earnings for a 42 h week; a 46 h week; a 50 h week.

11. Jacques earns $8.50/h for a 35 h week and time-and-a-half for any time above 35 h for the week. If *x* represents the number of overtime hours worked and *y* dollars represents his earnings, then an equation to represent his earnings during an overtime week is
    $y = (8.5)(35) + (1.5)(8.5)x$, or $y = 12.75x + 297.5$. Make a table to find Jacques's earnings for a 40 h week; a 45 h week; a 35 h week.

12. Marie earns $9.40/h for regular hours and time-and-a-half for any time above 40 h for the week. What are Marie's earnings for a 40 h week? a 46 h week? a 50 h week?

13. Using the same set of axes, graph the line represented by each equation. How are these lines related?
    a. $y = 2x$
    b. $y = 2x - 2$
    c. $y = 2x + 3$
    d. $y = 2x - 7$
    e. $y = 2x + 5$
    f. $y = 2x - 4.5$

14. Using the same set of axes, graph the line represented by each equation. How are these lines related?

   a. $y = x + 3$ **b.** $y = -x + 3$ **c.** $y = 3x + 3$

   d. $y = 2x + 3$ **e.** $y = -3x + 3$ **f.** $y = 3$

15. Plot each set of points and join the points to form a polygon. Find the area of each polygon by counting square units on the grid.

   a. $(2,2), (2,-3), (-3,-3), (-3,2)$

   b. $(2,6), (2,3), (-7,3), (-7,6)$

   c. $(2,1), (2,6), (5,1)$

   d. $(2,6), (-5,6), (-5,-4)$

   e. $(-2,-1), (-8,-1), (-6,-4), (0,-4)$

For exercises 16 to 21: choose two variables to represent the numbers that are asked for; write an equation relating the variables to the problem; use the equation to solve the problem.

16. A 10 m telephone pole was cut into two pieces. Find all possible whole numbers for the lengths of the two pieces, in metres.

17. At midnight on March 21, the temperature in Timmins was below zero, while the temperature in Windsor was above zero. If the temperature difference between the cities was 9°C, find all such possible pairs of temperature readings that are integers.

18. An isosceles triangle has a perimeter of 18 cm. Find all possible whole numbers for the lengths of the sides in centimetres. (*Hint*: The sum of the lengths of any two sides of a triangle must exceed the length of the other side.)

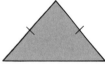

an isosceles triangle

19. A letter requires 90¢ postage. Only 15¢ stamps and 20¢ stamps are available. What combinations of these stamps can be used?

20. Kim works as a stereo salesperson, earning $150/week plus a commission of 2% of all sales. What are Kim's earnings when sales total $1500? $1750? $2350?

21. Leslie works as a miner in an ore mine, earning $275/week plus an incentive bonus of 3.5¢ for each tonne of ore mined. What are Leslie's earnings for a week when the amount of ore mined is 1000 t? 1500 t? 1600 t?

EXTRA

What postage of at least $2 can be made up with 17¢ and 24¢ stamps? In other words, for what values of x and y is $17x + 24y \geq 200$ for $x, y \in W$?

4–2 Graphing Pairs of Equations

In the lacrosse game during which Mick scored 6 points, he was involved in a total of 4 goals. How many goals and assists did he make?

A goal is worth 2 points, an assist 1 point.

Define the variables.	*Write two equations.*
Let x be the number of goals.	$2x + y = 6$
Let y be the number of assists.	$x + y = 4$

Graph the two equations for $x, y \in R$. Make a partial table of possible x and y values for each equation first.

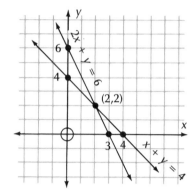

$2x + y = 6$

x	y
0	6
3	0
1	4

$x + y = 4$

x	y
0	4
4	0
2	2

The lines cross at the point (2,2).

The point (2,2) is a solution to *both* equations.

We say that (2,2) is a solution to the **system of equations**.

Check that (2,2) satisfies both equations.

For $2x + y = 6$, L.S. $= 2x + y$ For $x + y = 4$, L.S. $= x + y$
                       $= 2(2) + 2$ $= 2 + 2$
                       $= 4 + 2$ $= 4$
                       $= 6$ $=$ R.S. ✓
                       $=$ R.S. ✓

The point of intersection (2,2) indicates that Mick scored 2 goals and 2 assists.
Check: 2 goals give Mick 4 points and 2 assists give him 2 points;
          $4 + 2 = 6$ ✓

EXAMPLE 1: Student Council organized a school dance and sold tickets for $4 to students with student cards and for $6 to those without cards. They made $510 in ticket sales. They sold a total of 110 tickets. How many $4 and $6 tickets were sold?

Define the variables.	*Write two equations.*
Let x be the number of $4 tickets sold.	$4x + 6y = 510$
Let y be the number of $6 tickets sold.	$x + y = 110$

Graph the two equations assuming $x, y \in R$, and estimate the point of intersection.

Start by making a table of three possible solutions for each equation.

$4x + 6y = 510$ $x + y = 110$

x	y
3	83
45	55
15	75

x	y
10	100
50	60
60	50

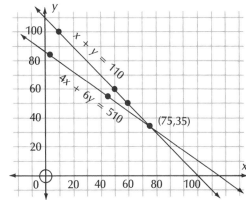

Reading from the graph, the solution appears to be (75,35) which, in this situation, would mean 75 tickets sold at $4 and 35 tickets sold at $6.

Check: 75 $4 tickets yield $300; 35 $6 tickets yield $210;
$300 + $210 = $510. ✓

A system of equations might not have *exactly* one solution.

EXAMPLE 2:   Graph the solution to $x - 2y = 4$ and $3x - 6y = 12$.

$x - 2y = 4$ $3x - 6y = 12$

x	y
0	−2
4	0
2	−1

x	y
0	−2
4	0
2	−1

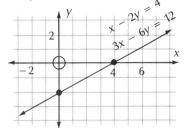

These two equations have the *same* graph; each solution of one equation is a solution to the other. The system of equations has an infinite number of solutions.

The two equations are *equivalent*. To see this is true, multiply each term of $x - 2y = 4$ by 3. The result is $3x - 6y = 12$.

EXAMPLE 3:   Graph the solution to $2x + y = 5$ and $4x + 2y = 4$.

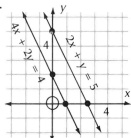

These two equations represent lines that never cross, or parallel lines. The system of equations has no solution, so we say the solution is the empty set ϕ.

To verify this, multiply both sides of the first equation by 2. The equations become $4x + 2y = 10$ and $4x + 2y = 4$. It is impossible to find any ordered pair (x,y) that will satisfy *both* $4x + 2y = 10$ *and* $4x + 2y = 4$.

99

EXERCISES

A 1. Estimate the solution of each system of equations graphed below. Test your answer.

a.

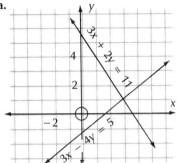

b.

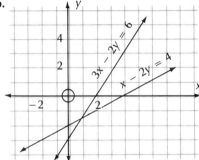

c.

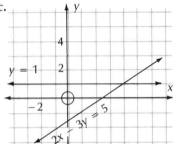

d.

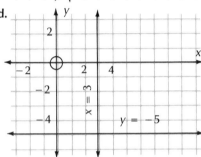

2. Determine whether the given ordered pair is a solution of the system of equations by substituting in both equations.

  a. (2,1): $3x - y = 5$
              $2x + y = 5$

  b. (−2,−4): $3x + y = -10$
                 $x - 2y = 2$

  c. (5,1): $x = 3y + 2$
              $y = x - 4$

  d. (−7,−3): $x - 2y = -1$
                 $y - 1 = 2x + 10$

3. Graph the line represented by the equation $3x - 5y = 15$.
  a. Draw a line whose equation has the solution $(-5, -6)$ in common with $3x - 5y = 15$.
  b. Draw a line whose equation has no solution in common with $3x - 5y = 15$.
  c. Draw a line whose equation has an infinite number of solutions in common with $3x - 5y = 15$.

4. Graph each system of equations and estimate the point of intersection.

  a. $x + y = 4$
        $x - y = 2$

  b. $3x + 2y = 6$
        $3x - 2y = -18$

  c. $x + 2y = 1$
        $x - y = -8$

  d. $3x + 2y = 1$
        $y = 2$

  e. $x = -2$
        $2x + 3y = 8$

  f. $2x + y = 1$
        $y = 1$

  g. $x = 7$
        $y = -3$

  h. $y = x$
        $y = 2x + 1$

  i. $y = 3x - 3$
        $x = 5$

100

B **5.** Solve each system of equations by graphing.

a. $y = 2x$
$2x + y = 8$

b. $3x + y = 6$
$3x + y = 3$

c. $4x - 2y = 10$
$y = 2x$

d. $7x - 2y = 14$
$3x - y = 5$

e. $2x + y = 12$
$2x - y = 14$

f. $5x - 2y = 20$
$4y = 10x - 50$

g. $5x + 2y = 10$
$10x + 4y = 20$

h. $5x + 2y = 15$
$y = 0$

i. $3x + 5y = 15$
$2x + 6y = 2$

6. A cash register contains 56 quarters and dimes with a total value of $8.60. How many quarters and dimes are there?
Let x be the number of quarters and y be the number of dimes.
Then $25x + 10y = 860$ represents the total value of the coins and $x + y = 56$ represents the number of coins. Find the solution of the pair of equations to solve the problem.

7. Thirty tickets were sold within six hours of announcing a concert. Adult admission is $3 and students are admitted for $2. If the total ticket sales were $78, how many of each ticket were sold?

8. Marion works a 40 h week. She is paid $10/h when she must supervise other employees and $8/h at other times. At the end of one week, she had earned $350. For how many hours had Marion supervised other employees?

9. Find a and b so that the given ordered pair is the solution to the system of equations. Graph the equations.

a. (3,5): $ax - y = 1$
$5x - by = 5$

b. (4, 10): $y = ax - 2$
$3x - by = -3$

c. (2, -5): $ax - 2y = 4$
$3x + by = -9$

d. (-4, -1): $5x + by = 15$
$ax - 2y = 14$

10. A bank deposit was to contain $3.20 in dimes and quarters. On the deposit slip, however, the numbers of dimes and quarters were accidentally reversed, showing a deposit of $3.80. How many dimes and quarters were actually in the deposit?

EXTRA

Buses leave every 10 min from the Kootenay Loop and travel down Hastings Street to the end of the route. The trip takes 55 min. The bus waits 15 min at the end of the route and travels back along the same route. On the route back to Kootenay Loop, how many buses will be passed going the opposite direction?

4–3 Line Segments on a Grid

Archaeological digs are often mapped on a coordinate grid so that the location of each find can be precisely identified. The graph below the photograph provides an example of such a map. The locations of finds and distances between various finds may give clues about the community that lived there long ago.

EXAMPLE 1: Find the distance between the bowl and the arrowhead.

The bowl is located at $P_1 (-2, -3)$. The arrowhead is at $P_2 (4, 1)$.

Apply the distance formula.

$$P_1P_2 = \sqrt{(x_2 - x_1)^2 + (y_2 - y_1)^2}$$

$$P_1P_2 = \sqrt{(4 - (-2))^2 + (1 - (-3))^2}$$

$$= \sqrt{6^2 + 4^2}$$

$$= \sqrt{36 + 16}$$

$$= \sqrt{52}$$

$$\doteq 7.21$$

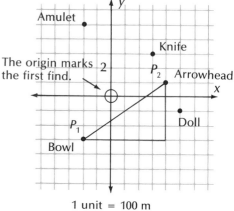

The origin marks the first find.

1 unit = 100 m

Each unit represents 100 m, so the distance is about 721 m.

EXAMPLE 2: As the dig continues, a student finds a small blade exactly halfway between the bowl and the arrowhead. At what point on the grid should the blade be marked?

In order for the midpoint M to be halfway between P_1 and P_2, its x-coordinate must be halfway between the x-coordinates of P_1 and P_2; its y-coordinate must be halfway between the y-coordinates of P_1 and P_2.

$$M = \left(\frac{(-2) + 4}{2}, \frac{(-3) + 1}{2}\right) \text{ or } (1, -1).$$

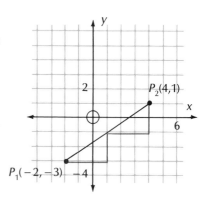

The calculation used in example 2 can be generalized.

> **The Midpoint Formula**
> The midpoint of the line segment joining $P_1(x_1, y_1)$, and $P_2(x_2, y_2)$ is:
> $$M = \left(\frac{x_1 + x_2}{2}, \frac{y_1 + y_2}{2}\right).$$

102

EXERCISES

A 1. Using the archaeological map on the previous page, find the distance between the given objects.
   a. the bowl and the amulet
   b. the bowl and the doll
   c. the amulet and the doll
   d. the arrowhead and the knife

B 2. Graph each segment with the given endpoints, then find its midpoint.
   a. (5,2), (9,6)
   b. (3,7), (11,15)
   c. (6,−1), (2,5)
   d. (−5,3), (−9,5)
   e. (−7,−8), (−3,−1)
   f. (1,6), (−3,−3)
   g. (5,−2), (5,−6)
   h. (5,−2), (9,−2)
   i. (3,8), (−2,1)

3. Graph each rectangle with the given vertices, then find the lengths of the two diagonals of each rectangle. What hypothesis can you make about the diagonals of a rectangle?
   a. $A(4,3)$, $B(8,3)$, $C(8,8)$, $D(4,8)$
   b. $I(−10,−3)$, $J(−5,−3)$, $K(−5,2)$, $L(−10,2)$
   c. $E(−7,3)$, $F(2,3)$, $G(2,6)$, $H(−7,6)$
   d. $M(−8,−6)$, $N(4,−6)$, $P(4,−4)$, $Q(−8,−4)$

4. Find the midpoint of the two diagonals of each rectangle you graphed in exercise 3. Make a hypothesis about the midpoints of the diagonals of rectangles.

C 5. Using a "generalized" rectangle with vertices $P(x_1,y_1)$, $Q(x_2,y_1)$, $R(x_2,y_2)$, and $S(x_1,y_2)$, prove your hypotheses from exercises 3 and 4.

6. Given the midpoint M and one endpoint of a line segment, find the other endpoint.
   a. $A(3,2)$, $M(5,6)$, $B(x,y)$
   b. $C(5,1)$, $M(6,5)$, $D(x,y)$
   c. $E(−4,6)$, $M(0,9)$, $F(x,y)$
   d. $G(8,5)$, $M(3,2)$, $H(x,y)$
   e. $I(3,−4)$, $M(4.5,−1.5)$, $J(x,y)$
   f. $K(−3,−1)$, $M(−7.5, 3.5)$, $L(x,y)$

EXTRA

Plot $\triangle XYZ$ with vertices $X(6,−2)$, $Y(8,6)$, and $Z(−8,8)$ on a large cardboard grid. Find the midpoints of the three sides and construct the **medians** (segments joining a midpoint to the opposite vertex). The three medians should meet at a single point called the **centroid** of the triangle. Cut out the triangle.

1. Place a pencil tip at the centroid of the cardboard triangle and try to balance the triangle, as shown.

2. Now place the pencil tip at several other places in the cardboard triangle. Can you balance the triangle?

3. The centroid of a triangle is sometimes called its "centre of gravity". Explain.

103

4–4 Calculating Slope

In many places, the law has specific requirements regarding the steepness of a wheelchair ramp, as a ramp that is too steep is very difficult to maneuver.

Suppose a wheelchair ramp rises 42 cm for every 560 cm of horizontal distance. The **slope** of the ramp is a measure of its steepness and is equal to the ratio $\dfrac{\text{Rise}}{\text{Run}}$.

$$\text{Slope} = \frac{\text{Rise}}{\text{Run}} = \frac{42}{560} = \frac{3}{40}$$

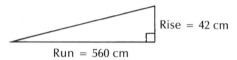

Rise = 42 cm

Run = 560 cm

To calculate the slope of a non-vertical line on a coordinate grid:
a. choose two points on the line;
b. determine the rise and the run between the two points;
c. find the rise-to-run ratio, expressed as a fraction.

EXAMPLE 1: a. Find the slope m of $\overleftrightarrow{AB}$.

For $\overleftrightarrow{AB}$, $m = \dfrac{\text{Rise}}{\text{Run}}$

$= \dfrac{4 - (-2)}{3 - (-1)}$

$= \dfrac{6}{4}$

$= \dfrac{3}{2}$

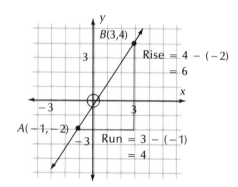

The slope is *positive*. It slants up and to the right.

b. Find the slope m of $\overleftrightarrow{PQ}$.

For $\overleftrightarrow{PQ}$, $m = \dfrac{\text{Rise}}{\text{Run}}$

$= \dfrac{3 - (-1)}{(-4) - 4}$

$= \dfrac{4}{-8}$

$= -\dfrac{1}{2}$

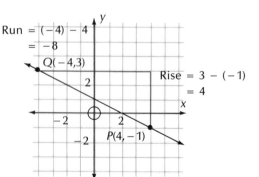

The slope is *negative*. It slants down and to the right.

The slope of a line can be calculated using the slope formula.

The Slope Formula
Given two points on a line $P_1(x_1, y_1)$ and $P_2(x_2, y_2)$:
Slope of $\overleftrightarrow{P_1P_2} = \dfrac{\text{Rise}}{\text{Run}} = \dfrac{y_2 - y_1}{x_2 - x_1}$.

EXAMPLE 2: Find the slope m of each line on the grid at the right.

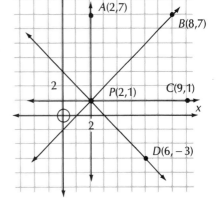

a. For $\overleftrightarrow{AP}$, $m = \dfrac{y_2 - y_1}{x_2 - x_1} = \dfrac{7 - 1}{2 - 2} = \dfrac{6}{0}$

The slope of a vertical line is undefined.

b. For $\overleftrightarrow{BP}$, $m = \dfrac{y_2 - y_1}{x_2 - x_1} = \dfrac{7 - 1}{8 - 2} = 1$

, c. For $\overleftrightarrow{CP}$, $m = \dfrac{y_2 - y_1}{x_2 - x_1} = \dfrac{1 - 1}{9 - 2} = \dfrac{0}{7} = 0$

The slope of a horizontal line is zero.

d. For $\overleftrightarrow{DP}$, $m = \dfrac{y_2 - y_1}{x_2 - x_1} = \dfrac{(-3) - 1}{6 - 2} = \dfrac{-4}{4} = -1$

The slope of a line is constant between any two points on the line. Thus, to determine if three or more points are **collinear** (lie in the same line), check that the slope between each and every pair of points is the same.

EXAMPLE 3: Are $A(3,1)$, $B(6,3)$, and $C(12,7)$ collinear?

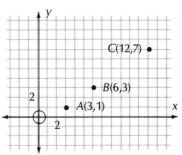

a. Find the slope m of $\overline{AB}$.
$$m = \dfrac{y_2 - y_1}{x_2 - x_1} = \dfrac{3 - 1}{6 - 3} = \dfrac{2}{3}$$

b. Find the slope m of $\overline{BC}$.
$$m = \dfrac{y_2 - y_1}{x_2 - x_1} = \dfrac{7 - 3}{12 - 6} = \dfrac{4}{6} = \dfrac{2}{3}$$

Since the slopes are equal, the three points are collinear.

105

EXERCISES

A 1. a. Which of the lines below have positive slope?
b. Which lines have negative slope?

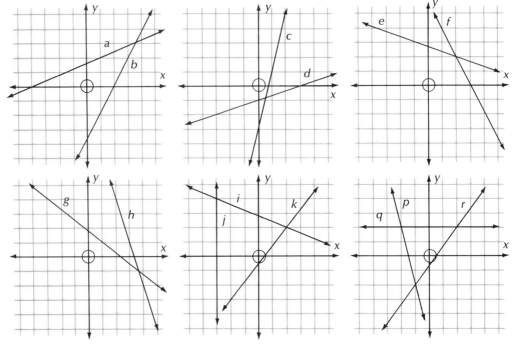

B 2. Find the slope of each line in exercise 1.

3. Find the slope of the line that passes through the given pair of points.
a. (2,3), (4,7)   **b.** (5,3), (3,9)   **c.** (−2,1), (1,10)
d. (3,−3), (5,3)   **e.** (−3,−2), (1,4) **f.** (5,−1), (5,20)
g. (8,2), (11,2)   **h.** (−6,1), (−5,0) **i.** (−5,−3), (−5,0)

4. For each item in exercise 3, state whether the line is horizontal, vertical, or slopes upward to the right or down to the right.

5. Which sets of points are collinear?
a. (3,4), (4,6), (8,14)   **b.** (3,7), (4,5), (8,−3)
c. (5,2), (2,6), (−1,10)   **d.** (0,1), (−10,−5), (−25,−14)
e. (−4,−2), (−10,−4), (0,−6)   **f.** (3,−2), (−6,4), (−3,2)

6. Find the point in the *x*-axis which is collinear with (0,−3) and (12,6).

7. Find *x* so that $A(x,5)$, $B(−4,2)$, and $C(4,−4)$ are collinear.

8. a. Find the midpoint of $\overline{AB}$ with endpoints $A(−3,5)$ and $B(7,−3)$.
b. Calculate the slope of $\overleftrightarrow{AB}$.

9. a. Find the midpoint of $\overline{PQ}$ with endpoints $P(−1,−7)$ and $Q(3,5)$.
b. Show that the endpoints and the midpoint are collinear.

10. The slope of the roof of an A-frame cottage is $\frac{3}{4}$. How high is the peak of the cottage, given that the total width of the cottage is 16 m?

11. A loading ramp at a grain elevator can be raised at an angle to enable trucks to empty their cargo. The slope of the ramp, when raised, is $\frac{5}{4}$. If the ramp is 4.2 m long, how high is its non-stationary end when the ramp is in the loading position?

12. A hill has a slope of 0.2 over a length of straight incline. If the run is 50 m, what is the length of the road going up the hill?

13. The sketch of a deck to be built at the side of a ravine is shown at the right. What is the required length for the exposed part of the two support posts?

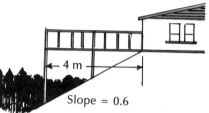

14. Shortly after take-off, a light airplane has a flight path that rises upward with a slope of 0.4. After the plane has travelled 300 m, how much higher is the plane off the ground? How far has the plane travelled along the flight path?

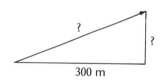

15. Rectangle $ABCD$ has vertices $A(5,9)$, $B(5,4)$, $C(2,4)$, and $D(2,9)$.
    a. Find the midpoint M of diagonal $\overline{AC}$.
    b. Show that M lies in diagonal $\overline{BD}$.

16. A 75 m stretch of mountain road has slope 0.35. What is the horizontal distance covered by the stretch of road? What is the rise of the stretch of road? Answer correct to two decimal places.

EXTRA

Logic Problems

Are the following statements *true* or *false*? Justify your answers.

1. If A, B, C, and D are collinear, then the slopes of $\overline{AB}$ and $\overline{CD}$ are equal.

2. If the slopes of $\overline{AB}$ and $\overline{CD}$ are equal, then A, B, C, and D are collinear.

3. If A, B, C, and D are not collinear, then the slopes of $\overline{AB}$ and $\overline{CD}$ are not equal.

4. If the slopes of $\overline{AB}$ and $\overline{CD}$ are not equal, then A, B, C, and D are not collinear.

4–5 Graphing and Slope

To determine the slope of a line, given its equation, find two points which lie in the line and then use the slope formula.

EXAMPLE 1: What is the slope of the line with the equation $3x - y = 5$?

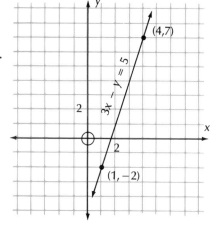

a. Find two solutions to the equation.

x	y
4	7
1	-2

b. Use the slope formula.

$$m = \frac{y_2 - y_1}{x_2 - x_1}$$

$$= \frac{(-2) - 7}{1 - 4}$$

$$= \frac{-9}{-3}$$

$$= 3$$

The slope of the line is 3.

If a point in a line and the slope of a line are given, the line may be constructed.

EXAMPLE 2: Construct the line with slope 3 and passing through $A(1, -1)$.

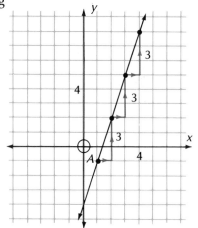

a. Plot the point $A(1, -1)$.

b. Slope $= 3$ or $\frac{3}{1}$

That is, $\frac{\text{Rise}}{\text{Run}} = \frac{3}{1}$, so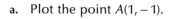

locate other points by moving from A to the right 1 and up 3, then repeating as shown.

c. Join the points to construct the line.

EXERCISES

A 1. Find the slope of each line graphed below.

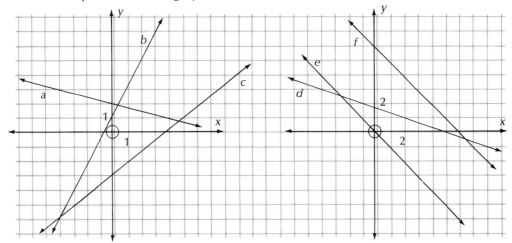

B 2. Find the slope of the line, given its equation.

a. $x + y = 5$ b. $x - y = 4$ c. $x + 3y = 8$

d. $x - 3y = 6$ e. $3x - 2y = 8$ f. $x + 3 = 2y$

g. $y = 3x - 1$ h. $2y = x + 4$ i. $y = -2x + 3$

j. $2x - 5y = 0$ k. $4x - 5 = 7$ l. $3y + 2 = 4$

3. Construct the line through the given point and with the given slope, m.

a. $(3,2)$, $m = 2$ b. $(3,-4)$, $m = 5$ c. $(-3,1)$, $m = \frac{2}{5}$

d. $(4,2)$, $m = -2$ e. $(-3,5)$, $m = -3$ f. $(-2,-3)$, $m = -\frac{3}{5}$

g. $(2,-5)$, $m = 1\frac{2}{3}$ h. $(-4,2)$, $m = -\frac{5}{2}$ i. $(5,-2)$, $m = -2\frac{1}{3}$

j. $(0,1)$, $m = \frac{5}{6}$ k. $(3,2)$, $m = 0$ l. $(-2,1)$, m undefined

4. Construct the line through the given point P, with the same slope as the line passing through the given points A and B.

a. $P(0,0)$, $A(1,-2)$, $B(3,2)$

b. $P(1,1)$, $A(3,-2)$, $B(5,3)$

c. $P(-2,1)$, $A(-6,2)$, $B(-9,3)$

d. $P(-1,-3)$, $A(-4,5)$, $B(0,1)$

e. $P(3,1)$, $A(6,-1)$, $B(-2,1)$

C 5. Find the missing coordinates, given the following pairs of points and the slope m of the segment between them.

a. $(3,5)$, $(4,y)$, $m = 3$ b. $(-1,3)$, $(x,-7)$, $m = 2$

c. $(2,7)$, $(x,1)$, $m = -3$ d. $(5,-2)$, $(3,y)$, $m = 0$

e. $(4,7)$, $(x,11)$, $m = \frac{2}{3}$ f. $(-4,1)$, $(x,-5)$, m undefined

g. $(5,2)$, $(-3,y)$, $m = -\frac{3}{4}$ h. $(-3,-2)$, $(x,-12)$, $m = -\frac{5}{3}$

i. $(2,1)$, $(-4,y)$, $m = \frac{3}{2}$ j. $(3,8)$, $(x,-2)$, $m = -\frac{5}{2}$

109

4–6 Parallel and Perpendicular Lines

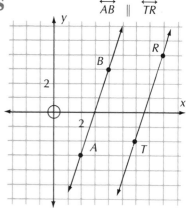

$$\overleftrightarrow{AB} \parallel \overleftrightarrow{TR}$$

The lines on the grid are parallel.
Find their slopes.

For $\overleftrightarrow{AB}$, $m = \dfrac{y_2 - y_1}{x_2 - x_1} = \dfrac{3 - (-3)}{4 - 2} = \dfrac{6}{2} = 3$

For $\overleftrightarrow{TR}$, $m = \dfrac{y_2 - y_1}{x_2 - x_1} = \dfrac{4 - (-2)}{8 - 6} = \dfrac{6}{2} = 3$

The slopes of $\overleftrightarrow{AB}$ and $\overleftrightarrow{TR}$ are equal.

> Parallel lines have equal slope. Two lines with equal slope are parallel.

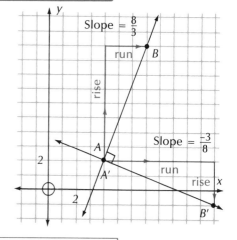

The lines on the grid at the right are perpendicular.
Find their slopes.

$\overleftrightarrow{AB}$ has been rotated 90° onto $\overleftrightarrow{A'B'}$.
The rise of $\overleftrightarrow{AB}$ became the run of $\overleftrightarrow{A'B'}$.
The run of $\overleftrightarrow{AB}$ became the rise of $\overleftrightarrow{A'B'}$.
For $\overleftrightarrow{AB}$, $m = \dfrac{8}{3}$; for $\overleftrightarrow{A'B'}$, $m = -\dfrac{3}{8}$.
The slopes of $\overleftrightarrow{AB}$ and $\overleftrightarrow{A'B'}$ are **negative reciprocals**.

$$\left(\dfrac{8}{3}\right)\left(-\dfrac{3}{8}\right) = -1$$

> Perpendicular lines have slopes that are *negative reciprocals*. Two lines with slopes that are negative reciprocals are perpendicular.

EXAMPLE 1:

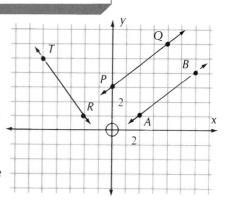

Prove that $\overleftrightarrow{AB}$ is parallel to $\overleftrightarrow{PQ}$ and perpendicular to $\overleftrightarrow{TR}$.
For $\overleftrightarrow{AB}$, $m = \dfrac{3}{4}$. For $\overleftrightarrow{PQ}$, $m = \dfrac{3}{4}$.
Since the slopes are equal, $\overleftrightarrow{AB} \parallel \overleftrightarrow{PQ}$.
For $\overleftrightarrow{AB}$, $m = \dfrac{3}{4}$. For $\overleftrightarrow{TR}$, $m = \dfrac{-4}{3}$.
Since the slopes of $\overleftrightarrow{AB}$ and $\overleftrightarrow{TR}$ are negative reciprocals, the two lines are perpendicular.

EXAMPLE 2: Construct the line that passes through $A(-2, -4)$ and is perpendicular to a line with slope $-\frac{2}{3}$.

a. The slope of the required line is $\frac{3}{2}$, the negative reciprocal of $-\frac{2}{3}$.

b. Plot point A. Locate other points on the line by moving to the right 2 and up 3.

c. Join the points to construct the line.

In the case of horizontal and vertical lines, which are perpendicular, the slopes are *not* reciprocals, since $m = 0$ or m is undefined.

EXERCISES

A 1. Give the negative reciprocal of each.

   a. $\frac{3}{4}$　　b. $\frac{5}{8}$　　c. $-\frac{5}{6}$　　d. -3　　e. $-1\frac{3}{4}$

2. Copy each diagram. Then construct the line through the point shown and parallel to the given line.

a.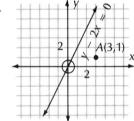

b.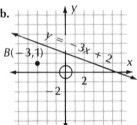

c.

d.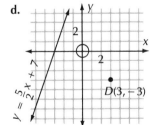

e.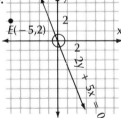

f.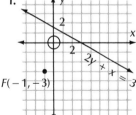

3. Repeat exercise 2, but construct the line through the point shown and perpendicular to the given line.

4. Lines k and l pass through the given pairs of points. Identify whether k and l are parallel, perpendicular, or neither.

   a. k: $(2,3)$, $(4,4)$　　　b. k: $(2,5)$, $(4,11)$　　　c. k: $(4,3)$, $(6,7)$
   　 l: $(3,6)$, $(-7,1)$　　　 l: $(0,4)$, $(-9,7)$　　　 l: $(-2,1)$, $(0,0)$

   d. k: $(-3,-7)$, $(9,-7)$　e. k: $(5,8)$, $(5,-2)$　　　f. k: $(-5,-1)$, $(-1,5)$
   　 l: $(3,5)$, $(-1,4)$　　　 l: $(-2,5)$, $(-2,-1)$　　 l: $(3,4)$, $(7,-2)$

111

B **5.** Construct the line that passes through the given point and is parallel to a line with the given slope, m.

a. $(3,2); m = 1$ b. $(4,5); m = -2$ c. $(-1,5); m$ undefined

d. $(-2,4); m = -\frac{1}{2}$ e. $(3,4); m = 0$ f. $(-5,-1); m = 0.4$

6. Construct the line that passes through the given point and is perpendicular to a line with the given slope, m.

a. $(2,1); m = -\frac{1}{3}$ b. $(4,3); m = -1.5$ c. $(3,5); m = 0.2$

d. $(-3,-2); m = 0$ e. $(-1,2); m = \frac{3}{4}$ f. $(5,-1); m$ undefined

7. What is the product of the slopes of two perpendicular lines, where neither slope is undefined?

8. Show that the quadrilateral with vertices $A(-4,-2)$, $B(-8,2)$, $C(10,2)$, and $D(14,-2)$ is a parallelogram. (Show $\overline{AB} \parallel \overline{CD}$ and $\overline{BC} \parallel \overline{AD}$.)

9. Use slopes to show that the triangle with vertices $F(1,-2)$, $G(3,0)$, and $H(3,-4)$ is a right-angled triangle. (Graph the triangle first.)

10. Which sets of points give the vertices of a right-angled triangle?

a. $(3,7)$, $(7,9)$, $(6,1)$ b. $(5,-6)$, $(8,-4)$, $(2,5)$
c. $(-5,-6)$, $(3,-4)$, $(7,-5)$ d. $(2,7)$, $(7,9)$, $(3,-1)$
e. $(-3,4)$, $(1,-10)$, $(8,-8)$ f. $(1,3.5)$, $(3.5,4.5)$, $(1.5,-0.5)$

11. Which sets of points give the vertices of a parallelogram?

a. $(4,3)$, $(-6,2)$, $(-2,-4)$, $(8,-3)$ b. $(5,1)$, $(1,4)$, $(0,-1)$, $(4,-4)$
c. $(2,2)$, $(-2,5)$, $(-4,1)$, $(1,0)$ d. $(-1,3)$, $(-7,6)$, $(0,-5)$, $(1,-3)$
e. $(5,1)$, $(3,4)$, $(-3,0)$, $(-1,-4)$ f. $(0,0)$, $(4,0)$, $(4,4)$, $(0,4)$

12. Show that the triangle with vertices $P(5,6)$, $Q(-9,4)$, and $R(-1,-2)$ is an isosceles right-angled triangle.

13. Given $A(-5,7)$ and $B(-5,-1)$ find the slope of a line perpendicular to $\overline{AB}$.

14. Given $P(4,-3)$ and $Q(7,-3)$ find the slope of a line perpendicular to $\overline{PQ}$.

C 15. Lines k and l containing the given points are parallel. Find the missing values.

a. k: $(2,5)$, $(8,14)$ b. k: $(-3,4)$, $(0,-2)$ c. k: $(-4,-7)$, $(-1,5)$
l: $(5,3)$, $(11,y)$ l: $(2,-2)$, $(0,y)$ l: $(2,8)$, $(x,-4)$
d. k: $(4,-1)$, $(13,5)$ e. k: $(5,8)$, $(26,14)$ f. k: $(3,7)$, $(5,y)$
l: $(-3,-5)$, $(x,1)$ l: $(-3,6)$, $(-24,y)$ l: $(-8,-16)$, $(6,5)$

16. Lines k and l containing the given points are perpendicular. Find the missing values.

a. k: $(3,4)$, $(5,8)$ b. k: $(0,2)$, $(9,-1)$ c. k: $(-3,-1)$, $(3,3)$
l: $(4,2)$, $(x,0)$ l: $(5,1)$, $(7,y)$ l: $(3,-4)$, $(5,y)$
d. k: $(-5,2)$, $(0,6)$ e. k: $(6,2)$, $(-1,6)$ f. k: $(x,1)$, $(2,2)$
l: $(4,7)$, $(x,12)$ l: $(-5,1)$, $(x,15)$ l: $(4,3)$, $(5,4)$

Review

1. Which of the ordered pairs listed are solutions to the given equation?
   a. $x - y = 0$ $(2,3), (8,8), (5,2), (-5,-5), (-7,1)$
   b. $2x + y = 7$ $(3,1), (7,0), (-1,9), (4,-1), (3.5,0)$

2. Graph the line with the given equation. Name the x- and y-intercept of each line.
   a. $3x - 4y = 12$ b. $y = 3x + 3$ c. $x = -2y - 3$
   d. $3x - 2y = -6$ e. $y = 5x - 5$ f. $2x - 3y = -24$

3. Estimate graphically the point of intersection of each pair of lines with the given equations.
   a. $2x - 3y = 2$ b. $x + y = 2$ c. $2x - y = 1$
      $y = x - 1$ $2x + 3y = 1$ $-3x + y = 0$

4. Find the midpoint M of $\overline{AB}$ with endpoints $A(3,-8)$ and $B(7,2)$. Use the distance formula to show that $AM = BM$.

5. Find the slope of each line which passes through the given pair of points.
   a. $(4,-9), (5,0)$ b. $(3,2), (-1,-9)$ c. $(2,1), (2,5)$
   d. $(3,1), (-5,8)$ e. $(2,-1), (7,-1)$ f. $(-2,-4), (-7,-1)$

6. Which sets of points are collinear?
   a. $(5,4), (-1,-8), (3,0)$ b. $(6,-9), (2,7), (4,-1)$ c. $(-3,1), (1,-2), (4,-1)$
   d. $(-2,-1), (-5,1), (-8,3)$ e. $(3,8), (18,3), (7,2)$ f. $(15,2), (-3,20), (4,13)$

7. Find a point in the x-axis collinear with $(1,3)$ and $(-4,-2)$.

8. Given that $A(-1,4)$, $B(1,y)$, and $C(2,-5)$ are collinear, find y.

9. Construct the line that passes through the given point and is parallel to a line with slope m.
   a. $(3,3); m = -1$ b. $(-1,-2); m = \frac{1}{2}$ c. $(2,-1); m = -\frac{3}{2}$

10. Construct the line that passes through the given point and is perpendicular to a line with slope m.
    a. $(-6,4); m = \frac{2}{5}$ b. $(6,-2); m = 0$ c. $(-2,2); m$ undefined

11. The students in class 10B held a car wash as part of a fund-raising drive. They charged $5 for all cars and $8 for vans and trucks. After washing 31 vehicles, they had made $179.
    a. Let x represent the number of cars washed, and let y represent the number of vans or trucks. Write an equation relating x and y to the total number of vehicles washed.
    b. Write an equation relating x and y to the total amount of money collected.
    c. Graph the two equations on the same grid.
    d. Estimate the number of each type of vehicle washed. Check your answer in the original word problem.

4–7 Slope-Intercept Form of a Linear Equation

Look at the lines and their equations on the grid at the right. The slope of each line is given beside its equation.

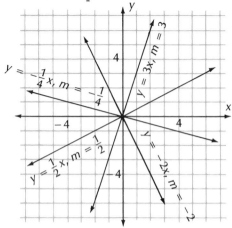

Note that, in each equation, the *coefficient* of x is equal to the *slope* of the line.

For example, two points that lie in $y = -2x$ are $(0,0)$ and $(-1,2)$. The calculated slope of $y = -2x$ is:

$$\frac{y_2 - y_1}{x_2 - x_1} = \frac{2 - 0}{(-1) - 0} = \frac{2}{-1} = -2.$$

> In general, any line of the form $y = mx$ has slope m.

The graph of each line at the right is given by an equation in the form $y = x + b$.

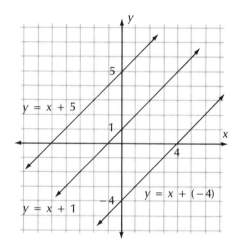

Note that the y-intercept of each line is the same as the numerical term in the equation.

For example, the graph of the line $y = x + 5$ crosses the y-axis at $(0,5)$; its y-intercept is 5.

> In general, any line of the form $y = x + b$ has y-intercept b.

The two observations above can be combined.

> **Slope-Intercept Form of a Linear Equation:** $y = mx + b$
>
> Given an equation in the form $y = mx + b$, the line represented by the equation has slope m and y-intercept b.

This result can be used to simplify graphing and to find and analyse equations of lines.

EXAMPLE 1: Graph the equation $3x + 2y = 6$.

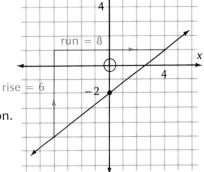

a. Rewrite the equation in slope-intercept form, $y = mx + b$.

$$3x + 2y = 6$$
$$2y = -3x + 6$$
$$y = -\frac{3}{2}x + 3$$

b. Read the slope and y-intercept.

$$y = \boxed{-\frac{3}{2}}x + \boxed{3}$$

slope, $m = -\frac{3}{2}$ y-intercept $= 3$

c. Graph the equation by plotting (0,3) and then moving to the right 2 and down 3 to locate other points on the line.

EXAMPLE 2: Find an equation of the graph at the right.

a. Determine the y-intercept, b.

The y-intercept is -2.

b. Determine the slope, m.

$$m = \frac{\text{rise}}{\text{run}} = \frac{6}{8} = \frac{3}{4}$$

c. Substitute m and b into the equation.
$$y = mx + b$$
$$y = \frac{3}{4}x + (-2)$$

The line can be represented by the equation $y = \frac{3}{4}x - 2$

EXAMPLE 3: Are the graphs of $3x - 2y = 8$ and $4x + 6y = 12$ parallel or perpendicular?

Rewrite in slope-intercept form to compare the slopes.

$$3x - 2y = 8$$
$$-2y = -3x + 8$$
$$y = \frac{3}{2}x - 4$$

$$4x + 6y = 12$$
$$6y = -4x + 12$$
$$y = -\frac{2}{3}x + 2$$

The slopes $\frac{3}{2}$ and $-\frac{2}{3}$ are negative reciprocals, so the lines are perpendicular.

115

EXERCISES

A **1.** Give the slope and *y*-intercept of the line with the given equation.

    a. $y = 3x + 2$ **b.** $y = \frac{1}{2}x + 4$ **c.** $y = -2x - 1$

    d. $y = -\frac{8}{5}x - 2$ **e.** $y = \frac{3}{7}x + \frac{1}{2}$ **f.** $y = 3x - \frac{1}{3}$

2. Determine an equation of the line with the given slope and *y*-intercept.
    a. slope 3, *y*-intercept 2   **b.** slope 2, *y*-intercept -4

    c. slope $-\frac{3}{4}$, *y*-intercept -1 **d.** slope $-\frac{5}{3}$, *y*-intercept $\frac{4}{3}$

3. Determine an equation of each line.

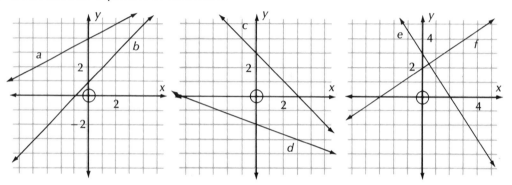

B **4.** Graph each equation without using a table of values.

    a. $y = 2x - 1$ **b.** $y = \frac{2}{3}x - 2$ **c.** $y = -\frac{5}{3}x + 2$

    d. $y = -3x - 1$ **e.** $y = 1.5x + 3$ **f.** $y = \frac{1}{6}x - 6$

5. Rewrite each equation in slope-intercept form.
    a. $x + y = 8$ **b.** $x - y = 3$ **c.** $2x - y = 3$
    d. $5x + 2y = 4$ **e.** $3x - 2y = 4$ **f.** $3x - 5y = 0$

6. Which pairs of equations represent parallel lines? perpendicular lines? neither?

    a. $y = 3x + 5$ **b.** $y = \frac{1}{2}x - 3$ **c.** $y = 5x - 2$
        $y = 3x - 1$ $y = -2x + 3$ $y = 3x - 1$

    d. $2x + 7y = 4$ **e.** $2x - 3y = 5$ **f.** $5x + y = 2$
        $7x = 2y + 3$ $2x + 3y = 4$ $x = 5y + 3$

7. Write an equation of the line with the given slope and *y*-intercept.
Give your answer in the form $ax + by = c$.

    a. $m = 3, b = 2$ **b.** $m = \frac{1}{2}, b = 2$ **c.** $m = -\frac{2}{5}, b = 2$

    d. $m = \frac{3}{4}, b = \frac{1}{2}$ **e.** $m = \frac{12}{5}, b = -7$ **f.** $m = \frac{1}{3}, b = -\frac{5}{6}$

8. The segment with the given endpoints is parallel to the line represented by the given equation. Find the missing values.
   a. $(2,5)$, $(4,a)$; $3x - y = 5$
   b. $(-3,1)$, $(b,-2)$; $x + 2y = 5$
   c. $(-3,-4)$, $(c,0)$; $y = \frac{2}{3}x + 4$
   d. $(0,8)$, $(8,d)$; $y = \frac{3}{4}x - 3$
   e. $(4,-3)$, $(-2,e)$; $y = 5$
   f. $(2,-1)$, $(f,3)$; $x = -3$

9. Find the equation of the line parallel to $5x - 7y = -4$, with a y-intercept of -2.

10. Find the equation of the line with slope $\frac{2}{3}$ and the same y-intercept as $3x - 4y = -12$.

11. Find the equation of the line parallel to the line represented by $4x - 2y = 3$, and with the same y-intercept as the line represented by $3x + 2y = 24$.

12. Find the equation of the line with the same y-intercept as the line represented by $-2x - 5y = 15$, and perpendicular to it.

C 13. A triangle is formed by the graphs of three equations:
   $3x - 2y = 6$, $2x + 3y = 17$, and $3x + 11y = 84$.
   Is the triangle a right-angled triangle? Show why or why not without graphing.

14. A parallelogram is formed by four lines with the given equations:
   $y = \frac{3}{4}x + 3$, $2x + 3y = -6$, $3x - 4y = 7$, and $y = mx + 5$.
   Find the value of m.

15. Without graphing, tell whether the pairs of lines with the given equations have no solution, one solution, or an infinite number of solutions.
   a. $2x - 3y = 8$
      $x + 2y = 5$
   b. $y = \frac{3}{5}x - 2$
      $3x - 5y = 7$
   c. $y = \frac{3}{4}x - 1$
      $3x - 4y = 4$
   d. $3x + y = 2$
      $y = -3x + 2$
   e. $y = \frac{5}{8}x + 3$
      $x = \frac{8}{5}y - 1$
   f. $y = 0.75x - 15$
      $x = -0.25y + 12$

EXTRA

Construct a quadrilateral by joining any four points in the coordinate plane, no three of which are collinear. Compute the midpoint of each side and construct the quadrilateral with the midpoints as vertices. Calculate the slopes of the sides of the quadrilateral constructed. Repeat this procedure with four new points a few times. What conjecture can you make?

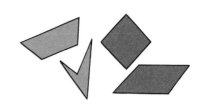

4–8 Point-Slope Form of a Linear Equation

Given the slope of a line and a point through which the line passes, you can find an equation of the line.

EXAMPLE 1: Find an equation of the line with slope $m = 3$ that passes through $T(1,4)$.

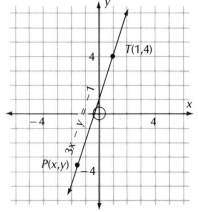

a. Choose any other point on the line and represent it as $P(x,y)$.
b. Substitute given values, $m = 3$ and $T(1,4)$, into the slope formula.

$$m = \frac{y_2 - y_1}{x_2 - x_1}$$

$$3 = \frac{y - 4}{x - 1}$$

$$3x - 3 = y - 4$$

$$3x - y = -1$$

An equation of the line is $3x - y = -1$.

The method used in example 1 can be generalized.

$$m = \frac{y - y_1}{x - x_1} \implies y - y_1 = m(x - x_1)$$

Point-Slope Form of a Linear Equation: $y - y_1 = m(x - x_1)$

Given the slope of a line, m, and a point in the line, (x_1,y_1), an equation of the line can be found by substituting the given values into the point-slope form of a linear equation: $y - y_1 = m(x - x_1)$.

Two points in a line are also sufficient to find an equation of the line.

EXAMPLE 2: Find an equation of the line through $A(1,2)$ and $B(5,-4)$.

a. Use points A and B to find the slope of the line, m.

$$m = \frac{y_2 - y_1}{x_2 - x_1} = \frac{(-4) - 2}{5 - 1} = \frac{-6}{4} = -\frac{3}{2}$$

b. Substitute m and $A(1,2)$ into the point-slope form.

$$y - y_1 = m(x - x_1) \implies y - 2 = -\frac{3}{2}(x - 1)$$

$$2y - 4 = -3x + 3$$

$$3x + 2y = 7$$

An equation of the line is $3x + 2y = 7$.

Example 3 illustrates an alternative method for finding an equation of a line.

EXAMPLE 3: Find an equation of the line through $A(-2, -1)$ that is parallel to the line with equation $2x + y = 3$.

a. Find the slope of the given line by transforming its equation to slope-intercept form, $y = mx + b$.

$$2x + y = 3 \quad \Longrightarrow \quad y = -2x + 3$$

The given line has slope -2. Since *parallel* lines have *equal* slope, the required line also has slope $m = -2$.

b. Substitute known values, $m = -2$ and $A(-2, -1)$, into $y = mx + b$ and solve for b.

$$y = mx + b \quad \Longrightarrow \quad \begin{aligned} -1 &= (-2)(-2) + b \\ -1 &= 4 + b \\ b &= -5 \end{aligned}$$

c. Having determined that $b = -5$, substitute the known values of m and b into $y = mx + b$.

$$y = mx + b \quad \Longrightarrow \quad y = -2x - 5$$

An equation of the line is $y = -2x - 5$.

EXAMPLE 4: A triangle has vertices $A(2,3)$, $B(5,9)$, and $C(9,5)$. Find an equation of the line through A and perpendicular to $\overline{BC}$.

a. Find the slope of $\overline{BC}$.

$$\text{For } \overline{BC}, m = \frac{y_2 - y_1}{x_2 - x_1} = \frac{5 - 9}{9 - 5} = \frac{-4}{4} = -1$$

Since the slopes of perpendicular lines are negative reciprocals, take the negative reciprocal of -1: $m - 1$.

b. Substitute $m = 1$ and $A(2,3)$ into the point-slope form.

$$y - y_1 = m(x - x_1) \quad \Longrightarrow \quad \begin{aligned} y - 3 &= 1(x - 2) \\ y - 3 &= x - 2 \\ -x + y &= 1 \end{aligned}$$

The line has equation $-x + y = 1$.

EXERCISES

A 1. A line with equation $y = 2x + b$ passes through the given point. Find the value of b.

a. $(1,3)$ b. $(2, -3)$ c. $(5,7)$ d. $(-1,3)$
e. $(-5, -7)$ f. $(-3,9)$ g. $(3, -1)$ h. $(2, -8)$

2. Find the slope of any line that is parallel to the line represented by the given equation.
   a. $2x - 5y = 8$ b. $3x + y = 7$ c. $y = -8x - 3$
   d. $y = -2x - 4$ e. $y = \frac{3}{4}x - \frac{1}{2}$ f. $4x - 7y = 14$

3. For each equation in exercise 2, find the slope of any line that is perpendicular to the line represented by the given equation.

4. Find the slope of any line parallel to the segment with the given endpoints.
   a. $(3,7)$, $(5,9)$ b. $(4,6)$, $(-3,9)$ c. $(7,-3)$, $(-2,-5)$

5. For each pair of points in exercise 4, find the slope of any line perpendicular to the segment with the given endpoints.

6. Find an equation of the line through $P(-3,5)$ and parallel to the following.
   a. the x-axis   b. the y-axis

7. Find the standard form equation of the line through the origin with a slope of $-\frac{2}{3}$.

B 8. Find an equation of the line through the given point and with slope m.
   a. $(-2,1)$, $m = 4$ b. $(3,-11)$, $m = -5$ c. $(8,-1)$, $m = \frac{3}{4}$
   d. $(0,5)$, $m = \frac{2}{5}$ e. $(-2,-3)$, $m = 7$ f. $(1,1)$, $m = \frac{1}{2}$

9. Find an equation of the line through A and perpendicular to $\overline{AB}$ if A is located at $(-3,4)$ and B is at $(5,7)$.

10. Find an equation of the line with an x-intercept of 5 and with a slope of $-\frac{1}{3}$.

11. Find an equation of the line parallel to $3y - 5x = -2$ and passing through the origin.

12. Find an equation of the line perpendicular to $3x - 2y = -4$ with a y-intercept of -2.

13. Find an equation of the line that passes through the given pair of points.
   a. $(2,-1)$, $(4,3)$ b. $(4,-3)$, $(-2,6)$ c. $(3,2)$, $(-3,0)$

14. Find an equation of the line through the given point and parallel to the line represented by the given equation.
   a. $(2,4)$; $5x - y = 3$ b. $(-3,1)$; $3x + y - 8 = 0$

15. Find an equation of the line through the given point and perpendicular to the line represented by the given equation.
   a. $(3,1)$; $2x + 7y = 4$ b. $(-2,5)$; $3x - y + 4 = 0$

16. Find an equation of the line parallel to $4x - 3y = -5$ and passing through the midpoint of $\overline{AB}$, with $A(-1,7)$ and $B(3,3)$.

C 17. A *median* of a triangle is a line segment joining a vertex to the midpoint of the opposite side. Find equations of the medians for $\triangle PQR$ if P is at $(4,-3)$, Q is at $(8,5)$, and R is at $(-4,3)$.

18. Three vertices of a rectangle are $Q(-8,2)$, $R(2,6)$, and $S(4,1)$. Find equations of the lines that contain the four sides of the rectangle.

19. Consider $\triangle ABC$ with $A(5,4)$, $B(-1,-6)$, and $C(7,2)$. Find the midpoints of $\overline{AB}$ and $\overline{AC}$ and call them M and N, respectively.
    a. Find the slope of $\overline{MN}$ and compare it to the slope of $\overline{BC}$.
    b. Find the length of $\overline{MN}$ and compare it to the length of $\overline{BC}$.
    c. What observation can you make?
    d. Repeat for any triangle of your choice.

Review

1. Graph the line represented by the given equation.
    a. $y = 5x$ b. $y = -2x - 5$ c. $y = 4$

2. Graph the line with the given slope and y-intercept. Write the equation of each line in slope-intercept form.
    a. $m = 3, b = 2$ b. $m = 2, b = -3$ c. $m = -5, b = -2$

3. Find an equation of the line with the given slope passing through the given point.
    a. $m = -\frac{5}{6}$; $(12,-3)$ b. $m = \frac{3}{2}$; $(-4,-2)$ c. $m = -\frac{5}{3}$; $(-9,7)$

4. Find an equation of the line through the given pair of points.
    a. $(5,1)$, $(-5,-3)$ b. $(-2,-4)$, $(1,-1)$ c. $(2,1)$, $(7,-3)$

5. Find an equation of the line through $P(1,-1)$ and parallel to the line represented by $2y - 5x + 6 = 0$. Find the line through P and perpendicular to the given line.

6. Find the missing values to make each pair of equations either parallel or perpendicular, as indicated.
    a. parallel: $5x + 3y - 2 = 0$ b. perpendicular: $2x - 3y + 5 = 0$
     $10x + by + 3 = 0$ $ax + by - 2 = 0$

    c. perpendicular: $y = 3x - 7$ d. parallel: $y = 1.5x - 3$
     $y = kx + 3$ $y = kx - 4$

    e. perpendicular: $-2x + y = 3$ f. perpendicular: $ax + by = 2$
     $ax + by = 10$ $5x + y = -3$

4–9 The Standard Form of a Linear Equation

The equation of a line can be written in many forms. The **standard form** of a linear equation is $Ax + By + C = 0$, where A, B, and C are real numbers. When a linear equation is written in standard form, fractions are usually eliminated, and the coefficient of x is positive.

EXAMPLES: **a.** $3x - 2y - 7 = 0$ **b.** $3x + 4y - 1 = 0$

A, B, and C can provide information about the slope and y-intercept of the line represented by $Ax + By + C = 0$.

Rewrite $Ax + By + C = 0$ in
slope-intercept form.
The line represented by $Ax + By + C = 0$
has slope $-\frac{A}{B}$ and y-intercept $-\frac{C}{B}$.

$$Ax + By + C = 0$$
$$By = -Ax - C$$
$$y = -\frac{A}{B}x - \frac{C}{B}$$

EXAMPLE 1: State the slope and y-intercept of the line represented by each equation.

a. $3x - 2y - 7 = 0$ Slope $= -\frac{A}{B}$ y-intercept $= -\frac{C}{B}$

$= \frac{3}{2}$ $= \frac{7}{2}$

b. $3x + 4y - 1 = 0$ Slope $= -\frac{A}{B}$ y-intercept $= -\frac{C}{B}$

$= -\frac{3}{4}$ $= \frac{1}{4}$

There are three special cases of a linear equation in standard form.

1. When $A = 0$, $B \neq 0$, the equation becomes $0x + By + C = 0$. The slope of the line is then $-\dfrac{0}{B}$ or 0.

> The graph of an equation in the form $By + C = 0$ is a horizontal line.

2. When $B = 0$, $A \neq 0$, the equation becomes $Ax + 0y + C = 0$. The slope of the line would be $-\dfrac{A}{0}$, which is undefined.

> The graph of an equation in the form $Ax + C = 0$ is a vertical line.

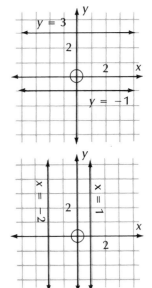

3. When $C = 0$, the equation becomes
$Ax + By + 0 = 0$. The y-intercept of its
graph is $-\dfrac{0}{B}$ or 0.

> The graph of an equation in the form
> $Ax + By = 0$ passes through $(0,0)$.

When $A = 0$ and $B = 0$, then $C = 0$.
No equation results.

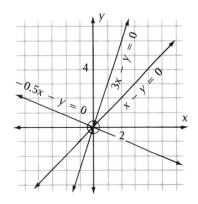

EXERCISES

A 1. Give the slope and the y-intercept of the line represented by the given
equation.

    a. $3x + y - 2 = 0$ **b.** $2x - 6y + 12 = 0$ **c.** $-x + 3y + 9 = 0$

    d. $2x + y - 4 = 0$ **e.** $3x - 2y + 5 = 0$ **f.** $x + 3y - 2 = 0$

B 2. Rewrite each equation in standard form. Then find the slope and the
y-intercept and graph.

    a. $3x + 2y = 6$ **b.** $y = -\dfrac{1}{2}x + 2$ **c.** $3x = y + 1$

    d. $y - 4 = \dfrac{3}{5}(x - 2)$ **e.** $3y + 3 = x$ **f.** $y = \dfrac{3}{4}x - 2$

3. Find the standard form equation of the line parallel to $4x + 5y + 7 = 0$
and having the same y-intercept as $5x - 2y + 10 = 0$.

C 4. Find the missing values, using the given information.

    a. $3x + By + 4 = 0;\ m = -1$ **b.** $Ax + 5y - 8 = 0;\ m = 1.6$

    c. $5x + By + 6 = 0;\ b = 3$ **d.** $2x + By + 8 = 0;\ b = -\dfrac{4}{3}$

    e. $Ax + 2y + 5 = 0;\ m = 2$ **f.** $Ax - 3y + C = 0;\ m = 2,\ b = 1$

EXTRA

A car starts 3 km from a point P and travels away from
the point at 30 km/h.

For this situation, let x be the number of hours travelled
and let y be the distance in kilometres from P at the time of x.
An equation to represent the situation is $y = 30x + 3$.

Graph the equation. What is the interpretation of the following?
1. the slope   **2.** the y-intercept

Graphing Systems of Equations

Use your algebra and graphing skills to solve the following problems involving situations that can be represented by two equations containing two variables.

1. Sylvia scored 11 points during a basketball game, some for baskets and some for foul shots. Each basket was worth 2 points and each foul shot was worth 1 point. Sylvia made a total of 7 successful shots during the game. How many were baskets and how many were foul shots? Write two equations to represent the information given, using x to represent number of baskets and y to represent number of foul shots. Graph the lines represented by the equations to find the whole-number solution.

2. Phil spent $12.50 on stamps. He bought 30 stamps altogether, some 35¢ stamps and some 45¢ stamps. How many of each type of stamp did he buy?

3. The yearbook editor approached several different printers for quotes for printing costs. Printer A quoted a flat fee of $2000 plus $5 per book. Printer B quoted $1500 plus $6 per book.
   a. For what number of books would the charges be equal?
   b. If 950 students have ordered yearbooks, which printer should the editor use?

4. Pat and Leslie both work as salespeople at a stereo shop. Pat makes $180/week plus 4% commission on sales. Leslie makes $150/week plus 6% commission.
   a. Write an equation for each of Pat and Leslie to show earnings per week according to sales for the week. Graph the lines represented by the equations.
   b. For what volume of sales do Pat and Leslie earn the same amount?
   c. If both Pat and Leslie had sold $1000 worth of merchandise one week, which one would earn more?

5. A taxi company charges its customers a flat fee, which is the same for all calls made. In addition, the taxi company charges a certain amount for each kilometre travelled. If the fare for 25 km is $23 and the fare for 15 km is $15, what is the flat fee and the charge per kilometre travelled?

6. An island ferry service provides reduced fares for children under 12, while infants under one year old may cross for free. Maria is bringing her seven-year-old twins and a ten-month-old infant across for a cultural festival. She pays $14. Jeff, a seventeen-year-old, pays $19 fare for his father and his younger brother, nine years old. What is the fare for adults? for children under 12?

Application

Graphs provide a valuable method for analysing data from an experiment. Meteorologists often use weather balloons to collect data. Graphing the data may reveal patterns or trends.

A weather balloon sent up on a calm day collected the temperature data recorded in the table below.

Altitude (kilometres)	0.5	1.0	1.5	2.0	3.0	5.0
Temperature (degrees Celsius)	16	14	10	6.5	0	− 12

Graphing the data reveals that the points fall roughly along a straight line.

Although it would be unwise to assume that the line extends past the known values, it would make sense to expect temperatures at altitudes from 0.5 km to 5.0 km to fit this same set of data.

Draw the "best-fit-line" along the data.

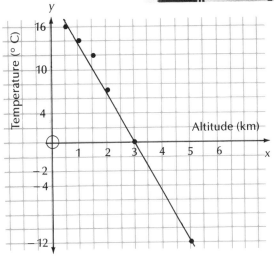

1. Using 2 points on the line, find an equation relating temperature (y) and altitude (x). Give the answer in standard form.

2. Use the equation to estimate the temperature to the nearest tenth at the given altitude.
   a. 2.5 km   b. 4.0 km   c. 4.75 km
   d. 0.75 km   e. 600 m   f. 1800 m

3. Rewrite the equation to isolate the variable representing altitude.

4. Apply the equation from exercise 3 to estimate the altitude at which the given temperature could be expected.
   a. 2° C   b. 12° C   c. 5° C
   d. 15° C   e. − 1° C   f. − 10° C

1. Which of the following are solutions to the equation $3x - 2y = -12$?
   a. $(0,6)$ **b.** $(-2,3)$ **c.** $(4,0)$

2. Copy and complete each table of values for the equation given.

   a. $x - 3y = 7$ **b.** $y = \frac{3}{2}x + 5$ **c.** $5x - 2y = -35$

x	y
1	?
?	2
?	0
-5	?

x	y
0	?
?	2
3	?
?	0

x	y
0	?
?	0
1	?
5	?

3. Give the x- and y-intercepts of the line represented by $2x + 3y = 6$. Find two other solutions and graph the line.

4. On the same grid as you used for question 3, graph the line represented by $x - y = 3$. Estimate the solution of the pair of equations.

5. Find the length of the segment with the given endpoints. Then find the midpoint of each.
   a. $(5,2)$, $(9,6)$ **b.** $(-7,-8)$, $(-3,-1)$ **c.** $(1,6)$, $(-3,-3)$

6. For each pair of points in question 5, find the slope of the segment with the given endpoints.

7. Rewrite the equation $4x + 3y = 6$ in slope-intercept form. Graph the line represented by the equation.

8. Graph the equation with slope $-\frac{3}{5}$ and y-intercept -3. Write an equation of the line.

9. Find an equation of the line for which:
   a. $m = -1$; $(3,-4)$ lies on the line.
   b. $(-2,-3)$ and $(5,-4)$ lie on the line.
   c. $(2,-3)$ lies on the line and is parallel to $2x + y = 7$.
   d. $(-1,1)$ lies on the line and is perpendicular to $5x - 2y = 4$.

10. Use the given information to find the missing values.
    a. $6x + By - 2 = 0$; $m = 2$ **b.** $Ax + 4y + C = 0$; $m = -2$; $b = \frac{3}{4}$

11. Find an equation of the line that passes through $A(5,9)$ and $B(2,6)$.

12. Find an equation of the line that passes through the origin and has slope $-\frac{1}{2}$.

Cumulative Review

1. Given $x = -4$, $y = -12$, $z = 3$, evaluate each expression.
   a. $x + y - z$
   b. $xy - z$
   c. xyz
   d. $5x - 2z$

2. Simplify each expression.
   a. $t^2r^3r^5$
   b. $(z^3)^2$
   c. $k^7 \div k^9$
   d. $(2b)^2$

3. Rewrite using scientific notation, then calculate.
   a. $49\,000\,000 \times 513\,000$
   b. $52\,000 \times 0.000\,12$
   c. $\dfrac{92\,000\,000 \times 0.012}{34\,000}$
   d. $\dfrac{(25\,000)^2}{0.000\,002}$

4. Evaluate each radical expression.
   a. $2\sqrt{2}\sqrt{2}$
   b. $3\sqrt{36}$
   c. $5\sqrt{7}\sqrt{28}$
   d. $11\sqrt{625}$

5. Simplify.
   a. $\dfrac{1}{\sqrt{5}}$
   b. $\dfrac{2}{\sqrt{6}}$
   c. $\dfrac{2\sqrt{3}}{\sqrt{5}}$
   d. $\dfrac{x\sqrt{y}}{\sqrt{2}}$

6. A shelf 20 cm deep is supported by a bracket attached 22 cm below the shelf and at the shelf edge. How long is the bracket, to the nearest tenth?

7. Find the length of each unknown side.

   a.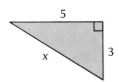
   b.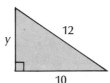
   c.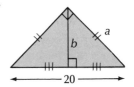

8. Find the distance between each pair of points, correct to two decimals.
   a. $(0, -1), (2, -3)$
   b. $(-1, -3), (-5, -7)$
   c. $(3,9), (-1,7)$

9. Solve and check.
   a. $4x + 7 = 3$
   b. $5t - 7 = 3t + 1$
   c. $4(x - 3) + 1 = 3(x + 2)$
   d. $\dfrac{t}{3} + \dfrac{t}{7} = \dfrac{1}{21}$
   e. $\dfrac{1}{4}x - 7 = \dfrac{1}{5}$
   f. $\dfrac{k}{2} + \dfrac{1}{4} = \dfrac{k}{5}$
   g. $\dfrac{2x - 3}{5} - \dfrac{x - 1}{3} = 1$
   h. $\dfrac{2}{3}(x + 1) - \dfrac{1}{6} = \dfrac{5}{9}(x - 2)$

10. Solve and check for one possible value.
    a. $3a - 7 < a + 2$
    b. $4j - 3 \geq 2(j + 1) - 5$
    c. $\dfrac{t}{2} \leq t + 7$

11. Solve for $x \in R$. Graph the solution set if it is not the empty set.
    a. $|x| = 15$
    b. $|x| - 2 = 7$
    c. $2|x| \leq 7$
    d. $|x - 7| \geq 12$
    e. $4|x + 1| - 5 > 9$
    f. $5|x + 3| \leq 2$
    g. $|1 - x| \leq 7$
    h. $3 + |7 - x| > 5$

5

Systems of Equations and Inequalities

5–1 Solving by Comparison

A grocery store received a shipment of 62 bags of potatoes and onions. Each bag of potatoes had a mass of 40 kg and each bag of onions had a mass of 20 kg. The shipment totalled 2000 kg. How many bags of onions and potatoes were there?

Define the variables.
Let x be the number of bags of potatoes.
Let y be the number of bags of onions.

Write two equations.
$x + y = 62$
$40x + 20y = 2000$

Estimate the solution by graphing.

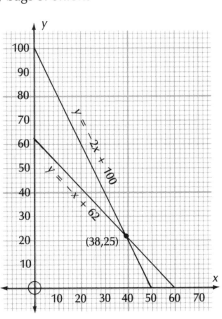

a. Rewrite the equations in slope-intercept form to simplify the graphing.
$x + y = 62 \quad \longrightarrow \quad y = -x + 62$
$40x + 20y = 2000 \longrightarrow y = -2x + 100$

b. The solution to the pair of equations *appears* to be $(x,y) = (38,25)$.

c. Check in the original problem: 38 bags of potatoes and 25 bags of onions totals 63. The estimated solution is *not* exact.

128

Solving a system of equations by graphing will not always yield exact solutions. There are *several* algebraic methods for solving a system of equations without using their graphs. One of these is the **comparison method**, illustrated below, which results in one equation in one unknown.

EXAMPLE 1: Find the intersection point of the graphs of $y = -x + 62$ and $y = -2x + 100$ algebraically.

a. Write an equation that equates the two expressions for y.
Then solve for x.

$$-x + 62 = -2x + 100$$
$$x + 62 = 100$$
$$x = 38$$

b. Solve for y by substituting $x = 38$ into one of the original equations.
Solution: $(x,y) = (38,24)$

$$y = -x + 62$$
$$y = -(38) + 62$$
$$y = 24$$

c. Check the solution in *both* equations.

For $y = -x + 62$:   For $y = -2x + 100$
R.S. $= -(38) + 62$ R.S. $= -2(38) + 100$
$= 24$ $= 24$
$=$ L.S. ✓ $=$ L.S. ✓

To use the comparison method, one can *equate* the two expressions for y (or for x). However, this sometimes creates an equation with fractions. It is usually easier to avoid fractions, if possible, as shown below.

EXAMPLE 2: Solve: $x + 4y = 17$; $3x + 2y = 6$.

a. Isolate the y terms in each equation. Write an equation *equivalent* to the second equation by multiplying both sides by 2.

$x + 4y = 17$ ⟶ $4y = 17 - x$
$3x + 2y = 6$ $2y = -3x + 6$
             $2(2y) = 2(-3x + 6)$ ⟶ $4y = -6x + 12$

b. Write an equation that shows both expressions for $4y$ as equal to each other. Then solve for x.

$$17 - x = 6x - 12$$
$$5x = -5$$
$$x = -1$$

c. Solve for y by substituting $x = -1$ into one of the equations.

Solution: $(x,y) = \left(-1, \frac{9}{2}\right)$

$$x + 4y = 17$$
$$(-1) + 4y = 17$$
$$4y = 18$$
$$y = \frac{9}{2}$$

d. Check the solution in both equations.

For $x + 4y = 17$:   For $3x + 2y = 6$:

L.S. $= (-1) + 4\left(\frac{9}{2}\right)$ L.S. $= 3(-1) + 2\left(\frac{9}{2}\right)$
$= 17$ $= 6$
$=$ R.S. ✓ $=$ R.S. ✓

EXERCISES

A 1. Which ordered pair is a solution of the given system of equations?

a. $2x + 3y = 2$ **i.** $(2,4)$ b. $3p + 2q = 4$ **i.** $(-2,5)$
   $3x - y = 14$ **ii.** $(4,2)$ $4p - q = -13$ **ii.** $(5,-2)$
                iii. $(4,-2)$ **iii.** $(-2,3)$

c. $4s - 2t = 20$ **i.** $(3,4)$ d. $6a - 5b = 4$ **i.** $(1,-2)$
   $2s + 3t = -6$ **ii.** $(3,-4)$ $3a - 2b = 1$ **ii.** $(2,-1)$
                iii. $(4,-3)$ **iii.** $(-1,-2)$

2. Estimate the solution by graphing the pair of lines.

a. $y = 4$ b. $x - y = 4$ c. $x - 2y = 4$
   $y = 3x - 8$ $2x + y = 5$ $3x - 6y = 12$

3. Solve each system of equations by the comparison method.

a. $y = 4x - 1$ b. $x = 2y - 6$ c. $y = -x + 8$
   $y = 3x + 4$ $x = 4y - 8$ $y = 2x - 7$

d. $x = 2y - 7$ e. $y = -2x + 9$ f. $y = 3x + 6$
   $x = 3y + 5$ $y = 3x - 1$ $y = 5x - 4$

B 4. Solve each system of equations. Check your solution.

a. $y = 4x - 1$ b. $x = 2y - 6$ c. $x - 3y = 6$
   $2y = 3x + 8$ $3x = 4y - 8$ $4x + 2y = 10$

d. $6x - y = 21$ e. $5m - 2n = 1$ f. $4a + 3b = 25$
   $2x + y = 11$ $m + 3n = 7$ $a - 2b = -2$

g. $2x + 6y = 7$ h. $4x + y = 7$ i. $3a + 4b = 5$
   $5x - 2y = 9$ $5x - 3y = 13$ $4a + b = -2$

j. $2x + 3y = 48$ k. $2p + q = -2$ l. $4m - n = 10$
   $x - 3y = 15$ $5p - 2q = -23$ $3m + 2n = 13$

5. The sum of two numbers is 42. One number is 4 more than the other. Let x be the lesser number and y be the greater. Then a pair of equations to represent the information is:

$$x + y = 42;$$
$$y = x + 4.$$

Solve the system of equations to find the numbers that satisfy the given conditions. Check your solution.

6. Anna is 5 years older than Bill. The sum of their ages is 37 years. If a represents Anna's age in years and b is Bill's age in years, then a pair of equations to represent the information is: $a + b = 37$; $a = b + 5$. Solve the pair of equations to find how old Anna and Bill are.

C **7.** Find the solution of each pair of equations algebraically.

a. $4x - 2y = 8$
$4y + x = 8$

b. $3x - y = 6$
$9x - 3y = 18$

c. $2x + 3y = 1$
$6y + 4x = 2$

d. $y + 2x = 9$
$4x - y = 12$

e. $2x - 4y = 3$
$2x - 4y = 7$

f. $4x = 3y + 9$
$8x + 2y = 18$

g. $3x + 5y = 10$
$5x = y + 12$

h. $2x + 6y = -13$
$x = 4y + 4$

i. $3x - y = -1$
$9x = 3y - 1$

j. $\frac{2}{3}x + y = -1$
$2x + 3y = -3$

k. $\frac{1}{2}x - 2y = 2$
$2y + 3x = 16$

l. $\frac{1}{3}y + \frac{1}{2}x = 4$
$3x - 4y = -12$

8. Twice Sue's age added to three times Tim's age is 44. Sue is two years older than Tim. Let s represent Sue's age in years and t represent Tim's age in years. Write a pair of equations to represent the situation. Then find Sue's and Tim's ages.

9. Tony ate two bananas and half a grapefruit. He ate 525 g of fruit altogether. The mass of the whole grapefruit was three times the mass of each banana. Let b represent the mass of a banana in grams and g represent the mass of a grapefruit in grams. Write a pair of equations to represent the situation. Then find the mass of each banana and the mass of the grapefruit.

EXTRA

Not all systems of equations have a solution.

At the right, the graphs of $2x + y = 4$ and $2x + y = 1$ do *not* intersect. They are *parallel lines*.

This system of equations has *no solution*.

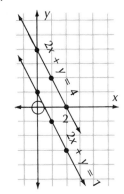

At the right, the graphs of $3x + y = -2$ and $6x + 2y = -4$ *coincide*. Every solution of either equation is a solution of the other. The equations are *equivalent*.

This system of equations has an *infinite* number of solutions.

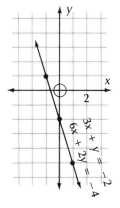

Give 3 examples of systems of equations having:
1. no solution.   **2.** an infinite number of solutions.

5–2 Solving by Substitution

A second algebraic method for solving two equations in two unknowns is by the **substitution** method, which yields one equation in one unknown.

EXAMPLE 1: Solve: $2x - 3y = 1$; $x + 2y = 18$.

a. Isolate the variable x or y in one of the equations.

$$x + 2y = 18$$
$$x = -2y + 18$$

b. Substitute the expression $-2y + 18$ for x in the other equation. Solve for y.

$$2x - 3y = 1$$
$$2(-2y + 18) - 3y = 1$$
$$-4y + 36 - 3y = 1$$
$$-7y = -35$$
$$y = 5$$

c. Solve for x by substituting $y = 5$ into one of the original equations.
Solution: $(x,y) = (8,5)$

$$x + 2y = 18$$
$$x + 2(5) = 18$$
$$x = 8$$

d. Check the solution in both equations.

For $2x - 3y = 1$:   For $x + 2y = 18$:
L.S. $= 2(8) - 3(5)$ L.S. $= (8) + 2(5)$
$= 1$ $= 18$
$=$ R.S. ✓ $=$ R.S. ✓

It is usually easier to avoid fractions when using the substitution method, as shown below.

EXAMPLE 2: Solve: $4x - 3y = 16$; $2x + 4y = -3$.

a. Isolate $2x$ in the second equation. Then write an *equivalent equation* by multiplying both sides by 2.
$$2x + 4y = -3 \longrightarrow 2x = -4y - 3 \longrightarrow 4x = -8y - 6$$

b. Substitute the expression $-8y - 6$ for $4x$ into the first equation. Solve for y.

$$4x - 3y = 16$$
$$(-8y - 6) - 3y = 16$$
$$-11y = 22$$
$$y = -2$$

c. Solve for x by substituting $y = -2$ into one of the original equations.

Solution: $(x,y) = \left(\frac{5}{2}, -2\right)$

$$4x - 3y = 16$$
$$4x - 3(-2) = 16$$
$$4x = 10$$
$$x = \frac{5}{2}$$

d. Check the solution in both equations.

For $4x - 3y = 16$:   For $2x + 4y = -3$:
L.S. $= 4\left(\frac{5}{2}\right) - 3(-2)$ L.S. $= 2\left(\frac{5}{2}\right) + 4(-2)$
$= 16$ $= -3$
$=$ R.S. ✓ $=$ R.S. ✓

132

EXERCISES

A **1.** Solve each system of equations by substituting the expression for x into the second equation.

  a. $x = 2y - 3$
   $2x + 3y = 22$

  b. $x = -y + 5$
   $x - 3y = 9$

  c. $x = 3y - 13$
   $2x + 3y = 1$

2. Solve each system of equations by substituting the isolated expression into the second equation.

  a. $4x = -6y + 6$
   $4x + 2y = 10$

  b. $10x = 2y - 3$
   $10x - 5y = 24$

  c. $5x = -2y - 32$
   $5x + 5y = -5$

B **3.** Solve and check.

  a. $x - 2y = 5$
   $3x - 4y = 9$

  b. $2a + 2b = 50$
   $a - b = 1$

  c. $x + y = 14$
   $3x + 2y = 48$

  d. $3x + y = 4$
   $2x + 4y = -4$

  e. $2x - y = 10$
   $2x + 3y = -6$

  f. $x - 3y = -14$
   $3x + 2y = 2$

  g. $5x + y = 18$
   $3x + 2y = -6$

  h. $2x - y = 26$
   $4x - 3y = 2$

  i. $2x + y = 10$
   $3x - 2y = 50$

  j. $2x + 3y = 3$
   $10x + 4y = 26$

  k. $3x + 6y = -2$
   $6x + 5y = 3$

  l. $2x + 7y = 5$
   $4x + 7y = -1$

4. Three times Marc's age less his father's age is 4. The sum of their ages is 52. If m represents Marc's age in years and f represents his father's age in years, then a pair of equations to represent the situation is:
$$3m - f = 4;$$
$$m + f = 52.$$
Solve the pair of equations to find the age of each. Check your result.

C **5.** Find the intersection point of the graphs of each pair of equations algebraically.

  a. $3x + y = 7$
   $4y + 10x = 26$

  b. $2x + 3y = -1$
   $2x + 3y = 4$

  c. $x + 4y = -5$
   $2y + 3x = 5$

  d. $\frac{1}{2}x + \frac{3}{4}y = -1$
   $2x + 3y = -4$

  e. $\frac{1}{4}x + \frac{1}{2}y = 8$
   $2x - y = 14$

  f. $\frac{1}{2}x + 3y = 12$
   $2x + 12y = 48$

6. Katrina has 14 coins, all nickels and dimes. The total value of the coins is one dollar. Let n represent the number of nickels and d represent the number of dimes. Write a pair of equations to represent the situation. Then find how many of each coin Katrina has.

7. The graphs of $x + 2y = 7$, $4x - y = 1$, and $6x + ay = 0$ intersect at the same point. Find a.

5–3 Solving by Adding or Subtracting

When two equations in two unknowns have *opposite* coefficients for the x or the y terms, a solution can be found by *adding* the right and left sides of the two equations. This eliminates one of the unknowns, leaving one equation in one unknown.

EXAMPLE 1: Solve: $x + 2y = 10$; $3x - 2y = 6$.

The variable y has *opposite* coefficients, 2 and -2.

a. Add the right and left sides of the two equations. The y terms will be eliminated. Then solve for x.

$$\begin{array}{rcl} x + 2y &=& 10 \\ 3x - 2y &=& 6 \\ \hline 4x &=& 16 \\ x &=& 4 \end{array}$$

b. Solve for y by substituting $x = 4$ into one of the original equations.

$$\begin{array}{rcl} x + 2y &=& 10 \\ (4) + 2y &=& 10 \\ 2y &=& 6 \\ y &=& 3 \end{array}$$

Solution: $(x,y) = (4,3)$.

c. Check the solution in both equations.

For $x + 2y = 10$:   For $3x - 2y = 6$:
L.S. $= 4 + 2(3)$ L.S. $= 3(4) - 2(3)$
      $= 10$ $= 6$
      $=$ R.S. ✓ $=$ R.S. ✓

When a system of equations has the *same* coefficients for either the x or the y terms, a solution can be found by *subtracting* the left and right sides of the two equations.

EXAMPLE 2: Solve: $3x + 4y = 1$; $x + 4y = -5$.

The variable y has the *same* coefficient in each equation.

a. Subtract the right and left sides of the two equations. The y terms will be eliminated. Then solve for x.

$$\begin{array}{rcl} 3x + 4y &=& 1 \\ x + 4y &=& -5 \\ \hline 2x &=& 6 \\ x &=& 3 \end{array}$$

b. Solve for y by substituting $x = 3$ into one of the original equations.

$$\begin{array}{rcl} 3x + 4y &=& 1 \\ 3(3) + 4y &=& 1 \\ 4y &=& -8 \\ y &=& -2 \end{array}$$

Solution: $(x,y) = (3,-2)$

c. Check the solution in both equations.

For $3x + 4y = 1$:   For $x + 4y = -5$:
L.S. $= 3(3) + 4(-2)$ L.S. $= 3 + 4(-2)$
      $= 1$ $= -5$
      $=$ R.S. ✓ $=$ R.S. ✓

The method of solution used in examples 1 and 2 is based on the addition property of equality: if $a = b$ and $c = d$, then $a + c = b + d$, and $a - c = b - d$.

Solving two equations in two unknowns can be applied to word problems.

EXAMPLE 3: Chris waited table one evening and made $55 in tips, all in bills with $1 and $2 denominations. There was a total of 42 bills. How many of each type of bill did Chris earn in tips?

Define the variables.
Let s be the number of $1 bills.
Let t be the number of $2 bills.

Write two equations.

$s + t = 42$ ←————— There are 42 bills altogether.
$s + 2t = 55$ ←——
                  The total value of the bills is $55.

Solve the system of equations by subtracting.

Eliminate s to solve for t.

$$s + 2t = 55$$
$$\underline{s + t = 42}$$
$$t = 13$$

Substitute $t = 13$ and solve for s.

$$s + t = 42$$
$$s + (13) = 42$$
$$s = 29$$

Solution: $(s,t) = (29,13)$
Chris had 29 one-dollar bills and 13 two-dollar bills from tips.

Check: 29 one dollar bills plus 13 two dollar bills are worth $29 + $26, or $55, which is the desired answer. ✓

EXERCISES

A **1.** Solve by adding. Check your solution.

a. $x + y = 7$
   $x - y = 3$

b. $2x + y = 3$
   $x - y = 12$

c. $x + y = 2$
   $-x + y = -4$

d. $-2x + 3y = -1$
   $2x - y = 5$

e. $4x + 2y = 3$
   $x - 2y = -2$

f. $x - 2y = -1$
   $2x - 2y = -2$

2. Solve by subtracting. Check your solution.

a. $5x + 2y = -6$
$3x + 2y = -2$

b. $-3x + y = 2$
$x + y = -2$

c. $x + 2y = 7$
$x - y = -2$

d. $2x + 7y = 14$
$2x + 2y = 4$

e. $x + 2y = -1$
$3x + 2y = -9$

f. $5x + 2y = 10$
$-4x + 2y = 1$

3. Would you add or subtract to obtain an equation in one variable?

a. $x + y = 13$
$2x - y = 11$

b. $2a + 3b = 16$
$5a - 3b = 19$

c. $p + 3q = 0$
$4p + 3q = -18$

d. $9x - 4y = 30$
$3x + 4y = -6$

e. $7s + 8t = 10$
$5s - 8t = -34$

f. $2m - 3n = 16$
$7m - 3n = 26$

B 4. Solve by adding or subtracting. Check your solution.

a. $2x + 3y = -2$
$4x - 3y = 50$

b. $2s - 4t = 0$
$4t + 3s = 10$

c. $4x + 5y = 11$
$7x + 5y = 8$

d. $2x + \frac{1}{2}y = 5$
$3x - \frac{1}{2}y = 4$

e. $3x + \frac{2}{3}y = -2$
$2x + \frac{2}{3}y = 0$

f. $0.6x + 0.5y = 27$
$-0.9y + 0.6x = -21$

g. $4m - 3n = 7$
$4m + 2n = 2$

h. $2a - 5b = 4$
$2a - b = -4$

i. $4s - 4t = -4$
$4t + s = -2$

5. The sum of two numbers is 54 and their difference is 16. What are the two numbers?

6. There are 962 students in a school. There are 28 more girls than boys. How many girls and boys are there?

7. The sum of Tanya's age and Rob's age is 36 years. Tanya is 4 years younger than Rob. How old are Rob and Tanya?

8. To fill two cars at a service station required 100 L of gasoline. The second car took 16 L less than the first. How many litres of gasoline did each car take?

9. Two apples and 3 pears cost $2.40. Five times the cost of an apple less three times the cost of a pear is 65¢. What is the unit cost of an apple and a pear?

10. Twice Kate's age added to half her mother's age is 48. Three times Kate's age decreased by half her mother's age is 27. How old are they?

11. The sum of two numbers is 61. Twice the lesser number is 7 less than the greater number. Find the two numbers.

12. Two meshing gears have a total of 89 teeth. One of the gears has 4 less than twice the number of teeth of the other gear. How many teeth does each gear have?

C 13. Find the intersection point of the graphs of each pair of equations algebraically. Use the method of your choice.

a. $3x + 2y = 7$
$6x + 5y = -2$

b. $3x + 2y = 5$
$6x + 4y = 10$

c. $4x - 2y = -2$
$y + 6x = 3$

d. $1.2x + 2.4y = -36$
$3.2x + 2.4y = 64$

e. $3x + 4y = 8$
$5x - 4y = 4$

f. $2x + 3y = 2$
$3y + 2x = -1$

14. The graphs of $5x - 3y = 35$, $7x - 3y = 43$, and $4x - ay = 61$ all intersect at the same point. Find a.

15. The given point P is the point of intersection of the graphs defined by the given equations. Find the value of k in each case.

a. $P(10,3)$: $x - y = 7$
$3x + ky = 5$

b. $P(-3, -5)$: $3x + 4y = -29$
$kx - 2y = -10$

c. $P(2,12)$: $kx - 3y = -16$
$y = 5x + 2$

d. $P(-1, -12)$: $y = 2x - 10$
$y = kx + 6$

16. Because of spoilage, a restaurant had to throw out 10 kg of food, 20% of a sack of potatoes and 40% of a bag of tomatoes. Later, they had to throw out 11 kg of food, 30% of a sack of potatoes and 20% of a bag of tomatoes. What is the mass of a sack of potatoes and a bag of tomatoes?

17. Ten boxes of nuts and 15 boxes of bolts have a mass of 14.75 kg. Twelve boxes of nuts and 10 boxes of bolts have a mass of 12.5 kg. What is the mass of a box of nuts? What is the mass of a box of bolts?

18. A financial advisor invested a total of $10 000, part at 7.5% per annum compounded annually, part at 8% per annum compounded annually. At the end of the first year, a total of $780 interest had been earned. How much had been invested at each interest rate?

EXTRA

One day, a radio station in Winnipeg announced the early-morning temperature. A listener in Fargo, North Dakota, phoned to inquire whether the announced temperature was in degrees Celsius or Fahrenheit. "It doesn't matter," said the station operator, "it is the same both ways." What was the announced early-morning temperature? (Hint: degrees Fahrenheit $= \frac{9}{5}$ degrees Celsius $+ 32$.)

5–4 The Addition Method

Adding or subtracting is not always immediately useful in solving a pair of equations. Consider the system of equations below.

$$2x + 5y = 4$$
$$-4x + 2y = 3$$

Neither the terms in x nor the terms in y have the same *absolute value*. Yet, notice what happens when an *equivalent* system of equations is made by multiplying both sides of the first equation by 2.

$$2x + 5y = 4 \longrightarrow 2(2x + 5y) = 2(4) \longrightarrow 4x + 10y = 8$$
$$-4x + 2y = 3 \longrightarrow \qquad\qquad\qquad\qquad\qquad\quad -4x + 2y = 3$$

Multiplying results in a system of **equivalent equations** with $4x + 10y = 8$ having the same graph as $2x + 5y = 4$.

Now the terms in x are opposites and the system of equations can be solved by adding.

Using multiplication, addition, or subtraction to solve a system of two equations in two unknowns is often referred to as the **addition** method.

EXAMPLE 1: Solve: $2x - 3y = 19$;
$\qquad\qquad\qquad 5x + 6y = 7.$

a. Multiply both sides of the *first* equation by 2 to get an equivalent system of equations that has opposite y coefficients.

$$2(2x - 3y) = 2(19) \longrightarrow 4x - 6y = 38$$
$$5x + 6y = 7 \longrightarrow \quad 5x + 6y = 7$$
$$\overline{\qquad\qquad\qquad 9x \qquad\quad = 45}$$

b. Eliminate y by adding. $\qquad\qquad\qquad\quad x = 5$

c. Solve for y by substituting $\qquad 2x - 3y = 19$
$x = 5$ into one of the $\qquad\quad 2(5) - 3y = 19$
original equations. $\qquad\qquad 10 - 3y = 19$
$\qquad\qquad\qquad\qquad\qquad\qquad\quad -3y = 9$

Solution: $(x,y) = (5, -3)$ $\qquad\qquad y = -3$

d. Check the solution in both equations.

For $2x - 3y = 19$: $\qquad\qquad$ For $5x + 6y = 7$:
L.S. $= 2(5) - 3(-3)$ $\qquad\qquad$ L.S. $= 5(5) + 6(-3)$
$\quad = 19$ $\qquad\qquad\qquad\qquad\qquad = 7$
$\quad = $ R.S. ✓ $\qquad\qquad\qquad\qquad = $ R.S. ✓

Sometimes you need to transform *both* equations by multiplication before you can eliminate either of the unknowns by adding or subtracting.

EXAMPLE 2:   Solve: $3x - 4y = 6$;
$$5x + 3y = -19.$$

a.   Since adding is easier than subtracting, try to obtain y terms with opposite coefficients so that addition can be used.

$$3(3x - 4y) = 3(6) \longrightarrow 9x - 12y = 18$$
$$4(5x + 3y) = 4(-19) \longrightarrow \underline{20x + 12y = -76}$$
$$29x \qquad\quad = -58$$

b.   Eliminate y by adding. $x = -2$

c.   Solve for y by substituting $3x - 4y = 6$
$x = -2$ into one of the $3(-2) - 4y = 6$
original equations. $-4y = 12$

Solution: $(x,y) = (-2, -3)$ $y = -3$

d.   The check is left to you.

In equations containing fractions, clear the fractions before solving.

EXAMPLE 3:   Solve: $\frac{1}{3}x - \frac{1}{2}y = 7$;
$$\frac{1}{4}x + \frac{1}{3}y = 1.$$

a.   Multiply by the LCD to clear all fractions.

$$6\left(\frac{1}{3}x - \frac{1}{2}y\right) = 6(7) \longrightarrow 2x - 3y = 42$$

$$12\left(\frac{1}{4}x + \frac{1}{3}y\right) = 12(1) \longrightarrow 3x + 4y = 12$$

Transform the equations again so the y terms have opposite coefficients.

$$4(2x - 3y) = 4(42) \longrightarrow 8x - 12y = 168$$
$$3(3x + 4y) = 3(12) \longrightarrow \underline{9x + 12y = 36}$$
$$17x \qquad\quad = 204$$

b.   Eliminate y by adding. $x = 12$

c.   Solve for y by substituting $2x - 3y = 42$
$x = 12$ into one of the $2(12) - 3y = 42$
equivalent equations. $3y = -18$
$$y = -6$$

Solution: $(x,y) = (12, -6)$

d.   The check is left to you.

EXERCISES

A **1.** Multiply one or both equations by numbers that make the coefficients of one variable have the same absolute value.

   a. $2x + y = 2$
        $3x - 2y = 10$

   b. $2p + 3q = 5$
        $4p + q = -5$

   c. $3m - 2n = 5$
        $4m + n = -8$

   d. $2x - 3y = 10$
        $3x + 2y = 5$

   e. $2p + 3q = -14$
        $4p + 5q = -22$

   f. $2a + 4b = 18$
        $5a - 3b = -20$

2. Transform the equations by multiplication so the addition method can be used.

   a. $\frac{1}{2}x + \frac{1}{3}y = -4$
        $x + y = -10$

   b. $\frac{1}{6}a + \frac{1}{4}b = \frac{3}{2}$
        $\frac{2}{3}a - \frac{1}{2}b = 0$

   c. $\frac{x}{15} + \frac{y}{5} = \frac{2}{3}$
        $\frac{x}{2} - y = 0$

3. Are the systems of equations equivalent?

   a. $\boxed{\begin{array}{l} 3x + 7y = -18 \\ 5x - 2y = -30 \end{array}}$ and $\boxed{\begin{array}{l} 6x + 14y = -36 \\ 35x - 14y = -30 \end{array}}$

   b. $\boxed{\begin{array}{l} \frac{1}{5}r - \frac{1}{2}s = \frac{3}{2} \\ \frac{1}{2}r - \frac{1}{3}s = 1 \end{array}}$ and $\boxed{\begin{array}{l} 2r - 5s = 15 \\ 3r - 2s = 6 \end{array}}$

   c. $\boxed{\begin{array}{l} \frac{1}{2}x + \frac{2}{3}y = 0 \\ \frac{4}{10}x + \frac{3}{10}y = \frac{7}{10} \end{array}}$ and $\boxed{\begin{array}{l} 3x + 4y = 0 \\ 4x + 3y = 7 \end{array}}$

   d. $\boxed{\begin{array}{l} 4a + 3b = -24 \\ 5a - 2b = -7 \end{array}}$ and $\boxed{\begin{array}{l} 8a + 6b = -48 \\ 15a - 6b = -21 \end{array}}$

B **4.** Solve by the addition method.

   a. $4a - 3b = 13$
        $2a + 4b = 12$

   b. $5x + 2y = 9$
        $10x - 3y = 4$

   c. $6s + 2t = 16$
        $3s + 5t = 4$

   d. $3x + 6y = -12$
        $2x - 3y = 34$

   e. $4c + 5d = 1$
        $3c - 10d = 97$

   f. $2m - 7n = 22$
        $6m + 3n = 18$

   g. $2s + 5t = 0$
        $3s - t = 17$

   h. $3x - 4y = 1$
        $4x + 2y = 16$

   i. $5x + 6y = 8$
        $2x - 3y = 14$

   j. $6s - 5t = 4$
        $2s + 4t = -10$

   k. $3m + 5n = -2$
        $4m - 2n = 32$

   l. $3x + 8y = -5$
        $-2x + 4y = -34$

   m. $3a + 2b = 4$
        $\frac{2}{3}a + \frac{1}{3}b = 1$

   n. $x - \frac{2}{3}y = -3$
        $3x - 3y = -9$

   o. $\frac{3}{8}p + \frac{1}{2}q = -\frac{1}{4}$
        $\frac{1}{2}p - \frac{3}{4}q = \frac{5}{2}$

5. Dan drew 2 bonus cards and 3 prize cards for a total of 14 points. Maria drew 5 bonus cards and 2 prize cards for a total of 24 points. What is the value of a bonus card and a prize card?

6. The sum of three times a number and twice a second number is 44. Twice the first number less four times the second is -24. What are the two numbers?

7. Larry used a total of 20 nickels and dimes to pay for a box of popcorn costing $1.25. How many of each type of coin did he use?

8. A waiter earned $55 in tips, all in $1 and $2 bills. There was a total of 38 bills. How many bills of each denomination were thre?

C 9. Find the intersection point of the graphs of each system of equations algebraically. Use the method of your choice.

a. $9x - 10y = 28$
$x - 5y = 7$

b. $8x - y = 12$
$4y + 3x = 92$

c. $2x - 3y = 2$
$-6y + 4x = 4$

d. $4x - 2y = -2$
$6x + y = 3$

e. $7x + 3y = 2$
$3y + 7x = 4$

f. $2x - 3y = 2$
$4x - 6y = 4$

g. $2y - 3x = -10$
$\frac{1}{2}x + \frac{1}{4}y = 11$

h. $\frac{1}{2}x + \frac{1}{3}y = 14$
$2x + y = 48$

i. $\frac{2}{3}x + \frac{1}{2}y = -2$
$3x - y = -22$

j. $\frac{1}{2}x + 2y = 0$
$2x + 8y = 0$

k. $\frac{1}{2}x + \frac{1}{3}y = \frac{5}{6}$
$\frac{1}{2}y + \frac{3}{4}x = \frac{5}{4}$

l. $x + 3y = 6$
$3x - y = \frac{4}{3}$

m. $4x - 2y + 4 = 0$
$2x + 3y - 2 = 0$

n. $2x + 3y = 0$
$3x - 2y + 65 = 0$

o. $5x - 2y + 7 = 0$
$2x + 3y - 1 = 0$

10. The graphs of $2x + 3y = 0$, $x + 5y = 7$, and $5x - ay = -27$ all intersect at the same point. Find a.

11. An excavation project required that 350 t of earth be removed. It took 97 truckloads to remove all the earth. Some truckloads were 2 t; others were 5 t. How many 2 t loads and 5 t loads were carried away?

12. Lisa earns an hourly wage plus tips waiting table. One week she worked 12 h and made $117 altogether. The next week she worked 10 h, earned the same amount in tips as the previous week, and made $110. What is Lisa's hourly wage?

13. The sum of the digits of a two-digit number is 11. The ones digit is 3 more than the tens digit. What is the number?

Using the Calculator

Use your calculator to find five consecutive numbers in which the sum of the squares of the first three numbers is equal to the sum of the squares of the last two numbers.

Writing Pairs of Equations

Many problems can be solved by writing two equations in two unknowns, then solving the system of equations to answer the problem.

EXAMPLE: To raise money for a class trip, students sold bags of mixed nuts and bags of dried fruit. Al sold 12 bags of mixed nuts and 10 bags of dried fruit and collected $54. Angie sold 8 bags of mixed nuts and 15 bags of dried fruit and collected $61. What price was charged for each item?

Define the variables.
Let m be the price of a bag of mixed nuts in dollars.
Let n be the price of a bag of dried fruit in dollars.

Write two equations.
$12m + 10n = 54$
$8m + 15n = 61$

Solve for n by adding.
$$2(12m + 10n) = 2(54) \longrightarrow 24m + 20n = 108$$
$$-3(8m + 15n) = -3(61) \longrightarrow -24m - 45n = -183$$
$$-25n = -75$$
$$n = 3$$

Solve for m.
$$12m + 10n = 54$$
$$12m + 10(3) = 54$$
$$12m = 24$$
$$m = 2$$

The solution is $m = 2$ and $n = 3$.

Check the solution in the original word problem.

Al sold 12 bags of mixed nuts (at $2) and 10 bags of dried fruit (at $3): $12(2) + (10)3 = 54$. ✓

Angie sold 8 bags of mixed nuts and 15 bags of dried fruit: $8(2) + 15(3) = 61$. ✓

The price for a bag of mixed nuts was $2 and for a bag of dried fruit was $3.

EXERCISES

A 1. The sum of two numbers is 120. Their difference is 14. What are the numbers?

2. Two mangoes and 3 kiwi fruit cost $4.35. Five mangoes and 3 kiwi fruit cost $7.32. Find the price of each fruit.

B 3. Marie paid for her $2.50 admission ticket with 13 dimes and quarters. How many of each coin did she use?

4. The length of a rectangle is 2 m more than its width. The perimeter is 52 m. Find the dimensions of the rectangle.

5. Jeff earned $74 over twenty hours, working part of the time at $3/h and part of the time at $4/h. How many hours did he work at each rate?

6. One week, a shop sold 42 boxes of stationery, some at $5 a box and some at $7 a box. The total value of the stationery sold was $246. How many boxes were sold at each price?

7. One day, an office mailed out 80 letters, some with 40¢ postage, some with 50¢ postage. The total postage was $35.20. How many letters were posted at each rate?

8. A construction company has 46 trucks, some of them dump trucks and some flatbed trucks. There are 8 more dump trucks than flatbed trucks. How many of each type of truck does the company have?

9. Find two numbers with a sum of −6 and a difference of 34.

10. On a test, some problems were worth 5 points and the others were worth 4 points. Myra solved 18 problems and got a mark of 83. How many 5-point problems did she solve?

11. The average of 2 numbers is 34. The difference of the numbers is 16. What are the numbers?

12. Four tapes and 3 records were sold for $67, and 2 tapes and 5 records were sold for $65. How much would it cost to buy 3 tapes and 4 records?

13. A man is three times as old as his son. In twelve years, he will be twice as old as his son. How old is each?

C 14. In a marathon race, Ted ran part of the 42 km at an average of 10 km/h, and walked the rest at an average of 6 km/h. He ran for 1 h more than he walked. How long did he take to finish the marathon?

15. A salesperson sold 12 television sets and video-cassette recorders in one week. The television sets sold for $500, and the video-cassette recorders, for $700. Total sales amounted to $7600.

   How many televisions and how many recorders did he sell? If he receives a commission of 8% on televisions and 5% on recorders, how much commission did he earn?

16. Andy and Beth each rode the roller coaster and the Ferris wheel for a total of ten times. The roller coaster rides cost $1.25 each and the Ferris wheel rides cost $0.75 each. Andy spent $11 and Beth spent $9.50. How many times did each ride on the roller coaster?

Rate and Mixture Problems

When a plane flies in a tailwind, its ground speed is the sum of its air speed (in calm air) and the speed of the tailwind. Against a headwind, its ground speed is decreased by the headwind speed.

EXAMPLE 1: Flying with a tailwind at a constant air speed, a plane makes a 2700 km trip in 4.5 h. The return trip against the same wind, at the same air speed, takes 6 h. What is the air speed of the plane (in calm air)? What is the speed of the tailwind?

Define the variables.
Let v_1 be the air speed of the plane in kilometres per hour.
Let v_2 be the tailwind speed in kilometres per hour.

Write two equations by using a table.

Speed × Time = Distance, or $vt = d$			
	Speed	Time	Distance
With the wind	$v_1 + v_2$	4.5	2700
Against the wind	$v_1 - v_2$	6	2700

$(v_1 + v_2)4.5 = 2700 \longrightarrow$ Divide each term by 4.5. $\quad v_1 + v_2 = 600$
$(v_1 - v_2)6 \;= 2700 \longrightarrow$ Divide each term by 6. $\quad\;\; v_1 - v_2 = 450$

Solve the system of equations.
Solve for v_1:
$$
\begin{aligned}
v_1 + v_2 &= 600 \\
v_1 - v_2 &= 450 \\
\hline
2v_1 \quad\;\; &= 1050 \\
v_1 &= 525
\end{aligned}
$$
Solve for v_2:
$$
\begin{aligned}
v_1 + v_2 &= 600 \\
(525) + v_2 &= 600 \\
v_2 &= 75
\end{aligned}
$$

Solution: $v_1 = 525$, $v_2 = 75$.

The air speed of the plane is 525 km/h and the tailwind speed is 75 km/h.

Check: For $vt = d$, or $(v_1 + v_2)t = d$: $(525 + 75)4.5 = 2700$ ✓
For $vt = d$, or $(v_1 - v_2)t = d$: $(525 - 75)6 = 2700$ ✓

Pure gold, at 24 karats, is too soft to be used in jewellery. Jewellers usually work with the following concentrations:

18 karat gold, which is $\frac{18}{24}$ pure gold;

14 karat gold, which is $\frac{14}{24}$ pure gold;

10 karat gold, which is $\frac{10}{24}$ pure gold.

EXAMPLE 2: A jeweller wants to make 144 g of 14 karat gold by melting 10 karat gold with 18 karat gold. How much of each should be used?

Define the variables.
Let x be the amount of 10 karat gold in grams.
Let y be the amount of 18 karat gold in grams.

Write two equations.

$$\frac{10}{24}x + \frac{18}{24}y = \frac{14}{24}(144) \longrightarrow 10x + 18y = 2016 \longrightarrow 5x + 9y = 1008$$

$$x + y = 144 \longrightarrow 5x + 5y = 720$$

Solve the system of equations.

Solve for y:

$$\begin{aligned} 5x + 9y &= 1008 \\ 5x + 5y &= 720 \\ \hline 4y &= 288 \\ y &= 72 \end{aligned}$$

Solve for x:

$$\begin{aligned} x + y &= 144 \\ x + 72 &= 144 \\ x &= 72 \end{aligned}$$

Solution: $x = 72$, $y = 72$.

The jeweller should use 72 g of each.

Check: For $\frac{10}{24}x + \frac{18}{24}y = \frac{14}{24}(144)$:

$$\text{L.S.} = \frac{10}{24}(72) + \frac{18}{24}(72) \qquad \text{R.S.} = \frac{14}{24}(144)$$
$$= 30 + 54 \qquad\qquad\qquad = 84$$
$$= 84 \qquad\qquad\qquad\qquad = \text{L.S.} \ \checkmark$$

EXERCISES

A 1. Aided by a tailwind, a Boeing 737 made the 1470 km flight from Seattle to Los Angeles in 1 h 45 min. Against the wind, the return trip took 2 h. What was the speed of the wind?

2. A jeweller wants to make 240 g of 18 karat gold by melting 14 karat gold with 20 karat gold. How much of each should be used?

B 3. Aided by a tailwind, a plane travelled 600 km in 2 h. The return trip against the wind took 3 h. Find the air speed of the plane and the speed of the wind.

4. In a silver shop, there are metal alloys containing 40% silver and others with 50% silver. A job order comes in calling for a 100 g bar with 44% silver. How much of each available silver alloy should be melted down and mixed to fill the order?

5. A broker invested $10 000 in two different stocks. On one investment, there was a profit of 12%, but on the other investment there was a loss of 3%. Net profit was $600. How much was invested in each stock?

6. Dried bananas sell at $4.59/kg and dried apricots sell at $6.59/kg. How many kilograms of each should be used to make a mixture of 50 kg of dried fruit to sell for $5.20/kg?

7. A submarine cruises underwater at 10 km/h and on the surface at 16 km/h. The submarine travels a distance of 160 km in 12.5 h. How long did it travel underwater? How long did it travel on the surface?

8. A flask contains 300 mL of a 30% acid solution. How much water must be added to reduce the acid strength to 20%?

9. A freight train and a passenger train are in stations 540 km apart. The freight train leaves a station at noon, travelling at an average speed of 60 km/h, and heading in the direction of the passenger train. One hour later, the passenger train leaves and heads towards the freight train at a speed of 90 km/h. At what time will the trains pass each other?

10. Doug swam ten lengths of a 50 m pool, some with the backstroke, the others freestyle. One length in backstroke takes him 60 s; one length in freestyle takes him 50 s. His total time for the ten lengths was 8 min 50 s. How many lengths did he swim with the backstroke?

11. A sum of money was invested in two stocks. The first investment earned an 8% return; the second earned a 12% return. The second investment earned twice as much as the first. The total amount earned was $1440. How much was invested in each stock?

C   12. Two alloys, one containing 20% gold and the other containing 30% gold, are to be mixed to make 400 g bars of alloy with 24% gold. There are 10 kg of the 20% gold alloy available. How many 400 g bars of 24% gold alloy can be made before the 20% gold alloy stock is depleted?

13. Two bus stations are 930 km apart. At midnight, buses leave each station, heading towards each other. The first bus travels 10 km/h faster than the second bus, but the first bus stops for one hour while the second bus travels non-stop. At 06:00, the buses meet at a station. How far is the station from each of the original points of departure?

14. On a canoe trip, two campers paddled a distance of 3 km. They paddled at a steady rate of 6 km/h, until they reached rapids, where they travelled at 12 km/h. The trip took 28 min. How long were the rapids?

15. At a dress shop, the regular price of a skirt and a blouse was $43. The price of the skirt was reduced by 20% and the price of the blouse was reduced by 25%, bringing the total cost down to $33.45.
    a. What were the regular prices of the skirt and blouse?
    b. If you decided to buy just the blouse, on sale, how much would it be? How much is the skirt?
    c. If you bought just the blouse, find the amount it would cost, including 5% sales tax.

Review

1. Solve each pair of equations by the comparison method.

   a. $y = 4x - 7$
   $y = -x + 3$

   b. $y = -2x - 1$
   $x + y = -9$

   c. $x = -3y - 3$
   $2x + 2y = 14$

2. Solve each pair of equations by the substitution method.

   a. $2x + y = -2$
   $y = -x - 5$

   b. $x = 7y - 3$
   $2x - 4y = -14$

   c. $x + y = -5$
   $3x = 2 - y$

3. Solve by the addition or subtraction method.

   a. $3x + 7y = 36$
   $7x - 7y = 14$

   b. $x + y = 5$
   $2x - 3y = -2$

   c. $2x + 5y = -3$
   $3x - 2y = -14$

4. Check the solution given for each pair of equations. Correct any incorrect solutions.

   a. $y = x - 7$
   $y = 2x + 3$
   $(x,y) = (-10, -17)$

   b. $x + y = -6$
   $2x + 3y = -1$
   $(x,y) = (-15, 10)$

   c. $x + 7 = 2y$
   $y - x = 3$
   $(x,y) = (4, 1)$

5. Solve, using the method of your choice. Check your solution.

   a. $y = -2x - 1$
   $y = 5x + 3$

   b. $x + 2y = 10$
   $y = x - 2$

   c. $2x + y = 4$
   $3x - 2y = 9$

   d. $-x - y = 7$
   $2x + y = 2$

   e. $y = 4x - 3$
   $y = -4x + 7$

   f. $y = -x + 1$
   $y = x - 4$

Solve by writing a system of equations to represent the situation.

6. The perimeter of a picture frame is 132 cm. The length is 6 cm more than the width. Find the dimensions of the frame.

7. At O'Riley's Drive-In, a customer placed an order for 6 hamburgers and 4 milkshakes and paid $14. The next customer ordered 5 hamburgers and 2 milkshakes and paid $10. A third customer ordered 2 hamburgers and a milkshake. How much did the third customer pay?

8. On a trip of 430 km, Kim drove part of the time at 80 km/h and the rest of the time at 100 km/h. The trip took 5 h. How much time did Kim travel at each speed?

9. Angie is 8 years older than her cousin Tony. In 3 years, she will be double his age. How old is Angie today? How old is Tony?

10. A mailroom clerk processes a package requiring $2.90 in postage, using stamps of 34¢ and 40¢ denominations. If a total of 8 stamps are used to give the exact postage, then how many of each denomination are used?

5–5 Graphing Linear Inequalities Containing Two Variables

The line represented by $y = 2x + 3$ divides the coordinate plane into three regions:

1. the points *in* the line;
2. the points *above* the line;
3. the points *below* the line.

The line forms a **boundary** between two **half-planes**.

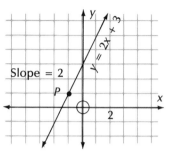

Consider any point P in the boundary line. Its coordinates satisfy $y = 2x + 3$. As you move downward from P, the y-coordinate *decreases*, giving $y < 2x + 3$. The lower half-plane, shaded at the right, represents the solution set of $y < 2x + 3$. Every point in the shaded region is a solution of $y < 2x + 3$.

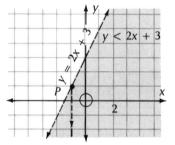

Again, consider a point P in the boundary line. Moving upward from P, the y-coordinate increases, giving $y > 2x + 3$.

The upper half-plane, shaded at the right, represents the solution set of $y > 2x + 3$. Every point in this region is a solution of $y > 2x + 3$.

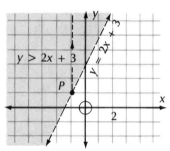

The broken lines in the graphs of the inequalities above indicate that y cannot *equal* $2x + 3$. The boundary line is *not* part of the graph. If the boundary line is *unbroken*, it is part of the graph, as shown below.

All points *in* or *above* the line are in the solution set of $y \geq 2x + 3$.

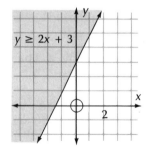

All points *in* or *below* the line are in the solution set of $y \leq 2x + 3$.

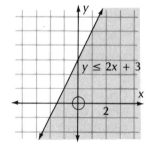

EXAMPLE 1:   Gerry has at most $20 to spend on ground pork and ground veal to make tourtière. The ground pork is $4/kg and the veal is $5/kg. What pork and beef combinations can he buy?

Define the variables.
Let x be the number of kilograms of pork bought.
Let y be the number of kilograms of veal bought.

Write an inequality.
$4x + 5y \leq 20$

Graph the solution set of the inequality to answer the question and make other observations.

Only the first quadrant is graphed, since it does not make sense to consider negative amounts of meat bought.

Since Gerry could spend the whole $20, an unbroken line is used along $4x + 5y = 20$.

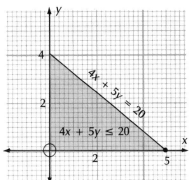

Solution set: The set of *all points* in the shaded region and in the line $4x + 5y = 20$.

Other observations:

a. What does the point (0,0) represent? ⟶ It represents a purchase of neither pork nor veal.

b. Could Gerry buy 2 kg each of pork and veal and stay under the $20 limit? ⟶ Yes, the point (2,2) lies in the shaded region.

c. What does the y-intercept represent? ⟶ It shows that Gerry could buy 4 kg of veal if he bought bought no pork.

d. What does the x-intercept represent? ⟶ It shows that Gerry could buy 5 kg of pork if he bought bought no veal.

e. Could Gerry buy 4 kg of pork and 2 kg of veal? ⟶ No, the point (4,2) lies outside the shaded region. Gerry would go over the $20 limit.

149

EXERCISES

A **1.** What is the inequality graphed? An equation of the boundary is given.

a.

b.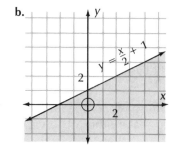

c.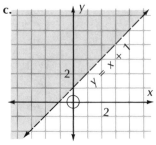

d.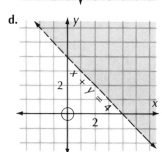

e.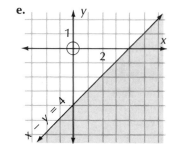

f.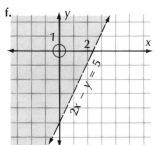

2. Identify the inequality associated with each graph. Then determine whether the given points are part of the solution set.

a. (20,40); (40,60); (70,80)

b. (6,9); (12,6); (24,0)

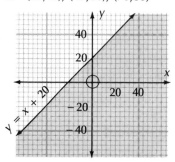

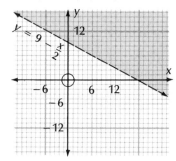

3. For each inequality, write an equation of the boundary of the graph, in $y = mx + b$ form.

    a. $x + y < 2$ **b.** $x - y \le 1$ **c.** $2x + 3y > 0$

B **4.** Graph the solution set of each inequality.

    a. $y \ge 2$ **b.** $x > 4$ **c.** $y < 0$ **d.** $x \le -3$

    e. $y \ge 3 - x$ **f.** $y < x + 4$ **g.** $y \ge 2x - 3$ **h.** $y \ge -5x - 2$

    i. $x + y < 9$ **j.** $2x + y > 8$ **k.** $x - y < 6$ **l.** $2x + 3y \le 18$

5. Graph an inequality to solve the following problem. A used-car lot has 1200 units of parking space. A compact car takes 3 units of space and a mid-size car takes 4 units of space.

   a. Could 400 compact cars be parked at the same time?
   b. Could 200 cars of each size be parked at the same time?
   c. If 200 compact cars were parked, how many mid-size cars could be parked?

   (Let x be the number of compact cars and y be the number of mid-size cars. An inequality to represent the situation is $3x + 4y \leq 1200$.)

C 6. The Drama Club costumers have a maximum of $270 to spend on fabric to make costumes for the club's annual Shakespearean play. The head costumer has decided on using broadcloth, at $5/m, and corduroy, at $6/m, for those costumes that will be sewn up.

   a. Could the costumers get 20 m of each fabric?
   b. Could they get 30 m of corduroy and 20 m of broadcloth?

   (Let x be the number of metres of broadcloth bought and y be the number of metres of corduroy bought. An inequality to represent the situation is $5x + 6y \leq 270$.)

   c. Identify the y-intercept. What does the y-intercept represent?
   d. What does the x-intercept represent?

7. Suppose the $270 had to cover, not only the fabric purchase, but also any items like thread, zippers, buttons, and trims. The head costumer estimates that $30 will be spent on these items. Rewrite the inequality to reflect this decision. Graph the inequality and answer questions **a** through **d** with respect to the new graph.

8. The limit on a salmon catch for a fishing boat was 1200 kg. If the average sockeye salmon has a mass of 2 kg and the average coho salmon has a mass of 5 kg, what are the possible legal catches of salmon? Graph your solution.

Using the Calculator

An astronomer once claimed that there are $2 \times 136 \times 2^{256}$ particles in the universe. If this were true, how many digits would there be in the number of particles written in standard form?

(Use the exponent key on your calculator to solve the problem. The answer will appear in scientific notation.)

5–6 Solving Systems of Linear Inequalities by Graphing

Schneider's Supermarket sold *more than* 200 kg of sugar in 2 kg and 4 kg bags. What are some possible numbers of each kind of bag sold?

Define the variables.
Let x be the number of 2 kg bags sold.
Let y be the number of 4 kg bags sold.

Write an inequality.
$2x + 4y > 200 \rightarrow y > 50 - \frac{x}{2}$

The shaded region in the graph illustrates the solution set of the inequality $y > 50 - \frac{x}{2}$.

Some possible amounts of sugar are in the table.

2 kg bags	20	80	40
4 kg bags	60	40	40

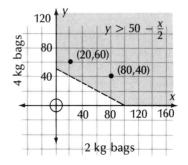

If further information is given about the sugar sales for that day, the new information could be represented on the same graph.

EXAMPLE 1: Schneider's Supermarket sold *more than* 200 kg but *less than* 300 kg of sugar in 2 kg and 4 kg bags. What are some possible numbers of each kind of bag sold?

Write a system of inequalities.
$2x + 4y > 200 \rightarrow y > 50 - \frac{x}{2}$

$2x + 4y < 300 \rightarrow y < 75 - \frac{x}{2}$

Graph the system of inequalities.

Solution: The set of all points between the lines in the doubly-shaded region satisfies the system of equations.

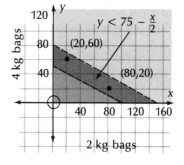

Some possible amounts of sugar are in the table.

2 kg bags	80	20	40
4 kg bags	20	60	40

Does (80,20) satisfy *both* inequalities?

For $y > 50 - \frac{x}{2}$:

L.S. = 20

R.S. = $50 - \frac{80}{2}$
= 10

L.S. > R.S. ✓

For $y < 75 - \frac{x}{2}$:

L.S. = 20

R.S. = $75 - \frac{80}{2}$
= 35

L.S. < R.S. ✓

152

In dealing with systems of inequalities, problems involving three inequalities, or even more, are possible.

Samples from an ore deposit indicate that *at most* 12% is copper and *at most* 9% is lead. Samples also indicate that there is *at least* a 15% copper/lead combination. If 300 t of ore are mined each day, what are some possible daily production levels for copper and lead?

Define the variables.
Let x be the amount of copper in tonnes produced daily.
Let y be the amount of lead in tonnes produced daily.

Write three inequalities.
$x \leq 36$
$y \leq 27$
$x + y \geq 45 \quad \rightarrow \quad y \geq 45 - x$

Graph the system of inequalities to find some possible solutions.

Solution: The set of all points in the darkest region and in the three boundary lines satisfy the system of inequalities.

Some possible daily production levels are shown in the table.

Copper (t)	36	36	18	30
Lead (t)	9	27	27	20

Check one of the solutions, say (36,9), in the three inequalities.

For $x \leq 36$:   For $y \leq 27$:   For $x + y \geq 45$:
L.S. = 36   L.S. = 9   L.S. = 36 + 9
R.S. = 36   R.S. = 27   = 45
L.S. $\leq$ R.S. ✓   L.S. $\leq$ R.S. ✓   R.S. = 45
                                         L.S. $\geq$ R.S. ✓

Note that *open dots* are used at the intersections of boundary lines that are *not* solutions of the system of inequalities.

The graph at the right shows the system of inequalities: $x < 36$;
$\qquad y < 27$;
$\qquad x + y > 45$.

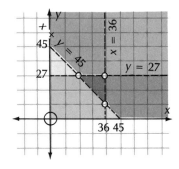

153

EXERCISES

A **1.** Match each system of inequalities with the appropriate graph.

a. 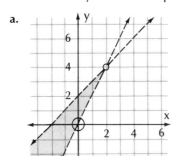   **b.** 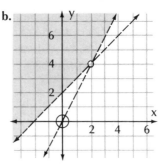   **c.**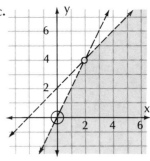

i. $y < x + 2$
   $y > 2x$

ii. $y < x + 2$
   $y < 2x$

iii. $y > x + 2$
   $y > 2x$

2. Name three possible integral solutions for each graph in exercise 1.

B **3.** Graph the solution set of each system of inequalities.

a. $y < 3 - x$
   $y > x$

b. $2y < x + 4$
   $y \geq 2 - x$

c. $y \leq x + 2$
   $y \geq 1 - x$

d. $x + y < 4$
   $y - 2x > 0$

e. $2x + y \leq 6$
   $x - y < 2$

f. $2x + 3y < 12$
   $x + y > 0$

g. $5x + 3y \geq 30$
   $y \geq 3x + 9$

h. $x + y > 5$
   $x > 3$
   $y < 4$

i. $x + 2y \leq 10$
   $x < 6$
   $y \geq 1$

4. Write a system of linear inequalities whose solution set is shown by the shaded region in each graph. Then write three possible integral solutions for each.

a. 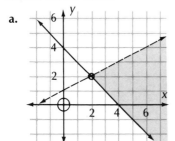   **b.** 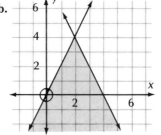   **c.**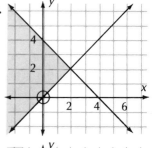

d. 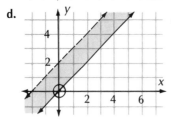   **e.** 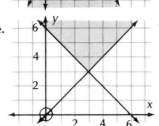   **f.**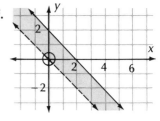

5. Write a system of linear inequalities whose solution set is shown by the shaded region in each graph.

a. 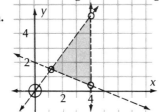 **b.** 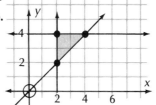 **c.**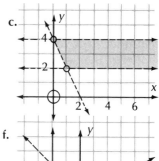

d. 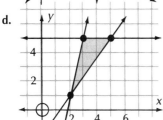 **e.** 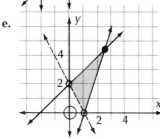 **f.**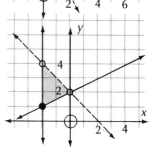

6. Graph each system of inequalities and identify the region representing the solution as a square, a rectangle, a trapezoid, or a parallelogram. Name the four intersection points of the boundary lines for each polygon.

a. $y < 5$
$y > 1$
$x > 3$
$x < 7$

b. $y > x$
$y > -x$
$y < x + 4$
$y < -x + 4$

c. $x > 1$
$x < 4$
$y > x$
$y < x + 3$

d. $y < x$
$y < 4$
$y > 0$
$x < 7$

e. $y \geq x$
$y \leq x + 6$
$y \leq -2x + 6$
$y > -2x$

f. $y \leq 2x$
$y \geq 3x$
$x \leq 5$
$x \geq 1$

g. $y > x + 1$
$y < x + 5$
$y > -x$
$y < -x + 2$

h. $y > 0$
$x > 0$
$y < 1$
$x < 1.5$

7. Write a system of inequalities that, when graphed, will yield a region of the given shape.
   a. right-angled triangle   **b.** square   **c.** parallelogram

8. A record shop sold more than 250 discounted records and tapes one day, with records selling for $8 and tapes for $5. The toal cash receipts on discounted items did not exceed $1750.
   a. Define variables and write two inequalities to represent the given information.
   b. Graph the solution set of the system of inequalities.

9. Samples from an ore deposit indicate that the deposit contains at most 19% copper and at most 11% lead. The samples also indicate that there is at least 25% of copper and lead combined.
   a. Define variables to represent the unknowns and write a system of three inequalities to represent the given information.
   b. Graph the system of inequalities.

5–7 Linear Programming

Linear inequalities have an extremely powerful application in business. Graphing inequalities helps businesses decide how much of their product to produce and market in order to maximize their profit or efficiency, and minimize their expenses. The process of using inequalities to optimize business opportunities is called **linear programming**.

EXAMPLE 1: A canning factory has 120 000 kg of peaches, to be packed in small and large cans. A case of small cans contains 4 kg of peaches; a case of large cans contains 8 kg. To meet incoming orders, at least 6000 cases of large cans and from 8000 to 15 000 cases of small cans must be canned. There is a 60¢ profit on each case of small cans and a dollar profit on each case of large cans. How many cases of each size can should be produced to maximize profit?

Define the variables.
Let x be the number of cases of small cans. Let y be the number of cases of large cans.

Write a system of inequalities.
$x \geq 8000$
$x \leq 15\ 000$
$y \geq 6000$
$4x + 8y \leq 120\ 000$

(That is, $x + 2y \leq 30\ 000$)

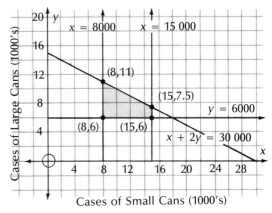

Graph the solution set of the system of inequalities.

Any point in the shaded region gives a possible solution to the system of inequalities. However, we need to find the point that gives a *maximum* profit. An equation to represent profit can be written from the problem:
Profit $= 0.6x + 1.0y$.

A theorem in linear programming establishes that a maximum or minimum value *must* occur at a vertex of the region. Check each vertex point, using the equation
Profit $= 0.6x + 1.0y$.

Point (thousands)	(8,6)	(15,6)	(8,11)	(15,7.5)
Profit (thousands)	10.8	15.0	15.8	16.5

A production of 15 000 cases of small cans and 7500 cases of large cans will bring maximum profit, $16 500.

EXAMPLE 2: An automobile corporation has two plants, A and B. The company needs to supply its dealerships with at least 60 000 compact cars and 40 000 mid-size cars. The table gives weekly production capacities and costs for the two plants.

Plant	Mid-Size Cars	Compact Cars	Production Costs
A	4000	3000	$500 000 000
B	2000	4000	$600 000 000

How many weeks should each plant operate in order to supply the dealership requirements with the least expense?

Define the variables.
Let x be the number of weeks that Plant A operates.
Let y be the number of weeks that Plant B operates.

Write a system of inequalities.

$4000x + 2000y \geq 40\,000$ $y \geq 20 - 2x$
$3000x + 4000y \geq 60\,000$ $y \geq 15 - 0.75x$

Graph the system of inequalities. There is no upper boundary for the region. The region reveals three vertex points to examine for minimum cost: (0,20); (4,12); (20,0). Which vertex gives minimum cost?

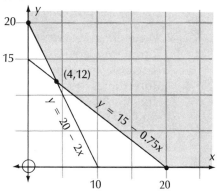

Cost = $5x + 6y$ ($\times$ $100 000 000)

Point	(0,20)	(4,12)	(20,0)
Cost	120	92	100

Operating Plant A for 4 weeks and Plant B for 12 weeks would minimize the cost of producing the required cars.

EXERCISES

A   **1.** For each system of inequalities graphed below, find the maximum profit P or the minimum cost C in each shaded region.

a. $P = 6x + 8y$

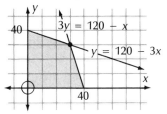

b. $C = 200x + 100y$

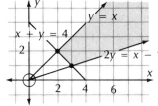

c. $P = 60x + 30y$

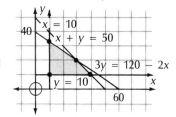

157

B **2.** Graph the solution set for each system of inequalities. For each region, determine the greatest and the least values of $3x + 2y$. All values of x and y are non-negative.

a. $x \le 5$
$y \ge 1$
$x + y \le 6$

b. $x \ge 3$
$y \le 6$
$y \ge x$

c. $x \ge 2$
$x \le 6$
$y \le x + 3$

d. $x \le 30$
$y \le 20$
$3x + 2y \ge 36$

3. Suppose the automobile corporation in example 2 also needed the cars to be produced within 10 weeks. This condition can be represented by adding the following equations to the system of equations used to solve example 2: $x \le 10$; $y \le 10$.

a. Graph the system of inequalities from example 2 together with the two inequalities above.
b. Name the three new vertices to be examined for cost.
c. Find the vertex that minimizes cost. Use the same equation for cost as was used in example 2. You will find that the minimum cost is now greater than the solution for example 2 was. However, since dealers without sufficient cars would be losing potential sales, the extra cost is probably justified.

C **4.** A supermarket has storage for 2400 kg of grapefruit and oranges. The profit from grapefruit sales is $0.50/kg and for oranges it is $0.20/kg. Because of customer demand, the amount of oranges is always at least three times the amount of grapefruit in stock. At least 400 kg of grapefruit must be stocked. If x represents number of kilograms of grapefruit and y represents number of kilograms of oranges, then a system of inequalities to represent the situation is:

$$x + y \le 2400;$$
$$x \ge 400;$$
$$y \ge 3x.$$

The problem also yields an equation for profit:
Profit $= 0.50x + 0.20y$.

a. Graph the system of inequalities and identify the region of the solution.
b. Name the three vertex points to examine for profit.
c. Find the point that will give maximum profit.

5. A contractor with two bricklayers on call has organized a construction project so that one week (up to 50 h) is allotted to bricklaying. Pat lays bricks at the rate of 50 per hour, earning $18/h. Chris lays bricks at a rate of 60 per hour, earning $21/h. The job requires that at least 4500 bricks be laid. If x represents Pat's hours and y represents Chris's hours, then a system of inequalities from the information is: $x \le 50$; $y \le 50$. An equation for cost is Cost $= 19x + 19y$.
Find the combination of hours for which the contractor will minimize costs.

6. An electronics company needs to supply its distributors with 60 000 to 72 000 calculators in regular and deluxe models. At least 36 000 must be regular models and at least 12 000 must be deluxe models. Write appropriate inequalities and graph the solution set. If the profit on a regular calculator is $2 and on a deluxe calculator is $3, find the greatest and the least possible profits, if all calculators are sold.

7. Dave and Melanie farm 120 ha of land for wheat and soybeans. They must plant at least 45 ha of wheat and at least 60 ha of soybeans. Costs for growing wheat are estimated at $240/ha and, for soybeans, at $160/ha. They can spend up to $24 000 in production costs. The profits are estimated at $300/ha for wheat and $200/ha for soybeans. How many hectares of each crop should Melanie and Dave grow?

Review

1. Graph the solution set of each inequality.
   a. $y \le -2x - 1$
   b. $y < 7x - 2$
   c. $y \le x - 4$
   d. $x + 2y > 7$
   e. $2x + y < 4$
   f. $2x + 5y > 5$

2. For each graph drawn in question 1, name three points that satisfy the inequality.

3. Graph each system of inequalities. Name three points that satisfy the system in each case.

   a. $y \le 4x + 2$
      $y < x + 3$

   b. $y > x + 1$
      $y > -x - 1$
      $y < x + 5$

   c. $y < 2x$
      $y < 6$
      $y > 0$
      $x < 6$

   d. $y \ge -2x - 7$
      $y < 3x$
      $x \le 0$

   e. $2x + 3y < 0$
      $x \ge 1$
      $x \le 9$

   f. $y > -2x$
      $y < -2x + 7$
      $y > -3$
      $y < x$

4. A car dealership sells compact and mid-size cars. They stock up to 30 cars, with at least 10 cars of each size. The dealership's cost for each compact car is $7500 and, for each mid-size car, $12 500. The value of the inventory must never exceed $300 000.

   a. Let x represent number of compact cars and y represent number of mid-size cars. Write appropriate inequalities for the information given. Graph the system of inequalities representing cars in stock.
   b. On the average, the dealership makes a profit of $600 on the sale of each compact car and $1500 on the sale of each mid-size car. Write an equation to represent potential profit.
   c. What is the greatest profit the dealership could earn if all cars in inventory were sold?

159

Using Graphs and Extreme Conditions

Problems involving linear relationships can be solved using graphs and extreme conditions. The following example shows you how.

EXAMPLE 1:   A handful of 20 nickels and dimes is worth $1.60. How many nickels and how many dimes are there?

Define the variables.
Let x be the number of nickels.
Let y be the number of dimes.

If all the coins were nickels, there would be 32 nickels, represented by point (32,0) on a coordinate grid.
If all the coins were dimes, there would be 16 dimes, represented by point (0,16) on a coordinate grid.

Plot the extreme conditions and join them with a straight line.

Write an equation for the number of coins and graph it. $x + y = 20$

The point of intersection of these two lines is the solution to the problem: (8,12).

There are 8 nickels and 12 dimes.

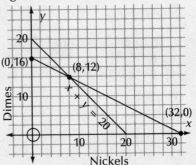

EXERCISES

Solve by using graphs and extreme conditions.

A **1.** Nadia can do a job in 3 h and Claude can do the same job in 6 h. They are working together on the job. Let x be Nadia's time and y be Claude's time.

   a. If Nadia worked by herself, how long would the job take? What is the point to represent this extreme condition?

   b. If Claude worked by himself, how long would the job take? What is the point to represent this extreme condition?

   c. Graph the extreme conditions from parts **a** and **b** and join the points with a line.

   d. If they are working together on the job, then they will spend equal time. Graph the equation $x = y$ with the extreme conditions to find how long they will take.

B **2.** Twenty-eight tickets, sold at $2 and $3 each, are worth $72 altogether. How many $2 and $3 tickets are there?

   3. Pipe A can fill a pool in 3 h and Pipe B can fill the pool in 5 h. At noon, pipe A is opened. One hour later, pipe B is also opened. At what time will the pool be filled?

Using the Computer

It is not possible to *graph* problems involving three or more variables. But, with computers, problems with many variables *can* be solved.

Problem:
A farmer wants to grow artichokes, beans, and cabbage on 60 ha of land. He wants between 5 ha and 10 ha of artichokes, between 25 ha and 35 ha of beans, and between 16 ha and 24 ha of cabbage. He wants to plant no more than 10 ha more of beans than cabbage. He estimates a profit of $400/ha for artichokes, $200/ha for beans, and $300/ha for cabbage. How many hectares of each vegetable should he grow for maximum profit?

Computer Program Solution:

```
10  REM  THIS PROGRAM SOLVES A FARMER'S PROBLEM
20  I = 0
30  FOR A = 5 TO 10
40  FOR B = 25 TO 35
50  FOR C = 16 TO 24
60  IF A + B + C < > 60 THEN  GOTO 140
70  IF B > C + 10 THEN  GOTO 140
80  I = I + 1
90  PRINT "A = ";A;
100  PRINT ", B = ";B;
110  PRINT ", C = ";C;
120 PROFIT = 400 * A + 200 * B + 300 * C
130  PRINT "  PROFIT(";I;") = $";PROFIT
140  NEXT C
150  NEXT B
160  NEXT A
```

The program prints out 21 possible combinations.

```
A = 5, B = 31, C = 24   PROFIT(1) = $15400
A = 5, B = 32, C = 23   PROFIT(2) = $15300
A = 6, B = 30, C = 24   PROFIT(3) = $15600
A = 6, B = 31, C = 23   PROFIT(4) = $15500
A = 6, B = 32, C = 22   PROFIT(5) = $15400
A = 7, B = 29, C = 24   PROFIT(6) = $15800
A = 7, B = 30, C = 23   PROFIT(7) = $15700
A = 7, B = 31, C = 22   PROFIT(8) = $15600
A = 8, B = 28, C = 24   PROFIT(9) = $15400
```

The farmer/user must read through the list and select the combination that gives maximum profit: 10 ha of artichokes, 26 ha of beans, and 24 ha of cabbage.

Modify the program as necessary to solve the same or similar problems.

1. The farmer decides to leave 10 ha for pasture. What will the maximum profit be, leaving the other conditions the same?

2. Suppose the farmer has 70 ha available, but decides to leave 10 ha for pasture. What will the maximum profit be?

3. A computer store keeps 60 computers in stock at all times. The manager wants to have 5 to 10 model A computers in stock, 25 to 35 model B computers, and 16 to 24 model C computers. She never wants to have more than 10 more model B computers than model C ones. There is a profit of $400 on each model A, $200 on each model B, and $300 on each model C. If all computers in inventory will be sold, what combination of computers will bring the greatest profit?

4. Question 3 is solved exactly by the program above. Write another problem, involving a different situation, which could be solved exactly by the program above.

Test   Unit 5

1. Solve each system of equations by any method.

   a. $3x + 6y = 9$
   $2x + y = 0$

   b. $2x - 3y = 12$
   $5x + 3y = 9$

   c. $2x - y = 5$
   $x + 3y = 13$

   d. $x + 4y = 7$
   $3x + 2y = 1$

   e. $3x + 4y = 5$
   $4x + 2y = 0$

   f. $2x - 5y = 19$
   $x + 2y = 23$

2. Graph the solution set of each inequality.

   a. $x + y < 5$

   b. $2x + y \geq 6$

   c. $y > \frac{x}{3} - 2$

3. For each graph, write the appropriate system of inequalities. Equations of the boundary lines are given.

   a.
   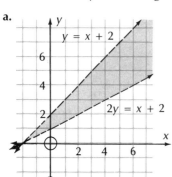

   b.
   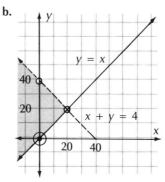

   c.
   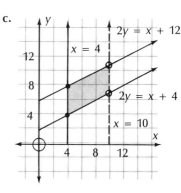

4. Graph the solution set of each system of inequalities.

   a. $y < x + 4$
   $x < 5$
   $y > 2$

   b. $x + y \leq 20$
   $y \geq x$

   c. $2x + y \geq 6$
   $y \geq x + 1$
   $y \leq 5$

5. For the shaded region in each graph, determine the greatest value of the function P, where P is given; or the least value of the function C, where C is given.

   a. $P = 4x - 3y$
   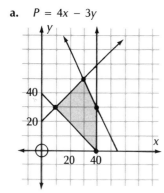

   b. $P = 20x + 3y$
   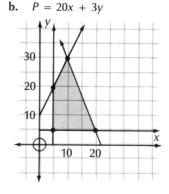

   c. $C = 6x + 4y$
   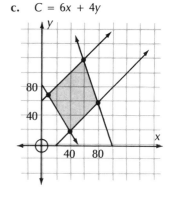

Cumulative Review

1. Simplify.

   a. $3x^2 - 6x + 4x^2 + 5x$

   b. $2xy - 3x(2y - 4) + 5x$

2. Evaluate for $x = 2$, $y = -3$, and $z = -1$.

   a. $2x^2 + 3y - 2z$

   b. $3xy + 4yz - 3x^2z$

3. Simplify.

   a. $2^3 - 3^2$

   b. $4^3 + \sqrt{81} - \sqrt[3]{27}$

   c. $(3^2 - 2^3)^2$

   d. $\sqrt{32} + 2\sqrt{72}$

   e. $3\sqrt{12} \times 4\sqrt{3}$

   f. $4\sqrt{50} \div \sqrt{2}$

4. Find each unknown measure.

   a.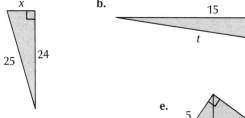

   b.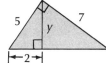

   c.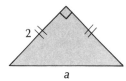

   d.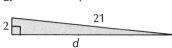

   e.

   f.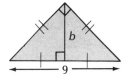

5. Find the distance between the points $A(2,3)$ and $B(14,8)$.

6. Solve each equation.

   a. $5x + 2 - 2x = -10$

   b. $2(5 - x) = 12$

   c. $3(2m + 4) = 4(m - 2)$

   d. $\frac{2x}{3} - 2 = \frac{4}{3}$

7. Find the solution set for each inequality and graph the solution.

   a. $2x + 1 < 7$

   b. $2(3x - 1) \geq 4x + 6$

   c. $x + 3 \leq 5$ and $x \geq 1$

   d. $x - 6 < 2$ or $x + 2 > 6$

8. Find the slope and the y-intercept of the line represented by the given equation. Graph the line.

   a. $3x + 2y = 8$

   b. $2x - 4y = 12$

9. Do the graphs of each pair of lines intersect in a single point, or are they parallel or identical?

   a. $x + 3y = 7$
      $3y = 12 - x$

   b. $2x + 3y = 7$
      $3x + 2y = 8$

   c. $2x = 3 + y$
      $4x - 2y = 6$

10. Find an equation of the line with the given characteristics.

    a. passes through $(2,6)$ and $(5,4)$

    b. passes through $(3, -2)$ and has slope 2

    c. passes through $(2,1)$ and is parallel to the line $2x + y = 7$

6 Polynomials and Factoring

6-1 Adding and Subtracting Polynomials

Number tricks are often based on simple algebra.

Think of a number.	x
Multiply by -4.	$-4x$
Add 8.	$-4x + 8$
Divide by 4.	$(-4x + 8) \div 4$
Add the number you started with.	$-x + 2 + x$
The result is 2.	2

By translating the instructions of the number trick into *algebraic expressions*, you can see why the result is *always* 2, no matter what the first number chosen is.

A single-term expression, like $-4x$, is a **monomial**.
An expression consisting of a sum of monomials is a **polynomial**.

A two-term polynomial, like $-4x + 8$, is a **binomial**.
A three-term polynomial is a **trinomial**.

The **degree** of a term is the sum of the exponents of the variables in the term. The **degree of a polynomial** is the greatest degree of any term within it. A polynomial in one variable is usually written in order of descending powers and is said to be in standard form.

Example	Degree
$3x^2$	2
$2xy^2z$	4
5	0
$2xy^2z - 3x^2$	4
$m^3n - mn$	4
$5a^2b - 3ab^2 + 2b^3$	3
$5x^5 - 3x^4y + 2x^3y^2 - 3y^3$	5

Given any polynomial, you can use the properties of real numbers to find an *equivalent* polynomial. For example, the distributive property was applied in both cases below.

$$-(x + 12) = -1(x + 12)$$
$$= -x - 12$$

$$5x^2y - 6x^2y = 5(x^2y) - 6(x^2y)$$
$$= (5 - 6)x^2y$$
$$= -x^2y$$

Polynomials can be added and subtracted by combining like terms.

EXAMPLE 1: Add $5x^2y + 2xy - 3y$ and $xy - y - 6x^2y$.

$(5x^2y + 2xy - 3y) + (xy - y - 6x^2y)$
$= 5x^2y + 2xy - 3y + xy - y - 6x^2y$ Apply the distributive property.
$= 5x^2y - 6x^2y + 2xy + xy - 3y - y$
$= -x^2y + 3xy - 4y$ The sum is a trinomial with degree 3.

EXAMPLE 2: Find the perimeter of the triangle.

$(3x^2 - 8x + 2) + (x^2 + 8x - 5) + (4x^2 - 12)$
$= 3x^2 + x^2 + 4x^2 - 8x + 8x + 2 - 5 - 12$
$= 8x^2 - 15$

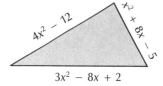

The triangle has perimeter $8x^2 - 15$.

EXAMPLE 3: Subtract $x + 12$ from $4x - 7$.

$(4x - 7) - (x + 12)$
$= 4x - 7 - x - 12$ Apply the distributive property.
$= 4x - x - 7 - 12$
$= 3x - 19$

EXAMPLE 4: A rectangular yard with perimeter $3ab + 5a - 2$ is going to be fenced on three sides, leaving one side, of length $6 + 3a - 2ab$, unfenced. What length of fencing is needed?

$(3ab + 5a - 2) - (6 + 3a - 2ab)$
$= 3ab + 5a - 2 - 6 - 3a + 2ab$
$= 3ab + 2ab + 5a - 3a - 2 - 6$
$= 5ab + 2a - 8$ $P = 3ab + 5a - 2$ $6 + 3a - 2b$

The length of fencing needed is $5ab + 2a - 8$.

EXAMPLE 5: Simplify. Give your answer in standard form.

$(8x^2 - 4 + 3x) - (-3 - 6x + 2x^2) + (x + x^2 + 1)$
$= 8x^2 - 4 + 3x + 3 + 6x - 2x^2 + x + x^2 + 1$
$= 8x^2 - 2x^2 + x^2 + 3x + 6x + x - 4 + 3 + 1$
$= 7x^2 + 10x$

165

EXERCISES

A **1.** Give the degree of each polynomial.

    a. $3x + 2x^2 - 5$ **b.** $4 - 3x + 2x^2$

    c. $4b^2 + 3 - 2a^2$ **d.** $5xy - 3ax + 2by$

    e. $7xy^2 + 3x^3 - 5x^2y - 2y^2$ **f.** $8a^2 + 4b^2 - 3ab$

    g. $-xyz + 3x^2y - 2y^2z + 2yz^2$ **h.** $3a^2b^2 - 2a^4 - 3b^4 + 5a^3b$

    i. $r^3s^2 - 2r^4s + 5s^3 - 3rs^2$ **j.** $3xz^2 - 2xyz + 5x^2y + 3y^3$

2. Add the following polynomials.

    a. $(7x + 3) + (3x + 5)$ **b.** $(2x + 8) + (4x + 3)$

    c. $(x + 7) + (3x + 4)$ **d.** $(4x - 3) + (3x + 2)$

    e. $(5x + 4) + (5 - 3x)$ **f.** $(4x^2 + 5x + 2) + (3x^2 + 2x + 7)$

    g. $(7x^2 + 4x + 5) + (2x^2 + 3x + 8)$ **h.** $(x^2 + 3x - 2) + (5x^2 - 5x + 3)$

    i. $(2x - 3x^2 - 2) + (2 + 5x^2 - 4x)$ **j.** $(-5x^2 + 2 - 6x) + (3x - 1 - x^2)$

3. Apply the distributive property.

    a. $-(x + 3)$ **b.** $-(2x - 3)$

    c. $+(x^2 - xy)$ **d.** $-(3x - 2y)$

    e. $-(3x^2 + 5x - 2)$ **f.** $+(2m^3 - 3m^2 - 2m)$

4. Subtract as indicated.

    a. $(5x + 6) - (2x + 5)$ **b.** $(3x + 6) - (x + 4)$

    c. $(x + 2) - (2x + 1)$ **d.** $(3x - 7) - (x - 3)$

    e. $(5x^2 + 6x + 3) - (2x^2 + 3x + 1)$ **f.** $(4x^2 + 7x + 6) - (x^2 + 5x + 3)$

    g. $(4x^2 + 2x + 3) - (x^2 + 4x + 1)$ **h.** $(x^2 + 2x - 3) - (5x^2 - 3x - 5)$

    i. $(x + 4x^2 - 3) - (3x - 4 - 2x^2)$ **j.** $(-3 - 5x^2 + 7x) - (x^2 - 5 - 3x)$

B **5.** Find the perimeter of each figure.

    a.   **b.**   **c.**

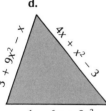

$2a + 7$ $5a - 12$ $3a + 11$

$x^2 + 8$ $x^2 + 5$ $2x^2 - 3$ $2x^2$

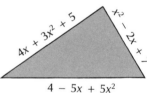

$4x + 3x^2 + 5$ $x^2 + 5$ $x^2 - 2x + 7$ $4 - 5x + 5x^2$

    d.   **e.**   **f.**

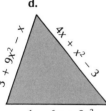 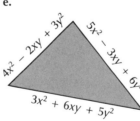 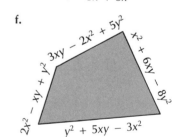

$3 + 9x^2 - x$ $4x + x^2 - 3$ $1 - 6x + 8x^2$

$4x^2 - 2xy + 3y^2$ $5x^2 - 3xy + 6y^2$ $3x^2 + 6xy + 5y^2$

$2x^2 - xy + y^2$ $3xy - 2x^2 + 5y^2$ $x^2 + 6xy - 8y^2$ $y^2 + 5xy - 3x^2$

6. What polynomial must be added to $x^2 - 2x - 1$ to obtain $4x^2 + 3x + 1$?

7. What polynomial must be subtracted from $2a - 3b - 5$ to obtain
$-4a + 4b - 3$?

166

8. Simplify.
   a. $(4x^2 + 6x + 8) - (2x^2 + 6x - 3) + (3x^2 + 4x + 6)$
   b. $(2x^2 - 5x - 9) + (5x^2 - 5x - 2) - (x^2 - 7x + 8)$
   c. $(3x^2 - xy - 3y^2) - (8x^2 + xy - 2y^2) + (3y^2 - 2x^2 + 9xy)$
   d. $(y^2 - xy + 7x^2) + (5x^2 - 5xy + 3y^2) - (2y^2 + 2x^2 - xy)$
   e. $(xy - 2x^2 + 6y^2) - (4x^2 + 3y^2 - xy) - (2xy - 9x^2 - 9y^2)$
   f. $(3ab^3 - 2a^2b + 2b^2) + (3a^3 - 2a^2b + 3b^2) - (ab^3 + a^3)$
   g. $(4m^2n + 3n^3) - (2m^3 + 3m^2n - 2n^3) - (m^2n + mn^2 + 3n^3)$
   h. $(5xyz + 2x^2y + 3xz) + (5xz - 2xy^2 + 4xyz) - (3x^2y - 2xz)$

9. Simplify. Then evaluate for $x = 2$, $y = -1$, and $z = -4$.
   a. $(3x - 2y + z) + (3y - z) + (2x + 3z)$
   b. $(3x^2 + 2x - 1) - (5x^2 - x + 3)$
   c. $(2y - z) - (3x + y) - (2x - z)$
   d. $(x^2 - 3xy + y^2) - (2x^2 + 5xy - 3y^2)$
   e. $(xz - 3x^2 - z^2) + (2x^2 - 3x + 7) - (2x^2 + 3x - 1)$

C 10. Solve each equation.
   a. $3x + 5 - 2x + 2 = 8$
   b. $5y - 3 + 4 + 4y = 19$
   c. $7x + 3 - 5x + 6 = x - 3$
   d. $(6x + 5) - (x - 2) = (3x + 7) + (x + 3)$
   e. $(a^2 + 3a - 5) - (a^2 + a + 7) = 0$
   f. $(x^2 - 3x + 4) - (x^2 + x + 2) = -2$
   g. $(3x^2 + 2x - 2) - (x^2 + 5x + 3) = (x^2 - 2x - 1) - (3x` - x^2 + 2)$

11. Find the missing values.
   a. $(3x^2 + 2xy - \blacksquare) + (\blacksquare x^2 + \blacksquare xy + 5) = 5x^2 - 3xy + 3$
   b. $(5a^3 - 3a^2b + \blacksquare ab^2 + \blacksquare b^3) + (\blacksquare a^3 + \blacksquare a^2b + 4ab^2 + b^3)$
      $$= 3a^3 - 2a^2b + ab^2 - 2b^3$$
   c. $(4x^2 - 3x + 2) - (\blacksquare x^2 + \blacksquare x + \blacksquare) = 5x^2 + 3x - 2$
   d. $(3a^2 - 2ab + \blacksquare b^2) - (\blacksquare a^2 + 3ab - b^2) - (2a^2 + \blacksquare ab + 2b^2) = 3a^2 - 2ab + b^2$
   e. $(3x^3 - \blacksquare x^2 + x - \blacksquare) + (\blacksquare x^3 + 5x^2 + 3x - 2) - (2x^3 - 3x^2 - \blacksquare x + 1)$
      $$= 5x^3 - 6x^2 - x$$

EXTRA

Calendar Math

Try this number trick on a friend.

On any calendar, have a friend choose a two-by-two array of four numbers and give you the number in the top left corner, say 17. Without looking at the calendar, you will announce the sum of the four numbers, 84 in this case.

This can be done with two quick mental calculations: multiply the given number by 4 and add 16.

JULY						
S	M	T	W	T	F	S
		1	2	3	4	5
6	7	8	9	10	11	12
13	14	15	16	17	18	19
20	21	22	23	24	25	26
27	28	29	30	31		

1. Use polynomials to show why the trick will always work, no matter what the two-by-two array is.

$17 \times 4 = 68$
$68 + 16 = 84$
(*Check*: $17 + 18 + 24 + 25 = 84$)

2. Find a similar rule for numbers in the following formations.
   a. four-by-one array
   b. three-by-three array

167

6–2 Multiplying Polynomials by Monomials

Carl Gauss illustrated his mathematical gifts at an early age. When he was about ten years old, his teacher, wanting to keep the class busy and quiet, assigned the task of adding all the numbers from 1 through to 100. Gauss immediately wrote 5050 on his slate while the remainder of the class struggled with the problem. Even after time was given for the other students to finish, Gauss alone had the correct answer, and with no calculation!

Carl Gauss 1777–1855

Gauss had mentally computed the sum by noting that $100 + 1 = 101$, $99 + 2 = 101$, $98 + 3 = 101$, and so on for 50 such pairs. Thus, he noted that the result is 50×101, or 5050.

Gauss's method: $1 + 2 + 3 + 4 + \ldots + 100 = \frac{1}{2}(100)(100 + 1) = 5050$

This method can be extended to give the sum of the first n consecutive numbers, where n is a whole number.

$$1 + 2 + 3 + 4 + \ldots + n = \frac{1}{2}n(n + 1) \qquad \text{Apply the distributive property.}$$
$$= \frac{1}{2}n^2 + \frac{1}{2}n$$

> To multiply a polynomial by a monomial, multiply *each term* of the polynomial by the monomial.

EXAMPLE 1: Multiply.

a. $3(x + 5) = (3)(x) + (3)(5)$
$= 3x + 15$

b. $5xy(3x - 2y - 4) = (5xy)(3x) + (5xy)(-2y) + (5xy)(-4)$
$= 15x^2y - 10xy^2 - 20xy$

EXAMPLE 2: Solve each equation.

a.
$3(x + 5) + 1 = 10$
$3x + 15 + 1 = 10$
$3x + 16 = 10$
$3x = -6$
$x = -2$

Check:
L.S. $= 3((-2) + 5) + 1$
$= 10$
$= $ R.S. ✓

b.
$\frac{2}{3}x + \frac{3}{4} = \frac{5}{8}$
$24\left(\frac{2}{3}x + \frac{3}{4}\right) = 24\left(\frac{5}{8}\right)$
$16x + 18 = 15$
$16x = -3$
$x = -\frac{3}{16}$

Check:
L.S. $= \frac{2}{3}\left(-\frac{3}{16}\right) + \frac{3}{4}$
$= \frac{5}{8}$
$= $ R.S. ✓

EXERCISES

A **1.** Multiply.

   a. $2(x + 2)$ **b.** $-2(y + 3)$ **c.** $4(5y + 3)$

   d. $7(x - 5y)$ **e.** $\frac{3}{4}(8x - 4y + 12)$ **f.** $-\frac{1}{5}\left(3x^2 - \frac{6}{5}x + \frac{9}{2}\right)$

2. Multiply.

   a. $x(x + 5)$ **b.** $3x(5x + 2y)$ **c.** $xy(3x + y)$

   d. $4x^2(5xy - 3y^2)$ **e.** $5x(3x^2 + 2x - 4)$ **f.** $-3y^2(2xy + y - 5)$

   g. $1.5x(0.2x^2 + 1.2xy - 0.6y^2)$ **h.** $-\frac{1}{3}ab(9a - 3b + 6)$

3. Solve each equation.

   a. $3(x - 2) = 12$ **b.** $5(x + 3) = -10$

   c. $4(x + 5) - 6 = 10$ **d.** $4(3x - 2) = 5(x + 3) - 2$

   e. $2(x - 5) = -(x + 1)$ **f.** $7(3 - x) + 5 = 3(x - 5) + 1$

B **4.** Simplify each expression.

   a. $3(x - 2) + 2(x + 5)$ **b.** $5(3 - x) + 4(2x - 5)$

   c. $2(5x + 3) - 7(2x + 1)$ **d.** $4(3x + 2y - 2) + 3(x - 5y + 3)$

   e. $a^2(3a + 5b - 2) + a(4a^2 - 2ab + 3a)$

   f. $2x(3x + 5y) - 2(x^2 + 3xy) - 5y(3x^2 - 2x)$

   g. $-(3a^2 - 2ab + b) + b(3a - 5b) - 2a(3a - b)$

   h. $5(3a - 2b) - [5a - (2a + b)]$

   i. $3x(2x + y) - 2x[3 - (2x + 4)]$

   j. $4a(3a^2 - 2a + 4) - 3a^2(2a - 5) + a[3a^2 - (a + 4)]$

5. Solve each equation.

   a. $\frac{3}{5}x - \frac{7}{10} = \frac{1}{2}$ **b.** $\frac{5}{8}x + \frac{3}{4} = \frac{1}{4}$ **c.** $\frac{5x - 4}{2} = \frac{3}{4}$

   d. $\frac{5}{6}(x - 3) = \frac{3}{4}(5 + x)$ **e.** $\frac{3(2x + 1)}{5} = \frac{x + 3}{2}$ **f.** $\frac{3x + 2}{3} = \frac{x + 2}{2} - 3$

C **6.** Find the area of each figure.

   a.   **b.**   **c.**   **d.**

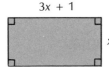

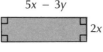

7. Find the volume of each solid.

   a.   **b.**   **c.**

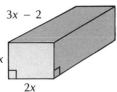

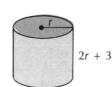

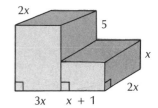

169

6–3 Multiplying Polynomials

Genetics is the study of inherited traits, passed on through the **genes**. Genetics provides an interesting application of multiplication of polynomials.

Brown eyes are a dominant trait. If a child inherits the dominant gene for brown eyes (call it *B*) from *either* parent, the child will have brown eyes.

The child will have eyes of a different colour only if a recessive gene (call it *b*) is inherited from *both* parents. The diagram illustrates the possible combinations if both father and mother have one dominant and one recessive gene.

	B	*b*
B	*BB*	*Bb*
b	*Bb*	*bb*

The possible combinations of inherited genes can also be written as a polynomial product.

$$(B + b)(B + b) = B^2 + Bb + Bb + b^2$$
$$= B^2 + 2Bb + b^2$$

An area *A* can be represented by a polynomial product of two factors.

EXAMPLE 1: Find the product and draw a diagram to illustrate it.

a. $(x + 2)(x + 3)$
$$= x^2 + 2x + 3x + 6$$
$$= x^2 + 5x + 6$$

b. $(a^2 + 3a + 1)(2a + 3)$
$$= 2a^3 + 3a^2 + 6a^2 + 9a + 2a + 3$$
$$= 2a^3 + 9a^2 + 11a + 3$$

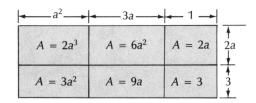

> To multiply a pair of polynomials, multiply each term of one polynomial by each term of the other.

EXAMPLE 2: Expand by multiplying and simplify if possible.

a. $(3x - 2)(2x + 5) = 3x(2x) + 3x(5) - 2(2x) - 2(5)$
$$= 6x^2 + 15x - 4x - 10$$
$$= 6x^2 + 11x - 10$$

b. $(2xy + 3x + 5)(x - 2)$
$$= 2xy(x) + 2xy(-2) + 3x(x) + 3x(-2) + 5(x) + 5(-2)$$
$$= 2x^2y - 4xy + 3x^2 - 6x + 5x - 10$$
$$= 2x^2y - 4xy + 3x^2 - x - 10$$

If both factors are binomials, you can save time by remembering **FOIL:** *First* terms; *Outside* terms; *Inside* terms; *Last* terms.

EXAMPLE 3: Multiply.

a. $(x + 7)(x - 2) = x^2 - 2x + 7x - 14$
$= x^2 + 5x - 14$

$(x + 7)(x - 2)$

b. $(2x - y)(x - 3y) = 2x^2 - 6xy - xy + 3y^2$
$= 2x^2 - 7xy + 3y^2$

$(2x - y)(x - 3y)$

To square a binomial, multiply it by itself.

EXAMPLE 4: Square each binomial.

a. $(x + 3)^2 = (x + 3)(x + 3)$
$= x^2 + 3x + 3x + 9$
$= x^2 + 6x + 9$

$(x + 3)(x + 3)$

b. $(b - 2d)^2 = (b - 2d)(b - 2d)$
$= b^2 - 2bd - 2bd + 4d^2$
$= b^2 - 4bd + 4d^2$

$(b - 2d)(b - 2d)$

Binomials can be squared *on sight* by writing a polynomial that contains the first term squared, double the product of the first and last terms, and the last term squared.

$$(a + b)^2 = a^2 + 2ab + b^2 \qquad (a - b)^2 = a^2 - 2ab + b^2$$

EXERCISES

A **1.** Draw a diagram to represent the given product.
   a. $(x + 3)(x + 7) = x^2 + 10x + 21$
   b. $(x + 5)(x + 2) = x^2 + 7x - 10$
   c. $(x + 3)(2x + y + 1) = 2x^2 + xy + 7x + 3y + 3$
   d. $(3x + 2)(x + 5z + 4) = 3x^2 + 15xz + 14x + 10z + 8$

2. Find each product of binomials.
   a. $(x + 4)(x + 7)$ b. $(a + 6)(a + 9)$ c. $(z - 2)(z + 3)$
   d. $(k + 8)(k - 3)$ e. $(t + 5)(t - 7)$ f. $(r - 3)(r - 5)$
   g. $(y - 9)(y - 1)$ h. $(x - 4y)(x - 6y)$ i. $(a - 8b)(a + 7b)$
   j. $(p + 5)(p - 5)$ k. $(d + 3)(d - 3)$ l. $(x + y)(x - y)$

3. Find each square.
   a. $(x + 5)^2$ b. $(t - 2)^2$ c. $(a - 4)^2$ d. $(2x + 1)^2$
   e. $(3j - 2)^2$ f. $(5p - 4)^2$ g. $(a + 2b)^2$ h. $(3x + 5y)^2$
   i. $(c - 2d)^2$ j. $(3a - b)^2$ k. $(6s + 2t)^2$ l. $(7k - 4m)^2$

171

B **4.** Solve each equation.

    a. $x^2 = (x - 2)(x + 3)$ **b.** $x^2 = (x + 6)(x - 2)$

    c. $t^2 = (t - 3)(t + 5)$ **d.** $v^2 = (v + 9)(v - 6)$

    e. $(2b - 1)(b + 3) = 2b^2$ **f.** $(m - 3)(5m + 6) = 5m^2$

5. Expand by multiplying and simplify if possible.

    a. $(3 - 5x)(x + 2)$ **b.** $(3x + 5)(x + 2)$

    c. $(2x - 3)(3x + 1)$ **d.** $(7a - b)(2a - 3b)$

    e. $(3x - 2y)(2x - 5y)$ **f.** $(2x^2 - 3)(3x + 1)$

    g. $(x + 1)(x^2 + x + 1)$ **h.** $(x + 3)(x^2 + 2x + 3)$

    i. $(x^2 - 2x + 3)(x - 1)$ **j.** $(a^2 - 5)(2a^2 - a + 3)$

    k. $(x + 3)(3x^2 + 2x + 3)$ **l.** $(5x + 2)(x^2 + 3x - 4)$

    m. $5(2x - 7)(x + 5)$ **n.** $x(2x - 3)(3x^2 - 5x - 1)$

    o. $8a(a + b)(a^2 - 2ab + b^2)$ **p.** $-2x(3x + y)(2x^2 - 5xy + 8y^2)$

6. Expand and simplify.

    a. $(x + 5)(x - 2) + (3x + 4)$ **b.** $(x - y)^2 + (x + y)^2$

    c. $8(5x - y)(x + y) - (3x - y)(x - y)$ **d.** $-x(x + 3) + (2x - 5)^2$

    e. $(x - 7)^2 - (3x + 4)^2$ **f.** $(x + 3)(2x - 5) - 8x(x + 3)$

    g. $(a + b)(5a - 2b) - 3a(a - b)$ **h.** $(x - 2y)(3x + y) - x(x + 5y)$

7. Solve each equation.

    a. $(x + 4)(x - 2) - x^2 = 3$ **b.** $(x + 5)(x - 3) - x(x + 4) = 5$

    c. $(5 - 4x)(2 - 3x) + (2x - 3)(1 - 6x) = -2$ **d.** $(x + 5)(x - 2) = (x + 1)(x - 1)$

    e. $x(x + 3) = (x - 1)(x + 5)$ **f.** $(3x - 8)(4 - 2x) = (4 - x)(6x + 4)$

8. Find the area of each figure.

    a. 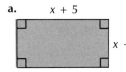   **b.**   **c.** 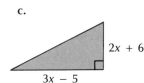   **d.**

9. Write an expression to represent the area of the given figure. Let w be width, h be height, and b be base length.

    a. a rectangle $3k$ units longer than it is wide

    b. a rectangle $5k$ units shorter than it is wide

    c. a rectangle with length $2b$ units more than triple its width

    d. a triangle with base $4d$ units longer than double its height

    e. a triangle with altitude $6k$ units shorter than the base

C **10.** A square concrete patio is extended 2 m in one direction and 3 m in the other. The new area is increased by 56 m². What are the original dimensions of the patio?

$(x + 2)(x + 3) - x^2 = 56$

11. A rectangular piece of sheet metal is twice as long as it is wide. When 5 cm are trimmed off the length and the width, the area decreases by 200 cm². What are the original dimensions of the sheet metal?

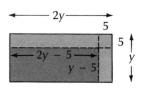

12. Simplify the following.
a. $(x - 2)(x + 3)(5 + x)$ **b.** $3(x + 1)(x - 2)(2x + 2) + (x - 3)(x + 5)$
c. $(x + 1)^3$ **d.** $(x + 1)^4$ **e.** $(x^2 - 1)(x^2 + 1)$
f. $(3x + 5)^3$ **g.** $(x^2 + x + 1)^2$ **h.** $(x^2 + x + 1)^3$

13. Give an expression for the area of each figure.
a.

b.

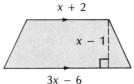

14. A farmer irrigates using rotating sprinklers. If the water pressure were increased a given amount, the water would travel an extra 3 m, increasing the total amount of area covered by one sprinkler by about 311 m². What distance does the water travel from the sprinkler now, at the lower water pressure?

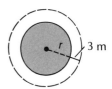

EXTRA

Earning Interest

The formula used to calculate the amount A of money accumulated when invested with *simple interest* is:

$A = P(1 + rn)$. P is the original principal;
                       r is the annual rate;
                       n is the number of years.

To calculate the amount A of money accumulated when invested with *compound interest*, the formula is:

$A = P(1 + r)^n$.

1. By expanding both formulas for $n = 1, 2, 3$, and 4 years, compare the potential amounts of money accumulated with simple interest and with compound interest.

2. When an investment is earning compound interest, then "interest earns interest". How is this shown in the expansion of $(1 + r)^n$?

173

6–4 Factoring Monomials

What are possible dimensions of the rectangle shown?

The monomial $2ab^2$ is the product of the following pairs
of factors.

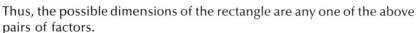

$1 \times 2ab^2$	$b \times 2ab$	$2b \times ab$
$a \times 2b^2$	$2 \times ab^2$	$2a \times b^2$

Thus, the possible dimensions of the rectangle are any one of the above
pairs of factors.

Note that some of the factor pairs above have *common factors*. For
instance, $2b$ and ab have a common factor of b, which is also the **greatest
common factor**, GCF, of the pair.

The GCF of a pair of monomials is the factor of each that has the greatest
degree and the greatest coefficient common to both.

The GCF of $2ab^2$ and $-6a^2b^2$ is $2ab^2$.

EXAMPLE 1:   Find the GCF of $24a^3b^2$ and $60ab^2c$.

    a. Find the GCF of the coefficients, 24 and 60, by writing their
prime factorizations.

$$
\begin{array}{l}
24 = 2 \times \boxed{2 \times 2 \times 3} \\
60 = \boxed{2 \times 2 \times 3} \times 5 \qquad 2 \times 2 \times 3 = 12
\end{array}
$$

The GCF of the coefficients is 12.

    b. Find the GCF of the variable parts, a^3b^2 and ab^2c, by
comparing the powers of each variable. Use the power
with the lesser exponent.

Compare a^3 and a.   Use a.
Compare b^2 and b^2.   Use b^2.
The variable c is not a common factor.

The GCF of $24a^3b^2$ and $60ab^2c$ is $12ab^2$.

EXAMPLE 2:   Find the GCF of $18x^3y^4$, $-36x^2y^2$, and $27x^2y^3$.

    a. Find the GCF of the numerical coefficients.
The GCF of 18, 36, and 27 is 9. (For -36, the negative
sign is ignored.)

    b. Find the GCF of the variable part by comparing the powers
of each variable.

Compare x^3, x^2, and x^2.   Use x^2.
Compare y^4, y^2, and y^3.   Use y^2.

The GCF of $18x^3y^4$, $-36x^2y^2$, and $27x^2y^3$ is $9x^2y^2$.

174

EXERCISES

A 1. Is the first monomial a factor of the second? Find the other factor if possible.
  a. a^3; a^5b^4
  b. $15x^3$; $5x^5y^2$
  c. m^7n^4; $m^{10}n^9$
  d. $3a^3b^5$; $12a^7b^{12}$
  e. $7a^2b$; $63a^3bc^4$
  f. 9; $36x^5y$

2. Give the set of factors of each monomial.
  a. x^2
  b. $3x^2$
  c. $6xy$
  d. x^2y
  e. $3x^2y$

B 3. Find each missing factor.
  a. $ab^3(\blacksquare) = a^5b^8$
  b. $(\blacksquare)x^3y^2z = x^3y^3z^3$
  c. $6x^2y(\blacksquare) = 24x^3y^5$
  d. $33x^3y^4 = -11xy(\blacksquare)$
  e. $2a^3b^5 = -a^2b^2(\blacksquare)$
  f. $(\blacksquare)(ab)^2 = a^4b^5$

4. Find the GCF of the given monomials.
  a. $16x^3y$, $20x^2y^2$
  b. $15ab$, $20a^2c$
  c. $32pq^2r$, $12p^2qr^2$, $20p^2q^2r$
  d. $25m^2n$, $35n^3p$, $45m^3n^2$
  e. $8xz$, $9y^2$, xy
  f. $a^5b^2c^3$, ab^2c, $a^2b^3c^2$
  g. $8p^3q^2r^5$, $5p^5q$, $7q^2r$
  h. $-21x^2y^5z$, $10x^3y^5z^3$, $15x^2y^4z^3$
  i. $6m^3n^2$, $24m^5n^3$; $3m^2n^2$
  j. $15a^2b^2c$, $21a^3c^4$, $18b^5c^3$

C 5. What are the dimensions of the largest square that will completely tile each rectangle? All variables are whole numbers.

a.
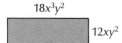
$18x^3y^2$
$12xy^2$

b.

$40a^2b$
$15ac^2$

c.
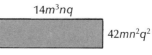
$14m^3nq$
$42mn^2q^2$

d.
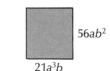
$56ab^2$
$21a^3b$

e.
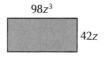
$98z^3$
$42z$

f.

$12rst$
$36r^2st^2$

6. Find the missing factors.
  a. $-4a^3b^2(\blacksquare)^2 = -16a^7b^8$
  b. $(\blacksquare)^25xy^3 = 45x^5y^9$
  c. $(\blacksquare)^210m^3n^2 = 40m^7n^{10}$
  d. $5ab^2(\blacksquare)^27ac = 140a^6b^2c^3$
  e. $(3xy)^2(\blacksquare)^22yz^2 = 450x^2y^5z^8$
  f. $2m^3(\blacksquare)^3 = -54m^6n^9$

EXTRA

Feeding Time

An attendant at the zoo has a bag of peanuts to feed the monkeys. If the nuts are shared equally among the 7 monkeys in the first room, or among the 11 monkeys in the second room, there will be 3 nuts left over. If the nuts are shared equally among the 13 monkeys in the third room, there will be 10 left over. But if the nuts are shared equally among all the monkeys in all three rooms, there will be none left over. How many peanuts does the attendant have?

6–5 Finding Common Factors of Polynomials

To find the surface area of metal used in the tin can, you could cut open the can and lay it out flat, then add the areas of the two circles and the rectangle.

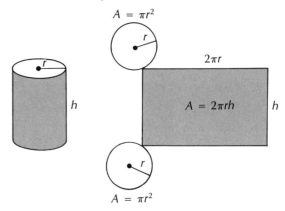

$A = \pi r^2$

$2\pi r$

$A = 2\pi rh$

h

$A = \pi r^2$

h

$$S A = 2\pi r^2 + 2\pi rh$$
$$= 2\pi r(r) + 2\pi r(h) \qquad \text{The GCF of the two terms is the monomial } 2\pi r.$$
$$= 2\pi r(r + h) \qquad \text{This is the factored form of the polynomial.}$$

To factor a polynomial, express it as a *product* of its **greatest monomial factor**, or GCF, and another polynomial whose GCF is 1.

EXAMPLE 1:　Factor $10x^2y + 5xy$.

The GCF of $10x^2y$ and $5xy$ is $5xy$.
Then, the polynomial is evenly divisible by $5xy$, assuming neither x nor y is equal to zero.

$$\frac{10x^2y + 5xy}{5xy} = \frac{10x^2y}{5xy} + \frac{5xy}{5xy}$$
$$= 2x + 1$$

Thus: $10x^2y + 5xy = 5xy(2x + 1)$ 　 *fully factored*

EXAMPLE 2:　Factor $8x^4y^2 - 12x^3y^3 + 20x^2y^4$.

The GCF of the trinomial is $4x^2y^2$.
Then, the polynomial is evenly divisible by $4x^2y^2$, assuming neither x nor y is equal to zero.

$$\frac{8x^4y^2 - 12x^3y^3 + 20x^2y^4}{4x^2y^2} = \frac{8x^4y^2}{4x^2y^2} - \frac{12x^3y^3}{4x^2y^2} + \frac{20x^2y^4}{4x^2y^2}$$
$$= 2x^2 - 3xy + 5y^2$$

Thus: $8x^4y^2 - 12x^3y^3 + 20x^2y^4 = 4x^2y^2(2x^2 - 3xy + 5y^2)$ 　 *fully factored*

The factorizations in the two examples can be checked by multiplying the resulting factors. The checks for examples 1 and 2 are left to you.

EXERCISES

A **1.** Divide each polynomial by its given GCF. Assume that no denominator equals zero.

a. $\dfrac{16x - 4}{4}$ b. $\dfrac{21x^2 - 14x}{7x}$ c. $\dfrac{15m^2 + 10mn}{5m}$

d. $\dfrac{24a^2b - 16ab^2}{8ab}$ e. $\dfrac{12x^2y^2 - 3xy^3 + 6xy}{3xy}$ f. $\dfrac{8a^3b^2 - 12a^2b^2 - 16ab^3}{4ab^2}$

2. Factor each polynomial, using the GCF.

a. $6x + 9$ b. $10m + 15$ c. $21a^2 - 7$ d. $12m^2 - 8$

e. $5x^2 - 10$ f. $3a^2 - 6a$ g. $14x - 2xy$ h. $5a^2 + 10ab$

i. $8m^2 + 4m$ j. $28m^2n - 16n^2$ k. $12ab^2 - 6ab$ l. $17xz^3 + 18xy$

3. Find the unknown dimensions in each rectangle. Assume no variables equal zero.

a.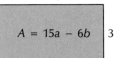
$A = 15a - 6b$ 3

b.
$A = 6c - 18$ 6

c.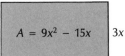
$A = 9x^2 - 15x$ 3x

d.
$A = 33ab - 22b^2$ 11b

e.
$A = 18xz^2 - 12xz$ 3xz

f.
$A = 10m^2n^2 + 15mn^2$ 5mn^2

B **4.** Divide each polynomial by its given GCF to write the numerator in factored form. Assume no variables are equal to zero.

a. $\dfrac{18m^5n^2 + 15m^2n^2 + 12m^3n}{3m^2n}$ b. $\dfrac{60x^2y^3z + 15x^2y^2z - 30x^2yz}{15x^2yz}$

c. $\dfrac{21x^3y^4z^4 + 18x^2y^3z^5 + 12x^2y^2z^2}{3x^2y^2z^2}$ d. $\dfrac{35m^3n^2t^2 + 25m^2n^2t^2 - 20mnt}{5mnt}$

e. $\dfrac{16x^5y^3z^2 + 18x^4y^2z^2 - 12x^3y^2z^2}{2x^3y^2z^2}$ f. $\dfrac{30r^2s^2t^2 + 45rs^2t^2 + 10rst^2}{5rst^2}$

5. Use factoring to simplify the given formula.

a. The perimeter of a rectangle is $l + w + l + w$.

b. The surface area of a square prism is $2b^2 + 4bh$.

c. The area of an annulus (the area between 2 concentric circles) is $\pi R^2 - \pi r^2$.

d. The surface area of a square pyramid is $b^2 + \frac{1}{2}sb + \frac{1}{2}sb + \frac{1}{2}sb + \frac{1}{2}sb$.

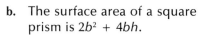

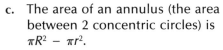

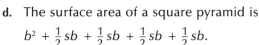

6. Factor each polynomial, using the GCF.

a. $15x^2 - 5x + 10$
b. $8x^2 + 6x - 12$
c. $3a^3 + 9a^2 - 6a$
d. $15m^3 - 30m^2 + 10m$
e. $a^2b^2 + a^2b - a^2$
f. $x^3y^2 + x^2y^3 - xy^4$
g. $7m^3n - 14m^2n^2 + 21mn^3$
h. $14x^5y - 21x^4y + 7x^3y$
i. $8m^5n^2 - 16m^3n^3 + 12m^2n^2$
j. $a^3b + 2a^2b^2 - ab^2$
k. $15x^2y - 10xy^2 + 30y^3$
l. $a^5b^2 - a^5b + a^5$
m. $8x^3y - 12x^2y^2 + 6xy^3 - 6xy$
n. $15a^3b^2c^3 + 18a^2b^2c^4 + 21a^2b^2c^3$
o. $21m^3n^2 + 14m^2n^3 - 35m^2n^2$
p. $24x^5y^3z^2 + 30x^3y^4z^2 - 18x^3y^3z^3$

7. Find each unknown dimension.

a.

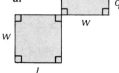

$18a^3b^3 - 6a^2b^2 + 9ab^2$ | $3ab^2$

b.

$16a^5bc + 32a^2b^2c^2 + 24a^2bc$ | $8a^2b$

c.

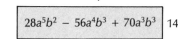

$28a^5b^2 - 56a^4b^3 + 70a^3b^3$ | 14a

8. Find a formula for the perimeter of the given figure, then simplify by factoring.

a.

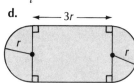

b.

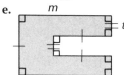

c.

d.

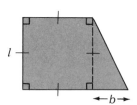

e.

f.

9. Find a formula for the area of each shaded region, then simplify by factoring.

a.

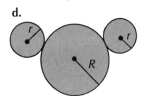

b.

c.

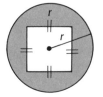

d.

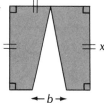

e.

f.

Biography **Roberta Bondar**

An advertisement in a newspaper in 1983 attracted the attention of Roberta Bondar, then assistant professor of medicine (neurology) at McMaster University and director of the Multiple Sclerosis Clinic for the Hamilton-Wentworth Region of Ontario. The National Research Council (NRC) was recruiting candidates for six positions on Canada's first astronaut team. For Dr. Bondar, the opportunity to join such a highly select team surpassed any daydreams she may have had as a young girl following early NASA space explorations.

Born in northern Ontario in 1945, Roberta was a bright and able student. Following high school, she attended the University of Guelph where she earned a degree in zoology and agricultural science. Encouraged by professors to continue her studies, Roberta went on to earn a master's degree in experimental pathology, and a doctorate in neurobiology in 1974. Attracted to the field of medicine, she enrolled in the program at McMaster University. She graduated as an M.D. in 1977, spending several of the following years doing postgraduate work in neurology.

As a member of Canada's astronaut team, Roberta Bondar must learn the technology and mechanics involved in the operation of the shuttle as well as assisting in preparations for every mission. Each astronaut also has a particular area of study he/she must focus on. In Dr. Bondar's case, this involves experiments on body organs, such as the eyes, that are responsible for balance. This system, known as the vestibular system, is one greatly affected by space flight and weightlessness. In more than 40% of astronauts, disturbance in this system results in travel sickness, a serious and dangerous event on a space flight. Dr. Bondar, with fellow astronauts Ken Money and Bob Thirsk, is currently devising experiments that will help to determine the specific causes of motion sickness in space.

Since the development and subsequent success of the Canadarm, more attention is being paid to the contributions that Canadians can make to space exploration. Roberta Bondar, chairperson of the Life Sciences Subcommittee for Space Station, will undoubtedly be one Canadian who will make noteworthy advances in space exploration.

6–6 Factoring $x^2 + bx + c$

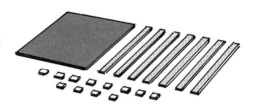

Phil is covering rectangular regions of a wall with decorative tiles. Each rectangle consists of one large square tile with an area of x^2; seven oblong tiles, each with an area of x; and twelve small square tiles, each with an area of 1. Therefore, the total area of each rectangular section is $x^2 + 7x + 12$. How can Phil arrange the tiles to fit into a rectangular section?

By trial and error, Phil can develop a diagram like the one at the right. The diagram shows that the dimensions for each rectangular section are $(x + 3)(x + 4)$.

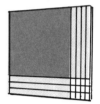

$x^2 + 7x + 12$ is called a **quadratic trinomial** since its term of greatest degree is 2. Phil actually factored this quadratic trinomial as he developed the diagram.

$$x^2 + 7x + 12 = (x + 3)(x + 4) \qquad \text{factored form}$$

Notice what happens when $(x + 3)$ and $(x + 4)$ are multiplied.

$$(x + 3)(x + 4) = x^2 + 7x + 12$$

The coefficient of the middle term is the *sum* of 3 and 4.

The last term is the *product* of 3 and 4.

Notice the pattern of coefficients formed when the binomials $(x + m)$ and $(x + n)$ are multiplied.

$$(x + m)(x + n) = x^2 + (m + n)x + mn$$
$$= x^2 + bx + c \qquad b = m + n;\ c = mn$$

As a first step in factoring a trinomial, examine the last term. If it is *positive*, then its factors have the *same sign*.

EXAMPLE 1: Factor $a^2 + 6a + 5$.

$a^2 + 6a + 5 = (a + \blacksquare)(a + \blacksquare)$

Find a pair of factors with a product of 5 and a sum of 6: 1 and 5.
$\therefore a^2 + 6a + 5 = (a + 1)(a + 5)$

Factors of 5	Sum
1 and 5	6
−1 and −5	−6

Check: $(a + 1)(a + 5) = a^2 + a + 5a + 5$
$$= a^2 + 6a + 5 \checkmark$$

EXAMPLE 2: Factor $p^2 - 6p + 8$.

$p^2 - 6p + 8 = (p + \blacksquare)(p + \blacksquare)$

Find a pair of factors with a product of 8
and a sum of -6: -2 and -4.

$\therefore p^2 - 6p + 8 = (p - 2)(p - 4)$

Check: $(p - 2)(p - 4) = p^2 - 2p - 4p + 8$
$= p^2 - 6p + 8 \checkmark$

Factors of 8	Sum
1 and 8	9
-1 and -8	-9
2 and 4	6
-2 and -4	-6

If the last term is *negative*, then its factors have *different signs*.

EXAMPLE 3: Factor $a^2 - 4ab - 21b^2$

$a^2 - 4ab - 21b^2 = (a + \blacksquare b)(a - \blacksquare b)$

Find a pair of factors with a product of -21
and a sum of -4: $+3$ and -7.

$\therefore a^2 - 4ab - 21b^2 = (a + 3b)(a - 7b)$

Factors of -21	Sum
-1 and 21	20
1 and -21	-20
-3 and 7	4
3 and -7	-4

Check: $(a + 3b)(a - 7b) = a^2 + 3ab - 7ab - 21b^2$
$= a^2 - 4ab - 21b^2 \checkmark$

To factor a trinomial fully, look for a common factor first.

EXAMPLE 4: Factor $3x^2 + 18x + 24$.

a. There is a common
factor of 3.
b. Notice that $x^2 + 6x + 8$ is a
quadratic trinomial. Find its
binomial factors.

$3x^2 + 18x + 24 = 3(x^2 + 6x + 8)$
$= 3(x + 2)(x + 4)$

EXAMPLE 5: Factor $-5a^3b^2 + 35a^2b^3 + 90ab^4$.

a. The GCF of each term is $5ab^2$.
Use the factor $-5ab^2$ to give a positive first
term in the trinomial.
b. Notice that $a^2 - 7ab - 18b^2$
is a quadratic trinomial.
Find its binomial factors.

$-5a^3b^2 + 35a^2b^3 + 90ab^4$
$= -5ab^2(a^2 - 7ab - 18b^2)$
$= -5ab^2(a - 9b)(a + 2b)$

Some trinomials cannot be factored. For example:

$x^2 - x + 10$

EXERCISES

A **1.** Find two integers with the given sum and product.

	a.	b.	c.	d.	e.	f.	g.	h.	i.	j.
Sum	5	10	−1	−7	5	6	−5	15	−12	−1
Product	6	9	−12	10	−24	5	−14	54	32	−20

2. Draw diagrams to show how each set of tiles can be arranged to form a rectangle.

a.
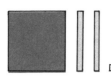

b.
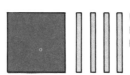

c.
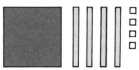

B **3.** Factor each trinomial.
a. $k^2 + 5k + 6$
b. $d^2 + 8d + 12$
c. $t^2 + 7t + 10$
d. $u^2 + 12u + 36$
e. $p^2 + 9p + 20$
f. $a^2 + 10a + 16$
g. $a^2 + 12ab + 20b^2$
h. $r^2 + 15rt + 36t^2$
i. $x^2 + 17xy + 30y^2$

4. Factor.
a. $m^2 - 3m + 2$
b. $n^2 - 8n + 15$
c. $t^2 - 10t + 25$
d. $x^2 - 7x + 12$
e. $y^2 - 10y + 16$
f. $b^2 - 9b + 20$
g. $a^2 - 13ab + 12b^2$
h. $x^2 - 11xy + 30y^2$
i. $t^2 - 8tv + 15v^2$

5. Factor and check by multiplying.
a. $a^2 - 3a - 10$
b. $m^2 - 9m - 36$
c. $y^2 + 3y - 18$
d. $x^2 + 5xy - 14y^2$
e. $a^2 - ab - 6b^2$
f. $a^2 + 3ab - 28b^2$
g. $p^2 - 4pq - 32q^2$
h. $r^2 + 5r - 14$
i. $m^2 - 10km - 39k^2$
j. $x^2 - 48x - 49$
k. $a^2 + a - 42$
l. $s^2 - 7st - 18t^2$

6. Factor if possible.
a. $x^2 - 3x + 8$
b. $a^2 - 2a - 10$
c. $r^2 + 3r - 40$
d. $y^2 + 7y - 30$
e. $x^2 - x + 1$
f. $a^2 - 3ab + b^2$
g. $x^2 + 3xy - 7y^2$
h. $s^2 + 2st - 24t^2$
i. $m^2 + 3mn - 15n^2$

7. Factor and check.
a. $x^2 + 5xy + 4y^2$
b. $a^2 - 17a + 60$
c. $n^2 + 12n - 45$
d. $10 - 7x + x^2$
e. $2m - 48 + m^2$
f. $4 + x^2 - 5x$
g. $3ab - 10b^2 + a^2$
h. $x^2 - 2xy + y^2$
i. $8 - 6s + s^2$
j. $-r^2 + 3r + 108$
k. $a^2 + 36 - 13a$
l. $-p^2 + 10q^2 - 3pq$
m. $24 - t^2 + 5t$
n. $45 - n^2 - 4n$
o. $k^2 + 35 + 12k$

8. Factor and check. Look for a greatest common monomial factor first.
a. $3x^2 + 24x + 21$
b. $4a^2 - 36a - 40$
c. $7x^2 + 35y^2 + 42xy$
d. $-84 - 16x + 4x^2$
e. $20ab + 4a^2 - 144b^2$
f. $5f^2 + 420g^2 - 95fg$
g. $60q^2 + 2pq - 2p^2$
h. $128 - 2x^2 - 24x$
i. $-8r - 2r^2 + 154$

182

9. Factor.
   a. $x^3 + 5x^2 + 6x$
   b. $x^4 + 13x^3 + 40x^2$
   c. $ax^2 + 6ax - 27a$
   d. $10ax^2 + 60ax - 160a$
   e. $7p^2q + 14pq^2 + 7q^3$
   f. $2xy^2 + x^2y^2 - 120y^2$
   g. $42ax^2 + 56ax + 7ax^3$
   h. $-90b^2c - 120b^2 - 15b^2c^2$
   i. $51m^2n^2 - 180mn^3 + 3m^3n$
   j. $-5s - 5st^2 + 10st$

C 10. What positive integer values of k will allow the given trinomial to be factored into a pair of binomials? (Answers are not unique.)
   a. $x^2 + kx + 6$
   b. $x^2 + kx + 10$
   c. $x^2 - kx + 31$
   d. $x^2 - kx + 21$
   e. $x^2 + 4x + k$
   f. $x^2 + kx + 35$

11. Factor.
   a. $(3x)^2 + 5(3x) + 6$
   b. $(8a)^2 - 2(8a) - 24$
   c. $(x^2)^2 + 3(x^2) + 2$
   d. $a^4 + 10a^2 + 9$
   e. $r^4 + 13r^2 - 30$
   f. $7t^4 + 21t^2 + 14$
   g. $(x + 1)^2 - 3(x + 1) + 2$
   h. $(2x)^2 + 3(2x)y - 28y^2$

12. Arrange each given set of tiles into a rectangle with the given area.

   a. $2x^2 + 7x + 3$
   b. $2x^2 + 7x + 6$

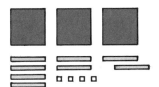 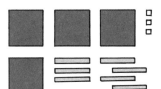

   c. $3x^2 + 8x + 4$
   d. $4x^2 + 7x + 3$

EXTRA

Prime Generators

In the past, mathematicians have tried to find a formula to generate prime numbers. It would seem logical to expect that an irreducible polynomial might yield prime numbers, but this isn't the case.

Two irreducible polynomials that do generate *many* prime numbers are:

$$x^2 - x + 41;$$
$$n^2 - 79n + 1601.$$

1. Substitute integer values for x and n to generate some prime numbers.

2. Then find the least integer for which the polynomials do *not* yield prime numbers. (Hint: For the first formula, the number is between 35 and 45. For the second, the number is between 75 and 85.)

6–7 Factoring $ax^2 + bx + c$

Notice what happens when $(3x - 10)$ and $(4x + 9)$ are multiplied.

$$(3x - 10)(4x + 9) = 12x^2 + 27x - 40x - 90$$
$$= 12x^2 - 13x - 90$$

The coefficient of the first term is the product of 3 and 4.

The middle term is the sum of $-40x$ and $27x$.

The last term is the product of -10 and 9.

Notice the pattern of the coefficients when $(rx + m)$ and $(sx + n)$ are multiplied.

$$(rx + m)(sx + n) = (rs)x^2 + (ms + rn)x + mn$$
$$= ax^2 + bx + c$$
$$a = rs; \qquad b = ms + rn; \qquad c = mn$$

With a trinomial of the form $ax^2 + bx + c$, where $a \neq 1$, there are many possibilities for the factors. Thus, to factor such a trinomial, it is helpful to look for clues in the *signs of the terms* and to make a *list of possible factors*.

EXAMPLE 1: Factor $2t^2 - t - 6$.

a. The first term, $2t^2$, indicates that $(2t + \blacksquare)$ and $(t + \blacksquare)$ are the only possible binomial factors.

b. List pairs of factors of the last term, -6: -1 and 6; 1 and -6; -2 and 3; 2 and -3.

c. Test the possible binomial factors until you find the pair that results in the correct middle term, $-t$.

Possible Factors	Middle Term
$(2t - 1)(t + 6)$	$11t$
$(2t + 1)(t - 6)$	$-11t$
$(2t + 6)(t - 1)$	$4t$
$(2t - 6)(t + 1)$	$-4t$
$(2t - 2)(t + 3)$	$4t$
$(2t + 3)(t - 2)$	$-t$

$\therefore 2t^2 - t - 6 = (2t + 3)(t - 2)$

Check by multiplying: $(2t + 3)(t - 2) = 2t^2 + 3t - 4t - 6$
$$= 2t^2 - t - 6$$

As you practise factoring, you will become more able to select the correct factors without writing all the possibilities.

EXAMPLE 2: Factor $10x^2 + 11x - 6$.

a. The first term, $10x^2$, indicates possible binomial factor pairs of $(10x + \blacksquare)(x + \blacksquare)$ and $(5x + \blacksquare)(2x + \blacksquare)$.

b. List pairs of factors of the last term, -6: -1 and 6; 1 and -6; -2 and 3; -2 and 3.

c. Test the possible binomial factors until you find the pair that results in the correct middle term, $11x$. Some of the possibilities are listed below.

Possible Factors	Middle Term
$(10x - 1)(x + 6)$	$59x$
$(10x + 6)(x - 1)$	$-54x$
$(10x - 6)(x + 1)$	$54x$
$(10x + 1)(x - 6)$	$-59x$
$(10x - 2)(x + 3)$	$28x$
$(10x + 3)(x - 2)$	$-17x$
$(10x + 2)(x - 3)$	$-28x$
$(10x - 3)(x + 2)$	$17x$

Possible Factors	Middle Term
$(5x - 1)(2x + 6)$	$28x$
$(5x + 6)(2x - 1)$	$7x$
$(5x + 1)(2x - 6)$	$-28x$
$(5x - 6)(2x + 1)$	$-7x$
$(5x - 2)(2x + 3)$	$11x$

$\therefore 10x^2 + 11x - 6 = (5x - 2)(2x + 3)$

Look for common monomial factors first to simplify the factoring process in questions like the one below.

EXAMPLE 3: Factor $10x^3y^2 - 65x^2y^3 + 105xy^4$.

a. There is a common factor of $5xy^2$.

$10x^3y^2 - 65x^2y^3 + 105xy^4 = 5xy^2(2x^2 - 13xy + 21y^2)$

b. Notice that $2x^2 - 13xy + 21y^2$ is a quadratic trinomial. Find its binomial factors.

The last term is positive, so its factors have the same sign. Since the middle term is negative, consider two negative factors of 21.

Possible Factors	Middle Term
$(2x - y)(x - 21y)$	$-43xy$
$(2x - 21y)(x - y)$	$-23xy$
$(2x - 3y)(x - 7y)$	$-17xy$
$(2x - 7y)(x - 3y)$	$-13xy$

$2x^2 - 13xy + 21y^2 = (2x - \blacksquare y)(x - \blacksquare y)$

$\therefore 10x^3y^2 - 65x^2y^3 + 105xy^4 = 5xy^2(2x - 7y)(x - 3y)$

Check by multiplying:

$$5xy^2(2x - 7y)(x - 3y) = 5xy^2(2x^2 - 7xy - 6xy + 21y^2)$$
$$= 5xy^2(2x^2 - 13xy + 21y^2)$$
$$= 10x^3y^2 - 65x^2y^3 + 105xy^4 \checkmark$$

EXERCISES

A 1. Multiply each pair of binomials.

  a. $(3x + 5)(2x + 3)$ **b.** $(2x + 7)(x + 9)$ **c.** $(5x - 4)(x + 3)$
  d. $(3x + 4)(2x - 7)$ **e.** $(7x - 6)(x - 4)$ **f.** $(4x + 5)(2x - 3)$
  g. $(6x - 1)(x + 8)$ **h.** $(3x - 4)(5x - 2)$ **i.** $(7x + 4)(3x - 5)$

2. By inspection, give the middle term of each of the following binomial products.

  a. $(x + 5)(3x + 2)$ **b.** $(2x + 9)(x + 7)$ **c.** $(3x - 5)(2x + 1)$
  d. $(4x - 3)(2x + 2)$ **e.** $(x - 8)(5x - 2)$ **f.** $(3x + 2)(5x - 3)$
  g. $(7x + 1)(4x - 2)$ **h.** $(8x + 2)(3x - 2)$ **i.** $(2x + 7)(3x - 10)$

3. For each quadratic trinomial, examine the three terms to indicate each of the following:

   i. all possible factors of the first term;
   ii. all possible factors of the last term;
   iii. the signs of the two factors of the last term.

  a. $2x^2 + 13x + 20$ **b.** $4x^2 - 8x + 3$ **c.** $3x^2 - 20x + 25$
  d. $4x^2 - 14x + 6$ **e.** $8x^2 - 12x - 36$ **f.** $3x^2 - 10x - 25$
  g. $6x^2 - 9x - 42$ **h.** $9x^2 + 3x - 6$ **i.** $15x^2 + 26x + 8$

4. What are all possible factors of the first term and the last term in each trinomial?

  a. $2x^2 + 11x + 15$ **b.** $3x^2 + 11x + 6$ **c.** $7x^2 + 12x + 5$
  d. $7x^2 - 2x - 5$ **e.** $4x^2 + 4x - 35$ **f.** $8x^2 - 61x + 35$
  g. $6x^2 - 13x - 5$ **h.** $9x^2 + 15x - 14$ **i.** $6x^2 - 7x - 20$

B 5. Factor each trinomial in exercise 3.

6. What are the values for the missing numbers?

  a. $6x^2 + 10x + 4 = (3x + 2)(\blacksquare x + \blacksquare)$
  b. $(3x + \blacksquare)(\blacksquare x + \blacksquare) = 12x^2 + 8x - 32$
  c. $10x^2 - 5x - 15 = (2x + \blacksquare)(\blacksquare x + 5)$
  d. $8x^2 + 38x + 42 = (2x + \blacksquare)(\blacksquare x + \blacksquare)$
  e. $(x + \blacksquare)(\blacksquare x + \blacksquare) = 12x^2 + 33x - 9$
  f. $(\blacksquare x + 7)(\blacksquare x + \blacksquare) = 6x^2 + 5x - 56$

7. Factor if possible.

  a. $3x^2 + 7x + 2$ **b.** $7x^2 + 10x + 3$ **c.** $2x^2 + 13xy + 15y^2$
  d. $11x^2 + 14xy + 3y^2$ **e.** $8k^2 - 5k + 1$ **f.** $7x^2 - 19x - 6$
  g. $15x^2 + 13xy + 2y^2$ **h.** $6x^2 - 7x - 3$ **i.** $3x^2 - 2xy - 8y^2$
  j. $3x^2 - 7x + 6$ **k.** $10 + 3y - y^2$ **l.** $5x^2 - 18x - 8$
  m. $y^2 - 5y - 30$ **n.** $12x^2 + 19xy - 18y^2$ **o.** $48m^2 - 13mn + n^2$
  p. $6x^2 + 17xy + 12y^2$ **q.** $10a^2 - 11ab - 6b^2$ **r.** $9x^2 - 9xy - 28y^2$
  s. $3x - 20 + 2x^2$ **t.** $20x + 4x^2 + 25$ **u.** $3xy + 15x^2 - 12y^2$
  v. $4x - 21 + 3x^2$ **w.** $6x^2 - 6x - 20$ **x.** $7mn - 3m^2 + 4n^2$

8. Factor if possible.

a. $18x^2 + 33x - 63$ b. $16x^2 - 36x + 18$ c. $6x^2 + 45x + 75$

d. $12x^2 + 12x - 45$ e. $16ax^2 + 8ax - 3a$ f. $5ax^2 - 16ax - 16a$

g. $10abc^2 + 17abc + 3ab$ h. $4x^2 - 2x - 42$ i. $9m^2n^2 - 6mn^2 - 3n^2$

j. $30x^2 + 95x + 40$ k. $18a^2 - 24ab - 42b^2$ l. $12x^2y - 2xy^2 - 24y^3$

m. $20 + 6x - 8x^2$ n. $16ab^2 - 12ab - 70a$ o. $90x^2yz + 180xyz + 80yz$

C 9. Factor and check by multiplying.

a. $-60x^2y^2 + 35xy^2 + 60y^2$ b. $-48ab^3c + 64ab^2c + 64abc$

c. $-105x^2 - 115x - 30$ d. $-32m^3n^2 - 72m^2n^2 - 16mn^2$

e. $12a(5y)^2 + 6a(5y) - 36a$ f. $24m^3y - 18m^3y^2 + 64m^3$

g. $21(2x)^2 + 70(2x) + 49$ h. $80a^3b + 18a^3bc - 18a^3bc^2$

i. $15(x - 2)^4 + 30(x - 2)^2 + 15$ j. $16a(b + 5)^2 - 16a + 24a(b + 5)$

k. $2(k - 1)^2 + (k - 1) - 21$ l. $6(d - 2)^4 + (d - 2)^2 - 2$

10. Arrange the given set of tiles into a rectangle with area $2x^2 + 22x + 30$.

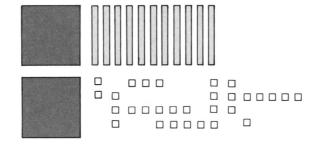

EXTRA

Another Factoring Method

To factor a trinomial like $2t^2 - t - 6$, consider the product of $2 \times (-6)$, or -12. Look for two factors whose product is -12 and sum is -1.

$$2t^2 - t - 6 \quad\quad\text{sum of } -1 \quad\quad\text{product of } -12$$

$(-4) \times 3 = -12$ and $(-4) + 3 = -1$

Rewrite the trinomial, using $-4t$ and $3t$ to replace $-t$. Factor as shown.

$2t^2 - t - 6 = 2t^2 - 4t + 3t - 6$ ← Note that 2 pairs of terms can be made.

$\qquad\qquad = 2t(t - 2) + 3(t - 2)$ ← By finding the GCF of each pair, a common *binomial factor* is revealed.

$\qquad\qquad = (2t + 3)(t - 2)$

Use this method to factor the following.

1. $6x^2 + 19x + 10$ 2. $3a^2 + 2a - 5$ 3. $9r^2 - 25rs - 6s^2$

6–8 Factoring Differences of Squares and Trinomial Squares

Notice what happens when you multiply the following binomials.

$(x + 4)(x - 4) = x^2 + 4x - 4x - 16 \qquad (3a + 5)(3a - 5) = (3a)^2 + 15a - 15a - 25$
$\qquad\qquad\qquad = x^2 - 16 \qquad\qquad\qquad\qquad\qquad = 9a^2 - 25$

In each case, the result is a squared term minus a squared term, or a **difference of squares.**

> In general: $(a + b)(a - b) = a^2 - b^2$

This result is useful when factoring the difference of two squares.

EXAMPLE 1:   **a.**   Factor $16x^2 - 25$.

$$16x^2 - 25 = (4x)^2 - (5)^2$$
$$= (4x + 5)(4x - 5)$$

        b.   Factor $x^4 - 81$.

$$x^4 - 81 = (x^2)^2 - (9)^2$$
$$= (x^2 + 9)(x^2 - 9) \qquad \leftarrow \text{Another difference of squares}$$
$$= (x^2 + 9)(x + 3)(x - 3) \quad \text{A } sum \text{ of squares cannot be factored.}$$

Now notice what happens when you square a binomial. The result is called a **trinomial square.**

$(x + 3)^2 = (x + 3)(x + 3) \qquad\qquad (x - 3)^2 = (x - 3)(x - 3)$
$\qquad\quad = x^2 + 2(3)(x) + 3^2 \qquad\qquad\qquad = x^2 - 2(3)(x) + 9$
$\qquad\quad = x^2 + 6x + 9 \qquad\qquad\qquad\qquad = x^2 - 6x + 9$

In each case, the first and last terms are *perfect squares*; the middle term is twice the product of the square roots of the first and last terms. $(\sqrt{9} = 3; \sqrt{x^2} = x)$.

> In general: $(a + b)^2 = (a + b)(a + b) \qquad (a - b)^2 = (a - b)(a - b)$
> $\qquad\qquad\qquad = a^2 + 2ab + b^2 \qquad\qquad\qquad = a^2 - 2ab + b^2$

This property can be used when factoring a trinomial square.

Look for the greatest monomial factor first.

EXAMPLE 2:   Factor $9x^2 + 12x + 4$.   **EXAMPLE 3:**   Factor $28am^2 - 84amn + 63an^2$.

$9x^2 + 12x + 4 \qquad\qquad\qquad\qquad\qquad 28am^2 - 84amn + 63an^2$
$= (3x)^2 + 12x + 2^2 \qquad\qquad\qquad\qquad = 7a(4m^2 - 12mn + 9n^2)$
$= (3x + 2)^2 \qquad\qquad\qquad\qquad\qquad\quad = 7a(2m - 3n)^2$

EXERCISES

A **1.** Which of the following are perfect squares? Give their square roots. Assume all variables are whole numbers.

    a. $36r^2$ **b.** $28x^2$ **c.** $25x^5$ **d.** m^2n^2 **e.** $49a^4b^6$

    f. $\frac{1}{9}s^2$ **g.** $32a^6$ **h.** $121a^8b^6$ **i.** $\frac{4}{25}t^2$ **j.** $0.01m^5$

2. Use the property for a difference of squares to find each product.

    a. $(x + 9)(x - 9)$ **b.** $(b + 6)(b - 6)$ **c.** $(r - 11)(r + 11)$

    d. $(7 - t)(7 + t)$ **e.** $(x + 3y)(x - 3y)$ **f.** $(x^2 + 2y)(x^2 - 2y)$

    g. $(m + 3)(m - 3)$ **h.** $(5k - 4)(4 + 5k)$ **i.** $(3a - 2b)(3a + 2b)$

3. Use the property for squaring binomials to find each product.

    a. $(x + 3)(x + 3)$ **b.** $(2x + 5)(2x + 5)$ **c.** $(2x - 5)(2x - 5)$

    d. $(4x + 7)^2$ **e.** $(5a - 3)(5a - 3)$ **f.** $(7a - 5)^2$

    g. $(5m^2 + 3)^2$ **h.** $(-2 + 3a)^2$ **i.** $(4mn - 5y^2)^2$

B **4.** Factor each difference of squares.

    a. $25a^2 - 49$ **b.** $36r^2 - 121$ **c.** $81m^2 - 4n^2$

    d. $9s^2 - 49t^2$ **e.** $169 - 121x^2$ **f.** $25r^2s^2 - 36t^2$

    g. $a^4 - 81d^4$ **h.** $4t^2 - 64v^2$ **i.** $2401j^4 - 625$

5. Factor each trinomial square.

    a. $x^2 + 6x + 9$ **b.** $25m^2 - 40m + 16$ **c.** $4r^2 - 20r + 25$

    d. $a^2 + 8ab + 16b^2$ **e.** $y^2 - 12y + 36$ **f.** $49r^2 - 42rt + 9t^2$

    g. $4x^2 - 20xy + 25y^2$ **h.** $9t^2 + 42tv + 49v^2$ **i.** $4a^2 - 44ab + 121b^2$

6. Factor.

    a. $121x^4 - 9y^4$ **b.** $b^6 + 22b^3 + 121$ **c.** $64a^2c^2 + 16abc + b^2$

    d. $m^2n^2 - 225$ **e.** $100y^4 - 9z^4$ **f.** $4x^6 + 60x^3 + 225$

    g. $9 - 6z^3 + z^6$ **h.** $x^6 - 10x^3 + 25$ **i.** $x^4y^4 - 625v^4$

7. Factor each polynomial.

    a. $4x^2 + 28x + 49$ **b.** $4x^2 - 2x - 30$ **c.** $16r^2 - 25s^2$

    d. $4x^2 - 13x + 3$ **e.** $9m^2 - 30m + 25$ **f.** $16a^2 + 24ab + 9b^2$

    g. $81x^6 - 1$ **h.** $25x^2 - 36$ **i.** $25x^2 + 36$

    j. $9x^2 - 12x + 4$ **k.** $5p^2 - 36pq + 36q^2$ **l.** $4z^4 + 36yz^2 + 81y^2$

C **8.** Factor.

    a. $4a^2 - (3a + 1)^2$ **b.** $7(2x^5)^2 + 40(2x^5) + 25$ **c.** $(a + b)^2 - 4(b + c)^2$

    d. $(x^2 - y^2)^2 - 2(x^2 - y^2) + 1$ **e.** $x^4 - 13x^2 + 36$ **f.** $x^8 - 1$

    g. $(2x - 5)^2 - 49x^2$ **h.** $(3x - 1)^2 - 16$ **i.** $25 - (2x + 3)^2$

EXTRA
                                         A Mathematical Application

Find the answer to the following computation. The numbers are too big for a calculator or for most microcomputers.

$$(987\ 654\ 322)^2 - (12\ 345\ 678)^2$$

6–9 Factoring to Solve Equations

An interior designer is using an oriental carpet in a 5 m by 7 m room so that an exposed strip of hardwood flooring is left around the carpet. The area of the carpet is 15 m². How wide is the exposed strip of hardwood?

Define a variable.
Let x be the width of the exposed strip in metres. Then the carpet dimensions in metres are $(7 - 2x)$ and $(5 - 2x)$.

Write an equation.
$(7 - 2x)(5 - 2x) = 15$ The area of the carpet
$35 - 24x + 4x^2 = 15$

Solve the **quadratic equation** $4x^2 - 24x + 35 = 15$.

a. Rewrite the equation so that R.S. = 0. $4x^2 - 24x + 20 = 0$
b. Factor the left side. $4(x - 1)(x - 5) = 0$
c. Since the product is equal to 0, at least one factor must be 0.

> *Zero-Product Property:* For all real numbers a and b:
> $ab = 0$ only if $a = 0$ or $b = 0$.

Solve for x by setting each factor $(x - 1) = 0$ or $(x - 5) = 0$
equal to 0. $x = 1$ $x = 5$

Solutions or **roots**: $x = 1$ and $x = 5$.

Check: If $x = 5$, then the carpet dimensions are $[7 - 2(5)]$ m by $[5 - 2(5)]$ m or (-3) m by (-5) m. Negative lengths and widths are inadmissible.
The solution $x = 1$ satisfies the conditions of the problem, making the exposed strip of hardwood 1 m wide and the carpet dimensions 5 m by 3 m.

Quadratic equations can be solved by factoring and then applying the zero-product property.

EXAMPLE: Solve the quadratic equation $2x^2 - 7x = 15$.

     a. Rewrite the equation so that R.S. = 0. $2x^2 - 7x - 15 = 0$
     b. Factor the left side. $(2x + 3)(x - 5) = 0$
     c. Set each factor equal to zero $(2x + 3) = 0$ or $(x - 5) = 0$
        and solve for x. $2x = -3$ $x = 5$

$$x = -\frac{3}{2}$$

The roots are $-1\frac{1}{2}$ and 5. You can check by substituting into the original equation.

EXERCISES

A 1. Give the root(s) of each equation by setting each factor equal to 0.
    a. $x(x - 1) = 0$
    b. $(x - 7)(x + 3) = 0$
    c. $(x + 7)(x + 9) = 0$
    d. $3(x - 4)(x + 4) = 0$
    e. $5x(x + 1) = 0$
    f. $(x - 3)(x + 9) = 0$
    g. $7(r + 5)(r - 8) = 0$
    h. $5(x - 8)(x - 8) = 0$
    i. $(x - 2)^2 = 0$

2. Find the root(s) of each equation.
    a. $(2x - 3)(x - 1) = 0$
    b. $(4x - 1)(x + 5) = 0$
    c. $(10x + 3)(2x + 5) = 0$
    d. $(x - 14)(x + 14) = 0$
    e. $\left(x - \frac{1}{2}\right)\left(x + \frac{3}{4}\right) = 0$
    f. $(2x - 1)(4x + 3) = 0$
    g. $(5x + 3)(5x + 3) = 0$
    h. $4(9x + 1)(2x - 7) = 0$

B 3. Factor and give the root(s) of each equation.
    a. $x^2 - 7x + 12 = 0$
    b. $b^2 - 9 = 0$
    c. $r^2 - 5r = 0$
    d. $t - 7t^2 = 0$
    e. $x^2 - 10x + 16 = 0$
    f. $9x^2 - 81 = 0$
    g. $x^2 - 3x - 18 = 0$
    h. $32a^2 - 50 = 0$
    i. $x^2 - 10x + 25 = 0$
    j. $4a^2 - 36a = 0$
    k. $5m^2 + 40m - 45 = 0$
    l. $r^2 - 7r - 8 = 0$

4. Factor and find the root(s).
    a. $6x^2 + x - 15 = 0$
    b. $4x^2 + 22x + 30 = 0$
    c. $4x^2 - 49 = 0$
    d. $15x^2 - 12x - 3 = 0$
    e. $25r^2 - 144 = 0$
    f. $3x^2 - 75 = 0$
    g. $49a^2 - 140a + 100 = 0$
    h. $16x^2 - 4x - 6 = 0$
    i. $8x^2 + 32x - 40 = 0$
    j. $16x^2 + 48x + 36 = 0$
    k. $18b^2 - 128 = 0$
    l. $30x^2 - 150x + 120 = 0$

5. Find the root(s) of each equation.
    a. $4x^2 = 64$
    b. $16y^2 = 25$
    c. $6x^2 = x + 1$
    d. $4x^2 = 8x + 5$
    e. $4t^2 = 8t$
    f. $3r^2 + 2r = 1$
    g. $f^2 = 24 - 5f$
    h. $6m^2 + 11m = 72$
    i. $2n^2 = 72$
    j. $3b^2 - 6b = 9$
    k. $32d^2 = 50$
    l. $4c^2 + 7 = 29c$
    m. $x^2 - 2x + 10 = 3x + 4$
    n. $x^2 - 9 = 8x$
    o. $2x^2 + 3x - 10 = x^2 - 2x + 4$
    p. $2x^2 + 7x - 9 = x^2 - 1$
    q. $6x^2 + 12x + 9 = 2x^2 + 24x$
    r. $(x + 2)(x + 1) = 20$
    s. $(x - 5)(2x + 1) = 40$
    t. $4x^2 + 4x + 49 = 5x^2 + 4x$
    u. $(x + 4)(x + 2) = x(4x + 1)$
    v. $(2x + 3)(x - 1) = (x - 1)^2$
    w. $(3x + 1)(2x - 5) = 2x^2 + 2x - 1$
    x. $(x + 4)(x - 2) = 10 - x$
    y. $(x + 3)^2 = (2x + 6)(x - 1)$
    z. $(2x + 1)(x + 4) = (x + 2)(x + 8)$

6. A number, x, added to its square, x^2, is equal to 20. What is the number?

7. The diagonal of a rectangle is 13 cm. The longer side is 2 cm longer than double the width. What are the dimensions of the rectangle? (Apply the Pythagorean Theorem.)

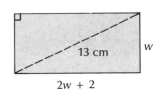
13 cm
w
$2w + 2$

8. A square is increased by 3 cm on one side and 5 cm on the other. The rectangle formed has an area of 120 cm². What were the dimensions of the original square?

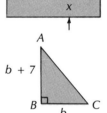

C 9. A rectangle is 5 cm longer than double its width. Its area is 75 cm². What are the dimensions of the rectangle?

10. A picture frame of uniform width surrounds a picture 25 cm by 40 cm. The total area of the picture and the frame is 1350 cm². What is the width of the frame?

11. *AB* is 7 cm longer than *BC*. The hypotenuse is 3 cm longer than double the length of *BC*. What are the dimensions of the triangle?

12. A building is bordered by a sidewalk on one side and a driveway on the other, as shown at the right. The driveway is 5 m wider than the sidewalk. The property is 15 m by 40 m; the area not covered by the sidewalk and the driveway is 429 m². Find the widths of the walk and the driveway.

EXTRA

Notice the following patterns as four consecutive integers are multiplied.

$1 \times 2 \times 3 \times 4 = 5^2 - 1$ $5 = 1(1 + 3) + 1 = 1 \times 4 + 1$
$2 \times 3 \times 4 \times 5 = 11^2 - 1$ $11 = 2(2 + 3) + 1 = 2 \times 5 + 1$
$3 \times 4 \times 5 \times 6 = 19^2 - 1$ $19 = 3(3 + 3) + 1 = 3 \times 6 + 1$
$4 \times 5 \times 6 \times 7 = 29^2 - 1$ $29 = 4(4 + 3) + 1 = 4 \times 7 + 1$

Each product can be expressed as one less than a perfect square.

1. Express each product as one less than a perfect square.
   a. $5 \times 6 \times 7 \times 8$ b. $6 \times 7 \times 8 \times 9$ c. $7 \times 8 \times 9 \times 10$ d. $8 \times 9 \times 10 \times 11$

2. Is the product of four consecutive integers *always* one less than a perfect square? The following equation represents the situation. Check that L.S. = R.S. to answer the question.

$$x(x + 1)(x + 2)(x + 3) = [x(x + 3) + 1]^2 - 1$$

Review

1. Simplify by combining like terms.
   a. $5x^2 + 6x + 3 - (2x^2 + 3x + 1)$
   b. $(k^2 + 2k - 3) - (5k^2 - 3k - 5)$
   c. $(t^2 - 1 - 3t) - (2 - t - 2t^2) - (2 + 6t + t^2)$
   d. $(3x^2 - 2xy + 9y^2) - (4x^2 + 3xy - 5y^2) - (8x^2 + 7xy + y^2)$
   e. $(xy - 2x^2 + 6y^2) - (4x^2 + 3y^2 - xy) - (2xy - 9x^2 - 9y^2)$
   f. $(3ab^3 - 2a^2b + 2b^2) + (3a^3 - 2a^2b + 3b^2)$

2. Find each product.
   a. $5(3x - 2)$
   b. $3x(2x - 3y)$
   c. $2y(3y - 4)$
   d. $2k(k + 2)$
   e. $5ab(2a^2 + 3b)$
   f. $7t(2 - 3t + 4r)$

3. Find each missing dimension. Assume no variable equals zero.
   a.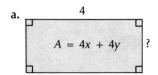
   b.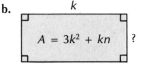
   c.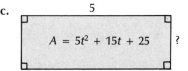

4. Find each product.
   a. $(2x + 7)(x - 4)$
   b. $(x - 3y)(2x + 3y)$
   c. $3(5a + 2b)(a - 4b)$
   d. $3x(x - 2)(x - 5)$
   e. $(x^2 - 2)(x^2 + 2)$
   f. $(x + 3)(x + 2)(x + 1)$
   g. $(2x - 3)^2$
   h. $(2xy + 5)^2$
   i. $3(5y - 3x)^2$

5. Factor each polynomial.
   a. $x^2 + 14x + 40$
   b. $x^2 - 11xy + 30y^2$
   c. $r^2 + 5r - 14$
   d. $k^2 - 4kn - 12n^2$
   e. $v^2 - 25w^2$
   f. $v^4 - w^4$
   g. $2a^2 + 13a + 20$
   h. $4b^2 - 14b + 6$
   i. $15k^2 + 26k + 8$
   j. $64r^2 - 9s^2$
   k. $144a^2b^2 - 81c^2$
   l. $2n^3 + 24n^2 - 90n$
   m. $64a^2 - 16ab + b^2$
   n. $y^4 + 10y^2 + 25$
   o. $10a^2 - 28ab - 6b^2$
   p. $(x - 3)^2 - 49$
   q. $a^2b^2 - 12ab + 36$
   r. $25x^2 - (x + 3)^2$

6. Solve each quadratic equation.
   a. $7x^2 - 14x = 0$
   b. $16x^2 + 48x + 36 = 0$
   c. $9v^2 = 169$
   d. $30x^2 + 120 = 150x$
   e. $72a^2 = 18$
   f. $24x^2 + 46x = -20$
   g. $(x + 3)^2 = 3x^2 - x - 6$
   h. $2x^2 + 28 = -18x$
   i. $9x^2 - 9 = -18x - 18$

7. The height of an object thrown up into the air can be approximated by the formula $d = vt - 5t^2$, where d is height in metres, v is initial velocity in metres per second, and t is time in seconds.

   a. A ball is thrown into the air at 16 m/s. At approximately what time will the ball be 12 m above the ground? (Interpret each of the two roots.)
   b. On Mars, the formula becomes $h = vt - 4t^2$. What would be the answer to part a if the ball is thrown on Mars?

8. A number is one greater than triple another number, n. The difference of the squares of the numbers is 45. What are the numbers?

6–10 Simplifying Rational Expressions

The force due to Earth's gravity decreases as an object moves away from the surface of the earth. Force of gravity can be found by a formula.

$$F_g = \frac{(4.0 \times 10^{14})M}{r^2}$$

M is the mass of the object in kilograms.
r is the distance from the centre of the earth in metres.
F_g is the force of gravity measured in Newtons (N).

For an 85 kg astronaut on Earth's surface (6.37×10^6 m from Earth's centre), the force of gravity is calculated below.

$$F_g = \frac{(4.0 \times 10^{14})(8.5 \times 10^1)}{(6.37 \times 10^6)^2} \doteq \frac{3.4 \times 10^{16}}{4.1 \times 10^{13}}$$
$$= \frac{3.4}{4.1} \times 10^3$$
$$\doteq 0.83 \times 10^3$$
$$= 830$$

The force of gravity on the astronaut on Earth's surface is about 830 N.

For the same astronaut, 3.6×10^7 m from Earth's centre, the force of gravity is calculated below.

$$F_g = \frac{(4.0 \times 10^{14})(8.5 \times 10^1)}{(3.6 \times 10^7)^2} \doteq \frac{3.4 \times 10^{16}}{1.3 \times 10^{15}}$$
$$= \frac{3.4}{1.3} \times 10^1$$
$$\doteq 2.6 \times 10$$
$$= 26$$

The force of gravity on the astronaut when 36 000 000 m from Earth's centre is about 26 N.

The expression on the right-hand side of the formula for force of gravity is called a **rational expression**. Since division by 0 is undefined, the denominator, r, cannot be 0. This restriction is natural, since r will never be 0 in any real application.

When rational expressions are simplified, you must restrict the variables in the denominator so it does not equal 0.

EXAMPLE 1:

a. $\dfrac{3x}{x + 5}$,

$x \neq -5$

b. $\dfrac{a + 6}{2a(a - 6)}$,

$a \neq 0, 6$

To simplify a rational expression, divide the numerator and denominator by all common factors. Be on the alert for common factors with terms in a different order, such as $(b + 9a)$ and $(9a + b)$.

EXAMPLE 2: Simplify $(10x + 2x^2) \div (3x^2 + 15x)$.
State any variable restrictions.

    a. Find the binomial factors.
    b. Look for the common factors.

$$\frac{10x + 2x^2}{3x^2 + 15x} = \frac{2\cancel{x}(5 + x)}{3\cancel{x}(x + 5)}$$

$$= \frac{2}{3}, \, x \neq 0, \, -5$$

EXAMPLE 3: Simplify $(x^2 - 3x - 10) \div (2x^2 + 3x - 2)$.
State any variable restrictions.

    a. Find the binomial factors.
    b. There is a common binomial factor, $(x + 2)$.

$$\frac{x^2 - 3x - 10}{2x^2 + 3x - 2} = \frac{(x - 5)\cancel{(x + 2)}}{(2x - 1)\cancel{(x + 2)}}$$

$$= \frac{x - 5}{2x - 1}, \, x \neq \frac{1}{2}, \, -2$$

EXAMPLE 4: The area of a triangle with base b and height h is $\frac{1}{2}bh$.

The area of a trapezoid with the same base and height is $\frac{1}{2}h(a + b)$.

Find the ratio of the area of the trapezoid to the area of the triangle.

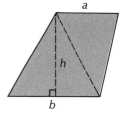

Look for common factors.

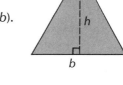

$$\frac{\frac{1}{2}h(a + b)}{\frac{1}{2}bh} = \frac{a + b}{b} \qquad (b \neq 0, \, h \neq 0)$$

The ratio of the area of the trapezoid to the area of the triangle is $(a + b):b$.

When you are simplifying, it will help you if you learn to recognize binomial factors that are negatives of each other.

    Factor   *Negative*
    $r - s$ $-(r - s)$, or $-r + s$, or $s - r$

EXAMPLE 5: Simplify $(3x^2 + 5x - 2) \div (5 - 14x - 3x^2)$.
State any variable restrictions.

    a. Find the binomial factors.
    b. Rewrite to reveal common binomial factors, since $(3x - 1)$ and $(1 - 3x)$ are negatives of each other.

$$\frac{3x^2 + 5x - 2}{5 - 14x - 3x^2} = \frac{(3x - 1)(x + 2)}{(1 - 3x)(5 + x)}$$

$$= \frac{-\cancel{(1 - 3x)}(x + 2)}{\cancel{(1 - 3x)}(5 + x)}$$

$$= -\frac{x + 2}{x + 5}, \, x \neq \frac{1}{3}, \, -5$$

EXERCISES

A 1. If the given variable expression were to appear in the denominator of a rational expression, what would the restriction(s) on the variable be?

    a. $r - 1$ **b.** $c + 1$ **c.** $d(d + 1)$ **d.** $x(2x - 9)$ **e.** $(a + b)(a - b)$

2. Divide all common factors from numerator and denominator. State the restrictions on the variable(s).

    a. $\dfrac{3x(x - 5)(x - 5)}{12y(x + 5)(x - 5)}$ **b.** $\dfrac{a(2a + 1)(2a + 1)}{9a(1 + 2a)}$ **c.** $\dfrac{4(x + 5)(x - 5)}{2x(5 + x)}$

    d. $\dfrac{3x - y}{2(y - 3x)}$ **e.** $\dfrac{(3 + s)(2 - s)}{(s + 2)(s - 2)}$ **f.** $\dfrac{(3 - b)(3 - b)}{(b + 3)(b - 3)}$

B 3. Express in simplest form and state any restrictions on the variables.

    a. $\dfrac{3m}{m^2 - m}$ **b.** $\dfrac{a^2 - ab}{a}$ **c.** $\dfrac{3xz - 6z}{3z}$

    d. $\dfrac{5k^2}{15k^2 - 5k}$ **e.** $\dfrac{2b + 4b^3}{6b}$ **f.** $\dfrac{8c^2d - 4cd}{2c}$

    g. $\dfrac{3t^3v + 6tv^2 + 12tv}{3t^2v}$ **h.** $\dfrac{3 - x}{x - 3}$ **i.** $\dfrac{a - 9}{9 - a}$

4. Simplify and state any restrictions on the variables.

    a. $\dfrac{(a - 8)(a + 3)}{(a + 3)(a - 5)}$ **b.** $\dfrac{6n + 12}{(n + 2)(n - 5)}$ **c.** $\dfrac{9a^2 - 18a}{6 - 3a}$

    d. $\dfrac{x^2 - 5x}{x^2 - 4x - 5}$ **e.** $\dfrac{t^2 + 2t - 8}{3t + 12}$ **f.** $\dfrac{x^2 + 8x + 15}{x^2 + 5x + 6}$

    g. $\dfrac{x^2 + 9x + 20}{x^2 + 7x + 12}$ **h.** $\dfrac{a^2 - 11a + 30}{a^2 - 3a - 10}$ **i.** $\dfrac{r^2 + 12r + 36}{36 - r^2}$

5. For a cone, the area of the base is πr^2 and the area of the remaining surface is πrs. What is the ratio of the lateral area to the base area?

6. The volume of the rectangular prism is $x(x + 1)(x + 5)$. The volume of the cube is $(x + 1)^3$. What is the ratio of the volume of the prism to the volume of the cube?

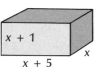

7. Simplify and state any restrictions on the variables.

    a. $\dfrac{2x^2 + 11x + 12}{2x^2 + 3x - 20}$ **b.** $\dfrac{5x^2 + 12x + 4}{x^2 + 5x + 6}$

    c. $\dfrac{6x^2 + 5x - 21}{10x^2 - 13x - 3}$ **d.** $\dfrac{6x + 8}{3x^2 + 10x + 8}$

    e. $\dfrac{3x^2 - 27}{x^2 - 2x - 15}$ **f.** $\dfrac{3m^2 + 9m - 30}{4 - m^2}$

    g. $\dfrac{4a^2 - 9a - 9}{3 + 8a - 3a^2}$ **h.** $\dfrac{a^2c - 3ac - 10c}{2a^2c^2 - 11ac^2 + 5c^2}$

    i. $\dfrac{3k^2 + k - 10}{3k(l + 2) - 5(l + 2)}$ **j.** $\dfrac{y^4 - 9}{y^2(y + 3) + 3(y + 3)}$

196

8. Simplify and state any restrictions on the variables.

a. $\dfrac{(x + 3z)(x - z)}{(x - z)(x + 2z)}$

b. $\dfrac{3r(r - s)}{(r + s)(r - s)}$

c. $\dfrac{x^2(x - 2z)^2}{3x(x - 2z)}$

d. $\dfrac{2m^2 - m - 6}{3m^2 - 6m}$

e. $\dfrac{a^2 + 2ab + b^2}{a^2 - b^2}$

f. $\dfrac{t^2 - v^2}{v^2 + tv - 2t^2}$

g. $\dfrac{m^3 - mn^2}{2m(n - m) + 4m^2(n - m)}$

h. $\dfrac{3x^2 + 14xz - 5z^2}{6x^2 + xz - z^2}$

i. $\dfrac{3t^3 + 3st^2 - 6s^2t}{6s^2 - 12st + 6t^2}$

j. $\dfrac{(a + b)^2 - 2b(a + b) + b^2}{(a + b)^2 - (a - b)^2}$

9. For each figure shown, write a rational expression to represent the unknown dimension, then simplify the expression and state any restrictions on the variables.

a.
$5y$
$A = 5x^2y + 15xy$?

b.
$a + 6$
$A = a^2 - 36$?

c.
$4t + 5$
$A = 16t^2 + 40t + 25$?

d.
$2n - 1$
$A = 6n^2 + 11n - 7$?

EXTRA

Why Astronauts Feel Weightless

A centrifuge is used to separate particles in a liquid such as raw milk or blood. As the centrifuge rotates at great speed, the heavier particles are separated from the fluid as they are forced away from the axis of rotation by a force called **centrifugal force**.

Astronauts orbiting Earth are like particles rotating around Earth at great speed, and a centrifugal force acting on them is directed away from Earth. When the centrifugal force on the astronaut equals the force of gravity (25 N), 3.6×10^4 km above the earth, then the astronaut becomes weightless.

By wearing suitable "wet gear", the buoyant force of water on a person can be made equal to the force of gravity and the person becomes weightless in a water environment. Astronauts can practise working in a weightless environment by using suitable wet suits and breathing apparatus in large tanks of water or swimming pools.

6–11 Multiplying and Dividing Rational Expressions

The following rule enables you to express a product of two rational expressions as a quotient.

> **Multiplication Rule for Fractions:** For any real numbers a, b, c, and d; $c \neq 0$ and $d \neq 0$: $\quad \dfrac{a}{c} \times \dfrac{b}{d} = \dfrac{ab}{cd}$

When multiplying rational expressions, the variable(s) in the denominator must be restricted, since dividing by zero is undefined.

EXAMPLE 1: Express each product in simplest terms. State any variable restrictions.

a. $\dfrac{8x^2}{5z} \times \dfrac{3z}{2x} = \dfrac{8x^{\cancel{2}}}{5\cancel{z}} \times \dfrac{3\cancel{z}}{2\cancel{x}}$

The denominators $5z$ and $2x$ must not equal zero.
$$= \frac{12x}{5}, \; x \neq 0, \; z \neq 0$$

b. $\dfrac{x^2 + 4x - 5}{x^2 + 3x} \times \dfrac{x^2 - 9}{1 - x} = \dfrac{(x - 1)(x + 5)}{x(x + 3)} \times \dfrac{(x - 3)(x + 3)}{-(x - 1)}$

The denominators $x^2 + 3x$ and $1 - x$ must not equal zero.
$$= \frac{\cancel{(x - 1)}(x + 5)(x - 3)\cancel{(x + 3)}}{-x\cancel{(x + 3)}\cancel{(x - 1)}}$$
$$= -\frac{(x + 5)(x - 3)}{x}, \; x \neq 0, \, 1, \, -3$$

Division of rational expressions involves multiplying by the reciprocal of the divisor.

> **Division Rule for Fractions:** For any real numbers a, b, c, and d; $b \neq 0$, $c \neq 0$, $d \neq 0$: $\quad \dfrac{a}{b} \div \dfrac{c}{d} = \dfrac{a}{b} \times \dfrac{d}{c}$

When dividing rational expressions, the variable(s) in the denominator for *each* step of the solution must be restricted.

EXAMPLE 2: Divide and simplify. State any restrictions on the variables.

$$\frac{x^2 + 4x - 5}{x^2 - 3x} \div \frac{x^2 - 1}{x^2 - 6x + 9} = \frac{x^2 + 4x - 5}{x^2 - 3x} \times \frac{x^2 - 6x + 9}{x^2 - 1}$$

$$= \frac{(x - 1)(x + 5)}{x(x - 3)} \times \frac{(x - 3)(x - 3)}{(x + 1)(x - 1)}$$

The denominators $x^2 - 3x$, $x^2 - 6x + 9$, and $x^2 - 1$ must not equal zero.

$$= \frac{\cancel{(x - 1)}(x + 5)(x - 3)\cancel{(x - 3)}}{x\cancel{(x - 3)}(x + 1)\cancel{(x - 1)}}$$

$$= \frac{(x + 5)(x - 3)}{x(x + 1)}, \; x \neq 0, \, 3, \, \pm 1$$

EXERCISES

A **1.** Express each product in simplest form. State any restrictions on the variables.

a. $\dfrac{3k}{8} \times \dfrac{2m}{9}$

b. $\dfrac{5}{y} \times \dfrac{3x}{10}$

c. $\dfrac{6}{x} \times \dfrac{5x^2}{2y}$

d. $\dfrac{5a^2b}{10a} \times \dfrac{6b}{4ab}$

e. $\dfrac{-10x^2}{9z^2} \times \dfrac{3z^2}{5x}$

f. $\dfrac{8m^2}{10n} \times \dfrac{5n^3}{6m^2}$

2. Express each quotient in simplest form. State any restrictions on the variables.

a. $\dfrac{8m}{9} \div \dfrac{2n}{3}$

b. $\dfrac{5a}{b} \div \dfrac{10}{7b}$

c. $\dfrac{3m^2}{n} \div \dfrac{2m}{n}$

d. $\dfrac{2r^2}{s} \div \dfrac{5r}{s^2}$

e. $\dfrac{9x^2z}{4} \div \dfrac{12z^2}{x}$

f. $\dfrac{-5a^3}{3b^2} \div \dfrac{10a^2b}{3b^2}$

3. Simplify. State any restrictions on the variables.

a. $\dfrac{a^2}{b} \times \dfrac{c}{a} \times \dfrac{b^2}{c^2}$

b. $\dfrac{3x}{z^2} \times \dfrac{2z}{9x^2z} \times \dfrac{z^2}{6z}$

c. $\dfrac{5mn}{2t^3} \times \dfrac{3t^2}{4m} \div \dfrac{12t^2}{10n^2}$

d. $\dfrac{12rt}{5s} \times \dfrac{10s^2t}{4r^2} \times \dfrac{6r^3}{t^3}$

e. $\dfrac{3ab}{c} \times \dfrac{c^2}{2a} \div \dfrac{b^2}{6}$

f. $\dfrac{r}{s^2t^3} \times \dfrac{3}{t} \div \dfrac{4r^5}{st}$

B **4.** Write in simplest form. State any restrictions on the variables.

a. $\dfrac{x^2}{x+5} \times \dfrac{x^2+10x+25}{3x^3}$

b. $\dfrac{x^2-1}{2x^2+3x+1} \times \dfrac{2x+1}{x+1}$

c. $\dfrac{3x-3}{x^2+5x+6} \times \dfrac{(x+3)^2}{1-x}$

d. $\dfrac{2x+6}{5y} \div \dfrac{6(x+3)}{y^2}$

e. $\dfrac{3x+9}{2x^4} \div \dfrac{x^2+5x+6}{4x^2}$

f. $\dfrac{2x^2-5x-3}{x+2} \times \dfrac{x^2-x-6}{2x+1}$

g. $\dfrac{r-2}{s^3} \div \dfrac{r^2-3r+2}{s^2}$

h. $\dfrac{n^2-2n-15}{12n+9} \div \dfrac{n+3}{6}$

5. Simplify. State any restrictions on the variables.

a. $\dfrac{3(x+5)}{2x+6} \times \dfrac{5(x+3)}{x^2+6x+5} \times \dfrac{4x+4}{3(x-2)}$

b. $\dfrac{7x+14}{x^2+3x-10} \times \dfrac{3x+15}{2x-7} \times \dfrac{2x-7}{2x+10}$

c. $\dfrac{x+1}{x^2-x-6} \times \dfrac{x+2}{x-1} \times \dfrac{x-3}{x^2+2x+1}$

d. $\dfrac{x^2-8x+15}{x-5} \div \dfrac{x^2-16}{6x-18} \times \dfrac{3x+12}{2x-10}$

C **6.** Simplify and state any restrictions on the variables.

a. $\dfrac{2x^2-3x-2}{6x^2-x-2} \times \dfrac{3x^2-5x+2}{4x^2-1} \div \dfrac{x^2-1}{6x^2+7x+2}$

b. $\dfrac{6m^2-7mn-3n^2}{4m^2+19mn-5n^2} \div \dfrac{9n^2-4m^2}{4m^2-1} \times \dfrac{8m^2+10mn-3n^2}{4m^2+4m+1}$

c. $\dfrac{x^2-xy-2y^2}{3x^2+5xy-2y^2} \times \dfrac{6x^2+xy-y^2}{x^2-y^2} \times \dfrac{2x^2+5xy+2y^2}{x^2-4xy+4y^2}$

d. $\dfrac{a^2-ab}{6a^2+11ab+3b^2} \div \dfrac{a^2-b^2}{2a^2-ab-6b^2} \div \dfrac{4a^2-7ab-2b^2}{3a^2+7ab+2b^2}$

6–12 Adding and Subtracting Rational Expressions

An airplane flew a given distance against the wind at speed v_1, and then returned the same distance with the wind at a different speed, v_2. The total time flown can be written as a rational expression by using the formula for speed, $v = \frac{d}{t}$, and isolating t.

$\therefore t = \frac{d}{v}$, where t is time, d is distance, v is speed

An expression to represent total time is: $\frac{d}{v_1} + \frac{d}{v_2}$.

These two rational expressions can be added together just like fractions.

a. Find the LCM of the denominators, v_1 and $v_2 \neq 0$.

b. Rewrite the expressions with their least common denominators.

c. Add the expressions with the LCD to simplify.

$$\frac{d(v_2)}{v_1(v_2)} + \frac{d(v_1)}{v_2(v_1)}$$

$$\frac{dv_2}{v_1 v_2} + \frac{dv_1}{v_2 v_1} = \frac{dv_2 + dv_1}{v_1 v_2}$$

The same rules apply if the denominators of two rational expressions to be added or subtracted are more complex.

EXAMPLE 1:   Add or subtract as indicated.

a. $\dfrac{x}{3} + \dfrac{5}{x}$ $x \neq 0$

$= \dfrac{x(x)}{3(x)} + \dfrac{5(3)}{x(3)}$ The LCD is $3x$.

$= \dfrac{x^2 + 15}{3x}$

b. $\dfrac{1}{m + 3} - \dfrac{m}{2}$ $m \neq -3$

$= \dfrac{1(2)}{(m + 3)(2)} - \dfrac{m(m + 3)}{2(m + 3)}$ The LCD is $2(m + 3)$.

$= \dfrac{2 - (m^2 + 3m)}{2(m + 3)}$

$= \dfrac{2 - m^2 - 3m}{2(m + 3)}$

Factor denominators if possible before looking for the LCD.

EXAMPLE 2:   Find the sum, given that $x \neq \pm 2$.

$$\frac{x + 1}{x^2 - 4} + \frac{2}{3x + 6} = \frac{x + 1}{(x + 2)(x - 2)} + \frac{2}{3(x + 2)}$$

$$= \frac{3(x + 1)}{3(x + 2)(x - 2)} + \frac{2(x - 2)}{3(x + 2)(x - 2)} \qquad \text{The LCD is } 3(x + 2)(x - 2).$$

$$= \frac{3x + 3 + 2x - 4}{3(x + 2)(x - 2)}$$

$$= \frac{5x - 1}{3(x + 2)(x - 2)}$$

200

EXERCISES

For all exercises, state any restrictions on the variables.

A **1.** Find the LCD of each pair of expressions.

  a. $\dfrac{x}{8}$, $\dfrac{x}{6}$

  b. $\dfrac{2}{a}$, $\dfrac{3}{a^2}$

  c. $\dfrac{x}{2y}$, $\dfrac{x+1}{3y}$

  d. $\dfrac{3}{x+1}$, $\dfrac{2}{x-1}$

  e. $\dfrac{4}{3(x+3)}$, $\dfrac{2x}{5(x+3)}$

  f. $\dfrac{3k}{2n(n-1)}$, $\dfrac{2k-1}{4n^2}$

2. Rewrite each pair of fractions with the common denominator given.

  a. $\dfrac{x}{6}$, $\dfrac{2x}{9}$; 18

  b. $\dfrac{2}{y}$, $\dfrac{3y}{5}$; 5y

  c. $\dfrac{x+1}{xy}$, $\dfrac{3}{y^2}$; xy^2

  d. $\dfrac{n+2}{3n^2}$, $\dfrac{n-1}{6n}$; $6n^2$

  e. $\dfrac{x+2}{2(x+1)}$, $\dfrac{x-3}{3(x+1)}$; $6(x+1)$

B **3.** Simplify.

  a. $\dfrac{5}{x} + \dfrac{3}{x}$

  b. $\dfrac{7}{2m} + \dfrac{3}{m}$

  c. $\dfrac{k}{2} - \dfrac{4}{3k}$

  d. $\dfrac{3a}{5} - \dfrac{7a}{10}$

  e. $\dfrac{4x}{3z} + \dfrac{z}{2x}$

  f. $\dfrac{3}{x} + \dfrac{2}{y}$

  g. $\dfrac{4a}{3b} - \dfrac{a}{2b}$

  h. $\dfrac{5a}{3b} + \dfrac{2}{5ab}$

4. Add or subtract as indicated. Simplify the answer if possible.

  a. $\dfrac{3x+4}{x+3} + \dfrac{5}{x+3}$

  b. $\dfrac{2x+3}{x-1} - \dfrac{5}{x-1}$

  c. $\dfrac{x}{x-4} + \dfrac{2}{x}$

  d. $\dfrac{z+1}{z-2} - \dfrac{2}{z}$

  e. $\dfrac{1}{x+2} + \dfrac{x}{1}$

  f. $3 - \dfrac{x}{x+3}$

  g. $\dfrac{x+3}{x+2} + \dfrac{x}{x-2}$

  h. $\dfrac{2x}{x+4} + \dfrac{3}{x+1}$

  i. $\dfrac{k}{k-1} + k$

5. Add or subtract as indicated.

  a. $\dfrac{5x+1}{3(x-2)} + \dfrac{x}{2(x-2)}$

  b. $\dfrac{x+4}{4(x+3)} - \dfrac{3}{6(x-2)}$

  c. $\dfrac{2x}{(x+1)(x+3)} + \dfrac{3}{x+3}$

  d. $\dfrac{3x}{(x-2)(x+1)} - \dfrac{2}{x(x+1)}$

  e. $\dfrac{x-2}{(x-3)(x+4)} - \dfrac{x+3}{(x-3)(x+1)}$

  f. $\dfrac{x+2}{(x+3)(x+5)} + \dfrac{x-1}{(x+3)(x-2)}$

  g. $\dfrac{x+3}{2x(x-1)} + \dfrac{x}{6(x+1)(x-1)}$

  h. $\dfrac{2}{(x+2)(x+2)} - \dfrac{3}{(x-1)(x+2)}$

C **6.** Add or subtract as indicated.

  a. $\dfrac{2}{3x+6} - \dfrac{3x}{2x+4}$

  b. $\dfrac{x+1}{x^2-3x} + \dfrac{x}{3x-9}$

  c. $\dfrac{x-3}{x^2+2x+1} + \dfrac{x}{x^2+3x+2}$

  d. $\dfrac{2x+1}{x^2-7x+12} - \dfrac{x}{x^2-3x-4}$

  e. $\dfrac{x-3}{x^2+4x+3} + \dfrac{2x}{x^2+5x+6}$

  f. $\dfrac{3x}{x^2+x-6} - \dfrac{2x+1}{x^2-4}$

  g. $\dfrac{a-b}{a^2-ab-2b^2} + \dfrac{a+b}{a^2+2ab+b^2}$

  h. $\dfrac{3x}{3x^2-12} + \dfrac{x-1}{x^2-4x+4}$

6–13 Solving Equations with Rational Expressions

A two-day mountain race was won by a cyclist who travelled 60 km each day, but with an average speed that was twice as fast the second day. The total time spent riding was six hours. What was the cyclist's rate for each day?

Define the variable.
Let v be the speed on the first day in kilometres per hour.
Let $2v$ be the speed on the second day in kilometres per hour.

Write and solve the equation.

$$\frac{60}{v} + \frac{60}{2v} = 6, v \neq 0$$

$$(2v)\left[\frac{60}{v} + \frac{60}{2v}\right] = (2v)6 \qquad \text{Clear the fractions by multiplying each side by } 2v.$$

$$120 + 60 = 12v$$
$$180 = 12v$$
$$v = 15$$
$$\therefore 2v = 30$$

The cyclist's rate the first day was 15 km/h and, the second day, 30 km/h.

Check: L.S. $= \frac{60}{(15)} + \frac{60}{2(15)}$ R.S. $= 6$
$\qquad \quad = 6 \qquad \qquad \qquad \qquad = $ L.S. ✓

Equations may also involve *quadratic trinomials*.

EXAMPLE: If the rider had finished the course in 5 h, averaging 10 km/h faster the second day, what would the speeds on the two days have been?

Define the variable.
Let v be the speed for the first day in kilometres per hour.
Let $v + 10$ be the speed for the second day in kilometres per hour.

Write and solve the equation.

$$\frac{60}{v} + \frac{60}{v + 10} = 5, v \neq 0.$$

$$v(v + 10)\left[\frac{60}{v} + \frac{60}{v + 10}\right] = v(v + 10)5 \qquad \text{Clear the fractions by multiplying each side by } v(v + 10).$$

$$\frac{[v(v + 10)]60}{v} + \frac{[v(v + 10)]60}{v + 10} = [v(v + 10)]5 \qquad \text{Multiply each side by } v(v + 10).$$

$$(v + 10)60 + 60v = 5v^2 + 50v$$
$$60v + 600 + 60v = 5v^2 + 50v$$
$$5v^2 - 70v - 600 = 0$$
$$5(v^2 - 14v - 120) = 0$$
$$5(v - 20)(v + 6) = 0$$

$$v - 20 = 0 \quad \text{or} \quad v + 6 = 0$$
$$v = 20 \qquad \qquad v = -6$$

The speed of -6 km/h is inadmissible.

Thus, the speed the first day was 20 km/h and the second day was 30 km/h.

$$\text{Check:} \quad \frac{60}{v} + \frac{60}{v + 10} = 5$$

$$\text{L.S.} = \frac{60}{(20)} + \frac{60}{(20) + 10}$$
$$= 5$$
$$\text{R.S.} = 5$$
$$= \text{L.S.} \; \checkmark$$

EXERCISES

A 1. Solve each equation.

   a. $\dfrac{x + 3}{4} = x - 3$

   b. $\dfrac{x + 5}{3} = \dfrac{x + 1}{2}$

   c. $\dfrac{3x - 1}{2} = \dfrac{5x + 1}{6}$

   d. $\dfrac{x - 3}{2} + \dfrac{x + 2}{4} = 5$

   e. $\dfrac{2x - 1}{3} - \dfrac{x + 3}{7} = 5$

   f. $\dfrac{x - 3}{4} = -\dfrac{3x - 5}{4}$

2. Solve each equation.

   a. $\dfrac{2}{x} + \dfrac{1}{3} = 1$

   b. $\dfrac{5}{x} - \dfrac{1}{3} = \dfrac{2}{3}$

   c. $\dfrac{1}{x} + \dfrac{1}{2x} = \dfrac{3}{4}$

   d. $\dfrac{1}{x} - \dfrac{1}{5x} = \dfrac{2}{5}$

   e. $\dfrac{3}{x} + \dfrac{1}{2x} = \dfrac{1}{2}$

   f. $\dfrac{4}{x} - \dfrac{3}{2x} = \dfrac{1}{2}$

   g. $\dfrac{3}{8} = \dfrac{2}{x} - \dfrac{1}{2x}$

   h. $\dfrac{5}{3x} - \dfrac{1}{3} = \dfrac{1}{x}$

   i. $\dfrac{5}{18} = \dfrac{1}{2} - \dfrac{2}{x}$

B 3. Solve and check.

   a. $\dfrac{x}{x + 2} = \dfrac{3}{5}$

   b. $\dfrac{x + 2}{3x} = \dfrac{1}{2}$

   c. $\dfrac{2x + 1}{5x - 1} = \dfrac{5}{9}$

   d. $\dfrac{4x}{x + 2} = 2$

   e. $\dfrac{3x + 1}{x - 1} = 4$

   f. $\dfrac{x + 7}{5 - x} = 5$

   g. $\dfrac{8}{x} + \dfrac{10}{2x + 1} = 6$

   h. $\dfrac{2}{x + 1} - \dfrac{x}{2x - 1} = 0$

   i. $\dfrac{x + 2}{10} = \dfrac{3}{x + 1}$

   j. $\dfrac{3}{2x + 2} + \dfrac{1}{x} = 1$

   k. $\dfrac{2x - 1}{2x + 1} = \dfrac{x + 2}{3x - 2}$

   l. $\dfrac{x + 2}{2x + 2} = \dfrac{5}{3x - 1}$

4. Bob cycled to the cottage, 90 km from his home, and returned by bus. He spent a total of eight hours travelling. The average speed of the bus was triple Bob's average cycling speed. What was Bob's average cycling speed?

5. To train for an upcoming marathon, Dawn ran a 15 km timed course once a week. At the end of her training period, she was running 2 km/h faster than at the beginning. The difference in her times on the course was $\dfrac{1}{4}$ hour. What was her final speed on the course?

6. Paula flew in a light plane, in still air, up to a summer camp 800 km away. On the return flight, a tailwind increased her speed by 40 km/h. Consequently, it took one hour less on the trip back than on the flight to the camp. What was the speed of the plane in still air?

Using the Calculator

The calculator can be used to reveal number patterns like the one illustrated below.

$$11^2 = 121$$
$$101^2 = 10\ 201$$
$$1001^2 = 1\ 002\ 001$$
$$10\ 001^2 = ?$$

Although this answer is too large for most calculator displays, you can *predict* an answer of 100 020 001.

The prediction can be *proven*, using a few algebraic skills. All of the squares above can be written as $(10^k + 1)^2$.

Squared Binomial: **Trinomial Square:**

$11^2 = (10^1 + 1)^2 = (10^1 + 1)(10^1 + 1) = 10^2 + 2(10) + 1 = \qquad 100 + 20 + 1 = 121$

$101^2 = (10^2 + 1)^2 = (10^2 + 1)(10^2 + 1) = 10^4 + 2(10^2) + 1 = \qquad 10\ 000 + 200 + 1 = 10\ 201$
$$\uparrow$$
$$1\ \text{zero}$$

$1001^2 = (10^3 + 1)^2 = (10^3 + 1)(10^3 + 1) = 10^6 + 2(10^3) + 1 = \qquad 1\ 000\ 000 + 2000 + 1 = 1\ 002\ 001$
$$\uparrow\ \uparrow$$
$$2\ \text{zeros}$$

$10\ 001^2 = (10^4 + 1)^2 = (10^4 + 1)(10^4 + 1) = 10^8 + 2(10^4) + 1 = \quad 100\ 000\ 000 + 20\ 000 + 1 = 100\ 020\ 001$
$$\uparrow\qquad \uparrow$$
$$3\ \text{zeros}$$
$$\vdots$$

$10\ldots 01^2 = (10^k + 1)^2 = (10^k + 1)(10^k + 1) = 10^{2k} + 2(10^k) + 1 = 10\ldots 20\ldots 1$
$$\uparrow\qquad \uparrow$$
$$k - 1\ \text{zeros}$$

---

1. Predict: **a.** $100\ 001^2$ **b.** $10\ 000\ 001^2$ **c.** $1\ 000\ 000\ 001^2$

2. **a.** Use a calculator to find a pattern for the following: $9^2, 99^2, 999^2, 9999^2, \ldots$
   b. Use the pattern to predict the values of $999\ 999^2$ and $9\ 999\ 999^2$.
   c. Use algebra to show why the pattern works.

3. Use a calculator to find a pattern for the following.

   $11^2, 111^2, 1111^2, \ldots$

4. The pattern in question 3 can be written out as follows.
   $$11^2 = (10 + 1)^2 = (10 + 1)(10 + 1)$$
   $$111^2 = (10^2 + 10 + 1)^2 = (10^2 + 10 + 1)(10^2 + 10 + 1)$$
   $$1111^2 = (10^3 + 10^2 + 10 + 1)^2 = (10^3 + 10^2 + 10 + 1)(10^3 + 10^2 + 10 + 1)$$

   a. Why would an algebraic proof be more difficult for this set? Expand the right-hand side of each equality and look for a pattern in the products.
   b. Predict $(111\ 111\ 111)^2$.
   c. What do you think happens for $(1\ 111\ 111\ 111)^2$?

204

Review

In each exercise, state any restrictions on the variables, where appropriate.

1. Simplify each rational expression.

   a. $\dfrac{(2n + 7)(n + 5)}{(3n + 2)(2n + 7)}$
   b. $\dfrac{x^2 + 2x - 8}{3x + 12}$
   c. $\dfrac{x^2 + 6x - 7}{x^2 - 49}$
   d. $\dfrac{x^2 + 12x + 36}{36 - x^2}$

2. Multiply or divide as indicated.

   a. $\dfrac{4(2x + 3)}{2x^3} \times \dfrac{3x}{2x + 3}$
   b. $\dfrac{3(x + 3)}{2x^4} \div \dfrac{x + 3}{4x}$

   c. $\dfrac{(x - 3)(x + 2)}{x - 1} \div \dfrac{(x + 1)(x + 2)}{x - 1}$
   d. $\dfrac{(x + 5)(x - 2)}{x - 3} \times \dfrac{(x + 4)(x - 3)}{x + 5}$

   e. $\dfrac{3a + 9}{2a - 4} \times \dfrac{a^2 - 8a + 12}{a^2 + 6a + 9}$
   f. $\dfrac{a^2 - 25}{a^2 - 10a + 16} \div \dfrac{5 - a}{a - 2}$

   g. $\dfrac{3n - 15}{4n^2 - 36} \times \dfrac{2n + 6}{n^2 - 2n - 15}$
   h. $\dfrac{(3m - 2)^2}{2m^2 + 5m - 25} \times \dfrac{4m^2 - 25}{9m^2 - 4}$

3. Find an expression to represent the unknown dimension.

   a.

   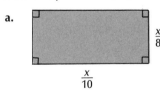

   b.

   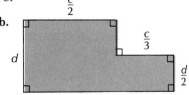

4. Add or subtract as indicated.

   a. $\dfrac{x}{x - 1} - \dfrac{x - 3}{x + 1}$
   b. $\dfrac{x + 2}{2x + 2} + \dfrac{x - 3}{3x + 3}$

   c. $\dfrac{3x + 9}{x^2 - 9} + \dfrac{2x - 8}{x^2 - 16}$
   d. $\dfrac{5x + 25}{(x + 5)(x - 2)} + \dfrac{2x - 8}{x^2 - x - 12}$

   e. $\dfrac{1}{m - 1} + \dfrac{1}{m + 1} + \dfrac{1}{m}$
   f. $\dfrac{3}{x^2 - 2x} - \dfrac{1}{x^2 - 2x - 3}$

5. Find the perimeter, P, and area, A, of each figure.

   a.

   b.

6. Solve each equation.

   a. $\dfrac{1}{2x} + \dfrac{1}{3x} = \dfrac{5}{12}$
   b. $\dfrac{3}{2x + 2} + \dfrac{1}{x} = 1$

   c. $\dfrac{3}{x - 1} - \dfrac{1}{x - 2} = \dfrac{5}{12}$
   d. $\dfrac{4}{x - 1} + \dfrac{x - 3}{2x + 3} = 1$

Using Factoring and Rational Expressions

The following problems can be solved using an algebraic approach.

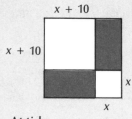

A **1.** A wall is tiled in a pattern like the one at the right. There are 500 white tiles in the pattern altogether, and the large white square has 10 more tiles along each side than the small white square does. How many grey tiles are there in the pattern?

B **2.** Denis travels in his boat 600 m from Lookout Point to Brock Bay. At tide change when the water is flowing at 2 m/s against the boat, it takes him 10 s longer. How fast does his boat travel?

3. An aircraft is making a round trip 800 km each way. On the outward leg of the trip, the aircraft encounters a headwind of 20 km/h but, on the way home, it benefits from a 20 km/h tailwind. The total flying time for the round trip is 9 h. What is the cruising speed of the aircraft in still air?

4. An oscillating lawn sprinkler irrigates a rectangular area which is twice as long as it is wide. If the water pressure is increased by a certain amount, then the irrigated area increases by 3 m in length and 1 m in width, and the total area irrigated doubles. What are the original dimensions of the rectangular area?

5. The resistance, in ohms (Ω), in a parallel circuit is calculated according to the following formula.

$$\frac{1}{R_T} = \frac{1}{R_1} + \frac{1}{R_2}$$ R_T is total resistance.

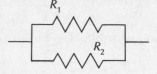

a. If the resistance in one circuit is 15 Ω and in the other circuit is 10 Ω, what is the total resistance in the circuit?
b. Calculate the total resistance in the circuit if there are three parallel branches and their resistances are 100 Ω, 50 Ω, and 200 Ω.
c. A resistance of 20 Ω is placed in one branch of a parallel circuit. What resistance should be placed in the other branch to give a total resistance of 15 Ω?
d. Rewrite the formula given above to isolate the variable R_T.
e. If a circuit has 40 Ω resistance in one branch, what resistance is needed in the second branch to increase the total resistance to 30 Ω?

6. A car travels 120 km at 110 km/h, and then travels another 120 km at 95 km/h.
a. What is the total time for the 240 km?
b. What is the average speed?

C **7.** A car travels d kilometres at 110 km/h, and then travels another d kilometres at 95 km/h. What is the total time taken and the average speed?

Application

Cameras, magnifying glasses, slide projectors, telescopes, and other optical instruments contain lenses to focus light. A lens that focusses light at a single point is called a **converging lens**.

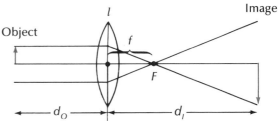

A converging lens, like the one at the right, transforms parallel rays of light so that they bend and coincide at a point, F, called the **principal focus** of the lens. The distance from the centre of the lens lying on line l, to the principal focus is called the **focal length**, f. The distance from the original object to the lens is d_O. The light rays continue past l to form an inverted image at a distance d_I from F.

The focal length determines where focussed images will be formed and how large the image will be according to the following formula.

$$\frac{1}{f} = \frac{1}{d_O} + \frac{1}{d_I}$$

1. Rewrite the formula to isolate the variable d_I, which represents the image distance.

2. Apply the formula to answer the following.
    a. An object is 75 mm from a converging lens with a focal length of 50 mm. How far from the centre of the lens will the image be formed?
    b. An object is 2.5 m from a converging lens with a focus length of 50 mm. How far from the centre of the lens will the image be formed?

A lens has a magnification factor of $M = \frac{d_I}{d_O}$.
This *ratio* is like a scale factor.
Each unit of length in the object is changed by a factor of M.

3. A slide projector has a lens with focal length 60 mm. It is constructed so that slides are placed 90 mm from the lens.
    a. How far from the lens will a properly focussed image be?
    b. What is the magnification of the image for this projector?
    c. If the slide is 3.5 mm wide, how wide will a properly focussed image be?

4. A magnifying glass has a focal length of 120 mm. Where is the image of a stamp 150 mm from the lens formed and what is its magnification?

5. A photographic enlarger has a lens with a focal length of 50 mm. A photographic negative is placed 60 mm from the centre of the lens. Where is the image focussed and what is the magnification?

Test

1. Combine like terms to simplify.
   a. $3x + 2y - 5x - 3y$
   b. $(4x^2 - 9x + 3) - (2x + 3x^2 - 2)$
   c. $(8a^2b + 3b^2) - (4a^3 + 5a^2b - b^3) - (a^2b + ab^2 + 2b^3)$

2. Expand and simplify.
   a. $3(x + 8)$
   b. $6x^2(2x + 3y)$
   c. $(x + 2)(x - 6)$
   d. $(x - 7)^2$
   e. $-3(4x^2 + 3)(3x^2 + 1)$
   f. $(4x - 5)(x + 2)$

3. Factor each polynomial, using the GCF.
   a. $13t - 26$
   b. $-12x^3 - 18x^2 - 24x$
   c. $44xy + 121y^3$
   d. $3x(x + 1) - 2(x + 1)$
   e. $30x^2y - 42xy + 6xy^2$
   f. $15m^2n + 45mn^2 - 90mn - 5n$

4. Factor completely.
   a. $x^2 + 6x + 9$
   b. $9x^2 - 49$
   c. $x^2 + 9x - 36$
   d. $x^2 - x - 12$
   e. $2x^2 + 5x + 3$
   f. $6x^2 - x - 1$
   g. $3x^2 - 30x + 27$
   h. $x^4 - 81$
   i. $3x^4 + 5x^2 - 8$
   j. $4x^2 - 36$
   k. $3x^2 - 27x + 30$
   l. $4x^3y + 12x^2y^2 + 8xy^3$
   m. $x^8 - 81$
   n. $3x^4 - 10x^2 - 8$

5. What must the value of k be for the following to be perfect square binomials?
   a. $x^2 + kx + 25$
   b. $x^2 - 14x + k$
   c. $9x^2 + 48x + k$

6. Solve and check.
   a. $x^2 - 6x + 8 = 0$
   b. $3x^2 - 2x - 5 = 0$
   c. $(x + 3)(x - 1) = (2x - 3)(x + 1)$
   d. $(x + 1)(x + 3) = (3x + 1)(x - 2)$

7. Simplify and state any restrictions on the variables.
   a. $\dfrac{5x}{x^2 - x}$
   b. $\dfrac{(a + 3)(a + 5)}{(a + 5)(a + 7)}$
   c. $\dfrac{m - 3}{9 - m^2}$
   d. $\dfrac{x^2 + 7x + 12}{x^2 + 6x + 9}$

8. Perform the indicated operations. State any restrictions on the variables.
   a. $\dfrac{3(x - 1)}{5x^2} \times \dfrac{10}{9(x - 1)}$
   b. $\dfrac{y^2 - y - 6}{y^2 - y - 30} \div \dfrac{y^2 - 9}{y^2 - 6y}$
   c. $\dfrac{5(y + 2)}{3y^3} \div \dfrac{3(y + 2)}{10y}$
   d. $\dfrac{(r + 3)(r - 7)}{(3r - 2)(r + 5)} \div \dfrac{(r - 7)(2r - 1)}{(2 - 3r)(r - 3)}$
   e. $\dfrac{x^2 - 3x - 10}{x + 2} \times \dfrac{x^2 - 4}{x^2 - 5x}$
   f. $\dfrac{2x^2 + 5x - 3}{x^2 - 6x + 5} \times \dfrac{x^2 - 2x + 1}{x^2 + 6x + 9}$
   g. $\dfrac{3}{x} + \dfrac{3}{y}$
   h. $\dfrac{2}{x + 3} - \dfrac{5}{x}$
   i. $\dfrac{7x}{x - 1} + \dfrac{4}{x(x - 1)}$
   j. $\dfrac{x + 3}{(x + 4)(x - 2)} - \dfrac{x - 3}{(x + 3)(x + 4)}$

9. Solve and check.
   a. $\dfrac{3}{2x} - \dfrac{1}{2} = \dfrac{1}{x}$
   b. $\dfrac{5}{x + 2} - \dfrac{1}{x - 1} = \dfrac{2}{x}$

208

Cumulative Review

1. Evaluate for $a = 2.5$, $b = -0.5$, $c = -3$.
   a. a^2b
   b. $ac - b$
   c. $\frac{ab}{c}$
   d. $a + b - c^2$

2. Simplify ($k \neq 0$).
   a. $\frac{1}{\sqrt{k}}$
   b. $\frac{3}{5\sqrt{2}}$
   c. $\frac{7}{3\sqrt{8}}$
   d. $\frac{9}{2\sqrt{2}}$

3. Find the unknown, correct to two decimal places. You may use a calculator.
   a.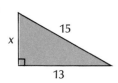
   b.
   c.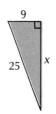

4. Which of the following are right-angled triangles?
   a.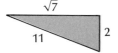
   b.
   c.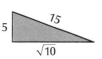

5. Solve and check.
   a. $x + 7 = 15$
   b. $3x - 9 = 12$
   c. $4(x - 1) = 2x + 8$
   d. $3x - 2 = 5(x + 1)$
   e. $9t = 7t - 2$
   f. $3k + 8 = 2(k - 1)$
   g. $-5(a + 2) = 3a + 4$
   h. $4b - 7 = \frac{1}{2}b$
   i. $\frac{2r}{3} + \frac{r}{2} = \frac{7}{4}$

6. Solve each inequality and graph its solution on a number line.
   a. $k + 2 \leq -3$
   b. $9 - t \geq 2t$
   c. $4 - 7c > 88$
   d. $-b \geq b + 32$
   e. $4 - 5m < 3m + 8$
   f. $4n - 5 \leq 5n$
   g. $|d - 6| < 4$
   h. $3|2 - a| \geq 15$
   i. $3 > |a + 3| - 4$

7. Find the slope of the line segment with the given endpoints.
   a. $A(4,8), B(9,-1)$
   b. $K(3,-5), J(-2,-8)$
   c. $M(2,0), N(2,-5)$

8. Graph the line represented by each equation.
   a. $y = 4x - 3$
   b. $y = 0.5x - 1$
   c. $x = 7$
   d. $2x + 3y = 36$

9. Find the point of intersection of each pair of equations.
   a. $x + y = 7$
      $x + 2y = 3$
   b. $y = 4x - 1$
      $x + y = 9$
   c. $x = 7$
      $2x + 3y = 11$
   d. $x = 7$
      $y = -2$

10. Graph each inequality.
    a. $y < x + 2$
    b. $y > 3x - 5$
    c. $y \geq -2x - 5$
    d. $2x + 3y \leq 12$

11. Graph each system of inequalities.
    a. $y < 4x + 1$
       $y < 2x$
       $y > x - 3$
    b. $x + y > 3$
       $2x + y < 12$
    c. $2x + y + 3 \leq 0$
       $x + y + 7 \geq 0$
       $x - y - 3 > 0$

7 Relations and Functions

7–1 Representing Relations

The yearbook editor approached several small printers to obtain quotes for printing the yearbook. The table gives the quotes from one of the printers.

Print Run	Cost of Run
1000	$4000
1500	$4500
2000	$5000

The table can also be written as a set of ordered pairs:

$$\{(1000,4000),\ (1500,4500),\ (2000,5000)\}.$$

A set of ordered pairs is a **relation**. The arrow diagram and the graph are alternative methods of representing the relation $\{(\text{print run, cost})\}$.

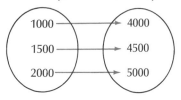

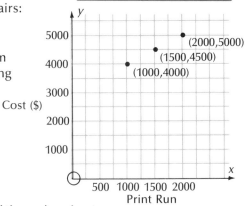

The **domain** of a relation is the set of first elements of the ordered pairs of the relation. The **range** of a relation is the set of second elements of the ordered pairs.

For the relation $\{(\text{print run, cost})\}$, the domain is $\{1000, 1500, 2000\}$ and the range is $\{4000, 4500, 5000\}$. Note that this relation has a *finite* number of elements in its domain and range.

The relation $\{(\text{print run, cost})\}$ can also be written in mathematical notation as:

$$\{(x,y)|y = x + 3000,\ x \in \{1000,1500,2000\}\}$$

Read: "The set of all ordered pairs, (x,y), *such that* $y = x + 3000$, and x is a member of the set $\{1000,1500,2000\}$.

EXAMPLE 1:   Find the domain and range of each of the following relations.

   a. $\{(x,y)|y = 2x - 1, x \in \{-1,0,1,2,3\}\}$
   The relation is $\{(-1,-3), (0,-1), (1,1), (2,3), (3,5)\}$.
   Domain $= \{-1,0,1,2,3\}$ and Range $= \{-3,-1,1,3,5\}$

   b. $\{(x, x^2 + 3)|x \in \{-2,-1,0,1,2\}\}$
   The relation is $\{(-2,7), (-1,4), (0,3), (1,4), (2,7)\}$.
   Domain $= \{-2,-1,0,1,2\}$ and Range $= \{3,4,7\}$

EXAMPLE 2:   Find the domain and range of each relation defined by the given graph.

a.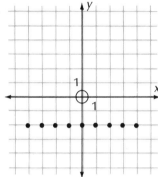

b.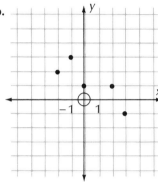

c.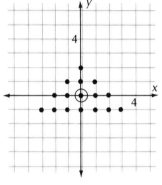

Domain $= \{-4,-3,-2,-1,0,1,2,3,4\}$
Range $= \{-2\}$

Domain $= \{-2,-1,0,2,3\}$
Range $= \{-1,1,2,3\}$

Domain $= \{-3,-2,-1,0,1,2,3\}$
Range $= \{-1,0,1,2\}$

EXAMPLE 3:   Find the domain and range of each relation defined by the given graph.

a.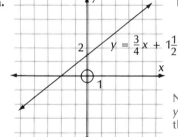

b.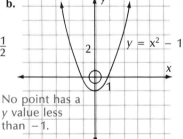

No point has a
y value less
than -1.

c.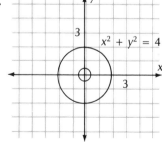

Domain $= \{x|x \in R\}$
Range $= \{y|y \in R\}$

Domain $= \{x|x \in R\}$
Range $= \{y \in R|y \geq -1\}$

Domain $= \{x \in R|-2 \leq x \leq 2\}$
Range $= \{y \in R|-2 \leq y \leq 2\}$

> Note: In this book, if the domain is not given, assume it is the set of real numbers.

211

EXERCISES

A **1.** Use the information given in the table below to write the indicated relation as a set of ordered pairs.

Team Member	Age	Position	Point Record Last Year
Chris	16	Centre	45
Pat	17	Left Wing	38
Kim	16	Right Wing	42
Terry	16	Left Defence	28
Robbie	15	Right Defence	13

    a. {(team member, age)}   **b.** {(team member, position)}

    c. {(team member, point record last year)}   **d.** {(position, point record last year)}

2. For each relation graphed below, write the relation as a set of ordered pairs (x,y). Give the domain and range of each relation.

a.
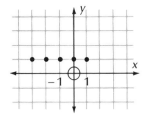

b.
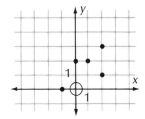

c.
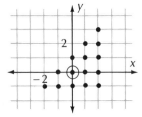

d.
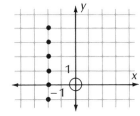

B **3.** Give the domain and range of the following relations.

    a. {(−10,4), (3,6), (7,8), (−4,−5)}   **b.** {(6,2), (7,2), (8,2), (9,2)}

    c. {(0,0), (1,1), (2,8), (3,27)}   **d.** {(−2,4), (−1,1), (0,0), (1,1), (2,4)}

4. Find the domain and range of the relation defined by the given graph.

a.
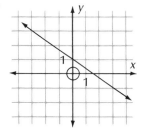

b.
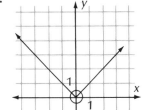

c.
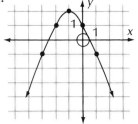

212

d. 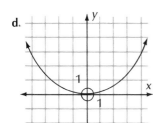 **e.** 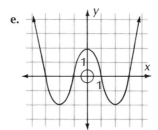 **f.**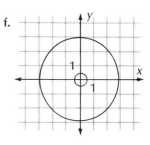

5. Find the domain and range of each relation defined below.

a. $\{(x,y)|y = x + 4, x \in \{0,1,2,3,4\}\}$

b. $\{(x,y)|x = 2y + 3, y \in \{-2, -1,0,1\}\}$

c. $\{(x,y)|y = 3x, x \in \{-2, -1,0,1,2\}\}$

d. $\{(x,y)|y = 3x - 4, x \in \{-2, -1,0,1\}\}$

e. $\{(x,y)|y = \dfrac{5x - 2}{3}, x \in \{4,1,-2,-5\}\}$

f. $\{(x,y)|y = x^3, x \in \{-2, -1,0,1,2\}\}$

g. $\{(x, \dfrac{1}{2}x - 4)| x \in \{0, \pm 2, \pm 4\}\}$

h. $\{(x, \dfrac{x - 5}{4})|, x \in \{0, \pm 1,2\}\}$

6. For each of the following relations, make a table of values, draw the graph, and state the domain and range.

a. $\{(x,y)|y = x - 2, x, y \in R\}$

b. $\{(x,y)|y = 2x + 1, x, y \in Z\}$

c. $\{(x,y)|x + 3y + 6 = 0, x, y \in R\}$

d. $\{(x,y)|x + y + 4 = 0, x, y \in R\}$

e. $\{(x,y)|x - y = 4, x, y \in R\}$

f. $\{(x,y)|y = \dfrac{1}{2}x - 1, x \in Z\}$

g. $\{(x, 2x + 2)| x \in R\}$

h. $\{(x, 3x - 1)| x \in R\}$

i. $\{(x, \dfrac{x + 1}{3})| x \in R\}$

j. $\{(\dfrac{1}{2}y + 1, y)| y \in R\}$

k. $\{(x,y)|y = 2, x, y \in R\}$

l. $\{(x,y)|x = -1, x, y \in R\}$

m. $\{(x,3)| x \in R\}$

n. $\{(x,y)|x - 3 = 0, x, y \in R\}$

C **7.** For domain $D = \{x \in Z \cdot | -6 \le x \le 6\}$, draw the graph of each given relation.

a. $y = |x|$

b. $y = |x - 3|$

c. $y = -|x + 5|$

d. $y = |x - 3| + 2$

e. $y = -|x + 3| + 2$

f. $|x| + y = 4$

EXTRA

Pennies for Penny

Penny devised a plan to get a bigger allowance for her work around the house. Instead of her parents' plan to pay an allowance of $50/month, Penny thought they should pay her 1¢ on the first day of the month, 2¢ on the second day, 4¢, 8¢, 16¢, . . . , on successive days for a total of 30 days. Why did Penny's parents not agree to her plan?

Consider the relation $\{(x,y)|y = 1 + 2 + 4 + 8 + \ldots + 2^{x-1}\}$.

1. Calculate how much Penny will get after 5 days, 10 days, 30 days.

2. Draw the graph of this relation.

213

7–2 Identifying Functions

A **function** is a special type of relation in which each element of the domain corresponds to exactly one element of the range.

Relation *A* is a function because each element of the domain corresponds to only one element of the range. Since the reverse is also true, relation *A* is a **one-to-one correspondence**.

Relation *B* is a function because each element of the domain corresponds to exactly one element of the range. Relation *B* is a **many-to-one correspondence**.

Relation *C* is *not* a function because "brown eyes" in the domain maps onto *two* elements in the range.

Relation A

Michael → age 16
Carole → age 13
Stephen → age 10

Relation B

Joe
Maria → grade 10
Lisa

Relation C

blue eyes → Kim
brown eyes → Rob
→ Ann

EXAMPLE 1:   Which of the relations listed are functions?

   a. $F = \{(3,7), (4,8), (5,9), (6,10)\}$
   b. $G = \{(-3,1), (4,7), (-3,2)\}$
   c. $H = \{(6,3), (8,3), (-1,3), (0,3)\}$

   Relations *F* and *H* are functions. Relation *G* is not.

Relation $F = \{(3,7), (4,8), (5,9), (6,10)\}$ above can be written in different mathematical notations, such as: $F = \{(x,y)|y = x + 4, x \in \{3,4,5,6\}\}$. It can also be written using mapping notation and a single letter to represent the function.

   $F:x \rightarrow x + 4$ Read, "The relation *F* maps *x* onto *x* + 4."

   $F(x) = x + 4$ Read, "The value of *F* at *x* is *x* + 4."

EXAMPLE 2:   List the elements of the range of the function $g:x \rightarrow 2x - 5$ if the domain $D = \{-1,0,1,2\}$.

Replace *x* with each element of D in a table of values to find the elements of the range R.

x	$2x - 5$
-1	$2(-1) - 5 = -7$
0	$2(0) - 5 = -5$
1	$2(1) - 5 = -3$
2	$2(2) - 5 = -1$

   $R = \{-7, -5, -3, -1\}$

EXAMPLE 3:   Given that $f:x \rightarrow 4x - 7$, find the following.

   a. $f(0)$ **b.** $f(-3)$ **c.** $f(14)$

   First write the relation as an equation: $f(x) = 4x - 7$.
   Now substitute the given values for *x*.

   a. $f(0) = 4(0) - 7$ **b.** $f(-3) = 4(-3) - 7$ **c.** $f(14) = 4(14) - 7$
   $= 0 - 7$ $= -12 - 7$ $= 56 - 7$
   $= -7$ $= -19$ $= 49$

214

You can tell whether a graph represents a function by the **vertical line test**.
If you can find a vertical line that crosses the graph at *more than one* point,
the relation is *not* a function.

EXAMPLE 4:   Which of the graphs below represent functions?

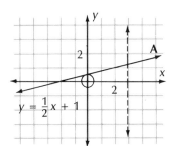
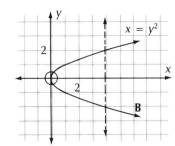
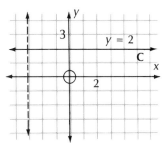

a.   Since a vertical line crosses the graph in at most *one point*,
the graphs labelled **A** and **C** are functions.
b.   The graph of $x = y^2$ in **B** is *not* a function, since we can
find two points in the curve with the same x-coordinate:
$(4,2)$, and $(4, -2)$.

EXAMPLE 5:   Which of the following represent functions?
The domain and range of each relation is the set of real numbers.

a. $\{(x,y)|y = 3x - 1\}$ b. $f:x \rightarrow 2x$ c. $\{(x, 2x + 2)\}$

Graph each relation and then use the vertical line test.

a.
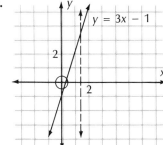

b.
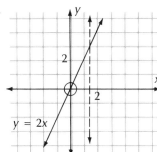

c.
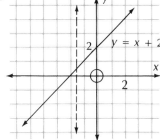

All of these relations are functions.
Since their graphs are straight lines, they are called **linear
functions**.

EXERCISES

A   1.   Which of the following are functions?
a. $\{(6,1), (7,10), (-1,4), (3,0)\}$ b. $\{(5,1), (6,1), (7,-2)\}$
c. $\{(0,0), (0,2), (7,9)\}$ d. $\{(-6,8), (-9,2), (0,0)\}$

215

2. Which of the following represent functions?

a. 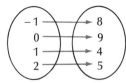 **b.** 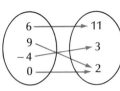 **c.**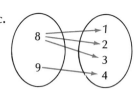

3. Which of the relations in exercises 1 and 2 are one-to-one correspondences?

4. Which of the following graphs represent functions?

a. 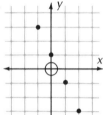 **b.** 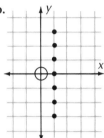 **c.** 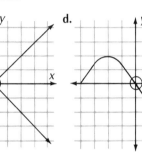 **d.**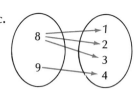

B **5.** For the students in your mathematics class, which of the following relations are functions?
  a. {(student, eye colour)} **b.** {(eye colour, student)}
  c. {(shoe size, student)} **d.** {(mathematics mark, student)}
  e. {(address, postal code)} **f.** {(parent, child)}

6. Make a table of values and state the range of each function.
  a. $f{:}x \rightarrow x + 5$, D $= \{0,1,2\}$
  b. $g{:}x \rightarrow 3 - x$, D $= \{-1,0,1\}$
  c. $F{:}x \rightarrow x^2$, D $= \left\{-\frac{1}{2}, 0, \frac{1}{2}\right\}$
  d. $G{:}x \rightarrow x^2 + 1$, D $= \{-1,0,1\}$
  e. $h{:}t \rightarrow 3t^2$, D $= \{0,1,2\}$
  f. $H{:}r \rightarrow r^2 + 3$, D $= \{-1,0,1\}$

7. State the range for each, given D $= \{-2,-1,0,1,2\}$. Which relations are functions?
  a. $f{:}x \rightarrow x^2 + 1$ **b.** $g{:}x \rightarrow 2^{x+2}$ **c.** $\left\{\left(x, \frac{x}{3}\right)\right\}$ **d.** $\{(x,y)|x = y^2 - 2\}$

8. Given the function $f(x) = 2x - 1$ with the set of real numbers as the domain, find the following values of f at x.
  a. $f(0)$ **b.** $f(-1)$ **c.** $f(1)$ **d.** $f(-2)$ **e.** $f(2)$ **f.** $f(6)$ **g.** $f(-4)$

9. Given the function $g(x) = x^2 - 2$ with the set of real numbers as the domain, find the following values of g at x.
  a. $g(1)$ **b.** $g(-1)$ **c.** $g(-3)$ **d.** $g(0)$ **e.** $g(-2)$ **f.** $g(-5)$ **g.** $g(8)$

10. For domain and range $\{-1,0,1,2,3\}$, make a table of values and graph each relation. Which are functions?

  a. $y = x$ **b.** $y < x$ **c.** $y > x$

C 11. Given that $f(x) = 3x^2$ and $g(x) = -2x^2$, find each of the following.

a. $\frac{1}{2}f(5)$ b. $2g(-3)$ c. $f(1) + g(1)$ d. $g(3) - f(3)$

12. Graph each relation over the given domain D. Which are functions?

a. $k{:}x \to x^2 - 2$, D $= \{-3, -2, -1, 0, 1, 2, 3\}$ b. $x = |y + 2|$, D $= \{0, 1, 2, 3\}$

c. $x = y^2 + 4$, D $= \{4, 5, 8, 13\}$ d. $f{:}x \to x^3$, D $= \{-3, -2, -1, 0, 1, 2, 3\}$

Biography   **René Descartes 1596–1650**

"Cogito, ergo sum." (I think, therefore I am.)

René Descartes, a brilliant French philosopher and mathematician, used this argument as the basis of his philosophic work. In addition to his philosophic writing, Descartes made many important contributions to mathematics. It was Descartes who originated the system of plotting points and curves on an *xy*-coordinate grid.

Born in La Haye (now La Haye-Descartes) in 1596, René Descartes was a sickly child. At the Jesuit school in La Flèche, he was often confined to his bed because of his poor health. It was a confinement Descartes came to enjoy: he made a lifelong habit of spending his mornings in bed. Descartes, who never married, maintained that the morning was his most productive time.

After leaving school, Descartes spent some time in Paris pursuing mathematical studies with contemporary scholars. In 1617, he joined the French army, a move which enabled him to devote considerable time to his philosophy, as he was not involved in any actual battles. After leaving the military, he spent several years travelling through Europe, and then settled for a short time in Paris. His large network of friends and acquaintances there, however, interfered with his writing. Descartes decided to move to Holland, where he lived and wrote for twenty years.

In 1649, René Descartes accepted an invitation to go to Sweden, where Queen Christina wanted to retain him as a philosopher with her court. Christina demanded much of Descartes. His grueling schedule contributed to his chronic state of poor health and, in the winter of 1650, Descartes contracted pneumonia and died. He left a legacy of personal notes and published works.

René Descartes signed his scholarly works with a Latinized version of his name, Renatus Cartesius. From this we have the *Cartesian coordinate system*, which is our current system of graphing on an *xy*-coordinate grid, as well as Cartesian thought, which can perhaps best be summed up in Descartes's own words: *"Cogito, ergo sum."*

7-3 Direct Variation

Philippe works part time at a fast-food stand for $4.10/h. His wages depend directly upon the number of hours he works.

Hours (x)	Wages ($) (y)	$\frac{y}{x}$
1	4.10	4.10
2	8.20	4.10
3	12.30	4.10
4	16.40	4.10

When Philippe's hours double, his wages double; when his hours triple, his wages triple; and so on. We say that *y* **varies directly** as *x*. We can write: $y \propto x$. ($\propto$ is the symbol for "varies directly as".)

In this example of direct variation, *y* is related to *x* by the *linear* equation $y = 4.10x$.

The graph of $y = 4.10x$ is a line that passes through (0.0).

The slope of the line is 4.10 and, for each pair (x,y) in the direct variation, the ratio $\frac{y}{x}$ is 4.10, a constant.

This constant is called the **constant of variation**.

The graph lies entirely in the first quadrant, since the number of hours Philippe works must be non-negative.

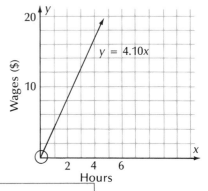

A direct variation is a function defined by an equation of the form $y = kx$, $k \neq 0$. The constant *k* is called the constant of variation. When the domain is *R*, the graph of a direct variation is a line with slope *k* that passes through (0,0).

EXAMPLE 1: Which of the following relations are examples of direct variation?

a. {(8,4), (10,5), (20,10), (9, 4.5)}

Since the ratio $\frac{y}{x}$ is constant for each ordered pair, $\left(\frac{y}{x} = \frac{1}{2}\right)$, this *is* an example of direct variation: $y \propto x$.

b. {(t,d)|d = 3.7t}
Since the equation is in the form $y = kx$, it defines a direct variation: $t \propto d$.

c. $\left\{(x,y)|x = \frac{12}{y}\right\}$
The table of values shows that, as |x| increases, |y| decreases. This is *not* a direct variation.

x	1	2	3	4	6	12	24
y	12	6	4	3	2	1	0.5

218

EXAMPLE 2:   As Chris cycles at a constant speed, the distance cycled varies directly as the time spent cycling. If Chris travels 37.5 km in 1.5 h, find k, the constant of variation.

Let d be the distance in kilometres and t be the time in hours. Since $d \propto t$, then $d = kt$.

Substitute $d = 37.5$ and $t = 1.5$ into $d = kt$.

$$d = kt$$
$$37.5 = 1.5k$$
$$25 = k$$

The constant of variation is 25, which is Chris's speed in kilometres per hour.

For any ordered pairs (x_1, y_1) and (x_2, y_2) in a direct variation, $\frac{y_1}{x_1} = k$ and $\frac{y_2}{x_2} = k$. Since *both* ratios are equal to k, a constant, the following must be true.

$$\frac{y_1}{x_1} = \frac{y_2}{x_2} \quad (= k)$$

When two ratios are equated, the resulting equation is called a **proportion**. For this reason, k is sometimes called the **constant of proportionality**, and y is said to be directly proportional to x.

EXAMPLE 3:   The amount of interest earned on savings is in direct proportion to the amount of money saved. If \$34 interest is earned on \$425, how much interest will be earned on \$700 in the same time period?

Let i, in dollars, be the interest on d dollars.
Then i_1 is 34, d_1 is 425, i_2 is unknown, and d_2 is 700.

There are two possible methods.

a. Write a proportion in the form $\frac{i_1}{d_1} = \frac{i_2}{d_2}$.

$$\frac{34}{425} = \frac{i_2}{700}$$
$$425 i_2 = 23\,800$$
$$i_2 = 56$$

b. Find the constant of proportionality k with the equation $k = \frac{i_1}{d_1}$.

$$k = \frac{34}{425}$$
$$= 0.08 \rightarrow \text{The constant of proportionality is } 0.08, \text{ which is the interest rate.}$$

Substitute $k = 0.08$ into the equation $i_2 = kd_2$.
$$i_2 = (0.08)700$$
$$= 56$$

By either method, \$56 interest will be earned on \$700.

EXERCISES

A 1. Which relations are examples of direct variaton? Give the constant of proportionality for each direct variation.

   a. $\{(0,0), (1,3), (2,6), (3,9)\}$ b. $\{(2,5), (3,7.5), (4,10), (6,15)\}$

   c. $\{(4,2), (6,3), (7,4), (9,5)\}$ d. $\{(8,5), (9,6), (10,7)\}$

2. Which equations represent examples of direct variation? Give the constant of proportionality for each direct variation.

   a. $C = 2\pi r$ b. $d = 3.4t$ c. $lw = 36$ d. $\frac{2}{3}x = y$

3. Find the missing value if (x_1,y_1) and (x_2,y_2) are ordered pairs of the same direct variation.

   a. $x_1 = 15, y_1 = 9$ b. $x_1 = 45, y_1 = ?$ c. $x_1 = 3.6, y_1 = 3$
   $\quad x_2 = 40, y_2 = ?$ $x_2 = 60, y_2 = 100$ $x_2 = ?, y_2 = 1$

   d. $x_1 = ?, y_1 = 7$ e. $x_1 = 10, y_1 = 100$ f. $x_1 = 5, y_1 = ?$
   $\quad x_2 = 7.65, y_2 = 9$ $x_2 = 5, y_2 = ?$ $x_2 = 3, y_2 = 9$

4. Given that $y \alpha x$, what is the effect on:
   a. x if y is doubled?   b. y if x is tripled?
   c. y if x is halved?   d. x if y is halved?

B 5. Given that y varies directly as x, and $y = 15$ when $x = 12$, find the constant of proportionality.

6. Given that $a \alpha b$, and that $a = 2.5$ when $b = 3$, find the value of a when $b = 9$.

7. Given that $p \alpha q$, and that $p = 16$ when $q = 10$, find the value of q when $p = 20$.

8. Given that $x \alpha y$, find y_2 if $x_1 = 6$, $y_1 = 8$, and $x_2 = 8$.

9. Given that $y \alpha x$ and $y = 15$ when $x = 10$, answer the following.
   a. Find the constant of proportionality.
   b. Find the equation relating x and y.
   c. Find x when $y = 16$.
   d. Find y when $x = 16$.
   e. Graph the equation and find its slope.
   f. Does the graph pass through the origin?

10. Given that $y \alpha x$, and that $x = 6$ when $y = 8$, answer the following.
    a. Find the equation relating x and y.
    b. Find x when $y = 4$.
    c. Find y when $x = 9$.
    d. Graph the equation and find its slope.
    e. Does the graph pass through the origin?

11. a. If $y \alpha x$, state the equation relating x and y.
    b. Describe the graph of the equation.

12. A soccer coach ordered three new uniforms for $48. Given that the cost varies directly as the number of uniforms ordered, answer the following. Let c be the cost in dollars and n be the number of uniforms ordered.
    a. Find the constant of proportionality.
    b. Find the equation relating c and n.
    c. How much would the coach pay for 12 new uniforms?

13. The number of words typed is directly proportional to the time spent typing. If Jim can type 225 words in five minutes, how long will it take him to type an essay 1125 words long?

14. Sales tax varies directly as the cost of an item. If $2 sales tax is added to the cost of a $25 item, what will be the sales tax charged on a $135 item?

15. The amount of oats needed in a cookie recipe is directly proportional to the amount of flour required. If the recipe calls for 750 g flour and 250 g oats, how much oats should be used with 325 g flour?

16. In a scale model of a sailboat, an object that is 2 m tall is represented by a figure 25 cm high. How tall should the mast of the sailboat be in the model if the actual mast of the sailboat is 12 m tall?

17. A sales representative for a cosmetics company, earning straight commission, makes $66.75 on sales of $1335. What is the representative's rate of commission? How much is earned on sales of $1750?

18. A labourer, earning a regular hourly wage, makes $318.75 in 25 hours. Find the length of time worked when the labourer has earned $459.

C 19. The shaded portion of the diagram at the right is equal in area to the inner circle.
    a. Prove that the area of the small circle is directly proportional to the area of the large circle.
    b. Does a vary directly as b? Explain.

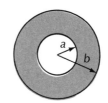

Using the Computer   A Program for Squares

Let N be a positive integer.

$f(N)$ is the sum of squares of digits of N, for example: $f(25) = 2^2 + 5^2 = 29$.
$g(N)$ is the sum of cubes of digits of N, for example: $g(25) = 8 + 125 = 133$.
$h(N)$ is the sum of fourth powers of digits of N, for example $h(25) = 16 + 625 = 641$.

Write a computer program in BASIC that will find all fixed points for f, g, and h. That is, find all N such that: **a.** $f(N) = N$;   **b.** $g(N) = N$;   **c.** $h(N) = N$.

7–4 Inverse Variation

Caroline cycles 36 km every Saturday as part of her fitness program. She realizes that if she doubles her speed, her time is cut in half; if she could triple her speed, her time would be one-third the original time.

Speed (km/h)	Time (h)	
(v)	(t)	vt
12	3	36
24	1.5	36
36	1	36

Since t decreases as v increases, we say that t **varies inversely** as v, or t is **inversely proportional** to v. In this example of inverse variation, v is related to t by the equation $vt = 36$. That is, the product of the variables involved is a constant, the constant of variation.

Since $vt = 36$ can also be written $t = \frac{36}{v}$, we can write: $t \alpha \frac{1}{v}$.

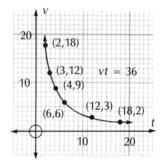

The graph of $vt = 36$ is *not* a straight line. It is part of a smooth curve called a **hyperbola**.

> In general, inverse variation is a function defined by an equation in the form $xy = k$, $k \neq 0$. The relation between the coordinates x and y is defined by the equation $y = \frac{k}{x}$,
>
> where k is the constant of proportionality and $x \neq 0$. If (x_1,y_1) and (x_2,y_2) are ordered pairs of the same inverse variation, then the coordinates satisfy the equation $xy = k$. Therefore, the equation $x_1y_1 = x_2y_2$ must be true.

Note that for direct variation, the *quotients* of the coordinates of an ordered pair are constant, and for inverse variation the *products* are constant.

EXAMPLE:
The thickness of a rubber sheet varies inversely as its area when it is stretched. If the thickness is 16 mm when its area is 25 m², what is the thickness when the rubber sheet is evenly stretched to an area of 100 m²?

Let t_1 and t_2 be the thickness of the sheet in millimetres.
Let A_1 and A_2 be the areas of the sheet in square metres.

There are two methods for solving for t_2 using $xy = k$.

a.
$$t_1A_1 = k$$
$$(16)(25) = k$$
$$k = 400$$
If $t_1A_1 = 400$, then $t_2A_2 = 400$
$$100t_2 = 400$$
$$t_2 = 4$$

b.
$$t_1A_1 = t_2A_2$$
$$(16)(25) = 100t_2$$
$$4 = t_2$$

The rubber sheet is 4 mm thick when its area is 100 m².

EXERCISES

A **1.** Which are examples of inverse variation? Explain.

    a. $xy = 8$ **b.** $m_1n_1 = m_2n_2$ **c.** $y = \frac{x}{k}$, $k \neq 0$ **d.** $\frac{x}{y} = 8$

    e. $\{(1,3), (2,6), (3,9), (4,12), (5,15)\}$ **f.** $\{(2,12), (3,8), (4,6), (6,4)\}$

B **2.** If x varies inversely as y, and $x = 5$ when $y = 3$, find y when $x = 15$.

3. Given that p varies inversely as q, and $p = 20$ when $q = 12$, answer the following.
    a. Find the constant of proportionality.
    b. Find the value of q when $p = 10$.
    c. Find the value of p when $q = 16$.

4. If x varies inversely as y, find the effect on x for the given condition.
    a. y is doubled.   **b.** y is halved.   **c.** y is tripled.

5. When the tension on the string of a harp is kept constant, the number of vibrations per second varies inversely as its length. A string vibrates at 480 vibrations per second when it is 0.9 m long. How long should the string be in order to vibrate at 360 vibrations per second?

6. Two masses, m_1 and m_2, can be balanced as shown. The mass required to balance one side of a lever is inversely proportional to its distance from the fulcrum. If a 30 g mass is 25 cm from the fulcrum, how far must a 10 g mass be placed from the fulcrum?

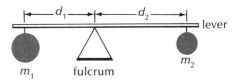

7. Travelling time varies inversely as the speed at which one travels.
    a. If a journey takes 3 h at 60 km/h, how long will it take at 80 km/h?
    b. What change in time occurs if the speed is doubled?

8. The value of a car varies inversely as its age.
    a. What is the value of a car at the end of three years if its value at the end of five years is $1500?
    b. Make a table of values and draw a graph to illustrate the relationship between the age of the car and its value.

Using the Computer

Identifying a Variation

Three ordered pairs from a relation are sufficient to determine whether they may result from a direct variation, an inverse variation, or neither. Write a program that accepts any three ordered pairs and determines whether they result from a direct or inverse variation. Run the program for the following sets of ordered pairs.

1. $\{(2,12), (-6,-4), (8,3)\}$ **2.** $\{(3,24), (-12,-6), (18,4)\}$

223

7–5 Partial Variation

The cost of having a luncheon catered at the Fireside Inn is $3.50 for each meal served plus a fixed $100 fee.

The cost consists of two parts: a *variable* fee which varies directly as the number of meals served; a *fixed* fee of $100. This is an example of **partial variation**.

The equation $c = 3.50m + 100$ defines the function. Note that the equation is in slope-intercept form, $y = mx + b$.

The graph illustrates that the function is linear. 3.50 is the slope and 100 is the y-intercept. Since the cost is written in terms of the number of meals served, the variable c is *dependent* on the variable m. Thus, m is the *independent* variable and is graphed on the horizontal axis.

Number of Meals Served (m)	Cost in Dollars (c)
20	20(3.50) + 100 = 170
40	40(3.50) + 100 = 240
60	60(3.50) + 100 = 310
80	80(3.50) + 100 = 380

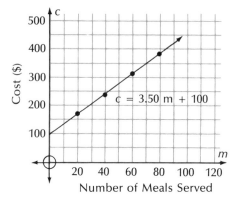

> Any two variables related by a linear equation $y = mx + b$, $b \neq 0$, are in partial variation.

EXAMPLE: Anita allows herself $24/month to spend on lunches from the school cafeteria. When she buys lunch at the cafeteria, she spends $1.50.
 a. How much money will Anita have after 7 school days?
 b. After how many school days will she have $15 left?

Let A be the amount of money in dollars Anita has left.
Let d be the number of school days that have passed.

Then $A = 24 - 1.50d$.

a. Substitute into the equation.
 $A = 24 - 1.50(7)$
 $= 24 - 10.50$
 $= 13.50$

 After 7 school days, Anita will have $13.50.

b. Graph the function $A = 24 - 1.50d$.

 Find a point on the graph that has 15 as its second element: (6,15).

 Anita will have $15 left after 6 school days.

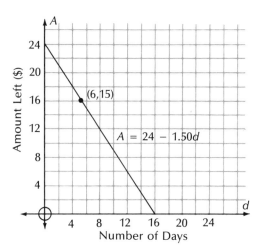

EXERCISES

A 1. If you booked a banquet for 65 people at the Fireside Inn, how much would it cost? Refer to the opening example for this lesson.

2. Which relations are examples of partial variation? (In all equations, k represents a constant.)

   a. $av = k$ b. $y = mx + k$ c. $x = \dfrac{k}{y}$

   d. $y = 3x - 2$ e. $x = -2y + 5$ f. $5x + 3y = -15$

3. The relation between a and b is given by $b = 3a + 4$.
   a. Find a when $b = -2$.   b. Find b when $a = 5$.

4. The equation $y = 2 - 6x$ represents a partial variation between x and y. Make a table of values and draw the graph of the relation.

B 5. Each of the graphs below represents a partial variation between x and y. Find an equation to represent each graph.

   a.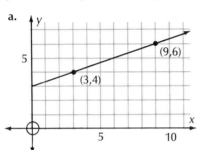

   b.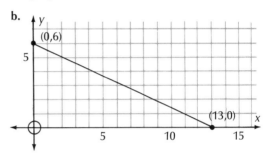

6. A limousine service charges a flat fee of $55 plus $14.50/h for Saturday rentals.
   a. Copy and complete the table to find an equation relating rental time and charge.

Rental Time in hours (t)	Charge in dollars (c)	Equation
1	$55 + 1(14.50) = 69.50$	
2		
5		
10		

   b. Graph the relation represented by the equation.
   c. Find the slope of the relation. In this situation, what does the slope represent?
   d. Find the vertical intercept of the relation. In this situation, what does the intercept represent?
   e. What is the charge for a rental time of 4.5 h?
   f. For how many hours was the limousine rented if the charge was $171?

7. A plumber charges a flat fee of $54 plus $24.50/h for service calls. A customer called the plumber for emergency repairs that took 4.5 h.
   a. Let x be time spent and y be charge. Write an equation to give the service charge for a call.
   b. Graph the relation represented by the equation.
   c. Find the slope and y-intercept of the relation. In this situation, what do the slope and intercept represent?
   d. Find the charge for a 4.5 h service call.

8. Bob works as a salesperson at a computer store, where he earns a fixed weekly salary of $150 plus a commission of 3% of all sales.
   a. How much does he earn if he sells $5000 in a week?
   b. How much must he sell in order to earn $390 in a week?

9. Janice works as a salesperson and earns a fixed weekly salary plus commission. One week, she earned $440 after selling $6000 worth of merchandise. In another week, she sold $7500 worth of merchandise and earned $500. Find her fixed weekly salary and rate of commission.

10. Bill and Jennifer bought personalized T-shirts with their first names on the back. The shirts cost a fixed amount and each letter printed on the shirt costs a certain amount. Bill's T-shirt cost $12.98; Jennifer's cost $15.98. Calculate the basic cost of the T-shirt and of each letter.

11. In the equation $y = 5x - 2$, y varies partially as x. If x increases from -6 to 8, what is the corresponding change in y?

C 12. At Arbour Inn, the cost of having a luncheon catered is $150 plus $3 for each meal served.
    a. Write an equation to represent the partial variation.
    b. Calculate the cost of serving 65 people.
    c. Determine, by graphing, the number of meals that must be served before it is more economical to have the banquet catered by Arbour Inn rather than Fireside Inn. Refer to the opening example.

13. Three car-rental companies are competing for the weekend market.

Company	Fixed Rate	Additional Cost per kilometre
Company A	$50	10¢
Company B	$30	15¢
Company C	$25	25¢

    a. For each company, find an equation relating total cost, c, to distance travelled, d.
    b. On the same grid, graph the relation represented by each equation.
    c. Discuss the circumstances under which it is to your advantage to rent from:
       i. Company A;   ii. Company B;   iii. Company C.

Review

1. Western High sent its top five track athletes to a county competition. Use the information in the table to write each indicated relation as a set of ordered pairs.

Athlete	100 m Dash	High Jump	Long Jump	Hurdles	Shot Put
Micki	14.3 s	1.51 m	6.09 m	18.7 s	12.2 m
Leslie	14.7 s	1.62 m	6.28 m	18.5 s	12.7 m
Pat	13.9 s	1.69 m	6.22 m	19.5 s	12.9 m
Jo	13.5 s	1.71 m	6.18 m	18.3 s	13.2 m
Bobbie	14.1 s	1.61 m	6.17 m	18.0 s	13.4 m

   a. {(athlete, 100 m dash time)}
   b. {(athlete, hurdles time)}
   c. {(athlete, shot put distance)}
   d. {(event, top athlete)}

2. State the domain and range of each of the following relations.
   a. {(2,4), (3,6), (4,8), (5,10)}
   b. $\{(x, 2x + 5)|x \in \{-2, -1, 0, 1, 2\}\}$

3. Which of the following relations represent functions?
   a. {(10, −3), (14,2), (10,0), (16,5)}
   b. {(4,8), (3,8), (5,0), (6,1)}
   c. $f:x \rightarrow 2x + 5$
   d. $g:x \rightarrow x^2 + 1$
   e. $\{(x,y)|x = 4, x,y \in R\}$
   f. $\{(x,y)|y = -2, x,y \in R\}$

4. Given the function $f(x) = x^2 + 2x$, with the set of real numbers as the domain, find the following.
   a. $f(0)$
   b. $f(-1.5)$
   c. $f(-15)$
   d. $f(\sqrt{5})$

5. Mary works at J-Mart part time. Her wages depend directly upon the number of hours she works. If she earns $145.25 for working 35 h, how many hours must she work to earn $215.80?

6. Given that $y \propto x$, and that $y = 12$ when $x = 15$, answer the following.
   a. Find the constant of proportionality.
   b. Find the value of y when x is 24.
   c. If x is increased by 15%, what is the effect on y?

7. Given that y varies inversely as x, and $y = 12$ when $x = 15$, answer the following.
   a. Find the constant of proportionality.
   b. Find the value of y when x is 24.
   c. If x is increased by 15%, what is the effect on y?

8. Travelling time varies inversely as the speed at which one travels. If a journey takes 3.5 h at an average speed of 80 km/h, how long will it take at an average speed of 70 km/h?

227

7–6 Graphing Non-Linear Relations

There are many examples in which a quantity varies either directly or inversely as the *square* of another quantity. For example, the area of a circle varies directly as the square of the radius: $A = \pi r^2$. *Pi* is the constant of proportionality.

This is an example of a **quadratic direct variation** in the form, $y = kx^2$, $k \neq 0$.

Circle	Area	Radius
x	78.5 mm²	5 mm
y	314 mm²	10 mm
z	706.5 mm²	15 mm

EXAMPLE 1:   As a rocket takes off and accelerates at a constant rate, the distance travelled varies directly as the time squared, at a constant acceleration rate. The relation is $d = \frac{1}{2}at^2$, where d is the distance in metres, t is the time in seconds, and a is the rate of acceleration. Find the distance travelled by a rocket, taking off at a constant acceleration of 25 m/s², after 6 s.

  a. Substitute $a = 25$ into the equation.

$$d = \frac{1}{2}at^2$$
$$= \frac{1}{2}(25)t^2$$
$$= 12.5t^2 \rightarrow \text{The constant is 12.5.}$$

  b. Substitute $t = 6$ in the relation.
$$d = 12.5(6)^2$$
$$= 450$$

The rocket will travel 450 m in the first 6 s.

Make a partial table of values and graph the relation.

Since the rocket is accelerating at a constant rate, we can assume a smooth progression from point to point. Join the points with a smooth curve.

t	d
0	0
1	12.5
2	50
3	112.5
4	200
5	312.5
6	450

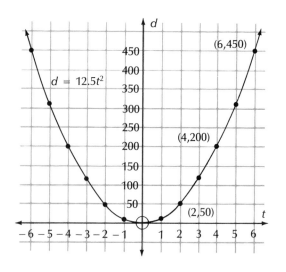

The graph of $d = 12.5t^2$ is a smooth curve called a **parabola**. Although the negative values are not appropriate in this situation, they are included to show the parabola.

In this situation, *d varies directly as t^2*.

If you double the distance between a table top and a lamp directly above it, the illumination is one fourth of what it was originally. If you triple the distance, the illumination is one ninth.

Illumination on a surface perpendicular to a light source *varies inversely* as the square of the distance from the light source. This is an example of **quadratic inverse variation**, in the form $y = \dfrac{k}{x^2}$, $x \neq 0$.

$E = \dfrac{I}{d^2}$, where E is the illumination measured in luxes, I is the intensity measured in candelas, and d is the distance in metres. Note that the *constant* in the inverse variation is the intensity.

The brightness, or intensity, I, of a light source is measured in units called candelas (cd). A 100 watt bulb gives about 130 cd. Illumination, E, is the amount of light energy per second that falls on a unit area. Illumination is measured in luxes (lx).

EXAMPLE 2:   a.   The illumination provided by a light on a desk top 2 m away is 16 lx. What is the intensity of the light source?

Solve for I using the formula

$$E = \dfrac{I}{d^2} \qquad 16 = \dfrac{I}{2^2}$$
$$I = 64$$

The intensity of the light source is 64 cd.

b.   For a 64 cd light source, find an equation relating illumination and distance from the light source for distances other than 2 m. Graph the relation represented by the equation.

$$E = \dfrac{I}{d^2} \text{ and } I = 64, \quad \text{so} \quad E = \dfrac{64}{d^2}$$

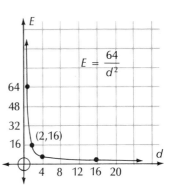

d	E
0	—
1	64
2	16
4	4
8	1
16	0.25
32	0.0625

Graph the points from the partial table of values.

A smooth curve joins the points.

Note that the curve does not cross either axis.

The graph shows that the further a surface gets from the source of light, the dimmer the illuminance on that surface becomes.

EXERCISES

A **1.** **a.** Make a table of values and graph the relation represented by $y = 3x^2$.
   b. Find the value of y when $x = 4$. Find the value of x when $y = 75$.

2. Given that $a \propto \frac{1}{b^2}$ and that $a = \frac{1}{2}$ when $b = 1$, find the value of a when $b = 4$. Find the value of b when $a = 8$.

3. Make a table of values and graph the relation represented by $y = 5\sqrt{x}$.

B **4.** Make a table of values of at least 8 ordered pairs and graph each relation on the same grid.

   a. $y = x^2$ **b.** $y = -x^2$ **c.** $y = 2x^2$
   d. $y = 0.5x^2$ **e.** $y = -0.5x^2$ **f.** $y = 5x^2$

5. Make a table of values of at least 8 ordered pairs and graph each relation on the same grid.

   a. $y = x^2 + 1$ **b.** $y = x^2 - 5$ **c.** $y = x^2 + 2$
   d. $y = x^2 + 0.5$ **e.** $y = x^2 - 1$ **f.** $y = x^2 - 3$

6. Make a table of values of at least 8 ordered pairs and graph each relation on the same grid.

   a. $y = \frac{1}{x}$ **b.** $y = \frac{1}{2x}$ **c.** $y = \frac{2}{x}$

   d. $y = -\frac{1}{x}$ **e.** $y = -\frac{24}{x}$ **f.** $y = \frac{1}{x^2}$

7. For each graph below, find the constant of proportionality, k. Find the defining equation of the relation.

a.

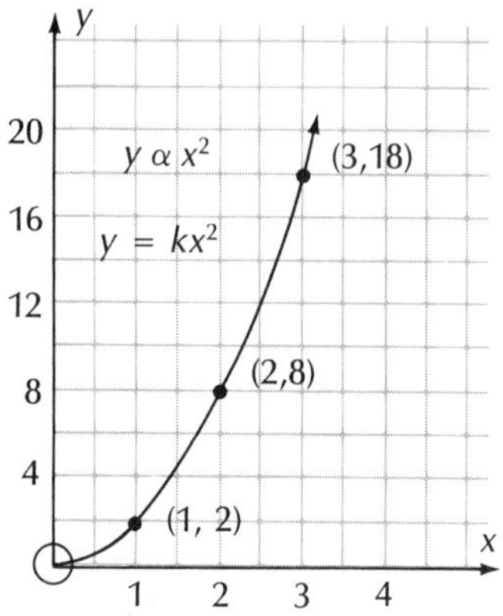

$y \propto x^2$
$y = kx^2$
(3,18)
(2,8)
(1, 2)

b.

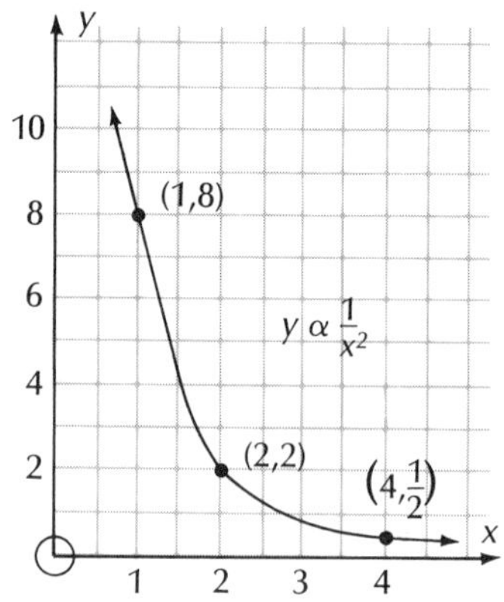

(1,8)
$y \propto \frac{1}{x^2}$
(2,2)
$\left(4, \frac{1}{2}\right)$

c.

(1,6)
$y \propto \frac{1}{\sqrt{x}}$
(4,8)
(16,4)

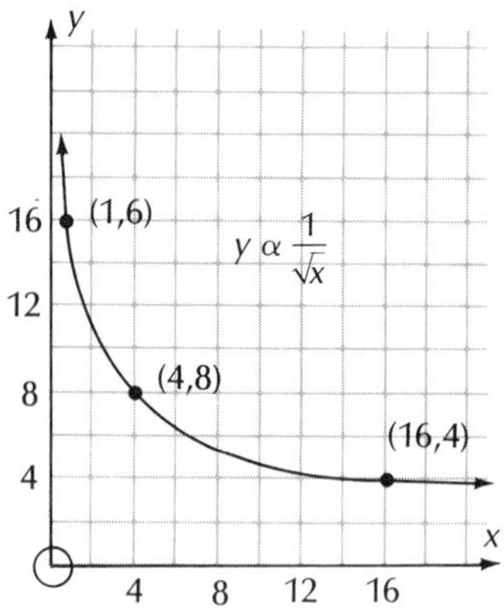

8. The area of a rectangle is 36 square units. This means that $xy = 36$, where x and y represent the lengths of the sides of the rectangle. Make a table of values and graph the relation.

9. Given that y varies directly as x^2, and that $y = 2$ when $x = 1$, answer the following.
   a. Find the constant of proportionality, k, in the equation $y = kx^2$.
   b. Write an equation relating x and y and make a table of values for x ranging from -5 to 5.
   c. Draw the graph of the relation represented by the equation.

10. Given that y varies directly as $\sqrt{x}$, and that $y = 12$ when $x = 4$, answer the following.
   a. Find the constant of proportionality and write an equation relating x and y.
   b. Make a table of values for $y \in \{0,6,12,18,24\}$.
   c. Graph the relation.

11. Given that y varies directly as x^3, and that $y = 0.25$ when $x = 0.5$, find the constant of proportionality and draw the graph of the relation.

12. Given that y varies inversely as x^2 and that $y = 8$ when $x = 4$, find the constant of proportionality and draw the graph of the relation.

13. As an object falls freely through the air, the distance travelled varies directly as the square of the time passed.
   a. Given that an object falls 19.6 m in 2 s, find an equation relating distance and time. Let d be the distance in metres and t be the time in seconds.
   b. Make a table of values and graph the relation represented by the equation.
   c. How far would an object fall in 1.5 s?
   d. How long would it take an object to fall 25 m?

14. The force due to gravity on an astronaut 6500 km above the centre of the earth is 600 N. Gravitational force varies inversely as the square of the distance to the centre of the earth. What is the force due to gravity on an astronaut 20 000 km above the centre of the earth? Answer correct to one decimal place.

Biography   **Hypatia of Egypt**

Hypatia (370 A.D. to 415 A.D.), from Alexandria, Egypt, was the first notable woman in mathematics. The daughter of Theon, also a mathematician and philosopher, she was well known for her beauty, her eloquence, and her remarkable intellect.

Hypatia devoted her time to studying astronomy and mathematics. Yet she lived in an environment where scholars were treated with great hostility by Christians, who considered learning and science to be pagan pursuits. Because of her interest in learning, Hypatia was barbarously murdered by a fanatical mob of Christians. Her murder initiated the departure of many scholars from Alexandria, and marked the beginning of the decline of Alexandria as a major centre of ancient learning.

7–7 Linear Interpolation

Students in a science lab recorded the temperature of a solution during the course of an experiment and graphed their results.

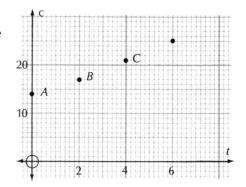

Time (*t* minutes)	Temp. (*c* degrees Celsius)
0 (Start)	14
2	17
4	21
6	25

The graph indicates that the temperature seemed to rise steadily. Although only four *exact* points are known, other values between the known points can be approximated from the graph.

EXAMPLE 1:   Approximate the temperature of the solution 3 min after the start of the experiment. That is, approximate the value of *c* when *t* = 3.

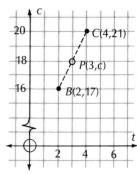

Even though the point (3,*c*) may not lie exactly in the line joining (2,17) and (4,21), it is nonetheless reasonable to expect it to be close to the line. Therefore a good approximation to the temperature at time 3 min is given by finding *c* so that *P*(3,*c*) is collinear with *B*(2,17) and *C*(4,21).

In this case, the value of *c* can be read directly from the graph: *c* = 19.

The solution temperature was about 19°C at time 3 min.

This method of approximating values, using a straight line joining two points, is called **linear interpolation**.

EXAMPLE 2:   Approximate the time at which the solution was 20°C. Find *t* so that *P*(*t*,20) is collinear with *B*(2,17) and *C*(4,21), the two points closest to *P*.

Since collinear points yield equal slopes:

Slope of $\overline{BP}$ = Slope of $\overline{BC}$ ⟹ $\dfrac{20-17}{t-2} = \dfrac{21-17}{4-2}$

$$\frac{3}{t-2} = 2$$
$$2(t-2) = 3$$
$$2t - 4 = 3$$
$$2t = 7$$
$$t = 3.5$$

The solution was 20°C about 3.5 min after the start of the experiment.

232

EXERCISES

A **1.** For each graph below, find the indicated value by reading from the graph.

a.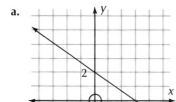

b.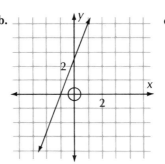

c.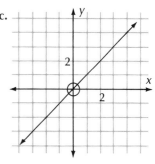

a.
  i. x when $y = 3$
  ii. y when $x = 2$

b.
  i. x when $y = 2$
  ii. y when $x = -1$

c.
  i. x when $y = 3$
  ii. y when $x = -4$

B **2.** Find the following.

  a. the value of x when $y = 2$
  b. the value of y when $x = -1$

Start by finding two ordered pairs on the graph.

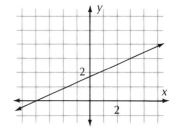

3. For the graph given at the right, use the slope formula to find the following.

  a. the value of x when $y = -2$
  b. the value of y when $x = 1$

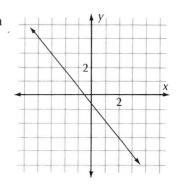

4. A line contains the points $A(5, -6)$ and $B(-1, 10)$. Find the value of y when x is 2.

5. **a.** Make a graph to illustrate the data in the table.
  b. Use linear interpolation to estimate Canada's population in 1955; in 1980.
  c. Approximate the time at which Canada's population was 20 000 000.

Canada's Population

Year	Population
1951	14 009 429
1961	18 238 247
1971	21 568 311
1981	24 343 181

C 6. The table gives average masses for North American males and females at ages from 12 to 65 years.

Age in years	12	14	16	18	25	45	65
Average Male Mass in kilograms	38.36	48.91	58.95	65.00	69.55	78.64	74.55
Average Female Mass in kilograms	39.82	49.27	53.18	54.55	56.36	63.18	60.91

   a. Graph the relations {(age, average male mass)} and {(age, average female mass)}.
   b. Use linear interpolation to estimate the average mass of males and females 20 years old.
   c. Use linear interpolation to estimate the average mass of males and females 50 years old.

7. A volcanic eruption creates one of the greatest releases of energy on Earth. The table gives the energy released by three volcanic eruptions, in Joules (J), and the mass of T.N.T. that would need to be exploded to achieve as great a release of energy. One megatonne (Mt) equals 1 000 000 t.

Eruption	Energy Released	T.N.T. Equivalent
Tambora, Indonesia, 1815	8×10^{19} J	20 000 Mt
Santorini, Greece, 1470 B.C.	3×10^{19} J	7500 Mt
Krakatoa, Indonesia, 1883	6×10^{18} J	1500 Mt

   a. Graph the relation {(energy released, T.N.T. equivalent)}.
   b. What is the T.N.T. equivalent of a volcano with an energy release of 6×10^{19} J?

8. The price of gasoline was 49.4¢/L on Saturday. On the following Wednesday, the price was 53.5¢/L. Can linear interpolation be used to determine the price of gasoline on Monday? Explain.

Historical Note

The Magic Square

Magic squares were originally thought to give protection against evil because of their special properties: the sum of each row, column, and diagonal is the same. Magic squares were even sold as good luck charms.

Use the magic square pattern at the right to devise your own good luck charm!

$a - x$	$a + x - y$	$a + y$
$a + x + y$	a	$a - x - y$
$a - y$	$a - x + y$	$a + x$

Review

1. Make a table of values and graph each of the following relations.

   a. $y = \frac{1}{2}x^2$ **b.** $x = 2y^2$ **c.** $y = 0.4x^2$

   d. $y = 2x^3$ **e.** $xy = 8$ **f.** $xy = 32$

2. For each relation in exercise 1, give its domain and range.

3. The area of a square varies directly as the square of its perimeter. If the area of a square is 36 cm² and its perimeter is 24 cm, find the area of a square with a perimeter of 44 cm.

4. Given that y varies inversely as x^2, and that y is 12 when x is 6, answer the following.

   a. Find the constant of proportionality.
   b. Find the value of y when x is 12.
   c. Find the value of x when y is 48.

5. The volume of a sphere varies directly as the cube of its radius. Given that a sphere of radius 3 cm has a volume of 36 cm³, answer the following.

   a. If x is the radius of a sphere and y is its volume, then $y = kx^3$. Find k, the constant of proportionality.
   b. Write an equation relating x and y.
   c. Graph the equation and give its domain and range.
   d. Find the volume of a sphere with a radius of 2.5 cm.
   e. Find the radius of a sphere with a volume of 288π cm³.

6. Find the indicated values.

   a.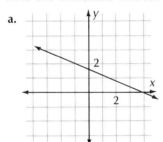
   i. y when $x = 1$
   ii. x when $y = 2$

   b.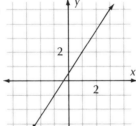
   i. x when $y = -2$
   ii. y when $x = -2$

   c.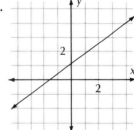
   i. x when $y = 3$
   ii. y when $x = -1$

7. A line contains the points $P(4,3)$ and $Q(0, -5)$. Find the value of y when x is 8.

EXTRA

A Construction Question

If three men can build three houses in three days, how many houses can seven men build in seven days?

235

Application

Investigating Models of Variation

Answer the following to investigate some concrete examples of variation.

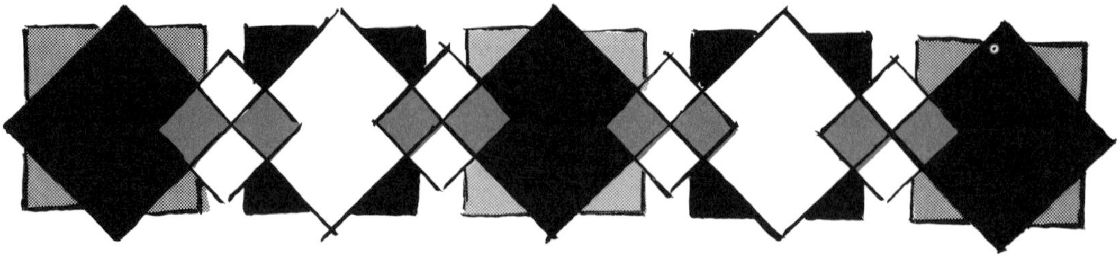

1. On a sheet of centimetre graph paper, draw squares that have side lengths of 1 cm, 2 cm, 3 cm, 4 cm, 5 cm, and 6 cm.

   a. Copy and complete the table below.

Side Length of Square	1 cm	2 cm	3 cm	4 cm	5 cm	6 cm
Perimeter of Square						
Area of Square						

   b. Graph the relation {(side length, perimeter)}.
   c. Graph the relation {(side length, area)}.
   d. Copy and complete the following statements.
   The perimeter of a square varies ______ its side length.
   The area of a square varies ______ its side length.

2. On a sheet of centimetre graph paper, draw 5 rectangles, each with an area of 36 cm^2.

   a. Copy and complete the table below.

Length					
Width					

   b. Graph the relation {(length, width)}.
   c. Copy and complete the following statement.
   If the area of a rectangle is constant, then the length varies ______ the width.

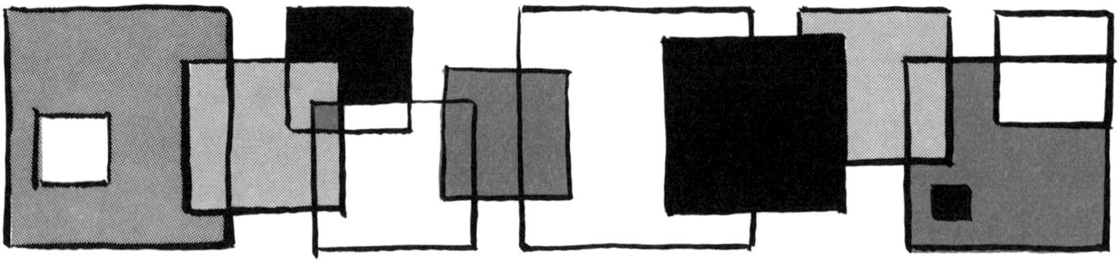

3. Using Plasticine, a heavy button, and 2.5 m of strong thread, set up a pendulum which can be varied in length. Using a stop watch, measure the time it takes the pendulum to go through five complete swings. Then divide this time by 5 to get an average time for one swing.

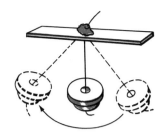

a. Copy and complete the table below.

Length of Pendulum	0.5 m	1.0 m	1.5 m	2.0 m
Time for One Swing (s)				

b. Graph the relation {(length of pendulum, time for one swing)}.
c. Copy and complete the following statement.
The time for one swing of a pendulum varies ▓▓▓▓▓▓▓▓ the length of the pendulum.

4. From the graphs at the bottom of this page, select the graph to fit into each part of the table below. You may want to copy the table into your notebook as a study guide.

Type of Variation	Symbolic Representation	Graph
Direct Variation	$y \propto x$	?
Inverse Variation	$y \propto \dfrac{1}{x}$	?
Quadratic Variation	$y \propto x^2$	?
Partial Variation	$y = mx + b$	?
Varying as the Square Root	$y \propto \sqrt{x}$	?

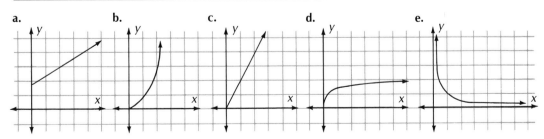

a.　　b.　　c.　　d.　　e.

Applying Relations

A **1.** Use the information in the flyer to answer the questions.

> ### PARTY FLAVOURS
>
> WE'LL DO THE PLANNING FOR YOU!
>
> The Sedate Dinner Party . . . . $150 plus $8.95 per person
> The Bridge Luncheon . . . . $55 plus $25 for a serving person
> Everyone Into the Pool! . . . . $122 plus 99¢ per person
> Quiet Evening at Home . . . .

    a. Select variables and write an equation to represent the cost for the Sedate Dinner Party.

    b. If you were planning a dinner party for 8 and wanted to use the services of Party Flavours, what would the charge be?

    c. If you were planning a dinner party for 15, but wanted to keep your expenses below $300, could you afford to use the services of Party Flavours? What would the charge be?

2. Use the information in the menu to answer the questions.

> ### ALFREDO'S PIZZA
>
> LUNCH MENU
>
> The Basic: pizza with tomato sauce $12.50
> (An additional 35¢ is charged for each topping.)
>
> The Special $13.65
> (mushrooms, green peppers, pepperoni, and cheese)

    a. Is the special a good buy?

    b. Under what conditions would a customer not want to order the special?

B **3.** Al cycles the same route every Saturday. The time it takes for him to complete the route varies inversely as his average speed. When his average speed is 12 km/h, it takes him 1 h 20 min.

    a. If Al increases his average speed to 15 km/h, how long will it take him to complete the route?

    b. How far does he cycle every Saturday?

4. The amount of time required to clear the tables in a restaurant varies inversely with the number of waiters, assuming that each waiter works at the same rate. If the tables can be cleared in 10 min by 3 waiters, how long would it take 4 waiters to clear the tables?

5. The cost of pies at a bake sale varies directly as the squares of their diameters. A pie with diameter 20 cm sells for $2.95.
   a. How much should be charged for a pie with a diameter of 25 cm?
   b. If a pie with diameter 23 cm is sold by the piece, with 6 pieces per pie, how much should be charged for each piece?

6. The kinetic energy of an object, measured in joules (J), varies directly as the square of its speed. An object with a speed of 5 m/s has a kinetic energy of 300 J. What is the kinetic energy of an object with a speed of 12 m/s?

7. The speed of a car varies directly as the square root of the distance required for it to stop. If a car takes 25 m to stop when it is travelling at a speed of 63 km/h, then how fast is a car going if, under the same conditions, it takes 36 m to stop?

8. The illuminance on a surface perpendicular to a light source varies inversely as the square of the distance from the light source. If the illuminance on a table 1 m directly under a lamp is 12 lx, what would the illuminance on the table be if the lamp were 2 m away?

9. The time required for one complete swing of a pendulum varies directly as the square root of its length. A pendulum 50 cm long takes 1.42 s to complete one swing. How long will it take for a 75 cm long pendulum to complete one swing?

C 10. Three women want to rent a cottage for a week. The rent for the cottage is $250/week and the women estimate that they will spend $15/day on food for the three of them over the seven days.
   a. Define variables and set up an equation that relates expenses for the week and number of days spent.
   b. Apply the equation to find the cost for one full week.
   c. How much would each girl's share be?
   d. The women decide that the cottage would cost too much for just the three of them. How many other women should they include in order that each person's share be a maximum of $100? Take into account that food allowance must increase if more people are included.

11. The volume of a cylinder, where the height is held constant, is directly proportional to the square of the radius. Two cylindrical glasses of the same height have diameters in the ratio 3:2. The larger glass has a volume of 342 cm³. What is the volume of the smaller glass?

Test

1. Make an arrow diagram for the relation given by $f{:}x \rightarrow 2x + 1$, for $x \in \{-1,0,1,2,3\}$. Determine whether f is a function and explain why or why not.

2. Graph each relation defined below. Which are functions?
   a. $\{(x,y)|y = 0.5x - 1, x,y \in R\}$
   b. $\{(x,x^2)|x \in R\}$
   c. $\{(x,y)|x + 3 = 0, x \in Z\}$
   d. $g{:}x \rightarrow 2x$

3. Give the domain and range of each relation in exercise 2.

4. For $g(x) = 3x - 5$, find the following.
   a. $g(0)$
   b. $g(-1)$
   c. $g(3.5)$
   d. $g(-17)$

5. Given that $y \propto x$, and that x is 12 when y is -5, find y when x is 7.

6. Given that p varies inversely as q, describe the effect on q when p is doubled.

7. Tony works as a salesperson. He has a fixed salary of $180/week, and earns 4% commission on all sales.
   a. How much does he earn if he sells $4500 worth of merchandise in a week?
   b. How much must he sell to earn $440 in a week?

8. For $f(x) = 2x^2$, find the following.
   a. $f(-2)$
   b. $f(2)$
   c. $f(0)$
   d. $f(-0.5)$

9. Using the function f given in exercise 8, make a table of values and graph f. Give the domain and range of f.

10. Make a table of values and graph each of the following relations.
    a. $x = y^2$
    b. $y = 3x^2$
    c. $y = 2x^3$
    d. $xy = 24$
    e. $xy = 15$
    f. $y = \frac{1}{4}x^2$

11. A line contains the points $A(-3,-5)$ and $B(6,3)$. Use linear interpolation to find the value of x when y is -2.

12. As a spherical balloon is inflated, its surface area varies directly as the square of its radius. A balloon with an initial radius of 25 cm is blown up so that its radius is 32 cm and its surface area is 4096π cm². Find the surface area of the balloon when the radius was 25 cm.

13. The wind pressure exerted on a flat surface varies directly as the square of the wind speed. If a 10 km/h wind exerts a pressure of 11.6 Pa, what wind speed will exert a pressure of 40 Pa?

Cumulative Review

1. Rewrite the following as entire radicals. Assume all variables are positive.
   a. $2\sqrt{3}$ b. $7\sqrt{7}$ c. $x\sqrt{3}$ d. $5\sqrt{k}$ e. $2y\sqrt{3z}$

2. Which of the following are right-angled triangles?

   a.   b.   c. 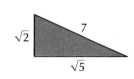   d.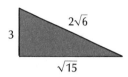

3. Solve and check.
   a. $3(x + 9) - 2 = 4$ b. $7(k + 6) - 20 = 22$ c. $2(b + 9) = 3(b + 7)$
   d. $\dfrac{2(m + 8)}{15} = \dfrac{8}{5}$ e. $7 + \dfrac{x}{2} = -\dfrac{2x}{3}$ f. $\dfrac{a}{5} - \dfrac{11}{2} = \dfrac{a}{3} - \dfrac{a}{2}$

4. Solve each inequality and graph the solution on a number line.
   a. $2x + 7 \le -3$ b. $14 > 3k - 2$ c. $-7 \le 4x + 5 \le 1$

5. Find an equation of the line containing the given pair of points.
   a. $P(4,2)$, $Q(-1,0)$ b. $A(7,-3)$, $B(4,-1)$ c. $J(3,2)$, $K(0,0)$

6. Use the given information to find the missing values in each.
   a. $Ax + 3y + 9 = 0$; $m = -\dfrac{2}{3}$ b. $5x + By + C = 0$; $m = -5$; $b = 3$

7. Solve each system of equations using the method of your choice.
   a. $2x + 8y = 14$ b. $4x + 3y = 5$ c. $5x - 2y = 22$
      $4x + 2y = 0$ $2y + 4x = 0$ $2x + y = 23$

8. Graph each inequality.
   a. $3x + 4y + 7 \le 0$ b. $y > 3x - 2$ c. $y < -\dfrac{1}{2}x - 2$

9. Graph each system of inequalities. Check for one point in the region in each case.
   a. $x \le y$ b. $x + y \le 1$
      $2y > x$ $2x - y \ge -3$
      $x \ge 0$

10. Solve and check each quadratic equation.
    a. $x^2 + 6x + 9 = 0$ b. $9x^2 = 49$ c. $6x^2 - x = 1$
    d. $30x = 3x^2 + 27$ e. $4x^2 + 10x + 6 = 0$ f. $4x^2 = 36$

11. Simplify and state any restrictions on the variables.
    a. $\dfrac{4xy}{x^2}$ b. $\dfrac{a + 5}{a^2 + 12a + 35}$ c. $\dfrac{k - 2}{4 - k^2}$ d. $\dfrac{d^2 + d - 2}{d^2 - 1}$

8 Statistics

8–1 Measures of Central Tendency

The students in a mathematics class received the marks shown at the right on a test. The list of marks is not organized in any apparent way. It is a set of **raw data**.

5, 7, 4, 6, 8,
10, 8, 9, 2, 5,
7, 9, 6, 4, 7,
8, 8, 6, 4, 6,
8, 9, 6, 6, 7

If a set of data must be characterized by a single representative value, then it would be appropriate to use one that is close to a central value of the set. The *mean*, *median*, and *mode* provide three different **measures of central tendency**.

1. The **mean** is the total of the values, divided by the number of values.

   Mean $= \dfrac{165}{25} = 6.6$ The mean of the set of test marks is 6.6.

2. The **median** is the middle value of the data listed in numerical order.

   Listed in descending order, the marks are:
   10, 9, 9, 9, 8, 8, 8, 8, 8, 7, 7, 7, 7, 6, 6, 6, 6, 6, 6, 5, 5, 4, 4, 4, 2.

   With 25 students altogether, the middle test mark occurs at the thirteenth position. The median is 7.

   $\dfrac{25 + 1}{2} = 13$

3. The **mode** is the most frequently occurring value.

   The mode is 6, since it is the test mark that occurred most frequently.

   In some situations, there may be one measure of central tendency that provides a more representative measure of the data than the others.

EXAMPLE: On a second test, the 25 mathematics students received the marks listed, in ascending order, at the right. Does the mean, median, or the mode best represent this set of data?

10,	13,	15,	21,	23,
50,	51,	53,	53,	58,
60,	60,	66,	66,	67,
67,	68,	69,	70,	71,
80,	80,	80,	82,	92

Mean = 57   Median = 66   Mode = 80

In this case, the median best represents the general performance of the class, since about half of the students are above the median mark and about half are below.

Note: To find the median of an *even* number of values, find the *two* middle values and calculate their mean.

EXERCISES

A 1. Find the mean, median, and mode of each of the following sets of data. Round to the nearest tenth if necessary.

    a. {37, 40, 38, 40, 42, 38, 40, 42, 44, 35, 38, 43, 39, 44, 40}
    b. {13, 11, 17, 16, 13, 18, 16, 19, 17, 13, 16, 12, 13, 11, 16, 13}
    c. {12.5, 11.0, 10.2, 11.6, 8.3, 8.5, 14.2, 9.1, 10.2, 10.7, 9.1, 10.2}
    d. {12, −8, 10, 6, −5, 15, 0, 3, −9, 2, 7, −4}

B

2. A survey of 25 gas stations was taken to find the price per litre of regular fuel. What are the mean and the median price?

53.8,	54.5,	54.1,	53.6,	53.8,
53.8,	54.1,	53.9,	53.9,	53.6,
53.8,	53.9,	53.6,	53.9,	53.6,
53.6,	53.9,	53.9,	54.1,	53.6,
53.8,	53.8,	53.9,	53.9,	53.6

3. Insert a new number into each set of data so that the mean becomes the given number.

    a. {4, 8, 15}; mean = 12   **b.** {4, 7, 11, 14}; mean = 8
    c. {4500, 3250, 3900}; mean = 3850   **d.** {45.3, 50.8, 41.9}; mean = 46.5

4. **a.** Find the mean, median, and mode of goals scored per game by each hockey team.
    b. For each team, which of the three measures of central tendency best represents the data? Why?

Team	Goals Scored Per Game
A	2 3 3 6 0 1 3 2
B	5 3 0 1 3 5 5 1
C	1 0 6 2 1 6 6 2

C 5. Joanna wants to complete the 6 laps of a race with a mean time not exceeding 1.25 minutes per lap. Her times in minutes for the first 5 laps were 1.15, 1.35, 1.20, 1.30, and 1.20.

    a. What time is needed in the last lap to attain the desired mean time?
    b. If, instead of a mean not exceeding 1.25 minutes per lap, Joanna wants a median time of 1.25 minutes per lap, how long must she take on the last lap?

243

8–2 Frequency Distributions

As part of its quality control, the Crisper Cracker Company selects samples of 20 boxes of crackers and counts the number of crackers in each box.

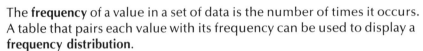

Sample K

108, 110, 109, 108, 111, 109, 109, 110, 107, 109, 111, 109, 108, 110, 108, 110, 109, 111, 109, 108

The quality control inspectors are interested in seeing how frequently each value in the list occurs.

The **frequency** of a value in a set of data is the number of times it occurs. A table that pairs each value with its frequency can be used to display a **frequency distribution**.

The data from sample K are listed in a frequency distribution table below.

Number of Crackers	Tally	Frequency
107	I	1
108	⊬⊬	5
109	⊬⊬ II	7
110	IIII	4
111	III	3
Total		20

Complete the tally column by reading through the sample and recording the occurrence of each value.

The first column shows that the *greatest* and *least values* in the set of data are 111 and 107. The difference between these two values is the **range**. In this case, the range is 111 − 107, or 4.

Frequency tables can easily be extended to simplify the calculation of the measures of central tendency. The frequency table for sample K is repeated below, with two additional columns.

Number of Crackers (x)	Frequency (f)	Cumulative Frequency	Subtotal ($x \times f$)
107	1	1	107
108	5	6	540
109	7	13	763
110	4	17	440
111	3	20	333
Total	20		2183

EXAMPLE 1: Find the mean, median, and mode of the quality control data collected in sample K.

a. In the Subtotal column, 2183 is the total number of crackers found in all 20 boxes.

Mean = 2183 ÷ 20
= 109.15

b. The Cumulative Frequency column shows that the tenth and eleventh positions, or the middle positions of the 20 ordered values, are held by 109 and 109. Thus, the median is 109.

c. The Frequency column shows that the value occurring most often is 109; the mode is 109.

When a set of data is very large, or when it involves real numbers rather than integers, data can be grouped into **intervals**.

EXAMPLE 2: A class survey revealed the data given at the right. Make a frequency table from the data, find the interval in which the median lies, and estimate the mean.

Notice that the heights range from 153 cm to 178 cm. If you made a table with an entry for each height in this range, you would need 25 entries in the table.

Student Heights (cm)
174, 162, 166, 171, 154,
155, 163, 168, 175, 156,
167, 178, 170, 165, 160,
158, 153, 161, 178, 170,
173, 169, 167, 170, 168

It is probably more efficient to group the data into intervals of 5 cm each. For the Subtotal column, the midpoint of the corresponding interval is used.

Height in centimetres	Tally	Freq. (f)	Cum. Freq.	Midpoint of Interval (x)	Subtotal (x × f)
150–154	II	2	2	152	304
155–159	III	3	5	157	471
160–164	IIII	4	9	162	648
165–169	IHI II	7	16	167	1169
170–174	IHI I	6	22	172	1032
175–179	III	3	25	177	531
Total		25			4155

The median height lies in the interval 165–169, since the thirteenth value is in that interval.

The mean can only be estimated, since grouping the data into intervals means that some of the detail of the raw data is lost. The *estimated* mean is 4155 ÷ 25, or 166.2 cm. (The exact mean is calculated using the total of all heights: 4151 ÷ 25, or 166.0 cm.)

EXERCISES

A **1.** For each set of data, make a frequency table, including columns for Cumulative Frequency and Subtotal. Use the table to find range, mean, median, and mode of the data.

  a. Numbers of family cars: 1, 2, 1, 3, 1, 2, 3, 4, 2, 2, 1, 2

  b. Test marks: 6, 7, 8, 6, 5, 10, 8, 4, 6, 7, 5, 7, 9, 8, 6, 7, 5, 6, 8, 8, 7, 7, 5, 6, 6, 7, 6, 7, 4, 7

  c. Gasoline prices per litre: 53.2¢, 54.1¢, 53.9¢, 54.1¢, 54.1¢, 53.8¢, 53.9¢, 53.8¢, 54.1¢, 53.2¢, 54.1¢, 53.9¢, 54.1¢, 54.1¢

  d. Home runs per season: 20, 22, 21, 24, 19, 22, 24, 25, 20, 20, 24, 19

  e. Tonnes of ore mined: 112, 113, 110, 116, 114, 111, 113, 112, 114, 118, 117, 115, 114, 112, 115, 114, 116, 115, 117, 111, 114

2. Copy and complete the table giving students' weekly earnings from part-time jobs.

Earnings	Frequency (f)	Cumulative Frequency	Midpoint of Interval (x)	Subtotal (x × f)
$30–$39.99	10	?	$34.50	?
$40–$49.99	13	?	$44.50	?
$50–$59.99	22	?	?	?
$60–$69.99	29	?	?	?
$70–$79.99	18	?	?	?
$80–$89.99	8	?	?	?

B **3.** Group the heights shown in example 2 into intervals of 10 cm and organize the data in a table.

  a. In what interval does the median lie?

  b. Estimate the mean height from the grouped data in the table. Explain why your result is not the estimate found in example 2.

4. Make a frequency table for the data given below. Use the table to find the range, mean, median, and mode of the data.

> **Total annual precipitation in centimetres for 30 years**
> 81, 80, 85, 77, 78, 81, 82, 81, 83, 78, 76, 81, 81, 82, 83, 80, 83, 81, 84, 85, 81, 78, 81, 80, 82, 83, 82, 78, 81, 83

5. a. Find the range, mean, median, and mode of the salaries in the table at the right.

  b. Which measure of central tendency would most favourably describe the data if you were a union worker for the company?

  c. Which measure would most favourably describe the data if you were the owner of the company?

Title	Number of Employees	Yearly Salary
Manager	1	$75 000
Assistant Manager	1	$68 000
Engineer	1	$36 000
Foreman	2	$25 000
Shipper	3	$21 000
Production Worker	9	$18 000

246

6. A company developed a new flavour of ice cream and conducted a taste test in a shopping mall. Responses were recorded as T (terrible), S (satisfactory), G (good), and F (fantastic).

Taste Test Results
S, G, G, T, F, G, T, S, S, G, S, T, T, G, S, G, G, T, S, F, T, G, T, S, T

a. Make a frequency table of the data.
b. What is (are) the mode(s) of the data?
c. Do you think the company should consider marketing their new flavour? Why?

7. Make a frequency table of the data below, including columns for Cumulative Frequency and Subtotal, grouping the data into intervals of 5 kg. Find the mean from the raw data and compare it to the mean as estimated from the grouped data.

Class 10B, Masses of Students (in kilograms)
55.3, 58.2, 47.1, 69.3, 52.9, 63.8, 68.5, 45.7, 51.0, 63.2,
66.1, 57.4, 48.9, 56.7, 46.3, 50.2, 61.3, 57.6, 48.7, 62.5

8. a. Copy and complete the table giving the results of car-tire tread-wear tests.

Tread Life in kilometres	Freq. (f)	Cum. Freq.	Midpoint of Interval (x)	Subtotal (x × f)
40 000–40 999	3	?	?	?
41 000–41 999	7	?	?	?
42 000–42 999	5	?	?	?
43 000–43 999	8	?	?	?
44 000–44 999	2	?	?	?
Total	?			?

b. From the table, estimate the mode, median, and mean of the data.

C 9. The table gives partial results of a survey of nine families on a suburban street. Copy and complete the table so that the mean, median, and mode are all equal.

Number of Children	Number of Families
0	
1	2
2	
3	
4	1

10. Under what conditions is it possible for the greatest number in a set of data to be the mean? the median? the mode?

11. Two classes were given the same test. The mean mark for the first class was 64, while the mean mark for the second was 60. Does this necessarily imply that the mean mark for all the students in the two classes was 62? Explain.

8–3 Bar Graphs and Histograms

Bar graphs are generally used to display sets of data with values in separate and distinct categories.

EXAMPLE 1: The yearly profits for Smith & Co. are shown in the table.

a. Display the data in a bar graph.
   Plot the profit in $10 000 intervals.

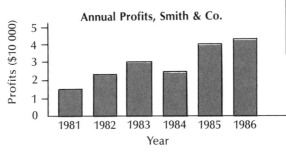

Annual Profits, Smith & Co.

Year	Profit
1981	$150 000
1982	$230 000
1983	$300 000
1984	$250 000
1985	$400 000
1986	$430 000

b. Is there any general trend apparent in the data?
   Except for 1984, the trend seems to be that profits are increasing.

Histograms are used to display frequency distributions. In a histogram, *no space* is left between the bars.

EXAMPLE 2: The frequency distribution at the right is a set of scores on a ten-point quiz.

a. Display the distribution in a histogram.
b. Find the mode from the histogram.
c. Find the median from the histogram.

Score	Frequency
4	2
5	4
6	7
7	9
8	11
9	5
10	4
Total	42

a.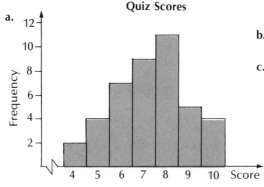

b. The mode occurs at the tallest bar. The mode is 8.

c. With 42 scores altogether, the median is the average of the twenty-first and twenty-second scores. Adding the heights of bars from left to right reveals that items 21 and 22 occur in the bar corresponding to a score of 7. The median is 7.

Large numbers of data often need to be grouped into intervals as they are included in a graph, as shown in the example below.

The plans for a sports-car engine call for a cylinder bore of 89.00 mm. The quality control engineers have selected a random sample of 25 motors and measured their cylinder bores to see how they conform to the specified size. The results of their measurements are shown at the right.

88.92, 89.13, 88.89, 88.86, 88.95,
89.03, 89.04, 89.08, 89.12, 89.04,
89.20, 89.06, 88.83, 88.91, 89.18,
88.98, 88.94, 89.23, 89.07, 89.13,
89.00, 89.24, 89.11, 88.87, 88.99

A histogram would give a good visual display of the data. The engineers could see general trends in the data and then possibly decide whether corrective action is needed in the manufacturing process.

In the frequency table, data has been grouped into intervals of 0.1 mm.

Intervals	Tally	Frequency
88.80–88.89	IIII	4
88.90–88.99	HHT I	6
89.00–89.09	HHT II	7
89.10–89.19	HHT	5
89.20–89.29	III	3

Graphing from the table results in the histogram shown at the right.

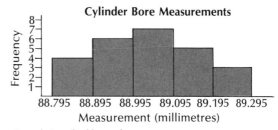

Cylinder Bore Measurements

Notice that the horizontal axis labels are the points lying halfway between consecutive intervals. This ensures that "borderline" values, like 88.89, clearly fall into the correct bar.

EXERCISES

A 1. Group each set of data into appropriate interval sizes.
   a. {64, 76, 45, 61, 59, 73, 58, 42, 53, 67, 48, 51, 43, 62, 55, 49, 42, 56, 72}
   b. {2.72, 1.95, 1.56, 3.45, 2.39, 4.14, 3.00, 2.89, 4.31, 2.68, 1.76, 3.85, 2.55}
   c. {2125, 5210, 3320, 3672, 5451, 4438, 4793, 3067, 4109, 2481, 2276, 3035}

B 2. Make a frequency table and a histogram for each set of data below, choosing appropriate interval sizes. Then find the interval containing the median of each set of data.

   a. **100 m Dash (in seconds)**
      12.1, 14.4, 13.8, 12.5, 12.8, 11.3, 10.8, 11.2, 12.6, 13.3,
      14.1, 13.9, 12.2, 11.0, 10.7, 12.2, 11.3, 13.6, 10.5, 11.9

   b. **200 m Dash (in seconds)**
      26.3, 24.1, 23.0, 24.7, 25.0, 27.1, 29.2, 26.4, 24.3, 23.5,
      23.2, 22.1, 27.8, 25.3, 23.8, 24.3, 28.0, 22.3, 26.9, 25.7

c. 400 m Dash (in seconds)
55.8, 61.0, 68.4, 57.0, 58.4, 54.7, 52.7, 55.1, 60.9, 62.4, 61.7, 66.3, 59.2, 54.1, 60.2, 50.8, 64.3, 57.5, 65.1, 56.3

d. 8 km Cross-country Run (in minutes)
30:17, 30:26, 30:49, 30:52, 31:05, 31:12, 31:18, 31:32, 31:10, 31:45, 31:51, 32:00, 32:11, 32:38, 32:47, 32:58, 33:07, 33:07, 33:21, 33:27, 33:39, 33:41, 33:50, 34:13, 34:35, 34:47, 35:02, 35:22, 35:31, 35:40

3. Make a bar graph to display the data at the right.
   a. What is the most popular sport?
   b. Compare the participation in fishing and hunting in the form of a ratio.
   c. Why does the total of all participants exceed the total combined population of Canada and the United States?

The Top Ten Leisure Sports in Canada and the U.S.

Sport	Participation
Swimming	775 000 000
Cycling	57 000 000
Camping	51 000 000
Fishing	50 000 000
Bowling	40 000 000
Weight Training	39 000 000
Running	32 000 000
Softball	26 000 000
Hunting	25 000 000
Hiking	23 000 000

4. Make a histogram from the frequency distribution table at the right.
   a. How many people surveyed receive 4 or more magazines?
   b. How many people were surveyed?
   c. What is the median of the data? the range? the mode?
   d. To the nearest tenth, what is the mean number of magazines received?

Magazine Subscriber Survey

Number of Magazines	Frequency
1	5
2	9
3	10
4	12
5	12
6	7
7	2

5. Refer to the double bar graph at the right.
   a. What major change has taken place in the Ontario work force from 1960 to 1980?
   b. What percent increase was there from 1960 to 1980 in male workers?
   c. By what percent of the 1960 figure has the female work force increased over the 20-year period shown?
   d. Express the number of female workers as a percentage of the labour force for each of the three years shown.

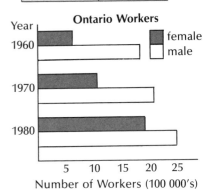

Ontario Workers

250

6. For each double histogram following, answer the questions.
   a. For native males, which age group makes up the greatest portion of the population?
   b. What percent of the female non-native population is between 40 and 44 years old?
   c. What percent of the non-native population is under age 25?
   d. List some reasons for the differences in the age distributions for the populations.

Native People Age-Sex Profile

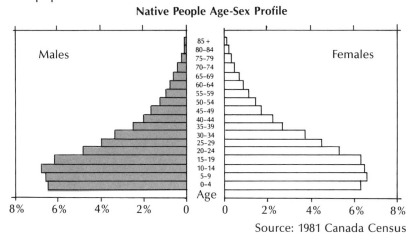

Source: 1981 Canada Census

Non-native People Age-Sex Profile

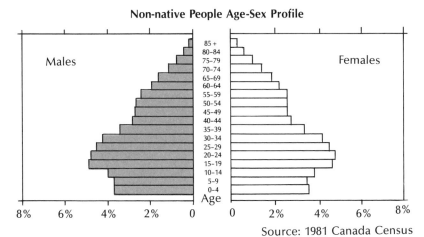

Source: 1981 Canada Census

7. a. Display the data at the right in a double bar graph.
   b. Which country had the largest relative increase in per capita income from 1973 to 1983?

National Per Capita Income

Country	Income ($1000 U.S.)	
	1973	1983
England	2300	7500
Canada	4000	11 000
Japan	3000	7700
United States	5000	13 900

8–4 Stretching the Truth

Many graphs in the media and advertising are skillfully arranged to present information in a favourable way. Altering the grouping, scale, or the data selected can change the impression made. The following brochure shows you some misleading graphs.

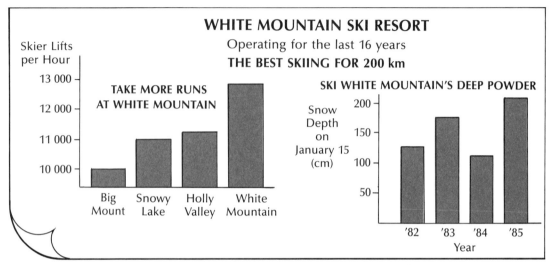

According to the advertising, White Mountain is a great place to ski, but a closer look at the data may show otherwise.

EXAMPLE 1:   a.   What impression is made by the first graph?

From the graph, it looks as if the lift capacity at White Mountain is double that of its nearest competitor. Reading from the graph, White Mountain's lift capacity is 13 000, while Holly Valley's is 11 000. These numbers are actually quite close.

b.   How is the impression created?

In this graph, the relative lengths of the bars have been distorted by breaking the scale on the vertical axis. If the scale *must* be broken because of space constraints, it should be visually indicated both on the axis *and* in each bar.

EXAMPLE 2:   a.   What impression is made by the second graph?

From the graph, it looks as if White Mountain always has lots of deep snow. At least, for the 4 years shown, White Mountain has had deep snow.

b.   What is misleading about the graph?

Read the brochure again: White Mountain has been open for the last 16 years. Why, then, are only 4 years shown in the second graph? Perhaps the figures before 1982 were very low. It would be useful to have more information.

EXERCISES

A 1. For each quote below, decide whether you would accept the statement as it is given. Would the quote influence you to purchase the item described? Explain your decision in each case.
  a. "Four out of five dentists recommend the use of Brand X toothpaste for their patients."
  b. "In five out of six blind taste tests, test subjects preferred the taste of Qualitee Ice Cream."
  c. "Over six million burgers served here."

2. Refer to the graph at the right to answer the following.
  a. By comparing the lengths of the vertical bars, comment on the improved circulation for the month of March.
  b. Redraw the histogram so that there is no break in the vertical scale. Comment on the circulation for March.

Newspaper Subscriber Survey

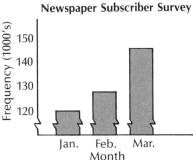

B 3. The pictograph at the right was used to display the profits of the National Investment Fund.
  a. What are the profits indicated for 1982 and 1985?
  b. Compare the 1985 profit and the 1982 profit as a ratio.
  c. Measure the heights of the coins for 1982 and 1985. Compare the heights as a ratio.
  d. How do the ratios in parts **b.** and **c.** compare?
  e. What impression is the advertisement trying to make?

National Investment Fund

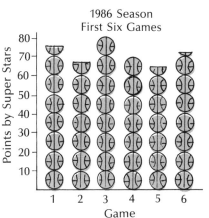

4. The coach of the City Super Stars basketball team made the graph at the right to show how consistently the team scores.
  a. What is the difference between the greatest and least scores?
  b. Express the difference as a percent of the least score.
  c. How has the coach arranged the presentation to make the scores *appear* more consistent?

**1986 Season
First Six Games**

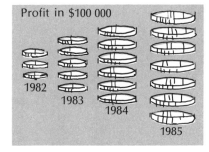

253

5. The mean February high temperatures at Sunny Sea Resort for the last 15 years are given below.

Mean February temperatures in degrees Celsius
25, 20, 15, 15, 25, 20, 25, 26, 20, 15, 21, 15, 22, 26, 25

Based on the data in the list above, Sunny Sea Resort used the histogram at the right as part of their advertising in a tourism magazine.

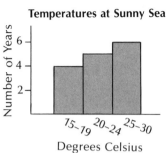

Temperatures at Sunny Sea

a. Calculate the mean, median, and mode from the set of raw data.

b. Using midpoints of the intervals, calculate the mean temperature indicated by the graph, and estimate the median. What is the most common temperature indicated?

c. How has the graph been presented to give a better impression of the data?

EXTRA

Breaking the Habit

The bar graph below is based on data from Health and Welfare Canada. Refer to the graph to answer the following questions.

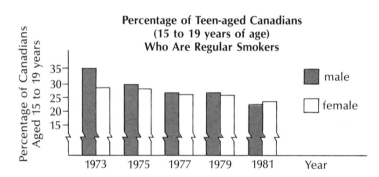

1. What has been the general trend in teen-age smoking over the years 1972 to 1981?

2. What are the differences between the trends for male and female teenagers?

3. Discuss possible reasons for these general trends.

4. Studies have shown that more smokers are breaking the habit. Suppose that over the years 1981 to 1986, about 16.0% of male smokers aged 20 to 24 years quit, while 19.0% of female smokers in the same age range also quit. Predict the percent of the population aged 20 to 24 years that would have been smoking in 1986 if there were no new smokers in the 20–24 age range.

254

Review

1. Calculate the mean and median of the following data:
   9, 27, 13, 19, 16, 23, 28, 11, 15, 18, 25, 14, 17, 10.

2. Sue attempted her figure skating program 11 times and her coach gave her the following scores: 5.1, 4.9, 5.2, 5.3, 5.0, 4.9, 5.3, 4.0, 5.3, 5.1, 5.2.
   a. Calculate her mean, median, and mode scores.
   b. Which number best represents the set of scores?

3. Copy and complete the table. Use the table to estimate the mean, and find the interval in which the median lies.

Growth Rates, Week 1, Puppy Group 7

Change in Height	Freq. (f)	Cum. Freq.	Midpoint of Interval (x)	Subtotal (x × f)
0 mm– 4 mm	2	2	2 mm	4
5 mm– 9 mm	4	?	?	?
10 mm–14 mm	3	?	?	?
15 mm–19 mm	8	?	?	?
20 mm–24 mm	6	?	?	?
25 mm–29 mm	1	?	?	?
Total	24			?

4. A survey of weekly spending allowances for Grade 10 students showed the following data.

   3.75 5.80 5.00 2.00 1.50 6.00 5.75 7.50 5.00 9.00 10.00
   8.00 11.00 9.50 12.50 5.00 3.00 14.75 5.75 4.50

   a. Group the data into $3.00 intervals, beginning with $0.01–$3.00, and make a frequency distribution table of the data.
   b. Draw a histogram of the data using this grouping.
   c. If you receive an allowance of $4.50, use a different grouping and scale to make a histogram that shows that most people get more money than you.

5. A survey of gasoline prices in a community produced the following results.

   48.8 51.3 49.6 48.7 47.5 49.0 50.3 52.1
   49.9 52.0 50.6 47.9 50.2 49.1 51.5

   a. Draw a histogram of the data, using intervals of 1 cent.
   b. Draw vertical lines on the histogram to represent the mean and the median of the data.

8–5 Making Predictions from Samples

The basketball coach tested 30 grade 10 students by giving each 5 shots from the free throw line. The table gives the results.

For this set of data, the mean is 2.3, the median is 2, and the mode is 2.

Number of Baskets	Frequency
0	2
1	7
2	10
3	5
4	3
5	3

The 30 students provide a **sample** of the total population of grade 10 students. Samples can be used to make predictions about a population, provided that the sample is representative of the population as a whole.

EXAMPLE 1:   Given that the sample of 30 students is representative, what would you expect the median score to be if all of the grade 10 students were tested on free throws?

Since the median of the sample was 2, you might expect a median of 2 for the total population.

The coach is interested in the proportion of students with a given score. Such a proportion is called the **relative frequency** of that score. The total of the relative frequencies of all numbers involved is always 1.

EXAMPLE 2:   Extend the table above, adding a column for Relative Frequency, expressed as a fraction *and* as a percent.

Number of Baskets	Frequency (*f*)	Relative Frequency $\left(\frac{f}{30}\right)$	(Percent)
0	2	$\frac{2}{30}$ or $\frac{1}{15}$	$6\frac{2}{3}$ %
1	7	$\frac{7}{30}$	$23\frac{1}{3}$ %
2	10	$\frac{10}{30}$ or $\frac{1}{3}$	$33\frac{1}{3}$ %
3	5	$\frac{5}{30}$ or $\frac{1}{6}$	$16\frac{2}{3}$ %
4	3	$\frac{3}{30}$ or $\frac{1}{10}$	10%
5	3	$\frac{3}{30}$ or $\frac{1}{10}$	10%
Total	30	$\frac{30}{30}$ or 1	100%

Predictions can be made based on relative frequency.

EXAMPLE 3:   If the total grade 10 population of 350 students were tested on free throws, how many might you expect to get a perfect score?

In the sample, 10% of the students made 5 baskets. In the total population, you should expect about the same proportion.

10% of 350 = 0.1 × 350
            = 35

If the sample of students is representative, then you should expect about 35 students out of 350 to get a perfect score.

EXERCISES

A 1. Use the data on the previous page to answer the following questions.
   a. What is the relative frequency of students who scored below the median?
   b. How many students might be expected to make 5 perfect shots if the total grade 10 population were 900?

2. The table gives the frequency distribution of ages of students in a secondary school.
   a. Copy and complete the table, giving relative frequencies correct to 3 decimal places.
   b. What proportion of the students are old enough to drive a car in your province?

Student Age	Frequency	Relative Frequency
13	26	?
14	239	?
15	253	?
16	218	?
17	187	?
18	94	?
19	3	?

B 3. A portion of highway was observed for a period of time and the makes of Japanese imports recorded. The graph displays the frequency distribution.
   a. Find the relative frequency of each make given.
   b. During a 24 h period, 357 Japanese imports pass the same point. How many would you predict to be Mazdas, assuming that the given sample is representative?

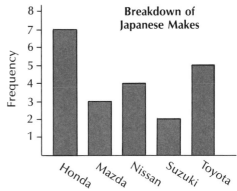

4. Ask any 5 students in your class how many pairs of running shoes they own. Record the data in a table.
   a. Find the median of the data.
   b. What proportion of the sample own 3 or more pairs?

5. Repeat exercise 4 with the total population of your class. How do the results of the sample compare to those of the population?

C 6. Earl Post was pleased to hear that an opinion poll placed him ahead in the mayor's race, with 35% of the sample supporting him, compared to 31% for Bob March and 29% for Kay Jones. The polling agency claims that the poll is accurate "within two percentage points", that is, the relative frequencies given can vary by 2% up *or* down.
   a. Seven of the respondents to the poll said they were undecided about how they would vote. Find the size of the sample polled.
   b. On election day, 17 592 city residents voted. Assuming that the poll was held sufficiently close to election day that it still reflected current opinion, calculate the range of votes you might expect for each of Post, March, and Jones.

8–6 Selecting an Unbiased Sample

While trying to convince her partners to open a music store in the west end of town, the manager of Best Tapes and Records claimed that, "The average student at Western High School buys 17 audio tapes a year."

Her partners may well question what "average" is being used, mean, median, or mode. Also, how were the data obtained? If a sample was used, how were the people selected?

EXAMPLE 1: Twenty students from a grade 12 class at Western High were asked how many tapes they had bought during the past year. Explain why the sample does not represent the total population of students at Western High.

Compared to the total student population, a larger proportion of grade 12 students would have part-time jobs and, therefore, more money to spend.

The sample in example 1 is a **biased sample**. For a *reliable* survey, the sample must be representative of the population.

A **random sample** is one in which all members of the population have an equal chance of being selected. A random sample is usually representative of the population.

A random number table like the one below, which consists of 500 digits randomly generated on a computer, can be used to select a random sample.

```
2 8 6 1 7 3 7 8 0 6 7 0 1 3 3 1 0 0 0 0 4 8 3 3 8 2 0 8 5 7 7 1 1 5 0 8 9 9 6 8 5 2 4 5 4 2 7 4 3 5
9 0 5 4 0 3 4 3 8 8 9 2 4 1 9 6 5 2 8 4 3 1 1 9 2 2 3 6 1 8 0 0 8 8 4 8 3 6 6 8 8 1 2 0 6 1 2 1 2 3
2 1 6 6 4 0 2 0 6 7 8 5 0 4 6 5 0 9 7 0 0 2 0 1 8 4 3 5 7 5 4 2 7 0 5 6 9 1 5 5 6 5 7 2 9 2 1 7 6 1
0 3 7 8 3 0 8 6 4 3 1 7 4 0 7 2 2 6 1 7 6 3 7 6 3 1 0 6 1 1 8 0 6 8 7 8 0 2 8 8 2 0 8 2 3 6 9 7 5 7
3 5 9 6 4 8 2 5 9 7 7 9 3 0 1 8 8 3 4 6 6 5 0 1 0 6 6 8 0 4 2 3 8 2 9 2 8 1 0 1 1 6 5 0 4 9 0 8 7 8
9 4 8 0 9 7 2 7 2 2 9 6 2 9 2 1 2 7 4 9 8 9 8 2 4 2 5 9 6 1 8 6 2 0 6 9 3 9 6 7 6 4 6 0 6 9 4 8 0 4
5 2 9 4 5 2 1 4 9 9 3 2 3 4 9 4 4 0 6 8 8 2 0 2 4 2 9 1 4 4 0 7 7 6 4 7 3 4 2 5 3 9 2 5 8 5 2 5 8 8
3 1 4 9 7 1 9 9 2 2 8 5 3 2 4 3 9 5 1 7 7 7 0 6 1 5 7 3 3 8 0 9 7 9 9 1 6 5 3 3 7 9 6 9 5 3 7 4 2 5
9 6 0 3 5 1 3 5 9 8 7 3 4 3 5 8 5 4 8 2 0 8 2 9 7 4 1 6 2 0 0 2 9 8 8 7 9 3 2 4 2 2 8 6 0 1 0 7 8 3
5 0 2 2 8 1 2 9 3 8 4 1 5 1 0 8 4 1 9 3 3 7 2 5 3 5 6 8 7 0 8 6 4 3 3 1 5 1 9 3 6 5 4 8 1 7 1 0 3 4
```

EXAMPLE 2: Given a complete list of the 1000 students attending Western High, how could you select a random sample of 20 students?

a. Number the students in the list from 1 through 1000.
b. Starting anywhere in the table, read 20 groups of three consecutive digits.
c. Match each of the 20 three-digit numbers to a student on the numbered list.

Since the selection of students is based on 20 *random* numbers, the sample will be **unbiased**.

Another way of ensuring an unbiased sample is to identify groups within the population, and randomly include individuals from each group in the same proportion as they appear in the population. Such a sample is a **stratified sample**.

EXAMPLE 3; The table gives the relative frequency of students in each grade at Western High. Find the number of students to select from each grade to give a stratified sample of 20 students altogether.

Grade	Relative Frequency
9	0.30
10	0.25
11	0.25
12	0.20

The sample should have the same proportion of students from each grade as appears in the population. The table summarizes the calculations to ensure this.

Grade	Relative Frequency	Rel. Freq. × 20
9	0.30	6
10	0.25	5
11	0.25	5
12	0.20	4
Total	1.00	20

For an unbiased stratified sample of 20, you should randomly choose 6 students from grade 9, 5 from grade 10, 5 from grade 11, and 4 from grade 12.

When working with a stratified sample, always keep in mind that it provides a good representation only if you have accurately identified groups within the population.

EXERCISES

A 1. Why is the sample described a biased sample?
   a. Interviews were conducted at the entrances to hockey arenas to determine Canadians' attitudes towards violence in hockey.
   b. High school students were interviewed to measure the popularity among teens of a new music star.
   c. Survey forms were mailed to randomly selected car owners to study the attitudes of Ontario residents towards new speed limits.
   d. To find the popularity of City Council, a poll was conducted by phoning people at numbers randomly selected from the phone book.
   e. A newspaper printed a survey form and counted the responses mailed in to determine Canadians' attitudes to capital punishment.

   2. A club has 20 male and 5 female members. If a committee of 5 is being formed, how many females should be on the committee to ensure their representation in proportion to the number of females in the club? A randomly chosen sample is quite likely to contain *no* females. In your view, what's the fairest way to select the sample?

3. The population of bighorn sheep in Alberta was estimated by dividing the province into sections of 1 km² and then randomly selecting 1000 of these sections to form a sample. Why would this provide a poor estimate?

B   4. Suppose the student list for Western High School were arranged with students 000 to 299 in grade 9, students 300 to 549 in grade 10, students 550 to 799 in grade 11, and students 800 to 999 in grade 12. Use the random number table to select a sample of 20 students and record the grade of each. How does your random sample compare to the stratified sample started in example 3?

5. Surveys were conducted in the girls' and boys' physical education classes to find the number of females in each student's family. The frequency table gives the results.

   a. For each sample, find the mean number of females per family.
   b. By how much do the means differ?
   c. Explain why you would in fact expect the two means to differ.

Number of Females	Frequency in Girls' Class	Frequency in Boys' Class
0	0	2
1	2	15
2	14	7
3	11	6
4	5	2
5	3	1
Total	35	33

6. This question, although based on a small population, exemplifies a sampling method that can be used with larger populations. The diagram shows the number of TV sets in each of ten houses with addresses from 1 to 10.

   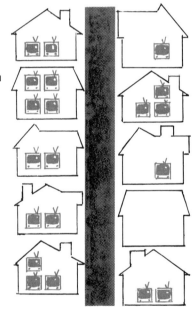

   a. Start at any point in the random number table and read 4 consecutive digits. Use these 4 digits as addresses to select 4 houses. Take 0 as 10 and read more digits along the line if there is repetition. Find the mean number of TV sets per house in the sample.

   b. Repeat the sampling procedure three more times. Then copy and complete the table.

Sample	A	B	C	D
Mean				

   c. Normally you cannot find the exact mean of a large population because of the volume of data involved, but here there are only 10 houses. Find the mean of the population. How does the population mean compare with the sample means?

   d. A better experimental mean can be found by taking the mean of the sample means. Find the mean of the four sample means. How does this number compare with the population mean?

7. The diagram shows a garden, 10 m by 10 m, marked off in units of 1 m². Each square can be named by a pair of coordinates. The dots represent bees in the garden. Follow the steps below to see how a researcher could estimate the size of the bee population in the entire garden.

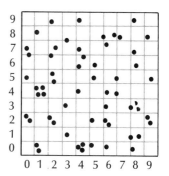

   a. Read 10 digits in a row from the random number table. The 10 digits give you 5 coordinate pairs, which indicate the squares of your sample. Count the bees in the 5 sample squares and find the mean number of bees in the sample.
   b. Use the mean of the sample to estimate the total number of bees in the garden of 100 squares.
   c. Repeat the experiment three more times using samples of 10, 15, and 20 squares. (In each sample, do not repeat squares. Instead, read more squares.)
   d. Find the actual number of bees in the entire garden. What happens to the accuracy of the estimate as you increase the sample size?

C 8. The duck population in a marsh is 55% teal, 25% black duck, and 20% mallard. A team of environmentalists capture 20 ducks in one day, tag them, and release them. To simulate the experiment:
   a. How could you use the random number table to select a "sample" of 20 ducks? Select such a sample and identify the numbers of each type of duck captured.
   b. The environmentalists capture 20 more ducks every day for the next 9 days. Repeat the sampling procedure 9 times. Record your results in a table.
   c. What was the mean number of each species taken per day?
   d. How does this compare with the composition of the duck population given originally?

Using the Computer

Random Number Table

The following program can be used to generate a random number table containing 100 digits.

```
10  INPUT "ENTER YOUR SEED NUMBER ";X
20  FOR I = 1 TO 10
30  FOR J = 1 TO 9
40  PRINT INT ( RND (X) * 10)" ";
50  NEXT J
60  PRINT INT ( RND (X) * 10)
70  NEXT I
80  END
```

The seed number is used to start the selection of digits.

Use this program to generate a random number table. Use the table to try exercise 6 again.

8–7 Scatterplots

The basketball coach at Chipawa High School appointed a student to act as team statistician. Her job was to compile data on each member of the team. Her data sheet for one game is given below.

Player	Minutes Played	Field Goals Made-Field Goals Attempted	Free Throws Made-Free Throws Attempted	Personal Fouls	Points Scored
Anne	32	5–13	4–6	2	14
Beth	30	4–10	3–3	3	11
Cecile	24	2–6	1–1	1	5
Dawn	29	1–3	2–4	1	4
Eliza	36	3–6	0–1	2	6
Fran	19	5–11	2–2	0	12
Gerry	12	0–3	0–4	3	0
Helen	21	1–5	1–2	1	3
Irene	18	3–5	1–5	2	7
Jane	19	3–7	2–6	2	8
Totals	240	27–67	16–28	18	70

You might expect that the player who attempts the most free throws would make the most free-throw points. You can check this using the statistician's data sheet. A more visual check would be provided by a **scatterplot**, which can give a picture of the relationship between number of attempts and number of successes for each player. To make a scatterplot, graph the ordered pair (free throws attempted, free throws made) for each player. Do not label any points.

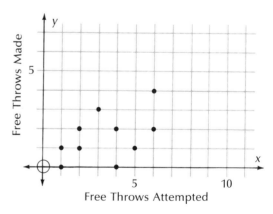

The scatterplot suggests, as expected, that the players who attempt more free throws make more free-throw points. We say there is a **positive correlation** between free throws attempted and free throws made. If the opposite were true (*more* attempts resulting in *fewer* successes), there would be a **negative correlation** between attempts and successes.

A player with a perfect free-throw record will be represented on the scatterplot by a point on the line through (0,0), (1,1), (2,2), ... The scatterplot shows that there are three players who achieved a perfect record. Players who are shooting foul shots poorly are represented by points far below this line.

EXERCISES

A 1. In each of following, state whether a positive, negative, or no correlation exists between the two quantities, and justify your answer with an example.
   a. hours of study and marks scored on an exam
   b. distance from Earth and force of gravity
   c. hours of typing practice and typing speed
   d. altitude and air pressure
   e. speed and air resistance

Use the Chipawa High School data for exercises 2 to 6.

2. Which player played the most minutes?

3. Conjecture why Gerry played for only 12 min.

4. If each team had 5 players on the floor, determine for how many minutes a game of basketball is played.

B 5. a. Make a scatterplot showing field goals made (*FG*) and field goals attempted (*A*).
   b. How would you determine if there are any perfect shooters?
   c. Is there a positive correlation between field goals attempted and field goals made? Explain.
   d. If a player had attempted 9 field goals, about how many successful field goals might she be expected to make?

6. a. Make a scatterplot showing time played and points scored by each player.
   b. Is there a correlation between time played and points scored? Explain.
   c. If a player had played 40 min, about how many points might she be expected to make?

7. The following table shows the Mathematics and Science marks for 12 students.

Mathematics	38	51	19	53	39	38	66	75	71	35
Science	50	72	36	64	52	56	80	85	61	40

   a. Make a scatterplot with Mathematics marks along the horizontal axis and Science marks along the vertical axis.
   b. How are Mathematics and Science marks correlated?
   c. If a student had 85 in Mathematics, about what mark might he or she be expected to have in Science?

8–8 Clusters and Trends

The Pythagoras Mathematics Contest is administered by the University of Waterford to grade 10 contestants in schools across Canada. To analyse one year's results, the contest officials categorized the schools as rural or urban. They obtained data on the percentage of grade 10 students in each school who competed in the Pythagoras contest and the mean contest score for the school. The following scatterplot was drawn from the data. Each point is identified as rural (R) or urban (U).

The scatterplot shows two groups or **clusters** of schools. Complete the following exercises to see how, by examining each cluster and comparing clusters, you can draw a number of conclusions from such a scatterplot.

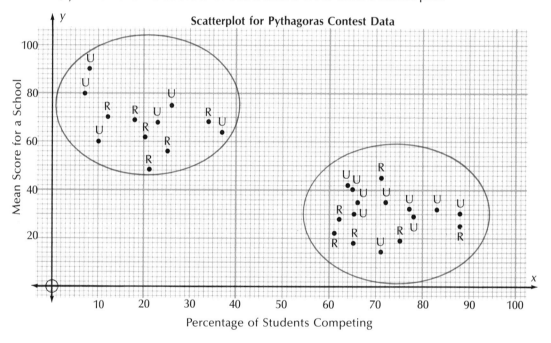

Scatterplot for Pythagoras Contest Data

EXERCISES

B 1. Use the scatterplot for schools competing in the Pascal contest to answer the following.

  a. In general, as a greater percentage of students enter the competition, what happens to the mean contest score for the school?

  b. Within each cluster, and for each category of school, determine if there is a positive, negative, or no correlation between the percentage of students competing and the mean score for the school.

  c. If the schools were rated by the scores of the best 10 students competing, would a rural or urban school be more likely to win the contest?

2. Using the masses and heights of 20 males in a large city, the following scatterplot was obtained.

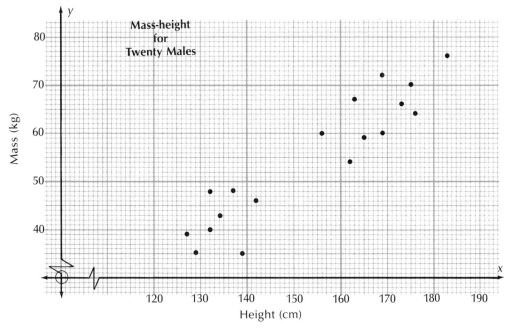

a. Identify two clusters and suggest a reason for the clusters occurring.
b. Describe the correlation between height and mass.
c. About what mass would you expect a male to have if his height is 165 cm?

3. Over a period of 10 years a record of the number of registered vehicles and the number of vehicle accidents was made, as given in the following table.

Year	Millions of Vehicles	Thousands of Accidents
1975	2.6	136
1976	3.1	163
1977	3.5	166
1978	3.7	153
1979	4.1	177
1980	4.4	201
1981	4.6	216
1982	4.9	208
1983	5.3	226
1984	5.8	238

a. Make a scatterplot of the data.
b. Describe the correlation between the number of vehicles and the number of accidents.
c. If the trend continues, how many vehicles and how many accidents might be expected in 1990?

8–9 Median Fit Line for Data

When there is a positive or negative correlation between variables, as illustrated in many scatterplots, it can be useful and informative to find a best-fitting line that can be used to represent the data. Such a line is called the **fitted line**.

To find the number of red blood cells in a sample using a microscope is not only awkward, but highly inaccurate as well. Another method, involving packed cell volume of the blood, simplifies the red blood cell count. To find a possible relationship between the number of red blood cells in a sample and the volume of the sample, blood samples were taken from 10 dogs and a scatterplot based on the data was made.

Packed Cell Volume (mm³)	Red Blood Count (millions)
45	6.53
42	6.30
56	9.52
48	7.50
42	6.99
35	5.90
58	9.49
40	6.20
39	6.55
50	8.72

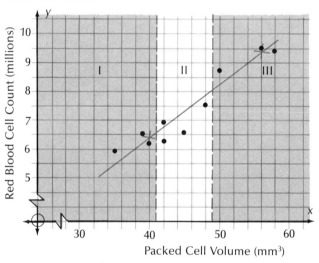

The scatterplot quite definitely displays a positive correlation.

To find the fitted line for the data, the graph is separated into three vertical regions, as shown. Each region contains about the same number of points. In this case, there are 4 points in the central region (II) and 3 points in each of the outer regions (I and III). Regions I and III are used to determine the fitted line, using the following steps.

1. Identify the coordinates of each point in Regions I and III.
   Region I: (35, 5.90), (39, 6.55), (40, 6.20)
   Region III: (50, 8.72), (56, 9.52), (58, 9.49)

2. Identify the median *x*-coordinate in each region.
   Region I: 39   Region III: 56

3. Identify the median *y*-coordinates.
   Region I: 6.20   Region III: 9.49

4. Plot the points (39, 6.20) and (56, 9.49). Join the points to form the fitted line, also called the **median fit line**.

Find the equation of the median fit line by calculating its slope, then substituting into point-slope form of a linear equation.

$$\text{Slope} = \frac{9.49 - 6.20}{56 - 39}$$

$$(y - 6.20) = 0.19(x - 39)$$
$$\text{or} \quad 0.19x - y = 1.21$$

$$= 0.19$$

This equation establishes a relationship between the number of red blood cells and the packed cell volume.

EXERCISES

B **1.** The table gives data for 17 father-and-son heights.

Father's Height (cm)	Son's Height (cm)
179	188
163	173
169	173
193	188
186	170
170	175
165	168
193	201
163	165
180	173
173	173
152	160
163	163
170	176
173	169
175	177
175	178

  a. Draw a scatterplot to represent the data.
  b. Divide the graph into 3 vertical regions containing 5, 7, and 5 points, respectively.
  c. Draw the median fit line.
  d. Find an equation of the median fit line.

2. In a laboratory an experiment was carried out on nine groups of locusts, each containing 120. The locusts were exposed to pesticides of different strengths and the deaths that resulted were recorded.

Concentration	1.2	1.3	1.4	1.5	1.6	1.7	1.8	1.9	2.0
Number Dead	38	45	52	49	46	58	76	69	66

  a. Draw a scatterplot to represent the data.
  b. Draw the median fit line.
  c. Find an equation of the line.

3. Social workers in a city identified ten depressed areas and conducted a survey to determine whether there was a relationship between the percentage of dwellings overcrowded (x) and infant mortality (y, given in deaths per 100 000). The results were recorded as follows.

x	13	33	12	40	12	5	20	4	15	26
y	124	151	124	156	128	78	127	109	127	144

  a. Make a scatterplot to represent the data.
  b. Draw a median fit line.
  c. Predict the infant mortality for a depressed area where 50% of the dwellings are overcrowded.

8–10 Smoothing Plots over Time

Some statistical graphs are made by making a scatterplot and then joining the data points in some order. For example, data may be collected on a yearly basis, and points for successive years joined. Such graphs are useful for illustrating annual statistics derived from such areas of concern as car accidents, car fatalities, break-ins, or murders.

The statistics for car accidents in a city were recorded as below.

Year	Number of Car Accidents (× 100)
1985	18
1984	16
1983	21
1982	21
1981	19
1980	25
1979	23
1978	28
1977	21
1976	18
1975	21
1974	17
1973	23
1972	26
1971	21

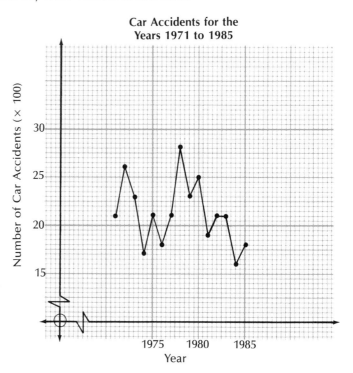

Car Accidents for the Years 1971 to 1985

The scatterplot fluctuates wildly; the highs and lows dominate our attention and mask any general trends in the data. To remove the large fluctuations from the data, a method called **smoothing** can be used. Smoothing is done by using the median of three successive values in a table in order to generate new values.

Follow the steps below to smooth the data in the accident table.

1. Leave the 1985 and 1971 values unchanged.

2. Starting with the 1984 value of 16, note the numbers before and after 16; 18 and 21.

3. Replace 16 by the median of 18, 16, and 21: 18.

4. Repeat for the remaining values in the table.

A table of smoothed values and its corresponding graph result.

Year	Number	Smoothed Number
1985	18	18
1984	16	18
1983	21	21
1982	21	21
1981	19	21
1980	25	23
1979	23	25
1978	28	23
1977	21	21
1976	18	21
1975	21	18
1974	17	21
1973	23	23
1972	26	23
1971	21	21

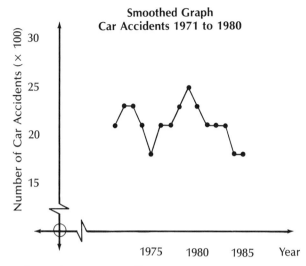

Smoothed Graph
Car Accidents 1971 to 1980

The smoothed graph reveals any general trends not originally apparent. For example, a dramatic decrease in accidents between 1979 and 1982 is now revealed. This decrease was probably due to the institution of a R.I.D.E. program in the city.

EXERCISES

B 1. The American League home run champions from 1901 to 1986 are shown in the following table. Use the data to answer the following questions.

Year	Player, team	No.	Year	Player, team	No.	Year	Player, team	No.
1901	Nap Lajoie, Phila.	13	1931	Lou Gehrig, N.Y., and		1961	Roger Maris, N.Y.	61
1902	Ralph Seybold, Phila.	16		Babe Ruth, N.Y.	46	1962	Harmon Killebrew, Minn.	48
1903	Buck Freeman, Bost.	13	1932	Jimmy Foxx, Phila.	58	1963	Harmon Killebrew, Minn.	45
1904	Harry Davis, Phila.	10	1933	Jimmy Foxx, Phila.	48	1964	Harmon Killebrew, Minn.	49
1905	Harry Davis, Phila.	8	1934	Lou Gehrig, N.Y.	49	1965	Tony Conigliaro, Bost.	32
1906	Harry Davis, Phila.	12	1935	Jimmy Foxx, Phila., and		1966	Frank Robinson, Balt.	49
1907	Harry Davis, Phila.	8		Hank Greenberg, Det.	36	1967	Carl Yastrzemski, Bost., and	
1908	Sam Crawford, Det.	7	1936	Lou Gehrig, N.Y.	49		Harmon Killebrew, Minn.	44
1909	Ty Cobb, Det.	9	1937	Joe DiMaggio, N.Y.	46	1968	Frank Howard, Wash.	44
1910	J. Garland Stahl, Bost.	10	1938	Hank Greenberg, Det.	58	1969	Harmon Killebrew, Minn.	49
1911	Franklin Baker, Phila.	9	1939	Jimmy Foxx, Bost.	35	1970	Frank Howard, Wash.	44
1912	Franklin Baker, Phila.	10	1940	Hank Greenberg, Det.	41	1971	Bill Melton, Chicago	33
1913	Franklin Baker, Phila.	12	1941	Ted Williams, Bost.	37	1972	Dick Allen, Chicago	37
1914	Franklin Baker, Phila., and		1942	Ted Williams, Bost.	36	1973	Reggie Jackson, Oak.	32
	Sam Crawford, Det.	8	1943	Rudy York, Det.	34	1974	Dick Allen, Chicago	32
1915	Robert Roth, Chi.-Cleve.	7	1944	Nick Etten, N.Y.	22	1975	Reggie Jackson, Oak., and	
1916	Wally Pipp, N.Y.	12	1945	Vern Stephens, St. L.	24		George Scott, Mil.	36
1917	Wally Pipp, N.Y.	9	1946	Hank Greenberg, Det.	44	1976	Graig Nettles, N.Y.	32
1918	Babe Ruth, Bost., and		1947	Ted Williams, Bost.	32	1977	Jim Rice, Boston	39
	Clarence Walker, Phila.	11	1948	Joe DiMaggio, N.Y.	39	1978	Jim Rice, Boston	46
1919	Babe Ruth, Bost.	29	1949	Ted Williams, Bost.	43	1979	Gorman Thomas, Milwaukee	45
1920	Babe Ruth, N.Y.	54	1950	Al Rosen, Cleve.	37	1980	Reggie Jackson, N.Y., and	
1921	Babe Ruth, N.Y.	59	1951	Gus Zernial, Chi.-Phila.	33		Ben Oglivie, Mil.	41
1922	Ken Williams, St. L.	39	1952	Larry Doby, Cleve.	32	1981*	Tony Armas, Oak., Dwight	
1923	Babe Ruth, N.Y.	41	1953	Al Rosen, Cleve.	43		Evans, Bost., Bobby Grich,	
1924	Babe Ruth, N.Y.	46	1954	Larry Doby, Cleve.	32		Calif., and Eddie Murray,	
1925	Bob Meusel, N.Y.	33	1955	Mickey Mantle, N.Y.	37		Balt. (tie)	22
1926	Babe Ruth, N.Y.	47	1956	Mickey Mantle, N.Y.	52	1982	Gorman Thomas, Mil., and	
1927	Babe Ruth, N.Y.	60	1957	Roy Sievers, Wash.	42		Reggie Jackson, Calif.	39
1928	Babe Ruth, N.Y.	54	1958	Mickey Mantle, N.Y.	42	1983	Jim Rice, Boston	39
1929	Babe Ruth, N.Y.	46	1959	Rocky Colavito, Cleve., and		1984	Tony Armas, Boston	43
1930	Babe Ruth, N.Y.	49		Harmon Killebrew, Wash.	42	1985	Darrell Evans, Detroit	40
			1960	Mickey Mantle, N.Y.	40	1986	Jesse Barfield	40

a. Make a scatterplot for home run records for the years 1920 to 1985 inclusive. Join the data points with line segments.

b. Smooth the graph from part **a** using the method described in lesson 8–10.

c. What world event happened around 1940 that may have affected the home run output by the champions at that time?

d. Study the smoothed graph to determine whether the following rule changes affected the yearly output of home runs by the champions.

1926: Fences must be more than 156 m from home plate for legitimate home runs.

1931: A fair ball that bounces over a fence will be counted as a double instead of a home run.

1956: Outfield fences in new ball parks must be at least 203 m down the foul line and at least 250 m in centre field.

1969: The pitcher's mound is lowered giving the hitter an advantage.

e. In 1981, the American League players went on strike, shortening the season. Does the original data show this? Does the smoothed data?

2. Make an example to illustrate if each of the following is true.

a. A peak will be smoothed out using the smoothing method.

b. A plateau will not be smoothed out using the smoothing method.

3. The following table shows the gold medal winners and the winning times for the men's 100 m dash in the Olympics from 1896 to 1984.

a. There are 3 gaps in the table when the Olympics were not held. Explain why they did not take place.

b. Make a scatterplot of the data.

c. Make a table of smoothed data and plot the smoothed data.

d. When did the greatest drop in winning time occur?

e. Make a prediction for the winning time in the 100 m dash at the 1988 Olympics.

Source: The 1986 Almanac, Houghton Mifflin Company

Men's 100 m Dash

1896	Thomas Burke, United States	12s
1900	Francis W. Jarvis, United States	10.8s
1904	Archie Hahn, United States	11s
1906	Archie Hahn, United States	11.2s
1908	Reginald Walker, South Africa	10.8s
1912	Ralph Craig, United States	10.8s
1920	Charles Paddock, United States	10.8s
1924	Harold Abrahams, Great Britain	10.6s
1928	Percy Williams, Canada	10.8s
1932	Eddie Tolan, United States	10.3s
1936	Jesse Owens, United States	10.3s[1]
1948	Harrison Dillard, United States	10.3s
1952	Lindy Remigino, United States	10.4s
1956	Bobby Morrow, United States	10.5s
1960	Armin Hary, Germany	10.2s
1964	Robert Hayes, United States	10s
1968	James Hines, United States	9.9s
1972	Valery Borzov, U.S.S.R.	10.14s
1976	Hasely Crawford, Trinidad and Tobago	10.06s
1980	Allan Wells, Britain	10.25s
1984	Carl Lewis, United States	9.99s

1. Wind assisted.

Review

1. A sample of 30 students in the school cafeteria were asked how much they had spent on lunch, with the following results.

   > 2.42, 2.65, 2.50, 2.38, 2.52, 2.70, 2.76, 2.80, 2.30, 2.27,
   > 2.45, 2.57, 2.65, 2.82, 2.89, 2.97, 2.75, 2.25, 2.55, 2.67,
   > 2.50, 2.95, 2.59, 2.25, 2.47, 2.75, 2.82, 2.55, 2.48, 2.73

   a. Group the data into 10-cent intervals, starting at $2.20–$2.29, and construct an extended frequency table for the survey.

   b. What is the relative frequency of students spending between $2.60 and $2.69?

   c. What is the relative frequency of students spending more than $2.49?

   d. Does the survey show that 20% of the students in the school spend at least $2.80 on lunch? Explain.

2. The Super Snack Shop wants to make a claim about their sizes of servings of French fries. During one hour, servings with the following numbers of fries were made up.

   > 40, 41, 40, 39, 37, 41, 38, 39, 42, 40, 38, 39, 40, 40, 41, 40, 39, 37, 38, 38,
   > 40, 41, 41, 42, 40, 40, 42, 42, 39, 39, 39, 40, 40, 41, 42, 40, 39, 40, 38, 42,
   > 41, 42, 40, 39, 37, 40, 42, 39, 39, 40, 40, 40, 39, 39, 38, 38, 37, 40, 40, 41,
   > 42, 41, 39, 38, 38, 37, 40, 40, 40, 39, 39, 42, 39, 39, 40, 37, 39, 41, 41, 41,
   > 40, 41, 41, 37, 39, 39, 41, 41, 40, 42, 41, 38, 39, 40, 41, 41, 42, 38, 40, 40

   a. Use the random number table on page 260 to select a sample of 10 customers to count their chips.

   b. What is the mean of the sample?

   c. Collect the results of the survey in a frequency table and draw a histogram of the data.

   d. Find the exact mean of the data.

3. The table at the right shows the gold medal teams for the women's 400 m relay, and their winning times, for the Olympics games from 1928 to 1984.

   a. Make a scatterplot of the data.

   b. Make a table of smoothed data and graph the smoothed data.

   c. Describe any general trends revealed by the graph of smoothed data. What factor(s) might have contributed to these trends?

Women's 400 m Relay

Year	Team	Time
1928	Canada	48.4s
1932	United States	47s
1936	United States	46.9s
1948	Netherlands	47.5s
1952	United States	45.9s
1956	Australia	44.5s
1960	United States	44.5s
1964	Poland	43.6s
1968	United States	42.8s
1972	West Germany	42.81s
1976	East Germany	42.55s
1980	East Germany	41.60s
1984	United States	41.65s

Source: The 1986 Almanac, Houghton Mifflin Company

Test

1. The masses in kilograms of the 24 babies in a hospital nursery were recorded at the time of their birth.

    2.51, 2.07, 3.25, 3.62,
    3.32, 4.68, 4.45, 3.41,
    3.10, 4.46, 3.59, 4.91,
    2.78, 4.12, 3.84, 5.23,
    2.43, 3.08, 1.83, 4.27,
    2.89, 3.36, 2.60, 3.92

    a. Select an appropriate interval size and record the data in a frequency table, extended to include columns for Cumulative Frequency and Subtotal.
    b. Estimate the mean of the data.
    c. Find the interval in which the median lies.

2. A record was kept of the ages of the mothers of the babies studied in question 1.

    21, 33, 26, 17, 22, 25,
    23, 28, 35, 27, 43, 25,
    36, 42, 20, 29, 18, 31,
    19, 28, 39, 22, 25, 38

    a. Organize the data in a frequency table.
    b. Select an appropriate interval size and make a histogram of the data.

3. a. Using the data from question 1, find the relative frequency of babies with masses less than 3.50 kg.
    b. Assuming that the nursery holds a representative sample of babies, about how many babies with masses less than 3.50 kg would you expect in the next 50 births without complication to take place at the hospital? (Since the sample is in the hospital nursery, we must consider that the babies are healthy, are not premature, and had safe deliveries.)

4. The histogram shows the results of a survey of 50 randomly selected homes in the city. Use the histogram to answer the following.
    a. What is the mean, median, and mode of the sample?
    b. What is the relative frequency of homes with 4 radios?
    c. If there are 10 200 homes in the city, and assuming the sample to be representative, how many homes would you expect to have 5 radios?

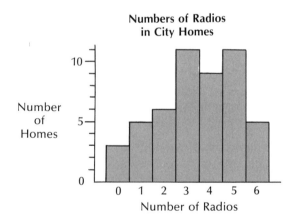

5. A survey of grade 10 students, studying how many pairs of jeans each student owned, yielded the following results: 1, 2, 1, 2, 3, 2, 3, 4, 3, 3, 2, 4, 2, 1, 2, 4, 5, 3, 2, 3, 3, 4, 3, 4, 3, 3, 5, 3, 5, 5, 4, 5, 4, 4, 4.
    a. Make an extended frequency table to find mean, median, and mode.
    b. Find the relative frequency of students with 2 pairs of jeans.
    c. If the class is taken as a sample of grade 10 students, then how many out of a population of 250 grade 10 students would you expect to own at least 3 pairs of jeans?

Cumulative Review

1. Define a variable in the appropriate units and write an expression to represent the given information.
   a. The rent was increased by 6%.
   b. The labourer earns $590/week plus $22.12/h for overtime hours.
   c. The cost of the meal was shared equally by two co-hosts.

2. Solve and check.
   a. $2(x + 1) = x + 9$
   b. $2x(x + 1) = 2x^2 - x - 9$
   c. $2x(x + 1) + 3x(x + 2) = 5(x^2 - 2) + 3x$
   d. $3x(x - 2) + 5 = 3x^2 - 7(x - 1)$

3. Find the length and the midpoint of each segment with the given endpoints. Answer correct to one decimal place.
   a. $R(5, -2), T(0, 7)$
   b. $A(-3, -2), B(5, 9)$
   c. $P(3, 3), Q(-1, 6)$
   d. $X(-5, -1), Y(2, -2)$

4. Find an equation in $y = mx + b$ form for each line described.
   a. has slope $\frac{1}{2}$ and y-intercept -3
   b. is parallel to the line represented by $y = 5x - 2$ and has y-intercept 7
   c. passes through $A(5, -2)$ and $B(-3, 7)$
   d. is perpendicular to a line with slope 4 and has y-intercept 1
   e. is perpendicular to the line represented by $2x + 3y = -9$, and has the same y-intercept as the line given by $y = 3x + \frac{1}{2}$

5. Solve each system of equations. Use the method of your choice.
   a. $y = 3x - 2$
      $y = x + 1$
   b. $2x - y = -8$
      $x + y = 2$
   c. $2x - 5y = 15$
      $3x + 5y = 30$
   d. $4x + 3y = 5$
      $2x + 4y = 0$
   e. $y = \frac{1}{3}x - 2$
      $x + y = -1$
   f. $y = \frac{1}{2}x - 3$
      $y = -\frac{2}{5}x + 1$

6. Graph the solution set of each inequality.
   a. $y \le 2x - 5$
   b. $y > -x - 1$
   c. $2x - y \ge -3$

7. What must the value of k be for the following to be perfect square binomials?
   a. $x^2 - kx + 36$
   b. $4x^2 + kx + 25$
   c. $kx^2 - 80x + 100$

8. Solve and check.
   a. $x^2 - 6x - 7 = 0$
   b. $x(x + 1) - 2 = 4$
   c. $2x^2 - 20x + 24 = x(x - 10)$

9. Graph each relation defined below. Identify those that are functions.
   a. $f(x) = 3x - 2$
   b. $f: x \rightarrow x^3$
   c. $f(x) = \frac{1}{2}x^2$
   d. $x = y^2$
   e. $xy = 24$
   f. $y = 2x - 3$

10. A line contains the points $A(3, 9)$ and $B(-7, -1)$. Find the value of y when x is 0.

9 Transformations

9–1 Transformations of Points

An amusement park provides many examples of situations that can be described by transformations, such as translation, reflection, rotation, and dilatation.

A **translation** provides a mathematical model of a *slide*: it describes the "before" and "after" positions of an object which has been moved a fixed distance along a straight line path. A translation is defined by a translation arrow or its ordered pair description.

EXAMPLE 1:   Find the image of point $A(-2, 3)$ under the translation given by the translation arrow on the grid below.

The arrow is defined by the ordered pair $[5, -2]$; the directed distance from the point to its image is 5 in the x direction and -2 in the y direction.

Under the translation $[5, -2]$, a point $P(x, y)$ will be mapped onto the point $P'(x + 5, y - 2)$.

Point $A(-2, 3)$ *maps onto* its image $A'(3, 1)$. We write: $A(-2, 3) \rightarrow A'(3, 1)$.

The mapping rule for $[5, -2]$ is written: $P(x, y) \rightarrow P'(x + 5, y - 2)$.

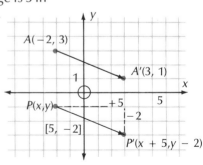

274

Geometric **reflection** provides a mathematical model of optical reflection in our everyday world. In each example below, the reflection line m represents a mirror. A point P (object) is mapped onto point P' (image) under a given reflection. Note that in each case the reflection line is the *perpendicular bisector* of $\overleftrightarrow{PP'}$.

EXAMPLE 2:   Find the image of point $A(-2, 3)$ under the given reflection in line m. Then write a general mapping rule for the reflection.

a. m is the x-axis.

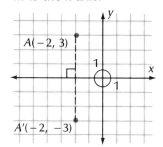

$A(-2, 3) \rightarrow A'(-2, -3)$

The mapping rule is:
$P(x, y) \rightarrow P'(x, -y)$.

b. m is the y-axis.

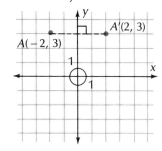

$A(-2, 3) \rightarrow A'(2, 3)$

The mapping rule is:
$P(x, y) \rightarrow P'(-x, y)$.

c. m is the line $y = x$.

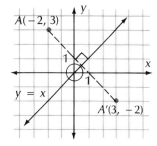

$A(-2, 3) \rightarrow A'(3, -2)$

The mapping rule is:
$P(x, y) \rightarrow P'(y, x)$.

A **rotation** provides a mathematical model of a turn; it describes the "before" and "after" positions of an object which is turned about a fixed point (the centre) through a specified angle. A *positive* angle of rotation describes a *counter-clockwise* turn.

EXAMPLE 3:   Find the image of point $A(-2, 3)$ under the given rotation about $(0, 0)$. Then write a general mapping rule for the rotation.

a. rotation of 90°

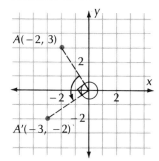

$A(-2, 3) \rightarrow A'(-3, -2)$

The mapping rule is:
$P(x, y) \rightarrow P'(-y, x)$.

b. rotation of 180°

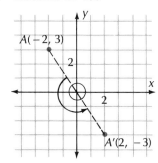

$A(-2, 3) \rightarrow A'(2, -3)$

The mapping rule is:
$P(x, y) \rightarrow P'(-x, -y)$.

c. rotation of 270°

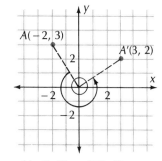

$A(-2, 3) \rightarrow A'(3, 2)$

The mapping rule is:
$P(x, y) \rightarrow P'(y, -x)$.

A **dilatation** provides a mathematical model for an *enlargement* or *reduction* in the size of an object. A dilatation with centre (0, 0) and scale factor k is defined by the mapping rule $P(x, y) \rightarrow P'(kx, ky)$.

EXAMPLE 4:   Find the image of point $A(-2, 3)$ under a dilatation with centre (0, 0) and scale factor k.

a. $k = \frac{1}{2}$

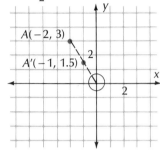

$A(-2, 3) \rightarrow A'(-1, 1.5)$

The mapping rule is:

$P(x, y) \rightarrow P'\left(\frac{1}{2}x, \frac{1}{2}y\right)$.

Note the image is *half* as far from the centre.

b. $k = 2$

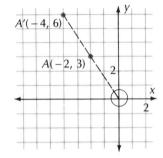

$A(-2, 3) \rightarrow A'(-4, 6)$

The mapping rule is:

$P(x, y) \rightarrow P'(2x, 2y)$.

Note the image is *twice* as far from the centre.

c. $k = -\frac{1}{2}$

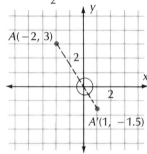

$A(-2, 3) \rightarrow A'(1, -1.5)$

The mapping rule is:

$P(x, y) \rightarrow P'\left(-\frac{1}{2}x, -\frac{1}{2}y\right)$.

Note the image is *half* as far from the centre.

EXERCISES

A **1.** What is the image of $G(5, -1)$ under the given translation?
   a. $(x, y) \rightarrow (x + 2, y - 3)$ **b.** $(x, y) \rightarrow (x, y + 1)$
   c. $(x, y) \rightarrow (x - 4, y)$ **d.** $(x, y) \rightarrow (x - 6, y - 6)$

2. What is the image of $Q(4, 3)$ under the given rotation about the origin?
   a. 90° rotation   **b.** 180° rotation   **c.** 270° rotation   **d.** −90° rotation

3. What is the image of $T(-1, 6)$ under the reflection in line m?
   a. m is the x-axis.   **b.** m is the y-axis.   **c.** m is the line $y = x$.

4. What is the scale factor of the given dilatation?

   a. $(x, y) \rightarrow (-3x, -3y)$ **b.** $(x, y) \rightarrow (4x, 4y)$ **c.** $(x, y) \rightarrow \left(\frac{2}{3}x, \frac{2}{3}y\right)$

B **5.** Copy and complete the table.

	Transformation	Original Point	Image Point
a.	Reflection in the x-axis	(5, −2)	?
b.	Translation [−3, 1]	(2, 1)	?
c.	Dilatation with $k = 3$ and centre (0, 0)	?	(12, −2)
d.	Rotation of 180° about (0, 0)	?	(6, −5)

6. Plot the image of the given point under the translation that maps $A(6, 8)$ onto $A'(2, -1)$.
   a. $B(0, 2)$ b. $C(-1, 3)$ c. $D(5, 4)$ d. $O(0, 0)$

7. What is the image of $A(5, -3)$ under the dilatation with centre $(0, 0)$ and the given scale factor, k?
   a. $k = 4$ b. $k = \frac{1}{4}$ c. $k = -4$ d. $k = -\frac{1}{4}$ e. $k = 1$

8. Find the image of the given point under the rotation of $90°$ about the origin.
   a. $A(5, 4)$ b. $B(-3, -1)$ c. $C(0, 6)$ d. $D(-2, -3)$ e. $E(a, b)$

9. Find the image of the given point under the rotation of $180°$ about $(0, 0)$.
   a. $A(2, 8)$ b. $B(-4, -3)$ c. $C(7, 0)$ d. $D(-3, 5)$ e. $E(a, b)$

10. What is the image of each given point in exercise 8 under the rotation of $270°$ about the origin?

11. What is the image of each given point in exercise 9 under reflection in the line $y = x$?

12. Describe three different transformations that have the effect of mapping $G(-3, 3)$ onto $G'(3, -3)$.

13. a. What is the image H' of $H(-1, 2)$ under the rotation of $90°$ about the origin?
    b. What translation maps H onto H'?
    c. What is the image G' of $G(3, -2)$ under the above rotation?
    d. What translation maps G onto G'?

C 14. Find the image of (a, b) under the given transformation.
    a. reflection in the x-axis   b. reflection in the y-axis
    c. reflection in the line $y = x$ d. dilatation with scale factor k
    e. rotation of $90°$ about $(0, 0)$ f. a half-turn about $(0, 0)$

15. Is there a rotation about the origin which maps $P(3, 4)$ onto $Q(-5, 6)$? Explain.

EXTRA

A Game of Angles

Picture a billiard table with a coordinate grid marked on it. A ball rolls at a $45°$ angle away from one side of the table. If the ball starts at point $(0, 1)$, it will eventually return to its starting point.

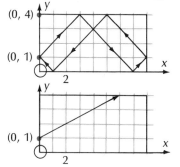

1. Would this happen if the ball started from any other point on the y-axis between $(0, 0)$ and $(0, 4)$?

2. Would this happen if the ball rolled at the angle shown in the second diagram?

9–2 Transformations of Geometric Figures

Under a translation, reflection, rotation, or dilatation, line segments map onto line segments. To determine the image of a line segment, it is sufficient to determine the image of each endpoint.

EXAMPLE 1: $\overline{PQ}$ has endpoints $P(-1, 1)$ and $Q(2, 2)$. Find the image of $\overline{PQ}$ under the given transformation.

a. translation $[3, -2]$

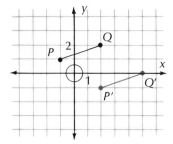

$P(-1, 1) \rightarrow P'(2, -1)$
$Q(2, 2) \rightarrow Q'(5, 0)$

The mapping rule is:
$(x, y) \rightarrow (x + 3, y - 2)$.

b. rotation of $90°$ about $(0, 0)$

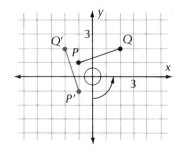

$P(-1, 1) \rightarrow P'(-1, -1)$
$Q(2, 2) \rightarrow Q'(-2, 2)$

The mapping rule is:
$(x, y) \rightarrow (-y, x)$.

c. reflection in line $y = x$

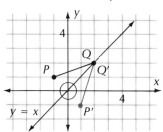

$P(-1, 1) \rightarrow P'(1, -1)$
$Q(2, 2) \rightarrow Q'(2, 2)$

The mapping rule is:
$(x, y) \rightarrow (y, x)$.

d. dilatation with $k = 2$ and centre $(0,0)$

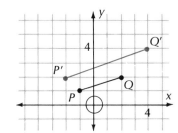

$P(-1, 1) \rightarrow P'(-2, 2)$
$Q(2, 2) \rightarrow Q'(4, 4)$

The mapping rule is:
$(x, y) \rightarrow (2x, 2y)$.

The *length* of $\overline{PQ}$ appears to be preserved in its image $\overline{P'Q'}$ under a translation, rotation, and reflection. That is, a segment and its image appear to be *congruent*. The *slope* of $\overline{PQ}$ appears to be preserved under a translation and a dilatation. Under these two transformations, $\overline{PQ}$ and its image appear to be parallel.

To determine the image of a polygon, it is sufficient to find the image of each vertex.

EXAMPLE 2: △*ABC* has vertices *A*(−3, 4), *B*(2, 1), and *C*(−2, 0).
Locate the image of △*ABC* under the given transformation.

a. translation [0, −3]

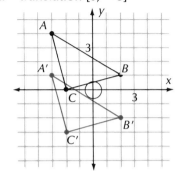

$A(−3, 4) → A'(−3, 1)$
$B(2, 1) → B'(2, −2)$
$C(−2, 0) → C'(−2, −3)$

The mapping rule is:
$P(x, y) → P'(x, y − 3)$

b. rotation of 180°

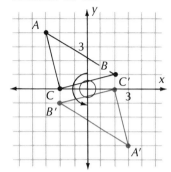

$A(−3, 4) → A'(3, −4)$
$B(2, 1) → B'(−2, −1)$
$C(−2, 0) → C'(2, 0)$

The mapping rule is:
$P(x, y) → P'(−x, −y)$.

c. reflection in *y*-axis

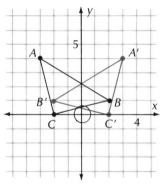

$A(−3, 4) → A'(3, 4)$
$B(2, 1) → B'(−2, 1)$
$C(−2, 0) → C'(2, 0)$

The mapping rule is:
$P(x, y) → P'(−x, y)$.

d. dilatation with *k* = 2 and centre (0, 0)

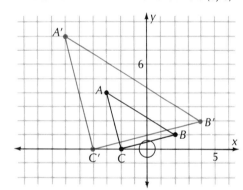

$A(−3, 4) → A'(−6, 8)$
$B(2, 1) → B'(4, 2)$
$C(−2, 0) → C'(−4, 0)$

The mapping rule is:
$P(x, y) → P'(2x, 2y)$.

The *side lengths*, the *angle measures*, and the *area measure* of △*ABC* appear to be preserved in its image △*A'B'C'* under a translation, rotation, and reflection. That is, the triangle and its image appear to be congruent. Note that the **orientation** of the image is *reversed* in a reflection only. (Orientation is reversed because, in moving from *A* to *B* to *C*, one moves clockwise, while in moving from *A'* to *B'* to *C'*, one moves counter-clockwise.)

EXERCISES

A **1.** Plot the segment with the given endpoints. Draw its image under the given transformation.

    a. $A(-2, 1)$, $B(3, 2)$; reflection in the x-axis

    b. $R(-2, 1)$, $T(2, -3)$; dilatation with $k = 3$ and centre $(0, 0)$

    c. $P(1, 2)$, $Q(4, 3)$; rotation of $90°$ about $(0, 0)$

    d. $C(-3, 4)$, $D(2, -1)$; reflection in the y-axis

    e. $J(-3, 2)$, $K(3, 1)$; $(x, y) \rightarrow (x - 2, y - 3)$

    f. $M(-4, 4)$, $N(-2, -1)$; reflection in $y = x$

B **2.** $\overline{PQ}$ has endpoints $P(4, 6)$ and $Q(1, -1)$.

    a. Locate the images of P and Q under $(x, y) \rightarrow (x - 2, y - 1)$. Then plot $\overline{PQ}$ and $\overline{P'Q'}$.

    b. Compare the slopes of $\overline{PQ}$ and $\overline{P'Q'}$.

    c. Use slopes to determine if $\overline{PQ}$ and $\overline{P'Q'}$ are parallel.

    d. Use the distance formula, $d = \sqrt{(x_1 - x_2)^2 + (y_1 - y_2)^2}$, to show that $PQ = P'Q'$.

3. $\overline{EF}$ has endpoints $E(-1, 0)$ and $F(4, -2)$.

    a. Locate the images of E and F under $(x, y) \rightarrow (3x, 3y)$. Plot $\overline{EF}$ and $\overline{E'F'}$.

    b. Compare the slopes of $\overline{EF}$ and $\overline{E'F'}$.

    c. Use slopes to determine if $\overline{EF}$ and $\overline{E'F'}$ are parallel.

    d. Make a statement about the lengths of $\overline{EF}$ and $\overline{E'F'}$ using the distance formula.

4. $\overline{RS}$ has endpoints $R(4, 3)$ and $S(-2, 1)$.

    a. Locate the images of R and S under a reflection in the y-axis. Plot $\overline{RS}$ and $\overline{R'S'}$.

    b. Compare the slopes of $\overline{RS}$ and $\overline{R'S'}$.

    c. Make a statement about the lengths of $\overline{RS}$ and $\overline{R'S'}$ using the distance formula.

5. $\overline{HM}$ has endpoints $H(-3, -1)$ and $M(4, 5)$.

    a. Locate the images of H and M under the rotation of $90°$ about the origin. Then plot $\overline{HM}$ and $\overline{H'M'}$.

    b. Compare the slopes of $\overline{HM}$ and $\overline{H'M'}$.

    c. What do the slopes reveal about $\overline{HM}$ and $\overline{H'M'}$?

    d. Rotate $\overline{HM}$ $-90°$ about the origin. What general property seems to be true for a line segment under a rotation of $\pm 90°$ about the origin?

6. $\triangle ABC$ has vertices $A(3, 4)$, $B(-1, 2)$, and $C(5, -2)$.

    a. Locate the vertices of $\triangle A'B'C'$ under $(x, y) \rightarrow (x + 3, y - 1)$.

    b. Compare the lengths of $\overline{AB}$ and $\overline{A'B'}$, $\overline{BC}$ and $\overline{B'C'}$, and $\overline{AC}$ and $\overline{A'C'}$.

    c. Compare the slopes of the three corresponding sides.

    d. Measure corresponding angles and compare their size.

    e. Measure to find the areas of $\triangle ABC$ and $\triangle A'B'C'$. Compare the areas.

    f. Describe the relationship between $\triangle ABC$ and $\triangle A'B'C'$.

7. $\triangle XYZ$ has vertices $X(-1, -2)$, $Y(1, 5)$, and $Z(6, 2)$.
   a. Locate the vertices of $\triangle X'Y'Z'$ under a rotation of $180°$ about the origin.
   b. Compare the lengths of the sides of $\triangle XYZ$ and corresponding sides in $\triangle X'Y'Z'$.
   c. Compare the slopes of the sides of $\triangle XYZ$ and corresponding sides in $\triangle X'Y'Z'$.
   d. Compare the angle measures of the three corresponding angles.
   e. Compare the area measures of $\triangle XYZ$ and $\triangle X'Y'Z'$.
   f. Describe the relationship between $\triangle XYZ$ and $\triangle X'Y'Z'$.

8. a. Locate the vertices of the image of $\triangle XYZ$ in exercise 7 under a reflection in the x-axis.
   b. Make the following comparisons of the sides of $\triangle XYZ$ and corresponding sides of $\triangle X'Y'Z'$: **i.** length; **ii.** slope.
   c. Compare the measures of corresponding angles.
   d. Compare the area measure of $\triangle XYZ$ and its image.
   e. Which properties of $\triangle XYZ$ are preserved in its image under this transformation? Which are not preserved?

9. Repeat exercise 8 using a reflection of $\triangle XYZ$ in the y-axis.

10. Square $DEFG$ has vertices $D(-1, 2)$, $E(2, 2)$, $F(2, -1)$, and $G(-1, -1)$.
    a. Locate the vertices of the image of square $DEFG$ under a dilatation with $k = 3$ and centre $(0, 0)$.
    b. Compare the square and its image with respect to the following.
       i. side lengths   **ii.** slopes of sides   **iii.** angle measures   **iv.** area

11. What general properties seem to be true about dilatations with centre $(0, 0)$ and the following scale factor?
    a. $|k| > 1$ **b.** $|k| < 1$ **c.** $|k| = 1$

12. Copy and complete the following summary table by writing *preserved*, *not preserved*, or *not always preserved*.

		Properties of Transformations			
		Translation	**Rotation**	**Reflection**	**Dilatation**
a.	Length				
b.	Slope				
c.	Angle Measure				
d.	Area Measure				
e.	Orientation				

C 13. Plot the image of $\triangle ABC$ in example 2 under reflection in the given line.
    a. reflection in $x = 2$ **b.** reflection in $y = 1$ **c.** reflection in $y = -x$

14. Trapezoid $TUVW$ has vertices $T(0,0)$, $U(1,3)$, $V(5,3)$, and $W(6,0)$.
    Locate its image under a dilatation with $k = 2$ and the given centre.
    a. centre at T **b.** centre at U **c.** centre at V **d.** centre at W

9–3 Glide Reflection

A **glide reflection** is the mapping that results from a reflection in line m followed by a translation parallel to line m.

EXAMPLE 1: Find the image of $\triangle ABC$ below under reflection in the y-axis. Then find the image of $\triangle A'B'C'$ under the translation defined by $[0, -4]$.

Note that the translation arrow defined by $[0, -4]$ is parallel to the reflection line.

The translation image of $\triangle A'B'C'$ is $\triangle A''B''C''$.

The mapping of $\triangle ABC$ onto $\triangle A''B''C''$ is called a *glide reflection*.

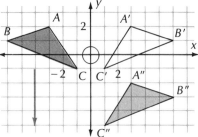

EXAMPLE 2: Find the image of $\triangle DEF$ below under reflection in the line $y = x$ and then translation parallel to $y = x$ by the translation arrow shown.

The two mapping rules are:
a. $(x, y) \rightarrow (y, x)$;
b. $(x, y) \rightarrow (x - 3, y - 3)$.

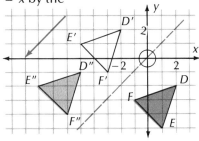

Note that, for a glide reflection, an object and its image appear to be congruent.

EXERCISES

A 1. $\triangle ABC$ maps onto $\triangle A'B'C'$ under the glide reflection illustrated below. Identify the following for each diagram.
  i. line of reflection
  ii. reflection mapping rule
  iii. line to which the translation is parallel
  iv. translation mapping rule

a.
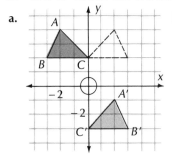

b.
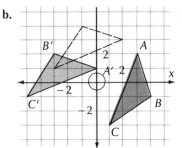

c.
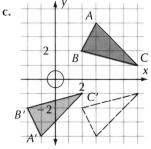

2. The statement refers to a glide reflection. Is the statement *true* or *false*?
  a. The given figure and its image are congruent.
  b. Corresponding sides of the object and image are parallel.
  c. The object and its image have the same orientation.

282

B **3.** Copy each diagram below. Then find the glide reflection image for the given reflection in line m and the given translation.

a.

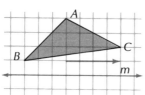

b.

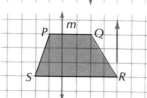

c.

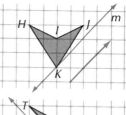

d.

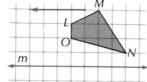

e.

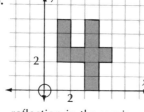

f.

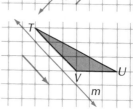

4. For the triangle with vertices $X(5, 9)$, $Y(0, 2)$, and $Z(1, -3)$, find its image under the given glide reflection. Draw the triangle and its image in each case.

   a. The mirror line is the y-axis; the translation is given by $[0, -2]$.

   b. The mirror line is the x-axis; the translation is given by $[-5, 0]$.

   c. The mirror line is given by $y = x$; the translation is given by $[-1, -1]$.

   d. The mirror line is given by $y = -x$; the translation is given by $[4, -4]$.

C **5.** Plot the image of the given figure under the glide reflection described.

a.

reflection in the y-axis;
then translation $[0, -4]$.

b.

reflection in the x-axis;
then $(x, y) \rightarrow (x - 5, y)$.

c.

reflection in $x = 3$;
then translation $[0, -6]$.

EXTRA

A Carpentry Application

A window is to be framed with moulding, as shown at the right. The moulding comes in long strips that are cut to fit the area to be framed. If the moulding is symmetric about the length, how could you make 45° cuts to yield the four required pieces, with the least amount of waste? How long must the piece of moulding be?

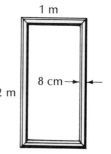

Test your answer by experimenting with a strip of paper "moulding" to frame a rectangular "window" 8 cm by 4 cm.

9–4 Properties of Glide Reflection

Complete the following exercises to discover some properties of glide reflection.

EXERCISES

B **1.** Perform the glide reflection in two ways:
   i. the reflection, then the translation;   **ii.** the translation, then the reflection.

   a. reflection in *x*-axis,
      translation $(x, y) \rightarrow (x + 2, y)$

   b. reflection in *y*-axis,
      translation $(x, y) \rightarrow (x, y - 3)$

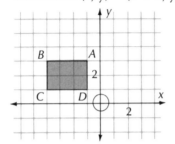

In a glide reflection, does the order in which the reflection and translation occur make a difference?

2. Under a glide reflection, do a figure and its image have corresponding sides of *equal length*? Find the glide reflection image of $\triangle ABC$ at the right and use the distance formula to help you answer the question.

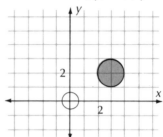

3. Under a glide reflection, do a figure and its image have corresponding sides that are *parallel*? Find the glide reflection image of $\triangle XYZ$ at the right. Then find the slopes of the corresponding sides to help you answer the question.

4. Under a glide reflection, are the *angles* of a figure and its image of the same size? To help you answer the question, find the glide reflection image of parallelogram *TUVW* at the right and measure the size of the corresponding angles.

5. Under a glide reflection, is the *area measure* of a figure and its image the same? Find the glide reflection image of rectangle *JKLM* at the right, then measure and calculate areas to help you answer the question.

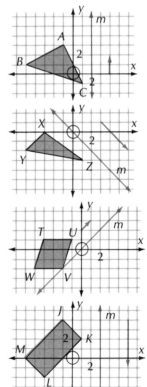

284

6. Under a glide reflection, is the *orientation* of a figure and its image the same or opposite? To help you answer the question, find the glide reflection image of pentagon *ABCDE* by reflection in the *x*-axis and then translation $(x, y) \rightarrow (x - 4, y)$.

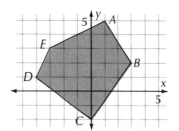

7. Copy and complete the following summary table by writing *preserved* or *not preserved*.

Properties of Glide Reflections	
a.	Length	
b.	Slope	
c.	Angle Measure	
d.	Area Measure	
e.	Orientation	

8. An object and its image under a glide reflection are given below. State the mapping for the translation and reflection of each.

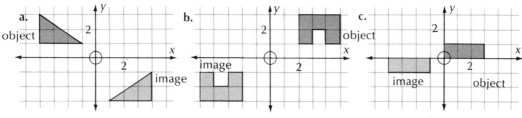

9. A glide reflection maps $\triangle PQR$ to $\triangle P'Q'R'$. Copy the diagram and locate the midpoints of $\overline{PP'}$, $\overline{QQ'}$, and $\overline{RR'}$. What seems to be true about these midpoints?

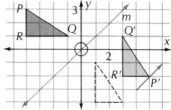

EXTRA

Isometries

An **isometry** is a transformation that preserves distance between points.

Let *P* and *Q* represent any two points in the plane and *P'*, *Q'* their images under a transformation.

> If $P'Q' = PQ$, then the transformation is an isometry.
> If the transformation is an isometry, then $P'Q' = PQ$.

Which of the transformations studied are isometries?

Review

1. $A(5, 2)$, $B(8, 6)$, and $C(1, 4)$ are the vertices of $\triangle ABC$. Plot $\triangle ABC$ and its image under the given transformation.

   a. $(x, y) \rightarrow \left(\frac{1}{2}x, \frac{1}{2}y\right)$ b. reflection in the line $y = x$

   c. 90° rotation about (0, 0)   d. $(x, y) \rightarrow (x - 6, y - 3)$

2. A translation maps $P(-5, 1)$ onto $P'(3, 4)$.
   a. What is the image of $Q(0, -3)$ under this translation?
   b. $K'(8, -3)$ is the image of what point under this translation?

3. Using the diagram at the right, give an example of a figure and its image under:
   a. a translation;
   b. a rotation;
   c. a reflection;
   d. a glide reflection.

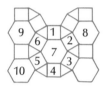

4. A circle with centre $C(-4, 2)$ passes through point $P(-1, 6)$. The circle is reflected in the x-axis. Find the coordinates of C' and P'. Draw the circle and its image.

5. Copy the graph, then find the image of the given figure under the transformation indicated.

   a. glide reflection   b. reflection in $y = x$ c. 90° rotation about (0, 0)

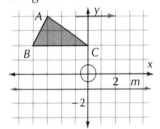 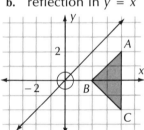 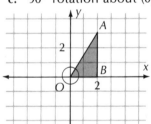

6. Plot $\triangle PQR$ with vertices $P(-7, 4)$, $Q(1, 6)$, and $R(-1, -6)$. Draw its image $\triangle P'Q'R'$ under the dilatation $(x, y) \rightarrow (2x, 2y)$.
   a. Compare the lengths of the corresponding sides.
   b. Compare the slopes of the corresponding sides.
   c. Show that P, O, and P' are collinear by calculating the slopes of OP and OP'.
   d. Measure and compare the sizes of the corresponding angles.
   e. Measure and compare the areas of $\triangle PQR$ and its image.

7. Repeat the steps you followed in exercise 6, using the dilatation $(x, y) \rightarrow (3x, 3y)$.

8. Repeat the steps followed in exercise 6, using the dilatation $(x, y) \rightarrow \left(\frac{1}{2}x, \frac{1}{2}y\right)$.

286

Application

A **pantograph** is a tool used to copy a plane figure to a desired scale. It consists of four jointed rods in the form of a parallelogram with extended sides. A pantograph can be made with 18 cm by 1 cm cardboard strips fastened together with pins or tacks that will allow the parallelogram to be non-rigid.

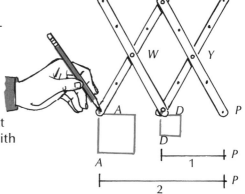

The four rods are pinned together so that a parallelogram is formed and points P, D, and A are collinear. Point P is fixed to the drawing board. To enlarge a figure, a marker at D traces the original figure so that the pencil at A draws the image.

The four rods in the diagram are fastened together at the midpoint of each rod, making an enlargement with a scale factor of 2. The ratio $PA : PD$ is 2 : 1. The ratio remains constant as the original is traced.

The scale factor can be changed by altering the hinges at points W and Y.

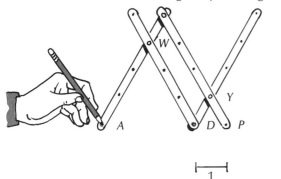

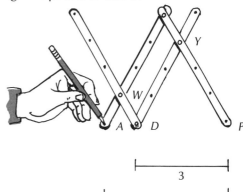

$PA : PD = 4 : 1$
The scale factor is 4.

$PA : PD = 4 : 3$
The scale factor is $\frac{4}{3}$.

1. Make a pantograph and enlarge some designs of your own choice. Experiment with different scale factors.

2. Explain what you would do to reduce a figure.

3. In each enlargement or reduction, can the original figure and its image be called similar? (Check the *Glossary* for a definition of similar figures.)

9–5 Composition of Reflections

The process of performing a transformation to produce image points, and then of performing a second transformation on the image points to produce a second set of image points, is called a **composition** of two transformations.

Composition of two reflections in parallel lines m_1 and m_2

Reflect E_1 in line m_1. Its image is E_2.
Now reflect E_2 in line m_2. Its image is E_3.

The process of performing two reflections in succession is called a **composition** of two reflections in parallel lines.

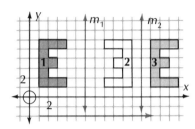

The mapping of E_1 directly onto E_3 is called a **composite** of two reflections in parallel lines. The composite is equivalent to a translation in which the translation arrow is perpendicular to m_1 and m_2 and its directed distance is *double* the distance from m_1 to m_2.

Composition of two reflections in intersecting lines m_1 and m_2

Reflect E_1 in m_1. Its image is E_2.
Reflect E_2 in m_2. Its image is E_3.

This process is called the composition of two reflections in intersecting lines.

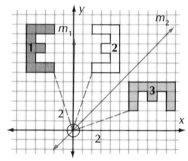

The mapping of E_1 directly onto E_3 is called a composite of two reflections in intersecting lines. The composite is equivalent to a rotation about O, with the angle of rotation *double* the angle measure from m_1 to m_2.

EXERCISES

A 1. Copy the diagram. Draw the images of the given figure under the composition of reflections in m_1 and m_2.

a.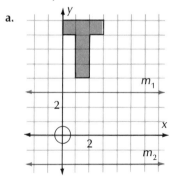

b.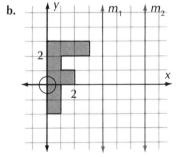

c.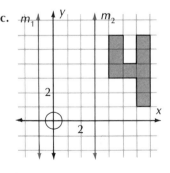

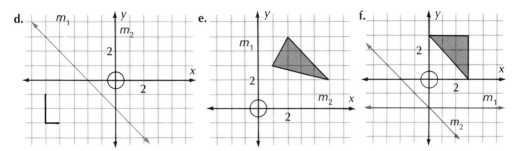

d. m_1 m_2

e. m_1 m_2

f. m_1 m_2

2. Repeat exercise 1, but this time reverse the order in which you perform the two reflections. Compare your results to those for exercise 1.

B 3. $\triangle ABC$ has vertices $A(1, 4)$, $B(-2, 2)$, and $C(2, 1)$.
   a. Plot its image under the composition of reflections in the line $x = 3$ and then in the line $x = -1$.
   b. Describe the composite of these two reflections.

4. $\triangle DEF$ has vertices $D(-1, 1)$, $E(-4, -1)$, and $F(3, -2)$.
   a. Plot its image under the composition of reflections in the line $y = 2$ and then in the line $y = -1$.
   b. Describe the composite of these two reflections.

5. $\triangle JKL$ has vertices $J(-3, -2)$, $K(-4, -4)$, and $L(2, -5)$.
   a. Plot its image under the composition of reflections in the line $x = 3$ and then in the line $y = -2$.
   b. Describe the composite of these two reflections.

6. Square $ABCD$ has vertices $A(2, 4)$, $B(4, 4)$, $C(4, 2)$, and $D(2, 2)$.
   a. Plot $ABCD$ and its image under the composition of reflections $(x, y) \rightarrow (x, -y)$ and then $(x, y) \rightarrow (y, x)$.
   b. Describe the composite of these two reflections.

C 7. $\triangle XYZ$ has vertices $X(-3, 5)$, $Y(-5, 1)$, and $Z(-1, 3)$.
   a. Plot $\triangle XYZ$ and its image $\triangle X'Y'Z'$ under reflection in the line $y = x + 3$.
   b. Draw the image of $\triangle X'Y'Z'$ under reflection in the line $y = -1$.
   c. Describe the composite of these two reflections.

8. Quadrilateral $ABCD$ has vertices $A(-5, 6)$, $B(-7, 4)$, $C(-7, 2)$, and $D(-2, 3)$.
   a. Plot quadrilateral $ABCD$ and its image under the composition of reflections in the y-axis and then in the line $y = x$.
   b. Describe the composite of these two reflections.

9. Triangle XYZ has vertices $X(1, -1)$, $Y(-1, -2)$, and $Z(0, 2)$. Plot $\triangle XYZ$ and its successive images under reflection in the x-axis, followed by reflection in $y = x$, followed by reflection in the y-axis. Describe the composite of these three reflections.

9–6 Composition of Isometries

Translation, reflection, rotation, and glide reflection are *isometries*; each transformation preserves distance between points.

The diagram at the right shows the composition of translation [8, 0] followed by reflection in the line $y = x$.

The mapping of E_1 onto E_3 is the composite of the translation and reflection.

The second diagram shows the composition of 90° rotation about A and then reflection in the line $x = -2$.

The mapping of T_1 onto T_3 is the composite of the rotation and reflection.

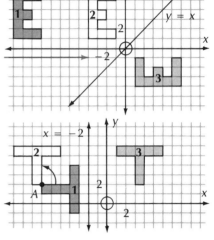

EXERCISES

A 1. Describe a transformation or composition of transformations that maps each figure onto its image.

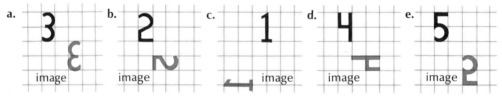

a. 3 image

b. 2 image

c. 1 image

d. 4 image

e. 5 image

B 2. a. By using two of each of the pieces shown at the right, a rectangle can be formed. One of the many possible solutions is given. Identify an isometry or composition of isometries that maps each numbered figure onto its congruent partner.

   b. Make cardboard pieces to help you find another solution. (There are approximately 800 solutions.)

3. Copy each diagram. Locate the image of $\triangle ABC$ under the composite of reflection in line m_1 and then in line m_2.

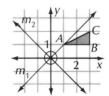

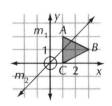

290

4. For each diagram in exercise 3, find the image of $\triangle ABC$ under the composite of reflections in line m_2 and then in line m_1.

5. $\triangle FGH$ has vertices $F(3, 5)$, $G(1, 3)$, and $H(-6, 2)$. Draw its image under the composite of reflections in $y = -1$ and then in $x = 3$.

6. $\triangle ABC$ has vertices $A(3, 5)$, $B(1, 3)$, and $C(5, 1)$.
   a. Plot its image under the composite of translation $[-3, 0]$ and then reflection in the line $y = 1$.
   b. Give the mapping rules of these two isometries.

7. Repeat exercise 6, but this time reverse the order of the isometries. Compare your answers.

8. $\triangle XYZ$ has vertices $X(-3, 3)$, $Y(-4, 0)$, and $Z(0, 1)$. Plot its image under the composite of reflection in the line $y = x$ and then a half-turn about the origin.

9. Repeat exercise 8, but this time reverse the order of the isometries. Compare your answers.

10. What isometry is equivalent to the composite of: translation and then reflection in a line parallel to the translation arrow? rotation and then reflection?

EXTRA
Frieze Patterns

Frieze patterns are generated by taking a single figure and performing repeated transformations to create a "ribbon" of pattern extending infinitely to the left and the right.

Frieze patterns can be classified by considering their symmetries, or the set of transformations that will map the entire pattern onto itself. If two frieze patterns have the same symmetries, they are considered to be essentially the same mathematically. The two patterns below are essentially the same.

 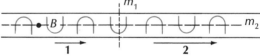

1. Give four different types of transformation to map each pattern above onto itself.

2. For each frieze pattern below, identify all of its symmetries. Which patterns can be classified in the same group?

a.    b.    c.

d.    e.    f.

3. How many different frieze patterns with repeated figure E can you find?

9–7 Congruence and Similarity

For two polygons to be congruent, all corresponding sides must be equal and all corresponding angles must be equal.

In previous lessons, we saw that translation, reflection, rotation, and glide reflection preserve length and angle measure; thus, they produce an image *congruent* to the original figure.

EXAMPLE 1:   A glide reflection maps $\triangle ABC$ onto $\triangle A''B''C''$. Show that $\triangle ABC$ and its image are congruent.

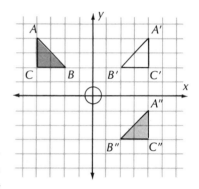

Since both the reflection and the translation preserve the lengths of corresponding sides and the size of corresponding angles, the following statements are true.

$AB = A'B' = A''B''$ $\angle A = \angle A' = \angle A''$
$AC = A'C' = A''C''$ $\angle B = \angle B' = \angle B''$
$BC = B'C' = B''C''$ $\angle C = \angle C' = \angle C''$

Thus, $\triangle ABC \cong \triangle A'B'C' \cong \triangle A''B''C''$. $\cong$ means *is congruent to.*

$\triangle ABC$ has clockwise orientation and $\triangle A'B'C'$ has counter-clockwise orientation. The triangles display **opposite congruence.**

$\triangle A'B'C'$ and $\triangle A''B''C''$ have the same orientation. They display **direct congruence.**

Two polygons are **similar** if the corresponding angles are equal and the corresponding sides are in the same ratio, or are proportional.

EXAMPLE 2:   The dilatation $(x, y) \rightarrow (3x, 3y)$ maps $\triangle ABC$ onto $\triangle A'B'C'$. Show that $\triangle ABC$ and its image are similar.

Compare the lengths of the corresponding sides.

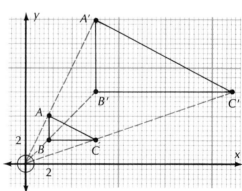

$AB = 2$ $A'B' = 6$
$BC = 4$ $B'C' = 12$
$AC = \sqrt{4 + 16}$ $A'C' = \sqrt{36 + 144}$
$\quad = \sqrt{20}$ $\quad = \sqrt{180}$
$\quad = 2\sqrt{5}$ $\quad = 6\sqrt{5}$

The corresponding sides are in the same ratio.
The scale factor is 3.

$$\frac{A'B'}{AB} = \frac{B'C'}{BC} = \frac{A'C'}{AC} = \frac{3}{1}$$

Thus, $\triangle ABC \sim \triangle A'B'C'$.

~ means *is similar to.*

In order to have two triangles that are similar, we need to know that *either* the corresponding angles are equal, *or* the corresponding sides are in the same ratio. You can find the lengths of sides in similar triangles by applying the proportionality of corresponding sides.

EXAMPLE 3: Given $\triangle PQR \sim \triangle HMC$ with side lengths as shown in the diagram, find the missing lengths in the smaller triangle.

Since the triangles are similar, the corresponding sides are in the same ratio.

$$\frac{PQ}{HM} = \frac{QR}{MC} = \frac{PR}{HC}$$

$$\frac{12}{c} = \frac{14}{h} = \frac{15}{5}$$

The unknown lengths are $c = 4$ and $h = \frac{14}{3}$.

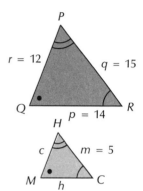

To identify corresponding sides, remember that corresponding sides are opposite corresponding equal angles.

EXERCISES

A 1. Given $\triangle ABC \cong \triangle PQR$, copy and complete the following statements.
   a. $\angle ABC = $ ■   **b.** $\angle BCA = $ ■   **c.** $\angle CAB = $ ■   **d** $BC = $ ■
   e. $AC = $ ■   **f.** $PQ = $ ■   **g.** $\triangle QPR \cong $ ■   **h.** $\triangle CAB \cong $ ■

2. Given $\triangle XYZ \rightarrow \triangle X'Y'Z'$ under a dilatation with scale factor 2, which of the following statements are true?
   a. $\angle X = \angle X'$ **b.** $\angle Z' = 2\angle Z$ **c.** $XZ = 2X'Z'$

   d. $YZ = 2Y'Z'$ **e.** $\frac{YX}{Y'X'} = \frac{1}{2}$ **f.** $\triangle XYZ \cong \triangle X'Y'Z'$

3. For $\triangle PQR$ and $\triangle XYZ$ as shown, which of the following statements are true?

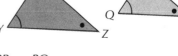

   a. $XZ = PR$ **b.** $\frac{XY}{PQ} = \frac{XZ}{PR}$

   c. $\triangle XYZ \sim \triangle PQR$ **d.** $\frac{YZ}{QR} = \frac{PQ}{XY}$ **e.** $\frac{PR}{XY} = \frac{PQ}{XZ}$ **f.** $QR = XZ$

4. $\triangle ABC$ maps onto $\triangle A'B'C'$ under a dilatation with scale factor 4. Given the following measures of the sides of $\triangle ABC$, find the length of each side of the image triangle.

   a. $AB = 7$ units   **b.** $BC = 5$ units   **c.** $AC = 8$ units

5. $\triangle PQR$ maps onto $\triangle P'Q'R'$ under a dilatation with scale factor 3. Given the following measures of the sides of $\triangle P'Q'R'$, find the length of each side of the original triangle.

   a. $P'Q' = 6$ units   **b.** $Q'R' = 8$ units   **c.** $P'R' = 9$ units

B 6. Identify at least 7 pairs of congruent figures and 4 pairs of similar figures in the diagram below. Write a congruence or similarity statement for each pair and justify each statement.

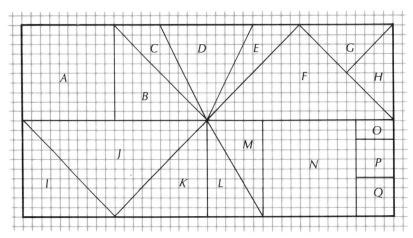

7. Draw $\triangle ABC$ with vertices $A(3, 5)$, $B(1, 2)$, and $C(6, 1)$. Draw its image under the transformation. Describe the nature of the transformation (direct congruence, opposite congruence, or similarity).

   a. $(x, y) \rightarrow (x + 2, y - 1)$
   b. reflection in the y-axis
   c. a half-turn about $(0, 0)$
   d. dilatation with scale factor 2 and centre $(0, 0)$
   e. reflection in the x-axis
   f. reflection in the y-axis and then translation $[0, -5]$

8. For each pair of similar triangles, find the lengths of the unknown sides.

   a.
   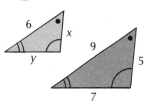

   b.
   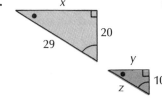
   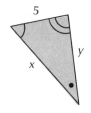

   c.

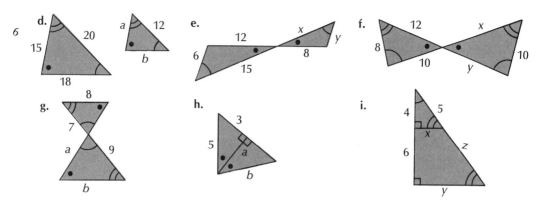

9. Draw △ABC with vertices A(−2, 4), B(0, 2), and C(−5, 1). Draw the image of △ABC under a dilatation with centre (0, 0) and scale factor −2.
   a. Is the orientation of the image the same as the orientation of the object?
   b. Is △ABC ∼ △A′B′C′? Explain.

C 10. Given △ABC ∼ △DEF and AB = 6 cm, DE = 4 cm, and the perimeter of △ABC is 14 cm, find the perimeter of △DEF.

11. Use similar triangles to show that $x^2 = ab$ in the diagram at the right.

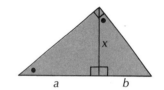

12. For figures ABCD and PQRS, show that:

    $$\frac{AB}{PQ} = \frac{BC}{QR} = \frac{CD}{RS} = \frac{AD}{PS}.$$

    Are the figures similar? Explain.

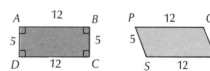

13. For figures ABCDE and PQRST, show that:

    $$\frac{AB}{PQ} = \frac{BC}{QR} = \frac{CD}{RS} = \frac{DE}{ST} = \frac{EA}{TP}.$$

    Are these figures similar? Explain.

14. △ABC maps onto △A′B′C′ under a dilatation.
    a. What is the scale factor of the dilatation?
    b. Find the area of each triangle.
    c. By what factor has the area been increased?
    d. By what factor would the area be increased if the scale factor of the dilatation were 3? 5? n? Draw △ABC and its various images under such dilatation factors to check your answer.

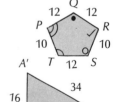

15. What would happen to the volume of a rectangular box if each side were made 2 times larger? 3 times larger? 5 times larger? Look for examples to check your answer.

Applying Similar Triangles

The properties of similar figures can be used to solve many problems that occur in practical situations. Lengths and distances that are difficult to measure directly, such as the height of a building, can be found by analysing mathematical models involving similar figures.

EXAMPLE: Carole, who is 165 cm tall, notices that her shadow is 750 cm long. At the same time of day, she notices that the shadow cast by a telephone pole on her street is 30 m long. How tall is the telephone pole?

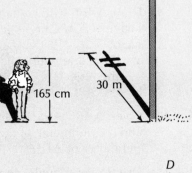

Define a variable.
Let e be the height of the telephone pole in metres.

Make a diagram to help you write a proportion involving similar triangles.

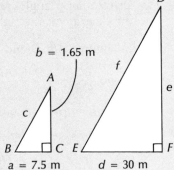

Because the shadows were measured at the same time of day, the sun is shining at the *same angle* on both Carole and the telephone pole. Thus, the corresponding angles of $\triangle ABC$ and $\triangle DEF$, below, are equal.

$\therefore \triangle ABC \sim \triangle DEF$

$a : b : c = d : e : f$

$\therefore \dfrac{b}{a} = \dfrac{e}{d} \rightarrow \dfrac{1.65}{7.5} = \dfrac{e}{30}$

$7.5e = 49.5$

$e = 6.6$

The telephone pole is 6.6 m tall.

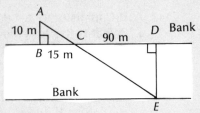

EXERCISES

A 1. To estimate the width of a river, a surveyor made the diagram shown. What is the approximate width of the river?

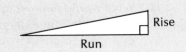

2. The steepness of a road is measured using its rise and run. If a road rises 9 m for a run of 126 m, what is its rise over a run of 2 m?

296

B 3. The shadow of a tree is 24 m long. At the same time, Mike, who is 180 cm tall, casts a shadow 27 m long. About how tall is the tree?

4. Maria is 1.75 m tall. To estimate the height of her school building, she measures the length of her own shadow and the length of the school building's shadow at the same time of the day. What is the approximate height of Maria's school?

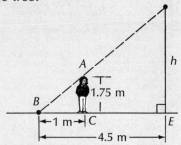

5. In order to estimate the distance across a pond, Jack makes the measurements shown in the diagram. What is the approximate distance from point *A* to point *B*?

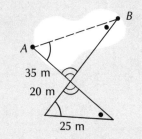

6. An article on safety procedures suggests that the base of a 5 m ladder should be 2.20 m from a wall in order that the ladder be stable. How far from the wall should the base of a 4 m ladder be placed?

7. Suppose you are flying a kite at an angle of 40° and have released 150 m of string. How high is the kite? Draw a triangle similar to the real triangle. Measure the height *b* of the scale triangle and use similar triangles to determine an approximate height *e* of the kite.

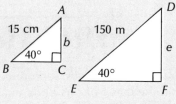

C 8. Hole 4 on Pat's local golf course is shown at the right. Pat decided that he could drive the ball across the stream instead of around it. In order to decide whether it was possible, he made the measurements shown. If Pat can drive the ball 200 m, can he reach the green in one shot? Use a scale diagram to justify your answer.

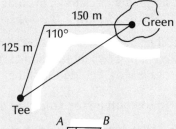

9. In order to estimate the distance across a river, a surveyor made the diagram shown and the following measurements: *DE* = 80 m; *CD* = 170 m; *AE* = 330 m. Approximate the distance, *AB*, across the river.

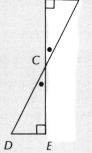

297

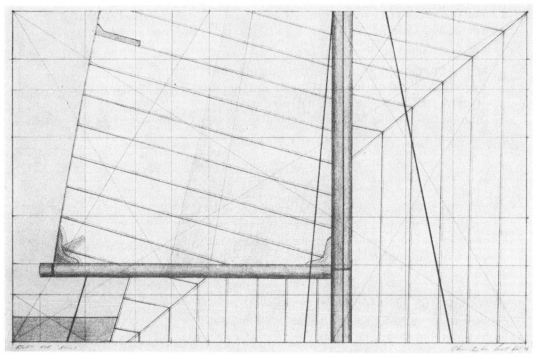

PRATT, Christopher *Study for Sails*, 1974

Application

Golden Rectangles

Both *Study for Sails*, reproduced above, and the print *Ocean Racer*, used on the cover of this book, make extensive use of the *golden rectangle*.

In a golden rectangle, the length *l* and width *w* satisfy the equation *l*:*w* = (*l* + *w*):*l*.

When a square is cut away from a golden rectangle, the remaining rectangle is similar to the original, and therefore is also a golden rectangle (that is, *l*:*w* = (*l* + *w*):*l*).

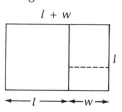

1. The outline for *Study for Sails* is a golden rectangle. Identify others.

2. How has the golden rectangle been used to create a focal point?

3. The numerical value of $\frac{l}{w}$ is $\frac{(1 + \sqrt{5})}{2}$. Use a calculator to evaluate the golden ratio as a decimal, correct to 4 decimal places.

4. In the Fibonacci sequence, 1, 1, 2, 3, 5, 8, 13, 21, 34, 55, 89, 144, ..., each number after the second is the sum of the preceding two numbers. Calculate the ratio of each member of the sequence to the preceding member. Compare your answer to the answer for question 3.

298

Review

1. For figure ABCD with vertices A(5, 9), B(−2, 3), C(−5, −7), and D(3, 0), find A'B'C'D' under the given composition of isometries. Draw ABCD and its image in each case.
   a. translation [−3, −1] followed by reflection in the y-axis
   b. reflection in the line y = x followed by reflection in the x-axis
   c. rotation of 90° about (0, 0) followed by reflection in the y-axis
   d. reflection in the line x = 5 followed by rotation of 180° about (0, 0)

2. Under a dilatation, is it possible for the image to be congruent to the object?

3. Find the missing measures which are represented by letters.

   a.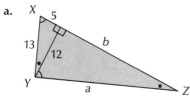

   b.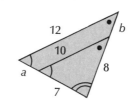

   c.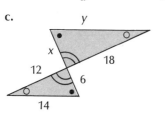

   d.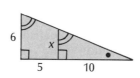

4. Under which transformations are a figure and its image related by:
   a. direct congruence?
   b. opposite congruence?
   c. similarity?

5. On a sunny day, a flagpole casts a shadow 3 m long while Doug, who is 180 cm tall, casts a shadow 2 m long. Apply similar triangles to estimate the height of the flagpole.

   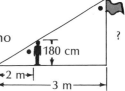

6. Given △ABC ~ △XYZ, find the following.
   a. the ratio of the perimeter of △ABC to the perimeter of △XYZ
   b. the ratio of the area of △ABC to the area of △XYZ

   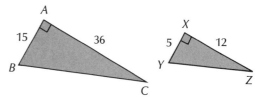

7. A rectangular living room with dimensions 8 m by 5 m has an area rug 6 m by 3.75 m. Show that the floor and the rug are similar in shape.

8. A room 10 m by 6 m has an area rug 6 m by 3.6 m. Are the floor and the rug similar in shape?

299

1. Find the image of $(5, -2)$ under the given transformation.
   a. $(x, y) \rightarrow (x - 3, y + 4)$
   b. reflection in the y-axis
   c. rotation of $90°$ about $O(0, 0)$
   d. reflection in $y = x$
   e. a half-turn about the origin
   f. dilatation $(x, y) \rightarrow (3.5x, 3.5y)$

2. $\overline{AB}$ has endpoints $A(5, -1)$ and $B(-6, -7)$. A translation maps A to $A'(-11, 4)$. What is the image of B under the translation?

3. $\triangle PQR$ has vertices $P(-7, 8)$, $Q(-2, 3)$, and $R(-4, 0)$. Find the image of $\triangle PQR$ under the given transformation.
   a. $(x, y) \rightarrow (2x, 2y)$
   b. $(x, y) \rightarrow (x + 2, y - 4)$
   c. reflection in the x-axis

4. For each glide reflection defined below, find the image of the figure graphed at the right.
   a. translation $[-2, 0]$; reflection in $y = -2$
   b. translation $[0, 5]$; reflection in $x = -3$
   c. reflection in $x = y$; translation $[-2, -2]$

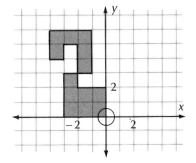

5. For which of the following transformations is the image congruent to the original object? Explain.
   a. translation
   b. dilatation
   c. rotation
   d. reflection
   e. glide reflection

6. Draw the image of figure F under the composite of reflections in m_1 and then m_2.

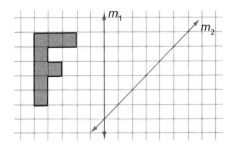

7. Give an example of a transformation in which an object and its image are:
   a. directly congruent;
   b. oppositely congruent;
   c. similar.

8. Find the value of each unknown.

a.
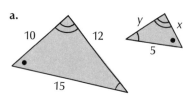

b.
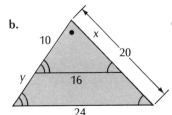

c.
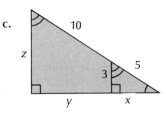

Cumulative Review

1. Given $\overline{AB}$ with endpoints $A(-7, -12)$ and $B(-8, 9)$, answer the following.
   a. Find the length of $\overline{AB}$.
   b. Find the midpoint M of $\overline{AB}$.
   c. Find the slope of $\overline{AB}$.

2. Rewrite the equation $4x - 3y = 15$ in slope-intercept form. Graph the line represented by the equation.

3. Find an equation of the line described.
   a. passing through $C(5, 3)$ and $O(0, 0)$
   b. passing through $K(-3, 4)$ and with slope -2
   c. passing through $T(2, 2)$ and parallel to the line represented by $y = x - 3$

4. Solve each system of equations, using the method of your choice.
   a. $x + y = 2$
      $3x - 2y = 1$
   b. $x + 2y = -1$
      $3x - y = 3$
   c. $2x - y = 8$
      $3x - 2y = 11$
   d. $x + y = -4$
      $2x - 3y = 2$
   e. $2x - 5y = -5$
      $3x - 2y = 20$
   f. $-2x + 6y = -14$
      $-3x - 5y = -22$

5. Graph each system of inequalities.
   a. $x \geq 7$
      $y \leq x$
   b. $y > -2$
      $y < 3x - 1$
      $x > 1$
   c. $x + y < 5$
      $2x + 3y \geq -4$
      $y \geq 5$

6. Factor.
   a. $x^2 - 4y^2$
   b. $x^2 + 5x - 14$
   c. $2x^2 + 5x - 3$
   d. $16x^4 - 81y^4$
   e. $3x^2 + x - 2$
   f. $2x^2 + 28x + 98$

7. Given that y varies directly as x, and that x is 22 when y is -2, find y when x is 3.

8. A line contains the points $R(5, 3)$ and $T(15, 28)$. Use linear interpolation to estimate the value of y when x is 10.

9. Use the data below to answer the following questions.

   Class 10D: Amount Collected in Walkathon

$25	$38	$28	$27	$35	$49	$32	$35
$27	$33	$26	$48	$33	$29	$42	$39
$22	$41	$33	$32	$40	$25	$33	$21
$15	$31	$39	$38	$59	$5	$23	$33

   a. Select an appropriate interval size for grouping the data.
   b. Make an extended frequency table of the data.
   c. Estimate the mean, median, and mode of the data.
   d. Display the data in a histogram.

301

10

Deductive Geometry

Pythagoras, a mathematician and philosopher of sixth-century Greece, had a large, almost cult-like following that flourished even after his death.

10–1 A Foundation for Rigour

Pythagoras, although best known today for the Pythagorean Theorem, made many contributions to the study of mathematics. Pythagoras put geometry on a scientific footing by insisting that logical, deductive reasoning be used in geometric proofs, claiming that the observation of several typical examples was not sufficient reason to make a generalized statement. Consider the following examples.

In each circle, the inscribed angle A is half the sector angle O. Is this always true?

  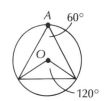

Although this question cannot be answered yet, the material in this unit will develop a number of stepping stones, one of which is the process of deductive reasoning, that can lead us to an answer. In deductive reasoning, we start with simple statements that can be readily accepted as true and, following rules of logical reasoning, we reach a valid **conclusion**. Deductive reasoning is the "bridge" from the known to the unknown.

The following set of statements provides an example of deductive reasoning.

All grade 10 students take Mathematics. ⎫ ← This is *known*.
Julie is a grade 10 student. ⎬ This conclusion was
Therefore Julie takes Mathematics. ← ⎭ formerly *unknown*.

EXAMPLES: For each set of statements, write a conclusion.

a. All insects have six legs.
A fly is an insect.

Conclusion: A fly has six legs.

b. All insects have six legs.
Some flying things are insects.

Conclusion: Some flying things have six legs.

c. All quadrilaterals have four sides.
All parallelograms are quadrilaterals.
Figure *WXYZ* is a parallelogram.

Conclusion: Figure *WXYZ* has four sides.

Deductive reasoning can be applied to the study of geometry. Euclid, a Greek mathematician of the third century B.C., sought to organize mathematical knowledge in a logical way in a collection of 13 books known as the *Elements*. Beginning with undefined terms, defined terms, and assumptions, and using the bridge of deductive reasoning, Euclid was able to prove a large number of propositions or theorems. The diagram illustrates the structure of deductive geometry.

An **undefined term** is a basic notion, so fundamental that it cannot be defined using other terms. A *point* is an undefined term in geometry.

A **defined term** is one that can be explained using previously defined terms.

A trapezoid is a quadrilateral ⟵――――― known set
with one pair of opposite sides parallel.

⬆
distinguishing property

A good definition places the term in a known set, and states the property which distinguishes it from the other members of the set.

An **assumption** is a statement so generally accepted that it need not be proved. Euclid described assumptions as **axioms** or **postulates**.

Input

Undefined Terms
Defined Terms
Assumptions
(Axioms and Postulates)

Process

Deductive Reasoning

Output

Deductions
Theorems

A **deduction** is a proof based on deductive reasoning. In a rigorous proof, underlying assumptions are stated for the reader, and the logical steps are explicitly displayed.

A **theorem** is a useful deduction which is specifically named and used as an authority in proving other deductions.

EXERCISES

A 1. State a conclusion from the given statements.

    a. All grade 10 students take Mathematics and Science.
        Andy is a grade 10 student.

    b. If you walk in the rain, you will get wet.
        James is walking in the rain.

    c. All babies sleep for several hours during the day.
        Anthony is a three-week-old baby.

    d. Any person suffering from myopia should wear corrective lenses.
        Claire suffers from myopia.

    e. Any person who exercises regularly will be fit.
        Al exercises regularly.

    f. Any triangle with two equal sides is isosceles.
        $\triangle ABC$ has two equal sides.

    g. The diagonals of a square bisect each other.
        The diagonals of square $ABCD$ cross at point M.

    h. All babies are vulnerable.
        All vulnerable creatures require nurturing and caring.
        Alicia is a newborn baby.

    i. All my dishes are made of clay.
        All things made of clay are easily broken if dropped.
        This saucer is one of my dishes.

    j. An elephant has a trunk.
        An animal with a trunk is a sight to be seen.
        Betsy is a circus elephant.

B 2. Does the given conclusion follow logically from the given statements?

    a. Some students study French and Spanish.
        Lisa studies French.
        Therefore Lisa also studies Spanish.

    b. Some mammals can fly.
        A butterfly can fly.
        Therefore a butterfly is a mammal.

    c. Some right-angled triangles are isosceles.
        An isosceles triangle has two equal sides.
        Therefore some right-angled triangles have two equal sides.

    d. Some students study Mathematics and Accounting.
        Some students study Mathematics and Computer Science.
        Therefore some students study Accounting and Computer Science.

    e. Some isosceles triangles are right-angled.
        An isosceles triangle has two equal sides.
        Therefore some right-angled triangles have two equal sides.

3. Identify a geometric figure defined by the given description.
   a. a quadrilateral with all sides equal
   b. a quadrilateral with all sides equal and at least one right angle
   c. a triangle with all sides equal
   d. a hexagon with all sides equal and all angles equal
   e. a triangle with one right angle
   f. a prism with square bases at right angles to the lateral edges
   g. a right prism with square bases and all edges equal in length

4. Explain the error in logical thinking.

   a. If Tom lives in Vancouver, he lives in British Columbia.
      Tom lives in British Columbia.
      Therefore Tom lives in Vancouver.
   b. All the girls in class 10A went to the school dance.
      Christine went to the school dance.
      Therefore Christine is in class 10A.
   c. At the provincial park, all dogs must be kept on a leash.
      Margaret keeps her pet, Oliver, on a leash.
      Therefore Oliver is a dog.
   d. All the angles of an acute triangle are less than 90°.
      In $\triangle ABC$, $\angle ABC = 60°$.
      Thefore $\triangle ABC$ is an acute triangle.
   e. When two lines intersect, opposite angles are equal.
      $\angle ABC = \angle XYZ$.
      Therefore $\angle ABC$ and $\angle XYZ$ are opposite angles.
   f. All rational numbers are real numbers.
      π is a real number.
      Therefore π is a rational number.

C 5. Some statements at first sight appear to be self-contradictory or absurd, but in reality contain an element of truth. Such a statement is called a **paradox**. Read the following statements. Is statement C true or false? Explain the paradox.

   A. Polar bears can fly.
   B. Mammals are birds.
   C. All of statements A, B, and C are false.

EXTRA

Who Shaves the Barber?

Terry is the only barber in the village of Pratt, where all of the men are clean-shaven, so Terry has put a sign in the shop window: "This barber shaves every grown man who does not shave himself."

Who shaves Terry?

What condition might make Terry's statement true?

10–2 Parallel Lines and Planes

Each window of the house suggests a geometric **plane**. Unlike a window, however, a plane has no thickness, and extends in all directions without ending. **Parallel lines** are suggested by the opposite sides of each window.

A plane is shown in a diagram by a four-sided figure representing part of the plane. Imagine it as extending forever in all directions. Planes are often named by a capital letter, and lines by a lower-case letter, or by two points in the line.

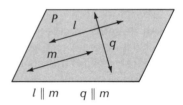

$l \parallel m \qquad q \parallel m$

Lines that lie in the same plane are **coplanar** lines. They either intersect in one point, or they are parallel, as illustrated in the diagram.

In the diagram at the right, l and m do not intersect, but they are not parallel. They are not coplanar, and are called **skew** lines.

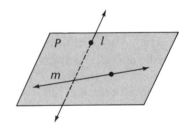

A line which intersects two or more lines is a **transversal** of these lines. When a transversal crosses two lines, the angles formed are categorized as follows.

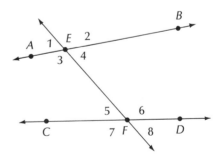

Interior angles: $\angle 3$, $\angle 4$, $\angle 5$, $\angle 6$
Exterior angles: $\angle 1$, $\angle 2$, $\angle 7$, $\angle 8$

Alternate angles (forming a $\mathbb{Z}$ pattern):
$\angle 3$ and $\angle 6$; $\angle 4$ and $\angle 5$

Corresponding angles (forming an F pattern):
$\angle 1$ and $\angle 5$; $\angle 3$ and $\angle 7$; $\angle 2$ and $\angle 6$; $\angle 4$ and $\angle 8$

Interior angles on the same side of the transversal (forming a $\mathbb{Z}$ pattern):
$\angle 3$ and $\angle 5$; $\angle 4$ and $\angle 6$

Planes which do not intersect are **parallel planes**. In a classroom, the floor and the ceiling suggest parallel planes. Imagine the floor and the ceiling extending forever; they would never intersect.

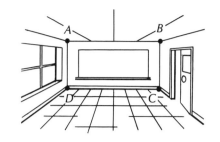

When two planes do intersect, they intersect in a line. Think of the line formed where two walls meet. $\overleftrightarrow{AD}$ is a line formed by the front wall meeting a side wall of the room.

A line can be parallel to a plane. Think of $\overleftrightarrow{AB}$ formed along the top of a wall. $\overleftrightarrow{AB}$ is parallel to the plane suggested by the floor.

EXERCISES

A 1. From the diagram at the right, name the following.

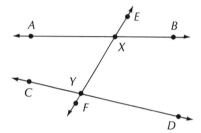

    a. four interior angles
    b. four exterior angles
    c. two pairs of alternate angles
    d. four pairs of corresponding angles
    e. two pairs of interior angles on the same side of the transversal

2. Use the diagram at the right to complete the following statements.

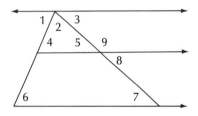

    a. ∠1 and ▆▆ are alternate angles. (Give two answers.)
    b. ∠3 and ▆▆ are corresponding angles.
    c. ∠7 and ▆▆ are alternate angles. (Give two answers.)
    d. ∠3 and ▆▆ are interior angles on the same side of the transversal.
    e. ∠5 and ▆▆ are corresponding angles.

B 3. Using the diagram of the shoe box, name the following.

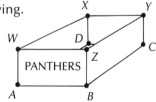

    a. four points on a plane parallel to the plane containing points W, X, Y, and Z
    b. six pairs of parallel line segments
    c. 12 pairs of line segments which are in skew lines

4. Name the following from the diagram.

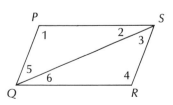

    a. three transversals that intersect $\overline{PS}$ and $\overline{QR}$
    b. all pairs of alternate angles formed by each of the transversals in part **a**
    c. three transversals that cross $\overline{PQ}$ and $\overline{SR}$
    d. all pairs of alternate angles formed by the transversals in part **c**

5. Using the diagram at the right, classify each pair of given angles as alternate, corresponding, interior angles on the same side of the transversal, or none of these.
    a. ∠2 and ∠10   b. ∠4 and ∠5
    c. ∠1 and ∠16   d. ∠5 and ∠15
    e. ∠7 and ∠13   f. ∠5 and ∠6
    g. ∠10 and ∠14   h. ∠4 and ∠13

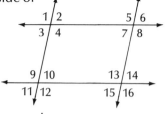

6. Draw two line segments in the same plane that do not intersect, but are not parallel.

7. True or false? If the statement is false, give an example.
    a. Two parallel lines are always coplanar.
    b. Two lines that are not coplanar never intersect.
    c. If a line is parallel to a plane *P*, then a plane containing that line is always parallel to plane *P*.
    d. If two lines are parallel to a third line, then they are parallel to each other.
    e. Two skew lines are sometimes parallel.
    f. If two lines are parallel to a third line, then all three lines are coplanar.

C 8. How many planes can contain:
    a. a given line?
    b. two given intersecting lines?
    c. two given skew lines?
    Give a description or a concrete example for each.

9. Through any three distinct non-collinear points, there is one and only one plane. The points **determine** the plane. How many planes are determined by four points in space, if all four are not coplanar?

10. Must a four-sided figure in space be a plane figure? Explain.

11. Draw diagrams to illustrate the following.
    a. Lines *x* and *y* are skew, lines *y* and *z* are skew, and *x*∥*z*.
    b. Lines *p* and *q* are skew, lines *q* and *r* are skew, and *p*⊥*r*.
    c. Lines *a*, *b*, *c*, and *d* are positioned so that every pair is parallel and no three are in the same plane.

EXTRA

Three-Dimensional Puzzles

1. Show how you could slice a cube by a plane in such a way that the cross section is a regular hexagon. Test your answer using a cube cut out of styrofoam.

2. Can a regular tetrahedron be sliced by a plane to give a square cross section? Explain.

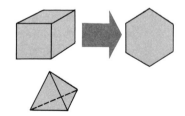

Historical Note

Planes, cylinders, and spheres are not the only surfaces in three-dimensional space studied by mathematicians. We can construct more unusual surfaces.

One of these oddities, the **Moebius strip**, was invented by the German mathematician Augustus Moebius in 1855.

To construct a Moebius strip, start with a long strip of plain paper, give it a half-twist, and tape the ends together.

1. To verify that the Moebius strip has only one side and one edge, trace a line along the middle of a Moebius strip with a pencil. You will come back to your starting point, having marked both "sides" without lifting your pencil from the strip. How many "sides" does this strip really have?

2. Use a pair of scissors to cut the Moebius strip along the line drawn for question 1. What result do you get? Cut this resulting strip lengthwise down the middle. What do you get?

3. Make another Moebius strip. Cut along a line marked one third of the way in from the edge. Describe the result.

4. Experiment with other possibilities. Try giving the paper two or even three twists before taping the ends, then cutting either along the centre or one third of the way in from the edge.

5. B.F. Goodrich Company has patented the use of the Moebius band as a conveyor or machinery belt. Explain why such a belt should last twice as long as a conventional belt.

EXTRA

1. Retrace the pattern shown in one continuous line, without lifting your pencil from the paper, and without going over any line segment twice.

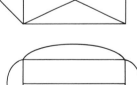

2. Perhaps you answered question 1 easily. If so, try the same thing with the figure at the right. (It can be done.)

10–3 Properties of Parallel Lines

The planter illustrated here has been constructed so that the plant remains level when it is raised or lowered.

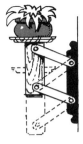

The planter provides a concrete example of the following theorem.

Parallel Lines Theorem (PLT) I

If two parallel lines are cut by a transversal, the following are true.

1. Alternate angles are equal.

   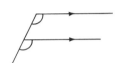

2. Corresponding angles are equal.

3. The sum of the interior angles on the same side of the transversal is 180°. (The angles are *supplementary*.)

   $x + y = 180$

The proof of this theorem is not possible at this time, as it involves material not yet covered. The theorem is to be considered a postulate at this stage.

EXAMPLE 1:   Apply PLT to find the size of each indicated angle.

a.
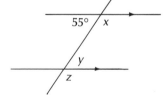

$x + 55 = 180$ (straight angle)
$\therefore x = 125$

$y = 55$ (alternate angles)

$z = 125$ (corresponding angles)

b.
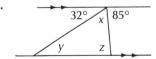

$x + 32 + 85 = 180$ (straight angle)
$\therefore x = 63$

$y = 32$ (alternate angles)

$z = 85$ (alternate angles)

Apply the following theorem to determine whether two given lines are parallel.

> **Parallel Lines Theorem (PLT) II**
>
> If two lines are cut by a transversal and one of the following is known to be true, then the lines are parallel.
>
> 1. Alternate angles are equal.
>
> 2. Corresponding angles are equal.
>
> 3. Interior angles on the same side of the transversal are supplementary.

EXAMPLE 2:   Are the lines parallel? Explain.

a.

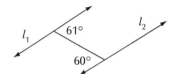

b.

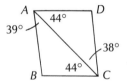

Lines l_1 and l_2 are *not* parallel, since 61° ≠ 60°.

$\overline{AD} \| \overline{BC}$, since alternate angles are equal; $\overline{AB}$ and $\overline{CD}$ are *not* parallel.

EXERCISES

A **1.** For the diagram at the right, name the following.
   a. two pairs of corresponding angles
   b. two pairs of alternate angles
   c. four exterior angles
   d. four interior angles
   e. two pairs of interior angles on the same side of the transversal
   f. all pairs of equal angles
   g. all pairs of supplementary angles

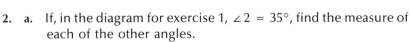

2. **a.** If, in the diagram for exercise 1, ∠2 = 35°, find the measure of each of the other angles.
   b. If ∠8 = 154°, find the measures of the other angles.

311

3. For the diagram at the right, answer the following.
   a. Name all angles equal to ∠4.
   b. Name all angles supplementary to ∠4.
   c. Find ∠10 if ∠2 = 80°.
   d. Find ∠15 if ∠16 = 115°.
   e. Find ∠10 if ∠5 = 75°.
   f. Find ∠11 if ∠7 = 82°.

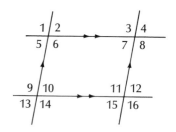

4. Find the size of each indicated angle.

   a.
   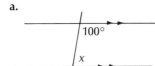

   b.
   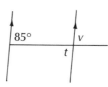

   c.

   d.
   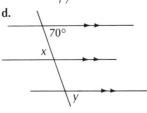

   e.
   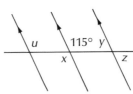

   f.

5. Use the following information to name the line segments, if any, that must be parallel.
   a. ∠1 = ∠5
   b. ∠4 = ∠7
   c. ∠6 = ∠2
   d. ∠5 = ∠6
   e. ∠1 + ∠2 + ∠3 + ∠4 = 180°.

   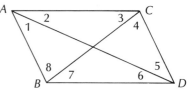

B 6. Find the size of each indicated angle.

   a.
   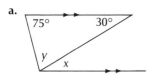

   b.
   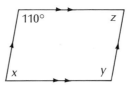

   c.
   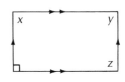

   d.
   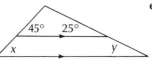

   e.
   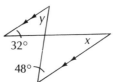

   f.
   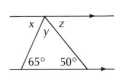

   g.
   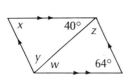

   h.
   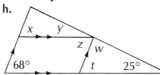

   i.
   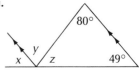

312

7. Find the value of x.

a.

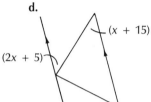

$(3x + 15)$

$2x$

b.

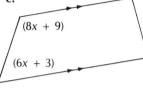

$7x$

$(2x + 18)$

c.

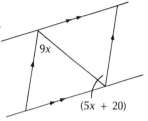

$(5x - 16)$

$(3x + 6)$

d.

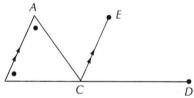

$(x + 15)$

$(2x + 5)$

e.

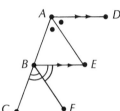

$(8x + 9)$

$(6x + 3)$

f.

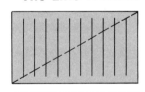

$9x$

$(5x + 20)$

8. A transversal t is perpendicular to two lines p and q. Show that p and q are parallel.

C 9. Given that $\overline{AD} \parallel \overline{BE}$, $\overline{AE}$ bisects $\angle DAC$, and BF bisects $\angle EBC$, show that $\overline{AE} \parallel \overline{BF}$.

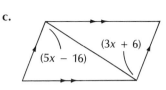

10. Given the information marked on the diagram, show that $\overline{CE}$ bisects $\angle ACD$.

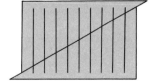

EXTRA

The Line Paradox

Draw a rectangle containing ten equal parallel line segments, like the one shown, and cut it out.

Cut the rectangle in half along the dotted line. Place the two pieces as shown. Count the line segments inside the figure.

Where did the tenth line segment go?

10–4 Intersecting Lines

Two intersecting lines form the angles shown.

Adjacent angles are two angles with a common vertex and a common side. The other sides are on opposite sides of the common side.

∠1 and ∠2 are adjacent angles.
∠2 and ∠3 are also adjacent angles.

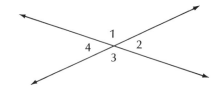

Supplementary angles are two angles whose measures total 180°.
∠1 and ∠2 are supplementary angles.

Opposite angles are two angles with a common vertex whose sides form intersecting lines.
∠1 and ∠3 are opposite angles; ∠2 and ∠4 are also opposite angles.

For the deck chair shown, the opposite angles marked 1 and 2 are always equal. As you open or close the chair, angles 1 and 2 increase or decrease together.

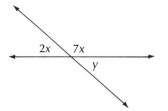

The deck chair provides a practical example of the following theorem for opposite angles.

The Opposite Angle Theorem (OAT)

When two lines intersect, opposite angles are equal.

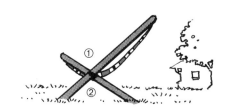

Given: Lines l and m intersect to form ∠1, ∠2, ∠3, and ∠4.

Prove: ∠1 = ∠3 and ∠2 = ∠4

Proof:
∠1 + ∠2 = 180°   (straight angle)
∠2 + ∠3 = 180°   (straight angle)
∠1 + ∠2 = ∠2 + ∠3 (Both L.S. and R.S. equal 180°.)
∴ ∠1 = ∠3   (Subtract ∠2 from each side.)

Use a similar method to prove ∠2 = ∠4.

EXAMPLE: Find the values of x and y.

$$2x + 7x = 180 \quad \text{(supplementary angles)}$$
$$9x = 180$$
$$\therefore x = 20$$
$$y = 2x \quad \text{(OAT)}$$
$$y = 2(20) \quad \text{(substitution)}$$
$$\therefore y = 40$$

314

EXERCISES

A Use the diagram at the right for exercises 1 to 3.

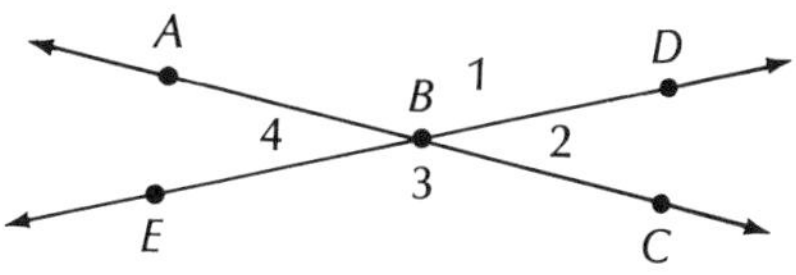

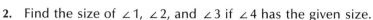

1. Name the following.
   a. two pairs of opposite angles
   b. four pairs of adjacent angles
   c. four pairs of supplementary angles

2. Find the size of $\angle 1$, $\angle 2$, and $\angle 3$ if $\angle 4$ has the given size.
   a. 32° b. 48° c. 54°

3. Complete each statement.
   a. $\angle 2$ is the supplement of [redacted] and of [redacted].
   b. $\angle 1$ and [redacted] are opposite angles.

B 4. Find the size of each unknown angle formed by intersecting lines.

a.
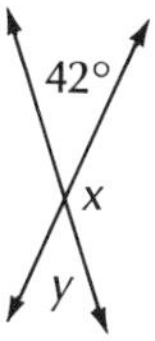

b.
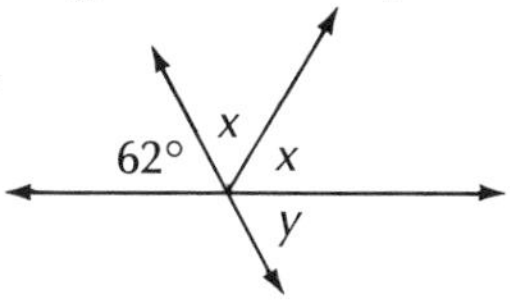

c.
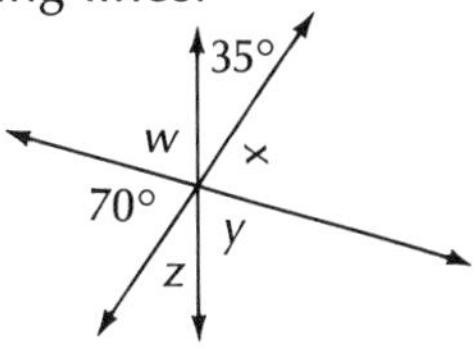

d.
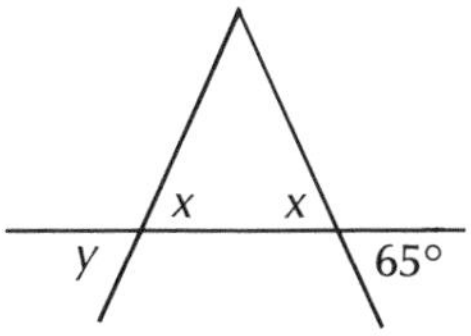

e.
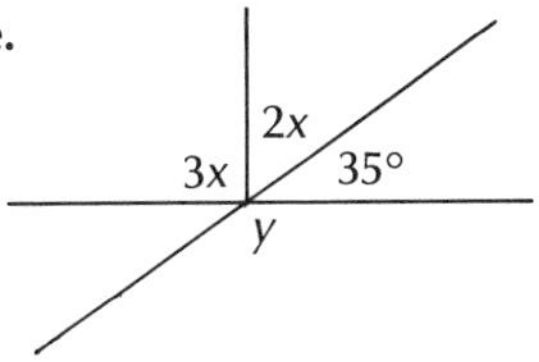

f.
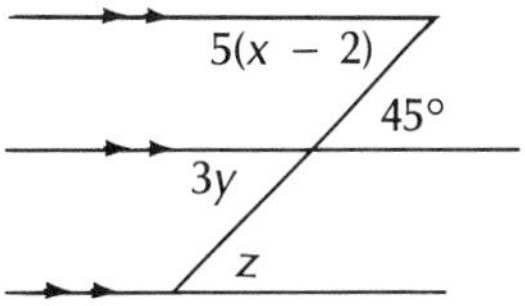

g.
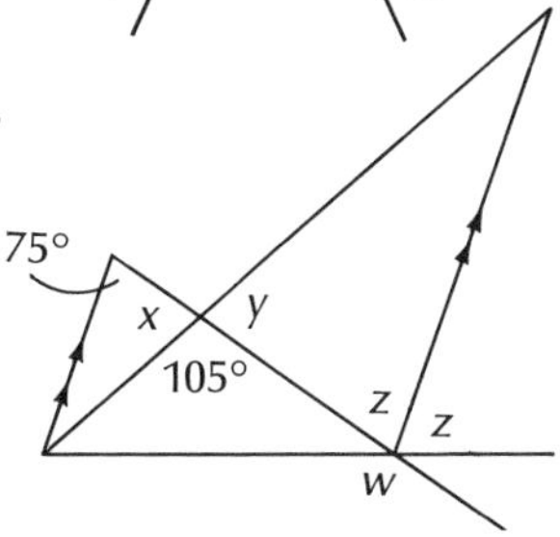

h.
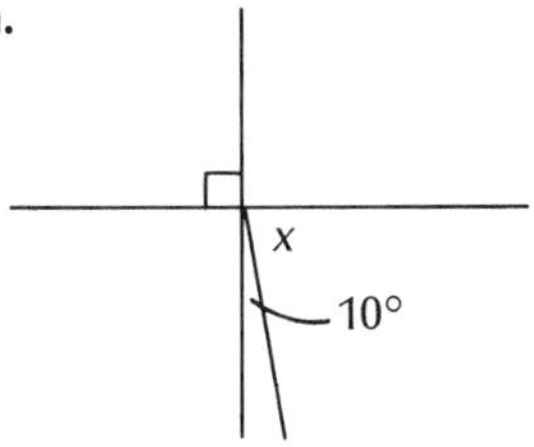

i.
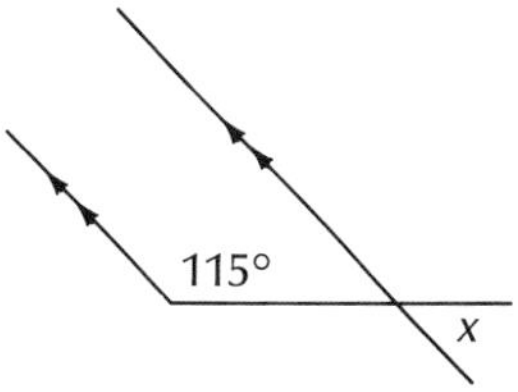

C 5. Prove that $\overleftrightarrow{AC} \parallel \overleftrightarrow{DF}$ if $\angle 1 = \angle 2$.

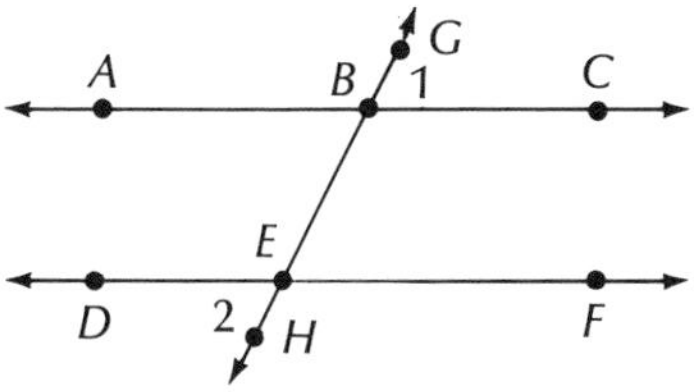

6. The diagonals of a trapezoid form two similar triangles.
   a. Name the similar triangles formed by the diagonals of trapezoid *WXYZ*.
   b. Prove that the triangles are similar by showing that corresponding angles are equal.

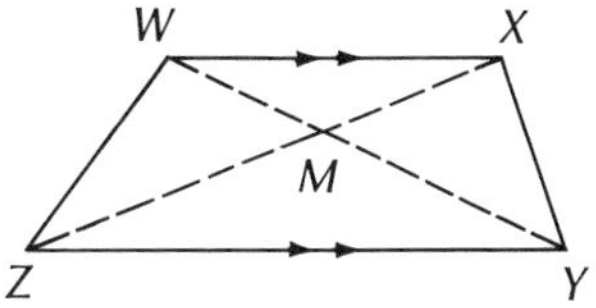

10–5 Sum of the Angles of a Triangle

Recall that the sum of the angles of a triangle is 180°. The diagram illustrates a special case. You can prove this concept using PLT.

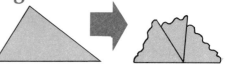

Angle Sum Theorem (AST)

The sum of the angles of a triangle is 180°.

Given: $\triangle ABC$
Prove: $x + y + z = 180$

Proof: Draw $\overleftrightarrow{DE}$ through A, parallel to $\overline{BC}$.

$\angle DAB = y$ (PLT: alternate angles)
$\angle EAC = z$ (PLT: alternate angles)

But $\angle DAB + x + \angle EAC = 180°$ (straight angle)
$\therefore \qquad y + x + z = 180$ (substitution)
or $\qquad x + y + z = 180$

EXAMPLE 1: Find the size of each unknown angle.

a.

$\angle A + \angle B + \angle C = 180°$ (AST)
$x + 65 + 85 = 180$
$x + 150 = 180$
$x = 30$
The size of $\angle A$ is 30°.

b.

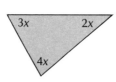

$3x + 2x + 4x = 180$ (AST)
$9x = 180$
$x = 20$

The sizes of the angles are 40°, 60°, and 80°.

c.

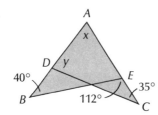

$\angle AEB = 68°$ (straight angle)
$\therefore x + 40 + 68 = 180$ (AST)
$x = 72$
$\therefore \angle BAE = 72°$

$x + y + 35 = 180$ (AST)
$72 + y + 35 = 180$ (substitution)
$y = 73$
$\therefore \angle ADC = 73°$

The Angle Sum Theorem can be used to prove the following theorem.

Exterior Angle Theorem (EAT)

An exterior angle of a triangle is equal to the sum of the two interior opposite angles.

Given: $\triangle ABC$ with exterior angle, $\angle ACD$
Prove: $\angle ACD = \angle A + \angle B$

Proof: $\angle A + \angle B + \angle ACB = 180°$ (AST)
  $\angle ACD + \angle ACB = 180°$ (straight angle)

  $\angle A + \angle B + \angle ACB = \angle ACD + \angle ACB$ (L.S. and R.S. both equal 180°.)
  $\therefore \qquad \angle A + \angle B = \angle ACD$ (Subtract $\angle ACB$ from each side.)

EXAMPLE 2: For the diagram at the right, find the values of x and y.

$x + y = 105$ (EAT applied to $\triangle ABC$)
But $x = 2y$ (EAT applied to $\triangle DAC$)
$\therefore 2y + y = 105$ (substitution)
  $3y = 105$
  $y = 35$

  $x = 70$

EXERCISES

A 1. Find the value of each unknown.

a.
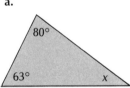
80°
63° x

b.
x
$3x$ $2x$

c.
$(4x + 2)$
$5x$
$(6x - 2)$

d.

$4x$
$2x$

e.
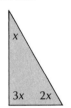
84°
x 38°

f.
52°
x
155°

g.
50°
x x

h.
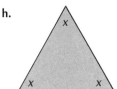
x
x x

i.
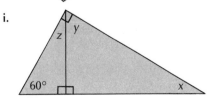
z y
60° x

317

B **2.** Find the size of each indicated angle.

a.
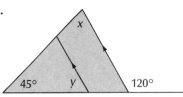

b.
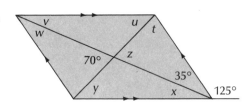

c.

d.
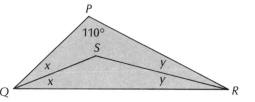

3. Find the size of ∠ QSR.

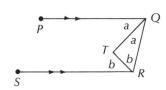

4. In the diagram at the right,
$\overline{PQ} \parallel \overline{SR}$ and the bisectors
of ∠ PQR and ∠ SRQ meet at T.
Prove that ∠ T = 90°.

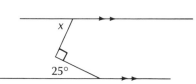

5. Calculate the value of x.

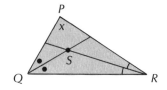

6. Prove that, if an angle of a triangle is equal to the sum of the other two angles, then the angle is a right angle.

C **7.** For the diagram at the right, prove that $\overline{DE} \parallel \overline{BC}$.

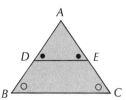

8. In △PQR, the bisectors of ∠ Q and ∠ R meet at a point S.

Prove that ∠ QSR = $\left(\dfrac{180 + x}{2}\right)^{\circ}$.

EXTRA

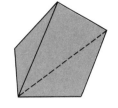

1. **a.** Draw a pentagon.
   b. From one vertex, draw diagonals to divide the pentagon into three non-overlapping triangles.
   c. What is the sum of the angles of each triangle?
   d. What is the sum of the angles of all three triangles?
   e. What is the sum of the angles of the pentagon?

2. Find the sum of the angles of each polygon.
   a. quadrilateral   **b.** hexagon   **c.** octagon
   d. decagon   **e.** a 15-gon   **f.** an *n*-gon

3. A regular polygon has all sides equal and all angles equal. Find the size of each angle of the given polygon.
   a. regular quadrilateral   **b.** regular pentagon
   c. regular octagon   **d.** regular hexagon

Review

1. List five practical examples of each of the following.
   a. a line
   b. a plane
   c. two parallel lines
   d. two parallel planes
   e. two skew lines

2. Find the value of each unknown.

   a.

   b.

   c.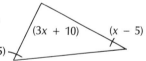

   d.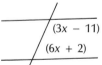

   e.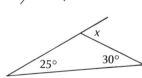

   f.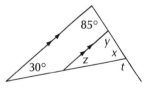

3. Identify parallel lines. Prove they are parallel.

   a.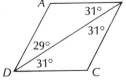

   b.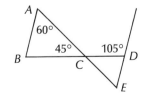

319

10–6 Congruent Triangles

The quilt pattern shown is made up entirely of congruent triangles.

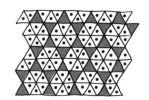

By definition, if two triangles are congruent, then their corresponding sides are equal and corresponding angles are equal. However, to prove two triangles are congruent, you do not need to know that *all* corresponding sides and *all* corresponding angles are equal.

There are three **congruence postulates**, given below, that can be used to prove two triangles congruent.

SAS Congruence Postulate

If two sides and the contained angle of one triangle are equal to two sides and the contained angle of another triangle, then the triangles are congruent.

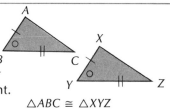

$$\triangle ABC \cong \triangle XYZ$$

EXAMPLE 1:

Given: $\triangle ABC$ and $\triangle DEF$, as shown
Prove: $\triangle ABC \cong \triangle DEF$

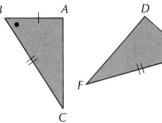

Proof: In $\triangle ABC$ and $\triangle DEF$:
  S $AB = DE$ (given)
  A $\angle B = \angle E$ (given)
  S $BC = EF$ (given)
  ∴ $\triangle ABC \cong \triangle DEF$ (SAS)

EXAMPLE 2:

Prove that the bisector of the vertical angle of an isosceles triangle bisects the base.

Given: $\triangle ABC$ with $AB = AC$, $\angle BAD = \angle CAD$
Prove: $BD = CD$

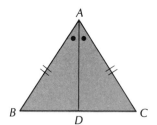

Proof: In $\triangle ABD$ and $\triangle ACD$:
  S $AB = AC$ (given)
  A $\angle BAD = \angle CAD$ (angle bisector)
  S $AD = AD$ (common side)
  ∴ $\triangle ABD \cong \triangle ACD$ (SAS)

  ∴ $BD = CD$ (congruent triangles)
  ∴ $\overline{AD}$ bisects $\overline{BC}$.

SSS Congruence Postulate

If three sides of one triangle are equal to three sides of another triangle, then the triangles are congruent.

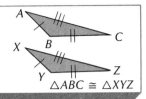

$\triangle ABC \cong \triangle XYZ$

EXAMPLE 3:

Given: Quadrilateral *XYWZ*, as shown
Prove: $\triangle XYZ \cong \triangle WYZ$

Proof: In $\triangle XYZ$ and $\triangle WYZ$:

   S $XY = WY$ (given)
   S $XZ = WZ$ (given)
   S $YZ = YZ$ (common side)

   $\therefore \triangle XYZ \cong \triangle WYZ$ (SSS)

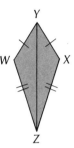

ASA Congruence Postulate

If two angles and the contained side of one triangle are equal to two angles and the contained side of another triangle, then the triangles are congruent.

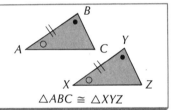

$\triangle ABC \cong \triangle XYZ$

EXAMPLE 4:

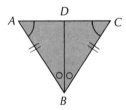

Given: $\triangle ABC$ with $\angle A = \angle C$, $AB = CB$, $\angle ABD = \angle CBD$
Prove: $\overline{BD} \perp \overline{AC}$

Proof: In $\triangle ABD$ and $\triangle CBD$:

   A $\angle A = \angle C$ (given)
   S $AB = CB$ (given)
   A $\angle ABD = \angle CBD$ (given)
   $\therefore \triangle ABD \cong \triangle CBD$ (ASA)

Then $\angle ADB = \angle CDB$ (congruent triangles)
and $\angle ADB + \angle CDB = 180°$ (straight angle)
$\therefore$ $\angle ADB = \angle CDB = 90°$
$\therefore$ $\overline{BD} \perp \overline{AC}$

EXERCISES

A **1.** Can the triangles be proven congruent? If so, what postulate applies?

a. 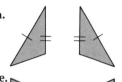   b.   c. 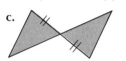   d.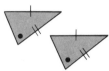

e.   f.    g.   h.

B **2.** Copy and provide a proof. List other pairs of equal sides and equal angles.

a. *Given:* $AB = CB$, $DB = EB$, $\overline{AC}$ intersects $\overline{ED}$ at B.
   Prove: $\triangle ABE \cong \triangle CBD$

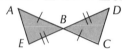

b. *Given:* $\angle YXW = \angle ZXW$, $\overline{XW} \perp \overline{YZ}$
   Prove: $\triangle XYW \cong \triangle XZW$

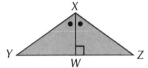

c. *Given:* $PQ = RS$, $QR = SP$
   Prove: $\triangle PQS \cong \triangle RSQ$

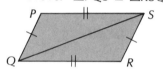

d. *Given:* $\overline{AE}$ intersects $\overline{DB}$ at C.
   Prove: $\triangle ABC \cong \triangle EDC$

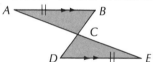

3. $ABCD$ is a quadrilateral with $AB = BC = CD = DA$. Make a sketch of $ABCD$ and prove the following.
   a. $\triangle ABD \cong \triangle CDB$ b. $\angle A = \angle C$

4. $\overline{AB}$ and $\overline{CD}$ are equal non-parallel chords of a circle with centre O. Prove that $\triangle ABO \cong \triangle CDO$.

5. $\overline{XY}$ and $\overline{PQ}$ bisect each other at O. Prove the following.
   a. $\triangle XOQ \cong \triangle YOP$ b. $\overline{XQ} \parallel \overline{YP}$

6. For each diagram below, with relationships among sides and angles as marked, prove the indicated deductions.

a.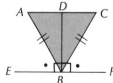

   i. $\triangle ADB \cong \triangle CDB$
   ii. $\overline{BD} \perp \overline{AC}$
   iii. $\overline{AC} \parallel \overline{EF}$

b.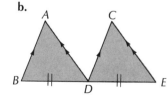

   i. $\triangle ABD \cong \triangle CDE$
   ii. $AD = CE$
   iii. B, D, E are collinear.

c.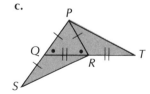

   i. $\triangle QSR \cong \triangle RPT$
   ii. $\angle QSR = \angle RPT$

7. Two circles with centres P and Q intersect at A and B. Prove the following.
    a. $\triangle APQ \cong \triangle BPQ$ b. $\angle APQ = \angle BPQ$

8. $\overline{AM}$ is a median of $\triangle ABC$ (M is the midpoint of BC) and $AB = AC$. Prove that $\overline{AM} \perp \overline{BC}$.

9. The diagram illustrates a method for constructing the bisector of $\angle ABC$. Prove that $\overline{BG}$ bisects $\angle ABC$.

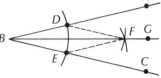

10. Quadrilateral $PQRS$ is a parallelogram. Prove the following.
    a. $\triangle PQS \cong \triangle RSQ$ b. $PS = RQ$ c. $PQ = RS$ d. $\angle P = \angle R$

C 11. For the diagram at the right, prove the following.
    a. $\triangle PQR \cong \triangle PSR$
    b. $\triangle PQT \cong \triangle PST$
    c. $\overline{PR} \perp \overline{QS}$

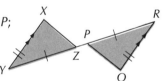

12. In quadrilateral $ABCD$, $\overline{AC}$ bisects $\angle BAD$ and $AB = AD$. Prove the following.
    a. $\triangle ABC \cong \triangle ADC$ b. $\overline{AC}$ bisects $\overline{BD}$.

13. Given: $XY = QR$; $\overline{XY} \parallel \overline{RQ}$; $YZ = RP$;
    $Y, Z, P,$ and R are collinear.
    Prove: $\overline{XZ} \parallel \overline{QP}$

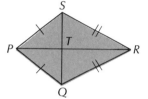

14. In $\triangle ABC$, P and Q are the midpoints of $\overline{AB}$ and $\overline{AC}$, respectively. $\overline{PQ}$ is extended to a point D so that $PQ = QD$. Prove the following.
    a. $\triangle APQ \cong \triangle CDQ$ b. $\overline{AB} \parallel \overline{CD}$

EXTRA

A tetrahedron with vertices $A, B, C,$ and D satisfies $AB = CD$, $AC = BD$, and $AD = BC$. Show that the four faces of the tetrahedron are congruent triangles.

(Hint: Open the tetrahedron onto a plane.)

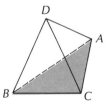

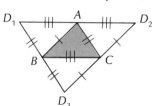

323

10–7 Isosceles Triangle Theorem

In deductive geometry, new theorems and deductions are proved using previously established postulates and theorems. The SAS Congruence Postulate can be used to prove the following theorem.

Isosceles Triangle Theorem (ITT)

In an isosceles triangle, the angles opposite the equal sides are equal.

Given: △ABC with $AB = AC$
Prove: $\angle B = \angle C$

Proof: Construct the bisector of $\angle BAC$ to meet $\overline{BC}$ at D.

In △ABD and △ACD:

  S $AB = AC$ (given)
  A $\angle BAD = \angle CAD$ (definition of angle bisector)
  S $AD = AD$ (common side)

  ∴   △ABD ≅ △ACD (SAS)
  ∴ $\angle B = \angle C$ (congruent triangles)

A **corollary** to a theorem is a new theorem which follows easily as an extension of the first theorem.

Corollary to ITT

An equilateral triangle is equiangular.

Given: △XYZ with $XY = YZ = XZ$
Prove: $\angle X = \angle Y = \angle Z$

Proof: In △XYZ:

      $XY = XZ$ (given)
  ∴ $\angle Y = \angle Z$ (ITT)
      $XZ = YZ$ (given)
  ∴ $\angle X = \angle Y$ (ITT)
  ∴ $\angle X = \angle Y = \angle Z$ (substitution)

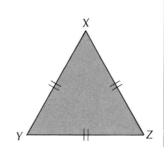

In the following examples, ITT and its corollary are used to find the sizes of angles in geometric figures and to prove deductions.

EXAMPLE 1: Find the size of each unknown angle.

a.

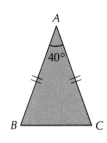

In △ABC:
    AB = AC (given)
∴ ∠B = ∠C (ITT)

But:
  ∠A + ∠B + ∠C = 180° (AST)
 40° + ∠B + ∠C = 180° (substitution)
∴   ∠B + ∠C = 140°
      ∠B + ∠B = 140° (substitution)
         2∠B = 140°
          ∠B = 70°
          ∠C = 70° (substitution)

b.

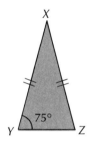

In △XYZ:
  XY = XZ (given)
  ∠Y = ∠Z (ITT)
∴ ∠Z = 75° (substitution)

But:
 ∠X + ∠Y + ∠Z = 180° (AST)
 ∠X + 75° + 75° = 180° (substitution)
     ∴ ∠X = 30° (subtraction)

EXAMPLE 2: For △PQR below, prove that PQ = PR.

Given: PA = PB, QA = RB
Prove: PQ = PR

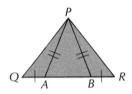

Proof: In △PAB:

               PA = PB   (given)
         ∴ ∠PAB = ∠PBA   (ITT)
    But ∠PAB + ∠QAP = 180°   (straight angle)
    and ∠PBA + ∠RBP = 180°   (straight angle)
  ∴ ∠PAB + ∠QAP = ∠PBA + ∠RBP
   ∠PBA + ∠QAP = ∠PBA + ∠RBP (substitution)
        ∴ ∠QAP = ∠RBP

In △PQA and △PRB:
S   PA = PB   (given)
A ∠QAP = ∠RBP (proved above)
S   QA = RB   (given)
∴   △PQA ≅ △PRB (SAS)
∴   PQ = PR   (congruent triangles)

EXERCISES

A 1. Find the size of each angle.

a.

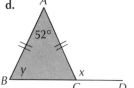

b.

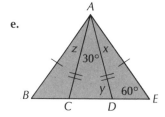

c.

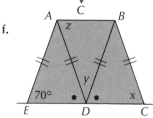

d.

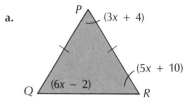

e.

f.

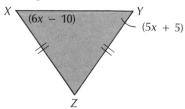

B 2. Calculate the value of x and the size of each angle.

a.

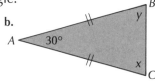

b.

3. The vertical angle of an isosceles triangle is the angle formed by the two equal sides. The base of an isosceles triangle is the side opposite the vertical angle. An altitude of a triangle is a perpendicular from one vertex to the opposite side. Prove the following deductions.

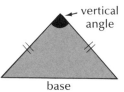

vertical angle

base

a. The altitude to the base of an isosceles triangle bisects the base.
b. The median to the base of an isosceles triangle is perpendicular to the base.
c. The bisector of the vertical angle of an isosceles triangle is the perpendicular bisector of the base.

4. For the diagram at the right, answer the following.
a. If ∠B = 30°, find the size of ∠BAD.
b. If ∠B = x°, find the size of ∠BAD.

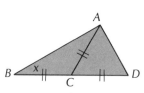

5. Using the diagram at the right, and given also that PQ = PR, prove that △TSU is isosceles.

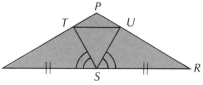

6. △*ABC* is an isosceles triangle in which *AB* = *AC*. *D* is in $\overline{AB}$ and *E* is in $\overline{AC}$, such that *DB* = *EC*. Prove the following.
    a. △*ADE* is isosceles.
    b. ∠*ADE* = ∠*B*
    c. $\overline{DE} \parallel \overline{BC}$

7. △*ABC* is an isosceles triangle in which *AB* = *AC*. $\overline{AB}$ is extended to *E* so that *AB* = *BE*. $\overline{BC}$ is extended to *D* so that *BC* = *CD*. Prove that *AD* = *EC*.

8. *D* is the midpoint of the base of isosceles triangle *ABC*, as shown. Prove that *D* is equidistant from the equal sides $\overline{AB}$ and $\overline{AC}$. (The distance from a point to a segment means the perpendicular distance.)

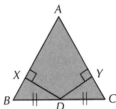

C 9. △*ABC* is an equilateral triangle with points *D*, *E*, and *F* on $\overline{AB}$, $\overline{BC}$, and $\overline{AC}$, respectively, so that *AD* = *BE* = *CF*. Prove that △*DEF* is equilateral.

10. For quadrilateral *ABCD* as shown, prove that ∠*A* = ∠*B*.

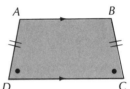

11. Two isosceles triangles, △*ABC* and △*DBC*, are on opposite sides of the same base, $\overline{BC}$. Prove that $\overline{AD}$ is the perpendicular bisector of $\overline{BC}$.

Historical Note

Bridge of Fools

Euclid's proof for the Isosceles Triangle Theorem was more complicated than the proof in lesson 10-7. The key steps of Euclid's proof are outlined below.

Draw △*ABC* with *AB* = *AC*.
Extend $\overline{AB}$ to *D* and $\overline{AC}$ to *E* so that *BD* = *CE*.
Join *C* to *D* and *B* to *E*.

First, prove that: △*ACD* ≅ △*ABE*
Then, prove: △*BDC* ≅ △*CEB*
Finally, show: ∠*ABC* = ∠*ACB*

Develop the proof from the outline above.

This proof was known as "pons asinorum", or "bridge of fools", probably because it separated the good students of the Middle Ages from the fools.

10–8 Theorems and Their Converses

Definitions, theorems, and postulates are frequently stated in the form, "If ... (*p*) ..., then ... (*q*) ...." A statement in this form is called a **conditional statement** or **implication**.

For example, ITT can be written as a conditional statement:
  "If *a triangle is isosceles*, then *its base angles are equal*."
The "*p*" statement, *a triangle is isosceles*, is called the **hypothesis** of the theorem; the "*q*" statement, *its base angles are equal*, is the **conclusion**.

To prove a theorem, we assume the hypothesis is true, and try to prove the conclusion using the hypothesis and previously developed knowledge of geometry.

Statements A and B illustrate a conditional statement and its **converse**.

  A. If my car is out of gas, then my car won't go.   If *p*, then *q*.
  B. If my car won't go, then my car is out of gas.   If *q*, then *p*.

Note that the converse of a true statement is not necessarily true.

A conditional statement and its converse can be combined in a single, **biconditional**, statement.

  C. My car won't start if and only if my car is out of gas.   *p* if and only if *q*

Note that statements A and B must *both* be true, in order for statement C to be true. In this case, statement C is false, as B is not necessarily true.

Some of the geometric theorems covered in this unit have true converses.

Isosceles Triangle Theorem (ITT) Converse

If two angles of a triangle are equal, then the triangle is isosceles.

Given: $\triangle ABC$ with $\angle B = \angle C$
Prove: $\triangle ABC$ is isosceles.

Proof: Construct $\overline{AD}$, the bisector of $\angle BAC$, to meet $\overline{BC}$ at D.

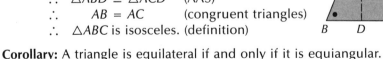

  In $\triangle ABD$ and $\triangle ACD$:
  A $\angle B = \angle C$ (given)
  A $\angle BAD = \angle CAD$ (definition)
  S $AD = AD$ (common side)
  $\therefore$ $\triangle ABD \cong \triangle ACD$ (AAS)
  $\therefore$ $AB = AC$ (congruent triangles)
  $\therefore$ $\triangle ABC$ is isosceles. (definition)

Corollary: A triangle is equilateral if and only if it is equiangular.

ITT and its corollary can be written as a biconditional statement: A triangle is isosceles if and only if the base angles of the triangle are equal.

To prove a biconditional statement true, you must prove that *both* conditional statements are true. The following theorems have been broken down into their two conditional statements. The proofs are to be established in the exercises.

Perpendicular Bisector Theorem (PBT)

A point is in the perpendicular bisector of a segment if and only if it is equidistant from the endpoints of the segment.

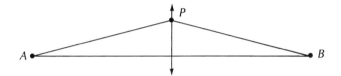

A. If a point is in the perpendicular bisector of a segment, then it is equidistant from the endpoints of the segment.

B. If a point is equidistant from the endpoints of a segment, then it is in the perpendicular bisector of the segment.

Angle Bisector Theorem (ABT)

A point is in the bisector of an angle if and only if it is equidistant from the arms of the angle.

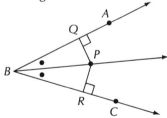

A. If a point is in the bisector of an angle, then it is equidistant from the arms of the angle.

B. If a point is equidistant from the arms of an angle, then it is in the angle bisector.

EXERCISES

A 1. State the converse of each statement.
    a. If it is raining, then the street is wet.
    b. If a triangle is isosceles, then it has two equal sides.
    c. If $x = 3$, then $x^2 = 9$.
    d. If $2x + 3 = 13$, then $x = 5$.
    e. If two numbers are odd, then their sum is even.

2. Which of the statements in exercise 1 have converses that are always true?

3. Rewrite each biconditional statement as two conditional statements.
    a. Two angles are supplementary if and only if their sum is 180°.
    b. Two lines are parallel if and only if alternate angles are equal.
    c. Two lines are parallel if and only if corresponding angles are equal.
    d. Two lines are parallel if and only if interior angles on the same side of the transversal are supplementary.

B 4. Complete parts a and b to give a proof of the Perpendicular Bisector Theorem.

    a. *Given:* $\overline{CE}$ is the perpendicular bisector of $\overline{AB}$;
                P is any point on $\overline{CE}$.
        Prove: $PA = PB$

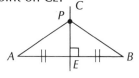

    b. *Given:* $PA = PB$
        Prove: $\overline{PE}$ is the perpendicular bisector of $\overline{AB}$.
        (Hint: Draw $\overline{PE}$ so that $AE = BE$.)

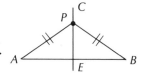

5. Complete the following proof of statement A of the Angle Bisector Theorem.

    Given: $\overline{PB}$ bisects $\angle ABC$;
               $\overline{PQ} \perp \overline{AB}$;
               $\overline{PR} \perp \overline{BC}$.
    Prove: $PQ = PR$

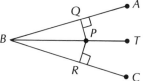

6. **a.** Prove △DBC is isosceles.

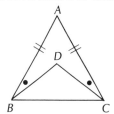

330

b. Prove $\overline{PQ}$ is the perpendicular bisector of $\overline{AB}$.

c. Prove $\triangle AXY$ is isosceles.

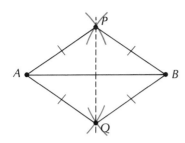

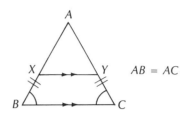

$AB = AC$

7. $ABCD$ is a quadrilateral with $AB = BC$ and $AD = CD$. Prove that $\overline{BD}$ is the perpendicular bisector of $\overline{AC}$.

8. For $\triangle ABC$ with exterior angle, $\angle ACD$, $\overline{CE}$ is the bisector of $\angle ACD$. If $\overline{CE} \parallel \overline{AB}$, prove that $\triangle ABC$ is isosceles.

9. For quadrilateral $PQRS$ as given, prove that $PQ = PS$.

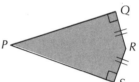

C 10. Prove that the centre of a circle lies in the perpendicular bisector of any chord of the circle.

11. Prove that the diagonals of the given quadrilateral are the perpendicular bisectors of each other.

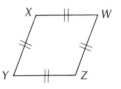

12. The bisector of $\angle R$ in $\triangle TRS$ intersects $\overline{TS}$ at B. The perpendicular bisector of $\overline{BR}$ intersects $\overline{TR}$ at A. Prove that $\overline{AB} \parallel \overline{RS}$.

EXTRA

1. Divide a circle into four parts of equal area by drawing three curved lines of equal length.

2. In square $ABCD$, P, Q, R, and S are the midpoints of $\overline{BC}$, $\overline{CD}$, $\overline{DA}$, and $\overline{AB}$, respectively. Prove that $TUVW$ is a square.

3. Copy and cut out square $ABCD$. Cut the square along the broken lines and arrange the pieces to form 5 congruent squares.

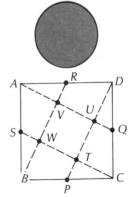

10–9 Proof of the Pythagorean Theorem

Now that you have learned some of the basic concepts of deductive reasoning in geometry, it is appropriate to consider how we might prove the Pythagorean Theorem.

Unfortunately, there is no record of Pythagoras's own proof. Yet many proofs have been given of the Pythagorean Theorem. One such proof is given here.

Pythagorean Theorem (PT)

If a triangle is right-angled with sides a, b and hypotenuse c, then $a^2 + b^2 = c^2$.

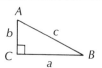

Given: $\triangle ABC$ with $\angle C = 90°$
Prove: $a^2 + b^2 = c^2$

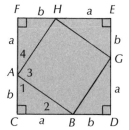

Proof: Consider a square $CDEF$ with the measure of each side $(a + b)$. The four triangles on the corners are all congruent to $\triangle ABC$, by **SAS**.

Because of the congruent triangles:
$AH = HG = GB = BA$.

Let the measure of each hypotenuse be c.

In $\triangle ABC$: $\angle 1 + \angle 2 + \angle C = 180°$ (AST)
But $\angle C = 90°$ (given)
$\therefore \qquad \angle 1 + \angle 2 = 90°$ (subtraction)
But $\angle 2 = \angle 4$ (congruent triangles)
$\therefore \qquad \angle 1 + \angle 4 = 90°$ (sustitution)
$\angle 3 + \angle 1 + \angle 4 = 180°$ (straight angle)
$\therefore \qquad \angle 3 = 90°$ (subtraction)
$\therefore \qquad \angle HAB = 90°$

In $AHGB$, all sides are equal and one angle is 90°.
$\therefore$ quadrilateral $AHBG$ is a square.

Now consider the areas, as follows.

Area of $CDEF$ = Area of $ABGH$ + 4 (Area of $\triangle ABC$)

$(a + b)^2 = c^2 + 4\left(\frac{1}{2} ab\right)$ (area formulas)

$a^2 + 2ab + b^2 = c^2 + 2ab$ (expansion)

$a^2 + b^2 = c^2$ (subtraction)

EXERCISES

A 1. Use the Pythagorean Theorem to find the value of x.

a.

b.

c.

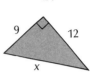

d.

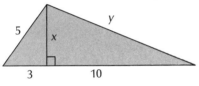

e.

f.

2. Which of the following sets of numbers are Pythagorean triples?
  a. 9, 40, 41   **b.** 7, 21, 24   **c.** 8, 15, 17
  d. 9, 12, 16   **e.** 20, 21, 29   **f.** 27, 36, 45

B 3. Calculate the values of x and y. Answer in simplest radical form.

a.

b.

4. a. Prove that if $a > b$, then $a^2 + b^2$, $a^2 - b^2$, and $2ab$ represent the sides of a right-angled triangle.
  b. Use the results of part a to generate five Pythagorean triples not discovered in exercise 2.

5. a. Write the converse of the Pythagorean Theorem.
  b. Complete the following proof of the converse.
    Given: $\triangle ABC$ in which $c^2 = a^2 + b^2$
    Prove: $\angle C = 90°$
    Proof: Consider $\triangle XYZ$ in which $XY = a$,
    $YZ = b$, and $\angle Y = 90°$.

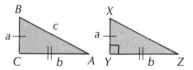

6. Use the results of exercise 5 to prove that $\angle P = 90°$.

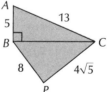

C 7. The diagram shows $\triangle ABC$, a right-angled triangle with $\angle ACB = 90°$ and sides a, b, c. Given that $ABDE$ is a square, and given parallel segments as marked, prove that $FGCH$ is a square with sides $(b - a)$ units long. Use this to obtain an alternative proof of the Pythagorean Theorem.

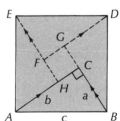

333

10–10 Proofs Using Transformations

The following examples show how transformations and their properties, studied in Unit 9, can be applied to give geometric proofs.

EXAMPLE 1: Prove that a quadrilateral with one pair of opposite sides both equal and parallel is a parallelogram.

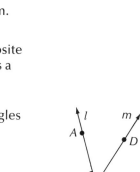

Given: Quadrilateral *PQRS* with $\overline{PS} \parallel \overline{QR}$ and *PS* = *QR*

Prove: Quadrilateral *PQRS* is a parallelogram.

Use a translation for this proof.
Under a translation, a segment is parallel to its image.

Proof: Under the translation defined by translation arrow *a*:

$$P \rightarrow S \quad \text{(definition of translation)}$$
$$Q \rightarrow R \quad \text{(definition of translation)}$$

or, $\overline{PQ} \rightarrow \overline{SR}$

∴ $\overline{PQ} \parallel \overline{SR}$ (property of translation)

and $\overline{PS} \parallel \overline{QR}$ (given)

∴ quadrilateral *PQRS* is a parallelogram.
(by definition)

Therefore, if a quadrilateral has one pair of opposite sides equal and parallel, then the quadrilateral is a parallelogram.

EXAMPLE 2: Prove that if two lines intersect, the opposite angles are equal.

Given: Lines *l* and *m* intersect at *O*.

Prove: ∠*AOC* = ∠*BOD*, ∠*AOD* = ∠*BOC*

Use a rotation of 180° about *O*. Under a half-turn about *O* a point *P*, its image *P'*, and *O* are collinear.

Proof: Under a half-turn about *O*:
ray *OA* → ray *OB*,
and *A*, *O*, and *B* are collinear. (property of half-turn)
ray *OC* → ray *OD*,
and *C*, *O*, and *D* are collinear. (property of half-turn)
or,   ∠*AOC* → ∠*BOD*
∴   ∠*AOC* = ∠*BOD* (property of rotation)

Similarly, ∠*AOD* = ∠*BOC*

Therefore, if two lines intersect, the opposite angles are equal.

EXAMPLE 3:   Prove that any point in the perpendicular bisector of a segment is equidistant from the endpoints of the segment.

Given: *m* is the perpendicular bisector of $\overline{AB}$; *P* is any point in *m*.

Prove: $AP = BP$

Proof: Under reflection in *m*:

$$A \to B \quad \text{(definition of reflection)}$$
$$P \to P \quad \text{(definition of reflection)}$$
or, $\overline{AP} \to \overline{BP}$
$$\therefore \ AP = BP \quad \text{(property of reflection)}$$

Therefore, a point lying in the perpendicular bisector of a segment is equidistant from the endpoints of the segment.

EXAMPLE 4:   Prove that, if the midpoints of two sides of a triangle are joined, then the segment formed is parallel to the third side and equal to half its length.

Given: $\triangle ABC$ as shown, with *P* the midpoint of $\overline{AB}$ and *Q* the midpoint of $\overline{AC}$

Prove: $\overline{PQ} \parallel \overline{BC}$ and $PQ = \frac{1}{2}BC$

Proof: Under the dilatation with centre *A* and scale factor 2:

$$P \to B \quad \text{(definition of dilatation)}$$
$$Q \to C \quad \text{(definition of dilatation)}$$
or, $\overline{PQ} \to \overline{BC}$
$$\therefore \ \overline{PQ} \parallel \overline{BC} \quad \text{(property of dilatation)}$$
and $PQ = \frac{1}{2}BC$ (property of dilatation)

Therefore, the segment joining the midpoints of two sides of a triangle is parallel to the third side and equal to half its length.

EXERCISES

A **1.** Describe four transformations under which *l* is mapped onto *m*, where *l* and *m* are parallel.

2. Under what four transformations is *l* mapped onto *m*?

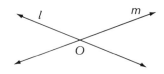

B Use transformations to prove the following deductions.

3. $\overline{AD}$ and $\overline{BC}$ are two diameters of a circle with centre *O*. Prove that $AB = CD$.

4. Prove that the angles opposite the equal sides of an isosceles triangle are equal.

5. Prove that, if a transversal crosses two parallel lines, then alternate angles are equal.

6. *P* is equidistant from the endpoints of segment $\overline{AB}$. Prove that *P* is in the perpendicular bisector of $\overline{AB}$.

7. Prove that $\triangle ACD \cong \triangle BDC$.

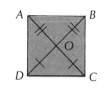

8. Given that $\overline{XV}$ and $\overline{WY}$ intersect at *Z*, prove the following.
   a. $XY = WV$
   b. $XW = YV$
   c. $\overline{XW} \parallel \overline{YV}$

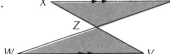

9. Given that $\angle A = \angle B$, prove that $\angle D = \angle C$.

C **10.** Use transformations to prove each of the three congruence postulates.
   a. If two sides and the contained angle of one triangle are equal to two sides and the contained angle of another triangle, then the triangles are congruent.
   b. If three sides of one triangle are equal to three sides of another triangle, then the triangles are congruent.
   c. If two angles and the contained side of one triangle are equal to two angles and the contained side of another triangle, then the triangles are congruent.

11. Let $\triangle ABC$ be an equilateral triangle. Choose *D* on $\overline{AB}$ and *E* on $\overline{AC}$ so $AD = AE$. Construct equilateral triangles *PCD*, *QAE*, and *RAB*, as in the diagram. Show that $\triangle PQR$ is equilateral. (Hint: Consider a $60°$ counter-clockwise rotation about *C* and show $BP = AD = AQ$; *R*, *B*, and *P* are collinear.)

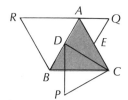

336

Review

1. *M* is the midpoint of line segment $\overline{AB}$. $\overline{CD}$ intersects $\overline{AB}$ at *M* so that $CM = DM$. Prove that $AC = BD$.

2. In quadrilateral *PQRS*, $PQ = PS$ and $QR = SR$. Prove the following.
   a. $\angle Q = \angle S$ b. $\overline{PR} \perp \overline{QS}$

3. $\triangle XYZ$ is isosceles with $XY = XZ$. $\overline{YZ}$ is extended to *V* and $\overline{ZY}$ is extended to *W* so that $WY = VZ$. Prove the following.
   a. $XW = XV$ b. $\angle WXY = \angle VXZ$

4. $\overline{AB}$ and $\overline{CD}$ bisect each other at *E*. Prove the following.
   a. $\triangle CEA \cong \triangle DEB$ b. $\overline{AC} \parallel \overline{BD}$

5. In $\triangle PQR$, $PQ = PR$. *T* is in the interior of $\triangle PQR$ such that $\angle PQT = \angle PRT$. Prove that $\triangle TQR$ is isosceles.

6. Prove that, in any parallelogram, the following are true.
   a. Opposite sides are equal.
   b. Opposite angles are equal.
   c. The diagonals bisect each other.

7. $\overline{AB}$ and $\overline{CD}$ are two equal chords in a circle with centre *O*. Prove that $\angle AOB = \angle COD$.

8. In quadrilateral *ABCD*, diagonals $\overline{AC}$ and $\overline{BD}$ bisect each other. Prove that *ABCD* is a parallelogram.

9. In quadrilateral *XYZW*, $XY = YZ = ZW = XW$. Prove that diagonals $\overline{YW}$ and $\overline{XZ}$ are the perpendicular bisectors of each other.

10. Two circles with centres *O* and *P* intersect each other at *A* and *B*. Prove that $\overline{OP}$ is the perpendicular bisector of $\overline{AB}$.

11. Find the value of *x*. Answer in simplest radical form as necessary.

   a. 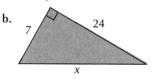   b.   c.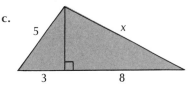

12. *Given:* $\overline{XY} \parallel \overline{ZW}$;
    $\overline{AB}$ bisects $\angle YAC$;
    $\overline{CB}$ bisects $\angle ACW$.
    Prove: $\angle ABC = 90°$

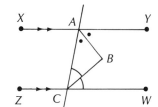

Solving Problems Involving Areas

The table below summarizes the area formulas for some plane figures.

Figure	Rectangle	Triangle	Parallelogram	Trapezoid
	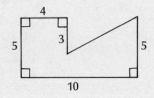			
Area Formula	$A = bh$	$A = \frac{1}{2}bh$	$A = bh$	$A = \frac{1}{2}(a + b)h$

EXAMPLE: A stained glass pattern uses a regular hexagon at its centre. Find the area of glass needed for the hexagon.

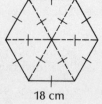

18 cm

A regular hexagon can be divided into six equilateral triangles.

a. Find the altitude of one of the triangles.

Apply the Pythagorean Theorem.

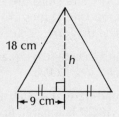

18 cm   h

9 cm

$$18^2 = 9^2 + h^2$$
$$324 = 81 + h^2$$
$$h^2 = 243$$
$$h = 15.59, \text{ to two decimal places}$$

b. Find the area of one triangle.

$$A = \frac{1}{2}bh$$

$$= \frac{1}{2}(18)(15.59)$$

$$= 140.31$$

c. Find the area of all six triangles in the hexagon.

$$A = 6 \text{ (Area of 1 triangle)}$$
$$= 6(140.31)$$
$$= 841.86$$

The hexagonal pane of glass has an area of about 841.86 cm².

EXERCISES

A 1. Find the area of the figure at the right.

4

5   3   5

10

2. Find the length of the altitude from Z to $\overline{XY}$.

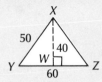

B 3. Find the area of the shaded portion. All angles are right angles.

a.

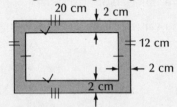

b.

4. Which has a greater area, and by how much: a rectangular lot 12 m by 36 m, or a square lot with the same perimeter?

5. Find the height of a triangle with area 45 cm² and base 15 cm.

6. Find the height of a trapezoid with area 162 mm² if its parallel sides are 14 mm and 22 mm.

7. A basketball court is rectangular in shape and has an area of 364 m². If its length is 26 m, what is its width?

C 8. A 10 kg bag of fertilizer covers 200 m² of lawn. How much fertilizer must be bought to fertilize a lawn 30 m by 65 m?

9. Ken is using driveway sealer to protect and restore the appearance of his driveway. A 2 L bottle of sealer covers approximately 46.5 m² and costs $11.99. If Ken's driveway measures 5 m by 30.5 m, what will it cost to seal the driveway?

10. The area of Canada is 9 976 139 km². Imagine that area being pushed into the shape of a square. What would be the length of one side of that square?

Using the Calculator

Maximum Area

A rectangle is to be formed from a piece of wire 12 m long.

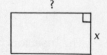

1. Let the width of the rectangle be x metres. Find an expression for the length of the rectangle.

2. Determine an expression for the area, A, of the rectangle.

3. Make a table of values for x and A for $x = 0, 0.5, 1.0, 1.5, \ldots, 6.0$.

4. Which rectangle has the greatest area?

5. Repeat for a piece of wire 20 m long; 30 m long; 40 m long.

6. What would be the dimensions of the rectangle of greatest area which could be formed from a piece of wire x metres long?

1. Explain the error in logical thinking.
   a. All doctors wear lab coats.
      This person is wearing a lab coat.
      Therefore this person is a doctor.
   b. Some students work part time.
      Kim is not a student.
      Therefore Kim does not work part time.

2. Calculate the values of the unknown angles.

   a.

   b.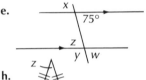

   c.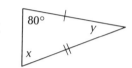

   d.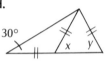

   e.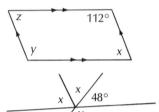

   f.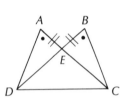

   g.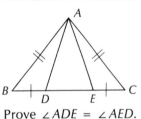

   h.

   i.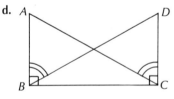

3. Prove the deduction given for each diagram.

   a.

   Prove △EDC is isosceles.

   b.

   Prove ∠Q = ∠S.

   c.

   Prove ∠ADE = ∠AED.

   d.

   Prove AC = DB.

4. The bisector of ∠XYZ in △XYZ meets $\overline{XZ}$ at Q. The perpendicular bisector of $\overline{YQ}$ meets $\overline{XY}$ at P. Prove that ∠PQX = ∠YZX and ∠QPX = ∠ZYX.

5. Give the converse of each statement. Is the converse necessarily true?
   a. If you live on your own then you're responsible for your rent.
   b. If you're a high school graduate then you've completed grade 12.
   c. If a triangle is equilateral then all of its angles are equal.
   d. If your new pet is a bird then it must have wings.
   e. If your new pet is a dog then it must have a wet nose.

Cumulative Review

1. Solve each system of equations, using the method of your choice.
   a. $y = 2x - 1$
      $y = -5x + 7$
   b. $3x + 2y = 6$
      $4x + y = 8$
   c. $2x + 7y = 42$
      $3x + 2y = 12$

2. Theatre tickets were sold at $5 for students and $7 for adults. One day, 576 tickets were sold for a total of $3382. How many of each type of ticket were sold?

3. Graph each inequality and test your answer for two points in the solution set.
   a. $y \geq 2x - 3$
   b. $y < -5x + 2$
   c. $y > -1$

4. Factor completely.
   a. $2x^2 - 14x$
   b. $6a^3b^2 - 6b^2$
   c. $3a^2 - 6a + 3$
   d. $t^4 - v^4$
   e. $x^2 + 6x - 7$
   f. $k^2 - 8k + 15$
   g. $12a^2 - 132a - 144$
   h. $2t^2 + 16t - 66$
   i. $6b^2 + 7b - 5$

5. Simplify each rational expression and state any restrictions on the variables.
   a. $\dfrac{x^2 + 2x + 1}{x + 1}$
   b. $\dfrac{x^2 + 3x + 2}{x + 2}$
   c. $\dfrac{x^2 + 2x - 15}{x^2 + x - 12}$

6. Make a table of values and graph each relation.
   a. $y = 3x - 7$
   b. $y = x^2 + 2$
   c. $xy = 36$

7. Given that $y \propto x$, and $y = 7$ when $x = 1$, find y when x is 2.5.

8. Given that $y \propto \dfrac{1}{x}$, and $y = \dfrac{1}{8}$ when $x = 2$, find y when x is 15.

9. The following set of data has a mean of 9.9. Find the value of x.

   Quiz Scores
   13, 5, 9, 11, 12, 14, 9, 8, 10, 14, 9, 10, x, 12, 15, 8, 7, x, 8, 11, 11, 9, 10, 4, 13, 13, 11, 6, 7, 10

10. Quadrilateral $ABCD$ has vertices $A(0, 1)$, $B(3, -1)$, $C(2, 5)$, and $D(-1, 4)$. Find the image of $ABCD$ under the given transformation.
    a. $(x, y) \rightarrow (x - 2, y + 3)$
    b. $(x, y) \rightarrow (y, x)$
    c. $(x, y) \rightarrow (-3x, -3y)$
    d. $(x, y) \rightarrow (-x, -y)$

11. For each pair of similar triangles, find the measures as represented by letters.
    a.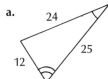
    b.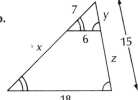

341

11 The Circle

11–1 Basic Geometric Constructions

This unit makes use of fundamental straightedge-and-compass construction methods in conjunction with the principles of deductive reasoning established in Unit 10. The fundamental constructions are reviewed below. Each method uses the fact that the points in the arc of a circle are equidistant from the centre of the circle. Each construction will be proved using deductive geometry in the exercises.

1. Construct an angle congruent to a given angle COD.

   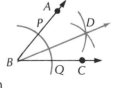

   Equal radii by construction:
   $RQ = OB = RP = OA$ and $PQ = AB$
   Result (to be proven): $\angle PRQ = \angle AOB$

2. Bisect a given angle ABC.

   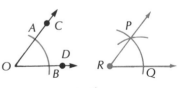

   Equal radii by construction:
   $BP = BQ$ and $QD = PD$
   Result (to be proven): $\overline{BD}$ bisects $\angle ABC$.

3. Construct a perpendicular to a given line l through a point P in the line.

   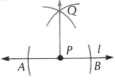

   Equal radii by construction:
   $PA = PB$ and $AQ = BQ$
   Result (to be proven): $\overline{QP} \perp \overline{AB}$

4. Construct a perpendicular to a given line *l* from a point *P* *not* in the line.

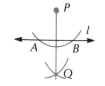

Equal radii by construction:
$PA = PB$ and $AQ = BQ$
Result (to be proven): $\overline{PQ} \perp l$

5. Construct the perpendicular bisector of a line segment *AB*.

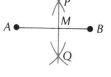

Equal radii by construction:
$AP = AQ = BP = BQ$
Result (to be proven): $\overline{PQ} \perp \overline{AB}$ and $AM = MB$

6. Construct a line parallel to a given line *l* through a point *P not* in the line.

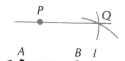

Equal radii by construction:
$AP = BQ$ and $PQ = AB$
Result (to be proven): $\overline{PQ} \parallel \overline{AB}$

EXERCISES

Use only a straightedge and a compass for each construction.

A 1. Draw a line segment *XY* and a point *P* not in $\overline{XY}$. Construct $\overline{PQ} \parallel \overline{XY}$.

2. **a.** Draw a line segment *AB* and a point *Y* in $\overline{AB}$. Construct $\overline{XY} \perp \overline{AB}$.
   b. Draw a line segment *AB* and a point *X* not in $\overline{AB}$. Construct $\overline{XY} \perp \overline{AB}$.

3. Draw an obtuse angle *PQR*. Construct its bisector.

B 4. Construct an angle of the given size.
   a. 90° **b.** 45° **c.** 22.5° **d.** 135°

5. Follow the diagram to construct an equilateral triangle.

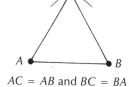

$AC = AB$ and $BC = BA$

6. Construct an angle of the given size.
   a. 60° **b.** 30° **c.** 15° **d.** 75°

7. The first fundamental construction is repeated at the right. Use one of the Congruence Postulates to prove that $\angle AOB = \angle PRQ$.

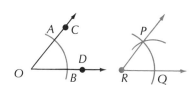

8. Prove the results of constructions 2, 3, 4, 5, and 6.

C 9. Construct parallelogram *ABCD* in which $AB = 5\,\text{cm}$, $BC = 8\,\text{cm}$, and $\angle ABC = 60°$.

10. Construct $\triangle PQR$ in which $PQ = 5\,\text{cm}$, $QR = 7\,\text{cm}$, and $PR = 8\,\text{cm}$. Construct the perpendicular bisector of $\overline{PR}$.

11–2 Basic Terminology

The circle is a common figure in the home, office, school, and playground. For example, the parts of the clock at the right suggest circles, tangents, chords, arcs, concentric circles, and congruent circles.

Some of the basic terminology of the circle is summarized in the table below.

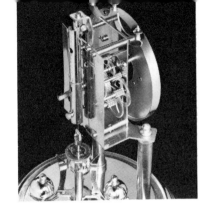

Term	Diagram	Definition
Circle	 $\overline{OA}$ is a radius.	A circle is a set of all points in a plane that are equidistant from a fixed point. The fixed point is the centre of the circle.
Centre		(Throughout this text, the centre of a circle is labelled O.)
Radius		A radius of a circle is a line segment joining the centre to a point in the circle.
Arc	 AB is an arc.	An arc AB of a circle consists of the points A and B and all points in the circle between A and B.
Chord	$\overline{CD}$ is a chord.	A chord CD of a circle is the line segment CD with endpoints C and D in the circle.
Diameter	$\overline{EF}$ is a diameter.	A diameter of a circle is a chord that passes through the centre.
Tangent	$\overline{GI}$ is a tangent. H is the point of contact.	A tangent of a circle is a line in the same plane as the circle that has one, and only one, point in common with the circle. The common point is called the point of contact.
Central (sector) Angle	∠JOK is a central angle.	A central (sector) angle is an angle formed by two radii.
Sector		A sector is a region bounded by an arc and two radii.
Segment	The shaded region is a segment.	A segment of a circle is a region bounded by an arc and a chord.

EXERCISES

A **1.** Identify the following in the diagram.
  - **a.** four radii
  - **b.** two diameters
  - **c.** a tangent
  - **d.** four chords
  - **e.** a point of contact
  - **f.** two sector angles

  2. From the diagram for exercise 1, identify the boundaries of the following.
  - **a.** four sectors
  - **b.** four segments

B **3.** **a.** When is a sector also a segment?
  - **b.** When is a segment also a semi circular region?

  4. ∠*AOA* is a complete rotation. What is its size?

  5. A **reflex angle** is an angle greater than half a rotation (180°) and less than a full rotation (360°). ∠*XOY* is a central angle of 62°. Find the size of reflex angle *XOY*.

  6. Find the angle between the minute hand and the hour hand of a clock at the given time.
  - **a.** 6:00
  - **b.** 3:00
  - **c.** 1:00
  - **d.** 7:00
  - **e.** 10:00

  7. **a.** Construct a circle with centre *O* and radius 3 cm.
  - **b.** Draw a central angle *AOB* of 60°.
  - **c.** Measure the length of chord *AB*.
  - **d.** What type of triangle is △*AOB*? Explain.

  8. ∠*AOC* is a central angle of a circle and *AB* is a diameter. Find the size of ∠*BOC* if ∠*AOC* = 125°.

  9. ∠*POQ* is a central angle of 112°. Find the size of ∠*OPQ*.

C **10.** Calculate the length of each indicated line segment.
  - **a.** chord *AB*
  - **b.** radius *OB*
  - **c.** diameter *AB*

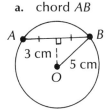
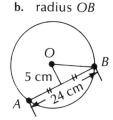
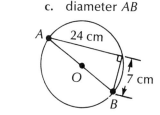

  11. Determine the area of the following sectors. Use π ≐ 3.14.
  - **a.** radius 5 cm, sector angle 90°
  - **b.** radius 3.5 cm, sector angle 55°
  - **c.** radius 6.2 cm, sector angle 115°

11-3 The Chord Property

In section 10-8, it was proved that a point is in the perpendicular bisector of a segment if and only if it is equidistant from the endpoints of the segment. This is the Perpendicular Bisector Theorem (PBT).

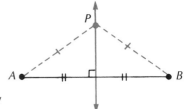

This theorem can be applied to a chord of a circle to show that the centre of a circle is equidistant from the endpoints of any chord.

The Chord Property

Let $\overline{AB}$ be a chord of a circle with centre O.

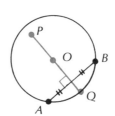

1. If $\overline{PQ}$ is the perpendicular bisector of $\overline{AB}$, then O lies in $\overline{PQ}$.

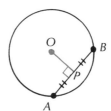

2. If $\overline{OP}$ is perpendicular to $\overline{AB}$, then $\overline{OP}$ bisects $\overline{AB}$.

The chord property has practical applications.

EXAMPLE 1: A fan-shaped piece of stained glass is going to be placed in the arch of the door shown. How could you find the centre of the circle that forms the arch?

Consider arc AC.

Let B be any other point on arc AC. Draw chords AB and BC. Construct the perpendicular bisectors of $\overline{AB}$ and $\overline{BC}$.

The centre of the circle is in each perpendicular bisector. Therefore, the point where they intersect is the centre O of the circle which contains arc AC.

(This could be verified by completing the circle.)

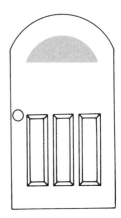

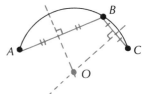

346

The chord property can be applied in geometric proofs.

EXAMPLE 2: **Concurrent lines** are two or more lines that intersect in one point.

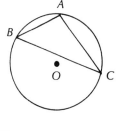

Given: *A*, *B*, and *C* are points in a circle, as shown.

Prove: The perpendicular bisectors of $\overline{AB}$, $\overline{AC}$, and $\overline{BC}$ are concurrent, and the point of concurrency is the centre of the circle *O*.

Proof: $\overline{AB}$ is a chord of the circle.   (by definition)
∴ centre *O* is in the perpendicular bisector of $\overline{AB}$.   (chord property)
∴ centre *O* is in the perpendicular bisector of $\overline{AC}$.   (chord property)
∴ centre *O* is in the perpendicular bisector of $\overline{BC}$.   (chord property)
∴ *O* is in the perpendicular bisectors of $\overline{AB}$, $\overline{AC}$, and $\overline{BC}$.
∴ The perpendicular bisectors of $\overline{AB}$, $\overline{AC}$, and $\overline{BC}$ are concurrent at point *O*.   (by definition)

EXAMPLE 3: A log of radius 13 cm is being cut into a rectangular beam. When the first cut is made, there is an exposed surface of 24 cm.

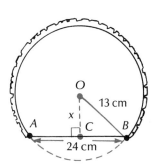

a. What is the distance from the centre of the circular cross section shown to the cut?

Let *x* centimetres be the perpendicular distance, *OC*, from centre *O* to the cut.

O lies in the perpendicular bisector of $\overline{AB}$.

∴ *CB* = 12 cm and △*OBC* is right-angled.

By the Pythagorean Theorem:
$$x^2 + 12^2 = 13^2$$
$$x^2 + 144 = 169$$
$$x^2 = 25$$
$$x = 5$$

The cut is 5 cm from the centre of the circular cross section.

b. If a second 24 cm cut is made parallel to the first cut on the opposite side of the log, what is the distance between the two cuts? If two more cuts are made to make a rectangular beam, what will be the dimensions of a cross section of the beam?

The total distance between the two cuts would be 10 cm. The dimensions of the rectangular beam would be 10 cm by 24 cm.

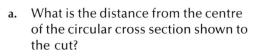

EXERCISES

A 1. Find the value of *x*. All linear measures are in centimetres.

a.

b.

c.

d.

2. Trace several large circular objects, like the end of a juice can or a plate. Apply the chord property to find the centre of each circle.

B 3. Find the value of *x*. All linear measures are in metres.

a.

b.

c.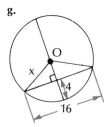

d.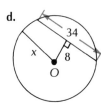

e.

f.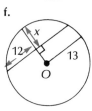

g.

h.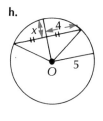

4. $\overline{AB}$ and $\overline{CD}$ are two equal chords of a circle. Prove that they are equidistant from the centre of the circle.

5. Two chords, $\overline{XY}$ and $\overline{PQ}$, are equidistant from the centre of a circle. Prove that $XY = PQ$.

6. **a.** Construct $\triangle XYZ$ so that $XY = 9$ cm, $YZ = 7$ cm, and $XZ = 8$ cm.
   b. Construct the perpendicular bisector of each side of $\triangle XYZ$.
   c. Construct the circle that has the sides of $\triangle XYZ$ as chords.

7. Apply exercise 6 to prove that any three non-collinear points are points on a circle.

8. Two circles with centres O and P intersect at X and Y. Prove that $\overline{OP}$ is the perpendicular bisector of $\overline{XY}$.

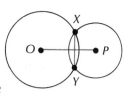

9. Two circles with centres P and Q intersect at A and B so that $AB = 24$ cm. If $AP = 13$ cm and $AQ = 15$ cm, find the length of $\overline{PQ}$.

10. A circle with radius 5 cm has two chords, $\overline{PQ}$ and $\overline{RS}$. If $PQ = 8$ cm and $RS = 6$ cm, which chord is closer to the centre of the circle? How much closer?

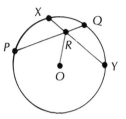

C 11. Two equal chords, $\overline{PQ}$ and $\overline{XY}$, of a circle with centre O, intersect at R. Prove that $\overline{RO}$ bisects $\angle PRY$.

12. What are the dimensions of a cross section of the largest square beam that can be cut from a circular log with a 13 cm radius?

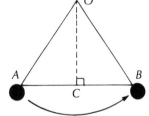

13. A pendulum $\overline{OA}$ swings from A to B.
    a. If $\angle AOB = 60°$ and $OA = 20$ cm, find AB.
    b. If $\angle AOB = 60°$ and $OA = 10$ cm, how far would it be from A to B?

14. The middle of the circular arch of a bridge across a river is 10 m above the water. The radius of the circle is 85 m. How wide is the river at the location of the bridge?

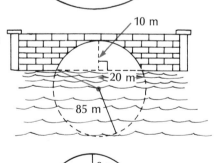

15. Rosanne wants to plant a flower bed in the shape of a segment of a circle. What is the radius of the circle she must use to construct the flower bed?

16. $\overline{AB}$ and $\overline{CD}$ are two parallel chords of a circle with centre O. E is the midpoint of $\overline{AB}$ and F is the midpoint of $\overline{CD}$. Prove that O lies in $\overline{EF}$.

11–4 Inscribed and Sector Angles

The owner of Martha's Marvellous Muffins designed a logo for use in correspondence and advertising. The design suggests two types of angles that occur in a circle.

An angle formed by the radii of a circle is a **sector angle**. An angle formed by chords of a circle is an **inscribed angle**.

$\angle BOC$ is a sector angle **subtended by** arc BC or by chord BC.

$\angle AFB$ is an inscribed angle subtended by arc AB or by chord AB.

$\angle CED$ is an inscribed angle subtended by arc CD or by chord CD.

Deductive geometry can be used to prove the following relationship between a sector angle and an inscribed angle subtended by the same arc or chord. The proof of one possible case is given below.

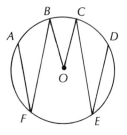

Inscribed Angle Theorem (IAT)

An inscribed angle in a circle is one half the sector angle subtended by the same arc.

Given: Circle with centre O, inscribed angle ABC, sector angle AOC
Prove: $\angle ABC = \frac{1}{2} \angle AOC$

Proof: Construct diameter BD.

In $\triangle AOB$: $OA = OB$ (equal radii)
  $\therefore \ \angle OAB = \angle OBA$ (ITT)

Let the size of $\angle OAB$ and $\angle OBA$ be $x°$.
  $\therefore \ \angle AOD = \angle OAB + \angle OBA$ (EAT)
  $\angle AOD = 2x°$ (substitution)

In $\triangle OBC$: $OB = OC$ (equal radii)
  $\therefore \ \angle OBC = \angle OCB$ (ITT)

Let the size of $\angle OCB$ and $\angle OBC$ be $y°$
  $\therefore \ \angle DOC = \angle OCB + \angle OBC$ (EAT)
  $\angle DOC = 2y°$ (substitution)

Now: $\angle AOC = \angle AOD + \angle DOC$
  $\therefore \ \angle AOC = 2x° + 2y°$ (substitution)
  $\therefore \ \angle AOC = 2(x + y)°$ (distributive property)
  $\therefore \ \angle AOC = 2(\angle OBA + \angle OBC)$ (substitution)
  $\therefore \ \angle AOC = 2\angle ABC$
or $\angle ABC = \frac{1}{2} \angle AOC$

There are two other possible cases. Their proofs are left to the exercises.

EXERCISES

A **1.** Name the following from the diagram.

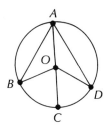

    a. three inscribed angles

    b. three sector angles

    c. two angles subtended by arc *BC*

    d. the inscribed angle and the sector angle

        subtended by arc *BC*

B **2.** Find the value of each unknown.

a.   **b.**   **c.**   **d.**

e.   **f.**   **g.**   **h.**

C **3.** Prove the Inscribed Angle Theorem (IAT) for the following cases.

a. 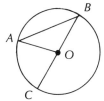   **b.**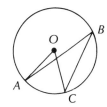

4. Find the value of each unknown.

a.   **b.**   **c.**   **d.**

e.   **f.**   **g.**   **h.**

351

11–5 Corollaries of IAT

The Inscribed Angle Theorem has two corollaries.

IAT Corollary 1

Inscribed angles subtended by the same chord or arc are equal.

Given: $\angle ABC$, $\angle ADC$, subtended by $\overline{AC}$
Prove: $\angle ABC = \angle ADC$

Proof: Construct sector angle, $\angle AOC$.

$$\angle ABC = \tfrac{1}{2}\angle AOC \quad \text{(IAT)}$$

$$\angle ADC = \tfrac{1}{2}\angle AOC \quad \text{(IAT)}$$

$$\therefore \angle ABC = \angle ADC \quad \text{(substitution)}$$

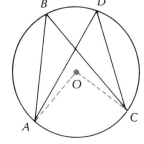

IAT Corollary 2

An angle inscribed in a semicircle is a right angle.

Given: $\angle ABC$ subtended by diameter AC
Prove: $\angle ABC = 90°$

Proof:

$$\angle ABC = \tfrac{1}{2}\angle AOC \quad \text{(IAT)}$$

$$\angle AOC = 180° \quad \text{(straight angle)}$$

$$\therefore \angle ABC = \tfrac{1}{2}(180°) \quad \text{(substitution)}$$

$$\text{or } \angle ABC = 90°$$

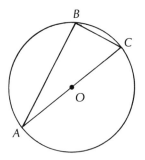

EXAMPLE 1: Find the value of each unknown.

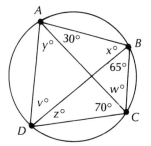

$$\angle ABD = \angle ACD \quad \text{(IAT Corollary 1)}$$
$$\therefore \quad x = 70 \quad \text{(substitution)}$$
$$\angle DAC = \angle DBC \quad \text{(IAT Corollary 1)}$$
$$\therefore \quad y = 65 \quad \text{(substitution)}$$
$$\angle BDC = \angle BAC \quad \text{(IAT Corollary 1)}$$
$$\therefore \quad z = 30$$

In $\triangle BDC$:
$$\angle BCD + \angle CDB + \angle DBC = 180° \quad \text{(AST)}$$
$$(w + 70) + 30 + 65 = 180 \quad \text{(substitution)}$$
$$w = 15$$
$$\angle ADB = \angle ACB \quad \text{(IAT Corollary 1)}$$
$$\therefore \quad v = w \quad \text{(substitution)}$$
$$v = 15 \quad \text{(substitution)}$$

An **inscribed quadrilateral** of a circle is a quadrilateral which has all four vertices in the circle. It is also called a **cyclic quadrilateral**.

EXAMPLE 2: Prove that in an inscribed quadrilateral of a circle the opposite angles are supplementary.

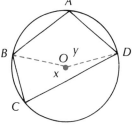

Given: Quadrilateral *ABCD* inscribed in a circle with centre *O*

Prove: $\angle BAD + \angle BCD = 180°$
$\angle ABC + \angle ADC = 180°$

Proof: Construct $\angle BOD$.
Inscribed angle *BAD* and reflex angle *BOD* are subtended by arc *BCD*.

The letter *x* marks reflex angle *BOD*.

$$\therefore \angle BAD = \tfrac{1}{2}x \qquad \text{(IAT)}$$

Inscribed angle *BCD* and sector angle *BOD* are subtended by arc *BAD*.

$$\therefore \angle BCD = \tfrac{1}{2}y \qquad \text{(IAT)}$$
$$\therefore \angle BAD + \angle BCD = \tfrac{1}{2}x + \tfrac{1}{2}y \quad \text{(substitution)}$$

But $x + y = 360°$ \qquad (complete rotation)

$$\therefore \angle BAD + \angle BCD = \tfrac{1}{2}(360°)$$
$$\angle BAD + \angle BCD = 180°$$

Similarly, it can be proved that $\angle ABC + \angle ADC = 180°$.

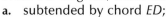

EXERCISES

A **1.** From the diagram, name the inscribed angles that are:
   a. subtended by chord *ED*;
   b. subtended by arc *AB*;
   c. subtended by chord *AE*;
   d. subtended by arc *DC*.

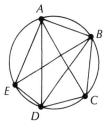

   2. Name all the inscribed quadrilaterals in the diagram given for exercise 1.

B **3.** Find the value of each unknown.

   a.   **b.**   **c.**   **d.**

e.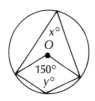

f.

g.

h.

4. Using the information shown in the diagram, prove the given deduction.

a.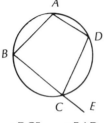

∠DCE = ∠BAD

b.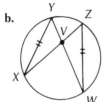

YW = ZX

c.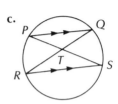

△PQT is isosceles.

d.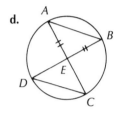

$\overline{AB} \parallel \overline{CD}$

5. For the diagram given, calculate the size of ∠YZW.

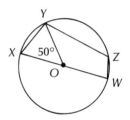

6. For the diagram given, with $\overline{PS}$ and $\overline{SR}$ diameters, prove that P, Q, and R are collinear.

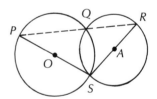

7. ABCD is a cyclic quadrilateral. $\overline{BD}$ and $\overline{AC}$ intersect so that ∠ACD = 21° and ∠ADB = 42°. Calculate the size of ∠BAD.

C 8. $\overline{PQ}$ and $\overline{XY}$ are equal chords in a circle with centre O. Prove that any inscribed angle subtended by $\overline{PQ}$ is equal to any inscribed angle subtended by $\overline{XY}$.

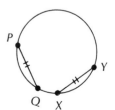

Review

1. Construct the perpendicular bisector $\overline{PQ}$ of a line segment AB, 10 cm in length. Prove that $\overline{PQ}$ is the perpendicular bisector of $\overline{AB}$.

2. Identify the following from the diagram.
   a. two radii
   b. a diameter
   c. a tangent
   d. a point of contact
   e. six inscribed angles
   f. two sector angles
   g. five chords
   h. the boundaries of two sectors
   i. the boundaries of five segments
   j. the boundaries of a semicircular region
   k. a right angle

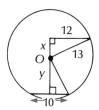

3. Find the value of each unknown. All linear measures are in centimetres.

   a.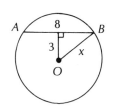
   b.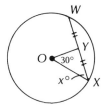
   c.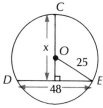
   d.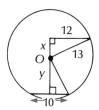

4. Find the value of each unknown.

   a.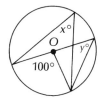
   b.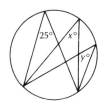
   c.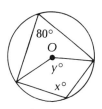
   d.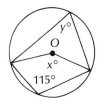

   e.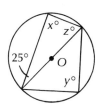
   f.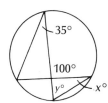
   g.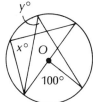
   h.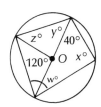

5. A, B, C, and D are points in a circle. $\overline{AD}$ and $\overline{BC}$ intersect at point E such that $\overline{AB} \parallel \overline{CD}$. Prove that $AE = BE$.

6. $PQRS$ is a quadrilateral inscribed in a circle. $\overline{PR}$ and $\overline{QS}$ intersect at T, $\angle RPS = 25°$, and $\angle PRQ = 62°$. Find the size of $\angle PTQ$.

7. $\triangle ABC$ is constructed in a circle with centre O and radius 5 cm so that $\overline{AB}$ is a diameter and $BC = 3$ cm. Find the length of $\overline{AC}$.

11–6 Tangent Properties

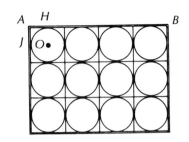

Juice glasses have been packed into partitioned boxes so that they will not touch during shipping. The partitions and the sides of the box suggest tangents to the circles of the glass rims. $\overline{AB}$ is *tangent* to the circle with centre O. H is a point of contact.

Imagine the radius $\overline{OH}$.
It can be shown that a tangent to a circle is perpendicular to the radius at the point of contact: $\overline{OH} \perp \overline{AB}$.

The proof of the tangent property is not included in this course. But see the EXTRA for this lesson for an experimental verification.

EXAMPLE 1: $\overline{PQ}$ is tangent to a circle with centre O. P is the point of contact.
If $PQ = 24$ cm and $OQ = 25$ cm, find the value of the radius of the circle.

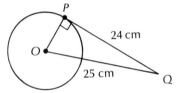

Since $\overline{OP} \perp \overline{PQ}$, apply the Pythagorean Theorem.

$$OP^2 + PQ^2 = OQ^2$$
$$OP^2 + 24^2 = 25^2$$
$$OP^2 = 625 - 576$$
$$= 49$$
$$OP = 7$$

The radius is 7 cm.

EXAMPLE 2:   Prove that tangent segments to a circle from an external point P are equal in length.

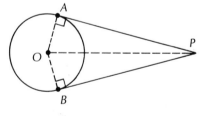

Given: $\overline{PA}, \overline{PB}$ are tangent segments with A, B points of contact

Prove: $PA = PB$

Proof: $\overline{OA} \perp \overline{PA}$ and $\overline{OB} \perp \overline{PB}$ (tangent property)
       $OA^2 + PA^2 = OP^2$ and $OB^2 + PB^2 = OP^2$ (Pythagorean Theorem)

But $OA = OB$ (equal radii)
and $OP = OP$ (reflexive property)
$\therefore PA^2 = PB^2$
and $PA = PB$

356

EXERCISES

A **1.** Find the values of x and y. $\overline{PA}$ and $\overline{PB}$ are tangent segments.

a.

b.

c.

B **2.** Two concentric circles have radii 5 cm and 3 cm. $\overline{AB}$ is a chord of the larger circle and is tangent to the smaller circle, with point of contact D. Find the length of $\overline{AB}$.

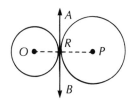

3. $\overline{PA}$ and $\overline{PB}$ are tangent segments to a circle with centre O. Prove the following.
   a. $\angle POA = \angle POB$ **b.** $\angle APO = \angle BPO$

4. A point C is 39 cm from the centre O of a circle with radius 15 cm. Find the length of tangent segment CA, where A is the point of contact.

C **5.** Two circles with centres O and P are tangent to line AB at R. Prove that O, R, and P are collinear. ($\overline{AB}$ is called a **common tangent** of the two circles.)

EXTRA

Paper Folding

By paper folding, you can experimentally test the accuracy of a tangent you have drawn by eye.

1. Draw a circle with centre O on a large piece of paper.

2. Mark a point P on the circle.

3. As best you can, draw a tangent APB to pass through P.

4. Fold the paper so that the crease passes through P and ray PB folds onto ray PA.

If your tangent is accurate, the crease will pass through the centre O and one half of the circle will fold onto the other half.

Test this technique several times.

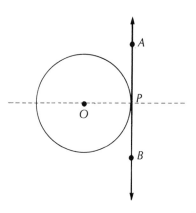

11–7 Tangent Constructions

The tangent property can be used to construct tangents to a circle.

EXAMPLE 1: Construct a tangent to a given circle with centre O through a given point P on the circle.

The required tangent must be perpendicular to line OP.

1. Draw the line OP.

2. Construct line PQ so that $\overleftrightarrow{PQ} \perp \overleftrightarrow{OP}$.

   $\overleftrightarrow{PQ}$ is the required tangent.

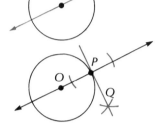

EXAMPLE 2: Construct both tangents to a circle with centre O from P, a point outside the circle.

1. Draw line OP.

2. Locate Q, the midpoint of $\overline{OP}$.

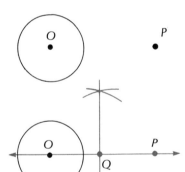

3. With centre Q and radius QO, draw a circle intersecting the given circle at R and S.

4. Draw lines PR and PS.

   $\overleftrightarrow{PR}$ and $\overleftrightarrow{PS}$ are the required tangents to the circle.

   The proof of this construction is required in the exercises.

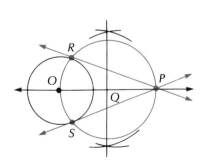

358

EXERCISES

A **1.** Make a similar diagram. Construct a tangent(s) to the given circle through point *P*.

a.

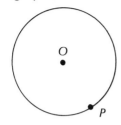

b.

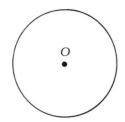

B **2.** Make a similar diagram by tracing a circular object. Locate the centre of the circle and construct the tangent to each circle through the given point *P*.

a.

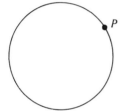

b.

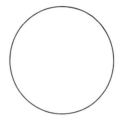

3. Prove that the construction described in example 2 produces two equal tangents to the circle.

4. Copy the diagram at the right. Construct tangent segments *SA* and *SB*. Prove that △*ASB* is isosceles.

EXTRA

Compass Designs

Try to draw these designs using a straightedge and a compass.

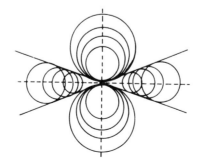
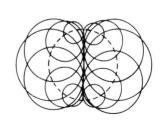

11–8 Circumscribed and Inscribed Circles

A **circumscribed circle** of a polygon, or **circumcircle**, is
a circle passing through the vertices of the polygon.
Not all polygons have circumscribed circles.

Circumcircles:

> For any triangle, there *is* a circumcircle.

Not Circumcircles:

The circumcircle of any given △*ABC* can be
constructed using the perpendicular bisectors of the
sides of the triangle. The perpendicular bisectors meet
at a single point, the **circumcentre** of the triangle.

Construction:

1. Construct the perpendicular
   bisectors of sides *BC* and *AC*. Label
   their point of intersection *O*.

2. With centre *O* and radius *OA*, draw
   a circle.

3. This circle passes through *A*, *B*, and
   C. It is the *circumcircle* of △*ABC*.

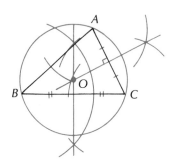

Proof:

O is in the perpendicular bisector of side *BC*. (by construction)
∴ *OB* = *OC* (PBT)

O is in the perpendicular bisector of side *AC*. (by construction)
∴ *OA* = *OC* (PBT)
∴ *OA* = *OB* = *OC* (substitution)

O is equidistant from *A*, *B*, and *C*.
∴ The circle with centre *O* and radius *OA* passes through
  A, *B*, and *C* and is the circumcircle of △*ABC*.

An **inscribed circle** of a polygon, or **incircle**, is a circle
tangent to each side of the polygon.

Incircles:

> For any triangle, there is an incircle.

Not incircles:

The incircle of any given △*ABC* can be constructed
using the angle bisectors of the angles of the triangle.
The angle bisectors meet at a single point, the **incentre**
of the triangle.

Construction:

1. Construct the bisectors of ∠ABC and ∠ACB. Label their point of intersection O.

2. Construct $\overline{OX} \perp \overline{BC}$.

3. With centre O and radius OX, draw a circle.

4. This is the incircle of △ABC.

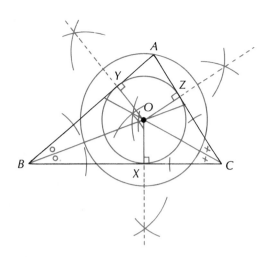

Proof:

Draw $\overline{OY} \perp \overline{AB}$ and $\overline{OZ} \perp \overline{AC}$.
OB bisects ∠ABC. (by construction)
∴ OY = OX   (ABT)

$\overline{OC}$ bisects ∠ACB. (by construction)
∴ OX = OZ   (ABT)
∴ OX = OY = OZ (substitution)
∴ The circle with centre O and radius OX passes through Y and Z; and $\overline{BC} \perp \overline{OX}$, $\overline{AB} \perp \overline{OY}$, and $\overline{AC} \perp \overline{OZ}$.

∴ Segments AB, AC, and BC are tangent to the circle.

EXERCISES

A 1. Draw a triangle similar to the given triangle, using half a page of your notebook. Construct its incircle.

a.   b.    c.

2. Draw a triangle similar to each triangle given in exercise 1. Construct its circumcircle.

B 3. The circle in the diagram is the incircle of △ABC with points of contact X, Y, and Z. Prove that AC + BY is half the perimeter of the triangle.

4. A circle which is tangent to one side and to two *extended* sides of a triangle is called an **escribed circle** of the triangle.
   a. Copy the construction shown at the right to produce an escribed circle.
   b. How many escribed circles does a triangle have?

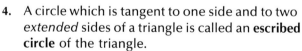

361

5. Find the measure of each angle in △XYZ.

6. Verify the following properties by drawing several examples.
   a. A circle can be drawn through the vertices of any triangle.
   b. A circle can be drawn through the vertices of a quadrilateral if and only if opposite angles of the quadrilateral are supplementary.
   c. A regular polygon can be circumscribed using the method for circumscribing a triangle.

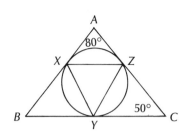

C 7. Construct the incircle of △ABC to touch $\overline{AB}$ at Q, and $\overline{AC}$ at P, with centre O. Locate the centre O of a circle through A, P, O, and Q to show that APOQ is a cyclic quadrilateral.

8. A circle is inscribed in quadrilateral ABCD as shown. If AW = 5, BX = 4, CY = 3.5, and DZ = 6, find the perimeter of quadrilateral ABCD.

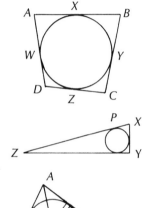

9. A circle inscribed in a right triangle XYZ is tangent to the hypotenuse XZ at P. If XP = 4 and PZ = 21, find the perimeter of △XYZ.

10. Show that the area of a triangle is equal to half the product of its perimeter and the radius of its incircle.
   (Look at △AOB, △AOC, and △COB.)

EXTRA

Inscribing Polygons

1. Follow the diagrams below as a guide to inscribe these regular polygons in circles. Use only a compass and a straightedge.

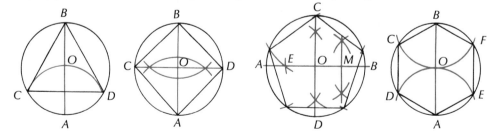

2. Find a method for inscribing a regular octagon.

362

Review

1. Find the value of each unknown. A and B are points of contact.

a.
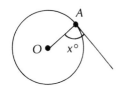

b.
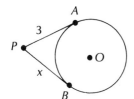

c.
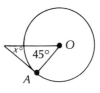

d.
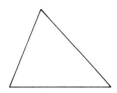

e.
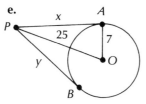

f.
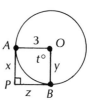

2. X, Y, and Z are points of contact.
   a. Find the values of p, q, and r.
   b. What is the perimeter of △ABC?
   c. If ∠BAC = 67° and ∠ACB = 54°, find the sizes of ∠AXY, ∠CBA, and ∠XZC.

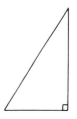

3. A is a point in a circle with centre O and radius 5 cm. Construct the circle and a tangent to the circle at A.

4. Draw a circle with centre O and radius 5 cm. Construct a tangent to the circle at point of contact A.

5. Draw a triangle similar to the given triangle. Construct its circumcircle.

a.
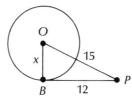

b.

c.
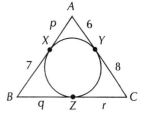

6. Draw a triangle similar to each triangle in exercise 5. Construct the incircle of each triangle.

7. $\overline{PA}$ and $\overline{PB}$ are tangent segments to a circle with centre O.
   a. If ∠APB = 74°, find the size of ∠PAB.
   b. If PO = 15 cm and PA = 12 cm, find the length of the radius of the circle.
   c. $\overline{PO}$ intersects $\overline{AB}$ at D. Prove that $\overline{PD}$ is perpendicular to $\overline{AB}$.
   d. Find the size of ∠AOD.

Tangent Circles

Problems involving tangent circles can lead to some interesting mathematical results.

1. Four congruent circles are positioned as shown, with each circle being tangent to two others. Prove that the four given segments joining the centres of the circles form a square.

   a. First, for each pair of touching circles, prove that the segments joining the centres also go through the point of contact.

   b. Then, prove that the quadrilateral formed has all sides equal.

   c. Finally, prove that one angle of the quadrilateral is 90°.

2. Three congruent circles of radius r are positioned so as to be tangent to each other. Prove that the three segments joining the centres of the circles form an equilateral triangle.

3. Suppose you packed the plane with congruent tangent circles using a square arrangement, as illustrated at the right. What percentage of the plane is covered? To answer this question, follow the steps below.

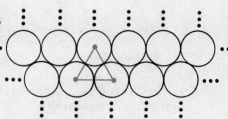

   a. Consider the smallest component of the pattern that, when repeated, will entirely cover the plane. This is the square shown at the right. Let the radius of each circle be r units. What are the dimensions of the square?

   b. Find the area of the square.

   c. Find the total area of the circular portions.

   d. What percentage of the square is taken up with portions of circles?

   e. What percentage of the plane is covered in a square arrangement used to pack the plane?

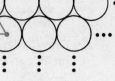

4. The diagram at the right shows a hexagonal packing of the plane. What percentage of the plane is covered?

   a. The smallest component of this pattern is the equilateral triangle shown at the right. Let the radius of each circle be r units. Find the area of the triangle and the total area of the circular portions.

   b. What percentage of the triangle is taken up with portions of circles?

   c. What percentage of the plane is covered when hexagonal packing is used?

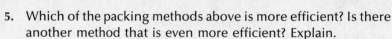

5. Which of the packing methods above is more efficient? Is there another method that is even more efficient? Explain.

Historical Note

Leonard Euler, born in Switzerland in 1707, was one of the most productive mathematical authors in history. Even though he became blind in about 1766, his output did not diminish. By dictating his material, he continued to write until his death in 1783, at the age of 76 years.

Euler's interests touched upon all areas of mathematics. Complete the following questions to learn about one of his geometric discoveries.

1. Draw a large scalene triangle *ABC*.

2. Construct the medians of each side to meet at *X*, the **centroid**.

3. Construct the altitude of each side to meet at *Y*, the **orthocentre**.

4. Construct the perpendicular bisector of each side to meet at *Z*, the *circumcentre*.

5. If your constructions were accurate, then *X*, *Y*, and *Z* should be collinear. Are they?

6. Construct the angle bisector of each angle of △*ABC* and determine if their intersection point, the *incentre*, lies in the same line.

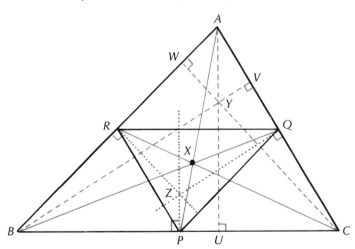

The line through the centroid, orthocentre, and circumcentre is called the **Euler Line**.

Test

1. Draw a line segment PQ and a point T in $\overline{PQ}$. Construct the perpendicular to $\overline{PQ}$ through T.

2. Draw a line segment AB and a point F not in $\overline{AB}$. Construct the line through F and parallel to $\overline{AB}$.

3. Construct an angle of the given size.
    a. 90°   b. 45°   c. 60°   d. 75°   e. 15°

4. Find the value of each unknown.

    a.   b.   c.   d.

    e.   f.   g.   h.

5. What are the indicated measures?

    a. 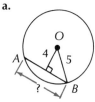   b.   c.   d.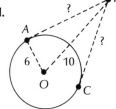

    $\overline{PA}$ and $\overline{PC}$ are tangent segments.

    A and C are points of contact.

6. Draw a circle with centre O and a point P outside the circle. Construct the two tangents to the circle that contain point P.

7. Draw an obtuse triangle and construct its circumcircle.

8. Draw a scalene triangle and construct its inscribed circle.

9. Using the information given in the diagram, prove $PT = ST$.

Cumulative Review

1. Solve each quadratic equation.
   a. $x^2 - 24 = 5x$
   b. $6x^2 + 20x + 25 = 2x^2$
   c. $3x^2 + 26x = 9$

2. Add or subtract as indicated. State any restrictions on the variables.
   a. $\dfrac{1}{x + 3} + \dfrac{1}{x - 4}$
   b. $\dfrac{t}{t - 7} - \dfrac{3 + t}{t}$
   c. $\dfrac{k + 1}{k^2 - 4} + \dfrac{k + 3}{k - 2}$

3. Give the domain and range for each graph illustrated below. Does the graph represent a function?

   a. 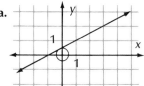   b. 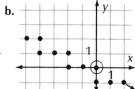   c. 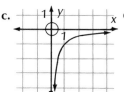   d.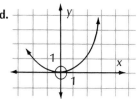

4. Given that y varies inversely as x, copy and complete the table below.

x	1	6				12	5	
y	24		6	3	2	-1			-5

5. For each sample selection described, explain why the population is not accurately represented.
   a. To assess student opinion at a high school, five students are selected from each home room.
   b. To assess community response to a proposed shopping complex, shoppers at a nearby mall are questioned.
   c. To assess community response to a news item, radio listeners are invited to telephone the radio station.

6. Quadrilateral $ABCD$ has vertices $A(5, 3)$, $B(0, 2)$, $C(-1, 2)$, and $D(-2, 3)$. Find the image of $ABCD$ under the rotation of $90°$ about $O(0, 0)$. Find the image of $A'B'C'D'$ under the dilatation with centre O and scale factor -3.

7. For the pair of similar figures at the right, find the values of x and y.

   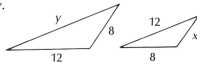

8. Find the value of each unknown.

   a. 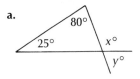   b.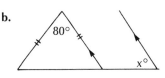

367

12

Three-Dimensional Geometry

Sphere with Angels and Devils, stained maple, 1942. By M.C. Escher.

12–1 Symmetry

The spherical wood carving shown above, by artist M.C. Escher, was an adaptation of his earlier illustration, shown below. This illustration displays two types of symmetry in two dimensions.

Escher's two-dimensional work displays **line symmetry**. The reflection lines *m*, marked on the illustration, map each figure onto itself.

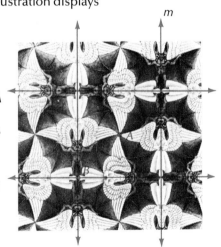

Escher's work also displays **rotational symmetry**. Point *A* is the **centre of rotation** and the **order** of rotational symmetry is 4, meaning the angel (or devil) figure maps onto itself four times under a complete rotation. Its smallest angle of rotation is $\frac{360°}{4}$ or 90°.

Point *B* is also a centre of rotation. The order of rotational symmetry about *B* is 2. Its smallest angle of rotation is $\frac{360°}{2}$ or 180°.

Angels and Devils, 1941, by M.C. Escher.

Three-dimensional figures, like Escher's *Sphere with Angels and Devils*, can also be examined for different kinds of symmetry.

A three-dimensional solid has **plane symmetry** if a plane cuts the object into two congruent halves. The solids shown below have plane symmetry. Each half maps onto the other half under reflection in the plane shown.

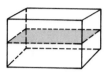
Rectangular Prism

Square Pyramid

Sphere

Cylinder

Cone

In this unit, "prism" and "pyramid" refer to *right* prism and *right* pyramid. "Cylinder" and "cone" refer to *right* cylinder and *right* cone.

Three-dimensional figures can have more than one plane of symmetry. The triangular prism below has four different planes of symmetry that map all points in one half onto corresponding points in the other half.

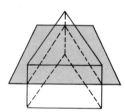
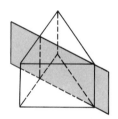
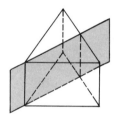
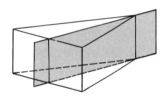

When a three-dimensional figure can be rotated about a centre **axis** so that the figure maps onto itself more than once under a complete rotation, it is said to have **rotational symmetry**.

A regular octahedron maps onto itself four times under a complete rotation about its centre axis. It has rotational symmetry of order 4 about that axis. The smallest angle of rotational symmetry is 90°. Can you find other axes of rotation for the regular octahedron?

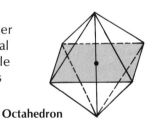
Octahedron

A regular tetrahedron displays rotational symmetry of order three about its centre axis. The smallest angle of rotational symmetry is 120°.

Tetrahedron or Triangular Pyramid

EXERCISES

A 1. Does the figure have line symmetry? If so, how many lines of symmetry does it have?

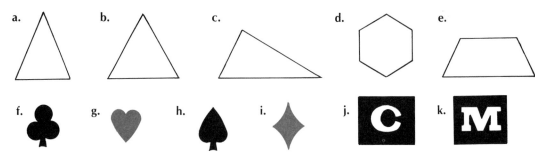

a.   b.   c.   d.   e.

f.   g.   h.   i.   j.   k.

2. **a.** Which of the figures in exercise 1 have rotational symmetry?
   b. State the order of rotational symmetry for each figure in exercise 1 with rotational symmetry.
   c. If a figure has line symmetry, what is the relationship between its number of lines of symmetry and its order of rotational symmetry?
   d. State the smallest angle of rotational symmetry for each figure with rotational symmetry in exercise 1.

B 3. Does the pentagonal pyramid have plane symmetry? If so, how many planes of symmetry does it have?

4. Does the rectangular prism have rotational symmetry? If so, how many axes of symmetry does it have?

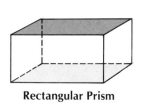

Rectangular Prism

Pentagonal Pyramid

5. The most ancient polyhedra are the set of five known as the **Platonic solids** or regular solids. They derive their name from the Greek philosopher, Plato, who described them in about 400 B.C. Each polyhedron has faces that are congruent, regular polygons.

   a. Does the tetrahedron have plane symmetry? If so, how many planes of symmetry does it have?
   b. Does the tetrahedron have rotational symmetry? If so, how many axes of symmetry does it have?
   c. What is the smallest angle of rotational symmetry for the tetrahedron?
   d. Does the hexahedron, or cube, have plane symmetry? If so, how many planes of symmetry does it have?
   e. Does the hexahedron have rotational symmetry? If so, how many axes of symmetry does it have?

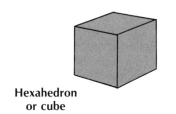

Tetrahedron

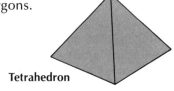

Hexahedron or cube

6. **a.** Do the regular octahedron (8 faces), regular dodecahedron (12 faces), and regular icosahedron (20 faces) have plane symmetry? If so, how many planes of symmetry does each figure have?

   b. Do they have rotational symmetry? If so, how many axes of symmetry does each figure have?

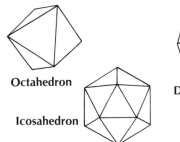

Octahedron

Dodecahedron

Icosahedron

Biography

Born in 1898 in Leeuwarden in the northern part of the Netherlands, Maurits Cornelis Escher was an artist whose work, though initially ignored by art critics, has captivated mathematicians, physicists, and crystallographers.

Trained in the graphic arts, Escher worked largely with woodcuts and lithographs. His early material, completed before 1937, is highly pictorial and realistic, usually depicting Italian landscape and architecture. (Escher lived in Rome from 1923 to 1935.) Yet, even within these works, Escher was able to introduce an element of fantasy, often by altering the perspective within the illustration, or by introducing a reflecting surface such as a mirror or a still pond. Escher's inspiration during this period stemmed from summer-long trips through the Italian countryside, where he made numerous sketches and took photographs for use in the winter months.

Self-portrait, woodcut, 1923

By 1935 the threat of war was already being felt in Europe. The political climate in Italy, under the leadership of Mussolini, became unbearable to Escher. He moved his family from Rome: first to Switzerland and then to Belgium, finally settling in Holland.

During the pre-war years Escher was able to make several trips along the Spanish coast, where he was fascinated by the Moorish mosaic tile patterns found in the country's architecture. These mosaic patterns later formed the foundation of Escher's studies in filling the plane with congruent figures. The illustration *Angels and Devils* is an example of such a study.

Escher's work after 1937 can be broadly characterized by his departure from the pictorial presentation of landscape and architecture. He began to pursue the themes of regularity and mathematical structure, continuity and infinity. Except for an illness in 1962, Escher continued to produce his captivating pieces of art until his death in 1972.

12–2 Surface Area and Volume of Prisms

Some geometric solids have **shells** which can be constructed out of thick paper by drawing a **net** of the figure. Each net below folds to make a prism.

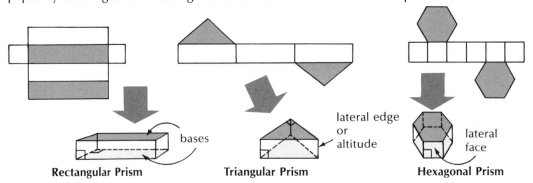

Rectangular Prism   Triangular Prism   Hexagonal Prism

The net of a prism shows all of its faces, and is therefore useful in calculating both surface area and lateral surface area. **Surface area** is the total area of all faces of an object; **lateral surface area** is the area of all lateral faces. **Volume**, or amount of space taken up by an object, can be found by a formula. (*h* is used to represent height.)

$$SA_{\text{prism}} = 2A_{\text{base}} + A_{\text{lateral faces}}$$

$$V_{\text{prism}} = A_{\text{base}} \times h$$

EXAMPLE:

A corner cabinet in the shape of a triangular prism is being built.

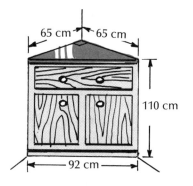

a. About how much wood is needed for the top, the bottom, and the sides?

$SA_{\text{prism}} = 2A_{\text{base}} + A_{\text{lateral faces}}$

$\phantom{SA_{\text{prism}}} = 2\left[\frac{1}{2}(65)(65)\right] + 2(110)(65) + (110)(92)$

$\phantom{SA_{\text{prism}}} = 2(2112.5) + 2(7150) + 10\ 120$

$\phantom{SA_{\text{prism}}} = 4225 + 24\ 420$

$\phantom{SA_{\text{prism}}} = 28\ 645$ (in square centimetres)

There are 28 645 cm² or about 2.9 m² of wood required.

b. What is the amount of space taken up by the cabinet?

$V_{\text{prism}} = A_{\text{base}} \times h$

$\phantom{V_{\text{prism}}} = \frac{1}{2}(65)(65)(110)$

$\phantom{V_{\text{prism}}} = 232\ 375$

The volume of the cabinet is 232 375 cm³ or about 232. 4 dm³.

EXERCISES

A **1.** Copy and complete.
   a. 350 000 cm² = ▪ m²   **b.** 98 m² = ▪ cm²   **c.** 17 820 cm² = ▪ m²
   d. 98 500 cm³ = ▪ m³   **e.** 4.2 m³ = ▪ cm³   **f.** 1 347 300 mm³ = ▪ cm³

2. Copy and complete the table, referring to the diagram at the right.
   All linear measurements are in centimetres.

	l	w	h	Lateral Area	Surface Area	Volume
a.	9	12	6	?	?	?
b.	3	5	?	32	?	?
c.	?	9	2	44	?	?
d.	5	5	?	?	?	400

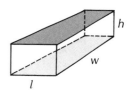

B **3.** Find the surface area of each figure described below.
   a. a rectangular prism 16 cm by 12 cm by 5 cm
   b. a square prism with base edge 7 cm and height 4 cm
   c. a triangular prism, with base triangle having a base 12 cm and a
       height of 8 cm, and with a height of 5 cm

4. Find the volume of each prism described in
   exercise 3.

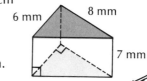

5. **a.** Find the volume of the triangular prism.
   b. Find its surface area.

6. A solid is completely submerged in a rectangular
   container, causing the water level to rise 3 cm. The
   base of the container is 25 cm by 40 cm. Find the
   volume of the solid.

7. Calculate the amount of air space per person in each tent.
   a. **3-person tent.** Floor measures 160 cm × 190 cm.
       Height 140 cm. Nylon/cotton interior.
       Flynet door. **69.95**

   b. **4-person tent.** Floor measures 210 cm × 270 cm.
       Full height 160 cm; side wall 50 cm.
       Laminated sheet floor. **74.99**

C **8.** **a.** If the edge of a cube is doubled, by how much is the
       surface area increased?
   b. If the edge of a cube is doubled, by how much is the
       volume increased?

9. A diagonal of a cube is $4\sqrt{3}$ cm long. What is the
   volume of the cube?

12–3 Surface Area and Volume of Pyramids

Each net below folds to make a pyramid. A **regular pyramid** is one whose base is a regular polygon. In a regular pyramid, each lateral face has the same height, called the **slant height**, s.

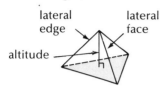

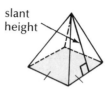

Triangular Pyramid   **Square Pyramid**

As with the nets of prisms, the nets of pyramids are useful in calculating surface area. Volume can be found by a formula. (h is used to represent height.)

$$SA_{\text{pyramid}} = A_{\text{base}} + A_{\text{lateral faces}}$$

$$V_{\text{pyramid}} = \tfrac{1}{3} A_{\text{base}} \times h$$

EXAMPLE:

Find the surface area and volume of the square-based pyramid shown.

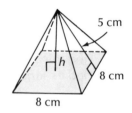

a. $SA_{\text{pyramid}} = A_{\text{base}} + A_{\text{lateral faces}}$

$= (8)(8) + 4\left[\tfrac{1}{2}(8)(5) \right]$

$= 64 + 80$

$= 144$

The surface area of the pyramid is 144 cm².

b. To find the volume of the pyramid, first use the Pythagorean Theorem to determine the height of the pyramid, h.

$h^2 + 4^2 = 5^2$

$h^2 = 25 - 16$

$h^2 = 9$

$h = 3$

Once the height is known, the volume can be calculated.

$V_{\text{pyramid}} = \tfrac{1}{3} A_{\text{base}} \times h$

$= \tfrac{1}{3}(64)(3)$

$= 64$

The volume of the pyramid is 64 cm³.

EXERCISES

A **1.** Draw the net of each pyramid below and label the dimensions of each face.

a.

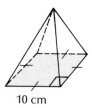

10 cm

Slant height is 16 cm.

b.

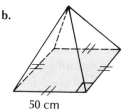

50 cm

Slant height is 42 cm.

c.

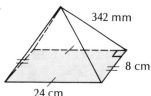

342 mm

8 cm

24 cm

2. Find the surface area of each pyramid in exercise 1.

3. Given the following height, h, find the volume of each corresponding pyramid in exercise 1.
  a. $h = 152$ mm   **b.** $h = 337$ mm   **c.** $h = 297$ mm

B **4.** Find the volume of each pyramid described below, in cubic centimetres.
  a. a square pyramid with height 12 mm and base edge 10 mm
  b. a rectangular pyramid with height 9 cm and a base 6 cm by 8 cm
  c. a triangular pyramid with height 3.5 cm and a regular base having edge 5 cm

5. Copy and complete the table for the square pyramid shown at the right. All measurements are in centimetres.

	h	s	b	x
a.	?	5	6	?
b.	12	13	?	?
c.	?	?	18	15
d.	?	24	?	25

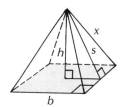

6. Find the surface area and volume of each pyramid tabulated in exercise 5.

7. The Great Pyramid of Cheops was originally 147 m high with a ground area of 53 095 m². Calculate its original volume.

C **8.** The Great Pyramid of Cheops was a square-based pyramid.
  a. Find the length of its base and its slant height.
  b. Find its surface area.

9. Find the surface area and volume of a regular hexagonal pyramid with base edge 14 cm and lateral edge 25 cm.

10. A square pyramid is inscribed in a cone with radius 6 cm and height 8 cm. Find its surface area and volume.

Application

For engineers and architects, a perspective drawing is not always as informative as their needs require. More information can be given by displaying three views of an object, the front view, top view, and side view. These three views are the **orthographic projections** of the object.

Below is a drawing of an object and its orthographic projections.

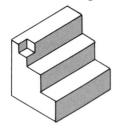

Front View   Top View   Side View

1. Which figure is formed by the given set of orthographic projections?

a. Front   Top   Side

A   B   C

b. Front   Top   Side

A   B   C

2. Draw the orthographic projections of each object illustrated.

a.   b.   c.   d.   e.

EXTRA

Each cube is made up of smaller cubes. Some of the smaller cubes have been removed to form tunnels. The surfaces of the cubes are painted, including inside the tunnels and the bottom. How many cubes have paint on 4 faces? 3 faces? 2 faces? 1 face? no faces?

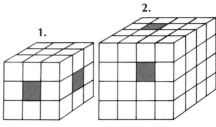

Review

1. Which objects have plane symmetry? How many planes of symmetry are there for those objects with plane symmetry?

a.    b.    c.    d.

2. Which objects illustrated in question 1 have rotational symmetry? Identify the axis of symmetry and state the order of rotational symmetry of each object which has rotational symmetry.

3. Find the volume and surface area of each figure.

a.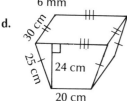
6 mm
6 mm
7 mm
6 mm

b.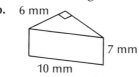
6 mm
7 mm
10 mm

c.
5 m
6 m
6 m

d.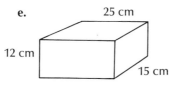
30 cm
25 cm
24 cm
20 cm

e.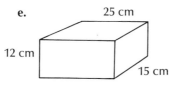
25 cm
12 cm
15 cm

f.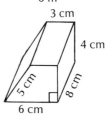
3 cm
4 cm
5 cm
8 cm
6 cm

4. Which takes up more space, the triangular corner cupboard or the rectangular bookcase?

   a. Corner Cabinet with engraved interior base, shelves. 76 × 175 cm high
      012 013 880 DLTJ — Each 199.98

   b. Hi-Boy Bookcase with 2 sliding doors, 4 shelves. 71 × 27 × 157 cm
      012 013 861 DLTJ — Each 149.98

depth 27 cm
175 cm
157 cm
76 cm
71 cm

5. Two wedges of cheese are cut as illustrated. Which contains more cheese?

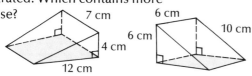
7 cm
6 cm
6 cm
4 cm
12 cm
10 cm

39 cm
61 cm
111 cm

6. Sandy decided to refinish the chest of drawers shown, and stain the top, front, and sides. What is the surface area to be stained?

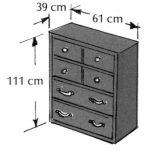

377

12–4 Surface Area of Cylinders and Cones

As with prisms and pyramids, the surface area formulas for the cylinder and the cone can be derived from their nets.

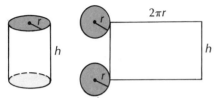

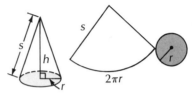

The circumference of each base is $2\pi r$.

The circumference of the base is $2\pi r$. The area of a sector with arc $2\pi r$ and radius s is πrs.

$$
\begin{aligned}
SA_{cylinder} &= 2(A_{base}) + A_{lateral\ face} \\
&= 2(\pi r^2) + (2\pi r)h \\
&= 2\pi r(r + h)
\end{aligned}
$$

$$
\begin{aligned}
SA_{cone} &= A_{base} + A_{lateral\ face} \\
&= \pi r^2 + \pi rs \\
&= \pi r(r + s)
\end{aligned}
$$

EXAMPLE 1: The outer surface of a cylindrical weight is to be coated so that it can be used in water. What is the surface area of metal to be coated?

$$
\begin{aligned}
SA_{cylinder} &= 2\pi r(r + h) \\
&\doteq 2(3.14)(5)(5 + 7) \\
&\doteq 376.8 \\
&\doteq 377 \text{ (to 3 significant digits)}
\end{aligned}
$$

About 377 cm² of surface needs to be coated.

EXAMPLE 2: Find the amount of surface in a conical top with a perpendicular height (depth) of 12 cm and a base diameter of 10 cm.

a. Use the Pythagorean Theorem to find the slant height.

$$
\begin{aligned}
h^2 + r^2 &= s^2 \\
12^2 + 5^2 &= s^2 \\
144 + 25 &= s^2 \\
s^2 &= 169 \\
s &= 13
\end{aligned}
$$

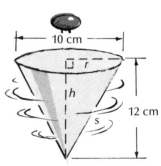

b. Find the surface area.

$$
\begin{aligned}
SA_{cone} &= \pi r(r + s) \\
&\doteq 3.14(5)(5 + 13) \\
&\doteq 282.6 \\
&\doteq 283 \text{ (to 3 significant digits)}
\end{aligned}
$$

The top has about 283 cm² of exposed surface.

EXERCISES

For the following exercises, use $\pi \doteq 3.14$ and round answers to three significant digits. Use a calculator where appropriate.

A 1. Find the surface area of a cylinder with the given height h, and radius r or diameter d.
   a. $h = 12$ cm, $r = 6$ cm   **b.** $h = 20$ cm, $d = 14$ m   **c.** $h = 50$ cm, $d = 12$ m

2. Find the surface area of a cone with the given slant height s, and radius r or diameter d.
   a. $s = 9$ cm, $r = 8$ cm   **b.** $s = 21$ m, $d = 180$ cm   **c.** $s = 24$ m, $r = 70$ cm

B 3. Find the surface area of each solid.

a. 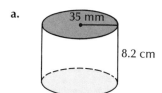   **b.** 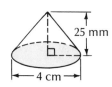   **c.**

4. A cylinder with height 14 cm has a lateral area of 56π cm². Find the radius of its base.

5. a. What are the approximate dimensions of a label for the can at the right? The label stops 5 mm away from the top and bottom of the can. Allow for 1 mm overlap of the label along its seam.
   b. How many labels can be cut from a piece of paper 1 m by 1.5 m?
   c. What area of metal would be needed to make the can?

C 6. A metal pipe 3.5 m long has a surface area of 10.99 m². Calculate its diameter.

7. A company wishes to paint the top and lateral face of a large cylindrical storage tank 28 m in diameter and 7.5 m high. A litre of paint covers 9 m² and costs $7.98. How much will it cost to paint the container?

8. A shade for a lamp is to be made in the shape of a truncated cone with dimensions as shown in the diagram. How much material will be used to make the shade? Allow for 0.5 mm overlap along the seam.

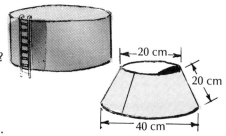

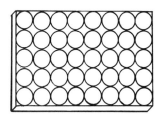

EXTRA

The Great Cola Company packs cola cans in cases that hold 40 cans packed side by side, as shown. Alicia discovered that 41 cans can be arranged in the case by simply rearranging the cans. How did she do it?

379

12–5 Volume of a Cylinder

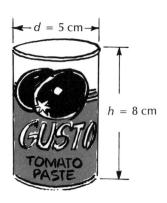

A canning factory uses its smallest cans for packaging tomato paste. A production manager would need to know the volume of material that would fit inside each can, in order to know the number of cans needed during a production run of tomato paste.

The volume of a cylinder is the product of the area of its base and its height.

$$V_{cylinder} = A_{base} \times h$$
$$= \pi r^2 h$$

EXAMPLE 1: Find the volume of tomato paste held by one can with inside dimensions as given in the diagram above.

$V = \pi r^2 h$
$\doteq (3.14)(2.5)^2(8)$
$= 157$ (to 3 significant digits)

Each can holds about 157 cm³ of tomato paste.
This means that a can holds about 157 mL.

EXAMPLE 2: Industrial engineers prepare cost reports on each item they design. To find the cost of the copper tube shown below, an engineer would first calculate the amount of copper needed to make the tube. How much copper would be needed?

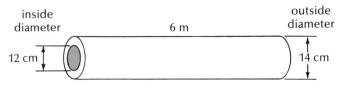

inside diameter   6 m   outside diameter

12 cm   14 cm

a. Find the volume of a cylinder with a 14 cm diameter and a cylinder with a 12 cm diameter.

For $d = 14$ cm: $V = \pi r^2 h$ For $d = 12$ cm: $V = \pi r^2 h$
$\doteq (3.14)(49)(600)$ $\doteq (3.14)(36)(600)$
$= 92\ 316$ $= 67\ 824$

b. Find the difference between the two volumes to find the total amount of copper in the tube.

$92\ 316 - 67\ 824 = 24\ 492$
$\doteq 24\ 500$ (to 3 significant digits)

The tube contains about 24 500 cm³ of copper.

EXERCISES

For the following exercises, use $\pi \doteq 3.14$ and round answers to three significant digits. Use a calculator where appropriate.

A 1. Find the volume of a cylinder with the given height h, and radius r or diameter d.

    a. $h = 3$ cm, $r = 5$ cm   **b.** $h = 24$ cm, $r = 0.8$ m

    c. $h = 0.2$ cm, $d = 12$ mm   **d.** $h = 10$ cm, $d = 0.23$ m

2. Find the height of a cylinder with a volume of 448π cm³, given that the radius of its base is 8 cm.

3. Find the radius of a cylinder 9 mm high, given that its volume is 1089π mm³.

4. Find the diameter of a cylinder 8 cm high, given that its volume is 1152π cm³.

B 5. The radius of cylinder B is double that of the radius of cylinder A, but their heights are the same. Describe the relationship between their volumes.

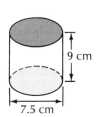

6. At 4° C, 1 L of water occupies 1000 cm³ and has a mass of 1000 g or 1 kg.

    a. What is the mass of water at 4° C, in kilograms, in a full aquarium measuring 25 cm by 50 cm by 25 cm?

    b. Find the mass of water, in metric tonnes, required to fill a cylindrical swimming pool 18 m in diameter and 3 m deep.

7. A restaurant serves soft drinks using glasses in either of the two shapes shown at the right. Which glass has the greater capacity? How much more does it hold?

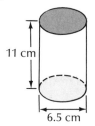

11 cm   9 cm

6.5 cm   7.5 cm

8. A cylindrical concrete pipe is 4 m long. It has an inside diameter of 0.8 m and an outside diameter of 0.9 m. How many cubic metres of concrete were needed to make the pipe?

9. At any given time, what amount of fluid could be flowing through the pipe described in exercise 8?

C 10. A can of condensed soup, Can A, is 10 cm high and 21 cm in diameter. To serve it, you add one full can of water and heat. Can B is 12 cm high and 32 cm in diameter and contains heat-and-serve soup: nothing is added. Which can yields more? How much more?

12–6 Volume of a Cone

The volume of a cone is one third the volume of a cylinder with the same base and the same height.

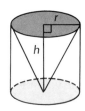

$$V_{cone} = \frac{1}{3} A_{base} \times h$$
$$= \frac{1}{3} \pi r^2 h$$

EXAMPLE 1:

What is the capacity in millilitres of the conical paper cup with dimensions as shown at the right?

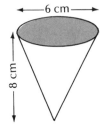

←——6 cm——→

8 cm

$$V = \frac{1}{3} \pi r^2 h$$
$$\doteq \frac{1}{3} (3.14)(9)(8)$$
$$= 75.36$$
$$\doteq 75.4 \text{ (to 3 significant digits)}$$

The paper cup has a volume of 75.4 cm³, to 3 significant digits. This means it holds about 75.4 mL of water.

EXAMPLE 2:

What is the maximum amount of grain, in cubic metres, that can be held by a conical grain bin with dimensions as shown at the right?

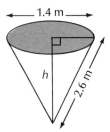

←——1.4 m——→

h

2.6 m

a. Apply the Pythagorean Theorem to find h.

$$(0.7)^2 + h^2 = (2.6)^2$$
$$h^2 = 6.76 - 0.49$$
$$h^2 = 6.27$$
$$h \doteq 2.503\ 996\ 805$$
$$h \doteq 2.50 \text{ (to 3 significant digits)}$$

b. Apply the formula for volume.

$$V = \frac{1}{3} \pi r^2 h$$
$$\doteq \frac{1}{3} (3.14)(0.49)(2.50)$$
$$= 1.282\ 167$$
$$\doteq 1.28 \text{ (to 3 significant digits)}$$

The grain bin can hold a maximum of 1.28 m³ of grain.

EXERCISES

For the following exercises, use $\pi \doteq 3.14$ and answer to three significant digits. Use a calculator where appropriate.

A **1.** Find the volume of the cone with the given height h, and radius r or diameter d.
  a. $h = 12$ cm, $r = 8$ cm   **b.** $h = 8$ m, $r = 12$ m
  c. $h = 5$ cm, $d = 20$ cm   **d.** $h = 12$ cm, $d = 0.4$ m
  e. $h = 0.12$ m, $r = 82$ m   **f.** $h = 10$ mm, $d = 1.8$ cm

B **2.** Find the volume of the cone with the given slant height s, and radius r or diameter d.
  a. $s = 5$ cm, $r = 3$ cm   **b.** $s = 25$ mm, $r = 24$ mm
  c. $s = 10$ mm, $d = 16$ mm   **d.** $s = 13$ cm, $d = 24$ cm

3. Find the volume of the cone with the given circumference of the base, C, and height h or slant height s.
  a. $C = 49\pi$ cm, $h = 9$ cm   **b.** $C = 121\pi$ cm, $h = 7.5$ cm
  c. $C = 800.7$ cm, $h = 6.2$ cm   **d.** $C = 50.24$ cm, $s = 10$ cm

4. A cone and a cylinder both have a radius of 7 cm and a height of 11 cm.
  a. Find the volume of the cylinder.
  b. Find the volume of the cone.
  c. If the radius of the cone were doubled while the cylinder remained unchanged, which solid would have the greater volume?
  d. If the height of the cone were doubled while the cylinder remained unchanged, which solid would have the greater volume?

5. A conical paper cup is 8 cm deep and has a diameter of 6.5 cm. What is its maximum capacity in millilitres?

C **6.** A square pyramid is inscribed in a cone with radius 6 cm and height 8 cm.
  a. Find the volume of the pyramid.
  b. Find the slant height of the pyramid.

7. A conical funnel, 6 cm in diameter and 8 cm deep, is filled with pepper to be transferred to a cylindrical pepper shaker. The shaker is 9 cm high with a diameter of 35 mm. If the funnel is completely filled with pepper, will it also reach the maximum capacity of the shaker?

8. Find the volume of a truncated cone with dimensions as shown in the diagram.

1.25 m

3 m

5 m

12–7 Surface Area and Volume of Spheres

The gold earrings shown are made from spherical beads of gold.

A **sphere** is the set of all points in space that are a given distance (the radius) from a fixed point (the centre).

The surface area of each bead would be important in costing the earrings if they were gold plated. The volume of each bead would be significant if the beads were 18 karat gold.

$$SA_{sphere} = 4\pi r^2$$
$$V_{sphere} = \frac{4}{3}\pi r^3$$

EXAMPLE 1: If beads with radius 4 mm were to be gold plated, what surface area of each bead would be plated?

$$SA = 4\pi r^2$$
$$\doteq 4(3.14)(4)^2$$
$$= 200.96$$
$$\doteq 201 \quad \text{(to 3 significant digits)}$$

About 201 mm² of each bead would be plated with gold.

EXAMPLE 2: How much gold would be required if each bead, with radius 4 mm, were 18 karat gold?

$$V = \frac{4}{3}\pi r^3$$
$$\doteq \frac{4}{3}(3.14)(4)^3$$
$$\doteq 267.95$$
$$\doteq 268 \text{ (to 3 significant digits)}$$

About 268 mm³ of 18 karat gold would be required.

EXERCISES

For the following exercises, use $\pi \doteq 3.14$ and answer to three significant digits. Use a calculator where appropriate.

A **1.** Find the volume of the sphere with the given radius r or diameter d.
   a. $r = 6$ cm   **b.** $r = 8.2$ cm   **c.** $d = 14$ mm   **d.** $d = 4.8$ m

2. Find the surface area of the sphere with the given radius r or diameter d.
   a. $r = 12$ mm   **b.** $r = 3.5$ cm   **c.** $d = 16$ cm   **d.** $d = 7.8$ mm

384

B **3.** Find the radius of the sphere with the given surface area *SA* or volume *V*.

 a. $SA = 256\pi$ b. $SA = 2500\pi$ c. $SA = \frac{196}{25}\pi$

 d. $V = \frac{500}{3}\pi$ e. $V = \frac{2048\pi}{3}$ f. $V = 4500\pi$

4. Which solid has the greatest surface area?

 a.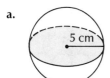

 b.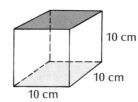

 c.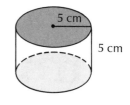

5. A cup in the shape of a hemisphere has a diameter of 9 cm. Find its full capacity in millilitres.

6. A spherical scoop of ice cream with diameter 6 cm is placed in a cone with base diameter 5 cm and depth 10 cm. Is the cone large enough to hold all of the ice cream if it melts?

7. A silo consists of a cylinder capped by a hemisphere. Its inside dimensions are given.

 a. Find the capacity of the cylindrical part of the silo.

 b. If 1 L of paint covers about 9 m², how many litres of paint are needed to cover the silo's interior?

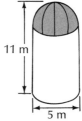

C **8.** By how much is the surface area of a sphere increased if the radius is doubled? tripled?

9. By how much is the volume of a sphere increased if the radius is doubled? tripled?

10. A spherical ball of yarn 5 cm in diameter sells for $3.99. How much should a ball of the same yarn cost if it has double the diameter?

11. The volume of Earth is about 1.08×10^{12} km³. Its diameter is about 3.67 times greater than the diameter of the moon. Assume Earth and its moon to be spheres to answer the following.

 a. Find the volume of the moon.

 b. Find the radius of Earth and its moon.

12. A sphere with radius 6 cm is inscribed in a cylinder to touch the lateral surface and top and bottom faces as shown.

 a. Find the volume of the cylinder.

 b. Show that the surface area of the sphere equals the lateral surface area of the cylinder.

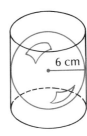

Application

Greengrocers often stack oranges in pyramids.
Consider a stack of oranges in the shape of a triangular pyramid. The
following diagrams show the number of oranges in each of the top five
layers.

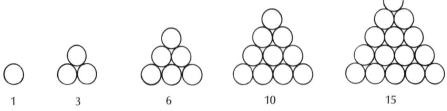

| 1 | 3 | 6 | 10 | 15 |

These numbers are known as **triangular** numbers. Now, look at the pyramids
from a top view.

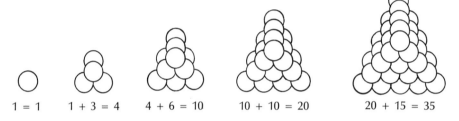

| 1 = 1 | 1 + 3 = 4 | 4 + 6 = 10 | 10 + 10 = 20 | 20 + 15 = 35 |

1. **a.** How many oranges will be in the bottom layer of a six-layer
      pyramid?
   b. What is the total number of oranges in a pyramid with six layers?

2. The number of oranges in a triangular pyramid with *n* layers is given
   by the following expression.

   $$1 + 3 + 6 + 10 + 15 + \ldots + \frac{n(n + 1)}{2} + \ldots = \frac{n(n + 1)(n + 2)}{6}$$

   a. Find the number of oranges in the bottom layer of a 15-layer
      pyramid.
   b. Find the number of oranges in a triangular pyramid with 15 layers.

3. Imagine a stack of oranges with a square base.
   The number of oranges in a layer or in the
   pyramid can be determined by using the
   diagrams.

   | 1 | 4 | 9 | 16 |

   a. How many oranges will be in the bottom
      layer of a 15-layer pyramid?
   b. How many oranges will be in a pyramid
      with 15 layers?

   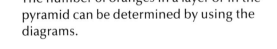

386

Review

For the following exercises, use $\pi \doteq 3.14$ and answer to three significant digits. Use a calculator where appropriate.

1. Find the volume and surface area of each of the following.

   a.

   −14 cm→

   b.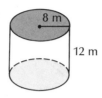

   8 m

   12 m

   c.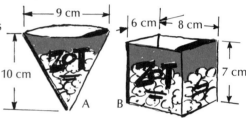

   ←14 cm→

   25 cm

2. Calculate the total surface area of the following.
   a. a cylinder, 8 cm in diameter and 65 mm high
   b. a cone, 10 cm in diameter and 15 cm high

3. A soft drink can has a radius of 3 cm and is 115 mm high. What is its capacity?

4. Popcorn is sold in two containers, with dimensions as shown. Container B costs twice as much as container A. Which is the better buy?

   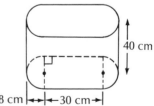

   ⊢— 9 cm —⊣   ⊢6 cm⊢← 8 cm→

   10 cm   7 cm

   A   B

5. How many cubic metres of water are needed to fill the swimming pools illustrated below?

   a.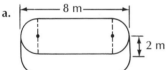

   ⊢— 8 m —⊣

   2 m

   The semi-circular ends have diameter 3 m.

   b.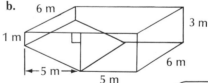

   6 m

   3 m

   1 m

   6 m

   ←5 m→   5 m

6. The base of the tub shown at the right is composed of a 30 cm by 16 cm rectangle with semicircular ends. If 20 L of water is poured into the container, what is the depth of the water?

   40 cm

   8 cm ⊢↔⊢← 30 cm →⊣

7. A farmer has two silos of the same height. One is cylindrical with a base 5.39 m in inside diameter. The other is a square prism with base of side length 4.78 m inside. Show that the two silos hold about the same amount of corn.

8. A sphere is inscribed in a cube with side length 10 cm. Find the amount of space in the cube which is not taken up by the sphere.

Test

For the following exercises, use $\pi \doteq 3.14$ and answer to three significant digits. Use a calculator where appropriate.

1. Discuss the symmetry of each object below. If the object has plane symmetry, identify one plane of symmetry. If the object has rotational symmetry, identify the axis of symmetry and state the order of rotational symmetry.

   a.   b.   c.

2. Find the volume and surface area of each figure.

   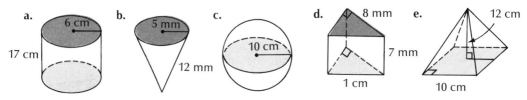

   a. 6 cm, 17 cm   b. 5 mm, 12 mm   c. 10 cm   d. 8 mm, 7 mm, 1 cm   e. 12 cm, 10 cm

3. The walls and ceiling of a rectangular room measuring 6.8 m by 4.5 m by 2.4 m are to be painted. Paint is sold in 4 L and 1 L cans at $24.99 and $8.99, respectively. If 1 L of paint covers 9.5 m², calculate the cost of painting the room. (Subtract 5 m² for doors and windows.)

4. The management at a movie theatre decided to introduce a new size of popcorn container. A box in the shape of a rectangular prism currently sells for $1.50. How much should a container in the shape of a rectangular pyramid sell for if the tops of the containers are the same size and the containers are the same height?

5. A sphere with radius 8 cm is inscribed in a cylinder. Find the volume of the cylinder.

6. A cylinder with a 12 cm height is inscribed in a sphere of radius 10 cm. Find the volume of the cylinder.

   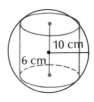

   10 cm
   6 cm

7. a. The surface area of Earth is about 510 070 000 km². Earth's surface is approximately 30% land and 70% water. Approximate the surface area covered by land.
   b. The diameter of Earth is approximately 3.67 times that of its moon. What is the approximate surface area of the moon?

Cumulative Review

1. Graph each function defined below and give its domain and range.
   a. $f: x \rightarrow x^2 + 4$ b. $f(x) = 2x - 3$ c. $f: x \rightarrow x^3$

2. When you are travelling at a given speed, the distance travelled varies directly as the length of time spent travelling. Leslie is driving at a constant speed and has gone 126 km in the past 1.5 h.
   a. Define variables for distance and time and find the constant of proportionality.
   b. Write an equation relating distance and time.
   c. How far would Leslie drive in 3.5 h?

3. In a random sample of 50 high school students, there are 21 who belong to at least one school club. If the sample is representative, then how many in the student body of 1124 would you expect to belong to at least one school club?

4. For the past 12 times that a pitcher has faced a full count (3 balls, 3 strikes), he has thrown the pitches shown in the table at the right.
   If you were the batter at a full count, what type of pitch would you expect to be most likely?
   (Assume the sample to be representative.)

Pitch	Frequency
Fast ball	4
Curve	5
Change-up	1
Slider	2

5. For $\triangle ABC$ with vertices $A(0,0)$, $B(-5,2)$, and $C(3,6)$, find the image of $\triangle ABC$ under the indicated transformation.
   a. rotation of $90°$ about $O(0,0)$
   b. translation $[-1, -2]$
   c. reflection in the line $x = y$
   d. dilatation with scale factor $-\frac{1}{2}$ about $O(0,0)$

6. In each diagram, identify a pair of congruent triangles and prove they are congruent.

   a.
   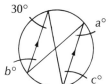

   b.
   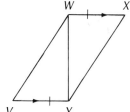

7. Find the measure of each indicated angle. T is a point of contact.

   a.
   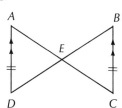
   b.
   c.

13 Vectors and Trigonometry

13–1 Vector and Scalar Quantities

A good sailboat navigator must ensure that the forces from any water currents, together with the force of the wind on the sails, add up correctly to result in the desired path for the boat. *Force*, measured in Newtons (N), is a physical quantity that has both **magnitude** (size) and direction.

A quantity with *both* magnitude *and* direction is called a **vector quantity**. A **scalar quantity** has magnitude only.

EXAMPLES: Does the sentence describe a vector quantity, a scalar quantity, or neither?

    a. The sailboat's navigator is 1.8 m tall.
    b. Andrea is sitting at Steve's right.
    c. The boat travelled 17 km to the southeast.

    a. The navigator's height is a magnitude. This sentence describes a scalar quantity.
    b. This sentence involves direction only. It describes neither a scalar nor a vector quantity.
    c. This sentence involves both magnitude (distance of 17 km) and direction (southeast). It describes a vector quantity.

There are some scalar quantities that have corresponding vector quantities from which they must be clearly distinguished.

Scalar Quantity	Vector Quantity
The wind speed is 12 km/h.	Its velocity is 12 km/h southwest.
The distance of the boat from the starting buoy is 3.5 km.	Its displacement after 15 min is 5 km due south.
The mass of its navigator is 78 kg.	His weight is 754.4 N.

In physics, **velocity** is defined to be speed in a given direction; **displacement** is defined as distance travelled in a given direction. **Weight** is force downwards due to gravity.

EXERCISES

A 1. Using the sailing photograph, give three examples of scalar quantities.

2. Is the given quantity scalar or vector?
   a. 1 dozen eggs
   b. 15 482 books in the library
   c. a 25 km/h wind from the northwest
   d. a 6 N force to the right
   e. a rise in temperature of 6°C
   f. a class of 31 students

B 3. Identify vector quantities and scalar quantities.
   a. the mass of a baseball
   b. the cost of a pair of Grey Cup tickets at centre field
   c. the velocity of a meteorite as it enters the atmosphere
   d. the average speed of Canada's Women's 400 m relay team
   e. the force required to pull a toboggan up a hill
   f. the speed of Wayne Gretzky as he swoops in on goal
   g. the instantaneous velocity of a puck as it leaves Mike Bossy's stick
   h. the weight of an airplane
   i. the mass of a helium balloon
   j. the distance of Suzanne's school from her home

4. For each practical situation, describe two possible vector quantities and two possible scalar quantities that would be present.
   a. An airplane is flying at a given altitude.
   b. A parachutist jumps from an airplane.
   c. A windsurfer skims along the water surface.

C 5. Identify each item as a scalar quantity, a vector quantity, or neither.
   a. the number of people on a flight to Florida
   b. a rise of 500 million dollars in the national debt
   c. the position of Peterborough, west of Kingston
   d. the volume of water going over Niagara Falls every minute
   e. the weight of an astronaut while in orbit
   f. the time required to run 5 km north along Keele Street
   g. the coordinates of a point on a coordinate grid
   h. Innisfail, Alberta is at 52° N latitude and 114° E longitude

13–2 Representing Vectors Geometrically

The windsurfer is using a northwesterly wind of 22 km/h to move through the water. (A northwesterly wind comes *out of the northwest* and is moving *to* the southeast.)

Although you cannot see the wind, you could draw an arrow to represent it.

A vector can be represented by an arrow drawn to scale. The magnitude of the vector is given by the length of the arrow; its direction is clearly given by the direction of the arrow. A vector is sometimes denoted by a single letter with an arrow symbol, such as $\vec{v}$, read "vector v". The magnitude of $\vec{v}$ is written $|\vec{v}|$.

EXAMPLE 1: Draw an arrow to represent a velocity of 22 km/h to the southeast, using a scale of 1 cm to represent 10 km/h.

Southeast can be represented by an arrow pointing down to the right, at a 45° angle to the horizontal. The arrow should be 2.2 cm long.

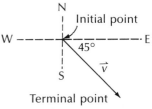

1 cm represents 10 km.

EXAMPLE 2: Interpret the vector represented below.

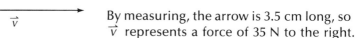

By measuring, the arrow is 3.5 cm long, so $\vec{v}$ represents a force of 35 N to the right.

1 cm represents 10 N.

Equivalent or **equal vectors** have the same magnitude and direction. It is not necessary that they have the same initial point or terminal point.

EXAMPLE 3: Compare the vectors $\vec{a}$ and $\vec{c}$, $\vec{a}$ and $\vec{b}$, and $\vec{a}$ and $\vec{d}$.

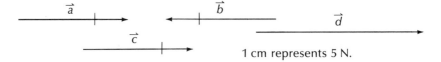

1 cm represents 5 N.

$\vec{a}$ and $\vec{c}$ are equal vectors because they have the same magnitude and the same direction.

$\vec{a}$ and $\vec{b}$ are not equal vectors because, although parallel, they point in different directions.

$\vec{a}$ and $\vec{d}$ are not equal vectors, even though they point in the same direction, because they do not have the same magnitude.

EXERCISES

A 1. Identify pairs of equal vectors.

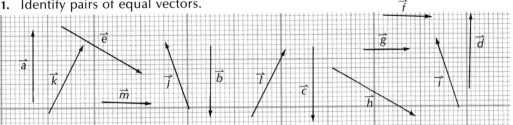

2. Given that 1 cm represents a force with a magnitude of 10 N, measure and state the magnitude of each of the following vectors.

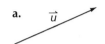   

a. $\vec{u}$ **b.** $\vec{w}$ **c.** $\vec{x}$ **d.** $\vec{y}$

3. Given that 1 cm represents 30 km/h, measure and state the magnitude of each vector below.

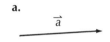

a. $\vec{a}$ **b.** $\vec{b}$ **c.** $\vec{c}$ **d.** $\vec{d}$

B 4. Using 1 cm to represent 10 N, draw a vector to illustrate each.
   a. a force of 48 N to the right   **b.** a force of 78 N upward
   c. a force of 36 N to the left   **d.** a force of 90 N downward

5. Using 1 cm to represent 20 km/h, draw a vector to illustrate each.
   a. a velocity of 48 km/h eastward   **b.** a velocity of 78 km/h north
   c. a velocity of 36 km/h west   **d.** a velocity of 90 km/h south

6. For each of the following, decide on a suitable scale and then draw a vector diagram to illustrate.
   a. a velocity of 525 m/s to the right   **b.** a displacement of 8 km west
   c. a force of 52 N upward   **d.** a weight of 675 N
   e. a northwest wind of 28 km/h   **f.** a force of 1500 N downward
   g. a force of 150 N exerted to pull a sled up a hill inclined at 30° to the horizontal
   h. an aircraft flying at 720 km/h in a direction of N 60° E (that is, 60° east of due north)

C 7. Two tractors, attached to a stump by chains, are being used to pull out the stump. One is pulling with a force of 4000 N due east. The other is pulling with a force of 4500 N northeast. Let point *P* represent the stump. Using a scale of 1 cm to represent 1000 N, with point *P* as the initial point of both vectors, draw a diagram to represent the combined forces of the two tractors acting on the stump.

13–3 The Triangle Law

The Trail Finders Club hiked in to a fishing camp along the path shown in the vector diagram. They walked 15 km N, then 9 km N 60° E.

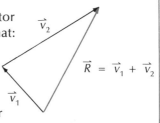

N 60° E means 60° east of a northerly direction. Measure 60° clockwise from the North ray.

The result of $\vec{v}$ followed by $\vec{u}$ is $\vec{R}$, the **resultant vector**.

Notice that $\vec{u}$, $\vec{v}$, and $\vec{R}$ form a triangle.

1 cm represents 6 km.

The Triangle Law of Vector Addition

Two vectors can be added by drawing a vector diagram to scale using a "head-to-tail" format: Draw one vector, $\vec{v}_1$, then draw the second vector, $\vec{v}_2$, so that its initial point is at the terminal point of $\vec{v}_1$.

The vector *sum* or *resultant*, $\vec{R}$, is the vector drawn from the initial point of $\vec{v}_1$ to the terminal point of $\vec{v}_2$.

$$\vec{R} = \vec{v}_1 + \vec{v}_2$$

EXAMPLE 1:

a. If the Trail Finders had wanted to follow a straight line to the camp, what direction should they have followed from their starting point?

By measuring, the angle between $\vec{v}$ and $\vec{R}$ is 22°. To measure angles in smaller diagrams, extend the rays to reach the protractor's edge.

Therefore, they could have walked N 22° E to follow a straight line to the camp.

b. If they had followed a straight path to the fishing camp, how far would the Trail Finders have walked?

Measure the length of $\vec{R}$ and apply the scale.

The arrow representing $\vec{R}$ is 3.5 cm long, and 3.5 × 6 = 21.
∴ $|\vec{R}| = 21$ km

The Trail Finders would have walked 21 km.

The diagram illustrates a resultant *displacement* of 21 km N 22° E.

EXAMPLE 2: To pull out a stump, chains are wrapped around the stump and attached to each of two tractors. One tractor exerts a force of 4500 N to the north while the other exerts a force of 5000 N to the northeast. Find the total force acting upon the stump.

A vector diagram to illustrate this situation has two vectors with the same initial point.

In order to apply the Triangle Law, draw $\vec{u}$ with its "tail" on the "head" of $\vec{v}$.

The resultant is $\vec{R}$.

By measuring, $\vec{R}$ represents 8800 N in a direction N 24° E.

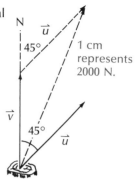

1 cm represents 2000 N.

EXERCISES

A **1.** Each diagram below represents the path followed by an orienteering team. By measuring, find the distance walked by each team, and find the distance from their starting point A to their resting point B.

a.

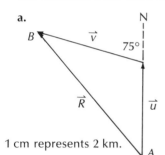

1 cm represents 2 km.

b.

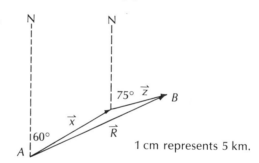

1 cm represents 5 km.

2. Measure to find the total displacement represented by each diagram in exercise 1.

3. Given that $|\vec{v}| = 24$ N in each case, find the scale that has been used in the diagram.

a.

b.

4. For each diagram below, first determine the scale used, then find $|\vec{x}|$ and $|\vec{y}|$.

a. $|\vec{R}| = 30$ N

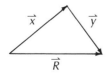

b. $|\vec{R}| = 56$ km/h

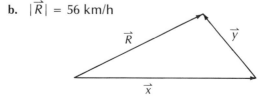

395

5. Select a suitable scale and draw a vector diagram to represent each pair of vectors. Draw the resultant.
   a. a force of 10 N upward and a force of 15 N to the right
   b. velocities of 45 km/h south and 9 km/h west
   c. a displacement of 36 m west and a displacement of 30 m south
   d. forces of 24 N upward and 19 N downward

6. Select a suitable scale and draw vector diagrams to find the resultant. Find the magnitude of the resultant and its direction relative to the first vector given.
   a. displacements of 15 km N and 7 km S 60° E
   b. velocities of 120 km/h N and 23 km/h N 60° W
   c. displacements of 34 m W and 9 m N 30° E
   d. velocities of 11 km/h S and 35 km/h N 60° E

7. Draw a vector diagram and find the magnitude of the resultant.
   a. forces of 3 N and 5 N at 60° to each other
   b. displacements of 15 m and 7 m at 120° to each other
   c. velocities of 5 m/s and 12 m/s at 90° to each other
   d. forces of 7 N and 7 N at 120° to each other

Construct scale diagrams to find solutions to the following problems.

8. Two tractors are used to pull out a stump, with each exerting a force of 5000 N on chains wrapped around the stump. If the angle between the two chains is 40°, find the magnitude of the total force acting on the stump.

9. An aircraft headed due west with a speed of 630 km/h encounters a jet stream coming from a direction S 30° W at 150 km/h. Find the resultant speed and direction of the aircraft.

10. In his rowboat, John heads directly across the North Saskatchewan River at 8 km/h. The river is flowing at a rate of 5 km/h.
    a. What angle will the resultant path of the boat make with the shoreline?
    b. If the river is 96 m wide, how far downstream will John land on the opposite shore?

11. In exercise 10, if John wanted to row directly across the river, then at what angle relative to the shore should he head?

12. An aircraft flies at 280 km/h in a direction N 40° E. After 1.5 h, how far is it north and east of its starting point?

13. A light aircraft with a cruising speed of 200 km/h, flying in still air, first flew east for 1 h 15 min, and then north for 3 h. If the pilot now flies directly back to the home airfield, on what bearing should the pilot fly, and how long will the flight take?

C **14.** A delivery van with three stops to make leaves the main office and drives east for 12 km, then north for 4 km, and finally west for 9 km. Draw a vector diagram to scale to find how far the van is from the main office.

15. An aircraft on patrol leaves the airport and flies 80 km N 30° E, then 150 km W, and finally 70 km N 30° E. Draw a vector diagram to find the straight-line distance back to the airport.

16. A training ship is directed to leave port and head south for 8 km, then go 15 km N 60° E, and finally go south for another 7 km.
   a. If the captain follows this set route correctly, how far will the ship be from the home port?
   b. What course should the ship follow to return to the home port directly?

17. A pilot wants to fly due north from London to Sudbury. If her cruising speed is 250 km/h and there is a west wind of 60 km/h, what course should she set?

18. A pilot wants to fly due north from Lethbridge to Camrose. If the cruising speed of his helicopter is 160 km/h and there is a wind of 40 km/h from the west, find his effective ground speed for the trip.

19. A pilot travels due north at an airspeed of 200 km/h for 1 h, then west at an airspeed of 225 km/h for 2 h. All this time, there is a wind of 15 km/h from the east. What is the resulting displacement?

20. A pilot wants to fly due east from Vermilion to Lloydminster, a distance of 80 km. She finds that she must head N 80° E in order to stay on course, because of a wind out of the north. If the flight takes 20 min, find the speed of the wind.

EXTRA   Applications in Three Dimensions

1. An airplane at an altitude of 5200 m is 7.5 km north and 3 km east of the Mirabel control tower. What is the straight-line distance from the control tower to the plane?

2. Joanne is sitting in a theatre so that she is in the centre of a row 16 m from the screen and on the same level as its bottom edge. If the screen is 12 m wide and 5 m high, how far is it from Joanne's seat to the upper right-hand corner of the screen?

3. An observer is 7.2 km west and 2.1 km north of a rocket site. If the rocket is shot straight up, what will be its altitude when the distance from the observer to the rocket is 10 km?

13–4 Representing Vectors Algebraically

Representing vectors on a coordinate grid enables you to use numerical and algebraic techniques to solve vector problems.

The vector $\vec{v}$, illustrated on the grid at the right, has a horizontal **component** of $+4$ and a vertical component of $+2$. We write: $\vec{v} = [4,2]$. Any initial point can be selected when representing a vector on a grid.

Note that square brackets are used to distinguish between vector $\vec{v} = [4,2]$ and point $P(4,2)$. Point P has position only, whereas $\vec{v} = [x,y]$ has both magnitude and direction.

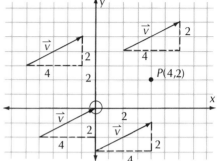

The magnitude of $[x,y]$ can easily be found using the Distance Formula. Its direction is determined by its slope m and the signs of its x and y components.

If both the x and the y components of a vector are positive, then the vector rises to the right. If the x component is negative and the y component is positive, then the vector rises to the left. Similar rules apply to the other two situations.

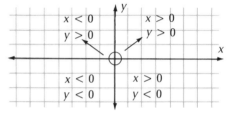

EXAMPLE 1: Find the magnitude and the slope of $\vec{u} = [-4, -2]$ and $\vec{v} = [2,1]$.

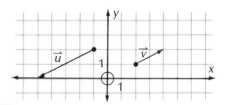

$$|\vec{u}| = \sqrt{(-4)^2 + (-2)^2} \qquad |\vec{v}| = \sqrt{2^2 + 1^2}$$
$$= \sqrt{20} \qquad\qquad\qquad = \sqrt{5}$$
$$= 2\sqrt{5}$$

$\vec{v}$ is half the length of $\vec{u}$.

For $\vec{u} = [-4,-2]$:   For $\vec{v} = [2,1]$:

$m = \frac{-2}{-4}$ $m = \frac{1}{2}$, pointing up

$= \frac{1}{2}$, pointing down   to the right
      to the left

Compare the slopes of $\vec{u}$ and $\vec{v}$ in example 1. Because $m = \frac{1}{2}$ for both $\vec{u}$ and $\vec{v}$, we know that the vectors are parallel; the signs of their x and y components show that they point in opposite directions.

EXERCISES

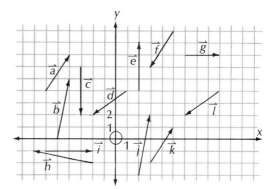

A 1. For each vector represented on the grid at the right, name the vector algebraically ($\vec{v} = [x,y]$).

B 2. There are three pairs of equal vectors in exercise 1. Identify them.

3. Represent each vector on a coordinate grid. Use the given point P as the initial point.
   a. $[3,-4]; P(-2,1)$ b. $[-4,-1]; P(1,3)$
   c. $[-2,5]; P(4,-2)$ d. $[4,-6]; P(-1,-1)$

4. Represent each vector on a coordinate grid. P is the terminal point.
   a. $[2,4]; P(1,-2)$ b. $[-3,5]; P(3,2)$
   c. $[-1,-6]; P(-2,-3)$ d. $[4,-1]; P(-4,1)$

5. Find the magnitude of each vector in exercise 4.

6. Draw the vector for which A is the initial point and B is the terminal point. Give its components.
   a. $A(-2,3), B(4,-2)$ b. $A(2,-5), B(-5,2)$ c. $A(3,4), B(1,-5)$

7. Find the slope of each vector in exercise 7, and describe its direction.

8. Find the terminal point B for each vector, given that the initial point is $A(1,-2)$.
   a. $[3,-4]$ b. $[-2,5]$ c. $[-4,-1]$ d. $[2,3]$ e. $[4,0]$

9. Find the initial point A for each vector, given that the terminal point is $B(1,-2)$.
   a. $[2,5]$ b. $[-1,3]$ c. $[4,-2]$ d. $[-3,-1]$ e. $[0,-3]$

10. For each of the following vectors, find its magnitude, give its slope, and show its direction ($\nearrow$, $\searrow$, $\swarrow$, $\nwarrow$, $\uparrow$, $\downarrow$, $\leftarrow$, $\rightarrow$).
    a. $[3,-4]$ b. $[5,12]$ c. $[-15,-8]$ d. $[-4,6]$ e. $[9,3]$
    f. $[5,-5]$ g. $[-5,5]$ h. $[0,-6]$ i. $[3,0]$ j. $[-3,-9]$

C 11. Copy and complete the table.

Slope of $\vec{v}$	Direction	x component	y component	$\vec{v} = [x,y]$	$|\vec{v}|$
$\frac{2}{3}$	$\nearrow$	6			
$-\frac{2}{5}$	$\searrow$		-8		
0	$\leftarrow$	-4			
$-\frac{3}{2}$	$\nwarrow$	-6			
$\frac{3}{4}$	$\swarrow$		-9		

13–5 Adding Algebraic Vectors

Applying the Triangle Law of Vector Addition to a pair of algebraic vectors on a coordinate grid yields an important result.

EXAMPLE 1: Find the sum of $\vec{w} = [3,1]$ and $\vec{u} = [2,4]$.

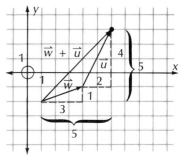

Any initial point may be selected. Select $A(1, -2)$ as the initial point for $\vec{w}$ and apply the Triangle Law.

$$\vec{w} + \vec{u} = [5,5]$$

Notice that the x component of the sum is the sum of the x components ($5 = 3 + 2$). The y component of the sum is the sum of the y components ($5 = 1 + 4$).

Adding Algebraic Vectors

Given $\vec{v}_1 = [x_1,y_1]$ and $\vec{v}_2 = [x_2,y_2]$, $\vec{v}_1 + \vec{v}_2 = [x_1 + x_2, y_1 + y_2]$.

Add algebraic vectors by adding their components.

EXAMPLE 2: Given that $\vec{v} = [3,1]$, find $\vec{v} + \vec{v}$.

$$\begin{aligned}
\vec{v} + \vec{v} &= [3,1] + [3,1] \\
&= [3 + 3, 1 + 1] \\
&= [6,2] \qquad \text{The } x \text{ and } y \text{ components both double.}
\end{aligned}$$

A natural way to write $\vec{v} + \vec{v}$ would be as $2\vec{v}$. Since the number 2 is a *scalar*, the calculation of $2\vec{v}$ is called **scalar multiplication**.

Scalar Multiplication of a Vector

Given a vector $\vec{v} = [x,y]$ and a scalar k, $k\vec{v} = [kx,ky]$.

EXAMPLE 3: For $\vec{w} = [-2,6]$, find and graph each of the following.

a. $\begin{aligned}[t] 3\vec{w} &= 3[-2,6] \\ &= [-6,18] \end{aligned}$

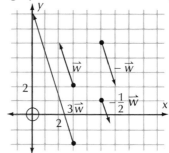

b. $\begin{aligned}[t] -\vec{w} &= (-1)[-2,6] \\ &= [2,-6] \end{aligned}$

Since no initial points are specified, any point may be selected.

c. $\begin{aligned}[t] -\tfrac{1}{2}\vec{w} &= -\tfrac{1}{2}[-2,6] \\ &= [1,-3] \end{aligned}$

Notice that $\vec{w}$ and $-\vec{w}$ in example 3 are parallel and congruent, *but* that they point in opposite directions. For any vector $\vec{v}$, then, we can find $-\vec{v}$. This leads to the following method for subtracting vectors.

EXAMPLE 4:   For $\vec{v} = [4,1]$ and $\vec{w} = [0,4]$, find and graph $\vec{v} - \vec{w}$.

$$\begin{aligned} \vec{v} - \vec{w} &= [4,1] - [0,4] \\ &= [4,1] + (-1)[0,4] \\ &= [4,1] + [0,-4] \\ &= [4,-3] \end{aligned}$$

EXAMPLE 5:   In the absence of any current, the wind will move a sailboat 3 km east and 1 km south during each hour the sails are up. In the absence of wind, the ocean current will move the boat 2 km east and 1 km north in an hour. If the navigator sails for 2 h, then lowers the sails to drift for the next 4 h, where will the boat be relative to its starting point? Graph the resultant.

As a convention, let a direction northward be represented by a positive y; direction east, by positive x; direction south, by negative y; direction west, by negative x.

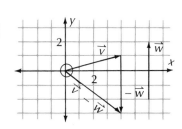

Let $\vec{w}$ be the wind vector: then $\vec{w} = [3,-1]$.
Let $\vec{c}$ be the current vector: then $\vec{c} = [2,1]$.

Write a vector $\vec{v}$ to represent the entire voyage.

$\vec{v} = 2\vec{w} + 4\vec{c}$ The wind acts for 2 h, the current for 4 h.

Substitute for $\vec{w}$ and $\vec{c}$ and evaluate $\vec{v}$.

$$\begin{aligned} \vec{v} &= 2\vec{w} + 4\vec{c} \\ &= 2[3,-1] + 4[2,1] \\ &= [6,-2] + [8,4] \\ &= [14,2] \end{aligned}$$

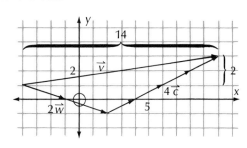

After sailing for 2 h and drifting for an additional 4 h, the boat will be 14 km east and 2 km north of its starting point.

EXERCISES

A **1.** Name $\vec{u}$, $\vec{v}$, and $\vec{R}$ in each case. Verify that $\vec{u} + \vec{v} = \vec{R}$ algebraically.

a.

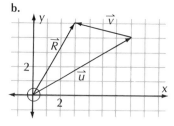

b.

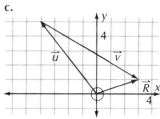

c.

d.

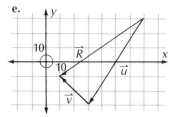

e.

f.

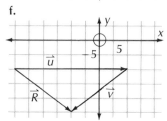

2. Draw vector diagrams to illustrate the following.
   a. $[3, -2] + [0, -3] = [3, -5]$ **b.** $[-4,2] + [-2, -5] = [-6, -3]$
   c. $[3, -5] + [1,2] = [4, -3]$ **d.** $[4,3] + [-7, -1] = [-3,2]$

3. Find each of the following sums algebraically.
   a. $[-5, -7] + [3, -2]$ **b.** $[4, -2] + [-4,5]$ **c.** $[-3,2] + [-1, -1]$
   d. $[5, -1] + [-2, -4]$ **e.** $[-4, -1] + [3, -3]$ **f.** $[2, -7] + [-9, -2]$

B **4.** Draw vector diagrams to illustrate the following.
   a. $[2, -4] + 3[1,2] = [5,2]$ **b.** $[3,1] + 2[-1,3] = [1,7]$
   c. $[1,4] + 3[-2, -2] = [-5, -2]$ **d.** $2[1,2] + 3[-1,0] = [-1,4]$

5. Find each of the following algebraically.
   a. $[2, -3] + 3[-2, -1]$ **b.** $[-3, -1] + 2[-1,4]$ **c.** $[3,2] + 2[-1, -2]$
   d. $2[3, -1] + \frac{1}{2}[-6, -4]$ **e.** $\frac{1}{3}[3,9] + 2[-7, -2]$ **f.** $\frac{1}{4}[8, -12] + \frac{1}{2}[-2,6]$

6. Write each of the following as a vector sum. Then draw vector diagrams to illustrate the resultant.
   a. $[4, -3] - [2,1] = [2, -4]$ **b.** $[-5, -1] - [-3,2] = [-2, -3]$
   c. $[3,4] - 2[1, -2] = [1,8]$ **d.** $[-3,1] - 3[-2, -1] = [3,4]$
   e. $[-5,6] - \frac{1}{2}[2,4] = [-6,4]$ **f.** $\frac{1}{3}[6, -9] - \frac{2}{5}[10, -15] = [-2,3]$

7. Find each of the following algebraically.
   a. $[2, -5] - [4, -2]$ **b.** $[-3, -1] - [-2,5]$ **c.** $[-3,4] - 2[-1, -4]$
   d. $[-1, -5] - 3[1, -1]$ **e.** $[7, -8] - [-1, -5]$ **f.** $[15,7] - [20, -5]$

8. Two forces in Newtons are represented by $[7,8]$ and $[-27,13]$. Find the magnitude of the resultant of the forces and measure the angle between the resultant and the x-axis.

402

9. A sailboat on the ocean is being affected by a wind that, in the absence of current, would move the boat 2.5 km east and 1 km south in an hour, and a current that, in the absence of wind, would move the boat 1.5 km due south every hour. The navigator lifts anchor and raises the sails for 2 h, then lets the boat drift for 1.5 h. Find the position of the boat relative to its starting point. Graph the resultant.

C 10. Draw vector diagrams to illustrate the following.
   a. $[6,3] + [-2,0] + [0,-3] = [4,0]$
   b. $[2,4] + [-5,1] - [1,1] = [-4,4]$
   c. $[2,-1] - [-3,4] - [2,-2] = [3,-3]$
   d. $[-4,2] + 2[3,1] - [-2,-3] = [4,7]$
   e. $[-1,-6] - 3[-1,2] - 2[-3,-2] = [-4,-8]$

11. Three forces in Newtons are represented by $[-5,4]$, $[15,18]$, and $[-2,-7]$. Find the magnitude of the resultant and measure the angle it makes with the x-axis.

12. By definition, if $[x_1,y_1] = [x_2,y_2]$, then $x_1 = x_2$ and $y_1 = y_2$. Use this concept to solve the following for a and b.
   a. $[3,a] = [b,-2]$
   b. $[3,a] + [b,-2] = [4,-5]$
   c. $[-4,5] + [a,b] = [0,0]$
   d. $[2,a] - 3[b,4] = [-7,3]$
   e. $[2a,5] - [1,-2b] = [-5,-3]$
   f. $[2a,3b] + [-3b,2a] = [-12,0]$
   g. $[a,b] - [-5,3] = [-b,a]$
   h. $a[-3,4] + [5,b] = [11,-5]$
   i. $\frac{3}{4}[a,-12] - \frac{2}{3}[3,b] = [4,-13]$

EXTRA

A vector can be named by first stating its initial point and then its terminal point. In parallelogram $ABCD$:

$$\vec{v} = \vec{BC} \text{ (or } \vec{AD})$$
$$\vec{u} = \vec{BA} \text{ (or } \vec{CD})$$

It follows that: $\vec{CB} = -\vec{v}$ and $\vec{AB} = -\vec{u}$.

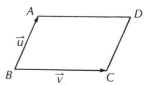

1. For the parallelogram above, name the following resultants using vertices.
   a. $\vec{u} + \vec{v}$ b. $\vec{u} - \vec{v}$ c. $-\vec{u} - \vec{v}$ d. $\vec{v} - \vec{u}$

2. In the diagram at the right below, $a\|b\|c$ and $l\|m\|n$. State a single vector equal to each of the following.
   a. $\vec{AB} + \vec{BE} + \vec{EF}$
   b. $\vec{AD} + \vec{FI} + \vec{GH}$
   c. $\vec{AC} + \vec{BE} - \vec{EF}$
   d. $\vec{AG} - \vec{FI} + \vec{AB}$
   e. $\vec{AB} - \vec{IH} - \vec{DA} - \vec{DF}$

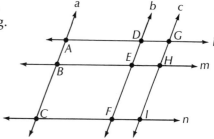

Sir William Rowan Hamilton, the most notable of Ireland's mathematicians, was born in Dublin in 1805. Orphaned at an early age, he was brought up by an uncle who ensured that he received a sound education in languages: by the time William was 13 years old, he could speak 13 languages. He first became intrigued with mathematics at the age of 15, when he witnessed a demonstration of the powers of a "human calculator", American Zerah Colburn. William began to read avidly and taught himself coordinate geometry and calculus.

Clearly a prodigy, Hamilton, while still in his teens, found an error in a work by a respected French mathematician, Pierre Laplace. At the age of 21, he was made professor of Astronomy at the University of Dublin, Director of the Dunsink Observatory, and Royal Astronomer of Ireland, in a unanimous decision by the university electors.

In 1833, Hamilton presented to the Irish Academy an algebra of complex numbers, a number system that includes the non-real number, $\sqrt{-1}$. This system used algebraic vectors to represent complex numbers. Two years after his presentation to the Irish Academy, Hamilton was knighted.

Hamilton published a major work dealing with the mathematics of vectors, *Treatise on Quaternions*, in 1853. He continued to write with the hope of a second major publication, *Elements of Quaternions*, but died before its completion.

Hamilton introduced a game to be played on a regular dodecahedron (12-sided solid). The diagram shows how he represented the dodecahedron in two dimensions. (The twelfth side is bounded by the large outside pentagon.)

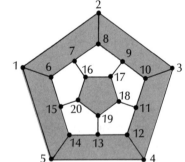

A **Hamilton Path** is one that starts at any vertex, passes through each of the remaining vertices only once, and returns to the original vertex. Place a piece of blank paper over the diagram and see if you can trace a Hamilton Path, starting at any vertex.

In the game, your opponent selects the first 5 vertices in a particular order; you must then complete the path.

Try to complete the following Hamilton Paths.

1. $1 - 6 - 7 - 16 - 17 -$
2. $1 - 6 - 15 - 14 - 5 -$
3. $1 - 2 - 8 - 7 - 6 -$

404

Review

1. Does the sentence describe a scalar or a vector quantity?
   a. A watermelon weighs 5.6 N.
   b. An astronaut in orbit has a mass of 78 kg.
   c. Today there is a west wind of 32 km/h.
   d. A ship is located 260 km east of Halifax.

2. Using 1 cm to represent 30 km/h, draw a vector to represent the given velocity.
   a. 102 km/h to the east
   b. 75 km/h to the northwest
   c. 48 km/h N 30° W
   d. 42 km/h S 55° E

3. For each of the following, select a suitable scale and draw vector diagrams to apply the Triangle Law of Vector Addition. Find the magnitude of the resultant in each case.
   a. displacements of 21 km W and 20 km N
   b. velocities of 80 km/h and 70 km/h at 60° to each other
   c. forces of 45 N and 70 N at 45° to each other

4. Graph and name the vector $[x,y]$ with initial point A and terminal point B. Calculate the magnitude of $[x,y]$.
   a. $A(-3,5)$, $B(-7,-2)$
   b. $A(4,3)$, $B(-4,5)$

5. Draw any vector on a coordinate grid and label it $\vec{v}$. Using this vector, draw vectors to represent the following.
   a. $3\vec{v}$
   b. $\frac{2}{3}\vec{v}$
   c. $-\vec{v}$
   d. $-2\vec{v}$

6. Two forces are given by $\vec{u} = [3,-2]$ and $\vec{v} = [-4,-3]$, in Newtons. Find the magnitude of $3\vec{u} - 2\vec{v}$.

7. If $\vec{v} = [-5,-1]$ is graphed with initial point $A(2,-6)$, find the terminal point.

8. If $\vec{u} = [2,-5]$ is graphed with terminal point $B(-4,3)$, find the initial point.

9. Given $\vec{w} = [6,-8]$, find the components of a vector with the given characteristics.
   a. 3 times as long as $\vec{w}$, in the same direction
   b. half as long as $\vec{w}$, in the opposite direction
   c. 1 unit long, in the same direction as $\vec{w}$
   d. 6 units long, in the opposite direction of $\vec{w}$

10. Solve for a and b.
    a. $[2a,3b] = [-4,5]$
    b. $[a+1,3] - [4,2+b] = [5,-3]$
    c. $a[2,-3] - 2[1,b] = [-8,11]$
    d. $[3a,-1] + 2[4,3] = [5,-1] - 2[3,b]$

13–6 Three Trigonometric Definitions

How can a surveyor find the distance across a marshy bog? How would you find the height of a tower without going to the top? How do astronomers calculate the distance to a star?

Trigonometry, meaning *triangle measurement*, developed as a method for calculating distances that cannot be measured directly. The word "trigonometry" derives from the Greek, as does the modern convention of frequently labelling angles using Greek letters: α (alpha); β (beta); ω (omega); θ (theta).

The trigonometry covered in this unit is based on angles in right-angled triangles, and requires some vocabulary not yet used.

For acute angle θ in the right-angled triangle shown, the **opposite** is the side opposite angle θ; the **adjacent** is the side adjacent to angle θ which is not the hypotenuse. The abbreviations **HYP**, **OPP**, and **ADJ** will be used for the hypotenuse, opposite, and adjacent, respectively.

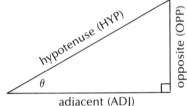

The diagram below shows several nested similar triangles, all with an acute angle of $\theta = 30°$.

Consider the value of $\dfrac{\text{OPP}}{\text{HYP}}$ in each triangle.

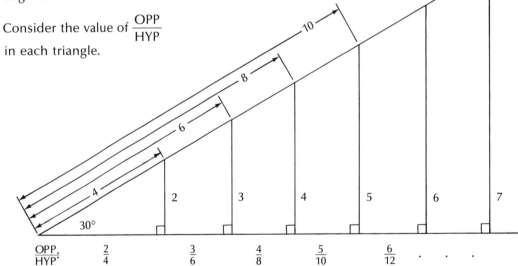

In each case, $\dfrac{\text{OPP}}{\text{HYP}}$ has a fixed value of $\frac{1}{2}$. Further work would show that, for these nested triangles, $\dfrac{\text{ADJ}}{\text{HYP}}$ and $\dfrac{\text{OPP}}{\text{ADJ}}$ also have constant values when $\theta = 30°$.

These ratios are in fact constant for *any* given angle θ in a right-angled triangle. Thus, they are considered to be *functions* of θ, and are named as follows.

The **sine** of angle θ is defined as the ratio of the length of the opposite to the length of the hypotenuse.

The **cosine** of angle θ is defined as the ratio of the length of the adjacent to the length of the hypotenuse.

The **tangent** of angle θ is defined as the ratio of the length of the opposite to the length of the adjacent.

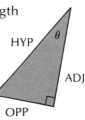

$$\sin \theta = \frac{OPP}{HYP} \qquad \cos \theta = \frac{ADJ}{HYP} \qquad \tan \theta = \frac{OPP}{ADJ}$$

EXAMPLE 1: Find $\sin \theta$, $\cos \theta$, and $\tan \theta$, expressed as a fraction, for the triangle given.

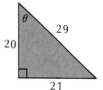

$$\sin \theta = \frac{OPP}{HYP} \qquad \cos \theta = \frac{ADJ}{HYP} \qquad \tan \theta = \frac{OPP}{ADJ}$$
$$= \frac{21}{29} \qquad\qquad = \frac{20}{29} \qquad\qquad = \frac{21}{20}$$

Scientific calculators can be used to evaluate trigonometric functions.

EXAMPLE 2: Use a calculator to find the sine, cosine, and tangent of 48°, correct to 4 decimal places.

Enter the given keystrokes for each calculation.

$\boxed{4}$ $\boxed{8}$ $\boxed{\sin}$ $\qquad$ $\boxed{4}$ $\boxed{8}$ $\boxed{\cos}$ $\qquad$ $\boxed{4}$ $\boxed{8}$ $\boxed{\tan}$

$\sin 48° \doteq 0.7431 \qquad \cos 48° \doteq 0.6691 \qquad \tan 48° \doteq 1.1106$

In *any* right-angled triangle with an angle $\theta = 48°$, the value of $\sin \theta = \dfrac{OPP}{HYP}$ is about 0.7431; $\cos \theta = \dfrac{ADJ}{HYP}$ is about 0.6691; $\tan \theta = \dfrac{OPP}{ADJ}$ is about 1.1106.

EXAMPLE 3:   **a.** Find $\sin \alpha$ and $\cos \alpha$ for the given triangle.

$$\sin \alpha = \tfrac{3}{5} = 0.6 \qquad \cos \alpha = \tfrac{4}{5} = 0.8$$

b. Find $\sin \beta$ and $\cos \beta$. Compare these values to those of $\sin \alpha$ and $\cos \alpha$, and explain the relationship.

$$\sin \beta = \tfrac{4}{5} = 0.8 \qquad \cos \beta = \tfrac{3}{5} = 0.6$$

$\alpha + \beta = 90°$

Notice that $\sin \alpha = \cos \beta$ and $\cos \alpha = \sin \beta$.
Because α and β are complementary angles in a right-angled triangle, the side that is *opposite* α is *adjacent* to β. Hence the result that $\sin \alpha = \cos \beta$. Similarly, the side that is *adjacent* to α is *opposite* β, so $\cos \alpha = \sin \beta$.

EXERCISES

A **1.** For each triangle, give the values for sin θ, cos θ, and tan θ, expressed as a fraction.

a.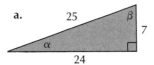

b.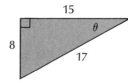

c.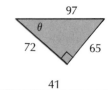

d.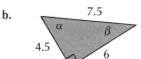

f.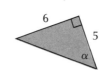

e.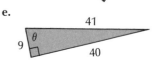

2. Find the following correct to 4 decimal places.
   a. sin 40°   **b.** tan 60°   **c.** tan 45°   **d.** cos 75°
   e. sin 37.8°   **f.** cos 6.08°   **g.** tan 78.25°   **h.** sin 3.12°

3. For each triangle below, give the sine, cosine, and tangent values for both α and β. Answer correct to 4 decimal places, where appropriate.

a.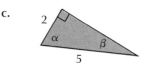

b.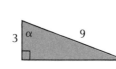

c.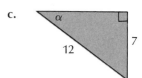

B **4.** For each triangle below, first find the length of the unknown side. Then find the cosine of α, correct to 4 decimal places where appropriate.

a. **b.** **c.**

5. Find the length of each unknown side, then find the sine of the indicated angle, expressed as a fraction. Rationalize the denominator where necessary.

a. **b.**  **c.**

6. Find the tangent of each indicated angle, expressed as a fraction. Rationalize the denominator where necessary.

a. 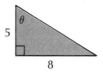 **b.** **c.**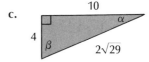

408

7. In $\triangle PQR$, $\angle R = 90°$, $PQ = 41$ units, and $PR = 9$ units. Draw $\triangle PQR$ and label $\angle PQR$ as θ. Then find the values of $\sin \theta$, $\cos \theta$, and $\tan \theta$, expressed as ratios.

8. In $\triangle XYZ$, $\angle Z = 90°$, $XZ = 40$ units, and $YZ = 42$ units. If $\angle YXZ = \theta$, then find the values of $\sin \theta$, $\cos \theta$, and $\tan \theta$, correct to 4 decimal places.

9. In $\triangle ABC$ with $\angle C = 90°$, $\cos A = \frac{80}{89}$. Draw and label $\triangle ABC$ to find $\sin A$ and $\tan A$.

10. In $\triangle PQR$ with $\angle R = 90°$, $\tan P = \frac{91}{60}$. Find the sine, cosine, and tangent of $\angle Q$.

C 11. a. Construct an isosceles right-angled triangle with an hypotenuse 10 units long. Measure as necessary to find the value of $\sin 45°$.
  b. Construct an isosceles right-angled triangle with an hypotenuse 14 units long. Measure again to find $\sin 45°$.
  c. If your constructions were accurate, your answers to **a** and **b** are the same. Explain why this is so.
  d. Check the accuracy of your constructions by evaluating $\sin 45°$ on a calculator.

12. Given that $\sin^2 \theta = (\sin \theta)^2 = (\sin \theta)(\sin \theta)$, evaluate each sum below.

  a. $\sin^2 17° + \cos^2 17°$ b. $\sin^2 31° + \cos^2 31°$ c. $\sin^2 48.7° + \cos^2 48.7°$

13. Make a conclusion based on inductive reasoning and your answers to exercise 12: for any θ, what is the value of $\sin^2 \theta + \cos^2 \theta$?

14. a. Find $\sin 30°$, expressed as a fraction.
  b. Explain the meaning of $\sin 30°$ as it relates to a ratio of lengths of sides of $\triangle ABC$.
  c. Given that $\overline{AC}$ is 4 units long, apply your answer to part **b** to find the length of $\overline{AB}$.
  d. If $\overline{AC}$ were 3 units long, find the length of $\overline{AB}$.
  e. If $\overline{AB}$ is 16 units long, how long is $\overline{AC}$? $\overline{BC}$?

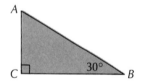

EXTRA

Slope and the Tangent Ratio

Recall that the formula for the slope of a line segment is:

$$m = \frac{y_2 - y_1}{x_2 - x_1}.$$

The diagram at the right illustrates that the slope of a line segment could also be interpreted as the tangent of the angle that the line makes with the x-axis.

Explain why this is so. Find the slope of $\overline{AB}$ and find $\tan \theta$.

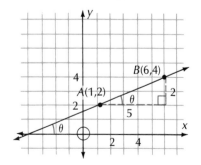

13–7 Finding Side and Angle Measures

The trigonometric functions provide a powerful tool for applications in mathematics and the practical world, as they can be used to solve for an unknown side or angle measure in a right-angled triangle.

EXAMPLE 1: Find the length of $\overline{BC}$, correct to 2 decimal places.

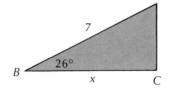

Identify the trigonometric function that involves the known angle, the known side, and the unknown side. Side $\overline{BC}$ is *adjacent* to $\angle B$ and side $\overline{AB}$ is the *hypotenuse*.

Therefore, apply $\cos \theta = \dfrac{\text{ADJ}}{\text{HYP}}$.

$$\cos \theta = \frac{\text{ADJ}}{\text{HYP}}$$

$$\cos 26° = \frac{x}{7} \qquad \text{Substitute.}$$

$$0.8988 = \frac{x}{7} \qquad \text{Evaluate } \cos 26°: \boxed{2}\ \boxed{6}\ \boxed{\cos}.$$

$$x \doteq 6.29 \qquad \text{Solve for } x.$$

Side $\overline{BC}$ is about 6.29 units long.

EXAMPLE 2: Find the measure of θ, correct to 2 decimal places.

Identify the function that involves the 2 known sides: $\overline{PR}$ is *opposite* θ and $\overline{PQ}$ is the *hypotenuse*.

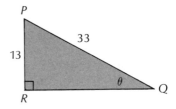

Therefore, apply $\sin \theta = \dfrac{\text{OPP}}{\text{HYP}}$.

$$\sin \theta = \frac{\text{OPP}}{\text{HYP}}$$

$$\sin \theta = \frac{13}{33} \qquad \text{Enter: } \boxed{1}\ \boxed{3}\ \boxed{÷}\ \boxed{3}\ \boxed{3}\ \boxed{=}$$

$$\therefore\ \sin \theta = 0.393\,939\ldots$$

When you have this repeating decimal on the calculator display, use one of the following keystrokes to find the value of θ.

The resulting display will be: 23.199 843 18.

For the triangle given, $\theta \doteq 23.20°$.

EXERCISES

In the following exercises, use a calculator as appropriate.

A **1.** Find the value correct to 4 decimal places.

    a. cos 48°   **b.** sin 72°   **c.** cos 29.5°   **d.** tan 37.25°

  2. For the given trigonometric value, find α correct to 2 decimal places.

    a. sin α = 0.0984   **b.** cos α = 0.2156   **c.** tan α = 0.8401

  3. Identify the function that involves all three of x, y, and z.

    a. 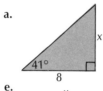   **b.** 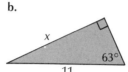   **c.**   **d.**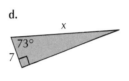

B **4.** Solve for x in each triangle, correct to 2 decimal places.

    a. 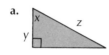   **b.** 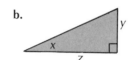   **c.** 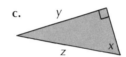   **d.**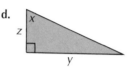

    e.   **f.** 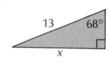   **g.**    **h.**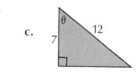

  5. For each triangle, find θ correct to 2 decimal places.

    a. 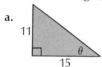   **b.**   **c.**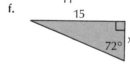

    d. 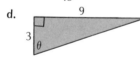   **e.**   **f.**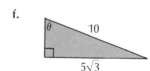

  6. Given that $\triangle XYZ$ is right-angled with $\angle Z = 90°$, answer the following.

    a. If XZ = 5 units and YZ = 7 units, find $\angle Y$. (Make a diagram first.)

    b. If XY = 5 units and $\angle X$ = 43°, find XZ.

    c. If XZ = 5 units and XY = 13 units, find $\angle Y$.

  7. Solve for each unknown correct to 1 decimal place.

    a. 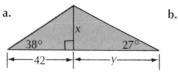   **b.** 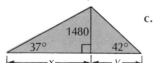   **c.**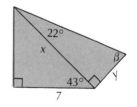

13-8 Applying Trigonometry

Trigonometry has many applications in engineering, design, surveying, and astronomy. The following examples illustrate some applications.

EXAMPLE 1: At its highest point, a cottage roof is 0.9 m above the ceiling. If the cottage is 8 m wide, what angle does the roof make with the ceiling? (The roof is symmetrical.)

Make a diagram to visualize the problem.

Write an equation using opposite and adjacent.

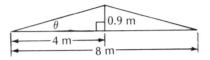

$$\tan \theta = \frac{0.9}{4} \quad \boxed{0}\ \boxed{.}\ \boxed{9}\ \boxed{\div}\ \boxed{4}\ \boxed{=}$$

$$\tan \theta = 0.225 \quad \boxed{\text{arc}}\ \boxed{\text{tan}}$$

$$\theta \doteq 12.68$$

The roof makes an angle of about 13° with the ceiling.

Surveyors use a measuring instrument called a **transit** to assist them in finding a **line of sight**, which makes an angle with the horizontal. This angle can then be applied in a right-angled triangle to solve for unknown measures. In this section, take the transit height to be 1.5 m.

A transit is equipped with a telescope, levels, and scales for measuring both vertical and horizontal angles.

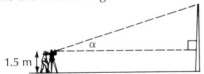

Sighting the top of a tower from the ground gives an **angle of elevation**.

Sighting a landmark from the top of a cliff gives an **angle of depression**.

EXAMPLE 2: From a point 60 m from the base of a tower, a surveyor measures the angle of elevation to the top to be 18°. Find the height of the tower.

Make a diagram.

Let x be the indicated measure.

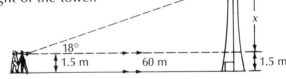

Write an equation.

$$\tan 18° = \frac{x}{60} \qquad \begin{array}{l} x = 60\ (\tan 18°) \\ x \doteq 19.5 \end{array}$$

Add 1.5 m for the height of the transit: 19.5 + 1.5 = 21.

The tower is about 21 m tall.

EXERCISES

Answer all questions correct to 2 decimal places, using a calculator as appropriate.

A 1. For maximum safety, a ladder should make an angle of 72° with the ground. If a ladder is 4 m long, how far will it reach up the wall?

2. A pendulum swings 18° to each side of the rest position. If the pendulum is 1.2 m long, how far does it swing to each side?

B 3. The angle of elevation to the top of a tree, measured on a transit 1.5 m tall from a distance of 30 m, is 15°. Find the height of the tree.

4. From a point 8 m from the base of an 11 m flagpole, David observed Polaris, the North Star, directly in line with the top of the flagpole. David is 2 m tall. Find the angle of elevation of Polaris. This angle will give David's latitude.

5. From the top of a 50 m building, the angle of depression to the centre of an intersection is 5.6°, measured on a transit 1.5 m tall. How far is the centre of the intersection from the base of the building?

6. Find the angle of elevation to the top of a 17 m tower from a point 12 m from its base. Disregard transit height.

7. From the top of a 35 m cliff, two boats in line are observed with angles of depression of 8° and 14°. How far apart are the two boats?

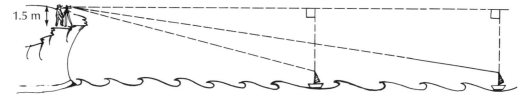

8. If a regular pentagon is inscribed in a circle with radius 18 cm, then what would be the length of each side of the pentagon?

9. How far does the tip of a 1.2 m pendulum rise as it swings 15° to one side?

10. From a point 150 m from the base of a building, with a transit 1.5 m tall, the angle of elevation to the top of the building is 46°. If the angle of elevation to the top of a flagpole on top of the building is 48°, find the height of the flagpole. Assume the flagpole is at the near edge of the building.

C 11. Two buildings are 30 m apart. From the top of the shorter building, the angle of depression to the base of the other is 53° and the angle of elevation to the top of it is 28°. Find the height of each building.

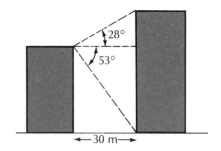

12. A regular pentagon with sides 8 cm long is inscribed in a circle. Find the radius of the circle and the area of the pentagon. Do not round off until the last step of your solution.

13. What is the measure of the longest metal rod that will fit inside a box that has a length of 30 cm, a width of 20 cm, and a height of 15 cm? What angle will the rod make with the bottom of the box?

14. If a pilot flies for 48 min in a direction of N 52° E at 270 km/h, how far will the plane be north and east of the starting point?

15. Find the area of a circle inscribed in an equilateral triangle with sides 10.4 cm long.

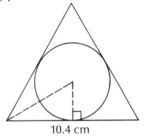

10.4 cm

Using the Calculator

Area of a Triangle

If 2 sides and the contained angle of a triangle are known, it is possible to find the area of the triangle using the following formula.

$$A = \frac{1}{2}ab(\sin C)$$

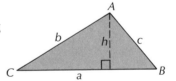

1. Prove the formula, using the fact that if you drop an altitude of length h from A to $\overline{BC}$, then h satisfies $\sin C = \frac{h}{b}$. (Solve for h and substitute into $A = \frac{1}{2}ah$.)

2. Apply the formula to find the area of each triangle.

a.

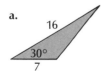

16
30°
7

b.

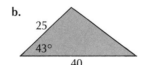

25
43°
40

c.

50
63°
40

414

Review

1. Solve for each unknown, correct to 2 decimal places.

a.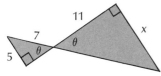

b.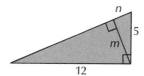

2. Solve for each unknown, correct to 2 decimal places.

a.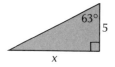

b.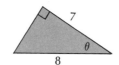

c.

d.

e.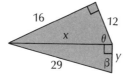

f.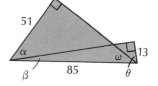

3. If $\cos \alpha = \frac{\sqrt{10}}{5}$, find $\sin \alpha$ and $\tan \alpha$.

4. If $\sin \theta = \frac{5}{17}$, use a calculator to find $\cos 2\theta$, correct to 4 decimal places.

5. When the sun is 38° above the horizon, the shadow of a tree is 7.81 m long. Find the height of the tree.

6. A camera lens has a 50° field of vision. A photographer wants to take a picture of a stadium that has a length of 150 m. If the photographer positions herself directly in front of the stadium, what is the closest she can stand and still have the entire stadium in the picture?

7. Draw $\triangle ABC$ with $\angle C = 90°$, $AB = 19$ units, and $BC = 14$ units. Solve for all unknown measures in $\triangle ABC$.

Using the Calculator

In each of the following, first find the measure of angle θ (do not record your answer), and then find the trigonometric value indicated, correct to 2 decimal places.

1. If $\sin \theta = \frac{\sqrt{3}}{2}$, find $\cos \theta$.

2. If $\cos \theta = \frac{24}{25}$, find $\tan \theta$.

3. If $\tan \theta = 0.225$, find $\sin \theta$.

4. If $\sin \theta = 0.923$, find $\tan \theta$.

Test

1. Draw scale diagrams and apply the Triangle Law of Vector Addition to find the magnitude of the resultant in each case.

   a. Forces of 40 N to the right and 60 N downward are acting on the same object.
   b. Displacements of 20 m and 45 m occur at 60° to each other.
   c. A velocity of 240 km/h N and a velocity of 60 km/h N 65° E.

2. Michel wants to row directly across a river 1.4 km wide that is flowing at a rate of 6 km/h. If he can row at 9 km/h in still water, then at what angle should he aim the boat relative to the straight-line distance across the river? What is his resultant speed and how long will it take him to cross?

3. If $\vec{u} = [1, -2]$ and $\vec{v} = [4,1]$, draw a vector diagram to illustrate $3\vec{u} - 2\vec{v}$ and find the magnitude of the resultant.

4. Solve for each unknown.

   a.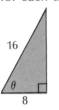

   b.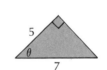

   c.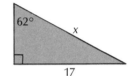

   d.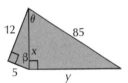

   e.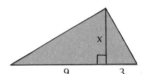

   f.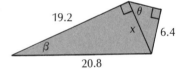

5. A pasture in the shape of a right-angled triangle has an hypotenuse of 750 m and one angle measuring 53°. Find the area of the triangle.

6. While standing 30 m from a ship in the Welland Canal, Graham observed the bow to be 38° to his left while the stern was 58° to his right. Find the length of the ship.

7. A guy wire 65 m long is anchored 56 m from the base of a radio tower. A second wire, also attached to the top of the tower, is 55 m long. How far is it anchored from the base of the tower, and what angle does it make with the ground?

8. Lauren and Elizabeth are standing at two points A and B on opposite sides of a mountain and at the same level 1740 m below the mountain peak. How far apart are Lauren and Elizabeth if the angles of elevation to the top of the mountain are 32° and 47°?

Cumulative Review

1. A survey of weekly salaries was taken in a company. The results of the survey for 20 warehouse staff and 20 secretarial staff are given below.

Weekly Salary, Warehouse Staff ($)
320, 259, 357, 410, 445, 340, 285, 342, 350, 418, 365, 430, 442, 380, 270, 425, 371, 393, 437, 335

Weekly Salary, Secretarial Staff ($)
315, 253, 369, 425, 400, 380, 322, 340, 343, 261, 289, 318, 355, 327, 334, 440, 277, 295, 392, 336

   a. Make a double histogram, choosing interval sizes appropriate to both sets of data.
   b. What is the median salary for the warehouse staff? for the secretarial staff?

2. For the pattern shown at the right below, describe a transformation or composition of transformations that will result in the given mapping.

   a. figure 1 to figure 20
   b. figure 8 to figure 5
   c. figure 10 to figure 17
   d. figure 17 to figure 18
   e. figure 3 to figure 19
   f. figure 12 to figure 19
   g. figure 4 to figure 7
   h. figure 11 to figure 10

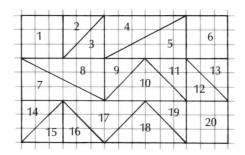

3. Use the information given in each diagram to prove the indicated result.

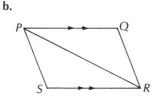

a. Prove △ADE ≅ △BCE.

b. Prove △PRS ≅ △RPQ.

c. 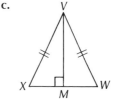 Prove △VXM ≅ △VWM.

4. A carpenter has a round sheet of wood to be used as the top of a table with a single pedestal stand. Explain how the carpenter can find the centre of the circle to ensure that the table top will be level when the stand is attached.

5. An above-ground pool, cylindrical in shape, has an inside diameter of 3.2 m and a height of 1.5 m. The owner must add 100 mL of pool chemical solution for every kilolitre of water in the pool. If the pool has just been filled with fresh water to a height of 1.4 m, how much solution must be added?

Appendix

Focus on: *Understanding the Problem*

1. The digits of the number 7194 are rearranged in descending order and then in ascending order. What is the difference of the two resulting numbers?

2. What is the smallest natural number by which 28 can be multiplied so that the result is a perfect cube?

3. How many vertices are there on a six-pointed star?

4. Which of the numbers 2025, 3025, and 4025 are square numbers?

5. The **factorial** symbol, !, is used to represent the product of a natural number n and all natural numbers less than n.
For instance, $5! = 5 \times 4 \times 3 \times 2 \times 1 = 120$.
Notice that the value of 5! ends in zero. How many zeros are at the end of the value of 31!?

6. The price of a soccer ball is reduced by one fourth during a sale. By what fraction must the sale price be increased to return to the original price?

7. Which pizza is the better buy, the regular, with a diameter of 30 cm, for $7, or the large, with a diameter of 40 cm, for $12?

8. Are all equilateral quadrilaterals equiangular? If not, give an example.

9. Are all equiangular quadrilaterals equilateral? If not, give an example.

10. How many different rectangles are there with whole-number dimensions and perimeter 36 units?

11. How can you make a number smaller by adding a number to it?

Focus on: *Guessing and Testing*

Guessing and testing is just one possible strategy for solving problems 12 to 19. There may be other strategies you'll prefer to use.

12. Find a two-digit number that is twice the product of its digits.

13. Phil's daughter Amy was born when he was 24 years old. When Amy is 3 times as old as she is today, Phil will be 3 times as old as Amy. How old is Phil today?

14. An open box can be constructed from a square piece of cardboard by cutting off square corners and turning up the sides. Starting with a 20 cm square, what size square should be cut from each corner to make a box with the greatest possible volume? Consider whole-number answers only.

 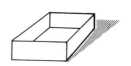

15. The four-digit number 8*AB*6 is a perfect square. Find $A + B$.

16. What is the largest prime number that, when multiplied by 6, gives a product less than 1000?

17. Using each of the digits 1, 2, 3, 4, and 5 exactly once, write two numbers that have a product of 11 342.

18. Copy the diagram. How would you place one of the numbers $\frac{1}{3}, \frac{2}{3}, 1, \frac{4}{3}, \frac{5}{3}, 2$, in each of the circles so that the two numbers at the ends of any line segment differ by more than $\frac{1}{3}$?

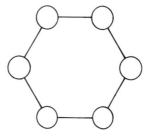

19. What is the minimum number of pitches possible in a complete nine-inning baseball game?

Focus on: *Making a List or Table*

Again, the strategy suggested here is just one possibility. You may want to try a different approach.

20. The members of the school band sold 240 tickets for the upcoming concert, for a total of $300. Tickets were priced at $1 for card-carrying students and $2 for non-students. How many $2 tickets were sold?

21. In the game of Math Blitz you can score 5, 4, 3, 2 or 0 points on any move. Leslie scored 30 points in 7 moves. Find all possible sets of individual scores that Leslie may have scored. (Order does not matter.)

22. A **palindromic** number is a number, like 157 751, whose digits read the same either backward or forward. Find the palindromic numbers less than 2000 that are perfect cubes.

23. A coin is tossed 5 times. What is the probability of getting more than 3 heads in the 5 tosses?

24. There are 5 male players and 5 female players on the Burnett School Badminton Team. The coach is establishing doubles teams for a district-wide tournament. How many doubles teams are possible? What percentage of them would be mixed doubles teams?

25. In a grocery store there is a manager, a cashier, and a clerk. Their names are Smith, Lee, and Gagné. The clerk, who is an only child, earns the least money. Smith, who is married to Lee's brother, earns more than the cashier. Name the person for each job.

26. The radiator of an automobile has been filled with 16 L of liquid, 8 L of which are water; the rest is antifreeze. Because of a leak, the radiator loses 2 L of liquid every month. This loss is replaced by water. After 3 months, how much antifreeze is in the radiator?

27. How many different licence plates for passenger vehicles can be made using 3 numerals followed by 3 letters? Zero is not used as a first numeral.

Focus on: *Finding Patterns*

28. Look for a pattern to find the missing numbers.
    a. 55, 45, ■, 28, 21
    b. 3, 7, 19, 55, ■
    c. 28, ■, 29, 35, 30, 34, 31
    d. 1, 4, 3, 16, 5, 36, 7, ■, ■, ■
    e. 6, 10, 19, 35, 60, ■, ■
    f. 17, 23, 40, 63, ■, ■

29. Find the value of the following expression.
    $(1 + 3 + 5 + \ldots + 49) - (2 + 4 + 6 + \ldots + 50)$

30. On his first math test of the year, Sam got 1 mark. On the second test he got 2 marks, on the third test he got 3 marks, and so on until he had written all 22 math tests scheduled for the year. The total number of marks possible on the tests was 500. Did Sam obtain a pass?

31. On what day of the week will Valentine's Day (February 14) fall in the year 2001?

32. For the number 1984, the product of the digits is 288. For what other years before 1984 do the digits of the year also yield a product of 288?

33. What is the ones digit in 8^{1001}?

34. Which whole numbers less than 1000 have an odd number of factors?

35. How many rectangles are there in the diagram at the right?

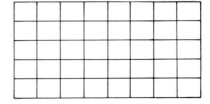

36. The illustrations below show three views of the same cube.

What is on the face opposite the face with the indicated figure?

a. 　　　　　b. 　　　　　c.

Focus on: *Solving a Simpler Problem or Working Backward*

37. A fence built to enclose a square garden is made of 48 posts placed 5 m apart. Find the area of the garden.

38. Given that X and Z represent single digits, and if $5X72 + 6578 = 12\,Z50$ and $12Z50$ is divisible by 9, what are the values of X and Z?

39. Convert x metres to centimetres. Convert z millimetres to centimetres.

40. A stock car racer drove 6 km around a track, driving the first 2 km at an average speed of 100 km/h, the next 2 km at an average speed of 200 km/h, and the final 2 km at an average speed of 300 km/h. Find the racer's average speed for the entire 6 km.

41. What is the greatest whole number n that, when substituted into the expression below, will yield a product less than 1 000 000?
$$(n)(n + 1)(n + 2)$$

42. How many digits are needed to write the standard form of 2^{50}?

43. For the concentric circles shown, the diameter of the inner circle is equal to the radius of the middle circle. The diameter of the middle circle is equal to the radius of the outer circle. What fraction of the largest circle is shaded?

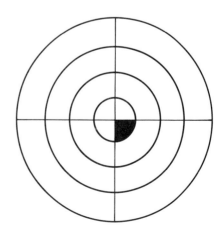

421

44. How many different line segments are determined by 6 collinear points?

45. The numbers from 1 to 40 are equally spaced, in consecutive order, around a circle. What number is opposite the number 9?

46. A soccer ball, dropped from the top of B.C. Place, bounces on the floor 60 m below. Each time the ball hits the floor, it rebounds upward to $\frac{2}{5}$ of its previous height. How high will the ball bounce after it hits the floor for the fourth time?

47. How many possible different triangles are there with whole-number dimensions x, $x - 2$, and $x - 3$, where $x < 10$?

48. Given 16 identical cubes, how many different rectangular solids can you make using all 16 cubes? How many can you make if you're allowed to use any number of the 16 cubes?

49. Draw a diagram to show how 10 students can be arranged in 10 rows with 3 students in each row.

50. An isosceles triangle with sides 10 cm, 10 cm, and 16 cm is folded in half. How long is the crease?

51. How many right-angled triangles can you form using the following points as vertices: $A(0,0)$, $B(0,1)$, $C(0,2)$, $D(1,0)$, $E(2,0)$, $F(1,1)$?

Focus on: *Extending and Generalizing Problems*

52. Of the pairs of integers that add up to 8, find the pair with the greatest product. Find a general rule for solving similar problems, where 8 is replaced by a different number.

53. How many angles are there in the diagram? Find a general rule for solving similar problems.

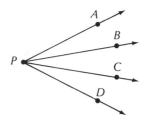

54. Six identical cubes are to be attached so that each cube shares at least one complete face with another cube. What arrangement of the six cubes will produce the least surface area to be painted? Predict the minimum surface area for a collection of 8 cubes using the same conditions.

55. Find the pattern: 3, 1, $\frac{1}{3}$, $\frac{1}{9}$, . . .

The 1st **term**, is 3; the 2nd term is 1; the third term is $\frac{1}{3}$. Find an expression to represent the nth term (the term occurring at position n). Verify that the expression holds for $n = 1$; $n = 2$; $n = 3$; $n = 4$.

56. Does there exist any even number that cannot be written as the sum of two prime numbers? If so, find an example.

57. In a 2-by-2 "checkerboard" there are 9 rectangles. In a 2-by-3 checkerboard, there are 18, and, in a 2-by-4 checkerboard, there are 30. How many rectangles are there in a 2-by-8 checkerboard? Can you generalize to an 2-by-n checkerboard?

58. There are 204 squares on a standard 8-by-8 checkerboard. How many rectangles are there on a checkerboard?

Focus on: *Selecting an Appropriate Strategy*

59. Find 4 consecutive integers that have a sum of -326.

60. Two students were playing chess and each of them played 5 games. How is it possible that each student won 4 games?

61. There are many ways to use all of the ten digits from 0 through 9 to make a total of 100. Find one way.

62. What is the maximum number of regions in which a square can be divided by drawing 5 straight lines?

63. Three single-digit whole numbers are pulled out of a hat. The sum of the numbers is the same as the product. What are the numbers?

64. Use nine line segments of the same length to form 5 equilateral triangles.

65. In the diagram at the right, 5 squares are formed using 12 equal line segments. Make 4 line segments so that there will be only 3 squares, all the same size.

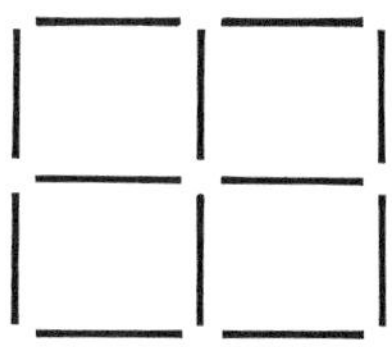

66. How would you move 2 line segments to yield 7 squares?

67. In one month a real-estate agent sold 3 houses at prices of $84 000, $72 000, and $116 000. Her commission is 4% of the selling price. How much did she earn in commission that month?

68. Season tickets for a concert series were discounted $31 off the total cost of the 6 individual concert prices. What would the season ticket prices be for a pair of tickets in each of the seat classifications shown below?

Seat Classification	Price per Concert
Orchestra	$24
Balcony 1	$19
Balcony 2	$15

69. Three neighbours are thinking of forming a car pool to commute to and from their work, 36 km from their neighbourhood. If each of them could drive every third work day, and if the average fuel economy for their three cars is 9.5 L/100 km, is it cheaper for them to have a car pool or to take public transportation at $1.25 each way? Assume a fuel cost of $0.59/L to derive an estimate on which to base your answer.

70. Carolyn worked at a Banff hotel one summer. One of her benefits was the offer of special half-rates on rooms for relatives of the working staff. Carolyn's parents visited for 6 nights, staying in a room with a regular rate of $85 per night. They also spent an average of $55/day on meals and miscellaneous expenses. How much did the Banff trip cost?

71. Two students, on holiday in Germany, went to a concert in Heidelberg. Their tickets cost 50 German marks. If the Canadian dollar was worth 2.1 marks, what was the cost for each student's ticket, in Canadian dollars?

72. If a biological culture increases its mass by 5% every minute, how large will a culture with an initial mass of 1 g be at the end of 1 h? 2 h? 5 h?

73. Kim obtained insurance on a new car with a basic cost of $942. Because of a safe driving record, the insurance company offered a discount of 35%. What is the discounted insurance cost?

74. Find a pattern and determine the next 3 numbers.

a. $\frac{1}{2}, -\frac{2}{3}, \frac{3}{4}, -\frac{4}{5}, \frac{5}{6}, -\frac{6}{7}, \ldots$ b. $1, \frac{1}{2}, \frac{1}{4}, \frac{1}{8}, \ldots$

c. $1, -1, 2, -\frac{1}{2}, 3, -\frac{1}{3}, 4, \ldots$

75. Points P, Q, and R mark 3 neighbouring rabbit holes in an open field.

a. Where should a fox stand to be the same distance from each hole?

b. By making a scale diagram, find the distance the fox must travel to reach any one of the 3 holes, if standing at the right position originally.

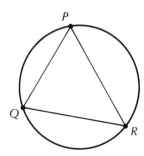

Glossary

Absolute value The positive distance of a number from zero. The absolute value of n is written $|n|$.

Acute angle An angle measuring less than $90°$.

Additive inverse The number which, when added to a given number, gives a sum of zero.

Adjacent (ADJ) For a given angle in a right-angled triangle, the side which is adjacent to the angle and is not the hypotenuse.

Adjacent angles Two non-overlapping angles that share a common side and vertex.

Algebraic expression A mathematical expression containing sums, products, differences, or quotients involving variables.

Alternate angles Angles on opposite sides of a transversal that cuts two lines.

Altitude (of a triangle) A perpendicular line segment drawn from a vertex to the opposite side.

Angle of depression The angle between the horizontal and the line of sight to a point below the horizontal.

Angle of elevation The angle between the horizontal and the line of sight to a point above the horizontal.

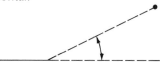

Arc A part of a circle's circumference.

Associative property The property stating that, when three or more numbers are added or multiplied, the operations can be performed in any order.
$$(a + b) + c = a + (b + c)$$
$$(a \times b) \times c = a \times (b \times c)$$

Assumption A statement that is generally accepted and need not be proved. (also **axiom** or **postulate**)

Axiom A statement that is generally accepted and need not be proved. (also **assumption** or **postulate**)

Bar graph A graph displaying data in which the length of each bar is proportional to the number it represents.

Base (in a power) The factor repeated in a power.

Base (of a polygon) Any face of a polygon.

Biased sample A sample that results from a sampling method in which not all members of the population have an equal chance of being selected.

Biconditional statement A conditional statement and its converse combined.

Binomial A polynomial consisting of two terms.

Bisect To divide into two congruent parts.

Box-and-whisker graph An arrangement of data which facilitates a quick summary by highlighting the median, the extremes, and the hinge points.

Capacity The maximum amount a container can hold.

Census An official, usually periodic, enumeration of a population.

Centi- A prefix meaning hundredth.

Central angle An angle with its vertex at the centre of a circle and bounded by two radii. (also **sector angle**)

Centre of a circle The point that is the same distance from all points in a circle.

Centre of rotation The point about which a figure is rotated.

Centroid The point where the medians of a triangle intersect.

Chord (of a circle) A line segment with endpoints in the circumference of a circle.

Circle The set of all points in a plane that are equidistant from a fixed point, the centre.

Circumcentre The centre of a circumcircle.

Circumcircle A circle that touches all the vertices of a polygon.

Circumference The perimeter of a circle.

Coefficient The numerical factor of an algebraic term.

Collinear points Points that lie in the same straight line.

Commutative property The property stating that two numbers can be added or multiplied in any order.

$a + b = b + a$
$a \times b = b \times a$

Complementary angles Two angles that have a sum of 90°.

Component (of a vector) A vector quantity which, with others, is equivalent to a given vector. The most useful pair is a pair at right angles lying along the x- and y-axes.

Composition of transformations The process of performing successive transformations one after another.

Concentric circles Circles that lie in the same plane and have the same centre.

Concurrent lines Two or more lines that intersect in one point.

Conditional statement A statement in the form "If...(p)..., then...(q)..." (also **implication**)

Cone A solid bounded by a circle and all line segments from a point outside the plane of the circle to all the points of the circle.

Congruent figures Figures with the same size and shape.

Consecutive numbers Numbers obtained by counting by ones from any given integer, such as 57, 58, 59, ...

Constant A quantity with a fixed value in a specified mathematical context.

Constant of proportionality The constant k in a direct, inverse, or partial variation.

Converse A statement in the form "If...(q)..., then...(p)...", given the original implication "If...(p)...,then...q...".

Coordinate plane A number grid on a plane with an x-axis and a y-axis.

Coordinates The two numbers in an ordered pair that locate a point on a grid.

Coplanar lines Lines that lie in the same plane.

Corollary A theorem which follows easily as an extension of another theorem and is deducible from the first theorem.

Correlation A term used to indicate an obvious relation between two variables of statistical data, as displayed by some scatterplots.

Corresponding angles For a transversal that cuts two lines, the angles on the same side of the transversal and on the same side of each line.

Cosine For a given angle in a right-angled triangle, the ratio of the length of the adjacent side to the length of the hypotenuse.

Cube (geometry) A regular polyhedron with six congruent square faces.

Cube (numeration) To raise a number to the third power.

Cube root The number which, when cubed, results in a given number.

$^3\sqrt{8} = 2$; 2 is the cube root of 8.

Cyclic quadrilateral A quadrilateral with all vertices in the circumference of a circle. (also **inscribed quadrilateral**)

Cylinder A three-dimensional figure with two parallel, congruent, circular bases.

Deca- A prefix meaning ten.

Deci- A prefix meaning tenth.

Defined term A term that can be explained using other terms.

Degree of a polynomial The greatest degree of any term within the polynomial.

Degree of a term The sum of the exponents of the variables in the term.

Dependent events Two or more events in which the result of one event affects the result of the event after it.

Diagonal A line segment joining any two non-adjacent vertices of a polygon.

Diameter A chord of a circle that passes through its centre.

Difference of squares A binomial consisting of a squared term minus a different squared term.

Dilatation A transformation for which the shape of the image is the same as the shape of the object but the image may be enlarged or reduced in size.

Direct congruence Having the same size, shape, and orientation.

Direct variation A function of two variables, say x and y, defined by an equation of the form $y = kx$, $k \neq 0$.

Disjoint sets Sets that have no elements in common.

Displacement The distance travelled in a given direction.

Distributive property The property that a product of a sum or difference can be written as a sum of or difference between two products.
$$a \times (b + c) = (a \times b) + (a \times c)$$
$$a \times (b - c) = (a \times b) - (a \times c)$$

Domain The set of the first elements of the ordered pairs of a relation.

Edge The intersection of two faces of a three-dimensional figure.

Entire radical A radical that contains no coefficients outside the radical sign.

Equation A mathematical statement showing two or more numbers or quantities equal.

Equilateral triangle A triangle with three congruent sides and three congruent angles.

Equivalent equations Equations that are obtained by performing the same operation on each side of a given equation.

Equivalent fractions Fractions that reduce to the same lowest terms.

Equivalent ratios Ratios that can be expressed as equivalent fractions.

Equivalent vectors Vectors that have the same magnitude and direction.

Escribed circle A circle drawn externally to a polygon to touch three consecutive sides with the first and third sides extended.

Event Any set of possible outcomes.

Experimental probability of an event The frequency of the occurrence of an event in a sample, divided by the total sample size.

Exponent (in a power) The number of times the base occurs as a factor.

Expression A combination of mathematical symbols, variables, and numerals.

Exterior angles Angles on the outside of two lines cut by a transversal.

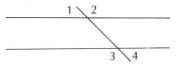

Extreme values The highest and lowest values in a set of numbers.

Face A flat surface of a three-dimensional figure.

Factor Any one of the numbers or expressions or variables used in multiplication to form a product.

Fitted line In a scatterplot displaying either positive or negative correlation, the best-fitting line about which the points seem to fall. (also **median fit line**).

Formula An equation that states a rule about quantities represented by variables.

Frequency The number of times a particular value in a set of data occurs.

Frequency distribution table A table that shows the frequencies of values in a set of data, often including columns for cumulative frequency, midpoint of interval, and subtotal.

Function A relation in which each element of the domain corresponds to exactly one element of the range.

Glide reflection A transformation that is the combination of a reflection in a line and a translation parallel to the line.

Greatest common factor (GCF) The largest number that is a factor of each of a set of numbers or the expression that has the greatest degree and numerical coefficient common to each of a set of expressions. (also **greatest monomial factor** when dealing with polynomials)

Greatest monomial factor The largest number that is a factor of each of a set of numbers or the expression that has the greatest degree and numerical coefficient common to each of a set of expressions. (also **greatest common factor**)

Half-turn symmetry A property exhibited in a figure for which there is a mapping that maps the figure onto itself under a rotation of 180°.

Hecto- A prefix meaning one hundred.

Height (of a polygon) The length of a perpendicular line segment from any vertex to the opposite side (or an extension of the opposite side).

Heptagon A polygon with seven sides.

Hexagon A polygon with six sides.

Histogram A graph used to display frequency distribution of data using touching bars and with the height of the bars representing frequencies and the width of the bars representing interval width.

Hyperbola The name of the shape of a graph of inverse variation which can be represented by an equation in the form $xy = k, k \neq 0$.

Hypotenuse (HYP) The side opposite the right angle in a right-angled triangle.

Hypothesis The "p" statement in a conditional statement.

Identity elements 0 in addition and 1 in multiplication.
$a + 0 = a$ and $a \times 1 = a$

Image The figure resulting from a transformation.

Implication A statement in the form "If...(p)..., then...(q)..." (also **conditional statement**)

Incentre The centre of an incircle.

Incircle A circle that touches each side of a polygon.

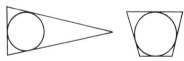

Independent events Events that have no effect on one another.

Inequality A mathematical statement that one quantity is greater than ($>$) or less than ($<$) another.

Inscribed angle An angle formed by two chords of a circle with a common vertex in the circle.

Inscribed quadrilateral A quadrilateral with all vertices in the circumference of a circle. (also **cyclic quadrilateral**)

Integers The set of numbers consisting of $\{..., -2, -1, 0, 1, 2,...\}$.

Integral exponent An exponent that is an integer.

Interior angles Two angles on the inside of two lines cut by a transversal, and on the same side of the transversal.

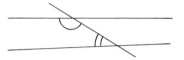

Interpolation Estimation of values between points of known values on a graph.

Intersecting lines Lines that have one point in common.

Interval (of statistical data) A set consisting of all the numbers between a pair of given numbers.

Inverse variation A function of two variables, say x and y, defined by an equation of the form $xy = k, k \neq 0$.

Irrational number A number that cannot be expressed as the quotient of two integers and whose decimal expansion neither terminates nor repeats.

Isolating a variable In a formula, solving for one variable in terms of the others.

Isometry A transformation that preserves distance between points.

Isosceles triangle A triangle with two congruent sides and two congruent angles.

Kilo- A prefix meaning one thousand.

Kilogram The basic unit of mass in the metric system.

Lateral surface area The area of all lateral faces (all the faces of a three-dimensional figure excluding the bases).

Least common multiple (LCM) The smallest non-zero number that is a multiple of each of two or more given numbers.

Like radicals Radicals that have the same radicand when in simplest form.

Line A set of points in a straight path extending infinitely in both directions.

Line graph A graph made up of line segments used to show data representing changes over a period of time.

Line of sight A direct (imaginary) line from an observer to a sighted object.

Line of symmetry A line that divides a figure into two congruent parts that are reflection images of each other.

Linear equation An equation of degree one that can be put into the form $Ax + By = C$ (A and B not both 0).

Linear function A function that is represented by a straight-line graph.

Linear programming The process of using inequalities to optimize business opportunites.

Linear relation A relation that is represented by a straight-line graph.

Litre The basic unit of capacity in the metric system.

Magnitude The absolute value of a number or a vector; size.

Many-to-one correspondence A relation in which more than one element in the domain corresponds to the same element in the range.

Mapping A correspondence of points or elements under some transformation or rule.

Mass The amount of matter in a body.

Mean The sum of a given set of values divided by the number of values.

Measure of central tendency A single value representative of a set of data, such as mean, median, or mode.

Median (of a triangle) A segment joining a vertex to the midpoint of the opposite side.

Median (statistics) The middle value of a set of data when the data are listed in numerical order.

Median fit line In a scatterplot displaying either positive or negative correlation, a fitted line found by dividing the graph into three regions and using the medians of x and y values in the outer regions.

Metre The basic unit of length in the metric system.

Micro- A prefix meaning millionth.

Midpoint The point in a line segment which bisects the line.

Milli- A prefix meaning thousandth.

Mode The most frequently occurring value in a set of data.

Monomial A single-term expression which is either a numeral, one or more variables, or a product of a numeral and one or more variables.

Multiple (of a number) The product of a given number and an integer.

Multiplicative inverse The number which multiplies by a given number to yield a product of one.

Mutually exclusive events Events which do not have common outcomes.

Nano- A prefix meaning billionth.

Natural numbers The set of all positive integers $\{1, 2, 3,...\}$.

Negative correlation A relationship between two statistical variables in which one variable tends to increase as the other decreases.

Negative reciprocals Two numbers whose product is -1.

Net A pattern that can be folded into a three-dimensional shell.

Nonagon A polygon with nine sides.

Obtuse angle An angle between 90° and 180°.

Octagon A polygon with eight sides.

Octahedron A polyhedron with eight faces.

One-to-one correspondence A relation in which each element of the domain corresponds to exactly one element of the range and each element of the range corresponds to exactly one element of the domain.

Opposite angles Angles formed by two intersecting lines which have a common vertex and are opposite to each other.

Opposite (OPP) For a given angle in a right-angled triangle, the side which is opposite the angle.

Order of rotational symmetry The number of times that the tracing of a figure fits onto the figure in one full turn.

Ordered pair A pair of numbers in which order is important. $(3, -2)$ and $(-2, 3)$ are different ordered pairs.

Orientation The determination of direction in terms of standard directions such as clockwise and counterclockwise, or north, east, south, and west.

Origin The point where the x-axis and the y-axis intersect.

Orthocentre The point where the altitudes of a triangle intersect.

Orthographic projections The drawings of the front, side, and top views of a three-dimensional figure.

Outcome The result obtained from an action or an experiment.

Pantograph A tool used to copy a plane figure to a desired scale.

Parabola The name of the shape of a graph of quadratic direct variation which can be represented by an equation in the form $y = kx^2$, $k \neq 0$.

Parallel lines Lines in a plane that do not intersect.

Parallel planes Planes in space that do not intersect.

Parallelogram A quadrilateral with opposite sides parallel.

Partial variation A function of two variables, say x and y, defined by an equation of the form $y = kx + b$.

Pentagon A polygon with five sides.

Perfect square A number whose square root is an integer.

Period (of a repeating decimal) The set of digits which repeat, indicated by a solid line over the period. The period of $\frac{4}{11} = 0.363\,636... = 0.\overline{36}$ is 36.

Periodic decimal A decimal fraction in which, after a certain decimal place, one digit, or a set of digits in the same order, is repeated indefinitely. (also **repeating decimal**)

Perpendicular bisector The line which bisects a segment and is perpendicular to it.

Perpendicular lines Lines that form 90° angles when they intersect.

Pi (π) The ratio of the circumference of a circle to its diameter.
$\pi \doteq 3.1416$.

Plane A flat surface that has no thickness, extends infinitely in all directions, and contains the whole of a straight line drawn through any two points in it.

Plane figure A set of points in a plane.

Plane of symmetry A plane that divides a three-dimensional figure into two congruent parts that are reflection images of each other.

Plane symmetry A three-dimensional figure has plane symmetry if it has at least one plane of symmetry.

Point A point has an exact position. It has neither magnitude nor direction and is shown by a dot.

Point-slope form of a linear equation The equation of a straight line written in the form $y - y_1 = m(x - x_1)$, where (x_1, y_1) is a point in the line and m is the slope.

Point symmetry A figure has point symmetry if there is a point O such that the figure maps onto itself under a rotation about O.

Polygon A closed figure whose sides are three or more line segments.

Polyhedron A three-dimensional figure whose faces are polygons.

Polynomial A monomial or a sum of monomials.

Population The entire set of individuals, items, or scores from which a sample is drawn.

Positive correlation A relationship between two statistical variables in which both variables tend to increase or decrease together.

Postulate A statement that is generally accepted and need not be proved. (also **assumption** or **axiom**)

Power A product of equal factors; for $216 = 6^3$, 216 is the third power of 6.

Principal Money on which interest is paid.

Principal square root (of a positive number) The positive square root.

Prism A three-dimensional figure whose bases are congruent polygons in parallel planes and whose faces are parallelograms.

Probability The ratio of the number of times a certain outcome can occur to the total possible outcomes.

Pyramid A three-dimensional figure whose base is a polygon and whose lateral faces are triangles.

Pythagorean triples Any three natural numbers a, b, and c satisfying the equation $a^2 + b^2 = c^2$.

Quadrant One of the four regions into which the coordinate axes separate the plane.

Quadratic direct variation A function of two variables, say x and y, defined by an equation of the form $y = kx^2$, $k \neq 0$.

Quadratic equation An equation of degree two that can be put into the form $Ax^2 + Bx + C = 0$ (A not 0).

Quadratic inverse variation A function of two variables, say x and y, defined by an equation of the form $x^2y = k$, $k \neq 0$.

Quadratic trinomial A three-term polynomial of degree two.

Quadrilateral A polygon having four sides.

Radical expression An expression containing a square root.

Radical sign The symbol $\sqrt{\ }$.

Radicand The expression below the radical sign.

Radius A line segment that joins the centre of a circle to any point in its circumference.

Random number table A table of the digits 0 through 9 in which each digit is equally likely to occur in any place in the table.

Random sample A sample in which each member of the population is equally likely to appear.

Range (of a relation) The set of the second elements of the ordered pairs of a relation.

Range (of statistical data) The difference between the smallest and largest values of a set of data.

Rational expression An expression that contains variables in the denominator.

Rational numbers The set of numbers that can be expressed as the quotient of two integers, the divisor not being zero.

Rationalizing the denominator The process of changing the denominator from an irrational number to a rational number.

Raw data Data that has not yet been organized.

Ray Part of a line extending without end in one direction only.

Real number Any number that is either a rational number or an irrational number.

Reciprocal The number which multiplies by a given number to yield a product of 1.

Rectangle A parallelogram with four right angles.

Rectangular prism A prism with two parallel congruent rectangular bases.

Rectangular pyramid A pyramid with a rectangular base.

Reflection A transformation that flips the points of a plane over a line.

Reflection line A line in which a figure is reflected (or mapped) onto its image.

Reflex angle An angle between 180° and 360°.

Regular polygon A polygon that is equilateral and equiangular.

Regular polyhedron A polyhedron whose faces are regular congruent polygons.

Relation A set of ordered pairs.

Relative frequency A ratio of the frequency of one element or interval of data to the total frequency.

Repeating decimal A decimal fraction in which, after a certain decimal place, one digit, or a set of digits in the same order, is repeated indefinitely. (also **periodic decimal**)

Replacement set (for a variable) The set of numbers which may be used to replace the variable.

Resultant vector The vector which is obtained by adding or subtracting two or more vectors.

Rhombus A quadrilateral with four congruent sides.

Right angle An angle measuring 90°.

Rotation A transformation in which the points of the plane are turned about a fixed point.

Rotational symmetry A figure has rotational symmetry if a tracing of the figure rotates onto itself in less than one full turn.

Sample A set of elements drawn from a population.

Scalar multiplication The multiplication of a vector quantity by a scalar quantity in order to change its magnitude or reverse its direction.

Scalar quantity A quantity with magnitude only.

Scale drawing A drawing of an object with all dimensions in proportion to corresponding actual dimensions.

Scale factor A number representing the amount by which the dimensions of an object are multiplied to get the dimensions of its image.

Scale ratio The ratio of the size of the enlarged or reduced image to the object in a scale drawing.

Scalene triangle A triangle with no congruent sides or angles.

Scatterplot A statistical graph displaying a two-variable set of data as a set of points on a coordinate grid.

Scientific notation A method of writing a number as the product of a power of ten and a number between one and ten.

Secant A line that contains a chord, as $\overleftrightarrow{AB}$.

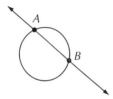

Sector (of a circle) A region bounded by an arc and two radii.

Sector angle An angle with its vertex at the centre of a circle and bounded by two radii. (also **central angle**)

Segment (of a circle) A region bounded by an arc and a chord.

Semicircle An arc which joins the endpoints of a diameter.

Set A group or collection of objects.

Shell A model of a solid whose interior is completely empty.

Similar figures Figures with the same shape but not necessarily the same size.

Sine For a given angle in a right-angled triangle, the ratio of the length of the opposite side to the length of the hypotenuse.

Skew lines Lines that are not parallel and do not intersect. The distance between any pair is defined by the length of the unique line that is perpendicular to both.

Slant height The height of a lateral face of a pyramid.

Slope-intercept form of a linear equation The equation of a straight line in the form $y = mx + b$, where m is the slope of the line and b is the y-intercept.

Slope formula The slope of a line is the ratio $\dfrac{y_1 - y_2}{x_1 - x_2}$ where (x_1, y_1) and (x_2, y_2) are points on the line.

Slope of a line The steepness of a line; the ratio of the rise of a line to its run.

Smoothing (of data) a method for removing extreme highs and lows in statistical data collected over time, by substituting the median of three consecutive values for each original value, excluding the first and last values.

Solid A three-dimensional figure whose inside is completely filled.

Solution set The set of values in the replacement set for a variable that make the sentence true.

Sphere The set of all points in space which are a given distance from a fixed point.

Square (geometry) A rectangle with four congruent sides.

Square (numeration) To raise a number to the second power.

Square root A number which, when multiplied by itself, results in the given number.

Standard form of a linear equation The equation of a straight line written in the form $Ax + By + C = 0$, where $A, B, C \in R$.

Statistics The study of methods of collecting and analysing data.

Stem-and-leaf graph An arrangement of data that facilitates the finding of the mean, median, and mode.

Straight angle An angle measuring $180°$.

Stratified sample A sample that randomly includes individuals from each of identified groups within the population in the same proportion as these groups appear in the population.

Subtend To be opposite to and to delimit, as chord AB or arc AB subtends $\angle APB$.

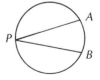

Supplementary angles Two angles that have a sum of $180°$.

Surface area The total area of the polygonal regions (faces) of a polyhedron.

System of equations A set of equations in the same variables.

Tangent (of a circle) A line in the same plane as the circle that has one, and only one, point in common with the circle. The common point is called the point of contact.

Tangent (trigonometry) For a given angle in a right-angled triangle, the ratio of the length of the opposite side to the length of the adjacent side.

Term A mathematical expression using numerals or variables or both to indicate a sum, difference, product, or quotient.

Tetrahedron A polygon with four triangular faces.

Theorem A statement that has been proved.

Theoretical probability The number of favourable outcomes divided by the number of possible outcomes.

Transformation A one-to-one mapping from the whole plane to the whole plane.

Transit An instrument equipped with a telescope, levels, and scales for measuring both vertical and horizontal angles.

Transversal A line crossing two or more lines.

Trapezoid A quadrilateral with one pair of opposite sides parallel.

Triangular prism A prism with two parallel, congruent, triangular bases.

Trigonometry An area of mathematical study involving the measurement of triangles.

Trinomial A polynomial consisting of three terms.

Trinomial square A three-term polynomial that is the product of squaring a binomial.

Unbiased sample A sample that gives a good representation of the group being studied.

Variable A letter used to represent an unknown quantity.

Vector quantity A quantity with both magnitude and direction.

Vector sum The vector which is obtained by adding two or more vectors.

Velocity Speed in a given direction.

Venn diagram A diagram used to show the relationship between two or more sets.

Weight Force downwards due to gravity.

Whole numbers The set of all natural numbers and zero. {0, 1, 2, 3,...}

x-axis The horizontal number line in a coordinate plane.

x-intercept The x-coordinate of a point where a graph crosses the x-axis.

y-axis The vertical number line in a coordinate plane.

y-intercept The y-coordinate of a point where a graph crosses the y-axis.

Answers to Exercises

Unit 1

Exercises, page 2
1. a. 3 **b.** 5 **c.** 1 **d.** $\frac{1}{2}$ **e.** $\frac{2}{3}$ **f.** 1 **g.** 0.2
h. 8.35 **2. a.** 2 **b.** 2 **c.** 3 **d.** 3 **e.** 2 **f.** 4
3. a. x **b.** a, b **c.** x, y **d.** m, n, r **e.** x, z **f.** r, s
4. a. 16 **b.** 3 **c.** 4 **d.** 5 **e.** 0 **f.** 17 **g.** 14
h. 5 **i.** 7 **j.** 4 **k.** 2 **l.** 1 **8. a.** $4s$ **b.** s^2
c. $2(l + w)$ **d.** lw **e.** bh **f.** $2(lw + lh + wh)$
g. $40r$ **h.** $0.02s$

Extra, page 3
a. $P = 3a$
$a = \frac{1}{3}P$
b. $C = 5p + 8$
$p = \frac{1}{5}C - \frac{8}{5}$
c. $t = \frac{d}{v}$
$d = tv$

Exercises, page 5
1. a. -7 **b.** 3 **c.** -10 **d.** 8 **e.** 6 **f.** 0
2. a. 7 **b.** -9 **c.** 0 **d.** 28 **e.** -16 **f.** -3
g. 14 **h.** -8 **i.** -8 **j.** 0 **3. a.** -5 **b.** 5 **c.** 7
d. -1 **e.** -3 **4.** positive **5.** negative **6. a.** 5
b. -5 **c.** -12 **d.** 4250 **e.** 58 **f.** 4 **g.** -3
h. 60 **i.** 450 **j.** 10 **k.** -60 **l.** 40 **m.** $-50\,000$
7. Answers will vary. **8. a.** -5 **b.** -12 **c.** -2
d. 6 **e.** -65 **f.** 27 **g.** -10 **h.** 13 **i.** -3
j. -15 **k.** 16 **l.** -3 **m.** -21 **n.** 32 **o.** -54
p. 35 **q.** 0 **r.** -60 **s.** -13 **t.** 3 **u.** -3
v. -7 **w.** 5 **x.** 5 **9. a.** -11 **b.** 24 **c.** -168
d. -4 **e.** 8 **f.** 72 **10. a.** -2 **b.** -5 **c.** 4
d. 3 **e.** 15 **f.** -12 **g.** 1 **h.** 240 **i.** 80 **j.** 18
k. -12 **l.** -12 **m.** -3 **n.** -8
11. a. $(-3509) + 8905 = 5396$
b. $468 \times 12 = 5616$ **c.** $2 \times 7 + 3 \times 2 = 20$
d. $4 \times 11 = 44$ **e.** $4 + 15 - 12 = 7$
f. $15 \times 8 - 5 \times 6 = 90$ **12. a.** 5 **b.** -14
c. 11 **d.** 9 **13. a.** $x \geq 0$ **b.** $x \leq 0$ **14. a.** 3
b. 1 **c.** 7 **d.** 15 **e.** 30 **f.** 10 **15. a.** 5 or -9
b. 7 or 3 **c.** 5 or -5 **d.** 3 or -4 **e.** -1 or -9
f. 4 or -4 **g.** 2 or -1

Extra, page 7
1. **2.**
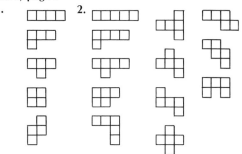

3. Answers will vary.

Exercises, page 8
1. a. 1 **b.** 32 **c.** 15 **d.** 4 **e.** 15 **f.** 4 **g.** 18
h. 8 **i.** 0 **j.** 2 **k.** 22 **l.** 7 **m.** 5 **n.** -27
o. -5 **p.** 0 **q.** 3 **r.** 3 **2. a.** -9 **b.** -13
c. -29 **d.** -2 **e.** -4 **f.** -17 **g.** -46 **h.** -5
i. -47 **j.** -5 **k.** 10 **l.** -26 **m.** 20 **n.** -72
o. 24 **p.** 8 **3. a.** -5 **b.** 15 **c.** 26 **d.** 5
e. 14 **f.** 5 **g.** 11 **h.** -1 **i.** -8 **4. a.** 1 **b.** 3
c. 80 **5. a.** $(3 + 5 - 8 \times 2 + 7) \div 2 = -\frac{1}{2}$
b. $\frac{7 - (3 - 2)}{4 + 8 \div 4} = 1$
c. $16 + 12 \times (18 - 20) = -8$
d. $5 \times (m + n) - 2 \times m = 30$ or
$5 \times m + (n - 2) \times m = 30$
e. $3 \times p + 2 \times (p - r) - q = 0$

Using the Calculator, page 9
1. 9 **2.** 2 **3.** 8 **4.** 3 **5.** 7

Exercises, page 12
1. a. \$2.89 **b.** \$0.63 **c.** \$1.53 **2. a.** 0.37
b. 0.375 **c.** -0.3125 **d.** $0.\overline{2}$ **e.** $-1.1\overline{6}$
f. $2.\overline{142\,857}$ **g.** $-3.\overline{615\,384}$ **h.** $4.708\overline{3}$ **i.** $-4.\overline{5}$
j. $-6.5\overline{1}$ **3. a.** $\frac{3}{20}$ **b.** $-\frac{1}{125}$ **c.** $\frac{3}{80}$ **d.** $-\frac{29}{50}$
e. $1\frac{39}{100}$ **f.** $-4\frac{11}{40}$ **g.** $-15\frac{1}{1000}$ **h.** $12\frac{7}{20}$
i. $-4\frac{1}{80}$ **j.** $3\frac{37}{40}$ **4. a.** $\frac{1}{6}$ **b.** $\frac{7}{12}$ **c.** $-1\frac{1}{8}$ **d.** $3\frac{35}{36}$
e. $\frac{11}{30}$ **f.** $-\frac{2}{21}$ **g.** $-4\frac{1}{10}$ **h.** $-1\frac{5}{6}$ **5. a.** $-\frac{3}{10}$
b. $\frac{3}{14}$ **c.** 2 **d.** $-1\frac{23}{27}$ **e.** $\frac{7}{9}$ **f.** $2\frac{1}{4}$ **g.** $\frac{6}{25}$ **h.** $4\frac{3}{7}$
6. a. $\frac{1}{40}$ **b.** 2 **c.** 5 **d.** $-\frac{7}{24}$ **e.** $1\frac{17}{35}$ **f.** $\frac{5}{9}$ **g.** 3
h. $6\frac{3}{4}$ **i.** 4 **7. a.** $1\frac{3}{10}$ **b.** $\frac{1}{4}$ **c.** $12\frac{31}{50}$ **d.** $28\frac{7}{20}$
e. $-1\frac{1}{4}$ **f.** $2\frac{9}{10}$ **g.** $1\frac{4}{5}$ **h.** 40 **i.** $\frac{1}{6}$ **8. a.** $\frac{7}{12}$
b. $1\frac{1}{12}$ **c.** $\frac{1}{12}$ **d.** $1\frac{1}{3}$ **e.** $5\frac{1}{3}$ **9. a.** $1\frac{3}{5}$ **b.** $-1\frac{1}{2}$
c. $-\frac{7}{10}$ **d.** $1\frac{11}{15}$ **e.** $\frac{21}{44}$ **10. a.** $\frac{4}{9}$ **b.** $\frac{1}{9}$ **c.** $\frac{9}{11}$
d. $\frac{29}{99}$ **e.** $\frac{385}{999}$ **f.** $-\frac{67}{99}$ **g.** $1\frac{39}{110}$ **h.** $-\frac{2713}{4995}$
i. $3\frac{224}{495}$ **j.** -1 **11. a.** 421.875 cm^3 **b.** 22.12 m^2

Review, page 13
1. a. $7; m$ **b.** $-2; x, y$ **c.** $1; a, b, c$ **d.** $-0.3; p$
e. $1; x, y$ **2. a.** 7 **b.** 3 **c.** 0 **d.** -7 **e.** 4
f. -9 **3. a.** -39 **b.** $\frac{7}{8}$ **c.** -15 **d.** $\frac{3}{32}$
e. -4.4 **f.** $1\frac{2}{7}$ **4. a.** -5 **b.** -4.2 **c.** -5.3

434

d. -0.2 **e.** $-\frac{1}{8}$ **f.** $-\frac{1}{2}$ **g.** $\frac{1}{10}$ **h.** $-1\frac{2}{5}$ **i.** $\frac{21}{100}$
j. $-8\frac{2}{7}$ **5. a.** 0.017 **b.** -0.072 **c.** $0.2\overline{7}$
d. $-2.\overline{27}$ **e.** $0.3\overline{1}$ **6. a.** $1\frac{19}{25}$ **b.** $-\frac{3}{40}$ **c.** $\frac{6}{11}$
d. $\frac{53}{165}$ **e.** $-4\frac{4}{11}$

Exercises, page 15

1. a. commutative; 21 **b.** associative; 38
c. distributive; 150 **d.** commutative; 17
e. commutative; 46.5 **f.** distributive; 7
g. associative; 640 **h.** commutative; 3.15
i. associative; 8 **j.** commutative; 17 **2. a.** 78
b. 340 **c.** 110 **d.** 12 **e.** 10 **f.** 14 **g.** 18
h. $\frac{7}{10}$ **i.** 12 **j.** 45 **3. a.** 3 **b.** $\frac{2}{25}$ **c.** 9
d. $-9\frac{1}{2}$ **e.** $\frac{1}{6}$ **f.** $-6\frac{1}{4}$ **g.** $2\frac{1}{52}$ **h.** 2 **i.** $-\frac{1}{10}$
4. a. -6 **b.** $3\frac{1}{2}$ **c.** $\frac{51}{70}$
d. $\frac{1}{2}$ **e.** 22 **f.** 15 **g.** 7 **h.** -30 **i.** $\frac{1}{2}$ **j.** $\frac{2}{5}$

5. a. i. distributive **ii.** commutative
b. iii. distributive **c. iv.** distributive
v. commutative **d. vi.** commutative
vii. distributive and commutative

Application, page 17

1. 0.0825; $31.35 **2.** 0.185; $1 422
3. 0.065; $272.75 **4.** 750 g for $3.45
5. 369 g for $3.29 **6.** 200 mL for $1.69

7. 325 mL for $2.09 **8.** $68\frac{3}{4}$% **9.** 0.397 **10.** 40
11. 60%

Exercises, page 18

1. a. -3 **b.** 2 **c.** 5 **d.** -0.4 **e.** $-4k$ **f.** $\frac{3}{7}$
g. $0.8m$ **h.** $5.9j$ **i.** 0 **j.** 1 **k.** $-xz - y$
l. $3x - 7$ **m.** $2xy + 5$ **n.** $\frac{3}{mn}$ **o.** $-1.3a - b$
2. a. $\frac{1}{a}$ **b.** $2\frac{2}{3}$ **c.** $\frac{k}{a}$ **d.** $-\frac{1}{9}$ **e.** $\frac{2}{b}$ **f.** $\frac{2}{7j}$
g. $\frac{1}{-2 + b}$ **h.** $1\frac{32}{67}$ **i.** $-\frac{9}{13}$ **j.** $\frac{1}{1 + 4k}$
k. $\frac{1}{m + 5n}$ **l.** $\frac{1}{mn - 7j}$ **m.** $\frac{1}{6ab + 7c}$
n. $-\frac{1}{3xy}$ **o.** $\frac{1}{4a}$ **p.** $-xy$ **q.** $-\frac{2}{3ab}$ **r.** $\frac{y}{5x}$
s. no reciprocal **t.** $-\frac{4y + 9}{13x}$ **3. a.** negative
b. negative **4. a.** $-xy$ **b.** $-2rt$ **c.** $4b$ **d.** m
e. r **f.** $3x$ **5. a.** -8 **b.** 3 **c.** $\frac{2}{3}$
d. -0.75 **e.** $-1\frac{3}{8}$ **f.** 5.9 **g.** $\frac{1}{7}$ **h.** $1\frac{1}{2}$ **i.** $-3\frac{1}{3}$
j. $\frac{1}{5}$ **k.** $1\frac{223}{777}$ **l.** $\frac{1000}{5999}$ **m.** $\frac{1}{5}$ **n.** $\frac{1}{2}$ **o.** -2
p. $1\frac{1}{4}$ **q.** $\frac{3}{4}$ **r.** $\frac{1}{9}$

Extra, page 19
1. 2 560 000 m^3 **2.** 3720 houses

Exercises, page 21

1. a. 8^5 **b.** 6^7 **c.** $(-2)^5$ **d.** 3^2 **2. a.** 9; 2; 9×9
b. -4; 5; $(-4)(-4)(-4)(-4)(-4)$
c. 6; 4; $-(6 \times 6 \times 6 \times 6)$
d. -3; 4; $(-3)(-3)(-3)(-3)$ **e.** 7; 3; $7 \times 7 \times 7$
3. a. 32 **b.** 256 **c.** -243 **d.** 1 **e.** 0 **f.** 1
g. -16 **h.** $\frac{1}{1000}$ **i.** -1 **j.** -1 **k.** $\frac{1}{3}$ **l.** $\frac{1}{49}$
m. 5 **n.** $-\frac{1}{4}$ **o.** $\frac{1}{9}$ **p.** $-\frac{1}{9}$ **q.** 1 **r.** $-\frac{1}{512}$
s. $\frac{1}{625}$ **t.** $-\frac{1}{27}$ **4. a.** 2^3 **b.** 3^3 **c.** 5^2 **d.** 10^2
e. 7^2 **f.** 6^3 **g.** 2^5 **h.** 5^3 **i.** 10^4 or 100^2 **j.** 10^5
5. a. -5^{-2} **b.** 2^{-3} **c.** 10^{-2}
d. 10^{-6} or 100^{-3} or 1000^{-2} **e.** 5^{-4} or 25^{-2}

6. 823 543 **7. a.** 17 **b.** 1100 **c.** $4\frac{1}{8}$ **d.** 200
e. $2\frac{1}{4}$ **f.** -1 **g.** -25 **h.** $\frac{1}{9}$ **i.** $\frac{17}{72}$ **j.** $\frac{1}{121}$ **k.** $\frac{1}{4}$
l. $\frac{1}{1000}$

Extra, page 21
1. $\frac{16}{25}, \frac{256}{625}$ **2.** $\left(\frac{4}{5}\right)^n$ **3.** about 20

Exercises, page 23

1. a. x^{10} **b.** m^{10} **c.** r^8 **d.** a^{14} **e.** y^{12} **f.** z^9
g. n^4 **h.** m^6 **2. a.** x^5 **b.** a^5 **c.** m^5 **d.** z^5 **e.** r
f. a^2 **g.** 1 **h.** b^{10} **3. a.** a^6 **b.** x^{10} **c.** b^8
d. z^{12} **e.** m^9 **f.** y^{14} **g.** 1 **h.** b^{12} **4. a.** s^5t^5
b. m^8n^8 **c.** $16a^4$ **d.** $125b^3$ **e.** $16x^4z^4$ **f.** $a^7b^7c^7$
g. 1 **h.** $25x^2y^2z^2$ **i.** $\frac{m^4}{n^4}$ **j.** $\frac{729a^6}{b^6}$ **k.** $\frac{8m^3}{27n^3}$
l. $\frac{x^3m^3}{27a^3b^3}$ **5. a.** 243 **b.** 64 **c.** 51 **d.** $-2\frac{2}{5}$
e. $\frac{9}{40}$ **8. a.** xy^{-1} **b.** m^3n^{-2} **c.** $2x^2y^{-4}z^{-3}$
d. $2a^2bc^{-3}$ **e.** $30m^{-3}$ **f.** x^3 **g.** $m^{-3}n^2$
h. $5x^2y^{-3}z^{-1}$ **9. a.** $\frac{b^2c}{a^3}$ **b.** $\frac{x^2}{y^3z^5}$ **c.** $\frac{x^4}{y}$
d. $\frac{n^2x^2}{m^3y}$ **10. a.** $8a^8b^5$ **b.** $225x^4y^{14}$ **c.** $8a^{17}b^{11}$
d. $-4a^7b^{20}$ **e.** $\frac{x^9}{y^6}$ **f.** $\frac{72y^{21}}{x}$ **g.** $-\frac{b^6}{27a^{12}}$
h. $\frac{2x^3}{y^5}$ **i.** $\frac{9a^5c^9}{b^2}$ **j.** $\frac{2}{y^5}$ **k.** m^7n **l.** $\frac{a^{10}b}{c^4}$
11. a. $\frac{8a^8}{9b}$ **b.** $-\frac{b^6}{27a^{12}}$ **c.** $\frac{256x^{11}}{z^5}$ **d.** $\frac{9}{t^4}$
e. $\frac{4y^2}{9x^2}$ **f.** $\frac{x^6z^6}{y^3}$ **g.** $\frac{27b^5}{2a^2}$ **h.** $\frac{z^2}{9x^2}$
12. a. $6\frac{1}{4}$ **b.** 36 **c.** $\frac{8}{9}$ **d.** 3 **e.** $\frac{9}{16}$ **f.** $1\frac{1}{9}$

435

g. $\frac{8}{27}$ h. 2 i. $\frac{5}{6}$ j. $1\frac{1}{2}$ 13. a. $135a^2b^2$

b. $\frac{12m^2}{n^2}$ c. $19x^2$ 14. a. $\frac{30a^3}{b^3}$ b. $20s^3$

Extra, page 25
1. 0.000 000 01 2. 0.0081 3. 0.000 002 56
4. 0.000 002 56 5. 0.000 000 01 6. 0.000 729
7. 0.000 064 8. 0.0256 9. 0.000 000 000 000 1
To find the product, ignore the decimal points and multiply the bases. Then, move the decimal point to the left, the number of places being equal to the power of the product.

Exercises, page 27
1. a. 5.9×10^3 b. 6.27×10^{-3} c. 3.6×10^7
d. 4.9×10^{-2} e. 9.6×10^{-1} f. 5.9×10 g. 3.5
h. 6.2×10^{10} i. 3.8×10^{-10} j. 4.6×10^5
k. 3.8×10^{-6} l. 3.5×10^{-6} m. 4×10^5
n. 3.7×10^{-2} o. 7.1×10^{-2} 2. a. 1 100 000
b. 0.000 489 c. 210 000 d. 0.034 11 e. 9.6
f. 88.1 g. 0.0474 h. 86 000 i. 0.000 000 287
3. a. 2 b. 2 c. 3 d. 3 e. 3 f. 3 g. 3 h. 4
i. 3 4. a. 24 000 000 b. 15.6 c. 0.01 d. 2300
e. 0.000 27 5. a. 3×10^9 b. 3.2×10^{-10}
c. 4×10^3 d. 2×10^{-6} e. 3.5×10^6
6. a. 4; 7; 11 b. 4; 2; 2 c. -3; 1.75; 2; -1
d. 1.26; 5; 2.8; -2; 7; 4.5; 6 7. a. 6×10^5
b. 8×10^{-5} c. 2×10^4 d. 3×10^{-1}
e. 3×10^5 f. 8×10^{-3} g. 4.2×10^7
h. 3.0×10^{-2} i. 3.8×10^{-5} j. 5.3×10^{-1}
8. a. 8.5×10^7 b. 1.9×10^5 c. 4.4×10^{-6}
d. 3.8×10^{-2} e. 5.9×10^2 f. 9.1×10^{-2}
g. 3.75×10^2 h. 1.3×10^{-3} i. 2.3×10^{-3}
j. 2.9×10^{10} 9. a. 1×10^{27} b. 1.3×10^9

Review, page 29
1. a. 7; $-\frac{1}{7}$ b. -0.75; $1\frac{1}{3}$ c. $1\frac{2}{7}$; $-\frac{7}{9}$ d. $-a$; $\frac{1}{a}$
e. $-xy$; $\frac{1}{xy}$ f. $-\frac{3}{8}$; $2\frac{2}{3}$ g. $3\frac{1}{3}$; $-\frac{3}{10}$ h. $-8x$; $\frac{1}{8x}$
i. $-\frac{3m}{n}$; $\frac{n}{3m}$ j. $-0.8x$; $\frac{5}{4x}$ 2. a. -3 b. -28
c. 21 3. a. 7; 6 b. -3; 3 c. 2; -5 4. $(-2)^6$
5. a. 81 b. 16 c. -25 d. $\frac{1}{49}$ e. $-\frac{1}{27}$
6. a. 6^2 b. 2^5 c. $\left(\frac{1}{10}\right)^2$ d. $\left(\frac{1}{5}\right)^2$ e. 0.1^3
7. a. x^2 b. m^2 c. $\frac{1}{x^6}$ d. $2x^4$ e. x^5 f. x^7
g. x^7y^3 h. a^{15} i. a^6b^{12} j. $81a^8$ k. $\frac{4}{9}$ l. $24x^{11}$
m. $\frac{3m^5}{n^5}$ n. $-30a^2b^3c^2$ o. $\frac{75}{x^5}$ 8. a. $3m^7n^{-4}$
b. $x^{-4}y^{-2}$ 9. a. 3.6×10^4 b. 1.8×10
c. 5×10^{-5} d. 3.6×10^{-6} e. 4.6×10

f. 3.93×10^{20} 10. a. 0.0037 b. 8 600 000
c. 0.43 d. 0.000 86 e. 43 900 f. 0.000 000 09
11. a. 1×10^4 b. 2×10^2 c. 4.5×10^6
d. 1.5×10^{10} e. 1×10^{-5} f. 5×10^{-4}

Problem Solving 1, page 30
1. a. 1.7 L b. \$11.98 2. 900 cm³ 3. 24 m/s
4. 68 m 5. a. 0.25 m b. 1 m c. 6.2 m
6. 19.4%

Problem Solving 2, page 31
1. 5×10^2 s 2. 9.45×10^{12} km
3. 4.1×10^{13} km 4. 4.9×10^{15} km
5. 1.6×10^5 light years 6. 4.0 people/km²
7. a. 9.4×10^8 km b. 1×10^5 km/h
8. a. 1.1×10^{21} m³ b. 6.0×10^{24} kg
c. 7.7×10^{22} kg 9. 3.7×10^7 beats
10. 2×10^{25} molecules 11. 1.2×10^7 pens

Using the Calculator, page 32
1. Take the square root of the number.
2. Take the cube root of the number.

Application, page 33
1. a. \$127.63 b. \$146.93 c. \$161.05 d. \$176.23
2. a. \$128.01; \$128.20; \$128.34
b. \$148.02; \$148.59; \$148.98
c. \$162.89; \$163.86; \$164.53
d. \$179.08; \$180.61; \$181.67
3. a. about 14.2 years b. about 9 years
c. about 7.3 years d. about 6.1 years

Historical Note, page 34
The older systems were incomplete because the variables were not specified. For example, $5x^3$ and $5g^3$ would both be written as $\overset{3}{5}$. Also, it would be impossible to denote terms with more than one variable such as $2xy$.

Extra, page 34
When the pieces are joined together, there is a space along the diagonal. The area of the space is responsible for the extra unit.

Test, page 35
1. a. -20 b. 13.2 c. -48 d. 25.8 e. 55
f. 416 2. a. 0.08 b. -0.04 c. 0.4375 d. $8.6\overline{3}$
e. $0.4\overline{6}$ 3. a. $3\frac{17}{25}$ b. $\frac{11}{200}$ c. $\frac{38}{99}$ d. $\frac{103}{330}$
e. $87\frac{5}{11}$ 4. a. -8 b. $-1.3x$ c. $\frac{1}{2}y$
d. $-4b + 5d$ 5. a. $1\frac{2}{5}$ b. $-\frac{3}{14}$ c. $\frac{1}{x}$ d. $\frac{2}{3}$
e. $\frac{2y}{3x}$ 6. a. x^{13} b. $6x^6$ c. $-90a^4b^2$ d. $\frac{6}{x}$
e. $9x^3$ f. $\frac{1}{27a^3}$ g. $\frac{3x^3}{2y^2}$ h. $\frac{3y^4}{2x^3z^3}$ i. $9a^4b^2c^6$

j. $\frac{3}{a^3}$ **k.** $27y^6$ **l.** $-8x^{16}y^9$ **7. a.** 3 **b.** 6.8×10^{-3}
c. 4.23×10^6 **d.** 8.1×10^{-9} **8. a.** 4500
b. 0.000 507 **c.** 0.000 000 064 **d.** 39 520
9. a. 9.0×10^6 **b.** 1.3×10^3 **c.** 7.0×10^{-2}
d. 1.3×10^{10} **10.** 2×10^3 h

Unit 2

Exercises, page 37

1. a, d, g **2. a.** 4 **b.** -5 **c.** 12 **d.** 6 **e.** -9
f. 10 **g.** 11 **h.** -1 **i.** 13 **j.** 3 **k.** -8 **l.** -14
m. -7 **n.** 15 **o.** -20 **p.** 16 **3. a.** 14
b. -30 **c.** 88 **d.** -35 **e.** -1 **f.** 1 **g.** -2.7
h. -0.005 **i.** 11 **j.** 1 **k.** 4 **l.** 3 **m.** 14
n. -12 **o.** -6 **p.** -2 **q.** -2 **r.** 17
4. 1.2 m $\times$ 1.2 m **5.** 300 tiles **6.** 37 m $\times$ 37 m
7. a. 6 **b.** 5 **c.** 1 **d.** 12 **e.** 28 **f.** 8 **g.** 2
h. 1 **i.** 5 **8.** 1.35 s **9.** 13.29 m/s **10. a.** x
b. $-x$ **11. a.** $-x$ **b.** x **12. a.** $x < 0$
b. $x > 0$ **c.** $x > 10$ **d.** $x < 10$

Extra, page 38

1. 3 **2.** 8 **3.** 10 **4.** 15 **5.** 49 **6.** 14 **7.** 17
8. 2500

Using the Computer, page 39

1. 13.416 **2.** line 150 **3. a.** 1.414 **b.** 4.472
c. 6.708 **d.** 8.544 **e.** 10.392 **f.** 11.180 **g.** 14.142
h. 22.361 **4. a.** $3\sqrt{15}$ **b.** $8\sqrt{21}$ **c.** $-126\sqrt{3}$
d. $40\sqrt{2}$ **e.** 200 **f.** $-120\sqrt{35}$ **g.** $126\sqrt{33}$
h. $-44\sqrt{6}$ **i.** $5\sqrt{5}$ **j.** 30 **k.** -10 **l.** $5\sqrt{5}$
m. $-6\sqrt{70}$ **n.** 180 **o.** $-150\sqrt{11}$ **p.** 10
q. -20 **r.** 2 **5. a.** 2.00 **b.** 2.24 **c.** 4.24
d. 2.20 **e.** 30.00 **f.** 18.00 **g.** 0.11 **6. a.** $10\sqrt{3}$
b. 10 **c.** $\dfrac{2}{5\sqrt{3}}$ **d.** $\dfrac{2\sqrt{5}}{\sqrt{6}}$

Exercises, page 40

1. a. rational **b.** irrational **c.** rational
d. rational **e.** irrational **f.** rational **g.** rational
h. irrational **i.** rational **j.** irrational
2. a. irrational **b.** rational **c.** irrational
d. rational **e.** rational **f.** irrational
g. irrational **h.** rational **i.** irrational **j.** rational
3. a. 0.5 **b.** irrational **c.** irrational **d.** 0.6
e. 0.9 **f.** irrational **g.** irrational **h.** 1.2 **i.** 0.3
j. irrational **4.** Answers will vary. **5. a.** 3.65
b. 7.35 **c.** 10.54 **d.** 8.41 **e.** 24.22 **f.** -2.46
g. 1.92 **h.** 2.21 **i.** 7.34 **6. a.** 12.71 **b.** 11.76
c. 11.53 **d.** 27 **e.** 50.35 **7. 1.** 1 is eventually
reached for all positive numbers entered because

the exponent $\left(\dfrac{1}{2}\right)^n$ approaches 0 as n increases.

Any non-zero number raised to a power of 0
equals 1.

8. a. $360x^4y^4\sqrt{2y}$ **b.** $14ab^3c^2\sqrt{3ab}$ **c.** $\dfrac{m^7n^3\sqrt{mp}}{p^2}$

Extra, page 43

1. 600 **2.** 0.0070 **3.** 800 000 **4.** 0.000 75
5. 660 **6.** 6100

Exercises, page 44

1.

		R	$\overline{Q}$	Q	Z	W	N
a.	6	Yes	No	Yes	Yes	Yes	Yes
b.	$\sqrt{5}$	Yes	Yes	No	No	No	No
c.	$\frac{7}{8}$	Yes	No	Yes	No	No	No
d.	$\sqrt{100}$	Yes	No	Yes	Yes	Yes	Yes
e.	$3\frac{1}{5}$	Yes	No	Yes	No	No	No
f.	-7.6	Yes	No	Yes	No	No	No
g.	0	Yes	No	Yes	Yes	No	No
h.	$\sqrt{48}$	Yes	Yes	No	No	No	No
i.	8.323 232	Yes	No	Yes	No	No	No
j.	0.312 131 4 ...	Yes	Yes	No	No	No	No
k.	4.876 4	Yes	No	Yes	No	No	No
l.	4.831 579 2 ...	Yes	Yes	No	No	No	No
m.	$\frac{\sqrt{5}}{2}$	Yes	Yes	No	No	No	No
n.	-1	Yes	No	Yes	Yes	No	No
o.	-12	Yes	No	Yes	Yes	No	No
p.	-4.6	Yes	No	Yes	No	No	No
q.	$-\sqrt{2}$	Yes	Yes	No	No	No	No
r.	$-0.\overline{12}$	Yes	No	Yes	No	No	No

2. a. T **b.** F **c.** F **d.** T **e.** T **f.** T **g.** T
h. F **i.** T **j.** F
3. No. A calculator cannot display an irrational
number exactly because an irrational number
never terminates. It goes on forever.
4. Only the square roots of negative numbers are
not real numbers. The square roots of all positive
integers are real numbers.
5. 0

Review, page 45

1. a. 4.47 **b.** 8.66 **c.** 7.28 **d.** 30.00 **e.** 8.25
2. a. 16 **b.** 11 **c.** 28 **d.** -15 **e.** 19 **f.** 30
g. 4 **h.** -3 **i.** 7 **3. a.** 10 **b.** 5 **c.** 7 **d.** 10
e. 6 **f.** $\sqrt{70}$ **4. a.** irrational **b.** rational
c. irrational **d.** rational **e.** rational
f. irrational **5. a.** 0.6 **b.** 1.5 **c.** 2.0 **d.** 6.2
e. 7.8 **f.** 1.0 **6. a.** $\sqrt{35}$ **b.** $\sqrt{3}$ **c.** $-4\sqrt{10}$
d. $24\sqrt{6}$ **e.** $-60\sqrt{3}$ **f.** $19\sqrt{23}$ **g.** $-2\sqrt{21}$

h. $2\sqrt{2}$ **i.** $\dfrac{2}{\sqrt{2}}$

Exercises, page 46

1. a. 25 **b.** 49 **c.** x^2 **d.** z^2 **e.** x^6 **f.** y^{10} **g.** a^4
h. $9b^2$ **i.** $4b^{10}$ **j.** $9a^2c^2$ **k.** $100b^4$ **l.** m^4n^2
m. $a^6b^2c^4$ **n.** $4x^2y^4$ **o.** $25m^6n^4$ **p.** $a^2b^6c^2$
q. $16s^6t^{10}u^2$ **r.** $121m^2n^4$ **s.** $49u^6v^2w^2$ **t.** $36r^4s^4t^2$
2. a. 9 **b.** 11 **c.** a **d.** x **e.** m^2 **f.** p^3 **g.** $2b$
h. $3m^4$ **i.** $10r^3$ **j.** $6m^5$ **k.** a^2b^3 **l.** x^4y
m. mn^5p^6 **n.** $4xy$ **o.** $5a^3b$ **p.** $12s^2t$ **q.** $7x^4y^3$

r. $9m^5n^4p^2$ **s.** $11uvw$ **t.** $15r^4u^5$ **3. a.** $\sqrt{18}$
b. $\sqrt{20}$ **c.** $\sqrt{12}$ **d.** $\sqrt{150}$ **e.** $\sqrt{160}$ **f.** $\sqrt{180}$
g. $\sqrt{300}$ **h.** $\sqrt{90}$ **i.** $\sqrt{63}$ **j.** $\sqrt{275}$ **k.** $\sqrt{48}$
l. $\sqrt{99}$ **m.** $\sqrt{216}$ **n.** $\sqrt{125}$ **o.** $\sqrt{98}$
4. a. $2\sqrt{10}$ **b.** $5\sqrt{3}$ **c.** $4\sqrt{5}$ **d.** $5\sqrt{2}$ **e.** $6\sqrt{2}$
f. $2\sqrt{3}$ **g.** $3\sqrt{5}$ **h.** $3\sqrt{10}$ **i.** $3\sqrt{11}$ **j.** $4\sqrt{11}$
5. a. $\sqrt{9x}$ **b.** $\sqrt{4y}$ **c.** $\sqrt{5x^2}$ **d.** $\sqrt{45x}$
e. $\sqrt{x^2y}$ **f.** $\sqrt{y^5}$ **g.** $\sqrt{x^2y^7}$ **h.** $\sqrt{9x^3y}$ **i.** $\sqrt{x^3y^4}$
j. $\sqrt{x^5y}$ **k.** $\sqrt{300m^3n^5p}$ **l.** $\sqrt{50a^2b^5c^7}$
6. a. $5\sqrt{x}$ **b.** $6\sqrt{y}$ **c.** $y\sqrt{7}$ **d.** $x\sqrt{y}$ **e.** $a^3\sqrt{11}$
f. $m^3n^2\sqrt{p}$ **g.** $ab^2c\sqrt{ab}$ **h.** $3x\sqrt{2xy}$ **i.** $5xy^3\sqrt{3}$
j. $6x^2\sqrt{2xy}$ **k.** $2xy^2\sqrt{5z}$ **l.** $30mn\sqrt{n}$
m. $3x^2y^3\sqrt{2xy}$ **n.** $-10a^2bc^2\sqrt{3b}$ **o.** $35rst^2\sqrt{rt}$
p. $32x^2y^2z^2\sqrt{2xy}$ **7. a.** $4\sqrt{3}$ **b.** $10\sqrt{2}$
c. $18\sqrt{10}$ **d.** 40 **e.** $-24\sqrt{7}$ **f.** $105\sqrt{2}$
g. $x\sqrt{y}$ **h.** $15mn^2\sqrt{m}$ **i.** $x^2y^3\sqrt{x}$
8. a. $360x^4y^4\sqrt{2y}$ **b.** $14ab^3c^2\sqrt{3ab}$ **c.** $\dfrac{m^7n^3\sqrt{m}}{p\sqrt{p}}$

Using the Calculator, page 47
1. 3 **2.** 2 **3.** 7 **4.** 6 **5.** 10 **6.** 5 **7.** 8 **8.** 11

Exercises, page 48
1. a. $\dfrac{\sqrt{5}}{5}$ **b.** $\dfrac{\sqrt{2}}{2}$ **c.** $\dfrac{3\sqrt{7}}{7}$ **d.** $\dfrac{2\sqrt{5}}{5}$
e. $\dfrac{\sqrt{10}}{10}$ **f.** $\dfrac{t\sqrt{3}}{3}$ **g.** $\dfrac{2\sqrt{6m}}{3m}$ **h.** $\dfrac{\sqrt{6a}}{6}$
i. $\dfrac{r\sqrt{5}}{5}$ **j.** $\dfrac{\sqrt{3mn}}{n}$ **2. a.** $\dfrac{2\sqrt{15}}{5}$ **b.** $\dfrac{3\sqrt{2}}{2}$
c. $\dfrac{\sqrt{130}}{20}$ **d.** $\dfrac{\sqrt{6}}{6}$ **e.** $5\sqrt{3}$ **f.** $\dfrac{4\sqrt{7}}{7}$ **g.** $\dfrac{\sqrt{2}}{6}$
h. $9\sqrt{3}$ **i.** $\sqrt{3}$ **j.** $\dfrac{\sqrt{14}}{2}$ **3. a.** 1
b. $2\sqrt{10}$ **c.** $\dfrac{40\sqrt{21}}{21}$ **d.** $\dfrac{3\sqrt{2}}{5}$ **e.** $\dfrac{4\sqrt{10}}{15}$
f. $\dfrac{5\sqrt{10}}{14}$ **g.** $\dfrac{3\sqrt{3}}{14}$ **h.** $\dfrac{3\sqrt{3}}{5}$ **i.** $\dfrac{8\sqrt{5}}{25}$ **j.** $\dfrac{2\sqrt{7}}{7}$
k. $\dfrac{9\sqrt{10}}{10}$ **l.** $\dfrac{4\sqrt{6}}{3}$ **m.** $\sqrt{2}$ **n.** $\dfrac{\sqrt{5}}{3}$ **o.** $\dfrac{\sqrt{10}}{4}$
4. a. $\dfrac{3\sqrt{2xy}}{y}$ **b.** $\dfrac{5\sqrt{6ab}}{2b}$ **c.** $\dfrac{3\sqrt{y}}{y}$ **d.** $\dfrac{2a\sqrt{7c}}{c^2}$
e. $\dfrac{5\sqrt{2mn}}{n}$ **f.** $\dfrac{\sqrt{6x}}{5y}$ **g.** $\dfrac{\sqrt{3xy}}{2x}$ **h.** $\dfrac{\sqrt{2xy}}{2y}$
i. $\dfrac{3\sqrt{x}}{5}$ **j.** $\dfrac{14y\sqrt{x}}{9x}$ **5. a.** $\dfrac{3\sqrt{5}}{10}$ **b.** $\dfrac{3\sqrt{2}}{2}$
c. $\dfrac{2\sqrt{7}}{7}$ **d.** $\dfrac{2\sqrt{6}}{3}$ **e.** $\dfrac{5\sqrt{30}}{18}$ **f.** $-4\sqrt{30}$
g. $-\dfrac{9\sqrt{6}}{16}$ **h.** $\dfrac{36\sqrt{35}}{25}$ **6. a.** $\dfrac{\sqrt{6}}{2}$ **b.** $\dfrac{\sqrt{6}}{8}$
c. $\sqrt{6}$

Extra, page 49
The doubling, addition of one and addition of the original number squared gives the following perfect square: $2x + 1 + x^2$, where x is the original number. This factors to give $(x + 1)(x + 1)$. Clearly, the square root is $x + 1$. When one is subtracted from $x + 1$, the original number is the result.

Exercises, page 50
1. b, c, e, f, g **2.** Answers will vary. **a.** $\sqrt{7}, 2\sqrt{7}$,
$3\sqrt{7}$ **b.** $\sqrt{2}, 2\sqrt{2}, 3\sqrt{2}$ **c.** $\sqrt{x}, 2\sqrt{x}, 3\sqrt{x}$
d. $3\sqrt{5x}, 4\sqrt{5x}, 5\sqrt{5x}$ **e.** $-\sqrt{mn}, 2\sqrt{mn}, 3\sqrt{mn}$
3. a. $9\sqrt{3}$ **b.** $4\sqrt{2}$ **c.** $-3\sqrt{7}$ **d.** $-3\sqrt{3}$
e. $-7\sqrt{11}$ **f.** $-3\sqrt{y}$ **g.** $8\sqrt{x} - 3\sqrt{z}$
h. $32\sqrt{6} + 5\sqrt{5}$ **i.** $-4\sqrt{x}$ **j.** $3\sqrt{b} + \sqrt{x}$
k. $5\sqrt{r} + 5\sqrt{tr}$ **l.** $3\sqrt{2} + 4\sqrt{x}$ **4. a.** $14\sqrt{2}$
b. $10\sqrt{5}$ **c.** $6\sqrt{6}$ **d.** $10\sqrt{5}$ **e.** $10\sqrt{7}$
f. $10\sqrt{10}$ **g.** $21\sqrt{2}$ **h.** $9\sqrt{6}$ **i.** $12\sqrt{3}$
5. a. $7\sqrt{x}$ **b.** $3\sqrt{y}$ **c.** $2m\sqrt{2n}$ **d.** $(3b - 50)\sqrt{a}$
e. $10y\sqrt{2x} + 20y\sqrt{x}$ **f.** $6mn\sqrt{n}$
g. $(4x - 4)\sqrt{xy}$ **h.** $25a\sqrt{a} - 3ab\sqrt{3a}$
6. a. $8\sqrt{2} + 3\sqrt{7}$ **b.** $5\sqrt{5} + \sqrt{6}$
c. $\sqrt{3} + 9\sqrt{2}$ **d.** $7\sqrt{5} + 2\sqrt{6}$ **e.** $2\sqrt{11} + 9\sqrt{2}$
f. $12\sqrt{2} + 5\sqrt{7}$ **g.** $5\sqrt{3} - 2\sqrt{10}$
h. $3\sqrt{5} + 9\sqrt{2}$ **i.** $4\sqrt{11} - 2\sqrt{15}$
j. $\sqrt{5} + 11\sqrt{3}$ **k.** $-\sqrt{2} + 4\sqrt{7} - 2\sqrt{3}$
l. $3\sqrt{15} + 5\sqrt{6} + 5\sqrt{5}$ **7. a.** $5\sqrt{m} - \sqrt{n}$
b. $-\sqrt{7ab} + 8\sqrt{c}$ **c.** $8x\sqrt{y} + 3\sqrt{15b}$
d. $4b\sqrt{3ab} + 9c\sqrt{d}$ **e.** $10y\sqrt{2x} + 3x\sqrt{y}$
f. $8a\sqrt{5ab} + 10mn\sqrt{3n}$

Exercises, page 54
1. a. 5 **b.** 12 **c.** 5.7 **d.** 11.2 **e.** 4.8 **f.** 10.3
g. 14.1 **h.** 6.7 **i.** 87.7 **2. a.** 5 **b.** $\sqrt{13}$
c. $\sqrt{61}$ **3.** a, c, d, e **4. a.** 15.0 **b.** 6.3 **c.** 4.5
d. 15.2 **e.** 10.8 **f.** 0.6 **g.** 2.1 **h.** 7.7 **i.** 14.6
5. 7.3 m **6.** 7.7 m **7.** 2.2 m **8.** 304 km **9.** a, c
10. 23.7 cm

Historical Note, page 55
$$\begin{aligned} \text{area} &= 4\left[\frac{1}{2}ab\right] + (a - b)^2 \\ &= 2ab + a^2 + b^2 - 2ab \\ &= a^2 + b^2 \\ \therefore \ c^2 &= a^2 + b^2 \end{aligned}$$

Exercises, page 57
1. a. $AB = 4$, $CD = 3\sqrt{2}$
b. $EF = 4$, $GH = 2\sqrt{5}$
c. $IJ = \sqrt{53}$
2. a. 4.5 **b.** 8.1 **c.** 6.7 **d.** 2.0 **e.** 5.8
f. 6.4 **g.** 9.1 **h.** 5.0 **i.** 11.0

3. a. ABC = 19.1; $DEFG$ = 16.5
b. HIJ = 13.2; KLM = 19.1
4. a. 2.1 **b.** 5.6 **c.** 7.4 **d.** 2.8 **5.** 3 or 11

Historical Note, page 58
1. The errors are in rows 2, 9, 13, and 15.

Review, page 59
1. a. $3x\sqrt{x}$ **b.** $6m\sqrt{6mn}$ **c.** $-a^2\sqrt{3a}$
d. $3.7m^3n^2p\sqrt{mnp}$ **2. a.** $\sqrt{4a^2b}$ **b.** $\sqrt{175cd}$
c. $\sqrt{64k^4}$ **d.** $\sqrt{405ab^3c^2}$

3. a. $\dfrac{5\sqrt{2}}{2}$ **b.** $\dfrac{\sqrt{7kt}}{7t}$ **c.** $\dfrac{3\sqrt{3}}{4}$ **d.** $\sqrt{3}$

4. a. $3.5\sqrt{2}$ **b.** $4\sqrt{2}$ **c.** $8\sqrt{3}$ **d.** $6\sqrt{14}$
5. a. 6.4 **b.** 7.9 **c.** 1.4 **d.** 11.4 **e.** 5.0 **f.** 15.0
6. 448.2 cm **7.** 32.1
8. a.

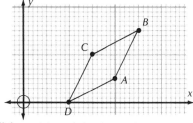

b. All four sides of the figure have length $\sqrt{5}$.

Problem Solving 3, page 60
1. a. 62.61 km/h **b.** 44.27 km/h **c.** 76.68 km/h
2. a. 44.72 km/h **b.** 31.62 km/h **c.** 54.77 km/h
3. 12.76 m; 25 m **4. a.** $135 **b.** $33.75
c. $21.60 **d.** $86.40 **5.** 80 km/h **6.** 118 km/h
7. a. 2 s **b.** 2.83 s **c.** 3.46 s **d.** 6.32 s
8. 0.25 m

Problem Solving 4, page 61
1. 123.8 m **2.** 60 m **3.** Yes **4.** 1.6 m **5.** 2.6 m
6. 9.5 km **7.** 39.4 m **8.** 2.8 km
9. 31.8 cm × 31.8 cm **10.** 37.4 cm

Test, page 62
1. a. 16 **b.** 11 **c.** -16 **d.** 11.5 **e.** -9.6 **f.** 5
2. a. 3 **b.** 4 **c.** 8 **3. a.** rational **b.** irrational
c. rational **d.** irrational **e.** rational **4. a.** 0.8
b. 1.3 **c.** 1.0 **d.** 8.8 **5. a.** $\sqrt{63}$ **b.** $\sqrt{320}$
c. $\sqrt{25x}$ **d.** $\sqrt{3x^3}$ **e.** $\sqrt{4x^2y^3}$ **6. a.** y^3

b. $5xy^2\sqrt{z}$ **c.** $5\sqrt{2}$ **d.** $7a^2\sqrt{2}$ **e.** $ab\sqrt{a}$ **f.** $\dfrac{\sqrt{5y}}{y}$

g. $\sqrt{3}$ **h.** $3\sqrt{2}$ **i.** $9\sqrt{2}$ **j.** $\dfrac{y\sqrt{3}}{3}$

7. a. 7.6 **b.** 13.9 **c.** 11.3 **d.** 5.0 **8.** No
9. 155 m **10. a.** 5.7 **b.** 10.8 **c.** 10.0
11. 776 m

Cumulative Review, page 63
1. a. -18 **b.** 13 **c.** -2 **d.** 4 **e.** -189 **f.** 0
g. -10 **h.** -2 **2. a.** -7 **b.** -4 **c.** -10
d. $-\dfrac{5}{7}$ **e.** -51 **f.** 43 **g.** -18 **h.** 21 **3. a.** $5x^5$
b. $3t^3$ **c.** $256k^4$ **d.** a^8b^{12} **e.** y^{10} **f.** 1 **g.** t^{14}
h. z^2 **4. a.** 1.958×10^{10} **b.** 1.92×10^{-7}
c. 3.7×10^{-5} **d.** 5.9×10^{11} **5. a.** 1.17×10^{11}
b. 7.1×10^6 **c.** 3×10^3 **d.** 2.3×10^{15}
e. 4×10^9 **f.** 4.3×10^2 **6. a.** 8.1 **b.** 7.1
c. 10.1 **7.** b, c **8. a.** 5 **b.** 3.2 **c.** 15 **d.** 8.2
e. 7 **f.** 8.9

Unit 3

Exercises, page 66
1. a. Add 4. **b.** Combine like terms.
c. Combine like terms. **d.** Add 6.
e. Subtract $3m$. **f.** Combine like terms.
g. Multiply by 10.
h. Apply the distributive property.
i. Multiply by 10.
2. a. 8 **b.** -2 **c.** 6 **d.** -21 **e.** 8 **f.** 7 **g.** 56
h. -6 **i.** 18 **3. a.** 4 **b.** 7 **c.** 2 **d.** 2 **e.** 15
f. 1 **g.** 3 **h.** -8 **i.** 2 **j.** 2 **k.** -7 **l.** 4

m. -9 **n.** 3 **o.** -1 **4. a.** $\dfrac{1}{2}$ **b.** -4 **c.** -16

d. $\dfrac{1}{9}$ **e.** 24 **f.** 2 **g.** 5 **h.** 7 **i.** 15 **j.** 22 **k.** 4

l. $-\dfrac{1}{2}$ **m.** 8 **n.** $-\dfrac{5}{6}$ **o.** 0 **p.** $-2\dfrac{2}{5}$ **5. a.** 1

b. -15 **c.** $-4\dfrac{1}{2}$ **d.** -14 **e.** $-4\dfrac{1}{2}$ **f.** 2 **g.** 21

h. $2\dfrac{1}{2}$ **i.** $-4\dfrac{4}{5}$ **j.** $-1\dfrac{2}{3}$ **6.** $9.15 **7.** $2 285

8. a. $w = \dfrac{A}{l}$ **b.** $c = 4A - a - b - d$ **c.** $t = \dfrac{I}{Pr}$

d. $l = \dfrac{P - 2w}{2}$ **e.** $E = \dfrac{I}{d^2}$ **f.** $h = \dfrac{V}{\pi r^2}$

9. $125 **10.** 19:00 **11. a.** 2 **b.** $\dfrac{1}{5}$ **c.** 0 **d.** 0

e. 16 **f.** -3 **12.** The coefficient of the first w is 7.

Extra, page 67

```
        ┌───┐
        │ 9 │
      ┌─┴─┬─┴─┐
      │ 7 │ 2 │
    ┌─┴─┐ └┬──┴┐
    │ 3 │   │ 4 │
  ┌─┴─┬─┴┐ ┌┴─┬─┴┐
  │ 1 │ 8 │ 6 │ 5 │
  └───┴───┴───┴───┘
```

Answers will vary.

Exercises, page 69
1. a. $11\dfrac{2}{3}$ **b.** 36 **c.** 15 **d.** $-\dfrac{3}{4}$ **e.** 9 **f.** -10

g. $\dfrac{1}{18}$ **h.** $19\dfrac{3}{5}$ **i.** $-1\dfrac{1}{3}$ **j.** 75 **k.** 4 **l.** $-\dfrac{5}{18}$

2. a. $9s - 8s = 72$ **b.** $9k - 90 = 5k$
c. $20z - 9z = 88$ **d.** $3(z - 2) + 2z = 64$
e. $16m - 3(3m - 4) = 4m$ **f.** $45 - 2r = 6(r + 2)$
g. $8t + 5 = 3t + 8$ **h.** $-4k = -3k - 2$
i. $6(z - 3) = 8(z - 3) - 13$ **3. a.** 4 **b.** 7 **c.** 3

d. $-\frac{1}{2}$ **e.** -3 **f.** $5\frac{1}{7}$ **g.** $-2\frac{5}{7}$ **h.** -2 **i.** 60

j. -2 **k.** -4 **l.** $1\frac{1}{5}$ **m.** $4\frac{1}{5}$ **n.** $3\frac{7}{25}$ **o.** $-20\frac{2}{5}$

p. $-2\frac{1}{3}$ **4. a.** 2 **b.** $35\frac{7}{10}$ **c.** $6\frac{12}{25}$ **d.** $5\frac{25}{26}$

e. $-2\frac{32}{75}$ **f.** 2 **g.** $-1\frac{18}{31}$ **h.** $3\frac{1}{6}$ **5.** 270 mL

6. $\frac{1}{10}$ of the liquid is 27 mL, so $\frac{7}{10}$ of the liquid is
$(7 \times 27 \text{ mL})$, and $\frac{2}{10}$ of the liquid is $(2 \times 27 \text{ mL})$.

Exercises, page 70

1. Let n be the number of nickels.
a. $3n$ **b.** $5n$ **c.** $10n$ **2. a.** $c + 3$ **b.** $c - 4$
c. $2c$ **3. a.** $4(c - 4) = 3c$ **b.** $(c + 3) + c = 35$
c. $2c - 8 = 3(c - 8)$
4. a. Let n be the number. $n + 7 = 26$
b. Let a be my age in years. $a - 6 = 14$
c. Let s be Suzanne's age in years. $s + 5 = 23$
d. Let l be the length. $2l - 8 = 32$
e. Let d be the number of dimes.
   $d + (d + 3) = 21$
f. Let d be the number of dimes.
   $10d + 5(d + 3) = 150$
5. a. $12d$ **b.** $4k$ **c.** $60x$ **d.** $35p$ **e.** $40b + 55p$
f. $32s + 11(s + 3)$ **6. a.** $x + 1$
b. $x - 1, x, x + 1$ **c.** $y + 2$
7. a. Let t be Tim's age in years. $5t = 85$
b. Let a be Anna's age in years. $a + (3 + a) = 35$
c. Let d be the number of dimes. $d + 2d = 33$
d. Let l be the Lions' score. $l + (l - 3) = 113$
e. Let a be Jay's age in years. $3a - a = 26$
f. Let x be one number and $(x + 1)$ be the other
   number. $x + (x + 1) = 75$
g. Let x be one number and $(x + 2)$ be the other
   number. $x + (x + 2) = 88$

Problem Solving 5, page 72

1. 324 tickets at $5 each and 41 tickets at $3.50
   each
2. Torches: 55 goals; Flames: 49 goals
3. $46.65 **4.** 45 wins and 28 losses
5. 12 days **6.** $84
7. 95 nickels, 190 dimes, and 240 quarters
8. Louise: 20 hours; Michelle: 10 hours;
   Penny: 8 hours
9. 7 points, 13 points, and 26 points
10. 24 m by 24 m; about 17.0 m by 33.9 m
11. 96 cm
12. Linda: 26 hours, $97.50; Larry: 30 hours, $97.50
13. 10 premium mufflers
14. 14 two-engine planes
15. Yes **16.** $4\frac{1}{2}$ hours
17. 12 years old **18.** about 3 hours

Extra, page 73

1.
2.5	1.5	2.9
2.7	2.3	1.9
1.7	3.1	2.1

2.
-17	8	-27
-22	-12	-2
3	-32	-7

3.
-1.6	-0.2	-1.2
-0.6	-1	-1.4
-0.8	-1.8	-0.4

Problem Solving 6, page 75

1. 125 kg of $8 coffee and 75 kg of $10 coffee
2. granola: 84 kg; raisins: 36 kg
3. peanuts: 45 kg; cashews: 15 kg
4. 30% copper: 160 kg; 48% copper: 80 kg
5. 18% acid: 100 mL; 42% acid: 100 mL
6. 75 mL **7.** 6 L **8.** 150 mL **9.** $3 600
10. 75 kg of $6 seeds and 45 kg of $10 seeds
11. 60 mL

Extra, page 75

1, 64, 729

Using the Computer, page 76

1. 240 g **2.** 105 mL **3.** $6400 at 6%; $3200 at 9%

Review, page 77

1. a. -5 **b.** 2 **c.** -3 **d.** 4 **e.** -7 **f.** 3
g. -5 **h.** 3 **2. a.** 14 **b.** 48 **c.** 12 **d.** 1 **e.** 7
f. -6 **g.** $-1\frac{3}{4}$ **h.** -5 **3.** Answers will vary.
4. a. $k + 11$ **b.** $\frac{1}{2}a$ **c.** $0.15l + l$ **5.** 352 tickets
6. 16 third places **7.** 18 suites **8.** 820 km/h
9. 840 quarters

Exercises, page 80

1. a. Let t be Tanya's height in centimetres.
   $t < 160$
b. Let m be the mass in kilograms. $m > 80$
c. Let r be the amount of rainfall in millimetres.
   $r \geq 120$
d. Let e be the elevator's load limit in kilograms.
   $e \geq 1500$
e. Let v be the speed in kilometres per hour.
   $v > 800$
f. Let p be the percentage of passes completed.
   $p \geq 50$
g. Let b be an excellent batting average.
   $b \geq 0.300$
h. Let n be the number of chocolates left.
   $n < 20$

2. a. $n < 5$
b. $n > 4$
c. $n > 4$

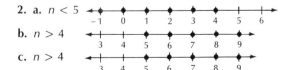

d. $n \geq \frac{1}{25}$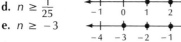

e. $n \geq -3$

f. $n > -1$

g. $n \leq -3\frac{1}{3}$

h. $n < -2$

i. $n \leq -2$

3. a. Let s be the cost of the skirt in dollars. $s > 30$

b. Let t be the time in hours required for lunch and gas. $t < 1.5$

c. Let p be the number of pages in the report. $p \geq 15$

d. Let m be the maximum mass of the bricks in tonnes. $m \leq 3.5$

e. Let t be the thawing time of the roast in hours. $t \geq 4$

f. Let v be my speed in kilometres per hour. $v \leq 90$

4. a. $\{\ldots, 5, 6, 7\}$ **b.** $\{-3, -2, -1, 0, 1, \ldots\}$

c. $\{2, 3, 4, \ldots\}$ **d.** $\{\ldots, 3, 4, 5\}$

e. $\{\ldots, -1, 0, 1, 2, 3\}$ **f.** $\{5, 6, 7, \ldots\}$

g. $\{3, 4, 5, \ldots\}$ **h.** $\{-1, 0, 1, \ldots\}$ **i.** $\{\ldots, -1, 0, 1\}$

5. a. $x > 1; B$ **b.** $x \leq -6; A$ **c.** $x > 7; D$

6. a. B, E **b.** A, D **c.** G, H **d.** C, F

7. a. Let g be the average number of goals per game. $g > 3.33$

b. Let h be the number of hours. $h > 2\frac{2}{3}$

c. Let t be the time in weeks. $t \geq 8$

8. a. $x \leq -1\frac{1}{3}$ **b.** $x \epsilon R$ **c.** $x \geq -5$ **d.** $x \leq \frac{3}{8}$

e. $x \leq 1\frac{2}{3}$ **f.** $x \leq 1$ **9.** more than 3 hours

Extra, page 81
Courier 26¢, Clarion 19¢, Crier 55¢

Exercises, page 83
1. a. $\{\ldots, -6, -5, -4, 3, 4, 5, \ldots\}$

b. $\{0, 1, 2, 3, 4, 5, 6\}$ **c.** $\{-3, -2, -1, 0, 1, 2\}$

d. $\{-2, -1, 0, 1, 2, 3, 4\}$

e. $\{\ldots, -7, -6, -5, 0, 1, 2, \ldots\}$ **f.** $\{0, 1, 2\}$

2. a. $-1 < x < 3$ **b.** $-1 \leq x \leq 2$

c. $-2 < x < 0$ **d.** $3 \leq x \leq 6$

e. $x \geq 3$ or $x < -3$ **f.** $x > 2$ or $x < -2$

3. a. Let a be Rita's age in years. $14 < a < 18$

b. Let l be the classroom's length in metres. $5 \leq l \leq 8$

c. Let t be the temperature in degrees Celsius. $-3 \leq t \leq 3$

d. Let c be the total cost in dollars. $30 < c < 35$

e. Let e be the effect on Pat's account. $-429 \leq e \leq 0$

f. Let v be Liz's speed in kilometres per hour. $80 \leq v \leq 100$

g. Let p be Paul's earnings in dollars. $30 \leq 2p \leq 40$

h. Let t be the temperature in degrees Celsius. $-5 \leq t \leq 9$

4. a. $5 < x < 8$ **b.** $-4 \leq x \leq 2$

c. $x > 0$ or $x < -4$ **d.** $1 \leq x \leq 3$

e. $x > 4$ or $x < 2$ **f.** $\frac{1}{3} \leq x \leq 2$

g. $5 \leq x \leq 7$ **h.** $x > -3$

i. $-2 < x < 2$ **j.** $-5 < x < 9$

k. no solution **l.** $x \epsilon R$ **m.** $-2 \leq x \leq 2$

n. no solution **o.** $x < -\frac{1}{4}$ **p.** no solution

q. $x < -2$ **r.** no solution **5. a.** $-1 < x < 3$

b. $x < 0$ or $x > 5$ **c.** $-3 \leq x \leq 3$ **d.** $2 < x \leq 6$

e. $-2 < x < 3$ **f.** $x < -1$ or $x \geq 0$

6. from 1075 points to 1200 points

7. between \$1860 and \$2110

Exercises, page 85
1. a. $b = 7$ or $b = -7$ **b.** $a > 2$ or $a < -2$

c. $m \leq 3$ and $m \geq -3$

d. $a - 5 < 4$ or $a - 5 > -4$

e. $n + 3 \geq 9$ or $n + 3 \leq -9$

f. $5x - 7 = 3$ or $5x - 7 = -3$

g. $\frac{m}{2} \leq 10$ and $\frac{m}{2} \geq -10$

h. $7b + 4 = 5$ or $7b + 4 = -5$

i. $2c - 8 \geq 6$ or $2c - 8 \leq -6$

2. a.

b.

c.

3. a. $-4 \leq x \leq 4$ **b.** $x > 3$ or $x < -3$

c. $x \geq 2$ or $x \leq -2$ **d.** $1 < x < 2$

e. $-1\frac{1}{3} \leq x \leq 2$ **f.** $x > 6$ or $x < -1$

g. $-7 < x < 0$ **h.** $x \geq 1\frac{1}{2}$ or $x \leq 0$

i. $-1 \leq x \leq -\frac{1}{5}$ **j.** $-7 \leq x \leq 7$

k. $y > 7$ or $y < -7$ **l.** $y > 2$ or $y < -2$

Using the Calculator, page 85
1. 64 **2.** 512 **3.** 4096 **4.** 32 768 **5.** 524 288

6. 33 554 432

Problem Solving 7, page 86
1. $8\frac{1}{3}$ hours **2.** at least 8 baskets

3. more than 2 games

4. at least \$1780; at most \$2848

5. more than $4\frac{1}{2}$ hours; less than 5 hours

6. at least 7 correct; at most 10 correct

7. more than $2\frac{2}{3}$ hours; less than $3\frac{1}{2}$ hours

8. less than \$2.10 **9.** 17 women

10. more than 667 g **11.** 249 adult tickets

12. 20 minutes **13.** 18 hours

14. at least 16 tapes; at most 20 tapes **15.** 30 m²

16. 7 km

17. 37 skilled workers and 111 unskilled workers

18. at least 225 minutes; at most 270 minutes

Extra, page 87

Start from the first row. The middle number in every other row is a perfect square.

Application, page 88

	Age	Maximum Heart Rate	Target Rate for Someone Who:		
			a. Has Been Exercising	**b.** Has Not Been Exercising	**c.** Is a Smoker
1.	20	200	150	140	130
2.	25	195	146.25	136.5	126.75
3.	30	190	142.5	133	123.5
4.	35	185	138.75	129.5	120.25
5.	40	180	135	126	117
6.	50	170	127.5	119	110.5
7.	60	160	120	112	104

Review, page 89

1. a. 5 **b.** 15 **c.** 6 **d.** -2 **e.** $-\frac{11}{4}$ **f.** $-1\frac{4}{7}$

g. $\frac{1}{3}$ **h.** $-1\frac{2}{7}$

2. $h = \dfrac{2A}{a+b}$ **3. a.** $x \le 4$ **b.** $x \ge -2$

4. a. $s < 7$ **b.** $s < -1$ **c.** $s \le -3$ **d.** $s \le -2$

5. a. $x \epsilon Z$ **b.** $\{0, 1, 2\}$ **6. a.** -11 or 11

b. -3 or 3 **c.** -7 or 21 **d.** $-6\frac{3}{4}$ or $\frac{3}{4}$

e. $-1\frac{2}{5}$ or $1\frac{2}{5}$ **f.** -4 or 8 **7. a.** $y > 4$ or $y < -4$

b. $-2 < m < 2$ **c.** $n \ge 4$ or $n \le -3$

d. $-3\frac{1}{2} < v < \frac{1}{2}$ **e.** $u \epsilon R$ **f.** $x > 7$ or $x < 1$

g. $k > 3\frac{1}{6}$ or $k < 1\frac{1}{2}$ **h.** $w \ge 5\frac{2}{3}$ or $w \le -1\frac{2}{3}$

i. $-2 \le t \le 2\frac{4}{5}$ **8.** 64 quarters, 36 dimes

9. 10 problems **10.** at least 1 250 000 records

11. 19 days

Test, page 90

1. a. -2 **b.** 3 **c.** 6 **d.** 5 **e.** -10 **f.** -27

g. 2 **h.** -1.3 **2. a.** $x \le -1$ **b.** $-2 \le x \le 2$

c. $x < -1$ or $x > 4$ **d.** $x < -2$ or $x > 0$

3. a. $x < -2$ **b.** $x \ge -2$ **c.** $x \le 2$

d. $-2\frac{2}{3} \le x < \frac{1}{3}$ **4. a.** $x \ge 3$ or $x \le -3$

b. $-5 < x < 2$ **c.** $-6 < x < 12$

d. $x \le 1$ or $x \ge 9$ **e.** $x \ge 2\frac{1}{2}$ or $x \le -3\frac{1}{2}$

f. $-4 \le x \le 12$ **5.** Answers will vary.

6. a. Let q be the number of quarters. $q + 7$

b. Let a be the kitchen area. $2a$

c. Let s be Jan's original salary per year in dollars. $s + 2800$

d. Let c be the cost of the pizza. $\frac{c}{5}$

7. $1\frac{1}{2}$ hours **8.** Marc: \$63; Steve: \$84 **9.** 100 mL

10. 84 dimes

Cumulative Review, page 91

1. a. -15 **b.** -22 **c.** $\frac{1}{2}$ **d.** -45 **e.** 8 **f.** 225

g. -9 **h.** -54 **2.** $\frac{5}{11}$ **3. a.** 4.4×10^{11}

b. 8.3×10^{17} **4. a.** 20 **b.** 15 **c.** 40 **d.** 9

5. a. $5\sqrt{2}$ **b.** $10\sqrt{3}$ **c.** $5\sqrt{5}$ **d.** $3\sqrt{6}$

e. $3xy\sqrt{x}$ **f.** $15a^2b^3\sqrt{a}$ **g.** $xy^2\sqrt{z}$ **h.** $4m\sqrt{6k}$

6. a. $2\sqrt{2}$ **b.** $\dfrac{\sqrt{3}}{2}$ **c.** $\dfrac{x\sqrt{7}}{7}$ **d.** $\dfrac{\sqrt{5}\,(t-1)}{15}$

7. 17 units **8. a.** $5\sqrt{2}$ **b.** $\sqrt{13}$ **c.** $\sqrt{34}$

d. $\sqrt{29}$

9.

t	$t \epsilon R$?	$t \epsilon \overline{Q}$?	$t \epsilon Q$?	$t \epsilon Z$?	$t \epsilon W$?	$t \epsilon N$?
2	Yes	No	Yes	Yes	Yes	Yes
$\sqrt{2}$	Yes	Yes	No	No	No	No
$-\sqrt{2}$	Yes	Yes	No	No	No	No
$\sqrt{-2}$	No	No	No	No	No	No
$\frac{4}{7}$	Yes	No	Yes	No	No	No
$\frac{5}{8}$	Yes	No	Yes	No	No	No
π	Yes	Yes	No	No	No	No
$\frac{3}{0}$	No	No	No	No	No	No
5.92	Yes	No	Yes	No	No	No
$3.\overline{1}$	Yes	No	Yes	No	No	No
9.121 121 112 …	Yes	Yes	No	No	No	No
$\frac{\pi}{4}$	Yes	Yes	No	No	No	No

Unit 4

Exercises, page 95

2. a. $x + 0y = 8$ **b.** $0x + y = -2$
c. $2x + 0y = 8$ **d.** $3x - y = 4$
3. a. (5,2), (0,7), (9,-2) **b.** (0,5), (2,-1), (1,2)
c. (2,0), (4,5), (-2,-10) **d.** (3,0), (6,4), (-3,-8)

4. a. linear **b.** not linear **c.** linear

d. not linear **e.** linear **f.** not linear

5. a.

x	y
0	5
5	0
3	2
7	-2

b.

x	y
0	-4
8	0
-6	-7
14	3

c.

x	y
0	8
-5	-2
1	10
-4	0

d.

x	y
3	0
-1	-2
9	3
0	$-1\frac{1}{2}$

6. a. x-intercept = -2; y-intercept = -2
b. x-intercept = 16; y-intercept = 16
c. x-intercept = -4; y-intercept = 4
d. x-intercept = 3; y-intercept = -6
e. x-intercept = -2; y-intercept = 3
f. x-intercept = -6; y-intercept = -8
g. x-intercept = 3; no y-intercept

h. x-intercept = $2\frac{1}{3}$; y-intercept = $3\frac{1}{2}$

i. no x-intercept; y-intercept = -1

8. a. x-intercept = -1; y-intercept = 3
b. x-intercept = 2; y-intercept = -4
c. x-intercept = 2; y-intercept = 3
d. x-intercept = -5; y-intercept = 2
e. x-intercept = -3; y-intercept = -3
f. x-intercept = -2; y-intercept = 1

10.

x	y
2	382.70
6	436.10
10	489.50

11.

x	y
5	361.25
10	425
0	297.50

12. 40 h week: $376; 46 h week: $460.60; 50 h week: $517

13. All the lines are parallel.

14. All the lines pass through the point (0,3).

15. a. 25 square units **b.** 27 square units
c. $7\frac{1}{2}$ square units **d.** 35 square units
e. 18 square units **16.** 1 m and 9 m; 2 m and 8 m; 3 m and 7 m; 4 m and 6 m; 5 m and 5 m
17. {(-8,1), (-7,2), (-6,3), (-5,4), (-4,5), (-3,6), (-2,7), (-1,8)}
18. 5 cm, 5 cm, and 8 cm; 6 cm, 6 cm, and 6 cm; 7 cm, 7 cm, and 4 cm; 8 cm, 8 cm, and 2 cm
19. 2 stamps at 15¢ and 3 stamps at 20¢; 6 stamps at 15¢
20. $180; $185; $197 **21.** $310; $327.50; $331

Extra, page 97

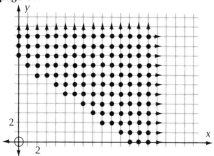

Exercises, page 100

1. a. (3, 1) **b.** $(1, -1\frac{1}{2})$ **c.** (4,1) **d.** (3,-5)
2. a. Yes **b.** No **c.** Yes **d.** Yes
3. a. Any line which goes through the point (-5,-6) is correct.
b. Any line which is parallel to $3x - 5y = 15$ is correct.
c. The line must be the same as $3x - 5y = 15$.
4. a. (3,1) **b.** (-2,6) **c.** (-5,3) **d.** (-1,2)
e. (-2,4) **f.** (0,1) **g.** (7,-3) **h.** (-1,-1)
i. (5,12) **5. a.** (2,4) **b.** ∅ **c.** ∅ **d.** (4,7)
e. $(6\frac{1}{2}, -1)$ **f.** ∅ **g.** infinite number of solutions
h. (3,0) **i.** (10,-3) **6.** 20 quarters and 36 dimes
7. 18 adult admissions and 12 student admissions
8. 15 hours
9. a. $a = 2$; $b = 2$ **b.** $a = 3$; $b = 3$
c. $a = -3$; $b = 3$ **d.** $a = -3$; $b = -35$
10. 12 dimes and 8 quarters

Extra, page 101
10 buses

Exercises, page 103
1. a. 800 m **b.** about 825 m **c.** 1000 m
d. about 224 m **2. a.** (7,4) **b.** (7,11) **c.** (4,2)
d. (-7,4) **e.** $(-5, -4\frac{1}{2})$ **f.** $(-1, 1\frac{1}{2})$ **g.** (5,-4)
h. (7,-2) **i.** $(\frac{1}{2}, 4\frac{1}{2})$ **3. a.** $AC = \sqrt{41}$; $BD = \sqrt{41}$
b. $IK = 5\sqrt{2}$; $JL = 5\sqrt{2}$

c. $EG = 3\sqrt{10}$; $FH = 3\sqrt{10}$

d. $MP = 2\sqrt{37}$; $NQ = 2\sqrt{37}$

The diagonals of a rectangle have the same length.

4. a. $(6,5\frac{1}{2})$ **b.** $(-7\frac{1}{2}, -\frac{1}{2})$ **c.** $(-2\frac{1}{2}, 4\frac{1}{2})$

d. $(-2, -5)$

The diagonals of a rectangle have the same midpoint.

5. $PR = \sqrt{(x_2 - x_1)^2 + (y_2 - y_1)^2}$

$SQ = \sqrt{(x_2 - x_1)^2 + (y_2 - y_1)^2}$

$\therefore PR = SQ$

midpoint of $PR = \left(\dfrac{x_1 + x_2}{2}, \dfrac{y_1 + y_2}{2} \right)$

midpoint of $SQ = \left(\dfrac{x_1 + x_2}{2}, \dfrac{y_1 + y_2}{2} \right)$

$\therefore$ midpoint of PR = midpoint of SQ

6. a. $(7,10)$ **b.** $(7,9)$ **c.** $(4,12)$ **d.** $(-2,-1)$

e. $(6,1)$ **f.** $(-12,8)$

Exercises, page 106

1. a. a, b, c, d, k, r **b.** e, f, g, h, i, p

2. slope of $a = \dfrac{2}{5}$ slope of $h = -3$

slope of $b = 2$ slope of $i = -\dfrac{2}{5}$

slope of $c = 4$ slope of j is undefined

slope of $d = \dfrac{1}{3}$ slope of $k = \dfrac{5}{4}$

slope of $e = -\dfrac{1}{3}$ slope of $p = -4$

slope of $f = -2$ slope of $q = 0$

slope of $g = -\dfrac{3}{4}$ slope of $r = \dfrac{4}{3}$

3. a. 2 **b.** -3 **c.** 3 **d.** 3 **e.** $\dfrac{3}{2}$ **f.** undefined

g. 0 **h.** -1 **i.** undefined

4. a. upward to the right **b.** down to the right

c. upward to the right **d.** upward to the right

e. upward to the right **f.** vertical **g.** horizontal

h. down to the right **i.** vertical

5. $a, b, c, d,$ and f **6.** $(4,0)$ **7.** -8

8. a. $(2,1)$ **b.** $-\dfrac{4}{5}$ **9. a.** $(1,-1)$

b. The slope between each pair of points is 3.

10. 6 m **11.** about 3.3 m **12.** about 51 m

13. 120 m; about 323 m **14.** 2.4 m

15. a. $(3\frac{1}{2}, 6\frac{1}{2})$ **b.** M is also the midpoint of $\overline{BD}$.

16. 70.79 m; 24.78 m

Extra, page 107

1. False

2. True

Exercises, page 109

1. slope $a = -\dfrac{1}{4}$ slope $d = -\dfrac{1}{3}$

slope $b = 2$ slope $e = -1$

slope $c = \dfrac{3}{4}$ slope $f = -1$

2. a. -1 **b.** 1 **c.** $-\dfrac{1}{3}$ **d.** $\dfrac{1}{3}$ **e.** $\dfrac{3}{2}$ **f.** $\dfrac{1}{2}$ **g.** 3

h. $\dfrac{1}{2}$ **i.** -2 **j.** $\dfrac{2}{5}$ **k.** undefined **l.** 0

5. a. 8 **b.** -6 **c.** 4 **d.** -2 **e.** 10 **f.** -4

g. 8 **h.** 3 **i.** -8 **j.** 7

Exercises, page 111

1. a. $-\dfrac{4}{3}$ **b.** $-\dfrac{8}{5}$ **c.** $\dfrac{6}{5}$ **d.** $\dfrac{1}{3}$ **e.** $\dfrac{4}{7}$

The slopes of the lines are given below.

2. a. $m = 2$ **b.** $m = -3$ **c.** $m = \dfrac{3}{2}$ **d.** $m = \dfrac{5}{2}$

e. $m = -\dfrac{5}{2}$ **f.** $m = -\dfrac{1}{2}$

The slopes of the lines are given below.

3. a. $m = -\dfrac{1}{2}$ **b.** $m = \dfrac{1}{3}$ **c.** $m = -\dfrac{2}{3}$

d. $m = -\dfrac{2}{5}$ **e.** $m = \dfrac{2}{5}$ **f.** $m = 2$

4. a. parallel **b.** perpendicular

c. perpendicular **d.** neither **e.** parallel

f. neither

The slopes of the lines are given below.

6. a. $m = 3$ **b.** $m = \dfrac{2}{3}$ **c.** $m = -5$

d. m is undefined. **e.** $m = -\dfrac{4}{3}$ **f.** $m = 0$

7. -1

8. slope of $\overline{AB} = -1$; slope of $\overline{CD} = -1$; $\therefore \overline{AB} \parallel \overline{CD}$

slope of $\overline{BC} = 0$; slope of $\overline{AD} = 0$; $\therefore \overline{BC} \parallel \overline{AD}$

9. slope of $\overline{FG} = 1$; slope of $\overline{FH} = -1$; $\therefore \overline{FG}$ is

perpendicular to $\overline{FH}$ and $\triangle FGH$ is a right-angled triangle.

10. $a, b,$ and e **11.** $a, b,$ and f

12. slope of $\overline{PR} = \dfrac{4}{3}$; slope of $\overline{QR} = -\dfrac{3}{4}$;

$PR = 10$; $QR = 10$; $\therefore \overline{PR}$ is perpendicular

to $\overline{QR}$, $PR = QR$, and the triangle is an isosceles

right-angled triangle.

13. 0 **14.** undefined

15. a. 12 **b.** 2 **c.** -1 **d.** 6 **e.** 0 **f.** 10

16. a. 8 **b.** 7 **c.** -7 **d.** 0 **e.** 3 **f.** 3

Review, page 113

1. a. $(8,8)$, $(-5,-5)$

b. $(3,1)$, $(-1,9)$, $(4,-1)$, $(3.5,0)$

2. a. x-intercept = 4; y-intercept = -3

b. x-intercept = -1; y-intercept = 3

c. x-intercept = -3; y-intercept = $-1\frac{1}{2}$

d. x-intercept = -2; y-intercept = 3

e. x-intercept $= 1$; y-intercept $= -5$
f. x-intercept $= -12$; y-intercept $= 8$
3. a. $(1,0)$ **b.** $(5,-3)$ **c.** $(-1,-3)$
4. $M = (5,-3)$

$AM = \sqrt{29}$; $BM = \sqrt{29}$

5. a. 9 **b.** $\frac{11}{4}$ **c.** undefined **d.** $-\frac{7}{8}$ **e.** 0

f. $-\frac{3}{5}$ **6.** $a, b, d,$ and f **7.** $(-2,0)$ **8.** -2

10. The slopes of the lines are given below.

a. $m = -\frac{5}{2}$ **b.** m is undefined. **c.** $m = 0$

11. a. $x + y = 31$ **b.** $5x + 8y = 179$
d. 23 cars and 8 vans or trucks

Exercises, page 116

1. a. $3; 2$ **b.** $\frac{1}{2}; 4$ **c.** $-2; -1$ **d.** $-\frac{8}{5}; -2$

e. $\frac{3}{7}; \frac{1}{2}$ **f.** $3; -\frac{1}{3}$ **2. a.** $y = 3x + 2$

b. $y = 2x - 4$ **c.** $y = -\frac{3}{4}x - 1$

d. $y = -1\frac{2}{3}x + 1\frac{1}{3}$ **3. a.** $y = \frac{1}{2}x + 4$

b. $y = x + 1$ **c.** $y = -x + 3$ **d.** $y = -\frac{1}{3}x - 2$

e. $y = -1\frac{1}{2}x + 3$ **f.** $y = \frac{2}{3}x + 2$

5. a. $y = -x + 8$ **b.** $y = x - 3$ **c.** $y = 2x - 3$

d. $y = -\frac{5}{2}x + 2$ **e.** $y = \frac{3}{2}x - 2$ **f.** $y = \frac{3}{5}x$

6. a. parallel **b.** perpendicular **c.** neither
d. perpendicular **e.** neither **f.** perpendicular
7. a. $3x - y = -2$ **b.** $x - 2y = -4$
c. $2x + 5y = 10$ **d.** $3x - 4y = -2$
e. $12x - 5y = 35$ **f.** $2x - 6y = 5$ **8. a.** 11

b. 3 **c.** 3 **d.** 14 **e.** -3 **f.** 2 **9.** $y = \frac{5}{7}x - 2$

10. $y = \frac{2}{3}x + 3$ **11.** $y = 2x + 12$

12. $y = \frac{5}{2}x - 3$

13. The slopes of the three lines are $\frac{3}{2}, -\frac{2}{3},$ and $-\frac{3}{11}$ respectively. Since $\frac{3}{2}$ and $-\frac{2}{3}$ are negative reciprocals, the lines are perpendicular and the triangle is a right-angled triangle.

14. $-\frac{2}{3}$

15. a. one solution **b.** no solution
c. infinite number of solutions
d. infinite number of solutions
e. no solution **f.** one solution

Extra, page 117
The quadrilateral with the midpoints as vertices is a parallelogram.

Exercises, page 119
1. a. 1 **b.** -7 **c.** -3 **d.** 5 **e.** 3 **f.** 15

g. -7 **h.** -12 **2. a.** $\frac{2}{5}$ **b.** -3 **c.** -8 **d.** -2

e. $\frac{3}{4}$ **f.** $\frac{4}{7}$ **3. a.** $-\frac{5}{2}$ **b.** $\frac{1}{3}$ **c.** $\frac{1}{8}$ **d.** $\frac{1}{2}$ **e.** $-\frac{4}{3}$

f. $-\frac{7}{4}$ **4. a.** 1 **b.** $-\frac{3}{7}$ **c.** $\frac{2}{9}$ **5. a.** -1 **b.** $\frac{7}{3}$

c. $-\frac{9}{2}$ **6. a.** $y = 5$ **b.** $x = -3$ **7.** $2x + 3y = 0$

8. a. $4x - y = -9$ **b.** $5x + y = 4$
c. $3x - 4y = 28$ **d.** $2x - 5y = -25$
e. $7x - y = -11$ **f.** $x - 2y = -1$
9. $8x + 3y = -12$ **10.** $x + 3y = 5$
11. $5x - 3y = 0$ **12.** $2x + 3y = -6$
13. a. $2x - y = 5$ **b.** $3x + 2y = 6$
c. $x - 3y = -3$ **14. a.** $5x - y = 6$
b. $3x + y = -8$ **15. a.** $7x - 2y = 19$
b. $x + 3y = 13$
16. $7x + 2y = 22; 5x - 8y = 0; x + 5y = 11$
17. $4x - 3y = -11$
18. $2x - 5y = -26; 5x + 2y = 22; 2x - 5y = 3;$
$5x + 2y = -36$
19. a. $M = (2,-1); N = (6,3);$ slope of $\overline{MN} = 1;$
slope of $\overline{BC} = 1$ **b.** $MN = 4\sqrt{2}; BC = 8\sqrt{2}$

c. Any line joining the midpoints of two sides of a triangle is parallel to and has half the length of the third side.

Review, page 121

2. a. $y = 3x + 2$ **b.** $y = 2x - 3$
c. $y = -5x - 2$ **3. a.** $5x + 6y = 42$
b. $3x - 2y = -8$ **c.** $5x + 3y = -24$
4. a. $2x - 5y = 5$ **b.** $x - y = 2$
c. $4x + 5y = 13$ **5.** $5x - 2y = 7; 2x + 5y = -3$
6. a. $b = 6$ **b.** $a = 3$ and $b = 2; a = -3$ and
$b = -2$ **c.** $k = -\frac{1}{3}$ **d.** $k = \frac{3}{2}$ **e.** $a = 1$ and
$b = 2; a = -1$ and $b = -2$ **f.** $a = 1$ and
$b = -5; a = -1$ and $b = 5$

Exercises, page 123

1. a. $-3; 2$ **b.** $\frac{1}{3}; 2$ **c.** $\frac{1}{3}; -3$ **d.** $-2; 4$

e. $\frac{3}{2}; 2\frac{1}{2}$ **f.** $-\frac{1}{3}; \frac{2}{3}$

2. a. $3x + 2y - 6 = 0; m = -\frac{3}{2}; b = 3$

b. $x + 2y - 4 = 0; m = -\frac{1}{2}; b = 2$

c. $3x - y - 1 = 0; m = 3; b = -1$

d. $3x - 5y + 14 = 0; m = \frac{3}{5}; b = 2\frac{4}{5}$

e. $x - 3y - 3 = 0; m = \frac{1}{3}; b = -1$

f. $3x - 4y - 8 = 0; m = \frac{3}{4}; b = -2$

3. $4x + 5y - 25 = 0$ **4. a.** 3 **b.** -8 **c.** -2
d. 6 **e.** -4 **f.** $A = 6; C = 3$

Extra, page 123
1. speed of the car
2. position before beginning to travel

Problem Solving 8, page 124
1. 4 baskets and 3 foul shots **2.** 10 stamps at 35¢ each and 20 stamps at 45¢ each
3. a. 500 books
b. printer A
4. a. Let x be sales for the week and y be the earnings per week in dollars. Pat: $y = \frac{1}{25}x + 180$; Leslie: $y = \frac{3}{50}x + 150$ **b.** $x = \$1500$ **c.** Pat
5. flat fee = \$3; charge per kilometre = \$0.80
6. adult: \$8; child: \$3

Application, page 125
1. $44x + 7y = 136$ **2. a.** $3.7°C$ **b.** $-5.7°C$
c. $-10.4°C$ **d.** $14.7°C$ **e.** $15.7°C$ **f.** $8.1°C$
3. $x = -\frac{7}{44}y + \frac{34}{11}$ **4. a.** 2.77 km **b.** 1.18 km
c. 2.30 km **d.** 0.70 km **e.** 3.25 km **f.** 4.68 km

Test, page 126
1. a and b

2. a.

x	y
1	-2
13	2
7	0
-5	-4

b.

x	y
0	5
-2	2
3	$9\frac{1}{2}$
$-3\frac{1}{3}$	0

c.

x	y
0	$17\frac{1}{2}$
-7	0
1	20
5	30

3. x-intercept = 3; y-intercept = 2 **4.** (3,0)
5. a. $4\sqrt{2}$; (7,4) **b.** $\sqrt{65}$; $(-5, -4\frac{1}{2})$
c. $\sqrt{97}$; $(-1, 1\frac{1}{2})$ **6. a.** 1 **b.** $\frac{7}{4}$ **c.** $\frac{9}{4}$
7. $y = -\frac{4}{3}x + 2$ **8.** $3x + 5y = -15$
9. a. $x + y = -1$ **b.** $x + 7y = -23$
c. $2x + y = 1$ **d.** $2x + 5y = 3$ **10. a.** $B = -3$
b. $A = 8; C = -3$ **11.** $x - y + 4 = 0$
12. $x + 2y = 0$

Cumulative Review, page 127
1. a. -19 **b.** 45 **c.** 144 **d.** -26 **2. a.** t^2r^8
b. z^6 **c.** $\frac{1}{k^2}$ **d.** $4b^2$ **3. a.** 2.5×10^{13} **b.** 6.2
c. 3.2×10 **d.** 3×10^{14} **4. a.** 4 **b.** 18 **c.** 70
d. 275 **5. a.** $\frac{\sqrt{5}}{5}$ **b.** $\frac{\sqrt{6}}{3}$ **c.** $\frac{2\sqrt{15}}{5}$ **d.** $\frac{x\sqrt{2y}}{2}$

6. 29.7 cm **7. a.** $\sqrt{34}$ **b.** $2\sqrt{11}$ **c.** $a = 10\sqrt{2}$; $b = 10$ **8. a.** 2.83 **b.** 5.66 **c.** 4.47 **9. a.** -1
b. 4 **c.** 17 **d.** $\frac{1}{10}$ **e.** $28\frac{4}{5}$ **f.** $-\frac{5}{6}$ **g.** 19
h. $-14\frac{1}{2}$ **10. a.** $a < 4\frac{1}{2}$ **b.** $j \geq 0$ **c.** $t \geq -14$
11. a. 15 or -15 **b.** 9 or -9 **c.** $-3\frac{1}{2} \leq x \leq 3\frac{1}{2}$
d. $x \geq 19$ or $x \leq -5$ **e.** $x > 2\frac{1}{2}$ or $x < -4\frac{1}{2}$
f. $-3\frac{2}{5} \leq x \leq -2\frac{3}{5}$ **g.** $-6 \leq x \leq 8$
h. $x > 9$ or $x < 5$

Unit 5

Exercises, page 130
1. a. iii **b.** i **c.** ii **d.** iii **2. a.** (4,4) **b.** (3,-1)
c. infinite number of solutions **3. a.** (5,19)
b. (-4,1) **c.** (5,3) **d.** (-31,-12) **e.** (2,5)
f. (5,21) **4. a.** (2,7) **b.** (4,5) **c.** (3,-1) **d.** (4,3)

e. (1,2) **f.** (4,3) **g.** $\left(2\frac{1}{2}\right)$ **h.** (2,-1) **i.** (-1,2)

j. (21,2) **k.** (-3,4) **l.** (3,2) **5.** 19 and 23
6. Anna: 21 years old; Bill: 16 years old

7. a. $\left(2\frac{2}{3}, 1\frac{1}{3}\right)$ **b.** infinite number of solutions

c. infinite number of solutions **d.** $\left(3\frac{1}{2},2\right)$

e. no solution **f.** $\left(2\frac{1}{4},0\right)$ **g.** $\left(2\frac{1}{2} 1\frac{1}{2}\right)$

h. $\left(-2, -1\frac{1}{2}\right)$ **i.** no solution

j. infinite number of solutions **k.** $\left(5\frac{1}{7} \frac{2}{7}\right)$

l. (4,6) **8.** Sue: 10 years old; Tim: 8 years old
9. banana: 150 g; grapefruit: 450 g

Extra, page 131
1. Answers will vary. **2.** Answers will vary.

Exercises, page 133
1. a. (5,4) **b.** (6,-1) **c.** (-4,3) **2. a.** (3,-1)

b. $\left(-2\frac{1}{10}, -9\right)$ **c.** (-10,9) **3. a.** (-1,-3)

b. (13,12) **c.** (20,-6) **d.** (2,-2) **e.** (3,-4)
f. (-2,4) **g.** (6,-12) **h.** (38,50) **i.** (10,-10)

j. (3,-1) **k.** $\left(1\frac{1}{3},-1\right)$ **l.** $\left(-3,1\frac{4}{7}\right)$

4. Marc: 14 years old; Marc's father: 38 years old
5. a. (1,4) **b.** no solution **c.** (3,-2)
d. infinite number of solutions **e.** (12,10)
f. infinite number of solutions
6. 8 nickels and 6 dimes **7.** -2

Exercises, page 135

1. a. $(5,2)$ **b.** $(5,-7)$ **c.** $(3,-1)$ **d.** $\left(3\frac{1}{2},2\right)$

e. $\left(\frac{1}{5},1\frac{1}{10}\right)$ **f.** $(-1,0)$ **2. a.** $(-2,2)$ **b.** $(-1,-1)$

c. $(1,3)$ **d.** $(0,2)$ **e.** $\left(-4,1\frac{1}{2}\right)$ **f.** $\left(1,2\frac{1}{2}\right)$

3. a. add **b.** add **c.** subtract **d.** add **e.** add
f. subtract **4. a.** $(8,-6)$ **b.** $(2,1)$ **c.** $(-1,3)$

d. $\left(1\frac{4}{5},2\frac{4}{5}\right)$ **e.** $(-2,6)$ **f.** $\left(16\frac{3}{7},34\frac{2}{7}\right)$ **g.** $(1,-1)$

h. $(-3,-2)$ **i.** $\left(-1\frac{1}{5},-\frac{1}{5}\right)$ **5.** 19 and 35

6. 495 girls and 467 boys **7.** Rob: 20 years old;
Tanya: 16 years old **8.** 58 L and 42 L
9. apple: 45¢; pear: 50¢ **10.** Kate: 15 years old;
Kate's mother: 36 years old **11.** 18 and 43
12. 31 teeth and 58 teeth **13. a.** $(13,-16)$

b. infinite number of solutions **c.** $\left(\frac{1}{4},1\frac{1}{2}\right)$

d. $(50,-40)$ **e.** $\left(1\frac{1}{2},\frac{7}{8}\right)$ **f.** no solution **14.** 9

15. a. $-8\frac{1}{3}$ **b.** $6\frac{2}{3}$ **c.** 10 **d.** 18
16. potatoes: 30 kg; tomatoes: 10 kg
17. nuts: 0.5 kg; bolts: 0.65 kg
18. $4000 at $7\frac{1}{2}$ %; $6000 at 8%

Extra, page 137
$-40°C = -40°F$

Exercises, page 140
There are other correct solutions.
1. a. $4x + 2y = 4$; $3x - 2y = 10$
b. $4p + 6q = 10$; $4p + q = -5$
or $2p + 3q = 5$; $12p + 3q = -15$
c. $3m - 2n = 5$; $8m + 2n = -16$
d. $6x - 9y = 30$; $6x + 4y = 10$
or $4x - 6y = 20$; $9x + 6y = 15$
e. $4p + 6q = -28$; $4p + 5q = -22$
f. $10a + 20b = 90$; $10a - 6b = -40$
or $6a + 12b = 54$; $20a - 12b = -80$

There are other correct solutions.
2. a. $3x + 2y = -24$
$3x + 3y = -30$ or $2x + 2y = -20$
b. $2a + 3b = 18$
$4a - 3b = 0$
c. $x + 3y = 10$
$x - 2y = 0$

3. a. No **b.** Yes **c.** Yes **d.** Yes **4. a.** $(4,1)$
b. $(1,2)$ **c.** $(3,-1)$ **d.** $(8,-6)$ **e.** $(9,-7)$
f. $(4,-2)$ **g.** $(5,-2)$ **h.** $(3,2)$ **i.** $(4,-2)$
j. $(-1,-2)$ **k.** $(6,-4)$ **l.** $(9,-4)$ **m.** $(2,-1)$

n. $(-3,0)$ **o.** $(2,-2)$ **5.** bonus card: 4 points;
prize card: 2 points **6.** 8 and 10
7. 5 dimes and 15 nickels
8. $1 bills: 21; $2 bills: 17 **9. a.** $(2,-1)$ **b.** $(4,20)$

c. infinite number of solutions **d.** $\left(\frac{1}{4},1\frac{1}{2}\right)$

e. no solution **f.** infinite number of solutions
g. $(14,16)$ **h.** $(12,24)$ **i.** $(-6,4)$
j. infinite number of solutions

k. infinite number of solutions **l.** $\left(1,1\frac{2}{3}\right)$

m. $\left(-\frac{1}{2},1\right)$ **n.** $(-15,10)$ **o.** $(-1,1)$ **10.** 6

11. 2 t loads: 45; 5 t loads: 52 **12.** $3.50 **13.** 47

Using the Calculator, page 141
$\{-2,-1,0,1,2\}$ or $\{10,11,12,13,14\}$

Problem Solving 9, page 142
1. 53 and 67 **2.** mango: 99¢; kiwi fruit: 79¢
3. 5 dimes and 8 quarters **4.** 12 m by 14 m
5. 6 h at $3/h and 14 h at $4/h
6. 24 boxes at $5 a box and 18 boxes at $7 a box
7. 40¢ postage: 48 letters; 50¢ postage: 32 letters
8. 27 dump trucks and 19 flatbed trucks
9. 14 and -20 **10.** 11 problems **11.** 26 and 42
12. $66 **13.** son: 12 years old; father: 36 years old
14. 5 h **15.** 4 televisions and 8 recorders; 440
16. Andy: 7 roller coaster rides; Beth: 4 roller
coaster rides

Problem Solving 10, page 145
1. 52.5 km/h
2. 80 g of 14 karat gold and 160 g of 20 karat gold
3. air speed of the plane: 250 km/h;
tailwind speed: 50 km/h
4. 60 g of 40% silver and 40 g of 50% silver
5. $6000 in the profitable stock and $4000 in the
losing stock
6. 15.25 kg of dried apricots and 34.75 kg of
dried bananas
7. 6 h and 40 min; 5 h and 50 min **8.** 150 mL
9. 16 : 12 **10.** 3 lengths
11. $6000 in the first stock and $8000 in the second
stock
12. about 41 bars
13. 450 km from the first station and 480 km from
the second one

14. $\frac{2}{5}$ km

15. a. skirt: $24; blouse: $19 **b.** $14.25; $19.20
c. $14.96

Review, page 147
1. a. (2,1) **b.** (8, −17) **c.** (12, −5) **2. a.** (3, −8)

b. $\left(-8\frac{3}{5}, -\frac{4}{5}\right)$ **c.** $\left(3\frac{1}{2}, -8\frac{1}{2}\right)$ **3. a.** (5,3)

b. $\left(2\frac{3}{5}, 2\frac{2}{5}\right)$ **c.** (−4,1) **4. a.** correct

b. (−17,11) **c.** (1,4) **5. a.** $\left(-\frac{4}{7}, \frac{1}{7}\right)$ **b.** $\left(4\frac{2}{3}, 2\frac{2}{3}\right)$

c. $\left(2\frac{3}{7}, -\frac{6}{7}\right)$ **d.** (9, −16) **e.** $\left(1\frac{1}{4}, 2\right)$

f. $\left(2\frac{1}{2}, -1\frac{1}{2}\right)$ **6.** 30 cm by 36 cm **7.** $4.25

8. $3\frac{1}{2}$ h at 80 km/h and $1\frac{1}{2}$ h at 100 km/h
9. 13 years old; 5 years old
10. 34¢ stamps: 5; 40¢ stamps: 3

Exercises, page 150

1. a. $y < x + 2$ **b.** $y \leq \frac{x}{2} + 1$ **c.** $y > x + 1$
d. $y > -x + 4$ **e.** $y \leq x - 4$ **f.** $y > 2x - 5$
2. a. $y \leq x + 20$; yes; yes; yes

b. $y > 9 - \frac{x}{2}$; yes; yes; yes **3. a.** $y = -x + 2$
b. $y = x - 1$ **c.** $y = -\frac{2}{3}x$

5. a. Yes **b.** No **c.** 150 **6. a.** Yes **b.** No
c. The y-intercept, 45, is the maximum number
of metres of corduroy that can be bought if no
broadcloth is bought. **d.** The x-intercept, 54, is
the maximum number of metres of broadcloth
that can be bought if no corduroy is
bought. **7. a.** Yes **b.** No
c. The y-intercept, 40, is the maximum number of
metres of corduroy that can be bought if no
broadcloth is bought. **d.** The x-intercept, 48, is
the maximum number of metres of broadcloth,
that can be bought if no corduroy is bought.

8. Let x be the number of sockeye salmon and
y be the number of coho salmon. The shaded
region represents the possible legal catches.

Using the Caculator, page 151
80 digits

Exercises, page 154
1. a. i **b.** iii **c.** ii **2.** Answers will vary.

4. a. $y < \frac{1}{2}x + 1$ **b.** $y \leq 2x$
$\quad\quad y \geq -x + 4$ $\quad\quad y \leq -2x + 8$
c. $y \leq -x + 4$ **d.** $y < x + 2$
$\quad\quad y \geq x$ $\quad\quad y \geq x$
e. $y \geq -x + 6$ **f.** $y > -x$
$\quad\quad y \geq x$ $\quad\quad y \leq -x + 2$

5. a. $y < \frac{4}{3}x$ **b.** $y \geq x$
$\quad\quad x < 4$ $\quad\quad y \leq 4$
$\quad\quad y > -\frac{2}{5}x + 2$ $\quad\quad x \geq 2$

c. $y \geq -2x + 4$ **d.** $y \geq \frac{4}{3}x - \frac{5}{3}$
$\quad\quad y < 4$ $\quad\quad y \leq 4x - 7$
$\quad\quad y > 2$ $\quad\quad y \leq 5$

e. $y \leq x + 2$ **f.** $y < -x + 2$
$\quad\quad y \geq -2x + 2$ $\quad\quad y \geq \frac{1}{2}x + 2$
$\quad\quad y \geq 3x - 3$ $\quad\quad x \geq -2$

6. a. square (3,1), (7,1), (3,5), (7,5)
b. square (0,0), (2,2), (0,4), (−2,2)
c. parallelogram (1,1), (4,4), (4,7), (1,4)
d. trapezoid (0,0), (7,0), (7,4), (4,4)
e. parallelogram (0,0), (2,2), (0,6), (−2,4)
f. trapezoid (1,2), (5,10), (5,15), (1,3)

g. rectangle $\left(-\frac{1}{2}, \frac{1}{2}\right)$, $\left(\frac{1}{2}, 1\frac{1}{2}\right)$, $\left(-1\frac{1}{2}, 3\frac{1}{2}\right)$, $\left(-2\frac{1}{2}, 2\frac{1}{2}\right)$

h. rectangle (0,0), $\left(1\frac{1}{2}, 0\right)$, $\left(1\frac{1}{2}, 1\right)$, (0,1)

7. Answers will vary.
8. a. Let x represent the number of discounted
records sold, y the number of discounted tapes:
$x + y > 250$; $8x + 5y \leq 1750$.
9. a. Let x represent the percentage of copper,
y the percentage of lead **b.** $x \leq 19$; $y \leq 11$;
$x + y \geq 25$.

Exercises, page 157
1. a. 420 **b.** 600 **c.** 2700
2. a. 17; 2 **b.** 30; 15 **c.** 36; 6 **d.** 130; 36

3. b. $\left(10, 7\frac{1}{2}\right)$, (10,10), $\left(6\frac{2}{3}, 10\right)$

c. At $\left(6\frac{2}{3}, 10\right)$, cost is about $9 333 333 333.

4. b. (400,1200), (400,2000), (600,1800) **c.** (600,1800)
5. Pat: 30 h; Chris: 50 h
6. greatest profit: $180 000; least profit: $132 000
7. 60 ha of wheat and 60 ha of soybeans

Review, page 159
2. Answers will vary.
4. a. $x + y \leq 30$ **b.** profit $= 600x + 1500y$
$\quad\quad x \geq 10$ **c.** $33 000
$\quad\quad y \geq 10$
$\quad\quad 7500x + 12 500y \leq 300 000$

Problem Solving 11, page 160
1. a. 3 h; (3,0) **b.** 6 h; (0,6)
d. 2 h **2.** $2 tickets: 12; $3 tickets: 16 **3.** 14 : 15

Using the Computer, page 161
1. $13 400 **2.** $16 400 **3.** 10 model As,
26 model Bs, and 24 model Cs
4. Answers will vary.

Test, page 162
1. a. $(-1,2)$ **b.** $(3,-2)$ **c.** $(4,3)$ **d.** $(-1,2)$
e. $(-1,2)$ **f.** $(17,3)$

3. a. $y < x + 2$ **b.** $y \geq x$
$\quad\quad y > \frac{x}{2} + 1$ $\quad\quad\quad\quad y < -x + 40$

c. $x \geq 4$
$\quad x < 10$
$\quad y \leq \frac{x}{2} + 6$
$\quad y \geq \frac{x}{2} + 2$

5. a. 160 **b.** 415 **c.** 320

Cumulative Review, page 163
1. a. $7x^2 - x$ **b.** $-4xy + 17x$ **2. a.** 1 **b.** 6
3. a. -1 **b.** $\frac{70}{}$ **c.** 1 **d.** $16\sqrt{2}$ **e.** 72 **f.** 20
4. a. 7 **b.** $\sqrt{229}$ **c.** $2\sqrt{2}$ **d.** $\sqrt{437}$ **e.** $\sqrt{21}$
f. $4\frac{1}{2}$ **5.** 13 **6. a.** -4 **b.** -1 **c.** -10 **d.** 5
7. a. $x < 3$ **b.** $x \geq 4$ **c.** $1 \leq x \leq 2$ **d.** $x \in R$
8. a. $-\frac{3}{2}; 4$ **b.** $\frac{1}{2}; -3$ **9. a.** parallel
b. intersect in a single point **c.** identical
10. a. $y = -\frac{2}{3}x + \frac{22}{3}$ **b.** $y = 2x - 8$
c. $y = -2x + 5$

Unit 6
Exercises, page 166
1. a. $2x^2 + 3x - 5; 2$ **b.** $2x^2 - 3x + 4; 2$
c. $-2a^2 + 4b^2 + 3; 2$ **d.** $-3ax + 2by + 5xy; 2$
e. $3x^3 - 5x^2y + 7xy^2 - 2y^2; 3$
f. $8a^2 - 3ab + 4b^2; 2$
g. $3x^2y - xyz - 2y^2z + 2yz^2; 3$
h. $-2a^4 + 5a^3b + 3a^2b^2 - 3b^4; 4$
i. $-2r^4s + r^3s^2 - 3rs^2 + 5s^3; 5$
j. $5x^2y - 2xyz + 3xz^2 + 3y^3; 3$ **2. a.** $10x + 8$
b. $6x + 11$ **c.** $4x + 11$ **d.** $7x - 1$ **e.** $2x + 9$
f. $7x^2 + 7x + 9$ **g.** $9x^2 + 7x + 13$
h. $6x^2 - 2x + 1$ **i.** $2x^2 - 2x$ **j.** $-6x^2 - 3x + 1$
3. a. $-x - 3$ **b.** $-2x + 3$ **c.** $x^2 - xy$
d. $-3x + 2y$ **e.** $-3x^2 - 5x + 2$
f. $2m^3 - 3m^2 - 2m$ **4. a.** $3x + 1$ **b.** $2x + 2$
c. $-x + 1$ **d.** $2x - 4$ **e.** $3x^2 + 3x + 2$
f. $3x^2 + 2x + 3$ **g.** $3x^2 - 2x + 2$
h. $-4x^2 + 5x + 2$ **i.** $6x^2 - 2x + 1$

j. $-6x^2 + 10x + 2$ **5. a.** $10a + 6$ **b.** $6x^2 + 10$
c. $9x^2 - 3x + 16$ **d.** $18x^2 - 3x + 1$
e. $12x^2 + xy + 14y^2$ **f.** $-2x^2 + 13xy - y^2$
6. $3x^2 + 5x + 2$ **7.** $6a - 7b - 2$
8. a. $5x^2 + 4x + 17$ **b.** $6x^2 - 3x - 19$
c. $-7x^2 + 7xy + 2y^2$ **d.** $10x^2 - 5xy + 2y^2$
e. $3x^2 + 12y^2$ **f.** $2ab^3 + 2a^3 - 4a^2b + 5b^2$
g. $-2m^3 - mn^2 + 2n^3$
h. $-x^2y - 2xy^2 + 9xyz + 10xz$ **9. a.** -3
b. -6 **c.** -11 **d.** 16 **e.** -40 **10. a.** 1 **b.** 2
c. -12 **d.** 3 **e.** 6 **f.** 1 **g.** 1 **11. a.** 2; 2; -5
b. $-3; -3; -2; 1$ **c.** $-1; -6; 4$ **d.** 2; $-2; -3$
e. 14; $-3; 4; -5$

Extra, page 167
1. Let x be the number in the top left corner of
the two-by-two array. Then the four numbers are
$x, x + 1, x + 7,$ and $x + 8$. Their sum is $4x + 16$.
2. a. Let y be the number in the top row of the
four-by-one array. Then the numbers are $y, y + 7$,
$y + 14,$ and $y + 21$. Their sum is $4y + 42$.
b. Let z be the number in the top left corner of
the three-by-three array. The sum of the nine
numbers is then $9z + 72$.

Exercises, page 169
1. a. $2x + 4$ **b.** $-2y - 6$ **c.** $20y + 12$
d. $7x - 35y$ **e.** $6x - 3y + 9$
f. $-\frac{3}{5}x^2 + \frac{6}{25}x - \frac{9}{10}$ **2. a.** $x^2 + 5x$
b. $15x^2 + 6xy$ **c.** $3x^2y + xy^2$ **d.** $20x^3y - 12x^2y^2$
e. $15x^3 + 10x^2 - 20x$ **f.** $-6xy^3 - 3y^3 + 15y^2$
g. $0.3x^3 + 1.8x^2y - 0.9xy^2$
h. $-3a^2b + ab^2 - 2ab$ **3. a.** 6 **b.** -5 **c.** -1
d. 3 **e.** 3 **f.** 4 **4. a.** $5x + 4$ **b.** $3x - 5$
c. $-4x - 1$ **d.** $15x - 7y + 1$
e. $7a^3 + 3a^2b + a^2$ **f.** $-15x^2y + 4x^2 + 14xy$
g. $-9a^2 + 7ab - 5b^2 - b$ **h.** $12a - 9b$
i. $10x^2 + 3xy + 2x$ **j.** $9a^3 + 6a^2 + 12a$ **5. a.** 2
b. $-\frac{4}{5}$ **c.** $1\frac{1}{10}$ **d.** 75 **e.** $1\frac{2}{7}$ **f.** $-5\frac{1}{3}$
6. a. $3x^2 + x$ **b.** $10x^2 - 6xy$ **c.** $7x^2 - x$
d. $30x^2 - 9x$ **7. a.** $6x^3 - 4x^2$ **b.** $2\pi r^3 + 3\pi r^2$
c. $8x^3 + 32x^2$

Exercises, page 171
2. a. $x^2 + 11x + 28$ **b.** $a^2 + 15a + 54$
c. $z^2 + z - 6$ **d.** $k^2 + 5k - 24$ **e.** $t^2 - 2t - 35$
f. $r^2 - 8r + 15$ **g.** $y^2 - 10y + 9$
h. $x^2 - 10xy + 24y^2$ **i.** $a^2 - ab - 56b^2$
j. $p^2 - 25$ **k.** $d^2 - 9$ **l.** $x^2 - y^2$
3. a. $x^2 + 10x + 25$ **b.** $t^2 - 4t + 4$
c. $a^2 - 8a + 16$ **d.** $4x^2 + 4x + 1$
e. $9j^2 - 12j + 4$ **f.** $25p^2 - 40p + 16$
g. $a^2 + 4ab + 4b^2$ **h.** $9x^2 + 30xy + 25y^2$
i. $c^2 - 4cd + 4d^2$ **j.** $9a^2 - 6ab + b^2$
k. $36s^2 + 24st + 4t^2$ **l.** $49k^2 - 56km + 16m^2$

449

4. a. 6 **b.** 3 **c.** $7\frac{1}{2}$ **d.** 18 **e.** $\frac{3}{5}$ **f.** -2

5. a. $-5x^2 - 7x + 6$ **b.** $3x^2 + 11x + 10$
c. $6x^2 - 7x - 3$ **d.** $14a^2 - 23ab + 3b^2$
e. $6x^2 - 19xy + 10y^2$ **f.** $6x^3 + 2x^2 - 9x - 3$
g. $x^3 + 2x^2 + 2x + 1$ **h.** $x^3 + 5x^2 + 9x + 9$
i. $x^3 - 3x^2 + 5x - 3$ **j.** $2a^4 - a^3 - 7a^2 + 5a - 15$
k. $3x^3 + 11x^2 + 9x + 9$ **l.** $5x^3 + 17x^2 - 14x - 8$
m. $10x^2 + 15x - 175$ **n.** $6x^4 - 19x^3 + 13x^2 + 3x$
o. $8a^4 - 8a^3b - 8a^2b^2 + 8ab^3$
p. $-12x^4 + 26x^3y - 38x^2y^2 - 16xy^3$
6. a. $x^2 + 6x - 6$ **b.** $2x^2 + 2y^2$
c. $37x^2 + 36xy - 9y^2$ **d.** $3x^2 - 23x + 25$
e. $-8x^2 - 38x + 33$ **f.** $-6x^2 - 23x - 15$
g. $2a^2 + 6ab - 2b^2$ **h.** $2x^2 - 10xy - 2y^2$

7. a. $5\frac{1}{2}$ **b.** -10 **c.** 3 **d.** 3 **e.** 5 **f.** 6

8. a. $x^2 + 3x - 10$ **b.** $9x^2 + 12x + 4$
c. $3x^2 + 4x - 15$ **d.** $x^2 + 2x - 15$
9. a. $w^2 + 3kw$ **b.** $w^2 - 5kw$ **c.** $3w^2 + 2bw$

d. $h^2 + 2hd$ **e.** $\frac{1}{2}b^2 - 3bk$ **10.** 10 m by 10 m

11. 15 cm by 30 cm **12. a.** $x^3 + 6x^2 - x - 30$
b. $6x^3 + x^2 - 16x - 27$ **c.** $x^3 + 3x^2 + 3x + 1$
d. $x^4 + 4x^3 + 6x^2 + 4x + 1$ **e.** $x^4 - 1$
f. $27x^3 + 135x^2 + 225x + 125$
g. $x^4 + 2x^3 + 3x^2 + 2x + 1$
h. $x^6 + 3x^5 + 6x^4 + 7x^3 + 6x^2 + 3x + 1$
13. a. $\pi x^2 + 6\pi x + 9\pi$ **b.** $2x^2 - 4x + 2$
14. about 15 m

Extra, page 173
1.

Year	Simple Interest	Compound Interest
1	$A = P + Pr$	$A = P + Pr$
2	$A = P + 2Pr$	$A = Pr^2 + 2Pr + P$
3	$A = P + 3Pr$	$A = Pr^3 + 3Pr^2 + 3Pr + P$
4	$A = P + 4Pr$	$A = Pr^4 + 4Pr^3 + 6Pr^2 + 4Pr + P$

2. Higher powers of r appear in the expansion of $P(1 + r)^n$ which do not appear in the expansion of $P(1 + rn)$, indicating that the accumulated interest is also earning interest.

Exercises, page 175
1. a. yes; a^2b^4 **b.** no **c.** yes; m^3n^5
d. yes; $4a^4b^7$ **e.** yes; $9ac^4$ **f.** yes; $4x^5y$
2. a. $\{1, x, x^2\}$ **b.** $\{1, 3, x, 3x, x^2, 3x^2\}$
c. $\{1, 2, 3, 6, x, y, 2x, 3x, 2y, 3y, xy, 2xy, 3xy, 6xy,$
$6x, 6y\}$
d. $\{1, x, xy, x^2, y, x^2y\}$
e. $\{1, 3, x, y, 3x, 3y, 3x^2, 3xy, x^2, xy, x^2y, 3x^2y\}$
3. a. a^4b^5 **b.** yz^2 **c.** $4xy^4$ **d.** $-3x^2y^3$
e. $-2ab^3$ **f.** a^2b^3 **4. a.** $4x^2y$ **b.** $5a$ **c.** $4pqr$
d. $5n$ **e.** 1 **f.** ab^2c **g.** q **h.** x^2y^4z **i.** $3m^2n^2$
j. $3c$ **5. a.** $6xy^2$ by $6xy^2$ **b.** $5a$ by $5a$
c. $14mnq$ by $14mnq$ **d.** $7ab$ by $7ab$ **e.** $14z$ by $14z$

f. $12rst$ by $12rst$ **6. a.** $2a^2b^3$ **b.** $3x^2y^3$ **c.** $2m^2n^4$
d. $2a^2c$ **e.** $5yz^3$ **f.** $-3mn^3$

Extra, page 175
465 peanuts

Exercises, page 177
1. a. $4x - 1$ **b.** $3x - 2$ **c.** $3m + 2n$
d. $3a - 2b$ **e.** $4xy - y^2 + 2$ **f.** $2a^2 - 3a - 4b$
2. a. $3(2x + 3)$ **b.** $5(2m + 3)$ **c.** $7(3a^2 - 1)$
d. $4(3m^2 - 2)$ **e.** $5(x^2 - 2)$ **f.** $3a(a - 2)$
g. $2x(7 - y)$ **h.** $5a(a + 2b)$ **i.** $4m(2m + 1)$
j. $4n(7m^2 - 4n)$ **k.** $6ab(2b - 1)$ **l.** $x(17z^3 + 18y)$
3. a. $5a - 2b$ **b.** $c - 3$ **c.** $3x - 5$ **d.** $3a - 2b$
e. $6z - 4$ **f.** $2m + 3$
4. a. $3m^2n(6m^3n + 5n + 4m)$
b. $15x^2yz(4y^2 + y - 2)$
c. $3x^2y^2z^2(7xy^2z^2 + 6yz^3 + 4)$
d. $5mnt(7m^2nt + 5mnt - 4)$
e. $2x^3y^2z^2(8x^2y + 9x - 6)$
f. $5rst^2(6rs + 9s + 2)$
5. a. $2(l + w)$ **b.** $2b(b + 2h)$ **c.** $\pi(R^2 - r^2)$
d. $b(b + 2s)$ **6. a.** $5(3x^2 - x + 2)$
b. $2(4x^2 + 3x - 6)$ **c.** $3a(a^2 + 3a - 2)$
d. $5m(3m^2 - 6m + 2)$ **e.** $a^2(b^2 + b - 1)$
f. $xy^2(x^2 + xy - y^2)$ **g.** $7mn(m^2 - 2mn + 3n^2)$
h. $7x^3y(2x^2 - 3x + 1)$ **i.** $4m^2n^2(2m^3 - 4mn + 3)$
j. $ab(a^2 + 2ab - b)$ **k.** $5y(3x^2 - 2xy + 6y^2)$
l. $a^5(b^2 - b + 1)$ **m.** $2xy(4x^2 - 6xy + 3y^2 - 3)$
n. $3a^2b^2c^3(5a + 6c + 7)$ **o.** $7m^2n^2(3m + 2n - 5)$
p. $6x^3y^3z^2(4x^2 + 5y - 3z)$
7. a. $6a^2b - 2a + 3$ **b.** $2a^3c + 4bc^2 + 3c$
c. $2a^4 - 4a^3b + 5a^2b$ **8. a.** $2(p + l + 2w)$
b. $6(b + s)$ **c.** $2\pi(r + R)$ **d.** $2r(\pi + 3)$
e. $2(m + 6t)$ **f.** $4(a + b)$ **9. a.** $x(x - \frac{1}{2}b)$

b. $l(l + \frac{1}{2}b)$ **c.** $\pi(R^2 - r^2)$ **d.** $\pi(2r^2 + R^2)$

e. $r^2(4 - \pi)$ **f.** $r^2(\pi - 1)$

Exercises, page 182
1. a. 3, 2 **b.** 9, 1 **c.** $-4, 3$ **d.** $-5, -2$ **e.** 8, -3
f. 5, 1 **g.** $-7, 2$ **h.** 9, 6 **i.** $-8, -4$ **j.** $-5, 4$
2. a. **b.** **c.**

3. a. $(k + 3)(k + 2)$ **b.** $(d + 6)(d + 2)$
c. $(t + 5)(t + 2)$ **d.** $(u + 6)^2$ **e.** $(p + 5)(p + 4)$
f. $(a + 8)(a + 2)$ **g.** $(a + 10b)(a + 2b)$
h. $(r + 12t)(r + 3t)$ **i.** $(x + 15y)(x + 2y)$
4. a. $(m - 2)(m - 1)$ **b.** $(n - 5)(n - 3)$
c. $(t - 5)^2$ **d.** $(x - 4)(x - 3)$ **e.** $(y - 8)(y - 2)$

450

f. $(b - 5)(b - 4)$ **g.** $(a - 12b)(a - b)$
h. $(x - 6y)(x - 5y)$ **i.** $(t - 5v)(t - 3v)$
5. a. $(a + 2)(a - 5)$ **b.** $(m + 3)(m - 12)$
c. $(y + 6)(y - 3)$ **d.** $(x + 7y)(x - 2y)$
e. $(a + 2b)(a - 3b)$ **f.** $(a + 7b)(a - 4b)$
g. $(p + 4q)(p - 8q)$ **h.** $(r + 7)(r - 2)$
i. $(m + 3k)(m - 13k)$ **j.** $(x + 1)(x - 49)$
k. $(a + 7)(a - 6)$ **l.** $(s + 2t)(s - 9t)$
6. c. $(r + 8)(r - 5)$ **d.** $(y + 10)(y - 3)$
h. $(s + 6t)(s - 4t)$ **7. a.** $(x + 4y)(x + y)$
b. $(a - 12)(a - 5)$ **c.** $(n + 15)(n - 3)$
d. $(x - 5)(x - 2)$ **e.** $(m + 8)(m - 6)$
f. $(x - 4)(x - 1)$ **g.** $(a + 5b)(a - 2b)$ **h.** $(x - y)^2$
i. $(s - 4)(s - 2)$ **j.** $(12 - r)(9 + r)$
k. $(a - 9)(a - 4)$ **l.** $(5q + p)(2q - p)$
m. $(3 + t)(8 - t)$ **n.** $(5 - n)(9 + n)$
o. $(k + 7)(k + 5)$ **8. a.** $3(x + 7)(x + 1)$
b. $4(a - 10)(a + 1)$ **c.** $7(x + 5y)(x + y)$
d. $4(x + 3)(x - 7)$ **e.** $4(a + 9b)(a - 4b)$
f. $5(f - 12g)(f - 7g)$ **g.** $-2(p + 5q)(p - 6q)$
h. $2(16 + x)(4 - x)$ **i.** $2(11 + r)(7 - r)$
9. a. $x(x + 3)(x + 2)$ **b.** $x^2(x + 8)(x + 5)$
c. $a(x + 9)(x - 3)$ **d.** $10a(x + 8)(x - 2)$
e. $7q(p + q)^2$ **f.** $y^2(x + 12)(x - 10)$
g. $7ax(x + 4)(x + 2)$ **h.** $-15b^2(c + 4)(c + 2)$
i. $3mn(m + 20n)(m - 3n)$ **j.** $-5s(t - 1)^2$
10. a. 5, 7 **b.** 7, 11 **c.** 32 **d.** 10, 22 **e.** 3, 4
f. 12, 36 **11. a.** $3(x + 1)(3x + 2)$
b. $8(2a + 1)(4a - 3)$ **c.** $(x^2 + 2)(x^2 + 1)$
d. $(a^2 + 9)(a^2 + 1)$ **e.** $(r^2 + 15)(r^2 - 2)$
f. $7(t^2 + 2)(t^2 + 1)$ **g.** $x(x - 1)$
h. $2(2x + 7y)(x - 2y)$

12. a.
   $x + 3$ **b.** $x + 2$
   $2x + 1$ $2x + 3$

c. **d.**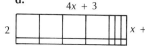
   $3x + 2$ $4x + 3$
   $x + 2$ $x + 1$

Extra, page 183
1. Answers will vary.
2. first polynomial: 41; second polynomial: 80

Exercises, page 186
1. a. $6x^2 + 19x + 15$ **b.** $2x^2 + 25x + 63$
c. $5x^2 + 11x - 12$ **d.** $6x^2 - 13x - 28$
e. $7x^2 - 34x + 24$ **f.** $8x^2 - 2x - 15$
g. $6x^2 + 47x - 8$ **h.** $15x^2 - 26x + 8$
i. $21x^2 - 23x - 20$ **2. a.** $17x$ **b.** $23x$ **c.** $-7x$
d. $2x$ **e.** $-42x$ **f.** x **g.** $-10x$ **h.** $-10x$ **i.** x

3. a. x, $2x$; 1, 2, 4, 5, 10, 20; both positive
b. x, $2x$, $4x$; 1, 3; both negative
c. x, $3x$; 1, 5, 25; both negative
d. x, $2x$, $4x$; 1, 2, 3, 6; both negative
e. x, $2x$, $4x$, $8x$; 1, 2, 3, 4, 6, 9, 12, 18, 36;
one positive and one negative
f. x, $3x$; 1, 5, 25; one positive and one negative
g. x, $2x$, $3x$, $6x$; 1, 2, 3, 6, 7, 14, 21, 42;
one positive and one negative
h. x, $3x$, $9x$; 1, 2, 3, 6; one positive and one negative
i. x, $3x$, $5x$, $15x$; 1, 2, 4, 8; both positive
4. a. x, $2x$; 1, 3, 5, 15 **b.** x, $3x$; 1, 2, 3, 6
c. x, $7x$; 1, 5 **d.** x, $7x$; 1, 5 **e.** x, $2x$, $4x$; 1, 5, 7, 35
f. x, $2x$, $4x$, $8x$; 1, 5, 7, 35 **g.** x, $2x$, $3x$, $6x$; 1, 5
h. x, $3x$, $9x$; 1, 2, 7, 14
i. x, $2x$, $3x$, $6x$; 1, 2, 4, 5, 10, 20
5. a. $(2x + 5)(x + 4)$ **b.** $(2x - 3)(2x - 1)$
c. $(3x - 5)(x - 5)$ **d.** $2(x - 3)(2x - 1)$
e. $4(2x + 3)(x - 3)$ **f.** $(3x + 5)(x - 5)$
g. $3(2x - 7)(x + 2)$ **h.** $3(3x - 2)(x + 1)$
i. $(5x + 2)(3x + 4)$ **6. a.** 2; 2 **b.** -4; 4; 8
c. -3; 5 **d.** 6; 4; 7 **e.** 3; 12; -3 **f.** 2; 3; -8
7. a. $(3x + 1)(x + 2)$ **b.** $(7x + 3)(x + 1)$
c. $(2x + 3y)(x + 5y)$ **d.** $(11x + 3y)(x + y)$
f. $(7x + 2)(x - 3)$ **g.** $(5x + y)(3x + 2y)$
h. $(3x + 1)(2x - 3)$ **i.** $(3x + 4y)(x - 2y)$
k. $(2 + y)(5 - y)$ **l.** $(5x + 2)(x - 4)$
n. $(4x + 9y)(3x - 2y)$ **p.** $(3x + 4y)(2x + 3y)$
q. $(5a + 2b)(2a - 3b)$ **r.** $(3x + 4y)(3x - 7y)$
s. $(2x - 5)(x + 4)$ **t.** $(2x + 5)^2$
u. $3(5x - 4y)(x + y)$ **w.** $2(3x^2 - 3x - 10)$
8. a. $3(6x - 7)(x + 3)$ **b.** $2(4x - 3)(2x - 3)$
c. $3(2x + 5)(x + 5)$ **d.** $3(2x + 5)(2x - 3)$
e. $a(4x + 3)(4x - 1)$ **f.** $a(5x + 4)(x - 4)$
g. $ab(5c + 1)(2c + 3)$ **h.** $2(2x - 7)(x + 3)$
i. $3n^2(3m + 1)(m - 1)$ **j.** $5(3x + 8)(2x + 1)$
k. $6(3a - 7b)(a + b)$ **l.** $2y(3x + 4y)(2x - 3y)$
m. $2(5 + 4x)(2 - x)$ **n.** $2a(4b + 7)(2b - 5)$
o. $10yz(3x + 4)(3x + 2)$ **9. a.** $-5y^2(4x + 3)$
b. $-16abc(3b + 2)(b - 2)$ **c.** $-5(7x + 3)(3x + 2)$
d. $-8mn^2(4m + 1)(m + 2)$
e. $6a(10y - 3)(5y + 2)$ **f.** $(2m^3(8 - 3y)(4 + 3y)$
g. $7(6x + 7)(2x + 1)$ **h.** $2a^3b(8 - 3c)(5 + 3c)$
i. $15[(x - 2)^2 + 1]^2$ **j.** $8a(2b + 9)(b + 7)$
k. $(2k + 5)(k - 4)$
l. $[3(d - 2)^2 + 2][2(d - 2)^2 - 1]$

Extra, page 187
1. $(3x + 2)(2x + 5)$ **2.** $(3a + 5)(a - 1)$
3. $(9r + 2s)(r - 3s)$

Extra, page 189
1. a. $6r$ **b.** not a perfect square
c. not a perfect square **d.** mn **e.** $7a^2b^3$ **f.** $\frac{1}{3}s$
g. not a perfect square **h.** $11a^4b^3$ **i.** $\frac{2}{5}t$

j. not a perfect square **2. a.** $x^2 - 81$ **b.** $b^2 - 36$
c. $r^2 - 121$ **d.** $49 - t^2$ **e.** $x^2 - 9y^2$ **f.** $x^4 - 4y^2$
g. $m^2 - 9$ **h.** $25k^2 - 16$ **i.** $9a^2 - 4b^2$
3. a. $x^2 + 6x + 9$ **b.** $4x^2 + 20x + 25$
c. $4x^2 - 20x + 25$ **d.** $16x^2 + 56x + 49$
e. $25a^2 - 30a + 9$ **f.** $49a^2 - 70a + 25$
g. $25m^4 + 30m^2 + 9$ **h.** $9a^2 - 12a + 4$
i. $16m^2n^2 - 40mny^2 + 25y^4$
4. a. $(5a + 7)(5a - 7)$ **b.** $(6r + 11)(6r - 11)$
c. $(9m + 2n)(9m - 2n)$ **d.** $(3s + 7t)(3s - 7t)$
e. $(13 + 11x)(13 - 11x)$ **f.** $(5rs + 6t)(5rs - 6t)$
g. $(a^2 + 9d^2)(a + 3d)(a - 3d)$
h. $4(t + 4v)(t - 4v)$ **i.** $(49j^2 + 25)(7j + 5)(7j - 5)$
5. a. $(x + 3)^2$ **b.** $(5m - 4)^2$ **c.** $(2r - 5)^2$
d. $(a + 4b)^2$ **e.** $(y - 6)^2$ **f.** $(7r - 3t)^2$
g. $(2x - 5y)^2$ **h.** $(3t + 7v)^2$ **i.** $(2a - 11b)^2$
6. a. $(11x^2 + 3y^2)(11x^2 - 3y^2)$ **b.** $(b^3 + 11)^2$
c. $(8ac + b)^2$ **d.** $(mn + 15)(mn - 15)$
e. $(10y^2 + 3z^2)(10y^2 - 3z^2)$ **f.** $(2x^3 + 15)^2$
g. $(3 - z^3)^2$ **h.** $(x^3 - 5)^2$
i. $(x^2y^2 + 25v^2)(xy + 5v)(xy - 5v)$ **7. a.** $(2x + 7)^2$
b. $2(2x + 5)(x - 3)$ **c.** $(4r + 5s)(4r - 5s)$
d. $(4x - 1)(x - 3)$ **e.** $(3m - 5)^2$ **f.** $(4a + 3b)^2$
g. $(9x^3 + 1)(9x^3 - 1)$ **h.** $(5x + 6)(5x - 6)$
i. cannot be factored **j.** $(3x - 2)^2$
k. $(5p - 6q)(p - 6q)$ **l.** $(2z^2 + 9y)^2$
8. a. $-(5a + 1)(a + 1)$ **b.** $(14x^5 + 5)(2x^5 + 5)$
c. $(a + 3b + 2c)(a - b - 2c)$ **d.** $(x^2 - y^2 - 1)^2$
e. $(x + 3)(x - 3)(x + 2)(x - 2)$
f. $(x^4 + 1)(x^2 + 1)(x + 1)(x - 1)$
g. $-5(9x - 5)(x + 1)$ **h.** $3(x + 1)(3x - 5)$
i. $4(1 - x)(x + 4)$

Extra, page 189
975 308 644 000 000 000

Exercises, page 191
1. a. 0; 1 **b.** 7; -3 **c.** -7; -9 **d.** 4; -4
e. 0; -1 **f.** 3; -9 **g.** -5; 8 **h.** 8 **i.** 2
2. a. $1\frac{1}{2}$; 1 **b.** $\frac{1}{4}$; -5 **c.** $-\frac{3}{10}$; $-2\frac{1}{2}$ **d.** 14; -14
e. $\frac{1}{2}$; $-\frac{3}{4}$ **f.** $\frac{1}{2}$; $-\frac{3}{4}$ **g.** $-\frac{3}{5}$ **h.** $-\frac{1}{9}$; $3\frac{1}{2}$ **3. a.** 3; 4
b. 3; -3 **c.** 0; 5 **d.** 0; $\frac{1}{7}$ **e.** 2; 8 **f.** 3; -3
g. 6; -3 **h.** $1\frac{1}{4}$; $-1\frac{1}{4}$ **i.** 5 **j.** 0; 9 **k.** 1; -9
l. 8; -1 **4. a.** $-1\frac{2}{3}$; $1\frac{1}{2}$ **b.** $-2\frac{1}{2}$; -3 **c.** $3\frac{1}{2}$; $-3\frac{1}{2}$
d. $-\frac{1}{5}$; 1 **e.** $2\frac{2}{5}$; $-2\frac{2}{5}$ **f.** 5; -5 **g.** $1\frac{3}{7}$ **h.** $\frac{3}{4}$; $-\frac{1}{2}$
i. -5; 1 **j.** $-1\frac{1}{2}$ **k.** $2\frac{2}{3}$; $-2\frac{2}{3}$ **l.** 1; 4 **5. a.** 4; -4
b. $1\frac{1}{4}$; $-1\frac{1}{4}$ **c.** $-\frac{1}{3}$; $\frac{1}{2}$ **d.** $2\frac{1}{2}$; $-\frac{1}{2}$ **e.** 0; 2
f. $\frac{1}{3}$; -1 **g.** -8; 3 **h.** $2\frac{2}{3}$; $-4\frac{1}{2}$ **i.** 6; -6

j. 3; -1 **k.** $-1\frac{1}{4}$; $1\frac{1}{4}$ **l.** $\frac{1}{4}$; 7 **m.** 2; 3 **n.** 9; -1
o. -7; 2 **p.** -8; 1 **q.** $1\frac{1}{2}$ **r.** -6; 3 **s.** $7\frac{1}{2}$; -3
t. 7; -7 **u.** $2\frac{2}{3}$; -1 **v.** -4; 1 **w.** $-\frac{1}{4}$; 4
x. -6; 3 **y.** 5; -3 **z.** 4; -3 **6.** -5 or 4
7. 5 cm by 12 cm **8.** 7 cm by 7 cm
9. 5 cm by 15 cm **10.** $2\frac{1}{2}$ cm
11. $AB = 12$ cm; $BC = 5$ cm; $AC = 13$ cm
12. sidewalk: 2 m; driveway: 7 m

Extra, page 192
1. a. $41^2 - 1$ **b.** $55^2 - 1$ **c.** $71^2 - 1$
d. $89^2 - 1$ **2.** Yes.

Review, page 193
1. a. $3x^2 + 3x + 2$ **b.** $-4k^2 + 5k + 2$
c. $2t^2 - 8t - 5$ **d.** $-9x^2 - 12xy + 13y^2$
e. $3x^2 + 12y^2$ **f.** $3a^3 - 4a^2b + 3ab^3 + 5b^2$
2. a. $15x - 10$ **b.** $6x^2 - 9xy$ **c.** $6y^2 - 8y$
d. $2k^2 + 4k$ **e.** $10a^3b + 15ab^2$
f. $14t - 21t^2 + 28rt$ **3. a.** $x + y$ **b.** $3k + n$
c. $t^2 + 3t + 5$ **4. a.** $2x^2 - x - 28$
b. $2x^2 - 3xy - 9y^2$ **c.** $15a^2 - 54ab - 24b^2$
d. $3x^3 - 21x^2 + 30x$ **e.** $x^4 - 4$
f. $x^3 + 6x^2 + 11x + 6$ **g.** $4x^2 - 12x + 9$
h. $4x^2y^2 + 20xy + 25$ **i.** $27x^2 - 90xy + 75y^2$
5. a. $(x + 10)(x + 4)$ **b.** $(x - 6y)(x - 5y)$
c. $(r + 7)(r - 2)$ **d.** $(k + 2n)(k - 6n)$
e. $(v + 5w)(v - 5w)$ **f.** $(v^2 + w^2)(v + w)(v - w)$
g. $(2a + 5)(a + 4)$ **h.** $2(2b - 1)(b - 3)$
i. $(5k + 2)(3k + 4)$ **j.** $(8r + 3s)(8r - 3s)$
k. $9(4ab + 3c)(4ab - 3c)$ **l.** $2n(n + 15)(n - 3)$
m. $(8a - b)^2$ **n.** $(y^2 + 5)^2$ **o.** $2(5a + b)(a - 3b)$
p. $(x + 4)(x - 10)$ **q.** $(ab - 6)^2$
r. $3(2x + 1)(4x - 3)$ **6. a.** 0; 2 **b.** $-1\frac{1}{2}$
c. $4\frac{1}{3}$; $-4\frac{1}{3}$ **d.** 1; 4 **e.** $\frac{1}{2}$; $-\frac{1}{2}$ **f.** $-1\frac{1}{4}$; $-\frac{2}{3}$
g. $-1\frac{1}{2}$; 5 **h.** -2; -7 **i.** -1

7. a. At $1\frac{1}{5}$ s, the ball is travelling up and is 12 m above the ground. At 2 s, the ball is falling down and is 12 m above the ground. **b.** 1 s; 3 s
8. $-2\frac{3}{4}$ and $-7\frac{1}{4}$; 2 and 7

Exercises, page 196
1. a. $r \neq 1$ **b.** $c \neq -1$ **c.** $d \neq 0, -1$
d. $x \neq 0, 4\frac{1}{2}$ **e.** $a + b \neq 0$; $a - b \neq 0$
2. a. $\dfrac{x(x - 5)}{4y(x + 5)}$; $x \neq 5, -5$; $y \neq 0$
b. $\dfrac{2a + 1}{9}$; $a \neq 0, -\frac{1}{2}$

c. $\dfrac{2(x-5)}{x}$; $x \neq 0, -5$ **d.** $-\dfrac{1}{2}$; $y - 3x \neq 0$

e. $-\dfrac{s+3}{s+2}$; $s \neq -2, 2$ **f.** $-\dfrac{3-b}{b+3}$; $b \neq -3, 3$

3. a. $\dfrac{3}{m-1}$; $m \neq 0, 1$ **b.** $a - b$; $a \neq 0$

c. $x - 2$; $z \neq 0$ **d.** $\dfrac{k}{3k-1}$; $k \neq 0, \dfrac{1}{3}$

e. $\dfrac{1+2b^2}{3}$; $b \neq 0$ **f.** $2d(2c-1)$; $c \neq 0$

g. $\dfrac{t^2+2v+4}{t}$; $t \neq 0$; $v \neq 0$ **h.** -1; $x \neq 3$

i. -1; $a \neq 9$ **4. a.** $\dfrac{a-8}{a-5}$; $a \neq -3, 5$

b. $\dfrac{6}{n-5}$; $n \neq -2, 5$ **c.** $-3a$; $a \neq 2$

d. $\dfrac{x}{x+1}$; $x \neq -1, 5$ **e.** $\dfrac{t-2}{3}$; $t \neq -4$

f. $\dfrac{x+5}{x+2}$; $x \neq -2, -3$ **g.** $\dfrac{x+5}{x+3}$; $x \neq -3, -4$

h. $\dfrac{a-6}{a+2}$; $a \neq -2, 5$ **i.** $\dfrac{r+6}{6-r}$; $r \neq -6, 6$

5. $\dfrac{2s}{r}$ **6.** $\dfrac{x(x+5)}{(x+1)^2}$ **7. a.** $\dfrac{2x+3}{2x-5}$; $x \neq 2\dfrac{1}{2}, -4$

b. $\dfrac{5x+2}{x+3}$; $x \neq -2, -3$ **c.** $\dfrac{3x+7}{5x+1}$; $x \neq -\dfrac{1}{5}, 1\dfrac{1}{2}$

d. $\dfrac{2}{x+2}$; $x \neq -1\dfrac{1}{3}, -2$ **e.** $\dfrac{3(x-3)}{x-5}$; $x \neq -3, 5$

f. $-\dfrac{3(m+5)}{m+2}$; $m \neq -2, 2$

g. $-\dfrac{4a+3}{3a+1}$; $a \neq -\dfrac{1}{3}, 3$

h. $\dfrac{a+2}{c(2a-1)}$; $a \neq \dfrac{1}{2}, 5$; $c \neq 0$

i. $\dfrac{k+2}{l+2}$; $k \neq 1\dfrac{2}{3}$; $l \neq -2$ **j.** $\dfrac{y^2-3}{y+3}$; $y \neq -3$

8. a. $\dfrac{x+3z}{x+2z}$; $x - z \neq 0$; $x + 2z \neq 0$

b. $\dfrac{3r}{r+s}$; $r + s \neq 0$; $r - s \neq 0$

c. $\dfrac{x(x-2z)}{3}$; $x \neq 0$; $x - 2z \neq 0$

d. $\dfrac{2m+3}{3m}$; $m \neq 0, 2$

e. $\dfrac{a+b}{a-b}$; $a + b \neq 0$; $a - b \neq 0$

f. $-\dfrac{t+v}{v+2t}$; $v + 2t \neq 0$; $v - t \neq 0$

g. $-\dfrac{m+n}{2(2m+1)}$; $m \neq 0, -\dfrac{1}{2}$; $n - m \neq 0$

h. $\dfrac{x+5z}{2x+z}$; $3x - z \neq 0$; $2x + z \neq 0$

i. $-\dfrac{t(t+2s)}{2(s-t)}$; $s - t \neq 0$ **j.** $\dfrac{a}{4b}$; $a \neq 0$; $b \neq 0$

9. a. $x^2 + 3x$; $y \neq 0$ **b.** $a - 6$; $a \neq -6$

c. $4t + 5$; $t \neq -1\dfrac{1}{4}$ **d.** $3n + 7$; $n \neq \dfrac{1}{2}$

Exercises, page 199

1. a. $\dfrac{km}{12}$ **b.** $\dfrac{3x}{2y}$; $y \neq 0$ **c.** $\dfrac{15x}{y}$; $x \neq 0$; $y \neq 0$

d. $\dfrac{3b}{4}$; $a \neq 0$; $b \neq 0$ **e.** $-\dfrac{2x}{3}$; $x \neq 0$; $z \neq 0$

f. $\dfrac{2n^2}{3}$; $m \neq 0$; $n \neq 0$ **2. a.** $\dfrac{4m}{3n}$; $n \neq 0$

b. $\dfrac{7a}{2}$; $b \neq 0$ **c.** $\dfrac{3m}{2}$; $m \neq 0$; $n \neq 0$

d. $\dfrac{2rs}{5}$; $r \neq 0$; $s \neq 0$ **e.** $\dfrac{3x^3}{16z}$; $z \neq 0$; $x \neq 0$

f. $-\dfrac{a}{2b}$; $a \neq 0$; $b \neq 0$

3. a. $\dfrac{ab}{c}$; $a \neq 0$; $b \neq 0$; $c \neq 0$

b. $\dfrac{1}{9xz}$; $x \neq 0$; $z \neq 0$

c. $\dfrac{25n^3}{16t^3}$; $m \neq 0$; $n \neq 0$; $t \neq 0$

d. $\dfrac{36r^2s}{t}$; $r \neq 0$; $s \neq 0$; $t \neq 0$

e. $\dfrac{9c}{b}$; $a \neq 0$; $b \neq 0$; $c \neq 0$

f. $\dfrac{3}{4r^4st^3}$; $r \neq 0$; $s \neq 0$; $t \neq 0$

4. a. $\dfrac{x+5}{3x}$; $x \neq -5, 0$ **b.** $\dfrac{x-1}{x+1}$; $x \neq -\dfrac{1}{2}, -1$

c. $-\dfrac{3(x+3)}{x+2}$; $x \neq -3, -2, 1$

d. $\dfrac{y}{15}$; $y \neq 0$; $x \neq -3$

e. $\dfrac{6}{x^2(x+2)}$; $x \neq 0, -2, -3$

f. $(x-3)^2$; $x \neq -2, -\dfrac{1}{2}$

g. $\dfrac{1}{s(r-1)}$; $s \neq 0$; $r \neq 1, 2$

h. $\dfrac{2(n-5)}{4n+3}$; $n \neq -3, -\dfrac{3}{4}$

5. a. $\dfrac{10}{x-2}$; $x \neq -5, -3, -1, 2$

b. $\dfrac{21(x+2)}{2(x+5)(x-2)}$; $x \neq -5, 2, 3\dfrac{1}{2}$

c. $\dfrac{1}{(x + 1)(x - 1)}$; $x \neq -2, -1, 1, 3$

d. $\dfrac{9(x - 3)^2}{(x - 4)(x - 5)}$; $x \neq -4, 3, 4, 5$

6. a. $\dfrac{(x - 2)(3x + 2)}{(2x - 1)(x + 1)}$; $x \neq -\dfrac{1}{2}, -\dfrac{2}{3}, -1, \dfrac{1}{2}, \dfrac{2}{3}, 1$

b. $-\dfrac{(3m + n)(2m - 1)}{(m + 5n)(2m + 1)}$; $4m - n \neq 0$;

$m + 5n \neq 0$; $3n + 2m \neq 0$; $3n - 2m \neq 0$;
$m \neq \dfrac{1}{2}, -\dfrac{1}{2}$

c. $\dfrac{(2x^2 + y)^2}{(x - y)(x - 2y)}$; $3x - y \neq 0$; $x + 2y \neq 0$;

$x + y \neq 0$; $x - y \neq 0$; $x - 2y \neq 0$

d. $\dfrac{a(a + 2b)}{(a + b)(4a + b)}$; $3a + b \neq 0$; $2a + 3b \neq 0$;

$a + b \neq 0$; $a - b \neq 0$; $a - 2b \neq 0$; $4a + b \neq 0$;
$a + 2b \neq 0$

Exercises, page 201
1. a. 24   **b.** a^2; $a \neq 0$ **c.** $6y$; $y \neq 0$
d. $(x + 1)(x - 1)$; $x \neq 1, -1$
e. $15(x + 3)$; $x \neq -3$ **f.** $4n^2(n - 1)$; $n \neq 0, 1$

2. a. $\dfrac{3x}{18}, \dfrac{4x}{18}$ **b.** $\dfrac{10}{5y}, \dfrac{3y^2}{5y}$; $y \neq 0$

c. $\dfrac{y(x + 1)}{xy^2}, \dfrac{3x}{xy^2}$; $x \neq 0$; $y \neq 0$

d. $\dfrac{2(n + 2)}{6n^2}, \dfrac{n(n - 1)}{6n^2}$; $n \neq 0$

e. $\dfrac{3(x + 2)}{6(x + 1)}, \dfrac{2(x - 3)}{6(x + 1)}$; $x \neq -1$

3. a. $\dfrac{8}{x}$; $x \neq 0$ **b.** $\dfrac{13}{2m}$; $m \neq 0$

c. $\dfrac{3k^2 - 8}{6k}$; $k \neq 0$ **d.** $-\dfrac{a}{10}$

e. $\dfrac{8x^2 + 3z^2}{6xz}$; $x \neq 0$; $z \neq 0$

f. $\dfrac{3y + 2x}{xy}$; $x \neq 0$; $y \neq 0$ **g.** $\dfrac{5a}{6b}$; $b \neq 0$

h. $\dfrac{25a^2 + 6}{15ab}$; $a \neq 0$; $b \neq 0$ **4. a.** 3; $x \neq -3$

b. 2; $x \neq 1$ **c.** $\dfrac{x^2 + 2x - 8}{x(x - 4)}$; $x \neq 0, 4$

d. $\dfrac{z^2 - z + 4}{z(z - 2)}$; $z \neq 0, 2$ **e.** $\dfrac{x^2 + 2x + 1}{x + 2}$; $x \neq -2$

f. $\dfrac{2x + 9}{x + 3}$; $x \neq -3$ **g.** $\dfrac{2x^2 + 3x - 6}{(x + 2)(x - 2)}$; $x \neq 2, -2$

h. $\dfrac{2x^2 + 5x + 12}{(x + 4)(x + 1)}$; $x \neq -4, -1$ **i.** $\dfrac{k^2}{k - 1}$; $k \neq 1$

5. a. $\dfrac{13x + 2}{6(x - 2)}$; $x \neq 2$

b. $\dfrac{x^2 - 14}{4(x + 3)(x - 2)}$; $x \neq -3, 2$

c. $\dfrac{5x + 3}{(x + 1)(x + 3)}$; $x \neq -1, -3$

d. $\dfrac{3x^2 - 2x + 4}{x(x - 2)(x + 1)}$; $x \neq -1, 0, 2$

e. $\dfrac{-8x - 14}{(x - 3)(x + 4)(x + 1)}$; $x \neq -4, -1, 3$

f. $\dfrac{2x^2 + 4x - 9}{(x + 3)(x + 5)(x - 2)}$; $x \neq -5, -3, 2$

g. $\dfrac{4x^2 + 12x + 9}{6x(x + 1)(x - 1)}$; $x \neq -1, 0, 1$

h. $\dfrac{-x - 8}{(x + 2)^2(x - 1)}$; $x \neq -2, 1$

6. a. $\dfrac{4 - 9x}{6(x + 2)}$; $x \neq -2$

b. $\dfrac{x^2 + 3x + 3}{3x(x - 3)}$; $x \neq 0, 3$

c. $\dfrac{2x^2 - 6}{(x + 1)^2(x + 2)}$; $x \neq -1, -2$

d. $\dfrac{x^2 + 6x + 1}{(x - 4)(x - 3)(x + 1)}$; $x \neq -1, 3, 4$

e. $\dfrac{3x^2 + x - 6}{(x + 3)(x + 1)(x + 2)}$; $x \neq -3, -2, -1$

f. $\dfrac{x^2 - x - 3}{(x + 3)(x + 2)(x - 2)}$; $x \neq -3, -2, 2$

g. $\dfrac{2a - 3b}{(a + b)(a - 2b)}$; $a - 2b \neq 0$; $a + b \neq 0$

h. $\dfrac{2x^2 - x - 2}{(x + 2)(x - 2)^2}$; $x \neq -2, 2$

Exercises, page 203
1. a. 5   **b.** 7   **c.** 1   **d.** 8   **e.** 11   **f.** 2
2. a. 3   **b.** 5   **c.** 2   **d.** 2   **e.** 7   **f.** 5   **g.** 4   **h.** 2
i. 9   **3. a.** 3   **b.** 4   **c.** 2   **d.** 2   **e.** 5   **f.** 3
g. $\dfrac{1}{3}, 2$ **h.** 1, 2   **i.** $-7, 4$ **j.** $-\dfrac{1}{2}, 2$ **k.** 0, 3
l. $-1\dfrac{1}{3}, 3$ **4.** 15 km/h   **5.** 12 km/h
6. 160 km/h

Using the Calculator, page 204
1. a. 10 000 200 001   **b.** 100 000 020 000 001
c. 1 000 000 002 000 000 001
2. a. $9^2 = 81$ **3.** $11^2 = 121$
     $99^2 = 9\ 801$ $111^2 = 12\ 321$
     $999^2 = 998\ 001$ $1111^2 = 1\ 234\ 321$
     $9999^2 = 99\ 980\ 001$
b. $999\ 999^2 = 999\ 998\ 000\ 001$
     $9\ 999\ 999^2 = 99\ 999\ 980\ 000\ 001$
c. Expand $(10^k - 1)^2$.

4. a. An algebraic proof is difficult because there are several terms to be multiplied in each expansion.
b. 12 345 678 987 654 321
c. 1 234 567 890 987 654 321

Review, page 205

1. a. $\dfrac{n + 5}{3n + 2}$; $n \neq -\dfrac{2}{3}, -3\dfrac{1}{2}$

b. $\dfrac{x - 2}{3}$; $x \neq -4$

c. $\dfrac{x - 1}{x - 7}$; $x \neq -7, 7$

d. $\dfrac{x + 6}{6 - x}$; $x \neq 6, -6$

2. a. $\dfrac{6}{x^2}$; $x \neq 0, -1\dfrac{1}{2}$

b. $\dfrac{6}{x^3}$; $x \neq 0, -3$

c. $\dfrac{x - 3}{x + 1}$; $x \neq -2, -1, 1$

d. $(x - 2)(x + 4)$; $x \neq 3, -5$

e. $\dfrac{3(a - 6)}{2(a + 3)}$; $a \neq 2, -3$

f. $-\dfrac{a + 5}{a - 8}$; $a \neq 2, 5, 8$

g. $\dfrac{3}{2(n + 3)(n - 3)}$; $n \neq -3, 3, 5$

h. $\dfrac{(3m - 2)(2m + 5)}{(m + 5)(3m + 2)}$; $m \neq -5, -\dfrac{2}{3}, \dfrac{2}{3}, 2\dfrac{1}{2}$

3. a. $9(k + 1)$; $k \neq -2$

b. $\dfrac{(2m + 3)(3 - m)}{(m + 2)(m - 1)}$; $m \neq -3, -2, 1, 3$

4. a. $\dfrac{5x - 3}{(x - 1)(x + 1)}$; $x \neq -1, 1$

b. $\dfrac{5x}{6(x + 1)}$; $x \neq -1$

c. $\dfrac{5x + 6}{(x - 3)(x + 4)}$; $x \neq -4, -3, 3, 4$

d. $\dfrac{7x + 11}{(x - 2)(x + 3)}$; $x \neq -5, -3, 2, 4$

e. $\dfrac{3m^2 - 1}{m(m + 1)(m - 1)}$; $m \neq -1, 0, 1$

f. $\dfrac{2x^2 - 4x - 9}{x(x + 1)(x - 2)(x - 3)}$; $x \neq -1, 0, 2, 3$

5. a. $P = \dfrac{9x}{20}$ $A = \dfrac{x^2}{80}$

b. $P = 2d + \dfrac{5c}{3}$ $A = \dfrac{2cd}{3}$

6. a. 2   **b.** $-\dfrac{1}{2}, 2$ **c.** $2\dfrac{4}{5}, 5$ **d.** $-3, 6$

Problem Solving 12, page 206

1. 400 grey tiles   **2.** 12 m/s   **3.** 180 km/h
4. 3 m by 6 m   **5. a.** 6 Ω   **b.** about 28.6 Ω   **c.** 60 Ω

d. $R_T = \dfrac{R_1 R_2}{R_1 + R_2}$ **e.** 120 Ω

6. a. about 2.4 h   **b.** about 102 km/h

7. $t = \dfrac{d(r_1 + r_2)}{r_1 r_2}$; $r_{ave} = \dfrac{2r_1 r_2}{r_1 + r_2}$

Application, page 207

1. $d_1 = \dfrac{f d_0}{d_0 - f}$

2. a. 150 mm   **b.** about 51 mm   **3. a.** 180 mm
b. 2   **c.** 7.0 mm   **4.** 600 mm; 4   **5.** 300 mm; 5

Test, page 208

1. a. $-2x - y$ **b.** $x^2 - 11x + 5$
c. $-4a^3 + 2a^2 b - ab^2 - b^3 + 3b^2$ **2. a.** $3x + 24$
b. $12x^3 + 18x^2 y$ **c.** $x^2 - 4x - 12$
d. $x^2 - 14x + 49$ **e.** $-36x^4 - 39x^2 - 9$
f. $4x^2 + 3x - 10$ **3. a.** $13(t - 2)$
b. $-6x(2x^2 + 3x + 4)$ **c.** $11y(4x + 11y^2)$
d. $(x + 1)(3x - 2)$ **e.** $6xy(5x - 7 + y)$
f. $15mn(m + 3n - 6)$ **4. a.** $(x + 3)^2$
b. $(3x + 7)(3x - 7)$ **c.** $(x + 12)(x - 3)$
d. $(x + 3)(x - 4)$ **e.** $(2x + 3)(x + 1)$
f. $(3x + 1)(2x - 1)$ **g.** $3(x - 1)(x - 9)$
h. $(x^2 + 9)(x + 3)(x - 3)$
i. $(3x^2 + 8)(x + 1)(x - 1)$ **j.** $4(x + 3)(x - 3)$
k. $3(x - 10)(x + 1)$ **l.** $4xy(x + 2y)(x + y)$
m. $(x^4 + 9)(x^2 + 3)(x^2 - 3)$
n. $(3x^2 + 2)(x + 2)(x - 2)$ **5. a.** 10   **b.** 49   **c.** 64
6. a. 2, 4   **b.** $1\dfrac{2}{3}, -1$ **c.** 0, 3   **d.** $-\dfrac{1}{2}, 5$

7. a. $\dfrac{5}{x - 1}$; $x \neq 1, 0$ **b.** $\dfrac{a + 3}{a + 7}$; $a \neq -5, 7$

c. $-\dfrac{1}{m + 3}$; $m \neq 3, -3$ **d.** $\dfrac{x + 4}{x + 3}$; $x \neq -3$

8. a. $\dfrac{2}{3x^2}$; $x \neq 0, 1$

b. $\dfrac{y(y + 2)}{(y + 5)(y + 3)}$; $y \neq -5, -3, 0, 3, 6$

c. $\dfrac{50}{9y^2}$; $y \neq -2, 0$

d. $-\dfrac{(r + 3)(r - 3)}{(r + 5)(2r - 1)}$; $r \neq -5, \dfrac{1}{2}, \dfrac{2}{3}, 3, 7$

e. $\dfrac{(x + 2)(x - 2)}{x}$; $x \neq -2, 0, 5$

f. $\dfrac{(2x - 1)(x - 1)}{(x - 5)(x + 3)}$; $x \neq -3, 1, 5$

g. $\dfrac{3x + 3y}{xy}$; $x \neq 0$; $y \neq 0$

h. $\dfrac{-3x - 15}{x(x + 3)}$; $x \neq 0, -3$

i. $\dfrac{7x^2 + 4}{x(x - 1)}$; $x \neq 0, 1$

j. $\dfrac{11x + 3}{(x + 4)(x - 2)(x + 3)}$; $x \neq -4, -3, 2$

9. a. 1 **b.** $\dfrac{1}{2}, 4$

Cumulative Review, page 209

1. a. -3.125 **b.** -7 **c.** $0.41\overline{6}$ **d.** -7

2. a. $\dfrac{\sqrt{k}}{k}$ **b.** $\dfrac{3\sqrt{2}}{10}$ **c.** $\dfrac{7\sqrt{2}}{12}$ **d.** $\dfrac{9\sqrt{2}}{4}$

3. a. 7.48 **b.** 6.40 **c.** 23.32 **4.** b **5. a.** 8

b. 7 **c.** 6 **d.** $-3\dfrac{1}{2}$ **e.** -1 **f.** -10 **g.** $-1\dfrac{3}{4}$

h. 2 **i.** $1\dfrac{1}{2}$ **6. a.** $k \leq -5$ **b.** $t \leq 3$

c. $c < -12$ **d.** $b \leq -16$ **e.** $m > -\dfrac{1}{2}$

f. $n \geq -5$ **g.** $2 < d < 10$ **h.** $a \geq 7$ or $a \leq -3$

i. $-10 < a < 4$ **7. a.** $-\dfrac{9}{5}$ **b.** $\dfrac{3}{5}$ **c.** undefined

9. a. $(11, -4)$ **b.** $(2, 7)$ **c.** $(7, -1)$ **d.** $(7, -2)$

Unit 7

Exercises, page 212

1. a. {(Chris, 16), (Pat, 17), (Kim, 16), (Terry, 16), (Robbie, 15)}

b. {(Chris, centre), (Pat, left wing), (Kim, right wing), (Terry, left defence), (Robbie, right defence)}

c. {(Chris, 45), (Pat, 38), (Kim, 42), (Terry, 28), (Robbie, 13)}

d. {(centre, 45), (left wing, 38), (right wing, 42), (left defence, 28), (right defence, 13)}

2. a. {$(-3,1), (-2,1), (-1,1), (0,1), (1,1)$}; domain = $\{-3, -2, -1, 0, 1\}$; range = {1}

b. {$(-1,0), (0,2), (1,2), (2,1), (2,3)$}; domain = $\{-1,0,1,2\}$; range = $\{0,1,2,3\}$

c. {$(-2, -1), (-1, -1), (-1,0), (0, -1), (0,0), (0,1),$ $(1, -1), (1,0), (1,1), (1,2), (2, -1), (2,0), (2,1), (2,2), (2,3)$}; domain = $\{-2, -1, 0, 1, 2\}$; range = $\{-1,0,1,2,3\}$

d. {$(-2, -1), (-2,0), (-2,1), (-2,2), (-2,3), (-2,4)$}; domain = $\{-2\}$; range = $\{-1,0,1,2,3,4\}$

3. a. domain = $\{-10, -4,3,7\}$; range = $\{-5,4,6,8\}$

b. domain = $\{6,7,8,9\}$; range = $\{2\}$

c. domain = $\{0,1,2,3\}$; range = $\{0,1,8,27\}$

d. domain = $\{-2, -1,0,1,2\}$; range = $\{0,1,4\}$

4. a. domain = $\{x | x \in R\}$; range = $\{y | y \in R\}$

b. domain = $\{x | x \in R\}$; range = $\{y | y \geq 0\}$

c. domain = $\{x | x \in R\}$; range = $\{y | y \leq 2\}$

d. domain = $\{x | x \in R\}$; range = $\{y | y \geq 0\}$

e. domain = $\{x | x \in R\}$; range = $\{y | y \geq -2\}$

f. domain = $\{x | -3 \leq x \leq 3\}$; range = $\{y | -3 \leq y \leq 3\}$

5. a. domain = $\{0,1,2,3,4\}$; range = $\{4,5,6,7,8\}$

b. domain = $\{-1,1,3,5\}$; range = $\{-2, -1,0,1\}$

c. domain = $\{-2, -1,0,1,2\}$; range = $\{-6, -3,0,3,6\}$

d. domain = $\{-2, -1,0,1\}$; range = $\{-10, -7, -4, -1\}$

e. domain = $\{-5, -2,1,4\}$; range = $\{-9, -4,1,6\}$

f. domain = $\{-2, -1,0,1,2\}$; range = $\{-8, -1,0,1,8\}$

g. domain = $\{-4, -2,0,2,4\}$; range = $\{-6, -5, -4, -3, -2\}$

h. domain = $\{-1,0,1,2\}$;

range = $\left\{-1\dfrac{1}{2}, -1\dfrac{1}{4}, -1, -\dfrac{3}{4}\right\}$

6. a. domain = $\{x | x \in R\}$; range = $\{y | y \in R\}$

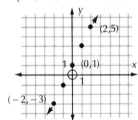

b. domain = $\{x | x \in Z\}$;

range = $\{\ldots, -5, -3, -1,1,3,5, \ldots\}$

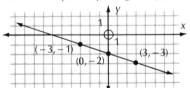

c. domain = $\{x | x \in R\}$; range = $\{y | y \in R\}$

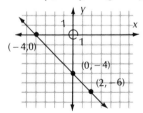

d. domain = $\{x | x \in R\}$; range = $\{y | y \in R\}$

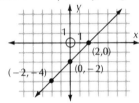

e. domain = $\{x \mid x \in R\}$; range = $\{y \mid y \in R\}$

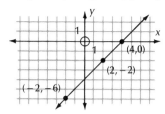

f. domain = $\{x \mid x \in Z\}$;

range = $\left\{ \ldots, -1\frac{1}{2}, -1, -\frac{1}{2}, 0, \frac{1}{2}, 1, 1\frac{1}{2}, \ldots \right\}$

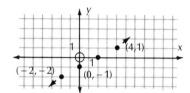

g. domain = $\{x \mid x \in R\}$; range = $\{y \mid y \in R\}$

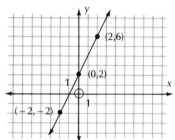

h. domain = $\{x \mid x \in R\}$; range = $\{y \mid y \in R\}$

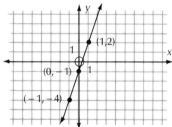

i. domain = $\{x \mid x \in R\}$; range = $\{y \mid y \in R\}$

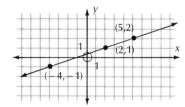

j. domain = $\{x \mid x \in R\}$; range = $\{y \mid y \in R\}$

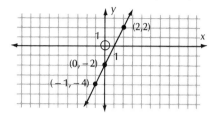

k. domain = $\{x \mid x \in R\}$; range = $\{2\}$

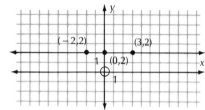

l. domain = $\{-1\}$; range = $\{y \mid y \in R\}$

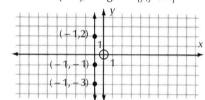

m. domain = $\{x \mid x \in R\}$; range = $\{3\}$

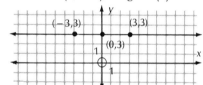

n. domain = $\{3\}$; range = $\{y \mid y \in R\}$

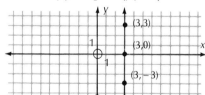

7. a.

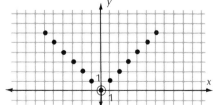

b.

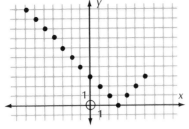

c.

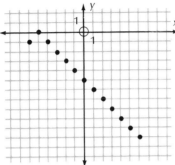

d.

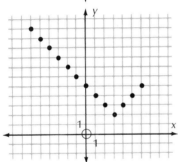

e.

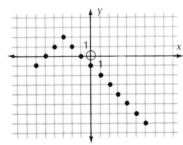

f.

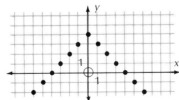

Extra, page 213
1. $0.31; $10.23; over $10 000 000

458

Exercises, page 215
1. *a*, *b*, and *d*
2. *a* and *b*
3. exercise 1: *a* and *d*; exercise 2: *a*
4. *a* and *d*
5. "e" is a function. Answers will vary for the other questions.

6. a.

x	$x + 5$
0	5
1	6
2	7

$R = \{5,6,7\}$

b.

x	$3 - x$
-1	4
0	3
1	2

$R = \{2,3,4\}$

c.

x	x^2
$-\frac{1}{2}$	$\frac{1}{4}$
0	0
$\frac{1}{2}$	$\frac{1}{4}$

$R = \left\{0, \frac{1}{4}\right\}$

d.

x	$x^2 + 1$
-1	2
0	1
1	2

$R = \{1,2\}$

e.

t	$3t^2$
0	0
1	3
2	12

$R = \{0,3,12\}$

f.

r	$r^2 + 3$
-1	4
0	3
1	4

$R = \{3,4\}$

7. a. $R = \{1,2,5\}$; function
b. $R = \{1,2,4,8,16\}$; function
c. $R = \left\{-\frac{2}{3}, -\frac{1}{3}, 0, \frac{1}{3}, \frac{2}{3}\right\}$; function
d. $R = \{-2, -\sqrt{3}, -\sqrt{2}, -1, 0, 1, \sqrt{2}, \sqrt{3}, 2\}$; not a function
8. a. -1 **b.** -3 **c.** 1 **d.** -5 **e.** 3 **f.** 11 **g.** -9 **9. a.** -1 **b.** -1 **c.** 7 **d.** -2 **e.** 2 **f.** 23 **g.** 62

10. a.

x	y
-1	-1
0	0
1	1
2	2
3	3

function

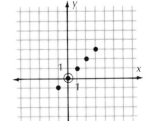

b.

x	y
−1	
0	−1
1	−1,0
2	−1,0,1
3	−1,0,1,2

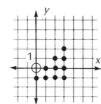

not a function

c.

x	y
−1	0,1,2,3
0	1,2,3
1	2,3
2	3
3	

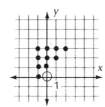

not a function

11. a. $37\frac{1}{2}$ **b.** −36 **c.** 1 **d.** −45

12. a. function **b.** not a function

c. not a function **d.** function

Exercises, page 220
1. a. direct variation; $k = 3$

b. direct variation; $k = 2\frac{1}{2}$

c. not a direct variation **d.** not a direct variation
2. a. direct variation; $k = 2\pi$
b. direct variation; $k = 3.4$
c. not a direct variation

d. direct variation; $k = \frac{2}{3}$

3. a. 24 **b.** 75 **c.** 1.2 **d.** 5.95 **e.** 50 **f.** 15
4. a. x doubles. **b.** y triples. **c.** y is halved.

d. x is halved. **5.** 1.25 **6.** 7.5 **7.** $12\frac{1}{2}$ **8.** $10\frac{2}{3}$

9. a. $1\frac{1}{2}$ **b.** $y = \frac{3}{2}x$ **c.** $10\frac{2}{3}$ **d.** 24

e. slope $= \frac{3}{2}$ **f.** Yes. **10. a.** $y = \frac{4}{3}x$ **b.** 3

c. 12 **d.** slope $= \frac{4}{3}$ **e.** Yes.

11. a. $y = kx, k \neq 0$
b. The graph is a straight line with slope k that passes through the origin.
12. a. 16 **b.** $c = 16n$ **c.** $192

13. 25 minutes **14.** $10.80 **15.** $108\frac{1}{3}$ g

16. 1.5 m **17.** 5%; $87.50 **18.** 36 h
19. a. small circle: $A = \pi a^2$
large circle: $A = \pi b^2$
shaded region: $A = \pi(b^2 - a^2)$
Given: $\pi(b^2 - a^2) = \pi a^2$
$\therefore b^2 - a^2 = a^2$
$b^2 = 2a^2$

large circle: $A = \pi(2a^2)$

$\therefore \dfrac{A_{\text{small circle}}}{A_{\text{large circle}}} = \dfrac{\pi a^2}{\pi(2a^2)}$

$= \dfrac{1}{2}$

$\therefore$ area of small circle $= \frac{1}{2}$ area of large circle

$\therefore$ area of small circle is directly proportional to area of large circle
b. Yes. a varies directly as b because $b = \sqrt{2}a$.

Exercises, page 223
1. a, b, and f **2.** 1 **3. a.** 240 **b.** 24 **c.** 15
4. a. x is halved. **b.** x doubles.
c. x is one-third its original value. **5.** 1.2 m

6. 75 cm **7. a.** $2\frac{1}{4}$ h **b.** Time is halved.

8. a. $2500 **b.** Let y be value of the car in dollars and x be age of the car in years.

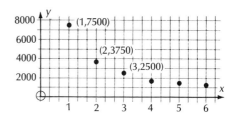

Exercises, page 225
1. $327.50 **2.** b, d, e, and f **3. a.** −2 **b.** 19

4.

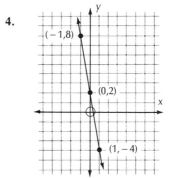

5. a. $y = \frac{1}{3}x + 3$ **b.** $y = -\frac{6}{13}x + 6$

6. a. $c = 14.5t + 55$
c. The slope, 14.5, is the rental fee per hour.
d. The vertical intercept would be 55 and would represent the flat fee. In this case, though, the point (0,55) does not really exist because there should be no charge if rental time is zero.
e. $120.25 **f.** 8 h

7. a. $y = 24.5x + 54$

459

c. The slope, 24.5, is the charge per hour. The y-intercept, 54, is the flat fee.
d. $164.25 **8. a.** $300 **b.** $8000
9. weekly salary = $200; commission rate = 4%
10. $9.98 for a T-shirt; $0.75 for a letter
11. y increases by 70.
12. a. $c = 3m + 150$ **b.** $345
c. more than 100 meals
13. a. company A: $c = \frac{1}{10}d + 50$;

company B: $c = \frac{3}{20}d + 30$;

company C: $c = \frac{1}{4}d + 25$

c. i. distance travelled is greater than 400 km
ii. distance travelled is between 50 km and 400 km
iii. distance travelled is less than 50 km

Review, page 227
1. a. {(Micki, 14.3), (Leslie, 14.7), (Pat, 13.9), (Jo, 13.5), (Bobbie, 14.1)}
b. {(Micki, 18.7), (Leslie, 18.5), (Pat, 19.5), (Jo, 18.3), (Bobbie, 18.0)}
c. {(Micki, 12.2), (Leslie, 12.7), (Pat, 12.9), (Jo, 13.2), (Bobbie, 13.4)}
d. {(dash, Jo), (high jump, Jo), (long jump, Leslie), (hurdles, Bobbie), (shot put, Bobbie)}
2. a. $D = \{2,3,4,5\}$; $R = \{4,6,8,10\}$
b. $D = \{-2,-1,0,1,2\}$; $R = \{1,3,5,7,9\}$
3. b, c, d, and f
4. a. 0 **b.** -0.75 **c.** 195 **d.** $5 + 2\sqrt{5}$
5. 52 h **6. a.** $\frac{4}{5}$ **b.** 19.2 **c.** y increases by 15%.
7. a. 180 **b.** 7.5 **8.** 4h

Exercises, page 230
1. a.

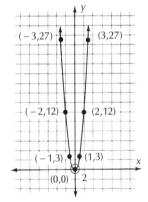

b. 48; 5 or -5
2. $\frac{1}{32}$; $\frac{1}{4}$ or $-\frac{1}{4}$

3.

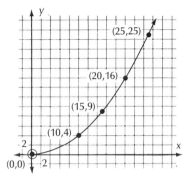

7. a. $k = 2$; $y = 2x^2$

b. $k = 8$; $y = \frac{8}{x^2}$

c. $k = 16$; $y = \frac{16}{\sqrt{x}}$

8.

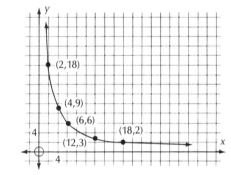

9. a. 2
b. $y = 2x^2$

x	y
-5	50
-4	32
-3	18
-2	8
-1	2
0	0
1	2
2	8
3	18
4	32
5	50

10. a. $k = 6$; $y = 6\sqrt{x}$
b.

x	y
0	0
1	6
4	12
9	18
16	24

11. 2; (relation: $y = 2x^3$)

12. 128; $\left(\text{relation: } y = \dfrac{128}{x^2}\right)$ **13. a.** $d = 4.9t^2$

c. 11.025 m   **d.** 2.26 s   **14.** 63.4 N

Exercises, page 233

1. a. i. $-1\frac{1}{3}$ **ii.** $\frac{2}{3}$ **b. i.** $-\frac{1}{3}$ **ii.** 0 **c. i.** 3

ii. -4 **2. a.** $\frac{2}{3}$ **b.** $1\frac{2}{7}$ **3. a.** $1\frac{1}{6}$ **b.** $1\frac{4}{5}$ **4.** 2

5. b. 1955: about 15 700 000; 1980: about 24 000 000

c. 1966

6. b. Males: 66.30 kg; Females 55.07 kg

c. Males: 77.62 kg; Females 62.61 kg

7. a. T.N.T Equivalent (10^3 Mt)

8. No. Fluctuations in gas prices do not follow a steady trend, (e.g., price wars).

Review, page 235

2. a. domain $= \{x|x \in R\}$; range $= \{y|y \geq 0\}$
b. domain $= \{x|x \geq 0\}$; range $= \{y|y \in R\}$
c. domain $= \{x|x \in R\}$; range $= \{y|y \geq 0\}$
d. domain $= \{x|x \in R\}$; range $= \{y|y \in R\}$
e. domain $= \{x|x \neq 0\}$; range $= \{y|y \neq 0\}$
f. domain $= \{x|x \neq 0\}$; range $= \{y|y \neq 0\}$

3. 121 cm² **4. a.** 432 **b.** 3 **c.** 3 **5.** $\frac{4\pi}{3}$

b. $y = \frac{4\pi}{3} x^3$

c. domain $= \{x|x \geq 0\}$; range $= \{y|y \geq 0\}$

d. $20\frac{5}{6}\pi$ cm³ **e.** 6 cm **6. a. i.** $1\frac{1}{5}$; **ii.** -1

b. i. $-1\frac{2}{3}$; **ii.** $-2\frac{1}{2}$ **c. i.** $2\frac{3}{5}$; **ii.** $\frac{3}{7}$

7. 11

Extra, page 235

$16\frac{1}{3}$ houses

Application, page 236

1. d. The perimeter of a square varies *directly* as its side length. The area of a square varies *directly as the square of* its side length.

2. c. If the area of a rectangle is constant, then the length varies *inversely* as the width.

3. a. Table is based on formula: $t = 2\sqrt{l}$.
Since this is an experiment, answers may vary.

c. The time for one swing of a pendulum varies *directly as the square root of* the length of the pendulum.

4. a. Partial Variation **b.** Quadratic Variation
c. Direct Variation **d.** Varying as the Square Root
e. Inverse Variation

Applying Relations, page 238

1. a. $C = 8.95p + 150$ (p is the number of people, C is cost)
b. $221.60 **c.** Yes. $284.25
2. a. Yes. **b.** If the customer does not want those toppings offered. **3. a.** 1 h 4 min **b.** 16 km
4. 7.5 min **5. a.** $4.61 **b.** $0.65 **6.** 1728 J
7. 75.6 km/h **8.** 3 lx **9.** 1.74 s
10. a. $E = 250 + 5dp$ (E is expenses for the week; d is number of days, p is number of people)
b. $355 **c.** $118 **d.** one **11.** 152 cm³

Test, page 240

1. f is a function because each value of x has only one value of y.

2. All are functions except for **c.**

3. a. domain $= \{x|x \in R\}$; range $= \{y|y \in R\}$
b. domain $= \{x|x \in R\}$; range $= \{y|y \geq 0\}$
c. domain $= \{x|x = -3\}$; range $= \{y|y \in R\}$
d. domain $= \{x|x \in R\}$; range $= \{y|y \in R\}$

4. a. -5 **b.** -8 **c.** 5.5 **d.** -56 **5.** $-2\frac{11}{12}$

6. 9 is halved. **7. a.** $360 **b.** $6500 **8. a.** 8
b. 8 **c.** 0 **d.** 0.5
9. domain $= \{x|x \in R\}$; range $= \{y|y \geq 0\}$

11. $\frac{3}{8}$ **12.** 2500π cm² **13.** 18.6 km/h

Cumulative Review, page 241

1. a. $\sqrt{12}$ **b.** $\sqrt{343}$ **c.** $\sqrt{3x^2}$ **d.** $\sqrt{25k}$
e. $\sqrt{12y^2z}$
2. b. and d. are right-angled triangles.
3. a. -7 **b.** 0 **c.** -3 **d.** 4 **e.** -6 **f.** 15

4. a. $x \leq -5$ **b.** $k < 5\frac{1}{3}$ **c.** $-3 \leq x \leq -1$

5. a. $2x - 5y + 2 = 0$ **b.** $2x + 3y - 5 = 0$
c. $2x - 3y + 0 = 0$ **6. a.** $A = 2$

b. $B = 1$; $C = -3$ **7. a.** $(-1, 2)$ **b.** $\left(2\frac{1}{2}, 5\right)$

c. $\left(7\frac{5}{9}, 7\frac{7}{9}\right)$

10. a. -3 **b.** $2\frac{1}{3}$ or $-2\frac{1}{3}$ **c.** $\frac{1}{2}$ or $-\frac{1}{3}$ **d.** 1 or 9

e. $-1\frac{1}{2}$ or -1 **f.** 3 or -3 **11. a.** $\frac{4y}{x}$; $x \neq 0$

b. $\dfrac{1}{a + 7}$; $a \neq -5$ or -7

c. $-\dfrac{1}{k + 2}$; $k \neq 2$ or -2

d. $\dfrac{d + 2}{d + 1}$; $d \neq -1$ or 1

Exercises, page 243

1. a. mean = 40; median = 40; mode = 40
b. mean = 14.6; median = 14.5; mode = 13
c. mean = 10.5; median = 10.2; mode = 10.2
d. mean = 2.4; median = 2.5; no mode
2. mean = 53.8; median = 53.8 **3. a.** 21 **b.** 4
c. 3750 **d.** 48
4. a. A: mean = 2.5; median = 2.5; mode = 3
B: mean = 2.9; median = 3; mode = 5
C: mean = 3; median = 2; mode = 6
b. The mean best represents the data for the three teams because it takes into consideration all of the data.
5. a. 1.3 min **b.** She could take 1.30 min or more.

Exercises, page 246

1. a. range = 3
mean = 2
median = 2
mode = 2

b. range = 6
mean = 6.6
median = 7
mode = 7

c. range = 0.9
mean = 53.9
median = 54
mode = 54.1

d. range = 6
mean = 21.7
median = 21.5
mode = 20 and 24

e. range = 8
mean = 114
median = 114
mode = 114

2.

Cumulative Frequency	Midpoint of Interval	Subtotal
10	34.50	345.00
23	44.50	578.50
45	54.50	1199.00
74	64.50	1870.50
92	74.50	1341.00
100	84.50	676.00

3. a. The median lies in the 160–169 cm interval.
b. mean estimate = 166.1 cm. This estimate is different from the estimate obtained in Example 2 because the intervals used are different.

4. range = 9 cm; mean = 81 cm; median = 81 cm; mode = 81 cm

5. a. range = $57 000; mean = $26 706; median = $18 000; mode = $18 000
b. The median. **c.** The mean.

6. b. T and G
c. No, because there were too many people that rated the ice cream flavour as Terrible.

7. mean = 56.54 kg; mean estimate = 56.70 kg
8. b. mode estimate = 43 499.5 km;
median estimate = 42 499.5 km;
mean estimate = 42 459.5 km

9.

Number of Children	Number of Families
0	1
1	2
2	3
3	2
4	1

10. The greatest number in a set of data can be the mean or median if the set has only one number (example: 20, 20, 20, 20). The greatest number in a set of data can be the mode if it is the most frequently occurring number (example: 18, 19, 20, 20).

11. No, the classes are not exactly the same size.

Exercises, page 249

1. a.

Interval	Data
40–49	42, 42, 43, 45, 48, 49
50–59	51, 53, 55, 56, 58, 59
60–69	61, 62, 64, 67
70–79	71, 73, 76

b.

Interval	Data
1.00–1.99	1.56, 1.76, 1.95
2.00–2.99	2.39, 2.55, 2.68, 2.72, 2.89
3.00–3.99	3.00, 3.45, 3.85
4.00–4.99	4.14, 4.31

c.

Interval	Data
2000–2999	2125, 2276, 2481
3000–3999	3035, 3067, 3320, 3672
4000–4999	4109, 4438, 4793
5000–5999	5210, 5451

2. a. Median is in the interval 12.0–12.9 s.
b. Median is in the interval 24.0–25.9 s.
c. Median is in the interval 58.0–61.9 s.
d. Median is in the interval 32:00–32:59 min.

3. a. Swimming **b.** Fishing: Hunting = 2:1
c. Because one person can participate in more than one sport.

4. a. 33 **b.** 57 **c.** median = 4; range = 6; mode = 4 and 5 **d.** mean = 3.8

5. a. The number of workers increased.

b. 47%   **c.** 157%   **d.** 1960: 29%; 1970: 34%; 1980: 42%   **6. a.** 10–14   **b.** about 2.5%
c. about 41.6%   **d.** Answers vary.

7. b. England

Exercises, page 253
2. a. The subscriptions seem to have tripled over the three-month period shown.
b. The circulation for the month of March has improved, but not as much as was led to believe.
3. a. The advertisement is trying to give the impression that profits quadrupled in the three-year period shown.
b. Profit for 1982: $300 000
Profit for 1985: $700 000.
c. (1982: 1985) 3:7   **d.** (1982: 1985) 1:4
e. The ratio in **c.** denotes a doubling in profit, but the ratio in **d.** denotes a quadrupling in profit.
4. a. 15   **b.** 23%
c. He has used circles (representing basketballs) in the graph and he has reduced the vertical axis.
5. a. mean = 21; median = 21; mode = 15 and 25
b. mean = 23; mode = 27; median = 22
c. The graph has been presented in a low number of intervals. Also, the month of February was not mentioned—it gives the impression that the temperatures are for the year.

Extra, page 254
1. The general trend is that teenage smoking has decreased in the 1972 to 1981 period.
2. Male teenagers were smoking more than female teenagers in the 1972 to 1979 period, but in 1981 there were more female teenagers smoking.
3. Some factors to consider: social pressures, job market.
4. 18% male smokers; 19% female smokers

Review, page 255
1. mean = 17.5; median = 16.5
2. a. mean = 5.0; median = 5.1; mode = 5.3
b. the median   **3.** mean estimate = 15.1

Exercises, page 257
1. a. $\frac{3}{10}$ or 30%   **b.** 90

2. a.

Student Age	Frequency	Relative Frequency
13	26	0.026
14	239	0.234
15	253	0.248
16	218	0.214
17	187	0.183
18	94	0.092
19	3	0.003

b. In Ontario (minimum age is 16): 49.2%
3. a. Honda: $\frac{1}{3}$ Mazda: $\frac{1}{7}$ Nissan: $\frac{4}{21}$ Suzuki: $\frac{2}{21}$
Toyota: $\frac{5}{21}$ **b.** 51
7. a. 140
b. Post: 5805 to 6509
March: 5102 to 5805
Jones: 4750 to 5454

Exercises, page 259
1. a. People who go to watch a hockey game are obviously not bothered by the violence.
b. High school students don't represent all teenagers.
c. Since only car owners were chosen, this leaves out a large population of people who don't own a car.
d. Not everyone is listed in the phone book.
e. Not everyone reads the same newspaper.
2. One; randomly select four males and randomly select one female.
3. because the bighorn sheep stays in clusters and does not spread out evenly over the province
5. a. mean (Girls' class) = 2.8
mean (Boys' class) = 1.8
b. 1   **c.** because the families of the girls have at least one girl
6. c. pop. mean = 2. The population mean can be obtained by rounding most of the sample means to the nearest integer.
d. The mean of the sample means should be very close to the actual population mean.
7. d. number of bees = 58. The accuracy increases with size of sample.
8. a. Choose two rows of twenty digits, each pair of digits being used for the sampling as follows:
　　　00 to 54 for teal
　　　55 to 79 for black duck
　　　80 to 99 for mallard
d. The means should correspond closely to the given composition.

Exercises, pages 263
1. Examples provided will vary.   **a.** positive
b. negative   **c.** positive   **d.** negative   **e.** positive
2. Eliza   **3.** Her statistics indicate that she is the weakest player.   **4.** 48   **5. b.** Look for points that lie along $y = x$.   **c.** yes   **d.** about 3 or 4
6. b. There is not a strong correlation.
c. anywhere from 6 to 15   **7. b.** positive correlation   **c.** about 85 to 90

Exercises, page 265

1. a. The mean score is pulled down when more students write. **b.** Within each cluster, there seems to be some negative correlation. However, any correlation is not strongly represented. More data may help. **c.** It isn't really possible to tell from the data given. **2. a.** One cluster occurs in the interval 120 cm to 150 cm, the other in the interval 150 cm to 200 cm. Probably due to the fact that sample may include boys as well as adult males. **b.** positive **c.** about 55 kg to 65 kg **3. b.** strong positive correlation **c.** about 7 000 000 vehicles, 270 000 accidents

Exercises, page 267

1. d. $x - y = -2$ **2. c.** $40x - y = 7$
3. c. about 170

Exercises, page 269

1. c. World War II, when many young men were overseas fighting or in training **d.** yes; no; no; no **e.** yes; no **2.** Answers will vary. **3. a.** World War I and II **4. d.** 1900 **e.** about 9.8 s

Review, page 271

1. a.

Lunch expense ($)	Tally	Freq.	Cumulative Freq.	Midpoint of Interval	Subtotal
2.20–2.29	III	3	3	2.245	6.735
2.30–2.39	II	2	5	2.345	4.69
2.40–2.49	IIII	4	9	2.445	9.78
2.50–2.59	JHT II	7	16	2.545	17.815
2.60–2.69	III	3	19	2.645	7.935
2.70–2.79	JHT	5	24	2.745	13.725
2.80–2.89	IIII	4	28	2.845	11.38
2.90–2.99	II	2	30	2.945	5.89

b. $\frac{1}{10}$ **c.** $\frac{7}{10}$
d. Yes, if the sample of 30 students was chosen randomly.

2. c.

Number of Fries	Tally	Freq.	Cumulative Freq.	Subtotal
37	JHT II	7	7	259
38	JHT JHT I	11	18	418
39	JHT JHT JHT JHT II	22	40	858
40	JHT JHT JHT JHT JHT IIII	29	69	1160
41	JHT JHT JHT IIII	19	88	779
42	JHT JHT II	12	100	504
Total		100		3978

d. mean = 39.77 **3. b.** The smoothed numbers are: 48.4, 47, 47, 46.9, 45.9, 44.5, 44.5, 43.6, 42.81, 42.81 42.55, 41.6, 41.65 **d.** The general trend is that of decreasing times. Contributing factors would include: changes/improvements in nutritional levels and growth rates over the past 60 years; changes in societal attitudes toward female athletes; popularization of track-and-field athletics.

Test, page 272

1. a.

Mass (kg)	Tally	Freq.	Cumulative Freq.	Midpoint of Interval	Subtotal
1.50–1.99	I	1	1	1.745	1.745
2.00–2.49	II	2	3	2.245	4.49
2.50–2.99	IIII	4	7	2.745	10.98
3.00–3.49	IIII I	6	13	3.245	19.47
3.50–3.99	IIII	4	17	3.745	14.98
4.00–4.49	IIII	4	21	4.245	16.98
4.50–4.99	II	2	23	4.745	9.49
5.00–5.49	I	1	24	5.245	5.245

b. mean estimate = 3.47 kg
c. median lies in the 3.00–3.49 kg interval

2. a.

1	7, 8, 9
2	0, 1, 2, 2, 3, 5, 5, 5, 6, 7, 8, 8, 9
3	1, 3, 5, 6, 8, 9
4	2, 3

b.

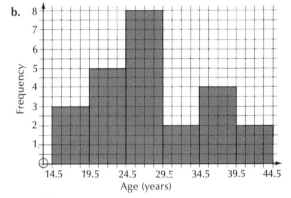

3. a. $\frac{13}{24}$ **b.** 27 **4. a.** mean = 3.42; median = 3.5; mode = 3 and 5 **b.** 18% **c.** 2244
5. a. mean $\doteq$ 3.17; median = 3; mode = 3
b. 20% **c.** about 178 students

Cumulative Review, page 273

1. a. $R = 0.06r + r$ (R = new Rent; r = old rent)
b. $S = 590w + 22.12h$ (S = salary; w = number of weeks; h = number of hours overtime)
c. $C = \frac{c}{2}$ (C = new cost; c = old cost) **2. a.** 7
b. -3 **c.** -2 **d.** 2 **3. a.** 10.3; (2.5, 2.5)
b. 13.6; (2, 3.5) **c.** 5; (1, 4.5) **d.** 7.1; $(-2.5, -1.5)$
4. a. $y = \frac{1}{2}x - 3$ **b.** $y = 5x + 7$
c. $y = -\frac{9}{8}x + 3\frac{5}{8}$ **d.** $y = -\frac{1}{4}x + 1$
e. $y = \frac{3}{2}x + \frac{1}{2}$ **5. a.** $\left(\frac{3}{2}, \frac{5}{2}\right)$ **b.** $(-2, 4)$
c. $\left(9, \frac{3}{5}\right)$ **d.** $(2, -1)$ **e.** $\left(\frac{3}{4}, -\frac{7}{4}\right)$ **f.** $\left(\frac{40}{9}, -\frac{7}{9}\right)$

6. a.

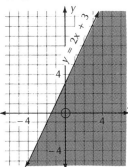

b.

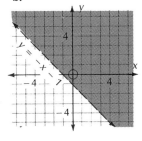

c.

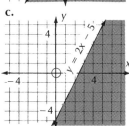

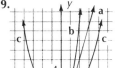

7. a. 12 **b.** 20 **c.** 16
8. a. 7 or -1
b. 2 or -3
c. 6 or 4

9.

10. 6

Unit 9

Exercises, page 276
1. a. $(7, -4)$ **b.** $(5,0)$ **c.** $(1, -1)$ **d.** $(-1, -7)$
2. a. $(-3,4)$ **b.** $(-4, -3)$ **c.** $(3, -4)$ **d.** $(3, -4)$
3. a. $(-1, -6)$ **b.** $(1,6)$ **c.** $(6, -1)$ **4. a.** -3
b. 4 **c.** $\frac{2}{3}$ **5. a.** $(5,2)$ **b.** $(-1,2)$ **c.** $\left(4, -\frac{2}{3}\right)$
d. $(-6,5)$ **6. a.** $(-4, -7)$ **b.** $(-5, -6)$ **c.** $(1, -5)$
d. $(-4, -9)$ **7. a.** $(20, -12)$ **b.** $\left(1\frac{1}{4}, -\frac{3}{4}\right)$
c. $(-20,12)$ **d.** $\left(-1\frac{1}{4}, \frac{3}{4}\right)$ **e.** $(5, -3)$

8. a. $(-4,5)$ **b.** $(1, -3)$ **c.** $(-6,0)$ **d.** $(3, -2)$
e. $(-b,a)$ **9. a.** $(-2, -8)$ **b.** $(4,3)$ **c.** $(-7,0)$
d. $(3, -5)$ **e.** $(-a, -b)$ **10. a.** $(4, -5)$ **b.** $(-1,3)$
c. $(6,0)$ **d.** $(-3,2)$ **e.** $(b, -a)$ **11. a.** $(8,2)$
b. $(-3, -4)$ **c.** $(0,7)$ **d.** $(5, -3)$ **e.** (b,a)
12. $(x,y) \rightarrow (x + 6, y - 6)$
$180°$ rotation about $(0,0)$
reflection in the line $y = x$
(also: dilatation with centre $(0,0)$ and $k = -1$)
13. a. $(-2, -1)$ **b.** $(x,y) \rightarrow (x - 1, y - 3)$ **c.** $(2,3)$
d. $(x,y) \rightarrow (x - 1, y + 5)$ **14. a.** $(a, -b)$ **b.** $(-a,b)$
c. (b,a) **d.** (ka,kb) **e.** $(-b,a)$ **f.** $(-a, -b)$
15. No, since a rotation about $(0,0)$ will always have
the same radius, e.g., $P(3,4)$ maps onto $P'(-4,3)$
after a $90°$ rotation.

Exercises, page 280
1. a. $A'(-2, -1)$, $B'(3, -2)$ **b.** $R'(-6,3)$, $T'(6, -9)$
c. $P'(-2,1)$, $Q'(-3,4)$ **d.** $C'(3,4)$, $D'(-2, -1)$
e. $J'(-5, -1)$, $K'(1, -2)$ **f.** $M'(4, -4)$, $N'(-1, -2)$
2. a. $P'(2,5)$, $Q'(-1, -2)$ **b.** same slopes
c. Yes, since slopes are equal.
3. a. $E'(-3,0)$, $F'(12, -6)$ **b.** same slopes **c.** Yes
d. $\overline{E'F'}$ is three times as long as $\overline{EF}$.
4. a. $R'(-4,3)$, $S'(2,1)$
b. $\overline{R'S'}$ has slope equal to the negative slope
of $\overline{RS}$. **c.** same lengths
5. a. $H'(1, -3)$, $M'(-5,4)$ **b.** The slope of $\overline{H'M'}$ is
equal to the negative reciprocal of the slope of
$\overline{HM}$. **c.** They are perpendicular. **d.** It becomes
perpendicular to the original segment and parallel
to the other $90°$ rotated segment.
6. a. $A'(6,3)$, $B'(2,1)$, $C'(8, -3)$
b. $AB = A'B'$, $BC = B'C'$, $CA = C'A'$
c. same corresponding slopes **d.** same
corresponding angles **e.** same area
f. congruent triangles
7. a. $X'(1,2)$, $Y'(-1, -5)$, $Z'(-6, -2)$
b. $XY = X'Y'$, $YZ = Y'Z'$, $ZX = Z'X'$
c. same corresponding slopes **d.** same
corresponding angles **e.** same area
f. congruent triangles
8. a. $X'(-1,2)$, $Y'(1, -5)$, $Z'(6, -2)$
b. i. $XY = X'Y'$, $YZ = Y'Z'$, $ZX = Z'X'$
ii. The slopes are opposites.
c. same corresponding angles **d.** same area
e. All properties except orientation are preserved.
9. a. $X'(1, -2)$, $Y'(-1,5)$, $Z'(-6,2)$
b. i. $XY = X'Y'$, $YZ = Y'Z'$, $ZX = Z'X'$
ii. The slopes are opposites.
c. same corresponding angles **d.** same area
e. All properties except orientation are preserved.
10. a. $D'(-3,6)$, $E'(6,6)$, $F'(6, -3)$, $G'(-3, -3)$
b. i. $D'E' = 3DE$, $E'F' = 3EF$, $F'G' = 3FG$, $G'D' = 3GD$

ii. same corresponding slopes **iii.** same angles
iv. Area of $D'E'F'G'$ is nine times the area of $DEFG$.
11. a. Image is bigger than original.
b. Image is smaller than original.
c. Image is the same as original.
12. a. preserved, preserved, preserved, not
always preserved **b.** preserved, not always
preserved, not always preserved, preserved
c. preserved, preserved, preserved, preserved
d. preserved, preserved, preserved, not always
preserved **e.** preserved, preserved, not
preserved, preserved.

13. a.

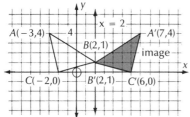

b.

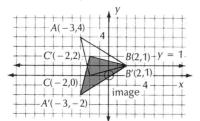

c.

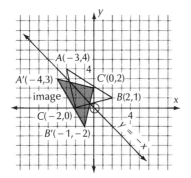

14. a. $T'(0,0)$, $U'(2,6)$, $V'(10,6)$, $W'(12,0)$
b. $T'(-1,-3)$, $U'(1,3)$, $V'(9,3)$, $W'(11,-3)$
c. $T'(-5,-3)$, $U'(-3,3)$, $V'(5,3)$, $W'(7,-3)$
d. $T'(-6,0)$, $U'(-4,6)$, $V'(4,6)$, $W'(6,0)$

Exercises, page 282
1. a. i. y-axis **ii.** $(x,y) \rightarrow (-x,y)$ **iii.** y-axis
iv. $(x,y) \rightarrow (x,y-5)$ **b. i.** $y = x$ **ii.** $(x,y) \rightarrow (y,x)$
iii. $y = x$ **iv.** $(x,y) \rightarrow (x-2,y-2)$ **c. i.** x – axis
ii. $(x,y) \rightarrow (x,-y)$ **iii.** x-axis **iv.** $(x,y) \rightarrow (x-4,y)$
2. a. True **b.** False **c.** False

3. a.

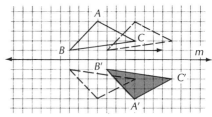

b.

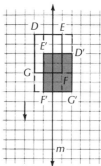

c.

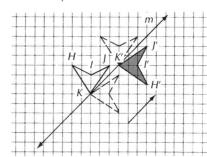

d.

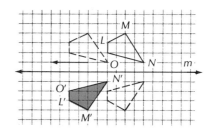

e.

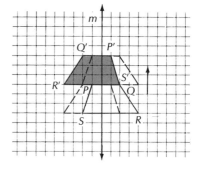

f.

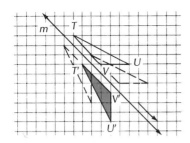

4. a. $X'(-5,7)$, $Y'(0,0)$, $Z'(-1,-5)$
b. $X'(0,-9)$, $Y'(-5,-2)$, $Z'(-4,3)$
c. $X'(8,4)$, $Y'(1,-1)$, $Z'(-4,0)$
d. $X'(-5,-9)$, $Y'(2,-4)$, $Z'(7,-5)$

5. a.

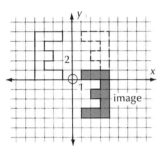

b.

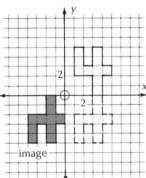

c.

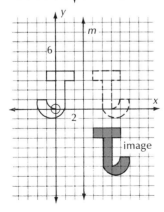

Extra, page 283
5.25 m

Exercises, page 284
1. No **2.** Yes **3.** No **4.** Yes **5.** Yes
6. Opposite **7. a.** Preserved **b.** Not preserved
c. Preserved **d.** Preserved **e.** Not preserved
8. a. $(x,y) \rightarrow (-x,y)$; $(x,y) \rightarrow (x,y-4)$
b. $(x,y) \rightarrow (x,-y)$; $(x,y) \rightarrow (x-7,y)$
c. $(x,y) \rightarrow (x,-y)$; $(x,y) \rightarrow (x-4,y)$
9. These midpoints, when joined, form a line parallel to line m.

Extra, page 285
translation, rotation, reflection, glide reflection

Review, page 286

1. a. $A'\left(2\frac{1}{2},1\right)$, $B'(4,3)$, $C'\left(\frac{1}{2},2\right)$

b. $A'(2,5)$, $B'(6,8)$, $C'(4,1)$
c. $A'(-2,5)$, $B'(-6,8)$, $C'(-4,1)$
d. $A'(-1,-1)$, $B'(2,3)$, $C'(-5,1)$
2. a. $Q'(8,0)$ **b.** $K(0,-6)$ **3.** Answers vary.
4. $C'(-4,-2)$, $P'(-1,-6)$

5. a.

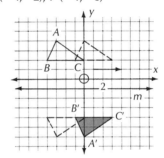

b.

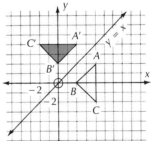

c.

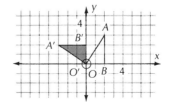

6. a. The sides of the image are twice as long as the corresponding sides of the object.
b. same corresponding slopes
d. same corresponding angles
e. The area of the image is four times bigger than the area of the object.

7. a. The sides of the image are three times as long as the corresponding sides of the object.
b. same corresponding slopes
d. same corresponding angles
e. The area of the image is nine times bigger than the area of the object.

8. a. The sides of the image are half as long as the corresponding sides of the object.
b. same corresponding slopes
d. same corresponding angles
e. The area of the image is four times smaller than the area of the object.

Application, page 287
1. Answers vary.
2. Make a pantograph with a scale factor of $\frac{1}{2}$, for example.
3. Yes

Exercises, page 288
1. a.

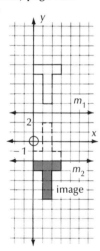

b.

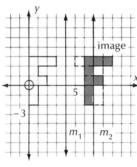

d.

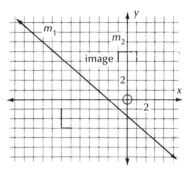

e.

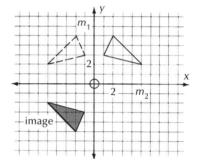

f.

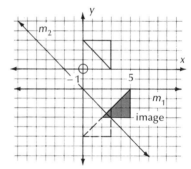

c.

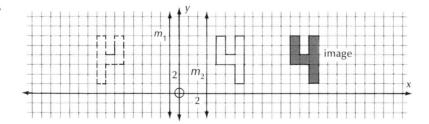

2. a.

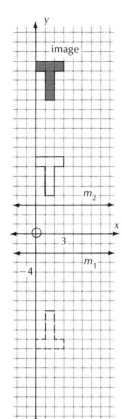

b.

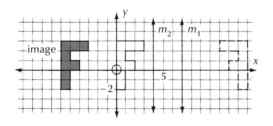

c.

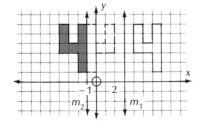

d.

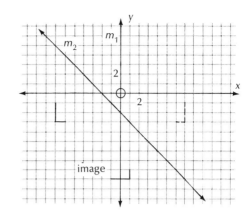

e.

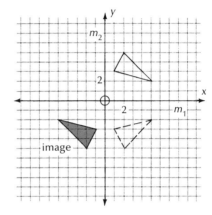

f.

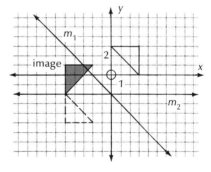

3. b. translation [−8,0] of object

4. b. translation [0,−6] of object

5. b. Answers vary.

6. b. Answers vary.

7. c. Answers vary.

8. b. Answers vary.

9. Answers vary.

Exercises, page 290

1. a. Note: Answers may vary for **1.a.** to **e.**

 180° rotation about *P* or reflection in line *m*, followed by reflection in line *n*

b.
 270° rotation about *Q*

c.
 translation *r*, followed by a reflection in line *m*

d.
translation *r*, followed by a reflection in line *m*

e.
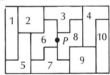 translation *r*, followed by a reflection in line *m*

2. a.

| 1 | 2 | 3 | 4 |

180° rotation about *P*

b. Answers vary.

3. a.
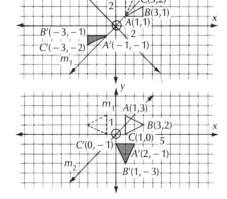

b.

4. a.
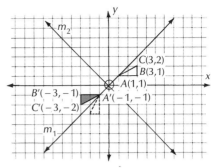

b.
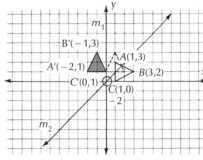

5.
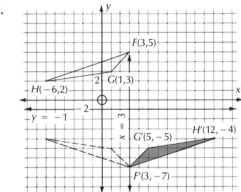

6. a.
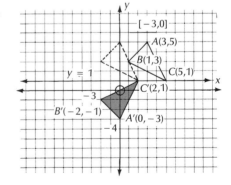

b. $(x,y) \rightarrow (x - 3, y)$
$(x,y) \rightarrow (x, -y + 2)$

470

7.

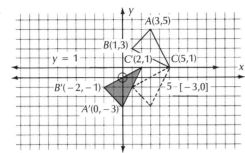

8.

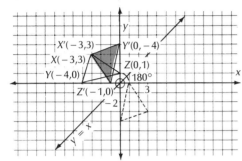

9.

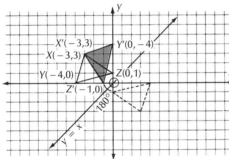

10. glide reflection; reflection

Extra, page 291

1. reflection in line m_1; translation 1 followed by reflection in line m_2; translation 2; 180° rotation about point B

Exercises, page 293

1. a. $\angle PQR$ **b.** $\angle QRP$ **c.** $\angle RPQ$ **d.** QR
e. PR **f.** AB **g.** $\triangle BAC$ **h.** $\triangle RPQ$
2. a., e. **3.** b., c. **4. a.** 28 units **b.** 20 units
c. 32 units **5. a.** 2 units **b.** $\frac{8}{3}$ units **c.** 3 units
6. $A \cong N$ $I \cong B$ $A \sim P$
  $J \cong F$ $K \cong B$ $A \sim Q$
  $I \cong K$ $L \cong M$ $N \sim P$
      $G \cong H$ $N \sim Q$

7. a.

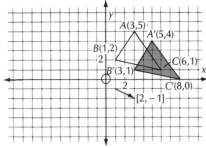

direct congruence

b.

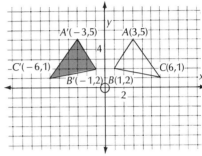

opposite congruence

c.

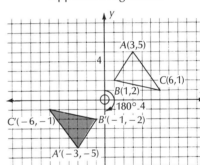

direct congruence

d.

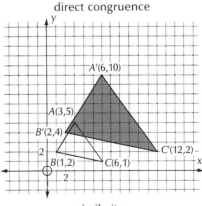

similarity

471

e.

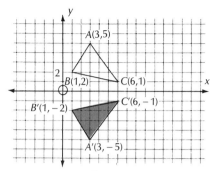

opposite congruence

f.

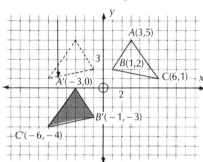

opposite congruence

8. a. $x = 3\frac{1}{3}$; $y = 4\frac{2}{3}$ **b.** $x = 21$; $y = 10\frac{1}{2}$; $z = 14\frac{1}{2}$

c. $x = 8\frac{3}{4}$; $y = 7\frac{1}{2}$ **d.** $a = 9$; $b = 10\frac{4}{5}$

e. $x = 10$; $y = 4$ **f.** $x = 15$; $y = 12\frac{1}{2}$

g. $a \doteq 7.7$; $b \doteq 10.3$ **h.** $a = 4$; $b = 5$

i. $x = 3$; $y = 7\frac{1}{2}$; $z = 7\frac{1}{2}$

9. a. Yes **b.** Yes, the corresponding angles are equal, and lengths of corresponding sides are in the same ratio.

10. $9\frac{1}{3}$ cm **11.** $\frac{x}{a} = \frac{b}{x}$ **12.** $\frac{12}{12} = \frac{5}{5} = \frac{12}{12} = \frac{5}{5} = 1$
No, the corresponding angles are not equal.

13. $\frac{6}{12} = \frac{6}{12} = \frac{5}{10} = \frac{6}{12} = \frac{5}{10} = \frac{1}{2}$
Yes, the corresponding angles are equal.

14. a. 2 **b.** area $\triangle ABC = 60$; Area $\triangle A'B'C' = 240$
c. 4 **d.** 9, 25, n^2
15. 8 times larger; 27 times larger; 125 times larger

Exercises, page 296

1. 60 m **2.** $\frac{1}{7}$ m **3.** 160 cm **4.** 7.875 m

5. 43.75 m **6.** 1.76 m **7.** 96.4 m
8. No, he has to drive the ball about 225 m.
9. 96 m

Review, page 299

1. a.

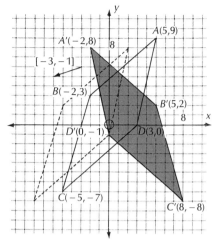

b.

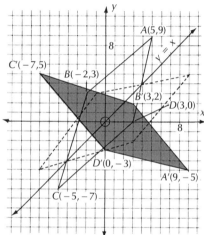

c.

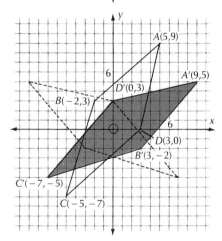

d.

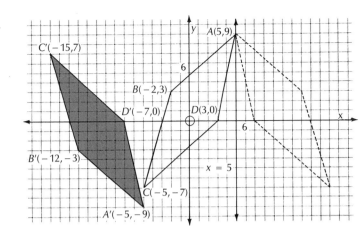

5. a., c., d., e., because each transformation preserves distance between points

6.

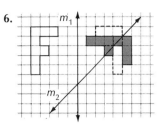

7. a. translation, rotation
b. reflection, glide reflection
c. dilatation

8. a. $x = 3\frac{1}{3}$; $y = 4$ **b.** $x = 13\frac{1}{3}$; $y = 5$
c. $x = 4$; $y = 8$; $z = 9$

2. Yes **3. a.** $a = 31\frac{1}{5}$; $b = 28\frac{4}{5}$
b. $a = 1\frac{2}{5}$; $b = 1\frac{3}{5}$ **c.** $x = 9$; $y = 21$ **d.** $x = 4$

4. a. translation, rotation
b. reflection, glide reflection **c.** none

5. 270 cm **6. a.** 3:1 **b.** 9:1 **7.** $\frac{8}{6} = \frac{5}{3.75} = \frac{4}{3}$

8. Yes

Test, page 300
1. a. (2,2) **b.** (−5,−2) **c.** (2,5) **d.** (−2,5)
e. (−5,2) **f.** (17.5,−7)
2. (−22,−2) **3. a.** $P'(−14,16)$; $Q'(−4,6)$; $R'(−8,0)$
b. $P'(−5,4)$; $Q'(0,−1)$; $R'(−2,−4)$
c. $P'(−7,−8)$; $Q'(−2,−3)$; $R'(−4,0)$

Cumulative Review, page 301
1. a. $AB = \sqrt{44.2}$ **b.** (−7.5,−1.5) **c.** −21
2. $y = \frac{4}{3}x − 5$ **3. a.** $y = \frac{3}{5}x$ **b.** $y = −2x − 2$
c. $y = x$ **4. a.** (1,1) **b.** $\left(\frac{5}{7}, −\frac{6}{7}\right)$ **c.** (5,2)
d. (−2,−2) **e.** (10,5) **f.** $\left(7\frac{3}{14}, \frac{1}{14}\right)$

4. a.

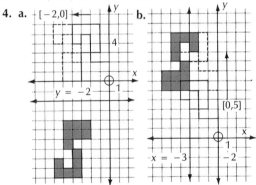

5. a.

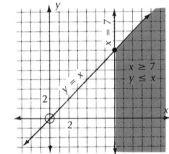

b.

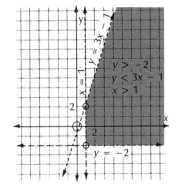

c.

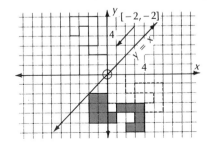

c.

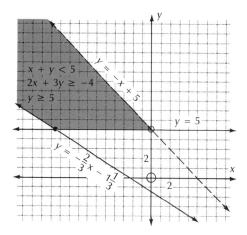

$x + y < 5$
$2x + 3y \geq -4$
$y \geq 5$
$y = -x + 5$
$y = 5$
$y = -\frac{2}{3}x - 1\frac{1}{3}$

6. a. $(x - 2y)(x + 2y)$ **b.** $(x + 7)(x - 2)$
c. $(x + 3)(2x - 1)$
d. $(4x^2 + 9y^2)(2x + 3y)(2x - 3y)$
e. $(x + 1)(3x - 2)$ **f.** $2(x + 7)^2$
7. $-\frac{3}{11}$ **8.** $15\frac{1}{2}$ **9. a.** $10

d.

Amount ($)	Freq.	Cum. Freq.	Midpoint of Interval ($)	Subtotal ($)
1–10	1	1	5.50	5.50
11–20	1	2	15.50	15.50
21–30	10	12	25.50	255.00
31–40	15	27	35.50	532.50
41–50	4	31	45.50	182.00
51–60	1	32	55.50	55.50

c. mean $\doteq$ $32.70;
median $\doteq$ $35.50;
mode $\doteq$ $35.50

b.

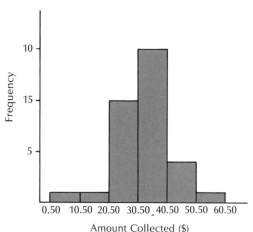

Frequency

Amount Collected ($)

Unit 10

Exercises, page 304
1. a. Therefore, Andy takes Mathematics and Science.
b. Therefore, James will get wet.
c. Therefore, Anthony sleeps for several hours during the day.
d. Therefore, Claire should wear corrective lenses.
e. Therefore, Al will be fit.
f. Therefore, $\triangle ABC$ is isosceles.
g. Therefore, the diagonals of square $ABCD$ bisect each other.
h. Therefore, Alicia requires nurturing and caring.
i. Therefore, this saucer is easily broken if dropped.
j. Therefore, Betsy is a sight to be seen.
2. a. No **b.** No **c.** Yes **d.** No **e.** Yes
3. a. rhombus **b.** square **c.** equilateral
d. regular hexagon **e.** right-angled triangle
f. cuboid **g.** cube
4. a. British Columbia is a big province, with more cities than just Vancouver.
b. Other girls also went to the dance; Christine may be one of them.
c. Oliver could be a cat that is kept on a leash.
d. What about the other angles?
e. $\angle ABC$ may be in one triangle and $\angle XYZ$ in another.
f. Not all real numbers are rational.
5. Neither true nor false.

Extra, page 305
Terry is a woman.

Exercises, page 307–308
1. a. $\angle YXA$, $\angle YXB$, $\angle XYC$, $\angle XYD$
b. $\angle AXE$, $\angle BXE$, $\angle FYD$, $\angle FYC$
c. $\angle YXA$ and $\angle XYD$, $\angle YXB$ and $\angle XYC$
d. $\angle AXE$ and $\angle XYC$, $\angle FYC$ and $\angle YXA$, $\angle BXE$ and $\angle XYD$, $\angle YXB$ and $\angle FYD$
e. $\angle XYC$ and $\angle YXA$, $\angle XYD$ and $\angle YXB$
2. a. $\angle 6$, $\angle 4$ **b.** $\angle 8$ **c.** $\angle 8$, $\angle 3$ **d.** $\angle 9$
e. $\angle 7$ **3. a.** A, B, C, and D
b. $\overline{XY} \parallel \overline{WZ}$, $\overline{DC} \parallel \overline{AB}$, $\overline{WX} \parallel \overline{ZY}$, $\overline{AD} \parallel \overline{BC}$, $\overline{WA} \parallel \overline{ZB}$, $\overline{XD} \parallel \overline{YC}$
c. $\overline{AD}$ and $\overline{BZ}$, $\overline{AD}$ and $\overline{YC}$, $\overline{WX}$ and $\overline{BZ}$, $\overline{WX}$ and $\overline{YC}$, $\overline{BC}$ and $\overline{WA}$, $\overline{BC}$ and $\overline{XD}$, $\overline{ZY}$ and $\overline{WA}$, $\overline{ZY}$ and $\overline{XD}$, $\overline{WZ}$ and $\overline{XD}$, $\overline{WZ}$ and $\overline{YC}$, $\overline{AB}$ and $\overline{XD}$, $\overline{AB}$ and $\overline{YC}$

*Note: Answers for **b.** and **c.** may vary.*
4. a. $\overline{QP}$, $\overline{QS}$, and $\overline{RS}$
b. $\angle 5$ and $\angle 3$, $\angle 2$ and $\angle 6$
c. PS, SQ, and QR
d. $\angle 5$ and $\angle 3$, $\angle 2$ and $\angle 6$

5. a. corresponding **b.** alternate
c. none of these **d.** none of these
e. interior angles on the same side of transversal
f. none of these **g.** corresponding
h. none of these
7. a. False **b.** False **c.** True **d.** True **e.** False
f. False **8. a.** an infinite number of lines
b. One **c.** Zero **9.** Four
10. No, the fourth point could be above or below
the plane containing the first three points.

Extra, page 308
1. slice down the cube, in the diagonal
2. Yes

Historical Note, page 309
1. Two
2. A strip with a double twist, twice as long as
Moebius strip; two strips hooked together.
3. A strip with a double twist, twice as long as the
Moebius strip with $\frac{1}{3}$ the width, and a Moebius
strip hooked on with $\frac{1}{3}$ the width of original.
5. Because it uses both sides.

Extra, page 309
1. Answers vary. **2.** Answers vary.

 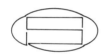

Exercises, page 311
1. a. $\angle 1$ and $\angle 5$, $\angle 2$ and $\angle 6$
b. $\angle 2$ and $\angle 7$, $\angle 5$ and $\angle 4$
c. $\angle 1$, $\angle 3$, $\angle 6$, and $\angle 8$
d. $\angle 2$, $\angle 4$, $\angle 5$, and $\angle 7$
e. $\angle 2$ and $\angle 5$, $\angle 4$ and $\angle 7$
f. $\angle 4$ and $\angle 5$, $\angle 5$ and $\angle 8$, $\angle 1$ and $\angle 5$, $\angle 1$ and
$\angle 8$, $\angle 4$ and $\angle 8$, $\angle 2$ and $\angle 7$, $\angle 3$ and $\angle 6$, $\angle 2$ and
$\angle 6$, $\angle 3$ and $\angle 7$, $\angle 5$ and $\angle 8$, $\angle 1$ and $\angle 4$, $\angle 7$ and
$\angle 6$, $\angle 2$ and $\angle 3$
g. $\angle 1$ and $\angle 3$, $\angle 1$ and $\angle 2$, $\angle 3$ and $\angle 4$, $\angle 5$ and
$\angle 6$, $\angle 7$ and $\angle 8$, $\angle 8$ and $\angle 6$, $\angle 7$ and $\angle 5$, $\angle 2$ and
$\angle 4$, $\angle 1$ and $\angle 7$, $\angle 1$ and $\angle 6$, $\angle 4$ and $\angle 7$, $\angle 4$ and
$\angle 6$, $\angle 2$ and $\angle 5$, $\angle 3$ and $\angle 5$, $\angle 2$ and $\angle 8$, $\angle 3$
and $\angle 8$

2. a. $\angle 1 = 145°$; $\angle 3 = 35°$; $\angle 4 = 145°$;
$\angle 5 = 145°$; $\angle 6 = 35°$; $\angle 7 = 35°$; $\angle 8 = 145°$
b. $\angle 1 = 154°$; $\angle 2 = 26°$; $\angle 3 = 26°$;
$\angle 4 = 154°$; $\angle 5 = 154°$; $\angle 6 = 26°$; $\angle 7 = 26°$

3. a. $\angle 2$, $\angle 10$, $\angle 12$, $\angle 15$, $\angle 7$, $\angle 5$, $\angle 13$
b. $\angle 8$, $\angle 3$, $\angle 11$, $\angle 16$, $\angle 1$, $\angle 6$, $\angle 9$, $\angle 14$
c. $80°$ **d.** $65°$ **e.** $75°$ **f.** $98°$

4. a. $x = 80°$; $y = 100°$ **b.** $t = 85°$; $v = 85°$
c. $x = 60°$; $y = 60°$ **d.** $x = 70°$; $y = 70°$
e. $x = 115°$; $y = 65°$; $z = 65°$; $u = 115°$
f. $t = 90°$; $u = 90°$; $v = 90°$
5. a. $\overline{AB} \parallel \overline{CD}$ **b.** none **c.** $\overline{AC} \parallel \overline{BD}$ **d.** none
e. $\overline{AB} \parallel \overline{CD}$
6. a. $x = 30°$; $y = 75°$
b. $x = 70°$; $y = 110°$; $z = 70°$
c. $x = y = z = 90°$ **d.** $x = 45°$; $y = 25°$
e. $x = 32°$; $y = 48°$ **f.** $x = 65°$; $y = 65°$; $z = 50°$
g. $w = 40°$; $x = 64°$; $y = 76°$; $z = 76°$
h. $t = 68°$; $w = 87°$; $x = 68°$; $y = 25°$; $z = 68°$
i. $x = 49°$; $y = 80°$; $z = 51°$
7. a. 33 **b.** 18 **c.** 11 **d.** 10 **e.** 12 **f.** 5
8.

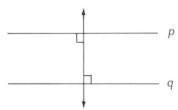

p and q are parallel because corresponding and
alternate angles are equal (also sum of interior
angles on the same side of the transversal is 180°)

Extra, page 313
The tenth line segment became one of the edges.

Exercises, page 315
1. a. $\angle 1$, $\angle 3$; $\angle 2$, $\angle 4$
b. $\angle 4$, $\angle 1$; $\angle 4$, $\angle 3$; $\angle 1$, $\angle 2$; $\angle 2$, $\angle 3$
c. $\angle 4$, $\angle 1$; $\angle 4$, $\angle 3$; $\angle 1$, $\angle 2$; $\angle 2$, $\angle 3$
2. a. $\angle 1 = 148°$; $\angle 2 = 32°$; $\angle 3 = 148°$
b. $\angle 1 = 132°$; $\angle 2 = 48°$; $\angle 3 = 132°$
c. $\angle 1 = 126°$; $\angle 2 = 54°$; $\angle 3 = 126°$
3. a. $\angle 1$, $\angle 3$ **b.** $\angle 3$
4. a. $x = 138°$; $y = 42°$ **b.** $x = 59°$; $y = 62°$
c. $w = 75°$; $x = 70°$; $y = 75°$; $z = 35°$
d. $x = 65°$; $y = 65°$ **e.** $x = 29°$; $y = 145°$
f. $x = 11°$; $y = 15°$; $z = 45°$
g. $w = 30°$; $x = 75°$; $y = 75°$; $z = 75°$
h. $x = 80°$ **i.** $x = 65°$

Exercises, page 317
1. a. $37°$ **b.** $30°$ **c.** $12°$ **d.** $15°$ **e.** $122°$
f. $103°$ **g.** $65°$ **h.** $60°$
i. $x = 30°$; $y = 60°$; $z = 30°$
2. a. $x = 35°$; $y = 35°$; $z = 30°$
b. $w = 32°$; $x = 84°$; $y = 84°$; $z = 64°$
c. $x = 75°$; $y = 60°$
d. $t = 75°$; $u = 50°$; $v = 20°$; $w = 35°$; $x = 20°$;
$y = 50°$; $z = 70°$
3. $145°$ **5.** $65°$

Extra, page 319
1. c. 180° **d.** 540° **e.** 540° **2. a.** 360°
b. 720° **c.** 1080° **d.** 1440° **e.** 2340°
f. $[(n - 2)180]°$ **3. a.** 90° **b.** 108° **c.** 135°
d. 120°

Review, page 319
1. Answers vary.
2. a. $x = 65°; y = 115°$
b. $x = 80°; y = 100°; z = 100°$ **c.** $x = 30°$
d. $x = 21°$ **e.** $x = 55°$
f. $t = 115°; x = 65°; y = 85°; z = 30°$

Exercises, page 322
1. a. No **b.** Yes: SSS **c.** No **d.** No **e.** No
f. No **g.** Yes: SAS **h.** Yes: ASA

Exercises, page 326
1. a. $x = y = z = 60°$ **b.** $x = y = 75°$
c. $x = 50°; y = 65°$ **d.** $x = 116°; y = 64°$
e. $x = 15°; y = 75°; z = 15°$
f. $x = 70°; y = 40°; z = 70°$
2. a. $x = 15°; \angle P = 40°; \angle Q = 70°; \angle R = 70°$
b. $x = 15°; \angle X = 80°; \angle Y = 80°; \angle Z = 20°$
4. a. 90° **b.** 90°

Exercises, page 330
1. a. If the street is wet, then it is raining.
b. If a triangle has two equal sides, then it is
isosceles. **c.** If $x^2 = 9$, then $x = 3$.
d. If $x = 5$, then $2x + 3 = 13$.
e. If the sum of two numbers is even, then they
are odd.
2. b. and d.
3. a. If two angles are supplementary, then their
sum is 180°. If the sum of two angles is 180°, then
they are supplementary.
b. If two lines are parallel, then alternate angles
are equal. If alternate angles are equal, then two
lines are parallel.
c. If two lines are parallel, then corresponding
angles are equal. If corresponding angles are
equal, then two lines are parallel.
d. If two lines are parallel, then interior angles on
the same side of the transversal are
supplementary. If interior angles on the same side
of the transversal are supplementary, then two
lines are parallel.

Extra, page 331
1. Draw a diameter and divide it into four equal
parts. Draw a semicircle on the top and bottom
of each segment of the diameter to create a
continuous curve at each segment.

Exercises, page 333
1. a. 5 **b.** 13 **c.** 25 **d.** 6 **e.** 72 **f.** 15
2. a., c., e., f. **3. a.** $x = 4, y = 2\sqrt{29}$
b. $x = 4\sqrt{3}, y = 2\sqrt{6}$
4. a. Prove: $(a^2 + b^2)^2 = (a^2 - b^2)^2 + (2ab)^2$
L.S. $= a^4 + 2a^2b^2 + b^4$

R.S. $= a^4 - 2a^2b^2 + b^4 + 4a^2b^2$
$ = a^4 + 2a^2b^2 + b^4$

L.S. = R.S.
b. Answers vary.
5. a. If $c^2 = a^2 + b^2$, then the triangle is a
right-angled triangle.

Exercises, page 335

1. a. Answers vary.

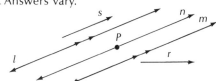

translation r
180° rotation about P
translation s, followed by reflection in line n
reflection in line n

2. Answers vary.

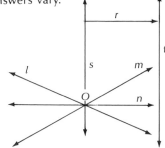

reflection in line n
45° rotation about O
translation r, followed by reflection in line t
reflection in line s

Review, page 337
11. a. 12 **b.** 25 **c.** $4\sqrt{5}$

Exercises, page 338
1. 41 **2.** 48 **3. a.** 220 cm² **b.** 112 cm²
4. A square lot; by 144 m². **5.** 6 cm **6.** 9 mm
7. 14 m **8.** 97.5 kg (10 bags) **9.** $47.96
10. 3158.5 km

Using the Calculator, page 339
1. Let the length be y; then $y = 6 - x$.
2. $A = x(6 - x)$

3.

x	A
0	0
0.5	2.75
1.0	5
1.5	6.75
2.0	8
2.5	8.75
3.0	9
3.5	8.75
4.0	8
4.5	6.75
5.0	5
5.5	2.75
6.0	0

4. 3 m × 3 m
5. 5 m × 5 m;
    7.5 m × 7.5 m;
    10 m × 10 m
6. $\frac{1}{4}x \times \frac{1}{4}x$

Test, page 340

1. a. not all people who wear lab coats are doctors
b. working part time is not restricted to people who are students
2. a. $x = y = 65°$ **b.** $x = 60°$
c. $x = 80°; y = 20°$ **d.** $x = y = 60°$
e. $w = 75°; x = 75°; y = 105°; z = 75°$
f. $x = 68°; y = 112°; z = 68°$
g. $x = 67°; y = 85°; z = 67°$
h. $x = 72°; y = 72°; z = 36°$
i. $x = 66°; y = 132°$
5. a. If you're responsible for your rent, then you live on your own. Not necessarily true.
b. If you've completed grade 12, then you're a high school graduate. True.
c. If all of a triangle's angles are equal, then it is equilateral. True.
d. If your new pet has wings, then it is a bird. Not necessarily true.
e. If your new pet has a wet nose, then it must be a dog. Not necessarily true.

Cumulative Review, page 341

1. a. $\left(1\frac{1}{7}, 1\frac{2}{7}\right)$ **b.** (2,0) **c.** (0,6)

2. 325 $5 tickets and 251 $7 tickets

3. a.

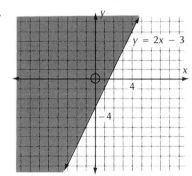

b.

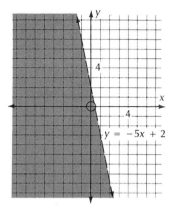

c.

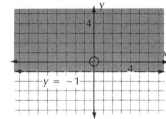

4. a. $2x(x - 7)$ **b.** $6b^2(a - 1)(a^2 + a + 1)$
c. $3(a - 1)^2$ **d.** $(t^2 + v^2)(t + v)(t - v)$
e. $(x + 7)(x - 1)$ **f.** $(k - 5)(k - 3)$
g. $12(a - 12)(a + 1)$ **h.** $2(t + 11)(t - 3)$
i. $(3b + 5)(2b - 1)$
5. a. $(x + 1); x \neq -1$ **b.** $(x + 1); x \neq -2$
c. $\dfrac{(x + 5)}{(x + 4)}; x \neq 3$ or -4

6.

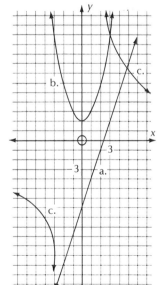

7. 17.5 **8.** $\frac{1}{60}$ **9.** 9

10. a. $A'(-2,4)$; $B'(1,2)$; $C'(0,8)$; $D'(-3,7)$
b. $A'(1,0)$; $B'(-1,3)$; $C'(5,2)$; $D'(4,-1)$
c. $A'(0,-3)$; $B'(-9,3)$; $C'(-6,-15)$; $D'(3,-12)$
d. $A'(0,-1)$; $B'(-3,1)$; $C'(-2,-5)$; $D'(1,-4)$

11. a. $x = 10$; $y = 10\frac{5}{12}$ **b.** $x = 14$; $y = 5$; $z = 10$

Unit 11

Exercises, page 343
4. a. bisect a straight angle
b. bisect a 90° angle (from a.)
c. bisect a 45° angle (from b.)
d. bisect a straight angle and then bisect the 90° angle formed on the left-hand side.

6. a. same as the method for constructing an equilateral triangle, leave out the third side.
b. bisect a 60° angle (from a.)
c. bisect a 30° angle (from b.)
d. construct a 90° angle and a 60° angle, bisect the 30° angle formed in between.

Exercises, page 345
1 a. $\overline{OB}$, $\overline{OA}$, $\overline{OC}$, $\overline{OD}$ **b.** $\overline{BD}$, $\overline{AC}$ **c.** $\overline{EF}$
d. $\overline{AB}$, $\overline{AD}$, $\overline{BD}$, $\overline{AC}$ **e.** C **f.** $\angle COD$, $\angle COB$
(Answers vary.)

2. a. $\overline{OA}$, $\overline{OB}$, arc AB; $\overline{OC}$, $\overline{OD}$, arc CD;
$\overline{OA}$, $\overline{OD}$, arc AD; $\overline{OB}$, $\overline{OC}$, arc BC; $\overline{OA}$, $\overline{OC}$, arc AC;
$\overline{OB}$, $\overline{OD}$, arc BD **b.** $\overline{AB}$, arc AB; $\overline{AC}$, arc AC;
$\overline{AD}$, arc AD; $\overline{BD}$, arc BD

3. a. when the angle is 180°.
b. when the chord is a diameter.

4. 360° **5.** 298° **6. a.** 180° **b.** 90° **c.** 30°
d. 150° **e.** 60°

7. d. Equilateral triangle, since $OA = OB$ and $\angle AOB = 60°$.
8. 55° **9.** 34° **10. a.** 8 cm **b.** 13 cm **c.** 25 cm
11. a. 19.63 cm² **b.** 5.88 cm² **c.** 38.56 cm²

Exercises, page 348
1. a. 4 **b.** 90 **c.** 4 **d.** 5 **3. a.** 8 **b.** 7 **c.** 10
d. 18.8 **e.** 4 **f.** 8 **g.** 10 **h.** 2 **9.** 14 cm

10. $\overline{PQ}$ by 1 cm **12.** 18.4 cm × 18.4 cm

13. a. 20 cm **b.** 5.8 cm **14.** 120 m

15. 13 m

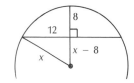

Exercises, page 351
1. a. $\angle DAB$, $\angle DAC$, $\angle CAB$
b. $\angle COB$, $\angle COD$, $\angle BOA$ (Answers vary.)
c. $\angle BAC$, $\angle BOC$

2. a. 110° **b.** 50° **c.** 140° **d.** 86°
e. $x° = 200°$; $y° = 160°$ **f.** 110°
g. $x° = 65°$; $y° = 230°$; $z° = 115°$
h. $x° = 50°$; $y° = 100°$

4. a. 45° **b.** 30° **c.** 25° **d.** 65° **e.** 50°
f. $x° = 80°$; $y° = 40°$; $z° = 80°$ **g.** $x° = y° = 40°$
h. $x° = 60°$; $y° = 30°$

Exercises, page 353
1. a. $\angle EBD$, $\angle EAD$ **b.** $\angle AEB$, $\angle ADB$, $\angle ACB$
c. $\angle ABE$, $\angle ADE$ **d.** $\angle DAC$, $\angle DBC$

2. $ABCD$, $ABDE$, $ACDE$, $BCDE$

3. a. 32° **b.** 90°
c. $x° = 65°$; $y° = 85°$; $z° = 30°$
d. $x° = y° = 90°$ **e.** $x° = 75°$; $y° = 105°$
f. $x° = 115°$ **g.** $w° = x° = y° = z° = 40°$
h. $x° = 35°$; $y° = 50°$ **5.** 115° **7.** 117°

Review, page 355
2. a. $\overline{OF}$, $\overline{OB}$ (Answers vary.) **b.** $\overline{CF}$ **c.** $\overline{DE}$
d. C
e. $\angle CAB$, $\angle FCB$, $\angle BAF$, $\angle CAF$, $\angle AFC$, $\angle ABC$
f. $\angle COB$, $\angle BOF$ (Answers vary.)
g. $\overline{CA}$, $\overline{AF}$, $\overline{CB}$, $\overline{AB}$, $\overline{CF}$
h. $\overline{OF}$, $\overline{OB}$, arc FB; $\overline{OC}$, $\overline{OB}$, arc CB (Answers vary.)
i. $\overline{CB}$, arc CB; $\overline{CF}$, arc CF; $\overline{CA}$, arc CA;
$\overline{AF}$, arc AF; $\overline{AB}$, arc AB
j. $\overline{CF}$, arc CF **k.** $\angle CAF$

3. a. $x = 5$ cm **b.** $x° = 60°$ **c.** $x = 32$ cm
d. $x = 5$ cm; $y = 12$ cm **4. a.** $x° = y° = 50°$
b. $x° = y° = 25°$ **c.** $x° = 100°$; $y° = 160°$
d. $x° = 130°$; $y° = 65°$
e. $x° = y° = 90°$; $z° = 65°$ **f.** $x° = 35°$; $y° = 65°$
g. $x° = 90°$; $y° = 50°$
h. $w° = 80°$; $x° = 90°$; $y° = 60°$; $z° = 60°$

6. 87° **7.** 9.5 cm

Exercises, page 357
1. a. 5 **b.** 12 **c.** $x = 12$; $y = 16$ **2.** 8 cm

4. 36 cm

Exercises, page 361
4. b. three

5. $\angle YXZ = 65°$; $\angle XZY = 65°$; $\angle ZYX = 50°$

7.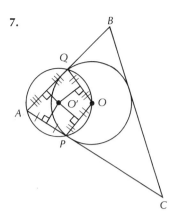

Construct perpendicular bisectors to $\overline{AP}$, $\overline{PO}$, $\overline{OQ}$, and $\overline{AQ}$. The point of intersection, O', is the centre of the circle with radius QO'. Construct this circle. It touches all vertices of quadrilateral $AQOP$, so $AQOP$ is cyclic.

8. 37 **9.** 56

10.

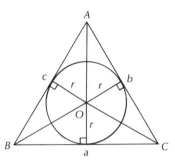

(Let r be the radius of the incircle.)

In $\triangle AOB$

Area $= \dfrac{1}{2}\,cr$

In $\triangle AOC$

Area $= \dfrac{1}{2}\,br$

In $\triangle BOC$

Area $= \dfrac{1}{2}\,ar$

$\therefore$ Area $\triangle ABC = \dfrac{1}{2}\,cr + \dfrac{1}{2}\,br + \dfrac{1}{2}\,ar$

$\qquad \therefore$ Area $= \dfrac{1}{2}\,r(a + b + c)$

Review, page 363
1. a. 90 **b.** 9 **c.** 45 **d.** 3 **e.** $x = y = 24$
f. $t° = 90°$; $x = y = z = 3$
2. a. $p = 6$; $q = 7$; $r = 8$ **b.** 42
c. $\angle AXY = 56.5°$; $\angle CBA = 59°$; $\angle XZC = 119.5°$
7. a. 69° **b.** 9 cm **d.** 69°

Exercises, page 364
3. a. $2r \times 2r$ **b.** $4r^2$ **c.** πr^2 **d.** 78.5%
e. 78.5% **4. a.** $\sqrt{3}r^2$; $\dfrac{1}{2}\pi r^2$ **b.** 90.6% **c.** 90.6%

5. Hexagonal packing. No other method is more efficient, since the triangle is the polygon with the least amount of sides.

Historical Note, page 365
6. No

Test, page 366
4. a. 42.5° **b.** 90° **c.** 60°
d. $x° = 52°$; $y° = 104°$ **e.** 90° **f.** 80° **g.** 140°
h. 60° **5. a.** 6 **b.** 24 **c.** 8 **d.** 8

Cumulative Review, page 367
1. a. 8 or -3 **b.** $-2\dfrac{1}{2}$ **c.** $\dfrac{1}{3}$ or -9
2. a. $\dfrac{(2x - 1)}{(x + 3)(x - 4)}$; $x \neq -3$ or 4
b. $\dfrac{(4t + 21)}{t(t - 7)}$; $t \neq 0$ or 7
c. $\dfrac{k^2 + 6k + 7}{(k + 2)(k - 2)}$; $k \neq -2$ or 2

3. a. D $= \{x | x \in R\}$; R $= \{y | y \in R\}$; Yes
b. D $= \{x | x \in I\}$; R $= \{y | y \in I\}$; No
c. D $= \{x | x > 0\}$; R $= \{y | y < 0\}$; Yes
d. D $= \{x | x \in R\}$; R $= \{y | y \geq 0\}$; Yes

4.

x	1	6	4	8	12	-24	12	5	$-4\frac{4}{5}$
y	24	4	6	3	2	-1	2	$4\frac{4}{5}$	-5

5. a. Each home form has a different number of students in it.
b. Shoppers will all be in favour of a new shopping complex (biased sample).
c. Not everyone listens to the same radio station.
7. $x = 5\dfrac{1}{3}$; $y = 18$ **8. a.** $x° = y° = z° = 120°$
b. $x° = 105°$; $y° = 75°$ **c.** $x° = 50°$

Unit 12

Exercises, page 370
1. a. Yes. 1 **b.** Yes. 3 **c.** No. **d.** Yes. 6
e. Yes. 1 **f.** Yes. 1 **g.** Yes. 1 **h.** Yes. 1 **i.** Yes. 2
j. No. **k.** Yes. 1 **2. a.** b, d, and i
b. figure b: order 3
figure d: order 6
figure i: order 2
c. The number of lines of symmetry is equal to the order of rotational symmetry.

d. figure b: 120°
figure d: 60°
figure i: 180°
3. Yes. 5 **4.** Yes. 2 **5. a.** Yes. 12 **b.** Yes. 4
c. 120° **d.** Yes. 12 **e.** Yes. 3
6. a. octahedron: Yes. 8
dodecahedron: Yes. 15
icosahedron: Yes. 15
b. octahedron: Yes. 9
dodecahedron: Yes. 6
icosahedron: Yes. 6

Exercises, page 373
1. a. 35 **b.** 980 000 **c.** 1.782 **d.** 0.0985
e. 4 200 000 **f.** 1347.3 **2. a.** 252; 468; 648
b. 2; 62; 30 **c.** 2; 80; 36 **d.** 16; 320; 370
3. a. 664 cm² **b.** 210 cm² **c.** about 268.1 cm²
4. a. 960 cm³ **b.** 196 cm³ **c.** 240 cm³
5. a. 168 mm³ **b.** 216 mm² **6.** 3000 cm³
7. a. about 709 333 cm³/person
b. about 1 488 375 cm³/person **8. a.** 4 times
b. 8 times **9.** 64 cm³

Exercises, page 375
2. a. 420 cm² **b.** 6700 cm² **c.** 1232 cm²
3. a. about 506.7 cm³ **b.** about 28 083.3 cm³
c. 1900.8 cm³ **4. a.** 0.4 cm³ **b.** 144 cm³
c. about 12.63 cm³ **5. a.** 4; $\sqrt{34}$ **b.** 10; $\sqrt{194}$
c. $3\sqrt{7}$; 12 **d.** $\sqrt{527}$; 14 **6. a.** 96 cm²; 48 cm³
b. 360 cm²; 400 cm³ **c.** 756 cm²; about 857 cm³
d. 868 cm²; about 1500 cm³ **7.** 2 601 655 m³
8. a. $b \doteq 230.42$ m; $s \doteq 186.77$ m
b. about 139 164.5 m²
9. about 1517 cm²; about 3516 cm³
10. about 225.7 cm²; 192 cm³

Application, page 376
1. a. A **b.** C

2. a.
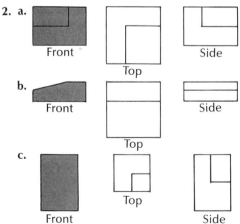
Front Top Side
b.
Front Top Side
c.
Front Top Side

480

d.
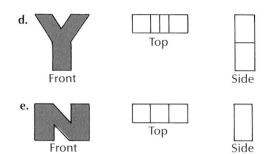
Front Top Side
e.
Front Top Side

Extra, page 376
1. 4; 16; 2; 0; 0 **2.** 0; 18; 30; 8; 0

Review, page 377
1. a. yes; an infinite number of planes
b. yes; one plane
c. yes; an infinite number of planes
d. yes; one plane
2. a. yes; axis, infinite order **b.** no
c. yes; axis 1, order 2; axis 2, infinite order **d.** no
3. a. 252 mm³; 240 mm² **b.** 168 mm³; 216 mm²
c. 48 m³; 96 m² **d.** 19 440 cm³; 4416 cm²
e. 4500 cm³; 1710 cm² **f.** 144 cm³; 180 cm²
4. rectangular bookcase
5. the one that is 4 cm by 12 cm by 7 cm
6. 17 808 cm²

Exercises, page 379
1. a. 678 cm² **b.** 317 m² **c.** 245 m²
2. a. 427 cm² **b.** 61.9 m² **c.** 20 700 m²
3. a. 257 cm² **b.** 113 m² **c.** 3270 mm²
4. 2 cm **5. a.** 9 cm by 22.1 cm
b. at most 70 labels **c.** 297 cm² **6.** 1 m
7. $1133.16 **8.** about 1900 cm²

Extra, page 379
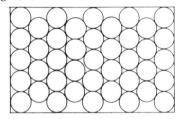

Exercises, page 381
1. a. 236 cm³ **b.** 482 000 cm³ **c.** 226 mm³
d. 4150 cm³ **2.** 7 cm **3.** 11 mm **4.** 24 cm
5. volume A: volume B = 1:4 **6. a.** 31.25 kg
b. about 763 tonnes
7. the glass with the height of 9 cm; about
32.6 cm³ more
8. 0.534 m³ **9.** 2009.6 L **10.** can B;
about 2720 cm³ more

Exercises, page 383
1. a. 804 cm³ **b.** 1210 m³ **c.** 523 cm³
d. 5020 cm³ **e.** 845 m³ **f.** 848 mm³
2. a. 37.7 cm³ **b.** 4220 mm³ **c.** 402 mm³
d. 754 cm³ **3. a.** 5650 cm³ **b.** 28 700 cm³
c. 105 000 cm³ **d.** 402 cm³ **4. a.** 1690 cm³
b. 564 cm³ **c.** cone **d.** cylinder **5.** 88.4 mL
6. a. 192 cm³ **b.** 10 cm **7.** No. **8.** 25.8 m³

Exercises, page 384
1. a. 904 cm³ **b.** 2310 cm³ **c.** 1440 mm³
d. 57.9 m³ **2. a.** 1810 mm² **b.** 154 cm²
c. 804 cm² **d.** 191 mm² **3. a.** 8 **b.** 25 **c.** 1.4
d. 5 **e.** 8 **f.** 15 **4.** b **5.** 191 mL **6.** No.
7. a. 167 m³ **b.** 21.4 L **8.** 4 times; 9 times
9. 8 times; 27 times **10.** $31.92
11. a. 2.18×10^{10} km³ **b.** 6370 km; 1730 km
12. a. 1360 cm³
b. surface area of sphere = 452 cm²;
lateral surface area of cylinder = 452 cm²

Application, page 386
1. a. 21 **b.** 56 **2. a.** 120 **b.** 680 **3. a.** 225
b. 1240

Review, page 387
1. a. 1440 cm³; 615 cm² **b.** 2410 m³; 1000 m²
c. 1230 cm³; 703 cm² **2. a.** 264 cm² **b.** 327 cm²
3. 325 cm³ **4.** container A **5. a.** 44.1 m³
b. 150 m³ **6.** 29.4 cm
7. Let h be the height of the silos.
cylindrical volume $\doteq$ 22.8h m³;
square prism volume $\doteq$ 22.8h m³
8. 477 cm³

Test, page 388
2. a. 1920 cm³; 867 cm² **b.** 314 mm³; 283 mm²
c. 4190 cm³; 1260 cm² **d.** 168 mm³; 216 mm²
e. 400 cm³; 360 cm² **3.** $58.97 **4.** $0.50
5. 3220 cm³ **6.** 2410 cm³
7. a. about 153 000 000 km²
b. about 37 900 000 km²

Cumulative Review, page 389
1. a. D = $\{x|x \in R\}$ R = $\{y|y \geq 4\}$
b. D = $\{x|x \in R\}$ R = $\{y|y \in R\}$
c. D = $\{x|x \in R\}$ R = $\{y|y \in R\}$
2. a. Let d be distance and t be time. Let the
constant of proportionality be v. $v = 84$
b. $d = vt$ **c.** 294 km **3.** about 472 students
4. curve
5. a. $A'(0,0)$; $B'(-2,-5)$; $C'(-6,3)$
b. $A'(-1,-2)$; $B'(-6,0)$; $C'(2,4)$
c. $A'(0,0)$; $B'(2,-5)$; $C'(6,3)$

d. $A'(0,0)$; $B'\left(2\frac{1}{2},-1\right)$; $C'\left(-1\frac{1}{2},-3\right)$
7. a. $a = 30$; $b = 30$; $c = 30$ **b.** $x = 90$
c. $y = 90$; $z = 50$

Unit 13

Exercises, page 391
1. The mass and length of the sailboat, the
temperature of the water are two possible answers.
2. a. scalar **b.** scalar **c.** vector **d.** vector
e. vector **f.** scalar **3.** vector: c,e,g,h
scalar: a,b,d,f,i,j
4. Answers may vary from those given below.
a. vector: the velocity and weight of the airplane;
scalar: the speed, mass, and altitude of the
airplane
b. vector: the velocity and weight of the airplane,
the velocity and weight of the parachutist;
scalar: the speed, mass, and altitude of the
airplane, the speed, mass, altitude, and height of
the parachutist;
c. vector: the velocity and weight of the
windsurfer;
scalar: the speed and mass of the windsurfer, the
temperature of the water
5. a. scalar **b.** vector **c.** vector **d.** scalar
e. vector **f.** scalar **g.** scalar **h.** neither

Exercises, page 393
1. a. $\vec{a}$ and d; b and c; $\vec{e}$ and $\vec{h}$; $\vec{f}$, $\vec{g}$ and $\vec{m}$; $\vec{i}$ and $\vec{j}$;
k and l **2. a.** 25 N **b.** 10 N **c.** 35 N **d.** 20 N
3. a. 69 km/h **b.** 45 km/h **c.** 69 km/h
d. 39 km/h

Exercises, page 395
1. a. 11 km; 9 km **b.** 20 km; 20 km
2. a. 9 km N 40° W **b.** 20 km N 66° E
3. a. 1 cm represents 4 N. **b.** 1 cm represents
8 N.
4. a. 1 cm represents 12.5 N; 17.5 N; 17.5 N.
b. 1 cm represents 14 km/h; 70 km/h; 32.2 km/h.
6. a. 13 km 28° clockwise from first vector
b. 133 km/h 9° clockwise from first vector
c. 31 m 15° clockwise from first vector
d. 31 km/h 78° counter-clockwise from first vector
7. a. 7 N **b.** 13 m **c.** 13 m/s **d.** 7 N
8. about 9400 N **9.** 570 km/h N 77° W
10. a. 122° **b.** 60 m **11.** 58°
12. about 321.7 km N and 270.0 km E
13. S 23° W, 3 h 15 min **14.** 5 km
15. 150 km **16. a.** 15 km **b.** N 60° W
17. N 14° W **18.** about 165 km/h
19. about 492 km N 66° W **20.** about 42.3 km/h

Extra, page 397

1. about 9600 m **2.** about 17.8 m
3. about 6.6 km

Exercises, page 399

1. $\vec{a} = [2,3]$; $\vec{b} = [1,5]$; $\vec{c} = [0,-4]$; $\vec{d} = [-3,-2]$;
$\vec{e} = [0,4]$; $\vec{f} = [-2,-3]$; $\vec{g} = [3,0]$; $\vec{h} = [-5,1]$;
$\vec{i} = [4,0]$; $\vec{j} = [1,5]$; $\vec{k} = [2,3]$; $\vec{l} = [-3,-2]$
2. a and k; b and j; d and l
5. a. $2\sqrt{5}$ **b.** $\sqrt{34}$ **c.** $\sqrt{37}$ **d.** $\sqrt{17}$
6. a. $[6,-5]$ **b.** $[-7,7]$ **c.** $[-2,-9]$
7. a. $-\dfrac{5}{6}$, pointing down to the right
b. -1, pointing up to the left
c. $\dfrac{9}{2}$, pointing down to the left
8. a. $(4,-6)$ **b.** $(-1,3)$ **c.** $(-3,-3)$ **d.** $(3,1)$
e. $(5,-2)$ **9. a.** $(-1,-7)$ **b.** $(2,-5)$
c. $(-3,0)$ **d.** $(4,-1)$ **e.** $(1,1)$ **10. a.** 5; $-\dfrac{4}{3}$; \
b. 13; $\dfrac{12}{5}$; ↗ **c.** 17; $\dfrac{8}{15}$; ↗ **d.** $2\sqrt{13}$; $-\dfrac{3}{2}$; \ **e.** $3\sqrt{10}$; $\dfrac{1}{3}$; \
f. $5\sqrt{2}$; -1; \ **g.** $5\sqrt{2}$; -1; \ **h.** 6; undefined; ↓
i. 3; 0; → **j.** $3\sqrt{10}$; 3; ↗

11.

Slope of $\vec{v}$	Direction	x component	y component	$\vec{v} = [x,y]$	$|\vec{v}|$
$\dfrac{2}{3}$	↗	6	4	$[6,4]$	$2\sqrt{13}$
$-\dfrac{2}{5}$	↘	20	-8	$[20,-8]$	$4\sqrt{29}$
0	←	-4	0	$[-4,0]$	4
$-\dfrac{3}{2}$	↘	-6	9	$[-6,9]$	$\sqrt{117}$
$\dfrac{3}{4}$	↙	-12	-9	$[-12,-9]$	15

Exercises, page 402

1. a. $\vec{u} = [2,3]$; $\vec{v} = [2,-2]$; $\vec{R} = [4,1]$
b. $\vec{u} = [7,4]$; $\vec{v} = [-4,1]$; $\vec{R} = [3,5]$
c. $\vec{u} = [-4,5]$; $\vec{v} = [7,-4]$; $\vec{R} = [3,1]$
d. $\vec{u} = [-5,-2]$; $\vec{v} = [-2,-4]$; $\vec{R} = [-7,-6]$
e. $\vec{u} = [-40,-60]$; $\vec{v} = [-20,20]$; $\vec{R} = [-60,-40]$
f. $\vec{u} = [40,0]$; $\vec{v} = [-20,-15]$; $\vec{R} = [20,-15]$
3. a. $[-2,-9]$ **b.** $[0,3]$ **c.** $[-4,1]$ **d.** $[3,-5]$
e. $[-1,-4]$ **f.** $[-7,-9]$ **5. a.** $[-4,-6]$
b. $[-5,7]$ **c.** $[1,-2]$ **d.** $[3,-4]$ **e.** $[-13,-1]$
f. $[1,0]$
6. a. $[4,-3] + [-2,-1] = [2,-4]$
b. $[-5,-1] + [3,-2] = [-2,-3]$
c. $[3,4] + [-2,4] = [1,8]$
d. $[-3,1] + [6,3] = [3,4]$
e. $[-5,6] + [-1,-2] = [-6,4]$
f. $[2,-3] + [-4,6] = [-2,3]$
7. a. $[-2,-3]$ **b.** $[-1,-6]$ **c.** $[-1,12]$
d. $[-4,-2]$ **e.** $[8,-3]$ **f.** $[-5,12]$

8. 29 N, 134°
9. The boat is 5 km east and 7.25 km south of its
starting point.
11. 17 N, 62°
12. a. $a = -2$; $b = 3$
b. $a = -3$; $b = 1$
c. $a = 4$; $b = -5$
d. $a = 15$; $b = 3$
e. $a = -2$; $b = -4$
f. $a = -3$; $b = 2$
g. $a = -4$; $b = -1$
h. $a = -2$; $b = 3$
i. $a = 8$; $b = 6$

Extra, page 403

1. a. $\overrightarrow{BD}$ **b.** $\overrightarrow{CA}$ **c.** $\overrightarrow{DB}$ **d.** $\overrightarrow{AC}$
2. a. $\overrightarrow{AF}$ **b.** $\overrightarrow{AH}$ **c.** $\overrightarrow{AE}$ **d.** $\overrightarrow{AE}$
e. $\overrightarrow{AD}$ or $\overrightarrow{BE}$ or $\overrightarrow{CF}$

Biography, page 404
These are some of the possible solutions.
1. 1-6-7-16-17-18-19-20-15-14-13-12-11-10-9-8-2-3-4-5-1;
1-6-7-16-17-9-8-2-3-10-11-18-19-20-15-14-13-12-4-5-1;
1-6-7-16-17-18-11-10-9-8-2-3-4-12-13-19-20-15-14-5-1;
2. 1-6-15-14-5-4-3-10-9-17-18-11-12-13-19-20-16-7-8-2-1;
1-6-15-14-5-4-12-13-19-20-16-7-8-9-17-18-11-10-3-2-1
3. 1-2-8-7-6-15-20-16-17-9-10-3-4-12-11-18-19-13-14-5-1;
1-2-8-7-6-15-14-13-12-11-18-19-20-16-17-9-10-3-4-5-1

Review, page 405

1. a. vector **b.** scalar **c.** vector **d.** vector
3. a. 29 km **b.** 130 km **c.** about 107 N
4. a. $[-4,-7]$; $\sqrt{65}$ **b.** $[-8,2]$; $2\sqrt{17}$ **6.** 17 N
7. $(-3,-7)$ **8.** $(-6,8)$ **9. a.** $[18,-24]$
b. $[-3,4]$ **c.** $\left[\dfrac{3}{5},-\dfrac{4}{5}\right]$ **d.** $\left[3\dfrac{3}{5},4\dfrac{4}{5}\right]$
10. a. $a = -2$; $b = 1\dfrac{2}{3}$ **b.** $a = 6$; $b = 4$
c. $a = -3$; $b = -1$
d. $a = -3$; $b = -3$

Exercises, page 408

1. a. $\sin\theta = \dfrac{3}{5}$; $\cos\theta = \dfrac{4}{5}$; $\tan\theta = \dfrac{3}{4}$
b. $\sin\theta = \dfrac{8}{17}$; $\cos\theta = \dfrac{15}{17}$; $\tan\theta = \dfrac{8}{15}$
c. $\sin\theta = \dfrac{65}{97}$; $\cos\theta = \dfrac{72}{97}$; $\tan\theta = \dfrac{65}{72}$
d. $\sin\theta = \dfrac{24}{25}$; $\cos\theta = \dfrac{7}{25}$; $\tan\theta = 3\dfrac{3}{7}$
e. $\sin\theta = \dfrac{12}{13}$; $\cos\theta = \dfrac{5}{13}$; $\tan\theta = 2\dfrac{2}{5}$
f. $\sin\theta = \dfrac{40}{41}$; $\cos\theta = \dfrac{9}{41}$; $\tan\theta = 4\dfrac{4}{9}$
2. a. 0.6428 **b.** 1.7321 **c.** 1 **d.** 0.2588
e. 0.6129 **f.** 0.9944 **g.** 4.8077 **h.** 0.0544

3. a. $\sin \alpha = 0.28$; $\cos \alpha = 0.96$; $\tan \alpha \doteq 0.2917$
$\sin \beta = 0.96$; $\cos \beta = 0.28$; $\tan \beta \doteq 3.4286$
b. $\sin \alpha = 0.8$; $\cos \alpha = 0.6$; $\tan \alpha \doteq 1.3333$
$\sin \beta = 0.6$; $\cos \beta = 0.8$; $\tan \beta \doteq 0.75$
c. $\sin \alpha \doteq 0.3714$; $\cos \alpha \doteq 0.9285$; $\tan \alpha \doteq 0.4$
$\sin \beta \doteq 0.9285$; $\cos \beta \doteq 0.3714$; $\tan \beta = 2.5$
4. a. 4; $\cos \alpha = 0.8$ **b.** $\sqrt{61}$; $\cos \alpha \doteq 0.6402$

c. $\sqrt{95}$; $\cos \alpha \doteq 0.8122$ **5. a.** 10; $\sin \alpha = \frac{3}{5}$

b. $6\sqrt{2}$; $\sin \beta = \frac{2\sqrt{2}}{3}$; **c.** $4\sqrt{2}$; $\sin \alpha = \frac{\sqrt{2}}{2}$

6. a. $\tan \theta = 2\sqrt{6}$ **b.** $\tan \theta = 1\frac{3}{5}$

c. $\tan \alpha = \frac{\sqrt{21}}{2}$; $\tan \beta = \frac{2\sqrt{21}}{21}$

7. $\sin \theta = \frac{9}{41}$; $\cos \theta = \frac{40}{41}$; $\tan \theta = \frac{9}{40}$

8. $\sin \theta \doteq 0.7241$; $\cos \theta \doteq 0.6897$; $\tan \theta = 1.05$

9. $\sin A = \frac{39}{89}$; $\tan A = \frac{39}{80}$

10. $\sin Q = \frac{60}{109}$; $\cos Q = \frac{91}{109}$; $\tan Q = \frac{60}{91}$

11. a. $\sin 45° \doteq 0.7071$ **b.** $\sin 45° \doteq 0.7071$
c. The triangles constructed in parts **a** and **b** are similar, so that the ratio $\frac{OPP}{HYP}$ for corresponding angles is constant.

12. a. 1 **b.** 1 **c.** 1 **13.** 1 **14. a.** $\sin 30° = \frac{1}{2}$
b. Since $\sin 30°$ is the ratio of opposite to hypotenuse, the ratio $\frac{AC}{AB}$ is $\frac{1}{2}$.
c. 8 units **d.** 6 units **e.** 8 units; $8\sqrt{3}$ units

Extra, page 409
In right-angled triangle *ABC* with vertex *C* at (6,2) and angle θ at *A* (1,2), the side *opposite* θ is the *rise* for segment *AB*; the side *adjacent* θ is the *run*.

Hence, $\dfrac{OPP}{ADJ} = \dfrac{rise}{run}$

slope $AB = \frac{2}{5}$; $\tan \theta = \frac{2}{5}$

Exercises, page 411
1. a. 0.6691 **b.** 0.9511 **c.** 0.8704 **d.** 0.7604
2. a. 5.65° **b.** 77.55° **c.** 40.03°
3. a. cosine **b.** tangent **c.** sine **d.** tangent
4. a. 6.95 **b.** 9.80 **c.** 5.66 **d.** 23.94 **e.** 11.52
f. 4.87 **g.** 12.05 **h.** 38.98 **5. a.** 36.25°
b. 43.81° **c.** 54.31° **d.** 71.57° **e.** 45° **f.** 60°
6. a. 35.54° **b.** 3.66 units **c.** 22.62°
7. a. $x \doteq 32.8$; $y \doteq 64.4$
b. $x \doteq 1964.0$; $y \doteq 1643.7$
c. $x \doteq 9.6$; $y \doteq 3.9$; $\beta = 68°$

Exercises, page 413
1. 3.80 m **2.** 0.37 m **3.** 9.54 m **4.** 48.37°
5. 525.24 m **6.** 54.78° **7.** 113.32 m **8.** 21.16 cm
9. 0.04 m **10.** 11.26 m **11.** 39.81 m and 55.76 m
12. 6.81 cm, 110.11 cm^2 **13.** 39.05 cm, 22.59°
14. about 132.98 km north and 170.21 km east
15. 28.32 cm^2

Using the Calculator, page 414
1. $\sin C = \frac{h}{b}$; $h = b \sin C$
Substitute in $A = \frac{1}{2} ah$ to get $A = \frac{1}{2} ab \sin C$.
2. a. 28 **b.** 341.0 **c.** 891.0

Review, page 415
1. a. $x \doteq 11.23$; $\theta \doteq 45.58°$ **b.** $m \doteq 4.62$; $n \doteq 1.92$
2. a. $x \doteq 9.81$ **b.** $\theta \doteq 28.96°$ **c.** $x \doteq 16.09$
d. $\theta \doteq 61.39°$ **e.** $x = 20$; $y = 21$; $\beta \doteq 43.60°$;
$\theta \doteq 53.13°$ **f.** $w \doteq 36.87°$; $\alpha \doteq 44.33°$; $\beta \doteq 8.80°$;
$\theta \doteq 44.33°$ **3.** $\sin \alpha \doteq 0.7746$; $\tan \alpha \doteq 1.2247$
4. 0.8270 **5.** 6.10 m **6.** 125.86 m
7. $AC = \sqrt{165}$ units, $<A \doteq 47.46°$, $<B \doteq 42.54°$

Test, page 416
1. a. about 72.1 N
b. about 57.7 m
c. about 270.9 km/h
2. 41.8°, about 6.7 km/h, about 12.5 min
3. $\sqrt{89}$
4. a. $\theta = 60°$ **b.** $\theta \doteq 44.42°$ **c.** $x \doteq 19.25$
d. $x = 13$; $y = 84$; $\beta \doteq 67.38°$; $\theta \doteq 81.20°$
e. $x = 5.20$ **f.** $x = 8°$; $\beta \doteq 22.6°$; $\theta \doteq 53.1°$
5. about 135 177.43 m^2 **6.** about 71.45 m
7. $AC = \sqrt{165}$ units, $\angle A \doteq 47.46°$, $\angle B \doteq 42.54°$

Cumulative Review, page 417
1. b. 368; 342.5 **2. a.** translation
b. rotation of 180° and reflection
c. glide reflection
d. glide reflection
e. rotation of 90° counter-clockwise and translation
f. rotation of 180° or reflection
g. glide reflection
h. rotation of 90° counter-clockwise and dilatation
4. Draw any two chords, *AB* and *CD*.
Construct their perpendicular bisectors.
The point where the perpendicular bisectors of *AB* and *CD* cross is the centre of the circle.
5. 1125.4 mL

483

Appendix: Mixed Problems

Understanding the Problem
1. 8262 **2.** 98 **3.** 12 vertices **4.** 2025; 3025
5. 7 **6.** $\frac{1}{3}$ **7.** large pizza
8. No. A rhombus is equilateral but not necessarily equiangular.
9. No. A rectangle is equiangular but not necessarily equilateral.
10. 9 rectangles. **11.** Add a negative number.

Guessing and Testing
12. 36 **13.** 28 years old **14.** 3 cm by 3 cm
15. 11 **16.** 163 **17.** 53 and 214

18. 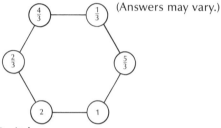 (Answers may vary.)

19. 52 pitches

Making a List or Table
20. 60 tickets
21. (5,5,4,4,4,4,4); (5,5,5,4,4,4,3); (5,5,5,5,4,3,3); (5,5,5,5,4,4,2); (5,5,5,5,5,3,2); (5,5,5,5,5,5,0)
22. 343; 1331 **23.** $\frac{3}{16}$
24. 45 doubles teams; 55.$\overline{5}$%
25. manager: Smith; cashier: Lee; clerk: Gagné
26. $5\frac{23}{64}$ L **27.** 15 818 400 licence plates

Finding Patterns
28. a. 36 **b.** 163 **c.** 36 **d.** 64; 9; 100
e. 96; 145 **f.** 103 **29.** -25 **30.** Yes.
31. Wednesday
32. 1948; 1894; 1849; 1498; 1489; 1668; 1686; 1866
33. 8
34. 1; 4; 9; 16; 25; 36; 49; 64; 81; 100; 121; 144; 169; 196; 225; 256; 289; 324; 361; 400; 441; 484; 529; 576; 625; 676; 729; 784; 841; 900; 961
35. 420 rectangles **36. a.** square or star
b. circle **c.** triangle

Solving a Simpler Problem or Working Backward
37. 3600 m^2 **38.** $X = 5$; $Z = 1$ **39.** 100x; 0.1z
40. about 164 km/h **41.** 99 **42.** 16 digits
43. $\frac{1}{64}$

Making a Diagram or Physical Model
44. 15 line segments **45.** 29 **46.** 1.536 m
47. 4 triangles **48.** 3 rectangular solids; 27 rectangular solids

49.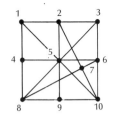

50. 6 cm **51.** 11 triangles

Extending and Generalizing Problems
52. 4 and 4; general rule: $\frac{n}{2}$ and $\frac{n}{2}$ (where n is the sum)
53. 6 angles; general rule: Let a be the number of points other than the main vertex. Then the number of angles formed is
$1 + 2 + 3 + ... + (a - 1)$.

54.

55. $\dfrac{3}{3^{n-1}}$ **56.** No. **57.** 108; $3x\left(\dfrac{n(n+1)}{2}\right)$
58. 1296

Selecting an Appropriate Strategy
59. -80; -81; -82; -83
60. Maybe the students did not play against each other. **61.** (Answers may vary.)
$(1 \times 9 - 2) \times 3 \times 4 - 5 + 6 + 7 + 8 + 0$
62. 16 **63.** 1, 2, and 3

64.   **66.**

65.

67. Orchestra: $226; Balcony 1: $166; Balcony 2: $118
68. $10 880 **69.** Car pool is cheaper. **70.** $585
71. $11.90
72. about 18.7 g; about 348.9 g; about 2 274 000 g
73. $612.30 **74. a.** $\dfrac{7}{8}$, $-\dfrac{8}{9}$, $\dfrac{9}{10}$
b. $\dfrac{1}{16}$, $\dfrac{1}{32}$, $\dfrac{1}{64}$
c. $-\dfrac{1}{4}$, 5, $-\dfrac{1}{5}$
75. a. The fox should stand at the centre of the circle. **b.** about 9 m

Symbols

=	is equal to	$a{:}b$	the ratio of a to b
≠	is not equal to	∅	empty set
>	is greater than	∪	union
<	is less than	∩	intersection
≤	is less than or equal to	ϵ	is an element of
≥	is greater than or equal to	∉	is not an element of
≐	is approximately equal to	/	such that
~	is similar to	∴	therefore
π	pi, ($\doteq$ 3.1416)	→	maps onto
≅	is congruent to	W	the set of whole numbers
⊥	is perpendicular to	Z	the set of integers
∥	is parallel to	Q	the set of rational numbers
$-a$	the opposite or additive inverse of a	$\overline{Q}$	the set of irrational numbers
$|a|$	the absolute value of a	R	the set of real numbers
$\frac{1}{a}$	the reciprocal or multiplicative inverse of a		

Formulas

Distance:	$d = vt$		Simple interest:	$I = Prt$
Speed:	$v = \frac{d}{t}$		Amount (total value):	$A = P$
Time:	$t = \frac{d}{v}$		Compound interest:	$A = P(1 + r)^n$

Perimeter of a rectangle:	$P = 2(l + w)$	Volume of a prism:	$V = Ah$
Circumference of a circle:	$C = \pi d$ or $2\pi r$	Volume of a pyramid:	$V = \frac{1}{3}Ah$
		Volume of a cylinder:	$V = \pi r^2 h$
Surface area of a cylinder:	$SA = 2\pi(r + h)$	Volume of a cone:	$V = \frac{1}{3}\pi r^2 h$
Surface area of a cone:	$SA = \pi r(r + s)$	Volume of a sphere:	$V = \frac{4}{3}\pi r^3$

Surface area of a sphere: $SA = 4\pi r^2$
Surface area of a prism and pyramid: SA = lateral area + area of base (s)

Metric Equivalents

Length
1 cm (centimetre)	= 10 mm (millimetres)
1 m (metre)	= 100 cm
1 km (kilometre)	= 1000 m

Mass
1 g (gram)	= 1000 mg (milligrams)
1 kg (kilogram)	= 1000 g
1 t (tonne)	= 1000 kg

Capacity
1 L (litre)	= 100 mL (millilitres)
1 kL (kilolitre)	= 1000 L

Area
1 cm² (square centimetre)	= 100 mm²
1 m² (square metre)	= 10 000 cm²
1 ha (hectare)	= 10 000 m²

INDEX

487

Photograph Credits

M.J. Bent/Bell Canada: 64
The Bettman Archive: 19, 39, 168, 217, 231, 302, 366
Dennis Broughton/Scarborough Board of Education: 76
Canada Post Corporation: 97
Canadian Yachting Magazine: 392
Canapress Photo Service: 17, 26, 72, 92, 102, 124, 125, 143, 144, 145, 200, 202, 213, 219, 228, 238
Chapman Photography: 32, 229
Collection Haags Gemeentemuseum — The Hague and M.C. Escher Heirs, courtesy of Cordon Art — Baarn — Holland: 368, 371
A.E. Cross Ltd. Studio: 28
Dept. of Regional and Industrial Expansion: 38, 53, 56
Eddie Black's Ltd.: 21
FAO Photo: 412
A. Gottlieb/Monkmeyer Press Photo Service: 72
Historical Picture Service, Inc.: 404
R. Kennedy/Canadian Yachting Magazine: 390
Laurence R. Lowry/Aerial Photo Service: 78
Masterfile: 342
Miller Services Ltd.: 36, 60, 74, 107, 125, 151, 210, 242, 274, 346
National Research Council: 164, 179, 194, 197
National Research Council, courtesy of RASC, Ottawa Centre: 31
C. Pearman: 30, 52
D. Reid/Monkmeyer Press Photo Service: 175
H. Rogers/Monkmeyer Press Photo Service: 1
Royal Bank: 33
Royal LePage Real Estate Services Limited: 306
Royal Ontario Museum: 30
Toronto Transit Commission: 101
Volkswagen Canada Ltd.: 60, 74, 86, 123
YMCA: 88

Photo Research: Joanne Close and Cynthia Pearman